Early Church Records of New Castle County, Delaware

Volume 2

The Records of Holy Trinity (Old Swedes) Church Wilmington Delaware

1713-1799
With Corrections Added

Translated from the Original Swedish by
Horace Burr
With an Abstract of the English Records

HERITAGE BOOKS
2007

HERITAGE BOOKS
AN IMPRINT OF HERITAGE BOOKS, INC.

Books, CDs, and more—Worldwide

For our listing of thousands of titles see our website
at
www.HeritageBooks.com

Published 2007 by
HERITAGE BOOKS, INC.
Publishing Division
65 East Main Street
Westminster, Maryland 21157-5026

Copyright © 1994 Horace Burr

All rights reserved. No part of this book may be reproduced or transmitted in any form or by any means, electronic or mechanical, including photocopying, recording or by any information storage and retrieval system without written permission from the author, except for the inclusion of brief quotations in a review.

International Standard Book Number: 978-1-58549-290-6

INTRODUCTION

Volume One of this series covers a number of church registers and other records discussed below. All births through 31 December 1800 were copied, regardless of the date of the baptism. The order of the records usually reflects the order of the "original" from which the transcriber worked. If the date of the baptism was not recorded one can guess that the event might have occurred sometime between the baptisms appearing before and after the given entry. In the case of most denominations the date of baptism usually indicates an approximate date of birth. This does not apply, of course, to the Baptists who baptized as adults. In addition to the church registers we have added other records which will be useful to genealogists, namely, marriage bonds, certificates of removal/letters of dismission and list of church members.

Volume Two is a reprint of the register of Old Swedes Church, taken from the translation by Horace Burr, published by Historical Society of Delaware in 1890, titled, *The Records of Holy Trinity (Old Swedes) Church As Translated By Horace Burr*, as amended by *Catalogue and Errata of The Records of Holy Trinity (Old Swedes) Church*, published by the Society in 1919.

Abbreviations:
MMtg - Monthly Meeting
dau - daughter
co. - county
Phila - Philadelphia
Wit: witness
hd - hundred

OLD SWEDES CHURCH

Among the original colony of Swedes who settled in Delaware and built Fort Christina in 1638 was Rev. Reorus Torkillus, who established religious worship in the fort, the first meeting-place for Christians on the

Delaware, and there it was continued until the church at Tinicum was erected in 1646. Crane Hook Church is said to have been built in 1667, probably by the united efforts of the Dutch congregation and the Swedes. It was used for public worship until the "Old Swedes' Church" was built in 1698 on the present site. Lutheran in denomination the church was the religious center for not only the Swedes but English and persons of various ethnicity and religious affiliation, as evidenced by the names of those who were baptized, married or buried. Eventually Swedish ministers were replaced by English ministers under cordial circumstances.

In using the records keep in mind the words of the translator, Horace Burr.

> "I have not attempted to render the old Swedish in which these records were written, into modern book English, but have made a very literal translation, following the style of the writer ... It would seem that the names of persons not Swedes have been spelt as they would sound to the Swedish ear, and many of them very differently from their proper English orthography."
>
> "The Bondê or agricultural population of Sweden has not sirnames at the time of the emigration, nor have they even now. The oldest son takes the father's name, as for instance, Johan the son of Johan, would be Johan Johansson, and all the other sons, Peter, Carl, etc., would be Peter Johansson, in English, Johnsson; and the daughters take dotter, as Brita Johansdotter.
>
> "After their settlement here among English and other nationalities, who had already adopted sirnames for all classes, the father's name naturally became the family name, but the peculiarity of spelling with two s' continued for a long time, and Paulsson

was the correct spelling until a quite
recent date."[1]

He and others cite various derivations of the
Swedish names, e.g.,
Didriksson became Derickson or Richardsson
and Poulson became Paulsson Justasson became
Justis or Justice.

From January, 1773 the records were written in
English. Mr. Burr omitted the names of
witnesses and sponsors. Burials were also
omitted "after the coming of Mr. Acrelius, as
they would add to the size of the work, and
are of less importance than births, baptisms
and marriages." We look forward to the time
when these are translated and published.[2]

SOCIETY OF FRIENDS (QUAKERS)

Friends began settling on the east side of the
Brandywine in New Castle County around 1682.
It was named the Newark Meeting and was
continued until 1754. In 1705 a meeting house
was built in New Castle which declined in
membership until it was finally discontinued
in 1758. Its members then attended the
meeting at Wilmington. A Monthly Meeting was
held in New Castle in 1686. In 1687 this
meeting decided that it was "more convenient
for the present that the meeting be held twice
on the other side of the Brandywine and the
third which will be the Quarterly Meeting at
New Castle." From 1689 to 1704 the Monthly
meeting seems to have been "held at Valentine
Hollingsworth's and other Friends' houses,"
and was called Newark Monthly Meeting. The
last monthly meeting held at Newark was in
1707. It was generally held at Centre though
sometimes at Kennett, from that date until
1760, when its name was changed to the Kennett
Monthly Meeting.

The Wilmington Preparative Meeting was
established in 1739. A Wilmington Monthly
Meeting was established in 1750 by Chester
(Concord) Quarterly Meeting out of Kennett

Monthly Meeting. It was in 1750 that the records begin. Wilmington Monthly Meeting included the particular meetings of Wilmington and New Castle at that time.

Records: Contained here are all the known records of Wilmington Monthly Meeting; the earlier Newark Monthly Meeting marriages are include insofar as one of the parties was from New Castle County. Copies of the records are found at Friends Historical Library of Swarthmore College, Swarthmore, Pennsylvania.

ANGLICANS (PROTESTANT EPISCOPAL)

See also Old Swedes' Church which became Holy Trinity Church.

The Emanuel Protestant Episcopal Church of New Castle was established in 1704. Rev. George Ross was sent by the Society for the Propagation of the Gospel in Foreign Parts as its first minister in 1705. In 1728 the pew holders were Richard Halliwell, Joseph Wood, John Strand, Samuel Kirk, Thomas Dakeyne, John Land, Peter Jaquett, Cornelius Kettle, Richard Grafton, William Read, Samuel Lowman, Yeates & Custis, Zophar Eaton, John Wallace, Thos. Gassel, Richard Reynolds, Peter Hance, James Sykes and John Cann. The records have been taken from Thomas Holcomb's works.[3]

St. Ann's was the earliest organized congregation in the southern portion of New Castle County. It was organized before 1704. The Anglican church at St. Georges was founded by Welsh families prior to 1707. In 1720 land was granted in Mill Creek Hundred for the use of St. James' Church. There are no known early registers surviving for any of these churches.

BAPTISTS

We have abstracted the records based on the published works, *Records of The Welsh Tract*

Baptist Meeting, Pencader Hundred, New Castle County, Delaware, 1701-1828. In Two Parts, published by the Historical Society of Delaware, Wilmington, 1904.

It was early in the 18th century that William Penn granted to David Evans and William Davis 30,000 acres of land to be divided and deeded to settlers from South Wales, some of whom had at that time settled in Radnor Township, Chester County, Penn. This grant, ever after known as "The Welsh Tract," is located partly in Pencader Hundred, New Castle County, Delaware and partly in Cecil County, Maryland. About one-fourth of the tract lay in Maryland. Thomas Griffith, their first minister, came from Pembroke and Carmarthenshire, South Wales in 1701, and soon after erected a long meeting house in which they worshiped until another structure was built in 1746. The original records for several years were kept in the Welsh language, afterwards in English.

Appearing in the minutes is this account of their arrival in this country:
"In the year 1701 some of us who were members of the churches of Jesus Christ in the countys of Pembroke and Caermarthen, South Wales in Great Britain, professing believers baptism; laying on of hands, election, and final perseverance in grace, were moved and encouraged in ... to come to Penn. Our number was sixteen, we sailed from Milford-haven in the month of June, 1701, in a ship named James and Mary and landed in Philadelphia 8 Sep following. Rec. [Received] by the congregation meeting in Philadelphia and Pennypack who held the same faith with us excepting the ordinance of laying on of hands on every particular members ...After our arrival during which time it pleased God to add to our number about 20 members, in which time we, and many other Welsh people purchased a tract of land in New Castle Co, on Delaware called Welsh tract, in the year

1703 we began to get our living out of it, and to set our meetings in order and build a place of worship, which was commonly known by the name of the Baptist meeting house by the Iron-hill."

Records: The records of the Welsh Tract Baptist Church were transcribed by Henry C. Conrad, Librarian, Wilmington, Del., October 1904.

The First Baptist Church of Wilmington, was established in 1785. We have no indication of the existence of these records prior to 1800. Bethel Baptist Church of New Castle Hundred was begun ca. 1786.

PRESBYTERIANS

The First Presbyterian Church of Wilmington took its beginning in 1737 when land was purchased. Three years later a church was erected at the present corner of 10th and Market Streets today. Rev. Robert Cathcart preached there every fourth Sunday until his death. The Second Presbyterian Church was formed by members from the First Church in 1774 with Rev. Joseph Smith as pastor. The name was changed to Christiana Church in 1787.

The only Presbyterian registers that we have for the 18th century are those of Pencader Presbyterian Church of Glasgow. According to J. Thomas Scharf, the Presbyterians of the Welsh Tract were constituted a church as early as 1710.[4] Rev. David Evans, son of David Evans, one of the grantees of the Welsh Tract, was the first pastor. Other ministers: Thomas Evans (1720-1743); Timothy Griffith (1743-1754); Alexander McDowell (1767-1773); Samuel Eakin (1776-1783); and Thomas Smith (1783-1801).[5]

Other Presbyterian churches founded in the 1700s include the following: Old Drawyers Presbyterian Church (ca. 1710); Presbyterian Church on Pigeon Run (ca. 1730); White Clay

Presbyterian Church (ca. 1721) in Mill Creek
Hundred; Presbyterian Congregation of Head of
Christiana Church (1708); Christiana
Presbyterian Church (1730-1738) in White Clay
Creek Hundred; Lower Brandywine Presbyterian
Church in Pencader Hundred (ca. 1720); St.
George's Presbyterian Church (early 1700s);
Red Clay Creek Presbyterian Church (1722);
Forest Presbyterian Church (1742).

METHODISTS

The Asbury Methodist Episcopal Church of
Wilmington began in 1766 with the sermon by
Captain Webb, a British army officer near what
is now the corner of King and 8th Streets. The
original members were John Thelwell and
Deborah his daughter, Henry Colesburg, Betsy
Colesburg, Sarah Colesburg, John Miller,
Thomas Webster, William Wood, J. Jaquet,
George Whitsill, David Ford, James Belt,
Patience Erwin and Sarah Wood. The church was
completed in 1789. There are no known 18th
century records extant.

Other Methodist churches which were
established in the late 1700s include the
following: White's Chapel in Appoquinimink
Hundred, Dickerson's Chapel near Dexter's
Corner and Bethel Church (Cloud's Chapel).

ROMAN CATHOLICS

There were few Catholics in New Castle prior
to 1800. Those who were here would have
sought the ministering of the Jesuits of Old
Bohemia in Cecil County, Maryland, or St.
Joseph's of Philadelphia.

The records of St. Peter's of Wilmington
appear just prior to 1800. After the French
Revolution, and the Negro insurrection in St.
Domingo, some distinguished French Catholic
families settled in the Wilmington area.

MARRIAGE BONDS

These were bonds are held in the collections of the Genealogical Society of Pennsylvania, Vol. 246, Phila. In 1910 Gilbert Cope deposited them with the Genealogical Society and made the following comments,

"When the county seat of New Castle County, Delaware, was removed from New Castle to Wilmington a great many of the old papers were placed in the attic of the new court house without any attempt to make them available for examination. About the only person who seemed to take much interest in them was Amos C. Brinton, the aged janitor of the building. He assorted them to some extent and picked out all the marriage license bonds noticed by him, and these he called my attention to in 1892. ... I went to Wilmington on the 26th of the same month and brought home the papers, which I put into twelve folio volumes. Before returning them I made a list of them for my own use.

"An examination of the numbers preserved for the different years (see page 221) will show that these form but a small part of those originally issued. For some reason not ascertained there are a considerable number from Sussex and a few from Kent County, and this suggests that some from New Castle may have gone astray elsewhere, but it is feared that these have shared the fate of other of the New Castle records, notably from the office of Register of Wills. The records of the Old Swedes' Church show that licenses for marriage were issued much earlier than the date of the oldest bond preserved.

"Those of early date specify the residence and occupations of the parties but after 1800 these facts are generally omitted. Much carelessness is also manifested in filling up these bonds.. When given in the bonds the residences will appear in the following pages, but the names of sureties and witnesses are mostly omitted after 1790. Gilbert Cope, West Chester, Pa. 1-15-1910."

End Notes

1. *The Records of Holy Trinity (Old Swedes) Church As Translated By Horace Burr*, as amended by *Catalogue and Errata of The Records of Holy Trinity (Old Swedes) Church*, published by the Society in 1919. See "PREFATORY REMARKS," pp. 3-8.

2. Records for burials of Old Swedes for the period, 1713-1765 were published by the Historical Society of Delaware in 1953.

3. Thomas Holcomb, Early Ecclesiastical Affairs In New Castle, Del. And History Of Immanuel Church, pp. 179-254.

4. J. Thomas Scharf, History of Delaware, p.955. Much of the information on the founding of churches in New Castle County was drawn from this source.

5. *Ibid.*, p. 955. The registers for the 1796 - 1800 are for marriages and baptisms performed by Rev. William Chealy. It is unclear why Scharff gives the minister's name for this period as Thomas Smith.

BIBLIOGRAPHY

Burr, Horace. *The Records of Holy Trinity (Old Swedes) Church As Translated By Horace Burr*, as amended by *Catalogue and Errata of The Records of Holy Trinity (Old Swedes) Church*, published by the Society in 1919.

Bicentennial Committee, Edward P. Bartlett. *Friends in Wilmington 1738-1938*. (copy at Historical Society of Delaware).

Colburn, Dorothy. *Old Drawyers. The First Presbyterian Church in St. Georges Hundred*. Odessa, Del (1989).

Craig, Peter Stebbins. *The 1693 Census of the Swedes On The Delaware, Family Histories of the Swedish Lutheran Church Members Residing in Pennsylvania, Delaware, West New Jersey and Cecil County, Maryland, 1638-1693*. Winter Park, FL: SAG Publications, (1993).

Descendants of Early Welsh Tract Families, Newark Delaware. Typed from handwritten manuscript, author unknown.

Eckert, Jack, Ed., *Guide to the Records of Philadelphia Yearly Meeting*. Haverford College, Records Committee of Philadelphia Yearly Meeting and Swarthmore College (1989).

Holcomb, Thomas. *Sketch of Early Ecclesiastical Affairs in New Castle, Delaware, and History of Immanuel Church*. Written By Request Of the Church Club, of Delaware. (1890).

Michener, Ezra. *A Retrospect of Early Quakerism*. Philadelphia (1860).

Rightmyer, Nelson Waite. *The Anglican Church in Delaware*. Philadelphia: The Church Historical Society (1947).

Scharf, J. Thomas. *History of Delaware. 1609 - 1888*. Westminster, Maryland: Family Line Publications (1991). With revised index by Historical Society of Delaware.

Springer, Courtland B. and Ruth L. Springer. "Burial Records, 1713-1756, Holy Trinity (Old Swedes) Church," *Delaware History*, vol. 5: p. 270; vol. 6: p.53, 140, 233, 307. Wilmington: Historical Society of Delaware (1953), 38 pp.

Two Hundredth Anniversary. First and Central Presbyterian Church of Wilmington, Del., Inc. 1737 - 1937. Published by the church (1937). The appendix contains a list of interments in the Old Church Cemetery.

Zepley, Frank R. *The Churches of Delaware*. Wilmington, DE (1947).

Inventory of Church Records of Delaware. Prepared by the Historical Records Survey, W.P.A. 1937.

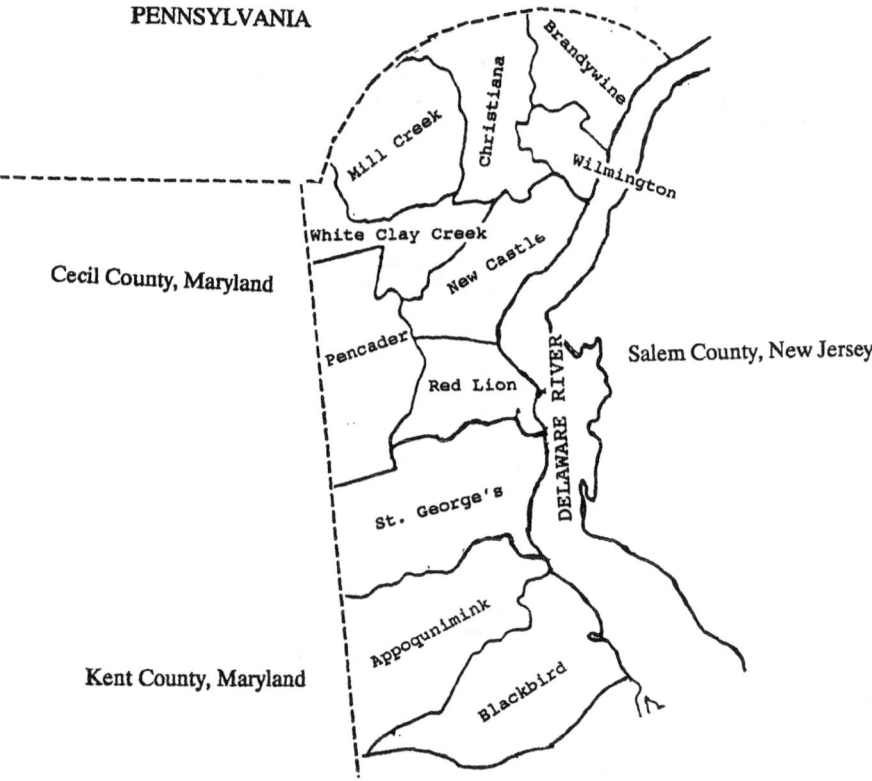

OLD SWEDES CHURCH

RECORD OF MARRIAGES IN CHRISTINA CONGREGATION.
IN THE YEAR OF OUR LORD 1713.

1st. Martin Gustaffson and Britta Walraven married the 18th of October.

2nd. Olof Mansson and Annika Tossawa married the 10th of November.

RECORD OF BAPTISM OF CHILDREN IN CHRISTINA
CONGREGATION IN THE YEAR 1713, WITH
NAMES OF PARENTS AND SPONSORS.

1st Zacharias Didriksson and wife Hellena's child Zacharias, baptized 25th of January, Sponsors, Cornelius Coineliisson, from the other side the river, Johan Peter Mansson, Peter Jaquettes wife Mariah and the late Johan Van de Ver's daughter Judith.

2nd. Mons Gustaff and wife Catharina's, child, Christina baptized 8th March, Sponsors, Jonas Walraven, Jesper Walraven, Johan Gustass's wife Britta and Britta Walraven.

3rd. Gustass Kock and wife Anna's child Francina, baptized Aril 5th, Sponsors, Johan Gioding, Philip Van de Ver, Mrs. Annika Gioding, and Mrs. Anna Kock.

4. Christian Joran and wife Elizabeth's, child Sophia, born May 6th, baptized May 15th, Sponsors Peter Anderson, Edward Robinson, Seneca's widow and Peter Anderson's wife Magdalena.

5. Staffan Tossawa and wife Catharina's, child Anders born March 1st, baptized May 24, Sponsors James Anderson, Anders Stalcop, James Anderson's wife and Johan Gustaf's wife Brita.

6. George Reed and wife Sara's, child Mary, born March 6th, baptized May 24th, Sponsor Jonas Walraven, Johan Skagen, Elizabeth Skagen and Mrs. Elibabeth Colesberg.

8. Johan Hendrickson and wife Brita's, child Susanna, born May 5th, baptized by Mr. Lidenius June 7th, Sponsors Pastor Magister Hessellius, Constantin, Mrs. Sara Hesselius and Maria Conrad's daughter.

8. Robin Clood and wife Gertrude's child Lydia, baptized June 14, eight months old, Sponsors Peter Mansson, Lars Persson from over the river, Margaretta Culen from Wicacoe congregation, and Maria Stedham.

9. James Watkins child John, born April 7th, baptized June 21st, Sponsors Lucas Stedpam, Lucasson, Timothy Lylofson Stedham, Mary Snecker and Conrad Constantine's daughter Mary.

10. Rev. Eric Biork's child Maria, born July 18, baptized July 19, Sponsors the Pastor Magister Hessellius, the Rev. Abraham Lidenius, Johan Stalcop, Martin Gustafsson, William Van de Ver's wife, Mrs. Helena Canpony and Ingeborg Stedham.

11. Olof Fransson's (from the other side,) child Peter, born July 28th, baptized the same day by Mr. Lidenius, Sponsors Anders Hendricson, Anders Seneca, Mrs. Brita Dunken and Mrs. Ingrid Peterson.

12. Samuel Hall's child Elizabeth, born June 15th, baptized August 2nd, Sponsors Johan Hindricson, Joseph Hedge, Johan Hindricsson's wife Brita, Gustaf Rock's wife Anna.

13. Robert Rekman's (other side of river,) child Thomas, baptized August 13th, five months old, Sponsors the Rev. Mr. Lidenius, George Morris, Anna Gioding and Anna Peterson.

14. John Casparsson's (over the river), Anthony, baptized 6 months old, Sponsors John Mink Olof Frantsson, Mary Carter and Catharina Ericsson from Chestnut Hook.

15. John Farr's of Chester County, child Catharina, born February, 14th, baptized September 13, Sponsors Hans Petersson, Capt. Johan Von Calen, Rebecca Redly, Elizabeth Cadie.

16. Olof Von Naeman's (over the river), child Elizabeth baptized by Mr. Lidenius, September 14, Sponsorr, Jacob Van de Ver, Gabriel Peterson, Mrs. Catharina Van de Ver, Virgin. Elizabeth Van Neeman.

OLD SWEDES CHURCH

17. Wm. Philpot's child Anna baptized by Mr. Lidenius,

18. Anders Cock's, child Annika, born September 15, baptized September 27, Sponsors Johan Hindricksson, Philip Van de Ver, Johan Hindresson's wife Brita and Hindri Hindersson's wife Judith. 19 Cornelius Walraven's child Elizabeth baptized by Mr. Lidenius, October 14, Sponsors, Matz Stark, Zackarias Bertetsson and his wife Sara, Carin Savoy.

20. Henrin Wainam's (over the river, child), Anna, baptized by Mr. Lidenius, October 4, Sponsors, Anders Hindriesson, Anders Seneke, Ingrid Hindriesson, Johan Hindersson's wife Beata.

21. Anders Johan (over the river), child, Margareta, baptized by Mr. Lidenius November 1, Sponsors, Thomas Guilliamson, Hans Sher, Beata Hinderson, Catharina Guilliamson.

22. Anders Seneke's, (over the river), child, Anders baptised by Mr. Lidenius November 17, Sponsors, Albert Bilterback, Johan Hindricsson, Jr., Ingrid Hindriesson, Catharina Vainam.

23. Albert Billerback (over the river), child, Daniel, baptized by Mr. Lidenius November 17, Sponsors, Anders Senekesson, Seneke Senekesoon, Anna Sher and Beata Hindersson.

24. Johan Mink's (over river) child Johan, baptized by Mr. Lidenius, November 25, Sponsors Lucas Petersson, Johan Von Neeman, Anna Frantssen, Christina Franssen.

RECORD OF COMMUNICANTS IN CHRISTINA CONGREGATION IN THE YEAR 1713.

May 23. Peter Anderson, Maslander's wife Helekin, Maria Stalcop

May 31. Anders Mink Grelsson, Eric Ericsson and his wife Emma, Goran Eictken and his wife Kerstin, Old Mrs. Annika and her daughter Kerstin, Brita Clemens, Thomas John's wife Anna.

June 7. Jonas Walraven and his wife Annika with their daughter Brita.

June 21. Johan Gioding and his wife Annika.

July 5. Provost Erick Biörk and his wife, Mäns Gustafsson and his wife Catharine.

July 19. Anders Gustafsson and his wife Brita.

August 2. Elizabeth Von Neeman with her daughter Elizabeth.

August 3. Pastor Hessellius and his wife Sara, Mr. Lidenius,

EARLY CHURCH RECORDS OF NEW CASTLE COUNTY

Brita Stalcop, Johan Von Culen, Kerstin Pälsson, Maria Pälsson.

October 18. Peter Mänssons wife Carin, Olof Mänsson, Annika Tassawa.

November 1, Conrad Constantin and his wife Kerstin.

November 8. Peter Canpony and his wife Helena.

November 22. Provost Eric Biörk and his wife, Pastor Magister Hessellius and his wife Sara, Maria Stalcop.

November 29. Judith Van de Ver in her sickness.

December 2. Johan Cock in St. Georges in his sickness.

December 25. Jacob Hinderson and his wife Maline, George Litien and his wife Kerstin, Jacob Van de Ver and his wife, Hans Peitterson and his wife Sara, Gabriel Peterson and his wife Kerstin, Hans Sher and his wife Anna, Henric Roisko, Christian Petersson, Olof Nilsson and his wife Margaretta, who all liveon the other side of the river, and were communicated by Mr. Lidenius.

December 26. Johan Gustafsson and his wife Brita, Mäns Gustafsson and his wire Catharina, Johan Van de Ver, Judith Van de Ver.

RECORDS OF DEATHS IN CHRISTINA CONGREGATION IN 1713.

1. Peter Canpony's child Anders, buried the 5th of April.
2. Matz Tosawa's child Maria, buried the 28th of July.
3. Peter Classon's wife Dorothea, buried the 22d of September.
4. Paul Paulson (in Crane hook Church yard) 25th of October.
5. Gertrude Mink buried by Mr. Lidenius over the river, buried the 6th of November.
7. Johan Cock of St. Georges, buried in his own garden on the 15th December.

RECORD OF MARRIAGES IN CHRISTINA CONGREGATION 1714.

1. Johan Culen, Miss Christina Pâlsson, married, January 6.
2. Johan Van de Ver, Miss Maria Stalcop, married January 14
3. Paul Gustafsson, Miss Carin Bethiem, married February 4.
4. Henric Garrison, Miss Kerstin Constantin, married April 3.
5. Thomas Johnsson, widow Margareta Samueldotter, married September 7.
6. Johannes Mânsson, Miss Ingeburg Stedham, married September 21.
7. Edward Robinson, Miss Margaretta Classon, married September 23.

OLD SWEDES CHURCH

RECORD OF MARRIAGES IN CHRISTINA CONGREGATION 1715.

1. Olof Palsson, widow Elizabeth Colesburg married February.
2. Revererd Abraham Lidenius, Miss Elizabeth Von Neeman married May 25.
3. Timotheus Lylofsson Stedham, Miss Elizabeth Van de Ver married June 7.
4. John Wright, Sarah Wright, from Maryland wedded with license of of the Governor, married June 20.
5. Lucas Lucasson Stedham, Miss Ingeburg La Quett, married October 26.
6. Enok Canly, widow Catharina Grantiem wedded in their house, married November 7.
7. Robin Peers, Miss Mary Simons, married November 25.
8. William Abraham, Miss Maria Constantin, wedded in the Parsonage, married December 1.

RECORD OF BAPTISMS WITH NAMES OF PARENTS AND SPONSORS IN THE YEAR 1714.

1. Richard Enos and wife, Susanna's child Joseph, a few months old, baptized January 17th, Sponsors Johan Von Culen and his wife Christina, Olof Pålson and Mariah Pälson.
2. Israel Petersson and wife, Marguretta's child Hans, born February 20th, baptized February 28th, Sponsors Pastor Hessellins Captain Hans Peterson, Mrs. Hellena Petersson, Stafan Tassawas wife Karin, and Miss Ingeborg Stedham.
3. Johan Tassawa and wife Annika's child Elias, born Jan. 21, baptized March 7th, Sponsors Wm. Van de Ver, Timotheus Bengtsson Stedham, Peter Petersson's wife Hellena and Miss Kiastin Conrad's dotter.
4. Aute Vainans and wife Marguretta's child Andreas, born February 2d, baptized March 21st, Sponsors Eskel Johansson, Miss Ingeberg Stedham and Miss Constantin.
5. Darby Whelan and wife Susa's child Richard, 4 months old, baptized April 18th, Sponsors Jacobus Van de Ver, Matthias Skagen, Olof Tossawa's widow Gertrude and Peter Mayer's wife Sara.
6. Regner Von Culen and wife Ingrid's child Kerstin, five months old, baptized April 25th, Sponsors Johan Von Culen, Peter Pálson, Mrs. Elizabeth Colesberg and Miss Magaretta Classon.

7. Peter Petersson Canpany and wife Hellena's child Johannes born June 3d, baptized June 6th, Sponsors Johannes Mánsson, Henrie Gruken, Máns Gustaf's wife Catharine, Miss Maria Snecker.

8. Edward Nelson and wife Sara's child Maria, born June 4th, baptized June 13th, Sponsors Peter Canpany, Jonas Stalcop, Samuel Stedham, Margaretta widow of Asmund, Miss Ingeberg La Quett, Miss Mary Skagan.

9. Staffan Cornelius and wife Wilhelmina's child Anders, born June 12; baptized June 20, Sponsors Peter Petersson from Brandywine, Conrad Constantine, Gustaf Cock's wife Anna.

10. Gustaf Gustafsson and wife Kerstin's child Nils, born June 19th, baptized June 27, Sponsors Martin Gustafsson, John Walraven, Anders Gustaf's wife Brita, Johan Gustaf's wife Brita.

11. Martin Gustafsson and wife Brita's child Jonas, born May 23th, baptized August 29th, Sponsors Pastor Hessellius, I Swedberg, Mrs Sara Hesellius, Mrs. Maria Braun.

12. Christiern Joransson and wife Elizabeth's child Christina born August 27, baptized August 29th, Sponsors Matz Petersson, Peter Canpony, Mrs. Kustin Constantine, Mrs. Brita Stalcop.

13. The young Peter Mänsson and wife Annika's child Olof, born August 20th, baptized August 30th, Sponsors Johannes Mânsson, Timotheus Benedictus Stedham, The senior Peter Mânsson's wife Karin and Olof Tossawa's widow Gertrude.

14. Johannes de Foss and wife Johanua's child Matthias, six months old, baptized September 5, Sponsors Conrad Constantin, Máns Gustafsson, Mrs. Kerstin Garrison and Miss Mary Constantin.

15. George Wilhelms and wife, Kustin, child, James 6 years old baptised September 7, Sponsors, Peter Mansson, Michael Mayer, Thomas Johnson and his wife Margaretta, Mrs. Helena Van de Ver.

16. Michael Meyers and wife Anna's, child, Christopher two weeks old, baptized September 7, Sponsors, Peter Mansson, Thomas Jamison and his wife Margaretta.

17. Zacharias Bertilson, (over the river) and his wife Sara's child William, baptized September 12, Sponsors, Olof Van Neeman, Johan Bertilsson, Miss Anna Perssen and Miss Magdalena Von Neeman.

18. Pastor Andreas Hessillius and wife Sara's child Andreas, born September 15, baptized by his father, September 19, Spon, sors, Bishop Swedburg (in his place responded) Charles Springer,

OLD SWEDES CHURCH

Col. John France, Jonas Walraven, Peter Canpany. The late Magister Hessellius' widow Maria Bergia, in Sweden, in whose place was Helena Canpony, Lucas Stedham's wife Karin and Anders Gustafs' wife Brita.

19. Timothens Adamsson Stedham and wife Engilke's child Maria born September 18, baptized September 26, Sponsors Capt. Hans Petersson, Anders Cock, Jacob Van de Ver, Hans Petersson's wife Annika, Anders Cock's wife Sara.

20. Peter Mansson and wife Annika's child Kerstin (from Prince Morris), one year old, baptized September 26, Sponsors Conrad Constantin, Jonas Walraven's wife Annika, Mrs. Kerstin Garrisson.

21. Joran Andersson and wife Maria's child Elizabeth(from St. Georges) 4 weeks old, baptized September 28, Sponsors Peter Andersson, Johan Ivarson's widow Elizabeth Ivarson who just after the birth had privately baptized the child, Peter Andersson's wife Magdalena.

22. Jons Anders Joransson and wife Sara's child Jons,(from St. Georges) 4 weeks old, baptized September 28, Sponsors John Ivarson, Matz Ericsson, Johan Ivarson's wife Maria, Miss Kasin Ivasson.

23. Alberti Volbach and wife Barbro's child Peters, born September 25, baptized October 3, Sponsors Peter Canpany in Matz Petersson's place; Hendric Hendricsson, Anders Gustaf's wife Brita.

24. Johan Stalcop and wife Maria's child Christina, born October 20, baptized October 24, Sponsors Matz Petersson, Swen Gustafsson and his wife Catharina, from Wicacoe, Johan Gustafsson's wife Brita, Miss Maria Petersson.

25. Mans Gustafsson and wife Catharina's child Maria, born November 4, baptized November 7, Sponsors Martin Gustafsson, Lucus Lucasson Stedham, Mrs. Maria Braun, Mrs. Helena Canpany.

26. Johan Didrick Elrod and wife Maria Magdalena's child, Agneta, born October 29, baptized November 8, Sponsors, Hans Piettersson, Peter Petersson from Brandywine, Hans Piettersson's wife Annika and Mrs. Brita Dunkin.

27. Johan Gustafsson and wife Brita's child Maria, born November 14, baptized November 17, Sponsors, Gustaf Gustafsson, Jr. Hindric Orban, Martin Gustaf's wife Brita, Miss Maria Petersson, Miss Maria Snecker.

28. Johan Johansson's child (over the river) Laurentz, baptized November 21, Sponsors, Olof Von Neeman, Martin Johnsson, Mrs. Anna Petersson, Mrs. Magdelena Von Neeman.

29. Lucas Petersson's child Abraham (over the river) baptized November 24, Sponsors Herr Abraham Lidenius, Johan Mink Elizabeth Mink 1715.

1715 1. William Maslander and wife Helena's child Maria, born October 27, 1714 baptized January 1st, Sponsors, Pastor Hesselius Jesper Walraven, Sara Hessellius, Miss Ingeborg Laquette.

2. Hendric Hendricsson and wife Judith's child Peter, born December 31, 1714, baptized January 3rd Sponsors, Pastor Hessellius and his wife Sara.

3. Bertil Johan and wife Maria's child from (Elk River) Maria 5 months old, baptized February 2nd at St. Georges, Sponsors, Matz Johansson, John Ivarsson and wife Maria and Walborg Ivarsdotter.

4. Måns Anderson and wife Elizabeth's child Matz (from St. Georges) born December 31, 1714, baptized February 2nd. Sponsors, Peter Holsten, Johan Anderson, James Anderson's wife Sara John Ivarsson's wife Maria.

5. Paul Gustafson and wife Karin's child Gustaf, 6 weeks old baptized, February 6th, Sponsors, Hendric Stedham, Timotheus Lylofson Stedham, Edward Robinson's wife Margaretta and Johan Tossawa's wife Annika.

6. William Van de Ver's old negro Christian, baptized February 20th, Sponsors, Jonas Stalcop and Miss Judith Van de Ver.

7. Hans Sher and wife Annika's child Isaiah (over the river) baptized April 10th, Sponsors, Rev. Abraham Lideuius, John Van Neemeen, Miss Catharina Stalcop, Miss Carin Guilliamson.

8. Johan Dickman's child, Mariah (over the river) baptized April 10th, Sponsors, Anders Hendricsson, Margaretta Billerback.

9. Samuel Hals and Anna Elizabeth's child George, born 2 weeks before Christmas, baptized April 17th after having been previously baptized from necessity by his mother, Sponsors, Carl Springer and his wife Maria, Miss Judith Van de Ver.

10. Simon Johansson and wife Annika's child Olof of Elk River, 5 months old baptized May 15th, Sponsors, Regner Von Culen, Jacob Hendricsson from Cranehook, Olof Pálsson's wife Elizabeth, Eric Ericsson's wife Annika.

11. Joseph Hodges and wife Catharina's child Joshua, born April 14th, baptized May 15th, Sponsors, Pastor Hessellius and his wife Sara, Anders Kock and Johan Henderson's wife Brita.

OLD SWEDES CHURCH

12. Robin Pickman and wife Sara's child Anna (over the river) baptized May 15th Sponsors, Abraham Savoy, Miss Anna Persson Miss Sara Bertilsson.

13. Cornelius Corneliisson's child Jacob (over the river) baptized May 15th, Sponsors, Jacobus Van de Ver Hindric Petterson, Miss Anna Frantssen, Miss Grenilla Bertilsson.

14. Philip Van de Ver and wife Elizabeth's child Peter born May 11th, baptized May 22nd, Sponsors. Timotheus Lylofsson Stedham, Jonas Stalcop, Coruelius Van de Ver, widow Margaretta, Miss Elizabeth Van de Ver.

15. Mâns Pâlsson and wife Margaretta's child Pâl, born May 18th, baptized May 29th, Sponsors, Margaretta Hessellins, Constantıns Constantin, Hans Pietterson's wife Anna.

16. Johan Classon's child Oney (over the river) baptized June 3rd, Sponsors, Jacobus Van de Ver, Jean Savoy, Miss Karin Guilliamson.

17. Hendric Vainam's child Lars , (over the river,) baptized June 3rd, Sponsors, Johan Hindricson, Martin Johnson, Ana Sher, Catharine Hendricson.

18. Johan Johanson and wife Hanna's child Lydia, (from Elk river,) 7 months old, baptized June 5th, Sponsors, Gustaf Gustafsson, Jr., Martin Gustafson, Jonas Walraven's wife Annika, Martin Gustafsson's wife Brita.

19. Jacob Stelle and wife Rebeca's child Maria, born June 22nd, baptized July. 3rd, Sponsors, Conrad Constantin, Martin Gustafsson and his wife Brita, Geisee the wife of Peter Pâlsson, Sen., Martin Gustaf's wife Brita.

20. Hugh Simons and wife Francina's child Christina, 16 years old, baptized July 8th, Sponsors, Carl Springer and his wife Maria.

21. Johan Oins and wife Elizabeth's child Catharine, 6 weeks old, baptized July 17th, Sponsors Peter Mânsson, Anders Stalcop, Miss Helena Petersson, Miss Sara Mânsson,

22. Hendric Garrisson and wife Kerstin's child Hendrick, born July 17th, baptized July 24th, Sponsors, Conrad Constantin, Johan Garresson, Peter Pâlsson's wife Geisie, Maria Constantin.

23. Hugh Simmons and wife Francina's daughter Mary, 20 years old, baptized July 31st, Sponsors, Anders Cock Staffen, Cornelius wife Willaminke.

24. Hugh Simmons and wife Francina's son Charles, 27 years old, baptized August 7th, Sponsors, Johan Gustafsson, Mâns Gustaf's wife Catharina.

25. Peter Meyer and wife Sara's child Abraham, born May 7th, baptized May 14th, Sponsors Pastor Hessellins and his wife Sara, Timotheus Lylofson Stedham, Annika the wife· of Peter Mnsson, Jr.

26. Ambrosius Loudon and wife Brita's child Jesper, born May 9th, baptized May 14th, Sponsors, Martin Gustafsson, Lucas Stedham, Jr., Mrs. Maria Braun, Miss Sara Jespesdotter Walraven.

27. Zackarias Didricsson and wife Helena's child Peter, born July 21st, baptized August 14th, Sponsors, Thomas Jansson, Michael Meyer, Thomas Johnson's wife Margareta, Timotheus Stedham's wife Elizabeth.

28. Edward Robinsson and wife Margaretta's child Richard, born August 30th, baptized September 11th, Sponsors, George Whiteside, Peter Classon, Mrs. Maria Braun, Mrs Walborg Classon.

29. Cornelius Walraven and wife Wolborg's child Johannas, (in St. Georges,) 5 weeks old, baptized October 4th, Sponsors, James Joransson Andersson, Mâns Andersson, Mrs. Maria Ivars, Miss Catharina Ivars.

30. Staffan Tossawa and wife Catharina's child Catharina, born September 30th, baptized October 9th, Sponsors, Israel Petersson, Timotheus Llyofson Stedham, Mrs. Helena Petersson, John Gustafsson's wife Brita.

31. Johanes Mânsson and wife Ingeborg's child Peter, born October 14th, baptized October 16th, Sponsors, Peter Mâusson, Christiern Brinburg, Lucas Stedham, Jr., Lucas Stedham's wife Carin, John Gustaf's wife Brita, Miss Sara Mânsson.

32. Johan Von Culen and wife Kerstin's child Johan, born October 19th, baptized October 23rd, Sponsors, Eric Erricson from Cranehook, Peter Classon and his wife Wolborg, Miss Mary Pâlsson.

33. Johan Link and wife Anna's child Johan, 2 years old, baptized November 5th, Sponsors, Johan Von Culen, Pâl Pâlsson and his wife Elizabeth.

34. Johan Grantrem's widow's children:

35. Carl, about 12 years old,
36. Helena, 7 years old,
37. Ambrosius, 5 years old,

baptized November 7th, Sponsors Enoch Canby, Peter Anderson's wife Magdalena, and Sara Hessellius for the youngest, in whose place stood Peter Anderson's wife Magdalena.

37. Anders Cock and wife Sara's child Brita, 7 weeks old,

OLD SWEDES CHURCH

baptized December 11th, Sponsors, Conrad Constantine, Timotheus Lylofsson Stedham, Eric Anderson's wife Brita, Miss Magdalena Petersdotter.

38. Jacob Van de Ver and wife Maria's child Jacob, born November 30th, baptized December 12, Sponsors, Pastor Hessellius, Peter Petersson, Miss Judith Van de Ver, Miss Magdalena Petersdotter.

39. Janson and wife Susanna's child Johan, 8 weeks old baptized December 8th, (of German birth and Presbyterians) Sponsors, Johan Willian Lerchenzciler, Anders Gustaf's wife Brita. (a)

RECORD OF BURIALS, 1714.

1. Thomas Jonsson's wife Anna, buried April 21st.
2. Staffan Cornelius' son Cornelius, buried January 2nd.
3. Joseph Clayton's wife Ella, buried July 11th.
4. Johan Anderson's wife Catharine, buried September 7th.
5. Johan Gustafsson's child Maria, buried December 5th.
6. Michael Meyer's child Christopher, buried December 22nd.

BURIALS, 1715.

1. Peter Petersson Canpany, buried February 6th.
2. Staffan Tossawa, buried February 8th.
3. Magdalena Stubby, buried March 6th.
4. Anders Gustafsson's child Johannes, buried March 11th.
5. Richard Mankin, buried March 18th.
6. Anton Vainam's mother Elizabeth, buried March 24th.
7. Morton Gustafsson's child Jonas, buried March 27th.
8. Peter Cock } buried in their garden at St. Georges
9. Magnus Cock } March 30th.
10. Hindric Johanson Orkan, buried April 3rd.
11. James Davis, buried April 3rd.
12. Albertus Wolback, buried April 4th.
13. Johan Iwarson, buried in his garden at St. George's, April 5th.
14. Edward Wilsson's wife Sara.
15. Wm. Skagan's widow Elizabeth, buried May
16. Johan the child of Peter Mânsson, Jr., buried May 16th.
17. Daniel, the servant of Peter Mânsson's son, buried June 29.
18. Johan Robinsson, buried August 3rd.

a. Hereafter the names of sponsors, etc., will be omitted. Also the record of communicants at each celebration of the communion.

19. Johan Stalcop's child Christina, buried September 12th
20. Johan Gustaf's child Swen, buried September 23rd.
21. Johan Oin's wife Elizabeth.

RECORD OF MARRIAGES 1716.

1. Anders Gustafsson Johan's Son and Miss Sara Månsson, married January 3d.

3. Jonas Stalcop and Miss Judith Van de Ver, married January 5th.

3. Hendric Stedham and Miss Elizabeth Tossawa, married January 26th.

4. Erasmus Stedham and widow Helena Petersson, married May 11th.

5. Jasper Walraven and Miss Maria Snecker, married May 24th.

6. Joseph Barker and Miss Johanna Clayton, married September 27th.

7. William Forehead and Miss Maria Stedham, married November 6th.

RECORD OF BAPTISMS 1716.

1. Gustaf Cock and wife Anna's child Catharina, born December 29th, 1715, baptized January 1st.

2. Peter Classon and wife Walborg's child Jesper, born February 21st, baptized February 27th.

3. William Abraham and wife Maria's child Joseph, born February 18th, baptized March 4th.

4. Ante Wainan and wife Margaretta's child Maria, born March 8th, baptized March 11th.

5. Martin Gustafsson and wife Brita's child Gustaf, born March 19th, baptized March 25th.

6. Olof Pålsson and wife Elizabeth's child Susanna, baptized April 4th, 3 weeks old.

7. Anders Loinan and wife Brita's child Joran, born May 19th, baptized May 27th.

8. Jonas Stalcop and wife Judith's child Johan, born May 26th, baptized June 3d.

9. Olof Månson and wife Anna's child Johannes, (in St. Georges) baptized June 5th.

10. Richard Enos and wife Susanna's child Elizabeth, born March 30th, baptized June 17th.

11. Lucas Lucasson Stedham and wife Ingeborg's child Peter, born June 16th, baptized June 24th.

12. Gustaf Hessellius and wife Lydia's child Andreas, born July 28th, baptized July 29th.

13. Israel Peterson and wife Margaeretta's child Lylof, born July 27th, baptized August 5th.

14. Staffan Cornelius and wife Williminka's child Gustaf, born August 3d, baptized August 5th.

15. Michael Meyers and wife Anna's child William, born July 16th, baptized August 12th.

16. Simon Johansson and wife Anna's child Maria, (in Elk River,) baptized August 12th, 8 weeks old.

17. William Maslander and wife Helena's child William born August 17th, baptized September 9th.

18. Johan Stalcop and wife Maria's child Matthias, born September 26th, baptized September 30th.

19. Bille Cock and wife Emma's child Johan, baptized October 21st, 10 months old.

20. Timotheus Adamsson Stedham and wife Engelke's child Magdalena, (necessary baptized September 4th.

21. Pastor Hessellius and wife Sara's child Petrus, born November 7th, baptized November 11th.

22. Hindric Garrisson and wife Kerstin's child Conrad, born November 16th, baptized November 18th.

23. Johannes de Foss and wife Hannah's child Anne, baptized November 25th, 10 months old, and only through the neglect of parents and contempt of all advice without the least excuse has been kept from baptism unto this day.

24. Mâns Gustafsson and wife Catharine's child Anders, born November 19th, baptized November 28th.

25. Erasmus Stedham and wife Helena's child Andreas, born November 22nd, baptized November 25th.

26. Isabel Atkinson baptized December 23, twenty-one years old.

BURIALS 1716.

1. Ante Vainan's child Staphan, buried March 30th.
2. Eric Ericson (from Crane hook,) buried November 8th.
3. Olof Tossawa's widow Gertrude, buried September 25th.
4. Pastor Hesselliu's child Petrus, buried November 25th.

In Holy Trinity Church close to Provost Biork's child Petrus which can be seen in the first church book page 89.

EARLY CHURCH RECORDS OF NEW CASTLE COUNTY

MARRIAGES, 1717.

1. Christopher Stedham and Miss Johanna Von der Culen, married Jan. 3.

2. Cornelius Ja Quette and Miss Maria Pâlsson, married May 14.
3. Anders Stalcop and Widow Barbro Wolback, married May 23.

4. Nathaniel Tucker and Mrs. Catharina Ivarsson, married October 31st.
5. Johan Oins and Miss Margaretta Stedham, married November 19th.

1717, June 17 - Mr. Gioding began holding school in Johan Gustafsson's house, ... the pastor examined the children as to their proficiency ...

1. Gustaf Johan Gustafsson, 9 years old, can read his catechism tolerably well, and also answers very well various questions of christian instruction.

2. Peter John Gustafsson, 7 years old, recites the ten commandments tolerably well.

3. Mary Geens, 9 years old, can read Swedish and say the ten commandments.

4. Gustaf Mâns Gustafsson, 7 years old, can read Swedish tolerably well

5. Mâns Gustaf's daughter Annika, 6 years old, can spell Swedish tolerably well.

6. Anders Gustaf's daughter Catherina, 12 years old, can read in a book, but must begin to learn to spell right.

7. Peter Stalcop Johansson's son, 5 years old, knows the letters.

8. Margaretta, the late Peter Stalcop's daughter, 11 years old, reads Swedish indifferently well, but must learn to spell anew.

9. Thomas Davis, 11 years old, can spell Swedish a little.

10. Annika, Anders Gustaf's daughter, 8 years old, can spell a little.

11. Ante Vainan's son Lars, 7 years old, knows the letters.

OLD SWEDES CHURCH

BAPTISMS 1717.

1st. Hindric Hindricsson and wife Judith's child Zacharias, born January 16th, baptized January 20th.

2. Philip Van de Ver and wife Elizabeth's child Maria, born January 20th, baptized January 27th.

3. Zacharias Didricsson and wife Helena's child Cornelius, born February 7th, baptized February 10th.

4. Henry Powell and wife Elizabeth Kent's child Anna Prudens, 6 years old, baptized February 9th.

5. William Forehead and wife Mary's child Margaretta, born February 19th, baptized March 4th.

6. Jacob Stille and wife Rebbecca's child Peter, born March 8th, baptized March 10th.

7. Christopher Meyer and wife Matta's child Margaretta, 7 weeks old, baptized March 10th.

8. Johan Stout and wife Anna's child Joseph, (from St. Georges,) 6 months old, baptized March 10th.

9. Christiern Joran and wife Elizabeth's child Margaretta, (from Fish point,) born November 26th, 1716, baptized Mar. 19.

10. Ambrosius London and wife Brita's child Ambrosius, born March 17th, baptized March 24th.

11. Rees Prees and his strumpet Eleonora Morris' illegitimate child Catharine, 11 months old, baptized in the house of Mr. Springer, April 8th.

12. William Howell and wife Margaretta's child Patience, 1 year old, baptized April 22nd.

13. Peter Mânson, Jr., and wife Anna's child Johannes, born April 22nd, baptized April 24th.

14. Bertil Johansson and wife Maria's child Susanna, (Elk river,) born March 17th, baptized May 5th.

15. Pâl Gustafsson and wife Catharina's child Peter, 8 weeks old, baptized May 19th.

16. The Quaker Oliver Matthews and wife Elizabeth's son William, 20 years old, baptized June 9th.

17. Gustaf Gustafsson and wife Kerstin's child Swen, born July 17th, baptized July 21st.

18. Johan Tossawa and wife Anna's child Hindric, born July 15th, baptized July 21st.

19. William Richardson and wife Mary's daughter Anna, 7 years old, the 5th of last April, baptized July 31st, in the house of Samuel Barker.

EARLY CHURCH RECORDS OF NEW CASTLE COUNTY

20. William Richardson and wife Mary's child Mary, one year old 17th of March last, baptized July 31st in the house of Samuel Barker.

21. William Hicks and wife Anna's child William, born December 17, 1715, baptized July 31st, in the house of Samuel Barker.

22. Samuel Hall and wife Anna Elizabeth's child Samuel 7 weeks old, baptized August 4th.

23. Matz Hamelin and his deceased wife Ingeborg's child Anna (in St. Georges,) born December 31, 1716, baptized in the house of Joran Anderson Sept 17th.

24. Hendrich Stedham and wife Elizabeth's child Johannes, born September 14th, baptized September 22nd.

25. Olof Pålson and wife Elizabeth's child Olof, born September 26th, baptized October 2nd.

26. Christopher Stedham and wife Johanna's child Catharina born September 26th baptized October 6th.

27. Lucas Stedham Jr. and wife Ingeborg's child Christina, born October 12th, baptized October 13th.

28. Johannes Mânson and wife Ingeborg's child Lucas, born October 13th, baptized October 20th.

29th. William Cleany and wife Maria's child Rebecca, born October 19th, baptized October 27th.

30. Anders Loinam and wife Brita's child Maria, born November 29th, baptized December 1st.

31. Anders Cock and wife Sara's child Helena born December 5th, baptized December 13th.

RECORD OF BURIALS 1717.

1. Johan Tossawa's child Hindric, buried September 15th.
2. William Abraham's wife Maria, buried September 15th.
3. Richard Enos' child Joseph buried at Cranehook October 2nd.
4. Hindric Stedham's wife Elizabeth, buried November 9th.
5. Anders Loinan's child Maria buried December 22nd.

RECORD OF MARRIAGES, 1718.

1. Mârtin Mârtinsson and Miss Kerstin Walraven, married May 8th.
2. Christopher Shegel and Miss Anna Maria Aistrin, married May 15th,

OLD SWEDES CHURCH

3. Johan Jaquett and Miss Hannah Ellis, married November 6th.

4. Johan Andersson (from St. Georges,) and Miss, Elizabeth Iwarssen, married November 12th.

5. Johan Eaton and Miss Mary Skagan, married November 30th.

6. Johnathan Otley and Miss, Debora Manly, married December 8th.

BAPTISMS 1718.

1. Johan Barnet and wife Margaretta's children Robert, 5 years old the 13th of March, baptized January 3rd.

2-3. Thomas and Jeremia twins, three years old the coming Easter, baptized same day.

4. Peter Classon and wife Walborg's child Margaretta, born March 3rd, baptized March 9th.

5. Anders Stalcop and wife Anna Barbro's child Catharina, born March 4th, baptized March 9th,

6. Johan Barnet and wife Margareta's child Carl, born March 8th, baptized March 16th.

7. Johan Didrick Elrod and wife Maria Magdalena's child Elizabeth, (from St. Georges,) born March 12th, baptized March 18th.

8. Jesper Walraven and wife Maria's child Elizabeth, born March 25th, baptized March 30th.

9. Thomas Elwood and wife Elizabeth's son William, (from Philadelphia,) 10½ years old, baptized April 16th.

10. Edward Robinsson and wife Margareta's child Jacob, 14 days old, baptized April 17th.

11. Anders Vainan and wife Margareta's child Peter, born April 17th, baptized April 20th.

12. Pastor Hessellius and wife Sara's child Emmanuel, born April 24th, baptized April 27th Sponsors, Mr. Gustaf Hessellius and his wife Lydia, *Herr Emmanuel Swedberg (in Sweden,) in whose place Christina Brunberg answered, Johan Stalcop, Jonas Walraven's wife Annika, Miss Mary Peterson.

13. Johan Barnet and wife Margareta's child Margareta, 9 years old, baptized May 11th.

14. Johannes de Foss and wife, Hanna's child Johan, born March 14th, baptized June 1st.

---

*Son of Bishop Swedberg, and founder of the New Church, called Swedenborgians.

17

15. Johan Eaton and the strumpet Elizabeth Nicssen's illegitimate child Maria, 3 months old, baptized June 1st.

16. Hâns Gustafsson and wife Catharina's child Catharina, born June 6th, baptized June 15th.

17. Cornelius Jaquett and wife Maria's child Johan, born June 24th, baptized July 20th.

18. Richard Enos and wife, Susanna's child Maria, 9 weeks old baptized August 17th.

19. Johan Stalcop and wife Maria's child Tobias, born September 29th, baptized October 5th.

20. William Maslander and wife Helena's child Abraham, born October 12th, baptized August 19th.

21. Johan Von Culen and wife Kerstin's child Maria, born October 3rd, baptized October 19th.

22. Jacob Van de Ver and wife Hana's child Magdalena, born November 5th, baptized November 11th.

23. The Indians Meckanappit and Gertrude Toene's child Philip, 8 years old last August 15th, Sponsors, Johan Hindricsson and his wife Brita, who had adopted the boy for their foster child.

24. Thomas Bird and wife Sara's child Elizabeth, born September 15th, baptized December 8th.

25. Israel Petterson and wife Margareta's child Petrus, born December 2nd, baptzied December 9th.

26. Philip Van de Ver and wife Elizabeth's child Cornelius, born December 2nd, baptized December 10th.

27. Jonas Stalcop and wife Judith's child Annika, born December 10th; baptized December 14th.

28. Hindric Garresson and wife Kerstin's child Maria, born December 12th, baptized December 14th.

29. Mârtin Gustafsson and wife Brita's child Beata, born December 8th, baptized December 14th.

30. Michael Meyers and wife Anna's child David, born December 10th, baptized December 16th.

31. Timotheus Adamsson Stedham and wife Engelke's child Israel, born December 11th, baptized December 20th.

OLD SWEDES CHURCH

BURIALS 1718.

1. Christopher Stedham's child Catharina, buried July 4th.
2. Cornelius Ja Quett's child Johan, buried September 4th.
3. William Van de Ver, buried October 11th.
4. Peter Mânsson, buried November 8th.
5. Philip Van de Ver's child Cornelius, buried December 19th.

MARRIAGES 1719.

1. Edward Brennen and Miss Mary Butcher, married January 7th.
2. Hans Piettersson Smith and Miss Elizabeth Oins, married February 5th.
3. John Wilder and Margaretta Van de Ver, married April 30.
4. Christiern Brynberg and Miss Maria Petersson, married July 2nd.
5. Samuel Stedham and Miss Annika Tossawa, married September 17th.
6. Hindric Stedham and Miss Catharina Van de Ver, married November 10th.
7. Jacobus Pâlsson and Miss Mary Davis, married Dec. 29th.

BAPTISMS, 1719.

1. Ambrosius London and wife Brita's child Helena, born January 1st, baptized January 11th.
2. Jacob Stille and wife Rebecca's child Susanna, born January 19th, baptized January 25th.
3. Niclas Bishop and wife Dorcas' child Johan, born October 6th, 1718, baptized January 28th.
4. Erasmus Stedham and wife Helena's child Israel, born February 12th, baptized immediately after birth.
5. Hendric Hendricsson and wife Judith's child Christina, born February 27th, baptized March 1st.
6. Anders Loinan and wife Brita's child Catharina, born March 6th, baptized March 8th.
7. William Cleany and wife Maria's child William, born April 22nd, baptized May 3rd.
8. Joseph Barker and wife Johanna's child Maria, born September 24, 1718, baptized May 17th.
9. Johan Stout and wife Anna's child Johan, born January 28th, baptized May 17th.

EARLY CHURCH RECORDS OF NEW CASTLE COUNTY

10. Mårten Mårtensson and wife Kersten's child Matthias, born May 14th, baptized May 18th.

11. William Forehead and wife Maria's child Johan, born May 27th, baptized May 31st.

12. Edward Branin and wife Mary's child Annika, born May 15th, baptized May 31st.

13. Paul Kilpos and wife Catharine's child Johan, born May 3rd, baptized June 7th.

14. Gustaf Pållsson and wife Marita's child Sara, born February 19, 1716, baptized June 7th.

15. Gustaf Pålsson and wife Marita's child, Debora, born January 14, 1718, baptized June 7th.

16. Olof Pålsson and wife Elizabeth's child Peter, born June 30th, baptized from necessity July 19th.

17. Joseph Coxe and wife Maria's child Margarita, 4 months and two weeks old, baptized July 19th.

18. Anders Stalcop and wife Barbara's child Andreas, born August 14th, baptized August 23rd.

19. Jesper Walraven and wife Maria's child Christina, born September 2nd, baptized September 24th.

20. Christopher Meyer and wife Matta's child Philip, born August 27th, baptized September 20th.

21. Christopher Stedham and wife Hanna's child Adam, born September 29th, baptized October 10th.

22. George Kraut and wife Anna Maria's child Johannes, 9 months old, baptized (at Amiasland) November 3rd.

23. Peter Månsson and wife Annika's child Bengt, born October 31st, baptized November 8th.

24. Philip Van de Ver and wife Elizabeth's child Andreas, born November 25th, baptized November 29th.

25. Cornelius Ja Quett and wife Maria's child Casparus, born November 14th, baptized November 29th.

26. Henry Fowler and wife Mary Andersson's child William, 13 days old, baptized December 6th.

27. Anders Cock and wife Sara's child Andreas born December 12th, baptized December 20th.

28. Christiern Brynberg and wife Karia's child Elizabeth, born December 14th, baptized December 20th.

OLD SWEDES CHURCH

BURIALS 1719.

1. Eramus Stednam's child Israel, buried February 15th.
2. Johan Wilhelm Lerchenzeiler's wife Susanna, buried July 14th.
3. Edward Brannin's child Annika, buried July 24th.
4. Aaron Johansson's widow Barbro buried September 20th.,
5. Matz Petersson buried September 27th.
6. Edward Robinsson's wife Margaretta, buried October 30th.
7. Pastor Hessellius' child Emmanuel, buried October 6th in the church close to his deceased brother Peter.
8. Casparus Palatinus buried November 29th.

RECORD OF MARRIAGES 1720.

1. Samuel Kirk and Mrs. Alice Van de Ver, married January 8th, with Governor's license.
2. Johan William Lerchenzeiler and widow Margareta Van de Ver, married April 19th.
3. Valentine Kock and widow Elizabeth Joransson, married April 20th.
4. William Ver de Man and Miss Magdalena Petersson, married April 21st.
5. Samuel Peterson and Kerstin Martens, married May 26th.
6. Pastor Herr Samuel Hessellius and Miss Brita Leikan, married June 9th, by license.
7. Israel Stalcop and Miss Sussanna Jaquett by license, married August 9th.
8. Johnathan Kirk and Miss Mary Andersson, by license married August 16th.
9. Johan Seeds and Miss Sara Jespersdotter Walraven, married August 22nd.
10. William Kellam and Miss Mary Reynolds by license, married August 23rd.
11. Edward Robinsson and Mrs Elizabeth Petersson by license, married October 18th.
12. Peter Pålsson of Sheephook and Miss Catharina Cock, married Oct. 20.
13. Hindrick Snicker and Miss Catharina Robinsson, married November 1st.
14. Jacob Jacobsson Van de Ver and Miss Margaret Mânsson, married November 2nd.
15. Johan Garrisson Frill and Miss Anna Pålsson, married November 15th.

EARLY CHURCH RECORDS OF NEW CASTLE COUNTY

BAPTISMS 1720.

1. Provost Magister Hessellius and wife Sara's child Jonas, born January 7th, baptized January 10th.
2. Anders Vainan and wife Margareta's child Jacob, born January 16th, baptized January 20th.
3. Johan Wilder and wife Margareta's child William, born January 30th, baptized February 7th.
4. John Cölen and wife Kerstin's child Jacob, born February 2nd, baptized February 21st.
5. Johannes Mânsson and wife Ingeborg's child Johannes, born March 4th, baptized March 8th.
6. Peter Ja Quett and wife Marta's child Maria, born March 12th, baptized March 19th.
7. William Cock and wife Emy's child Hanna, 1 year, 2 months, 3 day old, baptized April.
8. Gustaf Gustafsson and wife Kerstin's child Susanna, born March 25th, baptized April 3rd.
9. Peter Classon and wife Walborg's child Johannes, born April 2nd, baptized April 10th.
10. Joseph Cantrel and wife Catharina's child Hanna, born March 20th, baptized April 15th.
11. Mâns Gustafsson and wife Catharina's child Jesper, born May 22nd, baptized May 29th.
12. Timotheus Lylofsson Stedham and wife Elizabeth's child Cornelius, born May 22nd, baptized May 29th.
13. Olof Mânsson and wife Annika's child Abraham, born June 7th, baptized June 12th.
14. Gustaf Pâlsson Kilpos and wife Marta's child Peter, born June 26th, baptized July 13th.
15. The Quakers, Alphonsi Kirk and wife Abigail's son Jonathan, 21 years old, baptized in (*a*) St. James' Church, July 10th.
16. Stephen Cornelius and wife Wiliaminka's child Elizabeth, born July 6th, baptized July 10th.
17. Gustaf Cock and wife Annika's child Andreas, born May 23rd, baptized July 11th.
18. Johannes de Foss and wife Hanna's child Thomas, born May 12th, baptized August 21st.
19. Samuel Stedham and wife Annika's child Jacob, born September 19th, baptized September 25th.

a. The English Church at Stanton.

OLD SWEDES CHURCH

20. Johan Bateman and wife Susanna's child William, some months old, baptized at St. James' Church, October 9th.

21. Hans Jürgen Smith and wife Maria's child Peter, born October 12th, baptized October 14th. Sponsors, Herr Provost Eric Biörk, absent in Sweden, in whose place answered the Provost and Pastor in Christina, Mr. Andreas Hessellius, Johan Gustafs' son and his wife Brita, Mrs. Maria Stalcop.

22. Anders Loinan and wife Brita's child Andreas, born November 2nd, baptized November 8th.

23. Mr. Christiern Brynberg and wife Maria's child Swen, born November 17th, baptized November 20th.

24. Peter Meyer and wife Sara's child Aron, born November 8th, baptized November 22nd.

25. Abenezer Empson and wife Susanna's child Maria, born September 19, baptized November 9th.

26. Lucas Stedham Jr. and wife Ingeborg's child Maria, born December 2nd, baptized December 4th.

27. Christopher Hollin and wife Elizabeth's child Eleanor 3 months old, baptized December 11th, at St. James church.

s8. Hendrick Garissons and wife Kustin's child Johanney born December 14th baptized December 18th.

29. William Maslander and wife Helekin's child Elizabeth, born December 19th, baptized December 26th.

30. James Walter and wife Elizabeth's child Elizabeth, born December 22nd, baptized December 28th.

BURIALS 1710.

1. Johan Gioding buried January 2nd.
2. Christiern Brynberg's child Elizabeth buried January 29th.
3. Anders Vainan's child Jacob buried February 23rd.
4. Conrad Constantin's wife Kerstin buried March 12th.
5. Peter Ja Quett's child Maria buried in Peter Ja Quetts orchard March 31st.
6. Johannes de Foss' child Johannes buried April 19th.
7. Samuel Barker buried July 25th.
8. Anders Gustafson's daughter Brita 13½ years old, buried August 27th.

MARRIAGES 1721.

Joahn Twiggs to Helena Thomas, Feb. 16, 1721
Thomas Brackin to Martha Green, Dec. 21, 1721

EARLY CHURCH RECORDS OF NEW CASTLE COUNTY

RECORD OF BAPTISMS IN HOLY TRINITY AND ST. JAMES' (*b*)
CHURCHES, 1721.

1st Jeremy Ball & wife Mary's child William, born Dec. 16, 1720 bapt. Jan. 1, 1721. Sponsors, Thomas Ogle and Mary Ogle. (*c*)

2nd. William Howd and wife Margareta's child, Elizabeth, 2 years and 3 months old, bapt. Jan. 29.

3rd. Hans Petersson Smith and wife Elizabeth's child Maria, born Jan. 26, bapt. Jan. 29.

4. Mårten Gustafsson and wife Brita's child Jonas, born Jan. 25th, baptized Jan. 29th.

5. Mårten Mårtensson and wife Kerstin's child Jonas, born Jan. 31st, baptized Feb. 5th.

6. James Husten and wife Mary's child James, born Jan. 29th, baptized Feb. 12th.

7. Christopher Shligel and wife Mary's child Hanna, born Feb. 6th, baptized March 5th in St. James' Church.

8. Ambrosius Loodon and wife Brita's child Joseph, born Mar. 6th, baptized Mar. 12th.

9. Samuel Peterson and wife Kerstin's child Maria, born Mar. 7th, baptized March 12th.

10. Israel Petersson and wife Margareta's child Anders, born March 16th, baptized March 19th.

11. Johan Stalcop and wife Maria's child Catharina, born March 28th, baptized March 29th.

12. Richard Enos and wife Susanna's child Susanna, born Feb. 15th, baptized April 9th.

13. Jacob Stille and wife Rebecca's child Elizabeth, born April 3d, baptized April 10th.

14. Jacob Pålsson and wife Mary's child Peter, born April 8th, baptized April 10th.

15. Nicholas Bishop and wife Dorcas' child Susanna, born Jan. 24th, baptized May 7th.

16. Jonas Stalcop and wife Judith's child Carl, born May 8th, baptized May 14th.

17. Joseph Barker and wife Johanna's child Samuel, born March 30th, baptized May 21st.

18. James Robinson and wife Catharina's child Phœbe, born April 15th, baptized May 28th.

---

b. St. James, the English Church at Whiteley's Creek or White Clay Creek.

c. This was an English family.

OLD SWEDES CHURCH

19. Morgan Morgan and wife Catharina's child David, born May 12th, baptized May 28th.

20. Cornelius Ja Quett and wife Maria's child Maria, born June 1st, baptized June 4th.

21. William Kellam and wife Mary's child Parthenia, born June 13th, baptized June 15th.

22. Johan Montgomery and wife Anna Hallowday's child Anna 1 year old, baptized June 18th.

23. William McDonald and wife Mary's child Joseph, born April 24th, baptized June 18th.

24. William Cleany and wife Maria's child Carolus, born June 17th, baptized June 25th.

25. Hindrick Stedham and wife Catharina's child Hindrick, born June 20th, baptized June 25th.

26. Erasmus Stedham and wife Helen's child Maria, born June 23d, baptized June 25th.

27. Anders Stalcop and wife Barbro's child Philip, born June 20th, baptized June 25th.

28. Michael Meyer and wife Anna's child Margareta, born June 13th, baptized July 5th.

29. Israel Stalcop and wife Susanna's child Johan, born July 3d, baptized July 6th.

30. George Reed and wife Sara's child Sara, born June 11th, baptized Aug. 6th.

31. Johan Garretsson and wife Anna's child, Anna born Aug. 10 baptized August 13th.

32. Jacob Van de Ver and wife Maria's child Catharina, born August 20th, baptized August 27th.

33. Peter Palsson and wife Catharina's child Pawel, born August 14th, baptized August 27th.

34. Jesper Walraven and wife Maria's child Maria, born August 24th, baptized August 27th.

35. William Forehead and wife Maria's child Maria, born Aug. 13, baptized Sept. 24,

36. William Cann and wife Jane's child, William, 9 weeks old, baptised Oct. 1.

37. Thomas Perry and wife Mary's child Samuel, 4 weeks old, baptized in Great Arundal county, Maryland, Nov. 3.

38. Joathan Kirk and wife Mary's child James, 3 weeks old, baptized Nov. 19.

39. Joseph Champion and wife Mary's child, Mary, born Oct. 20, baptized Dec. 10.

EARLY CHURCH RECORDS OF NEW CASTLE COUNTY

40. Sanders McDuel and wife Jane's child Mary, 5 weeks old, baptized Dec. 31.

BURIALS 1721.

1. Ambrosius London's wife Brita, buried March 16.
2. Ambrosius London's child, Joseph, born March 6, buried March 29.
3. Johan Seed's wife Sara, buried April 4.
4. Jonas Stalcop's wife Judith, buried June 15.
5. Michel Meyer's child Margareta, buried July 11.
6. Erasmus Stedham's child, Maria, buried July 18.
7. Hindrick Garrisson's son, buried November 13.
8. Ambrosius London, buried December 4.
9. John Wilder's child, William, buried December 16.

MARRIAGES, 1722.

1. Joseph Pears to Mary Jackson, married Jan. 4th.
2. James Jordan to Hanna Brackin, married Feb. 2nd.
3. John Butcher to Sara Atkinson, married Aug. 15th.
4. Jonas Skagen to Annika Stedham, married Nov. 1st.
5. Van Holland to Sara Nicholas, married by Governor's license Nov. 13th.

RECORD OF BAPTISMS IN THE CHURCHES OF CHRISTINA, ST. JAMES (b) AND APPOQUINIMINK, (b) 1722.

1. George Jackson and wife Onar's daughter Mary, 20 years old, baptized January 1st.
2. Olof M nsson and wife Anna's child Susanna, born December 27th, 1721, baptized January 6th.
3. Henry Bradley and wife Catharina's child Elizabeth, 6 weeks old, baptized January 21st.
4. Johan Wilder and wife Margaretta's child William, born January 27th, baptized January 28th.
5 and 6. Anders Cock and wife Sara's children Adam and Catharina, born January 31st, baptized February 9th.
7. Johannes Mânson and wife Iugeborg's child Maria, born February 10th, baptized February 14th.
8. Johan Culen and wife Kerstin's child Anders, born February 5th, baptized February 18th.
9. Johan Didrick Elrod and wife Sara's child George Arendt, one month old, baptized in Appoquinimink Church, *March 4th.

(b) English churches. *Often spelt Apoquinimy.

OLD SWEDES CHURCH

10. Johan Cassel and wife Christina's child Johan, born January 25th, baptized in Appoquinimink Church March 4th.

11. Edward Hawkins and wife Ester's child Mary, born February 28th, baptized in Appoquinimink, March 4th.

12. George Williams and wife Sara's child Richard, born January 14th, baptized in Appoquinimink, March 4th.

13. Peter Mânsson and wife Margareta's child James from St. Georges, born January 3rd, baptized at Appoquinimink, March 4th.

14. William Monroe and wife Catharina's child Mary in St. Georges, 4½ years old, baptized at Bohemia at Isaac Von Bebber's, March 5th.

15. Christopher Stedham and wife Hanna's child Johan, 6 weeks old, baptized April 8th.

16. Joseph Cox and wife Mary's child Richard, 1½ years old, baptized April 28th.

17. Samuel Bushell and wife Alki's daughter Susanna, 14 years old, baptized at Bohemia, April 28th.

18. Samuel Bushell and wife Alki's daughter Catharina, 11¼ years old, baptized at Bohemia, April 28th.

19. Samuel Bushell and wife Alki's daughter Magdalena, 9½ years old, baptized at Bohemia, April 28th.

20. Samuel Bushell and wife Alki's daughter Ann, 6½ years old, baptized at Bohemia, April 28th.

21. Samuel Bushel and wife Alki's child Mary, born June 14th, 1720, baptized April 28th at Bohemia.

22. Johan Miller and wife Dorothy's child Killian, born January 8th, 1720, baptized in Bohemia, April 28th.

23. Johan Miller and wife Dorothy's child Johan, born November 8th, baptized April 28th at Bohemia.

24. Johan Sterling and wife Mary's child Rachel, 3½ years old, baptized September 28th at Bohemia,

25. Henry Skail and wife Alki's child Peter, 3½ years old, baptized April 28th at Bohemia.

26. Richard McCary and wife Esther's daughter Jane, 13 years and 4 months old, baptized April 29th at Bohemia.

27. Johan Smith and wife Charity's child Mary, 13 months old, baptized at Appoquinimink, April 29th.

28. Henry Skail and wife Alki's child Catharina, 16 months old, baptized May 27th at Bohemia.

29. Johan Bonny and wife Mary's child Johan, 1½ years old, baptized at Appoquinimink, May 27th.

30. Marten Sher and wife Maria's child Kerstin, born October 21st, 1721, baptized May 27th at Appoquinimink.

31. Johan Stout and wife Anna's child Cornelius, born December 2nd, 1721, baptized May 28th.

32. Augustin Cock and wife Anna's child Johan, born May 26th, baptized May 28th.

33. Lucas Stedham and wife Ingeborg's child Susanna, born June 28., baptized July 1st.

34. Peter Classon and wife Walborg's child Anna, born June 24th, baptized July 1st.

35. David Enoch and wife Helena's child Andreas, 6 months old, baptized July 1st.

30. Michal Meyer and wife Anna's child Maria, born July 3rd, baptized July 5th.

37. Johan Hayward and wife Margaretta Howel's child Rachel, born April 5, 1721 baptized July 5, 1722.

38. Mr. Dyer's child Henry, baptized at Appoquinimink, July 8th.

39. Johan Orchard and wife Margaretta's child Mary 3 months old, baptized at Appoquinimink, July 8th.

40. James Haley and wife Eleonora's child Mary, 3 months old, baptized at Appoquinimink, July 8th.

41. Marten Scottman and wife Elizabeth's child Mary, 6 months old, baptized July 8th.

42. Joseph Almond and wife Margaretta's son Solomon, 28 years old, baptized at Christina July 15th.

43. Henry Stedham and wife Catharina's child Margaretta, born July 29th, baptized August 5th.

44. Mans Gustafson and wife Catharina's child Sara, born August 3rd, baptized August 5th.

45. Aben Ezer Empson and wife Susanna's child Rebecca, born September 14th, baptized September 23rd.

46. Samuel Petersson and wife Kerstin's child Elizabeth, born September 23rd, baptized Semptember 30th.

47. Christian Brynberg and wife Maria's child Peter, born September 26th, baptized September 30th.

OLD SWEDES CHURCH

48. Sara Meyer's illegitimate child Jonathan, born October 2nd, baptized October 11th.

49. Philip Van de Ver and wife Elizabeth's child Tobias, born October 6th, baptized October 14th.

50. Robin Bird and wife Mary's child Rebecca, born October 13th, baptized October 21st.

51. Christopher Springer and wife Catharina's child Carolus born October 25th, baptized October 28th.

52. Thomas Harper and wife Elizabeth's child James born December 1st, baptized December 2nd in Bohemia.

53. Jacob Stille and wife Rebecca's child Margaretta, born December 18th, baptized December 23rd.

54. Johan Seed and wife Brita's child Joseph, born Decembe, 22nd, baptized December 25th.

55. Job Hill and wife Mary's child Mary, born October 8th, baptized December 30th at Appoquinimink.

56. Adam Leicestner and wife Magdalena's child Johannes, born November 29th, baptized December 31st, at Bohemia.

57. Donald Kirkpatrick, and strumpet Mary Tib's illegitimate child Adam, 2 weeks old, baptized December 31st, at Bohemia.

58. Hans George Smith and wife Mary's child Johan, born December 28th, baptized December 30th.

BURIALS, 1722.

1. Henry Garrisson, Jr., buried January 10th.
2. Widow Brita Dunken, buried January 13th.
3. Sara Reinhold, buried January 24th.
4. Henry Garrisson Jr's. son Hindrick, buried February 4th.
5. Johan Tossawa, buried March 25th.
6. Johan Garrisson, buried April 6th.
7. Olof Tossawa, buried April 25th.
8. Hindric Hindricsson's daughter Anna, buried May 9th.
9. Mr. Aben Ezer Empsson's child Rebecca, buried September 25th.

MARRIAGES, 1723

1. Gustaf Pålsson and Sara Thomas, married January 23.
2. Anders Pålsson and Elizabeth Berry, married February 21.
3. Richard Garrisson and Jane Carter. Government License, married Feb. 24, 1723
4. Thomas Scott and Catharina Justis, married July 30.
5. Peter Cordreat and Elizabeth Owin, in Appoquinimink with license, married August 4.

EARLY CHURCH RECORDS OF NEW CASTLE COUNTY

6. Anders Hindricksson and Maria Hindricksson, married November 6.
7. Lylof Stedham and Anna Garrisson, married Nov. 12.
8. Thomas West and Kerstin Tossawa, married November 20.
9. William Audersson and Rachael Mårten in New Castle, married November 21.
10. Michael Hamelin and Margareta Stannings, married November 26.
11. Johan Parker and Maria Rees at New Castle, married November 27.
12. Caleb Hall and Helena Hooker, married November 29.

BURIALS 1723.

1. Adam Stedham, buried January 9th.
2. Peter Månsson in St. Georges, buried January 29th.
3. Israel Petersson's child Hance, buried March 14th.
4. Peter Månsson in Bokton, buried July 14th.
5. Peter Månsson in Bokton, son Bengt, buried July 18th.
6. Johannes Månsson's son Petrus, buried August 17th.
7. Israel Petersson's child Susanna, buried September 13th.
8. Jesper Walraven's wife Maria, buried Nov. 12.
9. James Seneke's widow Darkish, buried November 13.
10. Margareta Stalcop's illegitemate child Joseph, buried November 21st.

BAPTISMS IN CHRISTINA AND APPOQUINIMINK.

1. The Provost Magister Andreas Hessellius and wife Sara's child Maria, born January 1st, baptized January 6th.
2. Garret Garrisson and wife Esther's child Elizabeth, ½ year old, baptized January 13th.
3. George Hugel's negress Alki's daughter Anna, a mulatto, 20 years old, baptized February 3d.
4. Peter Pålsson and wife Catharina's child Andreas, born January 21st, baptized February 3d.
5. Mårten Mårtensson and wife Kerstin's child Andreas, born March 11th, baptized March 15th.
6. William Cock and wife Emy's child Margareta, born January 20th, 1722, baptized March 14th, 1723.
7. Johan Clayton and wife Rosamunda's child Joseph, in Appouuimink, 2 months old, baptized March 24th.
8. Johan Sap and wife Martha's child Johan, in Apoquinimink 4 months old, baptized March 24th.

30

OLD SWEDES CHURCH

9. The pastor Herr Samuel Hessellius and wife Brita's child Anna Maria, born April 8th, baptized April 12th.

10. Israel Stalcop and wife Susanna's child Maria, born April 20th, baptized April 28th.

11. Gustaf Gustafsson and wife Kerstin's child Christina, born May 8th, baptized May 12th.

12. Hans Smith and wife Elizabeth's child Catharina, born May 28th, baptized June 2d.

13. Peter Månsson and wife Annika's child Maria, born June 3d, baptized June 5th.

14. Jonas Skagen and Elizabeth Kent's illegitimate child William about 2 years old, baptized June 10th.

15. Jonathan Kirk and wife Mary's child Elizabeth, born June 11th, baptized January 26th.

16. Edward Jones and wife Mary's child Elizabeth, in Appoquinimink, born May 8th, baptized June 23rd.

17. Timotheus Stedham and wife Elizabeth's child Lylof, born July 2nd, baptized July 7th.

18. Mårten Gustafsson and wife Brita's child Andreas, born July 9th, baptized July 12th.

19. Israel Petersson and wife Margareta's child Susanna, born July 10th, baptized July 14th.

20. Peter Holsten and wife Sara's child Maria, 2 months old baptized July 21st at Appoquinimink.

21. William Hacket and wife Sara's daughter Prudence, born in Sussex County, 16 years old, baptized July 27th, at Appoquinimink.

22. Carl Springer, Jr., and wife Margareta's child Maria, born July 25th, baptized July 28th.

23. Benjamin Allmond and wife Rachel's child Susanna, 5½ years old, baptized at Appoquinimink, August 4th.

24. Gabriel Clemens and wife Sara's child Joseph, in Elk River, born April 12th, baptized August 11th.

25. Johan Stalcop and wife Maria's child Ericus, born August 15th, baptized August 18th. Sponsors, The Provost in Fahlun, Herr Eric Biörk, in whose place stood the Provost Magister Andreas Hessellius.

26 and 27. Samuel Griffin and wife Margareta's sons at Dock Creek, William 18 years old, James 15 years old, baptized at Appoquinimink Church, September 1st.

28. George Von Culen and wife Margareta's child Helena, born September 7th, baptized September 13th.

29. Anders Loinan and wife Annika's child Johannes born September 8 th, baptized September 15th.

30. Jonas Skaggin and wife Annika's child Johan, born September 11th, baptized September 15th.

31. Olle Pâlsson and wife Elizabeth's child Jacob, born September 10th, baptized September 22nd.

32. William Clenny and wife Maria's child Jane, born September 23rd, baptized September 29th.

34. Jesper Walraven and wife Maria's child Jesper, born October 17th, baptized October 20th.

35. Johan Culen and wife Kerstin's child Christina, born October 20th, baptized October 27th.

36. Israel Robbesson and wife Elizabeth's child Anna, born November 1 , baptized November 27th.

37. Andreas Stalcop, Sr. and wife Anna Barbrie's child Maria Christina, born November 29th, baptized December 1st.

38. Johan Wilder and wife Margareta's child Richard, born December 14th, baptized December 15th.

39. Anders Pâlsson and wife Elizabeth's child Tobias, born December 9th, baptized December 15th.

Baptisms 1724.

1. Olle Mânsson and wife Annika's child Cartharina, born January 2, baptized January 5.

2. Cornelius La Quett and wife Maria's child Johannes, born December 26 1723, baptized January 12.

3. Elizabeth Ibard's illegitimate child Emmy, mulatto |girl born November 12, 1723 baptized January 19.

4. Hendrick Stedham and wife Catharina's child Maria, born January 21, baptized January 23.

5. Lucas Stedham Jr. and wife Ingeborg's child Jonas, born February 24, baptized March 1.

6. Jan Seeds and wife Brita's child Maria, born February 25, baptized March 1.

7. Robin Bird and wife Maria's child Susanna, born March 2, baptized March 8.

8. William Allen and wife Margaret's child Johan, born February 23, baptized March 15.

OLD SWEDES CHURCH

9. Johan Woodland and Gen Garden's illegitimate child Johan, born April 25, 1723, baptized March 15.

10, Jonas Stalcop and wife Helena's child Elizabeth, 6 weeks old, baptized March 29.

11. Lylof Stedham and wife Anna's child Hindric, born March 23, baptized March 29.

12. William Verdeman and wife Margareta's child Maria, born Apr. 1, baptized March 5.

13. George Anderson and wife Margareta's child (from Elk-river) Catharina, 10 weeks old, baptized Aprll 5.

14. Jacob Heine and wife Kerstin's child, Jacob born April 20, baptized April 26.

15, Peter La Quett and wife Marta's child Marta, born January 16, baptized May 10.

16. Elizabeth Calliert's illegitimate child Rebecca (a mulato) born November 13, 1723, baptized May 5.

17. Måns Gustafsson and wife Catharina's child Rebecca, born May 17, baptized May 24.

18. Thomas Scott and wife Catharina's child Maria, born May 23, baptized May 25.

19. Johannas Månsson and wife Ingeborg's child Catharina born June 3, baptized June 7.

20. Johan Dawson and Sara's child Maria, (from St. Georges), 7 months old, baptized June 21.

21. Michael Mayer and wife Annika's child Susanna, born July 10, baptized July 12.

22. Samuel Petersson and wife Kerstin's child Anna, born August 1, baptized August 16.

23. Christiern Brynberg and wife Maria's child Susanna, born August 15, baptized August 23.

24. Jonas Jespersson Walraven and wife Catharina's child Catharina, born August 12, baptized August 23.

26. Ebenezer Empsson and wife Susannas's child Susanna, several weeks old, baptized September 2.

26. Jacob Van de Ver and wife Maria's child Elizabeth, born September 10, baptized September 20.

27. Cornelius Walraven and wife Walborg's child Elizabeth (of St. George's) half year old, necessary baptism.*

---

*Previously baptized by some lay person for fear of death.

EARLY CHURCH RECORDS OF NEW CASTLE COUNTY

28. Jean Toiles and wife Anna's child Elizabeth, born August 31st, baptized October 7th.

29. Christopher Stedham and wife Johanna's child Margareta, born September 7th, baptized October 11th.

30. Anders Hindricksson and wife Maria's child Susanna, born October 20th, baptized October 25th.

31. Jean Griffis and wife Margareta's child Sara, born November 3d, baptized November 8th.

32. Anders Cock and wife Sara's children Carolus and Abigail, born November 8th, baptized November 11th.

33. Peter Classon and wife Walborg's child Maria, born November 12th, baptized November 15th.

34. Christopher Springer and wife Catharina's child Johan, born December, baptized December 20th.

RECORD OF BURIALS, 1724.

1. Johan Wilder's child Richard, buried January 2d.
2. Anders Stalcop, Sen.'s child Maria Christina, buried January 6th.
3. Olle Pâlsson's child Jacob, buried January 11th.
4. Johan Gioding's widow Annika, buried March 7th.
5. Jean Benjaminsson Pâlsson, buried March 7th.
6. Johanny Mânsson's child Maria, buried March 25th.
7. Lucas Stedham, Jr.'s child Maria, buried April 28th.
8. Erasmus Stedham's wife Helena, buried May 4th.
9. Jonas Stalcop's child Carl, buried May 21st.
10. The miller, Foster Pew, buried June 22d.
11. Widow Brita Gustafsson, buried August 22d.
12. Jonas Walraven, Sr., buried August 31st.

MARRIAGES, 1724.

1. Gustaf Pâulsson and Margaret Simpson, married March 8th.
2. William White and Miss Maria Ericsson, married April 30th.
3. Mâns Andersson and Miss Margaret Mans, married May 28th.
4. Timotheus Bengtsson Stedham and Miss Catharina Morse, married June 23d.
5. Jesper Walraven and widow Anna Garritsson, married August 6th.
6. David White and Miss Gierkie Cornelius, married September 17th.

OLD SWEDES CHURCH

7. William Evans and Anna Philips, married October 31st.

8. Anton Jaquett and Miss Catharina Gioding, married November 19th.

9. Garret Garretsson and Miss Elizabeth Ericsson, married December 3d.

10. Peter Petersson Canpany and Miss Magdalena Stedham, married December 3d.

11. Samuel Fowdrey and Anna Van de Ver, married December 8th.

12. Morgan Jones and Elinor Evans, married December 17th.

13. Lewis German and Margareta Jury, married December 31st.

BAPTISMS, 1725.

1. Philip Van de Ver and wife Elizabeth's child Elizabeth, born January 2nd, baptized January 3rd.

2. The negress Peggy's child Peter, (in the parsonage) born January 2nd, baptized January 3rd.

3. Israel Petersson and wife Margarita's child Regina, born January 25th, baptized January 17th.

4. William White and wife Maria's child Elizabeth, born January 31st, baptized February 3rd.

5. Benjamin Good and wife Ingrid's child Eschiel, born December 28th, baptized February 4th.

6. Peter Pålsson and wife Catharina's child Maria, born February 3rd, baptized February 14th.

7. Jacob Stille and wife Rebecca's child Rebecca, born February 4th, baptized February 14th.

8. Thomas Bird and wife Hanna's child Johan, born May 10th, 1723, baptized February 21.

9. Mâns Smith and wife Maria's child Tobias, born March 16 baptized March 21st.

10. Jonas Shagan and wife Annika's child Elizabeth, born March 16th, baptized March 28th.

11. Garrit Pålsson Garretsson and wife Ester's child Ester, born December 25th, 1724, baptized March 28th.

12. Anton Jaquet and wife Catharina's child Johan, born March 17th, baptized April 22nd.

13. James Owins and wife Dorothea's child Elizabeth, 3 months old, baptized May 23rd.

14. Brewer Seneke and wife Brita's child Anna, born May 23rd, baptized June 3rd.

15. Jesper Walraven and wife Anna's child Benjamin, born June 11th, baptized June 13th.

16. Anders Stalcop and wife Barbro's child Margarita, born June 17th, baptized June 20th.

17. Thomas Bird and wife Hannah's child Benjamin, born June 13th, baptized June 27th.

18. Mârten Mârtensson and wife Kerstin's child Sara, born June 21st, baptized June 27th.

19. Johan Wilder and wife Margarita's child Elizabeth, born June 22nd, baptized June 27th.

20. Peter Petersson Canpany and wife Magdalena's child Helena, born June 27th, baptized July 4th.

21. Joshua Robertsson and wife Maria's child Maria, 4½ years old, baptized July 7th.

22. Jonathan Kirk and wife Maria's child Jonathan, born May 28th, baptized July 11th.

23. David White and wife Gierkie's children Moses and Stephanius, born July 29th, baptized July 29th.

24. Capt. W. Battel and wife Cornelia's child France, 3 months old, baptized August 10th.

25. Carolus Springer, and wife Margarita's child Johan, born August 9th, baptized August 22nd.

26. Hindric Stedham and wife Elizabeth's child, Elizabeth, born September 6th, baptized September 12th.

27. Garrit Garrisson and wife Elizabeth's child Catharine born September 16th, baptized September 17th.

28. Hans Piettersson and wife Sara's child, Sara, born October 3rd, baptized October 20th.

29. Timotheus Benjamin Stedham and wife Catharina's child, Johan, 6 weeks old, baptized October 10th.

30. Johan Seed and wife Brita's child Johan, born October 11th, baptized October 13th.

31. Anders Loinan and wife Maria's child Maria, born October 18th, baptized October 24th.

32. Pastor Herr Magister Samuel Hesselius and wife Brita's child Sara, born October 23rd, baptized October 24th.

33. Cornelius JaQuett and wife Maria's child Petrus, born October 30th, baptized November 14th.

34. David Henock and wife Helena's child Annika, born October 30th, baptized November 14th.

OLD SWEDES CHURCH

35. Olle Mânson and wife Annika's child Petrus, born December 15th, baptized December 19th.

36. Johan Stalcop and wife Maria's child Israel, born December 24th, baptized December 26th.

MARRIAGES 1725.

1. William Jansson and Jane Jansson, married January 18th, (with Governor's license.)

2. David Harvey and Elizabeth Price, married September 20.

3. Rees Evans and Mary Welsh, married September 30th.

4. Walraven Walraven and Christina Kâlsberg married October 6th.

5. Isaac James and Rachel Rees, married November 4th.

6. Jesper Robesson and Magdalena Springer, married November 11th.

7. Johan Mârtensson and Margaretta Stalcop, (Governor's license,) married November 11th.

8. Peter Petersson Smith and Annika Mânson, married November 26th.

9. Matthias Stark and Brigitta Hindricsson, married November 28th.

10. Richard Williams and Elizabeth Brett, married December 14th.

BURIALS 1725.

1. Garret Garretsson's child Catharina, buried September 19th.

2. Israel Stalcop buried November 11th.

3. The late Jesper Walraven's widow Kerstin, buried December 20th.

BAPTISMS, 1726.

1. Lucas Stedham and wife Ingeborg's child Anna Maria, born January 4th, baptized January 9th.

2. Jacob Hein and wife Kerstin's child Cornelius, born January 4th, baptized January 9th.

3. George Reed and wife Sara's child Robert, born January 8th, baptized January 14th.

4. Samuel Hall and wife Anna Elizabeth's child Dina, 8 years old, baptized January 31st.

5. William Clenny and wife Maria's child Maria, born January 17th, baptized January 31st.

6. Hindric Snecker and wife Catharina's child Hindric, born February 7th, baptized February 8th.

7. Jonas Stalcop and wife Helena's child Israel, born February 19th, baptized the same day.

8. Jonas Jespersson Walraven and wife Catharina's child Maria, born February 21, baptized February 22d.

9. Johan Rais and wife Margareta's child Thomas, a half year old, baptized February 28th.

10. Johan Mâsten and wife Margareta's child Matthias, born February 5th, baptized March 6th.

11. Joseph Chantrill and wife Catharina's child John, one and one-half year old, baptized March 25th.

12. Lylof Stedham and wife Anna's child Lylof, born March 24th, baptized April 8th.

13. Gustaf Pâlsson and wife Margareta's child Elizabeth, 6 months old, baptized April 10th.

14. Samuel Fowdrey and wife Anna's child Susanna, born April 10th, baptized April 15th.

15. Peter Pâlsson and wife Ingeborg's child Susanna, Half yr old, baptized April 15th.

16. Israel Robbesson and wife Elizabeth child Carl, born April 11th, baptized May 1st.

17. Johan Von Culen and wife Kerstin's child Peter, born April 10th, baptized May 1st.

18. William Cock and wife Emy's child Regner Von der Culen, born January 15th, 1725, baptized May 4th.

19. Robert Ershelot and wife Margareta's child Samuel, born April 23rd, baptized May 8th.

20. Mârten Gustafsson and wife Brita's child Swen, born May 31st, baptized June 6th.

21. William Forehead and wife Maria's child Rebecca, a half year old, baptized June 12th.

22. Joseph Peersson and wife Maria's child Henry, born December 28th, 1725, baptized June 12th.

23. Joseph Peersson and wife Maria's child George, born Oct. 30, 1723, baptized September 10th.

OLD SWEDES CHURCH

24. Peter Petersson Smith and wife Annika's child Tobias, born September 5th, baptized September 10th.

25. Peter Tossawa and wife Margareta's child Johan, born September 13th, baptized September 17th.

26. Christiern Brynberg and wife Maria's child Matthias, born September 15., baptized September 25th.

27. Walraven Walravenand wife Kerstin's child Swen, born October 10th, baptized October 16th.

28. William White and wife Maria's child Maria, born November 13th, baptized November 16th.

29. Jasper Walraven and wife Anna's child Sara, born November 29th, baptized December 4th.

30. Hanna Matthew's illegitimate child Sara, 3 years old, baptized December 10th,

31. Joseph Chantrill and wife Catharina's child Joseph, a half year old, baptized December 10th.

32. Christopher Springer and wife Catharina's child Brita, born December 10th, baptized December 14th.

33. Thomas Bird and wife Rachael's child Johan, born November 22d, baptized November 15th.

34. Samuel Peterson and wife Kerstin's child Christina, born September 19th, baptized December 27th.

Burials, 1726.

1. Hans Piettersson's child Sara, buried January 11th.
2. Paul Månsson, buried January 25th.
3. George Reed's wife Sara, buried January 6th.
4. Johanneas Månsson's child Catharina Ester, buried January 17th.
5. Israel Stalcop's child Maria, buried January 31st.
6. William Robbersson, buried February 27th.
7. George Fisher's wife Elizabeth, buried March 21st.
8. Jesper Walraven's child Maria, buried September 27th.
9. Johannes Månsson, buried October 9th.
10. Josua Robbersson's child Maria, buried November 5th.
11. Garrit Garritsson's child, (had necessary baptism), buried November 16th.
12. William White's child Maria, (buried at Crane Hook), November 19th.
13. Edward Matthews, buried December 6th.
14. Lucas Stedham, Senior, buried December 8th.

15. Elias Nilsson, buried December 12th.
16. Johan Morriss' wife Helena, buried December 14th.
17. Mr. Ebenezer Empson's son Jonathan, buried December 16th.
18. Anders Cock's daughter Brita, buried December 16th.
19. Anders Cock's daughter Catharina, buried December 18th.
20. Hanna Mathew, buried December 18th.
21. Anders Stedham, buried December 2?d.
22. Johan Tossawa, buried December 17th.
23. Ebenezer Empson, buried December 18th.
24. Brita Jeans, buried December 19th.

Marriages, 1726

1. Thomas Martin and Elizabeth Issard, married February 6th.
2. Johan Williams and Mary Piggotte, married April 12th.
3. Richard Jefferis and Margaret Howl, married April 19th.
4. Thomas White and Rebecca Cloud, married May 7th.
5. Hindric Hindricsson and Maria Tossawa, married July 13th.
6. Johan Burns and Margaret Rickri, married July 25th.
7. Erasmus Stedham and Mary Littlejohn, (gov. license), married December 3d.
8. Johan Seneke and Ingeborg Tossawa, married December 9th.
9. Thomas Cordrey and Mary Matthews, married December 13th.

July 17, 1727. Anders Gustafsson was dismissed from the Churchwardenship for his disobedience and obstinacy, and Philip Van de Ver was elected in his place, and also Jacob Van de Ver was chosen in the place of Brewer Seneke.

Burials 1727.

1. Ebenezer Empsson's widow Susanna, buried January 2d.
2. Hindric Hindricsson's wife Maria, buried January 13th.
3. John Owin's daughter Sara, buried January 14th.
4. Olle Mânsson's child Susanna, buried January 24th.
5. Thomas Martin, buried February 26th.
6. Jonas Jespersson Walraven, buried March 11th.
7. Mr. Carl Springer's wife Maria, buried March 15th.
8. Jesper Robbesson, buried March 29th.
9. William Cock's child, Regner Von der Culen, buried April 18th.

OLD SWEDES CHURCH

10. Antille Stalcop's child Johannes, buried May 28th.
11. William Allen's child Jonas, buried October 12th.
12. Thomas Scott, buried November 13th.
13. Johan Wilder's child Margareta, buried December 16th.

BAPTISMS 1727.

1. Johan Rossen and wife Marget's child Maria, born December 25, 1720, baptized January 1st.
2. Peter Petersson and wife Anna's child Regner, born December 23d, baptized January 1st.
3. Thomas Bird and wife Maria's child Maria, born May 11, 1725, baptized January 1st.
4. Josia Wilson and wife Elizabeth's child Rebecca, born July 24, 1725, baptized January 1st.
5. Robbert Cloud and wife Sara's child Phœbe, born March 25, 1721, baptized January 1st.
6. Robbert Cloud and wife Sara's child James, born October 3, 1723, baptized January 1st.
7. Robbert Eckman and wife Christina's child Johan, born June 27, 1726, baptized January 1st.
8. Pâl Pâlsson and wife Catharina's child Richard, born February 5, 1726, baptized January 3d.
9. Pâl Pâlsson and wife Catharina's child Marget, born December 21, 1723, baptized January 3d.
10. Hans Petersson and wife Elizabeth's child Joseph, born December 25, 1726, baptized January 3d.
11. Mâns Gustafsson and wife Catharina's child Helena, born January 1st, baptized January 16th.
12. Edward Richardsson's child Sara, baptized January 6th.
13. The negress Peggy's child Elizabeth, born January 17th, baptized January 22nd.
14. Hindric Stedham and wife Catharina's child Catharina, born February 5th, baptized February 12th.
15. Anders Hindricsson and wife Maria's child Anders, born February 6th, baptized February 24th.
16. Anton Ja Quett and wife Catharina's child Elizabeth, born February 14th, baptized February 24th.
17. John Seed and wife Brita's child Rebecca, born February 26th, baptized February 27th.
18. Carolus Springer and wife Margareta's child Anna, born March 5th, baptized March 6th.
19. Christopher Stedham and wife Anna's child Zacharias, 5 weeks old, baptized March 12th.

20. Francis Chad and wife Grace's daughter Anna, 19 years old, baptized March 5th.

21. Richard Henock and wife Susanna's child Debora, 2 months old, baptized March 26th.

22. Robert Whittiker and wife Maria's child Anna, 2 months old, baptized March 26th.

23. Annika Likan's illegitimate child Elizabeth, 5 months old, baptized April 13th.

24. Breyer Meg Daniel and wife Catharina's child Catharina, 3 weeks old, baptized April 23rd.

25. John Pippin and wife Rebecca's child Joseph, 6 weeks old, baptized April 23rd.

26. Thomas Scott and wife Catharina's child Sara, born April 11th, baptized April 23rd.

27. Jacob Stille and wife Rebecca's child John, born April 22nd, baptized April 30th.

28. James Jordan and wife Anna's child Elizabeth, born February 8th, baptized May 21st.

29. Antilli Stalcop and wife Barbro's child Anders, born May 25th, baptized May 26th.

30. Antilli Stalcop and wife Barbro's child Anna Barbro, born May 25th, baptized May 26th.

31. Peter Classon and wife Walborg's child Joanna, born May 28th, baptized June 11th.

32. Peter Pålsson and wife Catharina's child Swen, born June 16th, baptized June 18th.

33. John Littlejohn and wife Maria's daughter Maria, 18 years old, baptized January 18th.

34. George Jackson and wife Honor's dau. Katharina, 15 years old baptized January 18th.

35. Jonathan Kirk and wife Maria's child Susanna, born July 24th, baptized August 13th.

36. Gustaf Pålssón and wife Margareta's child William, born August 22nd, baptized September 13th.

37. Edward Erby and wife Anna's child Susanna, born June 25th, baptized September 13th.

38. Hans Smith and wife Maria's child Fredric, born September 19th, baptized September 24th.

39. William Allin and wife Margaretta's child Jonas, 15 months old, baptized September 29th.

40. William White and wife Maria's child Susanna, born October 7th, baptized October 15th.

OLD SWEDES CHURCH

41. John Seneke and wife Ingeberg's child Darkis', born October 11th, baptized October 15th.

42. Brewer Seneke and wife Brita's child Brewer, born October 15th, baptized October 22nd.

43. Pastor Herr Magister Samuel Hessellius and wife Brita's child Christiern, born October 16th, baptized October 22nd, Sponsors, Pastor Herr Magister Petrus Tranberg and his wife Anna Catharine, Pastor Herr Magister Andreas Windrufwa and his wife Eliza-beth, Jacob Van de Ver, Anders Loinan, Hindric Gustafsson's wife Brita, Philip Van de Ver's wife Elizabeth.

44. Erasmus Stedham and wife Maria's child Erasmus, born October 20th, baptized October 24th.

45. Jesper Robbinsson and wife Magdalena's child Jesper, born October 23d, baptized October 28th.

46. Peter Petersson Canpany and wife Magdalena's child Maria, born November 18th, baptized November 19th.

47. Jonas Skaggen and wife Anna's child Jonas, born November 15th, baptized November 24th.

48. Cornelius JaQuett and wife Maria's child Susanna, born November 23d baptized December 3d.

49. James Canada and wife Tabitha's child George, born Nov. 25th, baptized December 3d.

50. John Wilder and wife Margareta's child Margareta, born December 7th, baptized December 8th.

51 and 52. Richard Certain and wife Ester's children Martha and Maria, born December 1st, baptized December 13th.

53. Richard Certain and wife Ester's child Emanuel, born January 5th, 1725, baptized December 13th.

54. Philip Van de Ver and wife Elizabeth's child Susanna born December 25th, baptized December 30th.

MARRIAGES, 1727.

1. Johannes JaQuett and Kerstin Barker, married January 26th.

2. Richard Certain and Ester Price, Governor's License, married March 17th.

3 John Greedy and Elizabeth Hooper, Governor's License, married March 21.

4. Richard Hanby and Elizabeth Wilsson, Governor License, married March 23d.

5. Nicolaus Cursine and Rebecca Bird, married April 5th.

6. Charles Empson and Mary Jeans, Governor's License, married April 19th.

7. John Davis and Anna Mackmath, Governor's License, married April 20th.

8. Jonas Stedham and Helena Dericsson, married May 10th.

9. Thomas Lobum and Elizabeth Cordery, married May 26th.

10. Edward Haley and Anna Cloud, married June 1st.

11. Thomas Wilcocks and Elizabeth Kohl, married June 3d.

12. Carl Springer and Annika Walraven, Governor's License, married June 15th.

13. William Trehearne and Catharine Rice, Governor's License, August 7th.

14. William Robbersson and Rachel Park, Governor's License, married August 11th.

15. Henry Wheatfield and Mary Blan, married September 1st.

16. John Right and Anna Tossawa, married September 22nd.

17. George Reed and Ingeborg Mânsson, married October 3rd.

18. Jonathan Waddington and Anna Waka, Governor's License, married October 12th.

19. *Magister* Andreas Windrufva and Elizabeth JaQuette, married November 9th.

20. William Wight and Elizabeth Few, married December 1st.

21. Jonas Walraven and Maria Justis, married December 1st.

22. William Van de Ver and Margareta Colesberg, married December 7th.

23. Robert Harper and Margareta Archer, married December 9th.

24. John Smith and Elizabeth Diricsson, married December 26th.

25. John Allower and Mary Rodgers, Governors License, married December 30th.

BAPTISMS 1728.

1. David Henock and wife Helena's child Hindric, born December 7th, 1727, baptized January 1st.

2. Timotheus Benjamin Stedham and wife Catharina's child Joseph, 7 weeks old, baptized January 1st.

3. Olle Mânssen and wife Annika's child Johan, born January 5th, baptized January 9th.

4. John Lewis and wife Elizabeth's child Sara, born December 27th, baptized February 10th.

5. Hans JaQuett and wife Kerstin's child Maria, 6 weeks old, baptized February 18th.

OLD SWEDES CHURCH

6. Garrit Garritfsson and wife Elizabeth's child John, born February 20th, baptized February 24th.

7. Garrit Pâlsson Garritsson and wife Ester's child Hindric, born January 28th, 1727, baptized February 26th.

8. Elizabeth Garritsson's illegiitmate child Rebecca, born March 3rd, 1727, baptized February 26th.

9. William Cock and wife Emi's child Regner, born February 20th, baptized February 27th.

10. Jacob Vandever and wife Maria's child Tobias, born February 20th, baptized February 27th.

11. William Kallom and wife Maria's child Benjamin, born January 17th, baptized March 3rd.

12. William Kallom and wife Maria's child John, born December 5th, 1725, baptized March 3rd,

13. Lucas Stedham and wife Ingeborg's child Sara, born March 11th, baptized November 27th.

14. William Forehead and wife Maria's child Samuel, born March 13th, baptized April 21st.

15. Jesper Walraven and wife Annika's child Margareta, born May 14th, baptized May 23rd,

16. William Justice and Elizabeth Witten's illegitimate child Isaac, born July 28th, 1723, baptized May 23rd.

17. Mârten Mârtensson and wife Kerstin's child Johannes, 6 weeks old, baptized May 31st.

18. Olle Tossawa and wife Maria's child Catharina, 4 weeks old, baptized June 16th.

19. Hindric Stedham and wife Catharina's child Cornelius, born May 31st, baptized June 16th.

20. Israel Petersson and wife Margaretta's child Magdalena, born July 14th, baptized July 21st.

21. Jonas Stedham and wife Helena's child Lucas, born July 29th, baptized August 4th.

42. Mâns Gustafsson and wife Catharina's child Swen, born August 1st, baptized August 4th.

23. George Reed and wife Ingeborg's child William, born August 4th, baptized August 10th.

24. John Right and wife Annika's child Sara, born August 21st, baptized August 19th.

25. Jonas Walraven and wife Maria's child Gustafsson, born September 7th, baptized September 15th.

96. John Seed and wife Brita's child Elizabeth, born September 7th, baptized September 15th.

45

27. Johannes Springer and wife Maria's child Carl, born July 21st, baptized September 25th.

28. Thomas Wort and wife Kerstin's child Judith, born March 14th, baptized September 15th.

29. Johannes de Foss and wife Hanna's child Elizabeth, born January 6, 1724 baptized September 25th.

30. Thomas Cordrey and wife Maria's child John, born December 24, 1727 baptized September 25th.

31. Adam Stole and wife Catharina's child Johannes, born September 22, baptized September 29th.

32. William Vandever and wife Margaretta's child Elizabeth, born October 1st, baptized October 5th.

33. John Dasson and wife Sara's child James, 6 months old, baptized October 5th.

34. William Clenny and wife Maria's child Hanna, 6 weeks old, baptized October 13th.

35. Peter Tossawa and wife Margaretta's child Elizabeth, born October 2nd, baptized October 13th.

36. John Crocker and wife Maria's child Anna, born June 5th, baptized November 3rd.

37–38. Peter Petersson and wife Annika's children Margaretta and Catharina, born November 2nd, baptized November 3rd.

39. John Mårten and wife Margaretta's child Christina, born November 13th, baptized November 24th.

40. John Dason and wife Sara's child John, 2 years old, baptized December 26th.

41. Carolus Springer and wife Margaret's child Carl, born December 17th, baptized December 22nd.

42. David White and wife Hierkie's child Carolus, born in August, baptized December 26th

MARRIAGES, 1728.

1. John Bush and Miriam Short, married January 6th.
2. John Crocker and Mary Neal, married February 1st.
3. Francis Laiton and Sarah Ford, married February 27th.
4. Thomas Clayton and Hanna Buckley, Governor's License married March 1st.
5. David Morgan and Jennet Mackelhenny, married April 1st.
6. Jacobus Dirixson and Annika Justice, Governor's License, married June 9th.
7. John Jackson and Rachel Grist, married June 17th.
8. Edward Cloud and Francis Bird, Governor's License, married June 19th.

OLD SWEDES CHURCH

9. William Lewis and Helena Welsh, Governor's License, married July 11th.
10. David Davis and Hanna Oborn, married August 22nd.
11. George Orson and Anna Macknel, married September 16.
12. Thomas Berry and Jean Beard, Governor License, married September 24th.
13. Peter Andersson and Elizabeth Dirixon, Governor's License, married October 5th.
14. Richad Hoe and Jean Pierce, Governor's License, married October 10th.
15. Regner Von Culen and Anna Skaggan, Governor License, married November 13th.
16. Pâl Pâlsson and Magdalena Robbisson, married November 19th.
17. Joseph Horsey and Sara de Foss, Governor'e License, married November 21st.
*18. Thomas Willing and widow. Catharine Scott, married December 5th.

BURIALS, 1728.

1. Olle Mânsson, buried January 1st.
2. Thomas Scott's child Sara, buried January 11th.
3. Philip Van de Ver's wife Elizabeth, buried February 5th.
4. Jonas Skaggen, buried February 11th.
5. Peter Pâlsson's wife Geikie, buried August 27th.
6. John Gustafsson's son Gustafwus, buried September 1st.
7. Berget Pâlsson's wife Margareta, buried September 9th.
8. Edward Robbesson's son Edward, buried September 10th.
9. Olle Mânsson's child Catharine, buried September 20th.
10. George Reed's child Robbert, buried September 29th.
11. Jacobus Diricson, buried October 1st.
12. Cornelius Ja Quett's child Susanna, buried October 13th.
13. Mâns Tossawa, buried November 24th.
14. Peter Petersson's child Catharina, buried November 30th.
15. John Smith, buried December 5th.
16. Conrad Constantin, buried December 11th.

BAPTISMS, 1729.

1. John Bird and wife Margareta's child Anna, 6 months old, baptized January 19th.
2. Walraven Walraven and wife Kerstin's child Maria, born January 23rd, baptized January 26th.

---
*The founder of Wilmington.

3. Samuel Fodrey and wife Anna's child Alis, 7 weeks old, baptized January 26th.

4. Edward Earby and wife Anna's child Maria, born October 13, 1728, baptized February 24th.

5. Christopher Springer and wife Catharina's child Peter, born March 9th, baptized March 16th.

6. Peter Pålsson and wife Catharina's child Catharina, born March 28th, baptized March 30th.

7. Thomas Martin and wife Elizabeth's child Susanna, 13 months old, baptized March 30th.

8. Christopher Stedham and wife Hunna's child Susanna, born Apr. 14th, baptized April 20th.

9. John Stalcop and wife Maria's child Annika, born April 12th, baptized April 20th.

10. John Wilsson and wife Margareta's child Maria, born April 25th, baptized May 11th.

11. Richard Hoe and wife Jean's child Anna, born June 3rd, baptized June 5th.

12. Lylof Stedham and wife Anna's child Elizabeth, 1 year old, baptized June 18th.

13. Anton JaQuett and wife Catharina's child Paulus, born May 30th, baptized June 9th.

14. Peter JaQuett and wife Marta's child Thomas, born July 14, 1728, baptized June 9th.

15. Anders Hindricsson and wife Maria's child Maria, born June 23rd, baptized June 29th.

16. Samuel Petersson and wife Kerstin's child Matthias, born August 1st, baptized August 3rd.

17. John York and wife Marget's child Maria, born June 26th baptized August 3rd.

18. David Henock and wife Helena's child Margareta, born July 29th, baptized August 10th.

19. Peter Anderson and wife Kerstin's child Jacobus, one week old, baptized Angust 17th.

20. Jonas Stalcop and wife Helena's child Maria, one week old, baptized September 28th.

21. Olle Andersson and wife Kerstin's child Brita, born October 7th, baptized October 12th.

22. Erasmus Stedham and wife Maria's child Maria, born October 8th, baptized October 26th.

23. Olle Tossawa and wife Maria's child John, born December 4th, baptized December 7th.

OLD SWEDES CHURCH

24. Regner Von Culen and wife Anna's child Margareta, born December 4th, baptized December 7th.

25. Timotheus Stedham and wife Elizabeth's, child Elizabeth, born December 15th, baptized December 21st.

26. Thomas Willing and wife Catharina's child Helena, born December 18th, baptized December 26th.

MARRIAGES, 1729.

1. William Justice and Elizabeth Base, Governor's License, married January 27th.

2. Wm. Croshee and Mary Littlejohn, married February 18th.

3. George Hudson and Mary Tatcher, married February 21st.

4. Daniel Rock and Elizabeth Carey, married March 25th.

5. Thomas Long and Jean Perkins, Governor's License, married March 30th.

6. John Littlejohn and Annika Petersson Canpany, married May 6th.

7. Richard Reinhold and Sara Pierce, married June 5th.

8. Thomas Bab and Sara Folek, Governor's License, married June 12th.

9. Hindric Månsson and Judith Justice, Governor's License, married June 26th,

10. John Chandler and Elizabeth Spragg, Governor's License, married July 13th.

11. Henry Johnson and Catharina Price, married October 14th.

12. Lars Vinan and Elizabeth Garritsson, married October 29th.

13. Joseph Ogle and Sara Winters, Governor's License, married December 4th.

14. John Green and Jean Perkins, married December 23rd.

15. Isaac Davis and Catharina Jacksson, Governor's License, married December 30th.

BURIALS 1729.

1 John Morris, buried January 18.

2. Olle Månsson's child, Peter, buried February 20.

3. Jesper Walraven's child, Benjamin, buried March 10.

4. Jesper Walraven's child, Sara, buried March 13.

5. Brewer Seneke's child, Brewer, buried April 10.

6. Peter Månssion's widow, Karin, buried June 9.

7. The late John Garritsson's child, Anna, buried August 15.

8. Peter Pålsson's child, Swen, buried August 18.

9. Anders Cock's wife, Sara, buried September 19.

10. Hindric Månsson, buried October 28.

EARLY CHURCH RECORDS OF NEW CASTLE COUNTY

Churchwardens
for Chester
{ RALPH PILE,
ALEXANDER HUNTER,
JOHN MATHER,
HENRY MUNDAY.

HENRY BOWRING,
JOHN PIKE,
WILLIAM PILE,
MATTHIAS MARTINS,
JOHN GARRET,
JOSEPH BOND,
HENRY GUEST,
THOMAS SILL,
JOHN WADE,
JOSEPH RICHARDS,
THOMAS GIFFING,
THOMAS BROOM,
STEPHEN COLE,
THOMAS CHESTER,
JOSEPH TOMPLEN.

JAMES WIDDOWS,
TIMOTHY CUMMINS,
BENJAMIN FORD,
EDWARD EARLY,
HENRY PIERCE, SEN.,
RICHARD HANBY,
HENRY PIERCE, JUNR.,
JOSEPH GRICE,
JOSEPH BAKER,
MICHAEL ATKINSON,
JAMES MATHER,
WILLIAM TREAHAME,
WILLIAM RASSEN,
GEORGE REED,

MARRIAGES, 1730.

1. James Senexon and Margaret Werdeman, married January 20th.
2. Anders Hannah and Margaret Shenan, married January 20th.
3. Samuel Strout and Hanna Talley, married January 27th.
4. Isachar Green and Sara Green, (gov. license), married April 26th.
5. John Garritsson and Elizabeth Cock, married May 14th.
6. Ambrous Clayton and Martha Barn, (gov. license), married May 27th.
7. Ralph Whithers and Mary Bird, (gov. license), married May 11th.
8. Pastor Magister Samuel Hessellius and Gertrude Stille, (gov. license), married July 1st.
9. Andrew Rossen and Sara Bloair, (gov. license), married July 28th.
10. Carl Cornelius and Annika Dirixon, married August 20th.
11. Anders Rinberg and Maria Likon, (gov. license), married August 14th.
12. Daniel Parsons and Brigget Fegen, (gov. license), married October 5th.

OLD SWEDES CHURCH

13. Edward Robbesson and Sara Bird, (gov. license), married December 9th.
14. Michael Padrick and Anna Robbesson, (gov. license), married December 26th.

BAPTISMS, 1730.

1. Peter Classon and wife Walberg's child Elizabeth, born December 18th, 1729, baptized January 1st.
2. James Canida and wife Jane's child, Wilyam, born December 28th, 1729, baptized February 15th.
3. Pâl Pâlsson and wife Magdalena's child Dorothea, born January 20th, baptized February 15th.
4. Hans Petersson and wife Elizabeth's child Rubin, born January 24th, baptized February 15th.
5. Christiern Brunberg and wife Maria's child John, born January 29th, baptized February 15th.
6. Lars Vinan and wife Elizabeth's child Hindric, 6 months old, baptized March 15th.
7. John Senepon and wife Ingeborg's child John, born February 28th, baptized March 29th.
8. Jacob Vandever and wife Maria's child Susanna, born March 20th, baptized March 29th.
9. Martin Kelle and wife Catharina's child Maria, born April 2d, baptized April 12th.
10. Lucas Stedham and wife Ingeborg's child Elizabeth, 2 months old, baptized April 12th.
11. William VandeVer and wife Margareta's child John, born April 26th, baptized April 29th.
12. Hindric Stedham and wife Catharina's child Adam, born April 23d, baptized May 10th.
13. William White and wife Maria's child Thomas, born March 30th, baptized May 10th.
14. Richard Madgier and wife Sara's child John, born May 3d, baptized May 17th.
15. Mårten Justice and wife Brita's child Lydia, born May 25th, baptized May 30th.
16. Patrick Done and wife Elizabeth's child Susanna, 1 year old, baptized June 14th.
17. Jonas Walraven and wife Maria's child Sara, born June 22d, baptized June 27th.
18. Thomas West and wife Kerstin's child Christina, born June 17th, baptized June 27th.

19. Jesper Walraven and wife Annika's child Jonas, born August 3d, baptized August 9th.
20. John Seed and wife Brita's child Susanna, born August 13th, baptized August 16th.
21. Peter Petersson Canpany and wife Magdalena's child Susanna, born August 12th, baptised August 16th.
22. Elizabeth Bryan's illegitimate child William, 9 months old, baptized August 16th.
23. John Right and wife Anna's child Matthias, born August 22, baptized August 30th.
24. Hindric Kålsburg and wife Elizabeth's child Maria, born September 25, baptized September 7th.
25. George Reed and wife Ingeborg's child Lydia, born September 5th, baptized October 2d.
26. Jones Stedham and wife Helena's child Christina, born October 31st, baptized November 8th.
27. Mårten Mårtensson and wife Kerstin's child Anna, 6 weeks old, baptized November 22d.
28. Adam Staal and wife Christina's child Adam, born December 2d, baptized December 6th.
29. Laughlin McLean and wife Anna's child Sara, 3 weeks old, baptized December 10th.
30. John Garritson and wife Elizabeth's child Thomas, some weeks old, baptized December 13th.
31. Brewer Seneke and wife Brita's child Brewer, born February 26th, baptized March 23rd.

BURIALS, 1730.

1. Pastor Herr Magister Samuel Hesselius' wife Brita, buried January 27th.
2. Peter Pålsson, senior, buried March 28th.
3. Jonas Stalcop, buried April 15th.
4. Christiern Brunberg's child Matthias, buried August 24th.
5. Peter Petersson Canpany's child Helena, buried August 27th.
6. Chrirtiern Brunberg's child John, buried August 29th.
7. Antilli Stalcop's step daughter Elizabeth,|buried September 9th.
8. Antilli Stalcop's son Andreas, buried September 15th.
9. Edward Robbesson's wife Elizabeth, buried September 23d.
10. Philip VandeVer's wife Brita, buried November 1st.

OLD SWEDES CHURCH

Marriages, 1731.

1. Thomas Grindall and Eleanor Cook, Governor's license, married January 25 th.
2. James Flannelkin and Jane Gelaspy, married January 28th;
3. William Haul and Catharina Mag Curde, (McGurdy) married February 25th.
4. David Bar and Anna Moose, Governor's license, married March 4th.
5. Tobias Hindricsson and Catharina Homspoker, Governor License, married March 15th.
6. Daniel Moloughny and Margaret Starret, married April 25.
7. Daniel Mickel and Grashon Durnal, married May 20th.
8. Thomas Neal and Susanna Quin, married May 30th.
9. George Linmeyer and Judith Mounsson, Governor's liceuse, married June 30th,
10. William Reily and Mary Hill, married August 1st.
11. John Hill and Sara Price, married August 2nd.
12. Rees Rees and Margaret Green, Governor License, married August 26th.

Baptisms, 1731.

1. Gustaf Pålsson and wife Marget's|child Maria, 8 weeks old, baptized January 1st.
2. Israel Robbisson and wife Elizabeth's child Elizabeth, born December 27, 1730, baptized January 1st.
3. Walraven Walraven and wife Kerstin's child Sara, born January 3d. baptized January 3d,
4. James Fitzsimmon and wife Marget's child Maria, 9 weeks old, baptized January 16th.
5. Wiljam Clenny and wife Maria's child Jane, 2 months old, baptized January 16th.
6. Hans Smith and wife Maria's child Andreas, born January 14th, baptized January 17th.
7. James Senexon and wife Margareta's child James, born Feb. 7th, baptized February 13th.
8. Israel Petersson and wife Marget's child Annika, born Feb. 6th, baptized February 14th.
9. Peter Petersson and wife Annika's child Susanna, born March 4th, baptized March 7th.
10. Carl Cornelius and wife Anna's child Andreas, born March 27th, baptized April 4th.

11. Thomas Clark and wife Annika's child Maria, one month old, baptized August 11th.

12. John Mårten and wife Margareta's child Petrus, born March 28th, baptized April 11th.

13. Gustaf Gustafsson and wife Kerstin's child Gustavus, born April 22nd, baptized April 26th.

14. Pastor Herr Magister Samuel Hessellius and wife Gertrude's child Samuel, born May 23rd, baptized May 29th.

15. Garrit Garritsson and wife Elizabeth's child Anna, born May 16th, baptized May 30th.

16. Peter Tossawa and wife Marget's child Anna, born June 20th, baptized June 27th.

17. Peter Pålsson and wife Catharina's child Elizabeth, 2 weeks old, baptized July 18th.

18. Matthias Mårtensson and wife Elizabeth's child Thomas, 4 weeks old, baptized July 13th.

19. Robert Robertsson and wife Catharine's child Elizabeth, born August 7th, baptized August 13th.

20. Samuel Lewis and wife Maria's child Wiljam, born May 20th, baptized September 4th.

21. Wiljam Tossawa and wife Maria's child Christina, born September 7th, baptized September 12th.

22. Samuel Mead and wife Anna's child Wiljam, 7 months old, baptized September 12th.

23. Wiljam Andersson and wife Kerstin's child Maria, born October 2nd, baptized October 10th.

24. Jonathan Kirk and wife Maria's child Josua, one year old, baptized October 11th.

25. David Enoch and wife Helena's child Gertrude, 3 weeks old, baptized November 9th.

25. Hendrick Stedham and wife Catharina's child Judith, born November 4th, baptized November 9th.

27. Christopher Springer and wife Chatarine's child Susanna, born November 10th, baptized November 21st.

28. Carl Springer and wife Marget's child Catharina born November 21st, baptized November 22nd.

29. Wiljam Vandever and wife Marget's child Cornelius, born December 1st, baptized December 12th.

30. Carl Morten and wife Marget's child Maria, about 8 years old, baptized December 12th.

OLD SWEDES CHURCH

Burials 1731.

1. Andreas Springer buried January 16th.
2. Israel Springer buried January 24th.
3. Sara Meyer buried February 21st.
4. John Pâlsson's wife Sophia, buried June 30th.
5. Hans Petersson Smith's child Reuben, buried July 6th.
6. Robert Robinsson's child Elizabeth, buried August 15th.
7. Pastor Mag. Samuel Hessellius' child Christina buried 21st.
8. Peter Pâlsson's child Andreas, buried September 19th.
9. Rener Kioln's children Jacob and Jonas, buried December 12th.

Baptisms, 1732.

1. Timotheus Stedham and wife Elizabath's child Marget, born December 1st, baptized December 2nd.
2. Samnel Fandric and wife Annika's child Maria, December 1st, baptized same day.
3. Cornelius Ket and wife Marick's child Judith, born November 1st, baptized January 1st.
4. Jacob Stille and wife Rebecca's child Leddie born Jannary 16th, baptized January 30th.
5. Peter Hindricsson and wife Anna's child Johan, born December 16th, baptized December 30th.
5. Jacob Rogis and wife Johanna's children Johanne's and Cornelius, born January 7th, baptized January 14th.
6. Johannes Springer and wife Maria's child Mary, born August 18, baptized January 31st.
6. James Senneckson and wife Margaret Werdman's child Henry born May 4th.
7. John Seed and wife Brita's child Nicklos, born January 30th, baptized January 31st.
8. Lucas Stedham and wife Ingeborg's child Ingeborg, born March 26th.
9. Peter Andersson and wife Kerstin's child Catharina, born January 16th, baptized March 26th.
10. Peter Classon and wife Walborg's child Israel, born April 7th, baptized April 23rd.
11. John Sennexen and wife Ingeborg's child Sara, born March 22nd.

55

12. Regner Culen and widow Annika's child William, born March 15th, baptized April 23rd.

13. Hance Petersson and wife Catharina's child, Jonas, born April 11th, baptized April 23rd.

14. Jonas Stedham and wife Helena's child Zacharias, born February 20th, baptized March 26.

15. James Fitzsimmons and wife Margaretta's child Elizabeth, born April 11th, baptized April 23rd.

16. Marten Justafsson and wife Brigitta's child Annika, born July 27th, baptized 3rd Sunday after Trinity.

17 Mâns Gustafsson and wife Catharina's child Mâns, born July 14th, baptized 9th Sunday after Trinity.

18. Joseph Springer and wife Annika's child, Charl born September 3rd, baptized September 18th.

19. Jacob Vandever Jr. and wife Maria's child Petrus, born May 11th, baptized May 20th.

20. Robert Robinsson and wife Catharina's child Eleonore, born May 2nd, baptized May 4th.

21. Charles Philips and wife Ann's child Susanna, born October 10th, baptized December 31st.

22. Henrick Colesberg and wife Elizabeth's child Elizabeth, born October 1st, baptized October 14th.

23. Samuel Petersson and wife Christina's child Sara, born July 26th, baptized June 1st.

BAPTISMS, 1733.

1. Jesper Walraven and Annika's children, Tobias and Anders born January 4, baptized January 8.

2. Walla Walraven and wife Kerstin's child Jonas, born February 5, baptized February 18.

3. Thomas Willing and wife Cathrina's child Rebecca, born February 8, baptized February 18.

4. Anders Hindricsson and wife Maria, Johan, born March 15, baptized March 18.

5. Israel Robinson and wife Elizabeth's child Maria, born February 25, baptized March 18.

6. Peter Petersson Canpany and wife Magdalena's child Andreas, born April 10th, baptized April 15th.

7. Jonathan Kirk and wife Maria's child Abigail, 5 months old, baptized May 27th.

8. Johan Bann, married a man, and Kerstin Mân's illegitimate child Johan, born April 10, baptized May 27th.

OLD SWEDES CHURCH

9. Gustaf Pâlson and wife Margareta's child Margareta, born May 20th, baptized June 3d.

10. John Seed and wife Brita's child Samuel, born July 1st baptized July 29th.

11. Olle Andersson and wife Kerstin's child Sara, born June 7th, baptized June 17th.

12. Marten Martensson and wife Kerstin's child Cornelius, born July 1st, baptized August 15th.

13. Peter Petersson, over Brandywine, child Andreas, born September 5th, baptized September 9th.

14. Hindrick Stedham and wife Gertrude's child Abraham, born September 25th, baptized September 31st.

15. Johan Mâsten and wife Marget's child Ledi, born September 30, baptized October 7th.

16. Brewer Seneke and wife Brita's child Maria, born October 5th, baptized October 7th.

17. James Springer and wife Maria's child Darkis, born October 17th, baptized October 21st.

18. Jonas Stedham and wife Helena's child Ingeborg, born October 14th, baptized October 28th.

19. Robert Robersson and wife Catharina's child Robert born November 11th, baptized December 2d.

20. Philip Vandever and wife Kerstin's child Susanna, born December 4th, baptized December 16th.

21. Peter Pâlsson and wife Catharina's child Kerstin, born December 19th, baptized December 23d.

22. Jacob Hein's son Nicklas, born in November, baptized December 25th.

23. Peter Andersson's child Brita, born in November, baptized November 25th.

24. Johan Stalcop and wife Maria's child Johan, born December 19th, baptized December 27th.

BURIALS, 1733.

1. Peter Classon, February 22, buried February 25.

2. Peter Pâlsson's son, Paulus Pâlsson, died February 27, buried March 1.

BURIALS, 1734.

1. Widow Maria Brown, died February 23, buried February 24.

2. Pâl Pâlsson's daughter Rebecca, died February 27, buried 28.

3. Peter Pâlsson's daughter, died February 10, buried February 11.

EARLY CHURCH RECORDS OF NEW CASTLE COUNTY

4. Elizabeth Garritson, died March 13, buried March 18.
5. Garritson's weakly child died March 22, buried March 24.
6. Carl Cornelius' weakly daughter, died July 17, buried July 18.
7. Josef Springer's son Andreas, died July 17, buried July 18,
8. Mârtin Mârtins' son, buried September 26.
9. Samuel Petersson's daughter, buried October 9.
10. Johan Stalcop's son Tobias, buried December 2.
11. Christopher Stedham's child.
12. Henrick.

BURIALS, 1735.

1. Christopher Stedham's child.
2. Israel Justis' child.
3. Henrick Stedham's wife, buried October 21.

BURIALS, 1736.

1. Cornelius Ja Quett's widow's little daughter, buried Febary 26.
2. Charles Springer Jr.'s child, buried March 7.
3. John Stalcop's eldest daughter, buried April 19.
4. Charles Cornelius' son, buried Jan. 7.
5. Mârtin Mârtin's little daughter, buried July 6.
6. Olle Walraven, buried August 4.
7. Peter Andersson's child, August 28.
8. Jonathan Stille's little daughter, October 5.

BURIALS, 1737.

1. Peter Petersson's wife, (over Brandywine), January 4.
2. William's child, May 4.
3. Anders Gustafsson's wife, buried January 27.
4. Adam and Jacob Vandever.
5. James Springer's child, died May 25.
6. Susanna Vandever.
7. 2 of Peter Petersson's children.
8. 2 of Samuel Frederick's girls, of dysentery.
9. Samuel Petersson's child.

BURIALS, 1738.

1. Elizabeth Stedham, buried March 6.
2. John Mârten's son, buried March 12.
3. Carl Christopher Springer, died May 26 and was buried May 28, 80 years old.
4. Robert Robertson, died August 22.
5. William Vandever's child, buried August 22.

OLD SWEDES CHURCH

6. Peter Andersson's buried October 11.
7. Bille Vandever's 2nd child.
8. Jesper Classon, Jr., buried December 15.

1739.

1. Margareta Petersson, died January 1, buried January 3.
2. Gustaf Justis, struck dead by ligtning in his own house, May 10, buried May 12.
3. Margaretta Jones.
4. Hindrick Stedham's two sons.
5. Olle Tossawa's son, died October 7th.
6. William Vandever, died Octoder 12th.
7. Kirsten Schaffenhauser, died November 15th.
8. Jacob Vandever, died November 16th.
9. Peter Pâlsson's wife, died November 18th.
10. Lars Petersson, 77 years old, died November 21st.

BURIALS 1740.

1. Olle Pâlsson, buried March 12th.
2. Stina Vandever. buried May 11th.
3. Peter Pâlsson's second child.
4. John Vanneman, killed by a weight falling on him, buried October 4th.
5. Hans Smith's little daughter, buried October 18th.
6. Ingeborg Read, buried October 30th.
7. Hans Smith's little son, buried November 16th.
8. Christopher Linmeyers's wife, buried November 25th.

BURIALS 1741.

1. Anders Loinan's wife, 61 years, buried September 2d.
2. Mârten Mârten's son, buried March 2d.
3. John Mârten's daughter, buried March 10th.
4. Andrew Hâka's little daughter, buried April 13th.
5. John Mârten's wife, buried May 12th.

MARRIAGES 1733.

1. Richard Morrow and Catharine Owen, married April 4th.
2. William Boulding and Elizabeth Potts, Governor's License, married April 4th.
3. William Petticrue and Margaretta Feer, married June 5th.
4. John Owen and Lille Hinston, married June 10th.
5. Humphrey Bates, and Margery Morlhousen, married Aug. 27th.
6. Eleizer Meyer and Marte Braun, married October 25th.

EARLY CHURCH RECORDS OF NEW CASTLE COUNTY

7. Nathaniel Carter and Anna Macfersson, married December 15th.

N.B.—All these are English.

MARRIAGES 1734.

1. Reynold Baudin and Maria Catharine Barrel, married February 26th.
2. William Gavin and Briget Canady, married April 23d.
3. James Armstrong and Mary Bird, married April 25th.
4. Francis Simonson and Jenny Coulter, married May 10th.
5. James Stoane and Mary Cowper, married June 14th.
6. Benjamin Williams and Anna Mannely, married June 19th.
7. Titus Early and Mary Aàr, married August 2nd.
8. Henry Damsel and Sara Nâdger, married August 11th.
9. John Whipple and Elizabeth Karlin, married September 9th.
10. John Degunn and Helena Price, married September 23d.
11. Thomas Chambell and Christina Ja Quett, married September 26th.
12. John Fletcher and Helena Heinman, married October 12th.
13. Thomas Measor and Elizabeth Teeth, married Oct. 14th.
14. Thomas Clark and Catharina Tossawa, married Oct. 27th.
15. John Ja Quette and Christina Stedham, married November 1st.
16. Robert Gordon and Pernilla Battel, married November 9th.
17. William Clark and Sara White, married November 14th.
18. Jacob Skute and Martha Turner, married November 21st.
19. James Bayley and Mary MacDaniel, married December 21st.
20. William Penn and Margaret Breyen, married December 26th.
21. Zacharias Kittel and Christine Justis, married December 26th.

MARRIAGES, 1735.

1. John Moore and Ann Robison, married January 16th.
2. John Day and Mary Mackluer, married January 30th.
3. Samuel Simmons and Jane Hamilton, married February 6th.
4. Martin Hius (Hughs) and Mary Jinkins, married February 15th.
5. John Evans and Rebecca Ley, married February 28.
6. Thomas Walker and Elizabeth Delany, married March 24th.
7. James Macgrau and Mary Dix, married March 25th.
8. Samuel Means and Grissel Ogle, married April 10th.

9. Jonathan Stille and Magdalena Vandever, married April 17th.
10. Samson Thomas and Hester Certain, married April 20th.
11. Garrit Garrisson and Mary Baudwin, married May 13th.
12. Asmond Stedham and Kerstin Hindricksdotter, married May 14th.
13. Wiljam Didrickson and Maria Petersson, married June 11th.
14. Moses Harper and Elizabeth Farlow, married July 6th.
15. James Mackmullen and Mary Mackdonald, married July 15th.
16. Edward Sergeant and Jane Read, married August 4th.
17. Denis Mackginley and Elsa Mackkarty, married August 10th.
18. John Robinson and Jeanet Mortol, married September 2nd.
19. Thomas Long and Martha Thatcher, married September 8th.
20. Elias King and Annika Tussey, (Tossawa) married October 22nd.
22. Anders Hindricsson and Kerstin Andersson, married December 3rd.
23. Jonas Andersson and Brita Loinan, married in my absence by Mr. Ross in New Castle, November 19th.
24. John Flintham and Abigail Green, married December 20th.
25. Neal Obiyan and Rachel Thomas, married December 24th.
26. John Poor and Mary Holoway. married December 25th.

Baptisms, 1734.

1. Hans Petersson and wife Chatrina's daughter Helena, born January 12th, baptized January 20th.
2. Caroli Springer and wife Marget's son Edward, born January 24th, baptized January 27th.
3. Pouel Poulsen and wife Magdalena's daughter Rebecca, born February 12th, baptized February 16th.
4. Christopher Springer and wife Catharine's son Solomon, born February 7th, baptized February 17th.
5. Garrit Garritssen and wife Elizabeth's daughter Maria, born March 6th, baptized March 10th.
6. William Vandewer and wife Marget's daughter Marget, born March 22nd, baptized March 24th.
7. John Seneck and wife Ingeborg's daughter Anna, born March 5th, baptized March 31st.

EARLY CHURCH RECORDS OF NEW CASTLE COUNTY

8. Mathew Morten and wife Bette's son Jacob, born February 17th, baptized March 31st.

9. James Seneck and wife Marget's son John, born April 17th, baptized April 21st.

10. Hans Georg Smith and wife Marias son Ericus, born May 31st, baptized June 3rd.

11. Peter Hendrickson and wife Anna's son Peter, born June 23rd, baptized June 30th.

12. Carl Cornelius and wife Nanne's daughter Elizabeth, born June 22nd, baptized June 30th.

13. Joseph Springer and wife Annika's son Andreas, born September 10th, baptized September 13th.

14. George Read and wife Ingeborg's son Charles, born September 24th, baptized September 29th.

15. Anders Polson and wife Elizabeth's son Andreas, born September 25th, baptized November 10th.

16. Henrick Colesburg and wife Bette's son Jacob, born October 29th, baptized November 10th.

17. Israel Peterson and wife Margaretta's son Jonas, born November 9th, baptized November 15th.

18. James Mechaslin and wife Annika's son James, born May 25th.

19. William Tossa and wife, Mary Shapenhoise's Sarah, born March 8th.

BAPTISMS, 1735.

1. William Cleneay and wife Maria's daughter Sarah, born December 14, 1734, baptized January 4th.

2. Samuel Peterson and wife Christina's daughter Susanna, born January 1st, baptized January 12th.

3. Walraven Walraven and wife Kirsten's daughter Elizabeth, born January 7th, baptized January 12th.

4. Timothei Stedham and wife Elizabeth's son Timotheus, born January 11th, baptized January 12th.

5. Robert Robinson and wife Catharina's daughter Anna, born February 16th, baptized February 23rd.

6. Olle Tusse and wife Maria's daughter Sara, born March 8th, baptized March 15th.

7. Henrick Stedham and wife Catharina's son Jacob, born March 17th, baptized March 23rd.

8. Rienold Baudin and wife Maria Chatrina's son Johan, born in March, baptized long Friday.

OLD SWEDES CHURCH

9. Pafuel Gustafson, (over Brandywine) son Joseph, more than a year old, baptized April 20th.

10. Joseph Pears and wife Mari's son Timotheus, born February 18th, baptized April 27th.

11. Hans Peterson and wife Elizabeth's (over Brandywine) son Johan, born March 22nd, baptized April 27th.

12. Jonas Stedham and wife Helena's son Johan, born January 2nd, baptized January 8th.

13. Andrew Hendrickson and wife Maria's son Israel, born June 8th, baptized June 15th.

14. Pafuel Pauelson and wife Magdalena's son Pafuel, born June 9th, baptized July 13th.

15. Israel Robesson and wife Elizabeth's son Joseph, born May 30th, baptized July 13th.

16. James Springer and wife Maria's son Charles, born August, baptized August 31st.

17. Ole Anderson and wife Kerstin's son James, baptized September 7th.

18. Carl Cornelii and wife Manni's son Samuel, born September 22d, baptized September 28th.

19. Peter Anderson and wife Kerstin's daughter Elizabeth, born October 7th, baptized October 19th.

20. Joseph Springer and wife Annika's daughter, born November 9th, baptized and called Beata November 22d.

21. William Didrickson and wife Maria's daugther Catharina, born November 22d, baptized November 26th.

22. Brewer Seneck and wife Brita's son James, born November 26th, baptized November 30th.

23. John Sead and wife Brita's son William, born October 1st, baptized November 23d.

24. Peter Polson and wife Catharina's son Ole, born December 4th, baptized December 14th.

BAPTISMS, 1736.

1. James Mechaslin and wife Annika's daughter Kethi, born January 1st, baptized January 3d.

2. Peter Petersson Conpony and wife Magdelena's daughter Anna, baptized January 11th.

3. Morten Morten and wife Kerstin's daughter Susanna, born Nov. 29, 1735, baptized January 8th.

4. Asmund Stedham and wife Kerstin's son Samuel, born January 14th, baptized February 8th.

5. Timotheus Stedham and wife Catharina's daughter Sara, born February 5th, baptized February 8th.

6. Hans Petersson and wife Catharina's son Petrus, born February 15th, baptized February 22d.

7. Walraven Walraven and wife Kerstin's son Johan, born February 27th, baptized February 29th.

8. Jonathan Stilley and wife Magdalena's daughter Rebecca, born January 23d, baptized February 29th.

9. William Vandever and wife Marget's daughter Catharina, born February 13th, baptized February 29th.

10. John Degnen and wife Helena's daughter Maria, born January 27th, baptized March 14th.

11. James Anderson and wife Brita's daughter Maria, born February 15th, baptized March 14th.

12. John Seneck and wife Ingeborg's daughter Catharina, born February 8th, baptized March 21st.

13. Robert Robesson and wife Câtharina son Israel, born March 31st, baptized April 11th.

14. Christiern Brynberg and wife Maria's son Matthew, born March 22d, baptized April 26th.

15. James Seneck and wife Marget's son James, born April 17th, baptized April 26th.

16. Garrit Garritsson and wife Maria's daughter Rebecca, born April 19th, baptized April 26th.

17. Gustaf Polsen and wife Marget's daughter Susanna born Nov. 23, 1735

18. Christopher Springer and wife Catharina's son Abraham, born April 25th, baptized May 16th.

19. Johannes Springer and wife Maria's son Joseph, born March 28th, baptized May 23d.

20. Morten Justis and wife Brita's son Johan, born May 26th, baptized May 30th.

21. Zacharias Didrickson, Jr. and wife Sara's son William, born June 4th, baptized June 13th.

22. Reinold Baudwin and wife Catharina's son Jacob, born June 13th, baptized June 20th.

23. John Von Niemen and wife Beata's son Johan, born December 11th, baptized December 25th.

24. Peter Petersson, Jr., and wife Annika's son Samuel, born December 23d, baptized December 25th.

OLD SWEDES CHURCH

25. Thomas Bord and wife Anna's daughter Anna, 2 years old; father ran away.
26. William Tossa and wife Mary's son Frederick, born December 23d.

MARRIAGES 1736.

1. Henrick Stedham and Margury Owens, by Mr. Backhouse, married January 8th.
2. James Lownes and Mattie Willey, license, married January 20th.
3. Augustine Pasmore and Judith Farlon, published, married January 22nd.
4. Joseph Bond and Susanna Cloud, published, married January 22nd.
5. Archibald Campbell and Marrian Ramage, married February 11th.
6. Charles Hedges and Mary Stilly, married February 12th.
7. James Cove and Isabel Kranston, published, married February 26th.
8. John Coln and Maria Pears, married March 28th.
9. William Gregory and Marget Lowe, married April 16th.
10. William Brown and Martha Dunn, married April 16th.
11. Jacob Harper and Sarah Hendrickson, married May 5th.
12. Samuel Hooton and Ann Goodbody, married May 8th.
13. Jonas Robertson and Rebecca Clenny, married May 19th.
14. James Flyed and Elizabeth Tobe, married June 6th.
15. John Martin and Judith Knight, published, married June 14th.
16. Benjamin Clark and Elizabeth Robinson, married June 28th.
17. Aaron Deveney and Margaret Stuerde, married July 26th.
18. Samuel Richie and Lydia Linvel, married August 10th.
19. Alexander Newden and Mary Tuckney, married August 10th.
20. Thomas Gregg and Esther Preis, married August 23rd.
21. Erasmus Morten and Ruth Roman, married August 29th.
22. Johannas Springer and Mary Demsy, married August 31st.
23. William Clark and Sarah Freeman, married September 4th.
24. John Sprus and Lydia Clayton, married September 14th.
25. Jeremiah Stârdger and Martie Wins, married September 14th.
26. ThollyMiller and MaryMackfadien, married September 19th.
27. John Halloer and Mary Griffis, married September 29th.

EARLY CHURCH RECORDS OF NEW CASTLE COUNTY

28. John Vandever and Mary Justice, married September 30th.
29. John Michel and Jane Noels, married October 3rd.
30. John Youngblood and Hannah Morsley, married October 25th.   Morsley/Mousley?
31. William Baxter and Elizabeth Miner, married October 29th.
32. Fenly Mackgreio and Elizabeth Lauris, married November 3rd.
33. William Green and Catherine Forkinear, married November 8th.
34. Thomas Brunton and Mary Leech, married November 8th.
35. David Black and Rachel Harris, married November 15th.
36. Elias Barns and Elizabeth Giarge, married November 27th.
37. Richard Graham and Hannah Kathi, married December 12.
38. Richard Groudt and Sarah Goun, married December 26th.
39. Joseph Jackson and Mali Vandever, marrried December 27th.

MARRIAGES 1737.

1. Elias Tossa and Christina King, married January 5th.
2. Charles steelman and Johanna Lawell, married February 3rd.
3. Thomas Anderson and Mary Winey, married April 12th.
4. Thomas Miner and Jane Wilson, married April 12th.
5. Francis Onayle and Anna Walker, married May 8th.
6. William Ford and Anna Ford, married May 9th.
7. John Creid and Anna Maken, married May 30th.
8. John Curtlo and Anna Wansford, married June 7th.
9. John Stardges and Mary Baid, married June 12th.
10. James Eldrich and Sarah Poil, married June 16th.
11. John Musgrave and Mary Brown, married June 18th.
12. John Justis and Kirstin Wa;raven, married July 30th.
13. Robert Skreen and Mary Baterten, married August 21st.
14. Conrad Garretson and Mary Johnson, married September 8th.
15. John Greer and Mary Blair, married September 26th.
16. David Nilson and Charity Peters, married September 29th.
17. Robert Babber and Catharine Tussy, married September 29th.
18. Owen Kynler and Sarah Weili, married October 10th.
19. John Crasher and Anna Curry, married November 26th.
20. Justas Justis and Susanna Stilley, married December 1st.

OLD SWEDES CHURCH

21. Peter Peterson and Brita Morten, married November 24th.
22. John Stefenson and Jane Thomson, married December 1st.
23. Michel Higgins and Frances Henrickson, married December 11th.
24. Peter Stalcop and Susanna Palson, married December 15th.
25. Thomas Wilson and Susanna Parker, married December 20th.
26. William Stewart and Mary Broom, married December 20th

MARRIAGES 1738.

1. Henry Lane and Hannah Kay, married New Year's Eve.
2. Joseph Williamson and Hannah Hays, married January 4th.
3. Arthur Lattimon and Rebecca Whiteside, married January 10th.
4. John Mahaffy and Jane Frey, married January 17th.
5. Benjamin King and Bathi Beheskei, married January 22nd.
6. Henry Maddock and Rebecca Sandelands, married February 8th.
7. Eliha Barns and Rachel Hollingsworth married February 12th.
8. Griffith Minshall and Sarah Minshall, married March 20th.
9. David Asbon and Catharina Walson, married April 3rd.
10. Jacob Yungblood and Mary Welsh, married April 10th.
11. Thomas Evans and Debora Harlin, married April 19th.
12. John Ford and Elizabeth Sincock, married April 24th.
13. John Gray and Barbara Boals, married May 15th.
14. William Stennop and Nannie Vainam, married May 22.
15. Joseph Simpson and Margaret Evans, married June 2nd.
16. Joseph Walter and Jane Branton, married June 6th.
17. Cornelius Vandever and Marget Morton, married June 22
18. John Nicklin and Sarah Nicklin, married August 3rd.
19. Mathiew Huston and Lydy Key, married August 6th.
20. John Tremble and Mary Langly, married August 23rd.
21. Bryan Macginnie and Sara Jones, married August 28th.
22. William Stoby and Nannie Gofard, married September 12th.
23. Bryan Culen and Sara Kelly, married October 12th.
24. Samuel Bane and Mary Brounfield, married October 2nd.
25. Michel Farlow and Mary White, married November 23rd.
26. Adolph Wulback and Catharina Vandever, married December 14th.

EARLY CHURCH RECORDS OF NEW CASTLE COUNTY

27. Andreas Stilly and Catharina Stalcop, married December 21st.
28. John Hedges and Susanna Hendrickson, married December 20th.
29. Peter Vandever and Margareta Hoppman, married December 28th.

MARRIAGES 1739.

1. Peter Anderson and Catharina Leina, married January 10th.
2. William Weily and Catharina Farlou, married February 5th.
3. James Robinson and Elizabeth Kiabbin, married February 6th.
4. James Nealy and Sarah MacMullin, married February 12th.
5. Abram Barnet and Elizabeth Chiafin, married March 1st.
6. Thomas Turner and Beata Justis, married April 4th.
7. Thomas Didrick and Eleanora Garron, married April 23rd
8. Thomas Jefferis and Cathreen Baldon, married May 6th.
9. John Isac and Eleanor Connelly, married May 14th.
10. Andrew Chalmers and Isabella Loftus, married May 14th.
11. Nater Raserman and Francis Macksen, married May 21st.
12. William Jones and Mary Branton, married May 28th.
13. Dennis Whealon and Anna Tounsen, married June 4th.
14. Christopher Hendricksson and Mary Robeson, married June 11th.
15. John Branden and Malii Cathi, married June 11th.
16. Edmund Burk and Rachel Howard, married June 25th.
17. Abraham Ford and Jane Ferris, married July 15th.
18. William Young and Susanna Boyd, married August 1st
19. Richard Buffington and Anna Morgan, married August 5th.
20. William Morgan and Anna Buffington, married August 5th.
21. Joseph Jaley and Letes Graims, married August 12th.
22. James Townsen and Sara Ward, married August 13th.
23. Moses Carshin and Jane Knochs, married August 20th.
24. Hugh Kirgian and Catharine Onail, married October 14th.
25. David Pouel and Elizabeth Chatson, married October 24th.
26. John Casper Lambert and Mary Snekins, married November 19th.

OLD SWEDES CHURCH

27. James House and Mary Wright, married November 25th.
28. Dan Beeby and Ann Tilton married December 4th.
29. Hugh Hallanger and Becky Henderson, married December 19th.
30. James Thompson and Hanna Armstong, married December 24th.
31. Robert Green and Anna Moore, married December 25th.

MARRIAGES IN 1740.

1. James Brucks and Mary Black, married February 1st.
2. Jacob Lachaerd and Mary Cunningham, married March 10th.
3. William Woods and Marth ι Macleclan, married March 25th
4. William Brown and Christina Mounson, married April 3d.
5. Ralph Williams and Martha Maccalshonder, married April 17th.
6. Arthur Donnelly and Mary Maccdade, married April 21st.
7. Thomas Wade and Anna Milleson, married April 28th.
8. John Crosby and Eleanor Culin, maried May 6th.
9. John Read and Hannah Belis, married May 11th.
10. Peter Sigfreedus Alrich and Susanna Stidham, married May 25th.
11. Richard Robinson and Susanna Justis, married May 27th.
12. Joseph Williamson and Judith Corner, married May 25th.
13. David Sharpless and Persilla Powel, married June 12th.
14. Peter Didrickson and Margareta Stilly, married June 19th.
15. Thomas Minshall and Jane Lalshield, married September 20th.
16. Joseph Tarrington and Jane Cooper, married November 2nd.
17. Anders Stiddom and Catharina Keen, married November 11th.
18. John McClary? and Jane Dads, married November 12th.
19. Thomas Ives and Rachel Brawn, married November 24th.
20. George Stroud and Elizabeth Cleaton, married December 7th.
21. Christopher Flinn and Rebecca Hossy, married December 26th.

EARLY CHURCH RECORDS OF NEW CASTLE COUNTY

MARRIAGES IN 1741.

1. Timotheus Steddom and Maria Vandever, married January 1st.
2. Nicol Bishop and Hester Smith, married January 1st.
3. Edward Seed and Abigail Buffington, married January 1st.
4. William Smith and Anne Lowry, married January 12th.
5th. Michael Morgan and Mary Buffington, married February 18th.
6th. John Welsh and Elizabeth Scott, married February 25th.
7. Henry Spragg and Elizabeth Lowry, married February 26.
8. Isaac Stroud and Sara Baker, married March 8th.
9th. Henry Simonson and Sussanna Tarrat, married March 9th.
10. John Wood and Martha Didrich, married March 27th.
11. James Biard and Jane Ross, married April 20th.
12. David Dutton and Mary Lind, married May 4th.
13. Myles Sweeney and Eleanor Champbell, married May 20th.
14. John Lawrence and Elizabeth Edwards, May 23d.
15. John Murphy and Catharine Spruce, married May 26th.
16. Joseph Been and Persanna Ellis, married May 29th.
17. James Milnor and Ester Vernon, married June 24th.
18. Joseph Brooks and Jane Deeble, married July 22nd.

RECORD OF BAPTISMS IN CHRISTINA, WITH THE NAMES OF THE PARENTS, 1737

1. Olle Tassa and his wife Maria's child Fredrick, born the 24th of December 1736, baptized the 2nd of January.
2. Samuel Fudrie and his wife Nanny's daughter, born 21st of January, baptized the 23rd of January.
3. Henrick Colesburg and his wife Elizabeth's son Swen, born the 27th of December 1736, baptized the 6th of March 1737.
4. John Stalcop and his wife Maria's child Andreas, born the 27th of January, baptized the 13th of March.
5. Charles Springer and his wife Margret's child Jacob, born the 9th of February, baptized the 20th of March.
6. Jones Stedham and his wife Helena's child Cornelius, born the 16th of March, baptized the 20th of March.
7. Peter Andersson and his wife Kerstin's child Eric, born the 19th of March, baptized the 27th of March.
8. Powel Pafwelson and his wife Magdalena' schild Carl, born the 10th of March, baptized the 11th of April.
9. William Clenny and his wife Kerston's child William, baptized the 25th of April.
10. Samuel Petersson and his wife Maria's child Samuel born the 2nd of April, baptized the 1st of May.

OLD SWEDES CHURCH

11. Jonas Robesson and his wife Rebecca's son Charles, born the 24th of April, baptized the 1st of May.
12. James Springer and his wife Maria's child Susanna, born the 26th of July, baptized the 31st of July.
13. Jonathan Stilly and his wife Magdalena's child Maria, baptized the 14th of August.
14. Elias Tossa and his wife Christina's child Alexander, born the 18th of September, baptized the 25th of September.
15. Robert Robeson and his wife Catharina's child Richard, born the 19th of September, baptized the 2nd of October.
16. John Mortin and his wife Marget's son Johan, born the 18th of September, baptized the 2nd of October.
17. John Senech and his wife Ingeborg's child Anna Ingeborg, born the 16th of September, baptized the 16th of October.
18. John Seed and his wife Brita's child Anna, born the 18th of October, baptized the 30th of October.
19. Joseph Springer and his wife Annika's child Maria, born the 27th of October, baptized the 30th of October.
20. Joseph Pears and his wife Maria's child Johan, born the 4th of November, baptized the 13th of November.
21. William Didrickson and his wife Maria's son Jacob, born the 10th of November, baptized the 20th of November.
22. Hans Smith and his wife Maria's child Jonas, born the 21st of November, baptized the 27th of November.
23. Erasmus Stedham and his wife Christina's child Adam, born the 17th of November, baptized the 2nd of December.
24. Andrew Hendrickson, senior, and his wife Maria's child Catharina, born the 29th of November, baptized the 6th of December.
25. James Anderssen and his wife Brita's child Catharina, born the 29th of November, baptized the 10th of December.
26. Ole Anderssen and his wife Kerstin's child Peter, baptized the 11th of December.
27. Joseph Jackson and his wife Malin's child George, born the 1st of November, baptized the 11th of December.
28. Morten Morten and his wife Kerstin's child Christina, born the 19th of December, baptized the 29th of December.
29. Robin Ford and his wife Mary's child Mary, born the 5th of March, baptized the 31st of December.

EARLY CHURCH RECORDS OF NEW CASTLE COUNTY

BAPTISMS IN 1738.

1. Reinold Baudwin and his wife Catharina's child Niclas, born the 17th of December 1737, baptized the 1st of January 1738.
2. William Vandever and his wife Margaretha's child Swen, born the 21st of December, baptized the 23rd of January.
3. James Macchaslin and his wife Annika's child Johan, born the 31st of December, baptized the 23rd of January.
4. Cunningham Walters and Agnes Andersson's child Edward, born the 11th of November, baptized the 3rd of February.
5. Christiern Brunberg and his wife Maria's child Christina, born the the 20th of January, baptized the 5th of January.
6. Hans Pettersson and his wife Catharina's child Elizabeth, born the 30th of March, baptized the 9th of April.
7. James Senecks and his wife Margaretha's child Susanna, born the 19th of March, baptized the 16th of April.
8. Peter Polson and his wife Catharina's child Peter, born the 30th of December, baptized the 12th of February.
9. Hans Petersson and his wife Catharina's child Susanna, born the 10th of May baptized the 18th of June.
10. Gustaf Justis, senior and his wife Susanna's child Maria, born the 1st of July, baptized the 16th of July.
11. Peter Petersson (over Brandywine) and his wife Brita's child Mathias, born the 2nd of September, baptized the 10th of September.
12. Christopher Springer and his wife Catharina's child Joseph, born the 19th of September, baptized the 8th of October.
13. Peter Anderson and his wife Kerstin's child Peter, born the 27th of September, baptized the 11th of October.
14. Morton Justis and his wife Brita's child Sara, born the 18th of September, baptized the 29th of October.
15. George Reed and his wife Ingeborg's child Elias, born the 30th of November, baptized the same day.

BAPTISMS IN 1739.

1. Peter Canpony and his wife Magdalena's child Catharina, born the 26th of November, baptized the 1st of January.
2. Henric Stedham and his wife Margaretta's child Sara, born the 27th of December, baptized the 1st of January.
3. Gustaf Palsson and his wife Margaretta's child Kerstin, born the 26th of November, baptized 21st of January.

OLD SWEDES CHURCH

4. Johan Justis and his wife Kerstin's child Susanna, born the 17th of December, baptized 21st of January.

5. James Springer and his wife Mary's child Mary, born the 13th of February, baptized the 18th of February.

6. Conrad Garritson and his wife Mary's child Christina, baptized the 25th of January.

7. Christ Lindmeyer and his wife's child Joran, born the 5th o February, baptized the 11th of March.

8. Cornelius Vandever and his wife Margaretta's child Susanna born the 6th of March, baptized the 3d of April.

9. William Tussy and his wife Maria's child Mathias, born the 1st of April, baptized the 4th of April.

10. Peter Stalcop and his wife Susanna's child Johan, born the 22nd of April, baptized the 29th of April.

11. Charles Springer and his wife Margaretta's child Gabriel, born the 11th of May, baptized the 10th of June.

12. Jonas Stedham and his wife Helena's child Helena, born the 14th of June, baptized the 17th of June.

13. Johan Neeman and his wife Beata's child Maria, born 31st of July, baptized the 12th of August.

14. Paul Pouelson and his wife Magdalena's child Petrus, born the 28th of July, baptized the 26th of August.

15. Joseph Jackson and his wife Malin's child Philip, born the 12th of August, baptized the 9th of September.

16. Thomas Bord and his wife Anna's child Rebecca, born the 29th of June, baptized the 9th of September.

17. Peter Vandever and his wife Margaret's child Andreas, born the 10th of September, baptized the 11th of September.

18. Henrick Colesburg and his wife Elizabeth's child Hendric, born the 17th of August, baptized the 20th of September.

19. Elias, Tassa and his wife Christina's child Anna, born the 30th of September, baptized the 8th of October.

20. Jonothan Stille and his wife Magdalena's child Jacob, born the 3d of September, baptized the 14th of October.

21. James Anderson and his wife Brita's child William, born the 2d of October, baptized the 14th of October.

22. Adolph Wuhlbach and his wife Catharina's child Maria, born the 14th of October, baptized the 15th of October.

23. Joseph Springer and his wife Annika's child Joseph, born the 17th of October, baptized the 21st of October.

24. Peter Polson and his wife Catharina's child Susanna, born the 13th of November, baptized the 25th of November.

EARLY CHURCH RECORDS OF NEW CASTLE COUNTY

25. Anders Stitly and his wife Catharina's child Maria, born the 5th of December, baptized the 9th of December.

26. William Anderson and his wife Kerstin's child William, born the 20th of November, baptized the 23d of December.

27. Johan Hedges and his wife Susanna's child Charles, born the 20th of December, baptized the 23d of December.

28. Joseph Peers and his wife Mary's child Richard, born the 24th of December, baptized January 1st, 1740.

29. Reynold Baudwin and his wife Catharina's child Fredrick, born the 4th of December, baptized the 17th of February, 1740.

RECORD OF BAPTISM, 1740.

1. Cornelius Vandever and his wife Margarita's child Brita, born the 31st of January, baptized 2d of March.

2. William Sloby and his wife Annika's child William, born the 16th of September, 1739, baptized the 30th of March, 1740.

3. John Senecks and his wife Ingeborg's child Susanna, born the 2d of April, baptized the 7th of April.

4. Andreas Stalcop, Jr. and his wife Johannes child Joanna, born the 13th day of May, baptized the 25th of May.

5. Henrich Stedham and his wife Margery's child Adam, born the 10th of August, baptized the 14th of September.

6. Peter Didrickson and his wife Margarita's child Jacob, born the 2d of September, baptized the 5th of October.

7. Hans Smit and his wife Maria's child Maria, born the 25th of September, baptized the 5th of October.

8. Gustaf Justison, Jr. and his wife Susanna's child Catharina, born the 1st of October, baptized the 12th of October.

9. Lucas Mânson and his wife Annika's child Jonathan, born the 9th of October, baptized the 12th of October.

10. Thomas Willing and his wife Catharina's child Anna, born the 22d of November, baptized the 4th of December.

11. Anders Hendrickson and his wife Maria's child Jonas, born the 18th of November, baptized the 13th of December.

RECORD OF BAPTISMS.

1. Peter Anderson and his wife Catharina's child Andreas, born the 7th of January, baptized the 9th of January.

2. Samuel Petersson and his wife Christina's child Jonas, born the 1st of March, baptized the 3rd of March.

3. Richard Robinson and his wife Susanna's child Margareta, born 11th of February, baptized immediately because of its weakness.

OLD SWEDES CHURCH

4. William Brown and Christina Mounson's child Abraham, born the 10th of March, baptized the 5th of April.

5. Cornelius Vandever and his wife Margret's child Jacob, born 31st of March, baptized the 3rd of May.

6. Christiern Brunberg and his wife Maria's child Elizabeth born 9th of April, baptized 5th of May.

7. Peter Peters Canpony and his wife Magdalena's child Johan, born the 10th of April, baptized the 5th of May.

8. Peter Hendrickson and his wife Anna's child David, born the 11th of April, baptized the 17th of May.

9. Thomas Turner and his wife Beata's child Maria, born the 23rd of April, baptized the 24th of May.

10. Augustus Constantine and his wife's child Maria, born in March, baptized the 24th of May.

11. Carolus Springer and his wife Margarita's child Margarita, born the 27th of May, baptized the 5th of June.

12. Peter Stalcop and his wife Susanna's child William, born the 27th of May, baptized the 27th of June.

13. Morten Morten and his wife Kerstin's child Johan, born the 5th of June, baptized the 19th of July.

14. John Hedges and his wife Susanna Hendrickson's child John, born the 25th of November.

15. Hans Peterson and his wife Catharina's child Andreas, born the 13th of August, baptized the 22nd of August.

August 9th 1743.—Timothy Lucas Stedham declared that he had sold to Timothy Lulofson Stedham and his heirs, the pew in Christina Church which he bought of Erasmus Stedham.

RECORD OF BAPTISMS, 1742.

1. James Anderson and Brita Loinan's child James, born the 25th of December, 1741.

2. William Von Culen and his wife Maria's child Andreas, born the 12th of March, 1742, baptized the 18th of April.

3. William Davis and his wife Grace's child Mary, born the 26th of June, baptized the 11th of September.

4. Joseph Cartmill and his wife Sara's child Hanna, born the 3d of October, baptized the 29th of December.

5. Morton Garrit's and his wife Annika's child Margaret, born the 13th of November, baptized the 29th of November.

6. Joseph Nowell and his wife Mary's child Christina, born the 8th of April, baptized the 20th of April.

EARLY CHURCH RECORDS OF NEW CASTLE COUNTY

7. Robert May and his wife Susanna's child Andrew, born the 2nd of October, baptized the 16th of October.

8. Niclos Turner and his wife Beata's child Mary, born the 23d of April, 1741, baptized the 26th of March, 1743.

9. John Stephanson and his wife Jane's child John, born the 8th of July, baptized the 31st of July.

10. Robert Smith and his wife Mary's child William, born April 30th, baptized the 31st April.

11. Asmund Stedham and his wife Christina Hindrickson's child Zacharias, born the 26th of April, baptized the 7th of June.

12. Justa Poulson and his wife Margret's child Catharine, born the 19th of July, 1741, baptized 1742.

13. Hans Petersson and his wife Catharina's child Andreas, born the 13th of August, 1741, baptized the 22nd of August.

14. Mathias Morten and his wife Elizabeth's child Elizabeth, born the 8th of September, baptized the 20th of September.

15. Joseph Springer and his wife Anna's child Catharina, born the 5th of October, 1741, baptized the 9th of October.

16. Christopher Springer and his wife Catharina's child Catharina, born the 20th of October, baptized the 26th of October.

17. Reinold Badin and his wife Catharina's child Maria, born the 10th of October, baptized the 8th of September.

17. Henry Colsberry and his wife Elizabeth's child William, born and baptized the 1st of November.

18. John Senecks and his wife Ingeborg's child Maria, born the 28th of November.

19. Peter Griffin and his wife Brigit's child Hannah, born the 8th of June, baptized the 12th of June.

20. Jonas Robeson's child Edward, born the 1st of December, baptized the 7th of December.

21. Peter Alldridge and his wife Susanna's child Mary, born the 4th of November, baptized the 8th of November.

22. James Seneck and his wife Margret's child Sara, born the 13th of June, baptized the 1st of July.

23. John Henricson and his wife Rebecca's child John, born the 22d of September, baptized the 30th of September.

24. William Dedrickson and his wife Mary's child Susanna, born the 31st of December, baptized the 8th of June.

25. An illegitimate child, laid to Robert Pierce, the name of the mother ——— Bird, born 1st of January.

OLD SWEDES CHURCH

26. Henry Stedham and his wife Margery's child Annika, born the 23d of November, baptized the 30th of November.

27. Peter Vandever and his wife Margarita's child Philip, born the 21st of May, baptized the 31st of ———.

BURIALS IN 1743.

Timotheus Stedham's two daughter's Elizabeth and Margaret died of dysentery.

Cornelius Vandever's daughter Brigitta, buried 7th October.

Andreas Stalcop died of consumption, buried 4th March.

Bartholomew Paulson's daughter Catharina, buried 22nd January.

RECORD OF BAPTISMS 1743.

1. Olle Monson's child Annika, born January, baptized the 30th of January.

2. Peter Paulson and his wife Mary's child Mary, born the 9th of January, baptized the 15th of January.

3. John Hedges and his wife Susanna's child Joseph, born the 7th of January, baptized the 11th of January.

4. Peter Garrisson and his wife Sara's child John, born the 6th of November, baptized the 20th of November.

5. Garret Garrison and his wife Mary's child Garret, born the 8th of March, baptized the 7th of November.

6. Israel Robeson and his wife Elizabeth's child Sara, born the the 15th of February, baptized the 21st of February.

7. Bartholomew Paulson and his wife Eleanor's child Mary, born the 2d of October, baptized the 7th of October.

8. Johan Hyland and his wife Mary's child Mary, born and baptized the 27th of August.

9. James Springer and his wife Mary's child Niclas, born the 5th, baptized the 8th of August.

10. Lulof Peterson's child Israel, born the 20th, baptized the 24th of July.

11. Carolus Springer and his wife Margret's child Rachel, born the 6th, baptized the 12th of June.

12. Joseph Springer and his wife Anna's child Sara, born and baptized the 26th of October.

13. Zachariah Dedrichson's child Ellinor, born the 24th of December.

14. William Stuby and his wife Anna's child James, born the 8th of January, 1743.

15. Augustin Constantin's child Sara, born the 10th, baptized the 15th of January.

16. Peter Stalcop and his wife Susanna's child Tobias, born the 1st, baptized the 6th of August.

17. Anders Henrickson and his wife Mary's child Leddy, born the 21st, baptized the 27th of January.

18. Anders Stalcop's child Mary, born the 2d of September, baptized the 3d of October.

19. Peter Anderson and his wife Catharina Lorena's child Christina, born and baptized the 27th of October.

20. William Tosawa and his wife Maria's child William, born the 22d, baptized the 28th of July.

21. Richard Robeson and his wife Susanna's child Andrew, born the 6th, baptized the 9th of March.

22. Thomas Badrill and his wife Maria's child Thomas, born the 1st, baptized the 6th of March.

23. Daniel Culen and his wife Elizabeth's child Daniel, born the 22nd of September, baptized the 10th of October.

24. Henry Tathen and his wife Elizabeth's child Andrew, born the 1st, baptized the 12th of October.

25. William Elly and his wife Margaret's child Benjamin, born the 27th of July.

26. Martin Ellet and his wife Jane's child Margret, born the 15th of December.

Pastor Peter Tranberg and his wife Catharina Rudman's child, born the 7th of January, 1736-7, and died.

BAPTISMS IN 1744.

1. William Culen and his wife Maria's child Rachel, born the 1st of October, baptized November 10th.

2. Philip Stalcop's child Andreas, born 29th October.

3. William Vaniman and his wife Magdalena's child, Catharina, born 28th April, baptised 29th May.

4. Jonathan Hille's child Elizabeth, born 18th, baptized 30th of July.

5. John Springer and his wife Mary's child John, born 18th of September, baptized the 1st of October.

6. Swen Justice and his wife Mary's child Christina, born 1st of Oct. baptized the 10th.

7. Jonas Stedham and his wife Helena's child Jonas, born the 11th of October, baptized the 19th.

OLD SWEDES CHURCH

8. Jesper Clawson and his wife Maria's child Elizabeth, born the 17th of September, baptized the 22nd.

9. Jacob Hynes' child Rebecca, born in November, baptized the 13th of December.

10. Nils Justice and his wife Mary's child Charles, born the 3rd of December, baptized the 12th.

11. Elias Tasse's child Ally, born and baptized the 12th of December.

12. Peter Henrichson's child Sara, born the 21st December, baptized the 28th.

13. Powel Powelson's child Sara, 6 years old, baptized the 28th of December.

14. James Anderson and his wife Brigitta's child Britta, born the 28th of March, baptized the 9th of April.

15. Lylof Stedham and his wife Jane's child Joseph, born the 5th, baptized the 10th of July.

16. William Stobby's child Magdalena, born the 1st, baptized the 10th of November.

17. Joseph Jackson and his wife Mary's child Elizabeth, born the 8th, baptized the 20th of April.

18. James Senecks and his wife Margaret's child Isaac, born the 12th of August, baptized the 9th of September.

19. Henry Colesberg and his wife Elizabeth's child Susanna, born and baptized the 28th of December.

MARRIAGES.

John Golfrey to Mary Perkins.
John Hopes to Ann Way.
John Reese to Marget McLaly.
James Floyd to Mary Barnet.
John Smith to Ann Springer.
Joseph Abraham to Margaret Farrys.
James Hamilton to Mary Lammon.
John Johnstone to Margaret Hogg.
Patrick Monagan to Sara Crafford.
Charles Hall to Hannah Hall.
Philip Stalcop to Susanna Brunberg.
John Cooper to Rachel Thompson.
David Turns to Sara James.
John Whelch to Marget Hillyard.
Henry Stedham to Mary Griffy.
Johan Vanneman to Rebecca Stille.

EARLY CHURCH RECORDS OF NEW CASTLE COUNTY

Joseph Willis to Hanna House.
James Miller to Mary Miller.
Daniel Lawson to Hanna Flemmen.
Elias Humphreys to Elizabeth Harris.
Edward Millegan to Mary Savage.
Nail MacGeary to Ann Docherty.
Cornelius Cabner to Catharina Spark.
Mathew Long to Ellenor Burnside.
Edward Harris to Margaret Cartell
John Garrison to Ann Glinn.
Archibald Cannady to Catharina Jordon.
William Lampligh to Rebecca Wilson.
Francis Henekly to Ellenor Necklyn.
Joseph Thomason to Susanna Edmundson.
Richard Nicles to Catharine McGery.
David Bradford to Rosannah Shepard.
Joseph Williams to Martha Baldwin.
Thomas Knot to Margret Mayer.
Edward Carrel to Susanna Barker.
Jonas Tungberg to Johanna Heart.
Lars Holsten to Mary Pidget.
John Wolsten to Elizabeth Packerton.
Josiah Ramsey to Elizabeth Holleys.
Benj. Underwood to Lara Nicher.
Robert McCartsy to Elizabeth Plate.
Cornelius O'Bryan to Mary Crockert.
Joseph Carter to Elizabeth Moulders.
Thomas Thornberg to Debora Bruse.
Charles Tassy to Marjory Knot.
George Kock to Mary Miller.
William Vanneman to Mary Scott.
Thomas Cohoon to Mary Gragan.
Benjamin Cook to Mary Gibs.
John Walker to Hannah White.
John Harrison to Ann McFarlen.
John Beard to Susanna Futtrey
James Whitecker to Hannah Davis.
John Dully to Miriam Bush.
George Miller to Susanna Bird.
Thomas Smith to Elizabeth Ammet.
Jacob Mote to Mary Ammet.
Archibald Taylor to Catharine Richards.

OLD SWEDES CHURCH

Benj. Beason to Elizabeth Pohlson.
Gasper Trayner to Elizabeth McGuky.
Jassay Falkner to Martha Smith.
Even Lewis to Liddy Litler.
Archibald Armstrong to Mary Fresher.
James Dicky to Isabel Hodgeson.
Richard Folton to Isabel McChestney.
Wm. Brackstine to Margery Cregg.
Thomas Bellef to Ann Bates.
Samuel Land to Catharine Davis.
David Lewis to Marj. Morris.
Arthur Graham to Mary Simson.
James Lee to Rachel Jones.
John Pile to Sara Baldwin.
Philip Vandever to Beata Vanneman.
Richard Grimes to Ann Buckley.
Archibald Hamilton to Judith Fewler.
Marris Ward to Elizabeth Hasford.
Robert Baty to Elizabeth Forgeson.
Patrick Oreton to Rachel Reece.
James Ellet to Jane Sharp.
Peter Dobbin to Mary Robeson.
Hugh Martin to Mary Corry.
Jonas Justis to Mary Walraven.
Richard Dilworth to Susanna Honk.
Thomas Veals to Mary Meam.
John Link to Mary Kirk.

MARRIAGES IN 1745.

JANUARY.

1. Elias King to Mary Beans.
3. Robert Macarther to Alie Buffinton.
11. James Guest to Phœbe Evanson,
John Welch to Elizabeth Vandevoir.
James Vathan to Brita Peterson.
28. Thomas Curle to Sara Anstel.

FEBRUARY.

Joshua Focker to Margret Webb.
William Klenny to Mary Thomson.
Daniel Kelly to Ann Royly.
23. James Dilworth to Liddy Martin, 11 years, 4 months and 23 days old.

EARLY CHURCH RECORDS OF NEW CASTLE COUNTY

26. Joseph Gorby to Mary Loan.

MARCH.

In Lent, none.

APRIL.

17. John Linan to Catharina Robinson.
21. William Cochran to Mary Humahrg.
19. Andrew Morton to Johanna Withal.
30. Samuel Smith to Rebecca Colter.

MAY.

4. Thomas Foster to Esther Morschey.
6. Hugh Carrel to Mary Fips.
7. Richard Adkis to Mary Atherson.
11. Richard Fassal to Rachel Agorsen.
16. Archibald Crackon to Hanna George.
16. Elias Walraven to Christina Walraven.
23. Richard Durrom to Margret Dawson.

JUNE.

Mounce Hopman to Britta Matson.
Thomas Canady to Mary Stolt.
William Dackeyne to Ann Hance.
Thomas Jones to Mary Ladly.
Johan Cornelius to Catharina Stedham.
Benjamin King to   Foremer.
Barney Hughes to Elizabeth Wolters.
John Williams to Mary Garrison.

JULY.

Abel Whittaker to Mary Lofton.
Josua Newbrough to Hanna Collier.
Mathias Morton to Rebecca Evars.
Valentin Bratson to Rebecca Hall.
Wm. Beard to Mary Lockhart.
Thomas Daniel to Johanna Milove.
Samuel Branton to Elizabeth Blager.
Henry Towel to Dorothy Ballman.
James McFarn to Mary Mills.

AUGUST.

Elia Bradford to Susanna Peters.
Samuel Harlan to Elizabeth Hallingsworth.

OLD SWEDES CHURCH

James Ellet to Mary Bell.
Samuel Cabner to Sara Dockria.
Peter Bricker to Barbara Meyer.
Wm. Beard to Margret Gordon.
John Steel to Susanna Kaglay.
Wm. Floyd to Ann Foston.
David Evans to Ann Borch.
Benjamin England to Susanna Collier.
Mordecay Vernon to Mary Ellet.

SEPTEMBER.

Patrick Glason to Cicily Graves.
John French to Sarah Clark.
John Stein to Jane McCoy.
William Anderson to Jane Kalton.
Cadwalet Griffith to Jane McKey.
Nathan Frame to Catharine Chalfant.

OCTOBER.

Alexander Lindsey to Latisha James.
John Price to Elizabeth Wollows.
Samuel Gothrey to Margaret Kanots.
John Moore to Elizabeth McCarty.
Jacob Long to Ann Yung.
Edward Parker to Mary Kiser.
Wm. Marsh to Mary Jefrys.
Jerem Godfrey to Mary Williams.
James Downart to Mary Thomson.
Joseph Powel to Mary Peast.

NOVEMBER.

Wm. Quighly to Jane Glansy.
Wm. Dixon to Mary Collins.
George Colter to Agnes Miller.
John Harday to Catharine Close.
Robert Turner to Elizabeth Andrew.
George Dickey to Mary Baker.
Francis Elliott to Jane Legare.
Mortin Mac Gra to Judith Cory.
James Bird to Mary Ashford.
Joseph Thomson to Isabel Bristol.

DECEMBER.

John Lathemore to Elizabeth Smith.

Michel Montgomery to Ann McDoel.
Thomas Bowles to Elizabeth Latty.
Samuel Petles to Ellinor Reough.
Wm. Montgomery to Amy McDoel.
Charles Ahlford to Elizabeth Laughton.
Joseph Grubb to Hanna Foard.
John Hogly to Eliza Dawsy.
James Goldsmit to Susanna Ashton.
Edward Duckerty to Elizabeth Carrel.
James Crowley to   Newport.
Thomas Bowels to Elizabeth Latty.

BAPTISMS.

1. Andreas Stille and his wife Catharina's child Jacob, born and baptized the 22nd of January.

2. Michael Genny and his wife Susanna Morton's child Jacob, born the 1st of April, baptized the 20th of May.

3. Anders Hendrickson's child Sarah, born and baptized 15th of April.

4. Samuel Peterson and his wife Mary's child Andrew, born the 8th of May, baptized 9th of June.

5. John Hedges and his wife Susanna Hendrickson's child Sara, born and baptized 11th of May.

6. Peter Anderson and his wife Catharina Loinan's child Margrita, born 12th May.

7. Peter Vandever and his wife Margarita's child Elizabeth, born the 11th baptized the 30th of May.

8. William Tossa and his wife Mary Scapenhois's child Mary, born the 14th of May, baptized the 9th of June.

9. Philip Vandever and his wife Beata Hoffman's children Rachel and Rebecca, born and baptized the 27th of September.

10. Richard Robinson and his wife Susanna Justice's child Mary, born and baptized the 16th of December.

11. Joseph Mortenson and his wife Regina Peterson's child Joshua, born and baptized the second of April.

12. Zacharias Hindrickson and his wife Elizabeth Howel's child William, born the 14th, baptized 22d of September.

13. Joseph and Margret Abraham's child Mary, born and baptized 16th of November.

14. Joran and Catharina Loinan's child Brita, born 11th of March.

OLD SWEDES CHURCH

MARRIAGES IN 1746.

JANUARY.

Thomas Huston to Ellinor Taylor.
John Durrham to ———— McLaghlin.
John Cowins to Margret Creig.
Wm. Griffy to Catharina Morphey.
Jonas Morton to Sara Justice.
Robert More to Mary Roads.

FEBRUARY.

John Shuggart to Susanna Talkinton.
Edward Haggorn to Mary Black.
Cornelius Clark to Jane Conri.
Joseph Rotheram to Catharine Jacobs.
Robert Baverlin to Susan Goldtrop.
Wm. Baldwin to Ruth Barns.
Wm. Voniman to Christina King.
John Martin to Margret Knocks.
Samuel Hayes to Eliz. Hearney.
John Bodly to Ann Fitchgirl.
Andrew Bartelson to Catharine Hossman.
Robert Reed to Lucy Barden.

MARCH.

Daniel Avery to Judith Jackson.
John Carter to Jane Black.
Muxtey Handly to Sara Tate.
Eric Stalcop to Mary Twigs.
Cornelius Reyon to Ann Wilkinson.
Henry Holyday to Mary Fail.
James Kirk to Mary Walker.
Patrick More to Mary Brown.
Wm. Price to Eliz. Camel.
John Jackson to Margret McTear.
Aaron Harlay to Sara Hollingsworth.   Harley/Harlog?
Wm. Henry to Hanna Tanner.
John Powel to Ellinor Bloomer.

APRIL.

Niclas Corsine to Magdalena Senecks.
Hugh Bryarly to Rebecca Forwood.

EARLY CHURCH RECORDS OF NEW CASTLE COUNTY

John Brand to Margret Nicolson.
Thomas Lion to Mary Aly.
Edward Bennet to Patience Niclan.
Hugh Romage to Jane Adare.
Samuel Hall to Elizabeth Wellcock.
John Kampster to Martha Collier.
Richard Woodward to Mary Yetman.
Isaac Barbor to Jane Henry.

MAY.

Ezekiel Wintworth to Mary Gilborg.
George McCleave to Elizabeth Portman.
Richard Cornelius to Susanna Philips.
John Walraven to Sara Stedham.
Cornelius McOllern to Christina Supingam.
Benjamin Jackson to Prishilla Vernon.

JUNE.

Abel Morgan to Elizabeth Howels.
John Bishop to Elizabeth Jordan.
Nathaniel Canada to Mary Wood.
Benjamin Moore to Ann Roads.
Samuel Read to Ann Harper.
James Bullerward to Catharine Hopman.
Richard Bartelson to Jean Grooms.
Michel Cleester to Jane Colberson.
Wm. Miller to Jane Maggee.
Joseph Elwill to Mary Jaquet.
Joseph Jones to Ann Latton.
Charles Bark to Sara McCormick.

JULY.

James Hall to Mary Clenny.
Peter Brunberg to Ann Owens.

AUGUST.

Patrick to McCarter.
Richard Egleston to Margret Shannon
John Gibson to Ruth Martin.
Francis Baldwin to Margret Little.

OLD SWEDES CHURCH

John Vouman to Mary Ford.
Immanuel Barns to Mary Miller.
George Crow to Mary Gandouct.
Josua Roman to Rachel Pile.
John Misman to Margret Swan.

SEPTEMBER.

Sept. 2 Amos Richards to Elizabeth Reece.
Sept. 3 Joseph Holland to Jane Young.
Sept. 10 Robert Ketrick to Isabella Hall.
Amos Earby to Rachel Bayly.
Sept. 7 William Croker to Ellenor Hoslip.
Joseph Eldare to Sara Luffirty.
Abram Barbor to Mary Michel.
Robert Piles to Mary Roman.
Joseph Heald to Hannah Hild.

OCTOBER.

Cornelius McSweany to El'enor Birk.
Nail Morns to Margret Tuffs.
Darby Morgon to Elizabeth Clatt.
Samuel Finley to Sara Witterton.
John Theals to Margret Sarr.
Dennys Sallovain to Mary Leat.

NOVEMBER.

Thomas Hagton to Mary Dakrill.
James Bredin to Susanna Mullin.
John King to Magdalena Peterson.
Peter Peterson to Magdalena Voniman.
John Gardner to Margret Newwork.
John McWilliams to Mary Blak.
John Borom to Ann Vansant.
Francis Baldwin to Charity Hackney.
John Hanson to Ellenor Lewis.

DECEMBER.

James Donn to Jean Farrel.
Jacobus Heirs to Mary Blew.

EARLY CHURCH RECORDS OF NEW CASTLE COUNTY

BAPTISMS IN 1746.

1. Pastor Peter Tranberg and his wife Catharina Rudman's child Theophilus, born 9th of March, baptized and died 9th of May.
2. Carolus Springer and his wife Margret Robinson's child Rebecca, born and baptized the 2nd of July.
3. James Senecks and his wife Margret Werdeman's child Margret, born and baptized the 6th of July.
4. Michel Sigmund and his wife Elizabeth Walraven's child John William, born and baptized 11th of July.
5. Peter Smith and his wife Eliz. Wandewer's child Mary, born the 19th, baptized 22nd of June.
6. James Anderson and his wife Brita Loinan's child Lady, born and baptized 5th of August.
7. Nils Justis and his wife Maria Springer's child Justa, born the 14th of September, baptized 21st of September.
8. Joseph and Margret Abraham's child Agnes, born and baptized 12th of October.
9. William and his wife Magdalena's child Rachel, born and baptized the 20th of March.
10. James McGennis and his wife Laddy Kobb's child William, born 15th of December, baptized 12th of June.
11. Joran and Catharine Loinan's child Elizabeth, born and baptized 10th of July.
12. Asmund Stedham and his wife Christina Hendrickson's child Sara, born the 15th, baptized the 19th of November.
13. Peter Peterson and his wife Rebecca Hoffman's child Maria, born the 19th, baptized 26th of December.

MARRIAGES IN 1747.

JANUARY.

Henry Robinson to Margaret Dennys.
Ebenezer Wolleston to Catharine Ogden.
Henry Peaxe to Ann Bayly.
John McRichy to Mary Williamson.
Joseph Wilson to Ann Woodward.

FEBRUARY.

1. Wm. Bean to Margaret Evans.
2. Wm. Reily to Ann Beaty.

OLD SWEDES CHURCH

5. Wm. Wolleston to Sarah Ball.
13. James Hollingsworth to Mary Harvey.
13. Samuel Lewis to Ann Armer.
16. John Hannons to Rachel Martin.
19. David Whitleta to Mary Morten.
21. Peter Ganthony to Hannah Broom.
24. William Smith to Ann McClare.
26. Thomas Veal to Mary Gothrey.
26. Hugh McConnel to Elizabeth White.

MARCH.

10. Uria Blew to Mary Jordon.
11. N. McConnel to Isabella Bell.
12. Robert Whiterous to Elizabeth Evans.
15. James Webb to Mary Hurfurd.
26. Thomas Harvey to Mary Armstrong.
26. Daniel Mackarfoss to Liddy Hall.
26. William Capon to Christina Swanson.

APRIL.

21. Charles Laughead to Elizabeth McNail.
23. John Dobson to Hannah Fail.
24. Henry Dearon to Elizabeth Stedham.
29. Henry Burnet to Margaret Adare.

MAY.

3. John McGinnys to Martha More.
7. Thomas Flaregan to Mary Scoggen.
14. Lewis Resse to Sarah Lewis.
14. William Thomas to Catharina Johns.
14. James Elders to Elizabeth Polson.
25. Samuel Moore to Sarah Wilson.
8. Henry Badden to Hannah Bean.
13. James Baxter to Elizabeth Clark.
25. Erasmus Morton to Martha Ronolls.
28. William Denney to Esther Bischop.

JUNE.

1. Daniel King to Rebecca Chambers.
5. John Plummer to Elizabeth Barber.
12. Daniel Bean to Mary Meredith.

EARLY CHURCH RECORDS OF NEW CASTLE COUNTY

20. Israel Stedham to Elizabeth Batson.
21. James Mackever to Mary Owens.
25. Cornelius Clark to Ann Hudgeson.
25. David Ogle to Margaret Hall.

JULY.

5. John Bard to Anna Briond.
6. Wm. McFarson to Margaret Trego.
14. Thomas Ellet to Brigita Mortin.
20. John Jones to Ellenor Hooper.
22. Garsheam Alexander to Jana Thomas.
23. George White to Susanna Cloud.
30. Timothy Morphy to Ann Anderson.

AUGUST.

1. Niclas Fling to Sara Bettel.
2. Patrick Cafford to Magdalen Dame.
12. Brice Collins to Elizabeth Bradley.
14. John Folton to Mary Crafford.
14. Peter Jacquet to Elizabeth Jacquet.
25. Hugh Morgan to Catharina Weight.
25. Isaac Witocck to Martha Bean.
30. James Hersman to Hannah Dyke.

SEPTEMBER.

6. Wm. Cross to Rachel Welk.
8. Andrew More to Elizabeth
11. Philip Culford to Easter
13. John McGrub to Joan Baxter.
14. Wm. Collet to Mary
24. John McBright to Mary White.
24. John Litle to Jane Mollin.
24. Abraham Twigg to Sara Bird.

OCTOBER.

1. Charles Collet to Elizabeth Neals.
12. John Walraven to Hannah Gravenrod.
29. Jacob Kidd to Elizabeth Smith.
29. Henry Vandever to Sara Barber.
29 Alexander Davidson to Ann Denny.

OLD SWEDES CHURCH

NOVEMBER.

4. Peter Boon to Debora Monde.
24. Wm. Armstrong to Ready Armstrong.
20. John Springer to Mary Welsh.
16. Robert Chalfon to Sara Cloud.
23. Frances McFall to Sara McGarvy.
20 James Canady to Christian Meason.
24. Cain Wholohan to Martha Kelley.
24. Jeremiah Gran to Susanna Thomson.
25. Isaac McDowal to Elizabeth Littol.
13. Samuel Harper to Mary Butler.
30. Adam Steward to Sara Hamilton.

DECEMBER.

1. James Danally to Mary Morrow.
5. Martin Justice to Magdalena Pohlson.
10. Claytor Buddle to Anne Bird.

BAPTISMS IN 1747.

1. Carolus Springer and his wife Margaret Robinson's child Elizabeth, born and baptized 18th of February.

2. Wm. Van Neman and his wife Mary Scott's child Abraham born and baptized 17th of March

3. John Springer and his wife Mary's child Margarita, born and baptized 25th of March.

4. John Walraven and his wife Sara Stedham's child Jonas, born 29th of May, baptized 8th of June.

5. Joseph Springer and his wife Anna Justice's child Anna, born and baptized 18th of June.

6. Cornelius Stedham and his wife Susanna's child Mary, born and baptized 27th of August.

7. Wm. Castan and Christina Swensson's child Andreas, born and baptized 10th of November.

8. Henric and Anna Pierce's child Joseph.

MARRIAGES IN 1748.

JANUARY.

John Jaquet to Johanna Clawson.
John Knotts to Elizabeth Taknet.

EARLY CHURCH RECORDS OF NEW CASTLE COUNTY

Daniel Sharpley to Catharine Robeson.
Wm. Patton to Agnis Boyd.
Daniel Done to Mary James.
Moses White to Ann Cann.
Thomas Chalfon to Margret Green.

FEBRUARY.

Samuel Wright to Jane Morney.

MARCH.

Alexander Harper to Sara Patton.
James Alexander to Mary Gray.
Timothy Canners to Catharine Hays.
Henry Hollis to Ann Harvey.
Thomas Ogle to Elizabeth Robeson.
Andrew Cox to Mary Link.
Wm. Sharpley to Susanna Earby.
Thomas Vickry to Sara Sinex.
Samuel Jones to Mary Correl.

APRIL.

Robert Rea to Sara Parker.
James Pyle to Sara Harlon.
James Carson to Mary Espy.
Giles Sankey to Margaret Calhoun.
Charles Springer to Mary Ball.
Charles Pierce to Ann Austle.
John Way to Mary Pierce.
Jonnathan Jordan to Mary Vaugham.

MAY.

1. James Ottlay to Anne Pierce.
3. Robert McGarrout to Agnes Ketly.
5. John Philpot to Ann Roberts.
6. Wm. Bork to Susanna Hosen.
16. Thomas Downs to Judy McFall.
16. John Tinn to Mary McGee.
18. James Stevenson to Elizabeth Weldin.
19. John Cox to Ellenor Elnes.
26. Zachrison Didrickson to Elizabeth Polson.
29. Swen Justis to Mary Jones.
30. Charles Gollfey to Margret Elleson.

OLD SWEDES CHURCH

JUNE.

5 John Norman to Prishilla Besly.
14 John Montgomery to Charity Reed.
15. Patrick Burns to Rose Inglisby.
20 Edward Ogle to Margret Howard.
21 John Heeld to Margret Davis.

JULY.

1. Isaac Baily to Ellinor Cohoon.
1. John Kelly to Sara Welldon.
10. Wm. Ruledson to Martha Evans.
3. Barney Rice to Mary Hooper.
11. Daniel Show to Catharina Burns.
12. Lulof Stedham to Mary Rotter.
13. Jacob Vandevoir to Mary Cannaway.
18. John Fillpot to Ann Casparson.
20. James Steward to Hannah Woolcocks.
20. John Berry to Catharina Anhedson.
20. Thomas Singleton to Mary McDoul.
25. Thomas Giffing to Hannah Bell.
26. John Mahan to Ellinor Caby.
27. Wm. Farniss to Mary Dowling.
28. Robert Hueston to Jane Crafford.
25. Wm. Hall to Elizabeth Reyal.

AUGUST.

8. John Dolboy to Hannah Williams.
13. Thomas Thomason to Elizabeth Camel.
14. David Bush, Esq., to Ann Welsh.
18. Jonathan Gust to Elizabeth Catori.
23. Peter Jaquet t' Jean Crafford.
30. Hugh Cummins to Ellinor Laughton.
23. John Pedrick to Rachael Grubb.
25. Wm. Reed to Elizabeth Duglas

SEPTEMBER.

Philip Taylor to Mary Riley.
Zacheus Kay to Sarah George.
Robert Bolton to Elizabeth Thomson.
James Maxwell to Margret Bullock.

EARLY CHURCH RECORDS OF NEW CASTLE COUNTY

OCTOBER.

3. Archdibald McDunold to Elizabeth Johnston.
6. John Hopes to Rachael Barns.
3. Wm. Follis to Sara Maker.
28. Nathan Cloud to Ann Smith.
6. Jonathan Kirk to Dorothy More.
19. Isaac Allen to Liddy Jackson.
23. Hugh Laughlin to Mary Evans.
24. Cornelius Gutrey to Jane Peterson.
17. John Allen to Lucretia Loyd.

BAPTISMS, 1748.

1. Joseph Jackson and his wife Mary's child Benjamin, born and baptized 11th of January.
2. Philip Van de Weer and his wife Beata Hoffman's child Rebecca, born and baptized 30th of January.
3. John Hedges and his wife Susanna Hindricsson's child Samuel, born and baptized 1st of February.
4. John Smidt and his wife Anna Springer's child Rachel, born the 7th, baptized 13th of March.
5. Peter Anderson and his wife Catharina Loinan's child Mary, born and baptized 2nd of April.
6. Asmund Stedham and his wife Christina Hindrickson's child Cornelius, born 12, baptized 18th of June.
7. Joseph and Margaret Abraham's child Sara, born and baptized 12th October.
8. Henry Darran and his wife Elizabeth Stedham's child Susanna, born 19th of September, baptized in October.
9. Nils Justice and his wife Mary Springer's child Christina, born 4th of November, baptized 13th of November.
10. Joran and Catharina Loinan's child Anders, born 25th of October.

BAPTISMS 1749.

1. Thomas Natt and his wife Margareta Mayer's child Johanna, born and baptized 20th of January.
2. Andrew Hendrickson and his wife Maria's child Tobias, born 26th, baptized 30th of January.
3. Joseph Jackson and his wife Mary's child John, born 17th January, baptized 2nd of April.
4. James Minzi and his wife Ellenor Willing's child Edai, born and baptized 30th of May.

OLD SWEDES CHURCH

5. Joseph Mortenson and his wife Regina Peterson's child Mary, born and baptized 1st of June.

6. Olaf Tossa and his wife Mary Schapenhois' children Isaac and Rebecca, born and baptized 16th of September.

7. James Anderson and his wife Brigita Loinan's child Andrew, born 15th of October, baptized 18th of November.

8. Peter Peterson and his wife Rebecca Hoffman's child Rachel, born 24th of October, baptized 18th of November.

9. Peter Stedham and his wife Isabella Hare's child William, born 30th September, baptized 30th of November.

10. Michael Sigmund and his wife Elizabeth Walraven's child Cornelius, born and baptized 6th of December.

11. James Seneck and his wife Margaret Werdeman's child Morina, born 26th October, baptized 26th November.

12. Hans Gorgen Rushocken and his wife Mary Frey's child Catharina, born 15th of November, baptized 10th December.

13. The child Phœbe, born 9th of January, baptized 18th of December, the parents negroes.

14. John Dilmore and his wife Elizabeth Aldrichson's child Edward, born 14th June, baptized 14th December.

15. Swen Walraven and his wife Catharina Hindrickson's child Johannes, born 21st December, baptized 24th December.

16. John Racen and his wife Anna Petersson's child Andrew, born 25th, baptized 31st December.

BURIALS.

Andrew Cock died the 8th of December, buried 10th December.

Johannes Walraven buried 30th December.

MARRIAGES.

William Glinn to Mary Tool, the 30th November, of New Castle County and Brandewyn Hundred.

Thomas Corcoran to Prudence Foresides, 26th of December, of Brandewyn Hundred.

Wm. Strode to Deborâh Woodward. the 28th of December, both of Chester County and East Bradford Township.

On the 8th of November, 1748, Pastor Peter Tranberg resigned his soul to his Saviour's hand, to be transferred to the Heavenly joy. He took his leave of this world from the other side of the river in the house of Mr. William Von Neman, where he had gone to bury his (Mr. Von Neman's) parents, Mr. Olle Von Neman and his wife Magdalena Von Dever, who had died in Penn's Neck four days previously.

Baptisms in the year 1750, by the Rev. Israel Acrelius. Those designated by a star are of the Christina Congregation.

Child Isabella, born December, baptized January 1st; parents, John and Mary Greenup.

Child William, born December, baptized January 31st; parents, William and Catharine McLacklon.

*Child Lucas, born December 30, 1749, baptized February 4th; parents, John Wallace and Sarah Stedham.

*Child William, born December 22d, baptized February 15th; parents, Wm. Van Neman and Mary.

Child Charles, born February 10th, baptized February 18th; parents, Thomas and Jane Philips.

Child Prudence, born December 23, 1749, baptized February 28th; parents, Thomas and Sara Mehan.

Child James, born January 18th, baptized February 18th; parents, Robert and Jane Mellor.

*Child Swen, born February 22d, baptized same day; parents, Nils and Mary Springer Justis.

*Child Jacob, born February 10th, baptized February 23d; parents, Jacob and Mary Bishop Springer.

*Child Prudence, born January 26th, baptized February 25th; parents, John and Mary Mortonson Spari.

*Child Elizabeth, born February 15th, baptized February 25th; parents, John and Susanna Hindrickson Hedge.

*Child John, born February 27th, baptized March 11th; parents, Zacharias and Elizabeth Howell Hindrickson.

*Child Sarah, born October 30, 1749, baptized March 11th; parents, Niclas and Magdalena Stedham Curseng.

Child William, born May 15, 1747, baptized March 12th; parents, Robert and Mary Congttun.

*Child Marta, born February 2d, baptized March 25th; parents, Henry and Elizabeth Colesberg.

Child John, born October 28, 1749, baptized March 25th; parents, William and Mary Fellows.

Child Jacob, born March 1st, baptized April 1st; parents, Saul and Barbro Haussman.

OLD SWEDES CHURCH

*Child Rachel, born April 5th, baptized April 8th; parents, Joseph and Anna Justis Springer.

*Child John, born March 12th, baptized April 13th; parents, Andrew and Dorothea Paulson Justice.

Child John, born December 26, 1745; child Elizabeth, born January 24, 1747; child Nannie, born May 12, 1749; baptized April 22d; parents, Johannes and Emma Kallamiller Gassert.

Child Andrew, born November 15, 1749, baptized April 29th; parents, Johannes and Susanna Boman.

*Child Philip, born February 26th, baptized April; parents, Cornelius and Margaret Morton Vanderweer.

*Child Jacob, born September 27, 1749, baptized April 30th; parents, Samuel and Elizabeth Peterson Riard.

Child Elizabeth, born May 17, 1749, baptized April 30th; parents, Thomas and Sarah Ly (Lee).

*Child Eric, born April 27th, baptized May 2d; parents, Olle and Christeen Andersson.

*Child Andrew, born May 1st, baptized May 6th; parents, John and Mary Springer.

Child Tobias, born April 26th, baptized May 20th; parents, Asmund and Christeen Hendrickson Stedham.

*N. B.—Hannah, 18 years old, parents, Quakers, baptized May 21st, and immediately married to John Boggan; names of her parents, Jacob and Hannah Grist.

Child Josiah, born May 19th, baptized May 27th; parents, Jonathan and Dorothea Kirk.

*Child Helena, born May 25th, baptized May 28ht; parents, Marten and Magdalena Springer Justice.

*Child John, born April 13th, baptized June 5th; parents, Carl and Johanna Lavel Stillman.

Child Sarah, born March 25th, baptized June 13th; parents, Henry and Dorothea Powel.

Child John, born December 6, 1749, baptized June 16th; parents, David and Mary McKelwhay.

Child Mary, born March 5th, baptized June 16th; parents, Simon and Elizabeth Thetford.

Child Eleonora, born June 25th, baptized July 6th; parents, Robert and Elizabeth Robinson Armstrong.

*Children Michael and Susanna, the former born July 2d, and the latter born July 3d; parents, Michael and Susanna Morton Gennett.

EARLY CHURCH RECORDS OF NEW CASTLE COUNTY

*Child Peter, born June 25th, baptized July; parents, Peter and Catharine Loinan Andersson.

*Child Maria, born July 1st, baptized September 2d; parents, Conrad and Maria Johnson Garitsson.

Child Rebecca, born November 6, 1749, baptized September 8th; parents, John and Eliza King.

*Child Samuel, born August 18th, baptized September 9th; parents, Christopher and Eleonora Hindricksson.

Child Thomas, born June 8th, baptized September 14th; parents, Thomas and Jennet Hamilton Johnsson.

Child Anna, born April 10, 1749, baptized September 15th; parents, Joseph and Sarah Gepson Cartmell.

Child William, born March 28, 1748, baptized September 20th; parents, William and Margaret Townsend Donaldson.

Child Francis, born March 29th, baptized September 20th; parents, William Hay and wife.

Children William and Stephen, born September 17th, baptized September 26th; parents, David and Mary Kein Withetan.

Child Jacob, born July 14th, baptized September 30th; parents, Rudolph and Margaret Thespen Hweitman.

*Child John, born September 30th, baptized October 22; parents, William and Margaret Almond.

Child Enoch, born September 26th, baptized October 31st; parents, James and Elizabeth Lewis.

Child Barbro, born November 1st, baptized November 8th; parents, Henry and Barbro Sorborg.

*Child Rebecca, born October 30th, baptized November 9th; parents, Jesper and Susanna Hindricksson Justice.

Child Mary, born October 9th, baptized November 11th; illegitimate; of Richard Frest and Mary Ann McMary.

*Child James, born July 6th, baptized November 18th; parents, Andrew and Sarah Peterson.

Child Rachel, born October 8th, baptized November 25th; parents, John and Elizabeth Taylor.

*Child Isabelle, born November 13th, baptized November 26th, parents, Willian and Anna Ifvarson Stoubei.

*Child Rebecca, born December 12th, baptized December 13th; parents, John and Anna Springer Smidt.

Child Anne, born February 12, 1749, baptized December 26th; parents, James and Lady Kob McGennis.

NOTE.—The star denotes children of members of the Swedish Church.

OLD SWEDES CHURCH

Child Rachel, born September 2d, baptized December 30th ; parents, John and Mary Correll.

1751.

Child Lewis, born October, 8, 1750, baptized January 1st ; parents, David and Anne Bush.

*Child Margret, born October 21, 1750, baptized January 1st ; parents, Henry and Elizabeth Stedham Darrayn.

*Child Philip, born January 9th, baptized January 20th ; parents, Goran and Margret Stalcop Loinan.

*Child Rachel, born December 23, 1750, baptized February 2d ; parents, Joseph and Mary Vanderweer Jacksson.

,Child John, born October 5, 1750, baptized February 3d ; parents, Abraham and Sarah Twiggs.

*Child John, born January 3d, baptized February 3d.; parents, John and Elizabeth Stedham Paulsson.

*Child Rachel, born February 9th, baptized February 17th ; parents, Jesper and Mary Walraven.

Child Mary, born August 23, 1745, } parents, Benjamin and
Child Jesper, born September 23, 1748, } Eliz. Paulsson Bisen.

*Child Swen, born February 20th, baptized February 24th ; parents, Nils and Mary Springer Justice.

Child Johanna, born December 12, 1744, } baptized February
Child Hannah, born February 21, 1747, } 24th, parents, Elias
Child Thomas, born July, 1749, } and Eliz. Humpries.

Child Mary, born January 27th, baptized March 14th; parents, William and Elizabeth Patersson.

*Child Jacob, born February 12th, baptized March 17th ; parents, Garrit and Mary Garitsson.

*Child Sarah, born March 6th, baptized March 17th ; parents, Thomas and Beata Turner.

*Child Rebecca, born February 11th, baptized March 24th ; parents, Jonas and Sarah Mortensson.

*Child Dina, born February 27th, baptized March 31st; parents, Jonathan and Magdalena Vanderveer Stille.

Child John, born February 15th, baptized April 3d; parents, John and Elizabeth Tummelsson.

*Child Dorothea, born March 24th, baptized April 5th; parents, Philip and Susanna Brunberg Stalcop.

Child Roda, born December 19, 1750, baptized March 14th ; parents, Lanty and Margaret Jonston.

EARLY CHURCH RECORDS OF NEW CASTLE COUNTY

*Child Margaret, born December 14, 1750, baptized April 21st; parents, Joseph and Margaret Abraham.

Child Martha, born November 8, 1750, baptized April 29th ; parents, James and Mary McChever.

The following 12 were all baptized the same day in the Marlborough Church.

Boy Robert, 11 years old, born July 22, 1740, baptized May 1st; parents, Robert and Margret Aggor.

Child Sarah, born October 5, 1746, baptized May 1st; parents, the last named.

Child Margret, born July 5, 1750, baptized May 1st; parents, John and Jane Little.

Child William, born June 25, baptized May 1st; parents, John and Mary Thompson.

Child Mary, born April 1, 1750, baptized May 1st; parents, Thomas and Mrs. Bowles.

Child John, born December 2, 1749, baptized May 1st; parents, John and Marget.

Child Edward, born January 20th, baptized May 1st; parents, same as last.

Child Samuel, born February, 1750, baptized May 1st; parents, John and Walled King.

Child Marget, born February, 1749, baptized May 1st; parents, same as last.

Child Joseph, born November, 1750, baptized May 1st; parents, John and Jane Woods.

Child Nelly, born March 20th, baptized May 1st; parents, Thomas and Mary Baret.

Child Elizabeth, born August 15th, baptized May 1st; parents, William and Mary Braun.

Child Rebecca, born March 29th, baptized May 12th; parents, Adolph and Catharine Wolfsbach.

Child ———, born February 24th, baptized May 12th; parents, John and Jane Jaquette.

Child Henry, born April 23d, baptized May 18th; parents, Henry and Mary Bishop.

Child Sarah, born April 24th, baptized May 18th; parents Peter and Mary Galloway.

Child James, born February 14th, baptized May 27th; parents, Matthews and Elizabeth Grew.

Child Elizabeth, born May 24th, baptized May 27th; parents, Elias and Elizabeth Humphreys.

OLD SWEDES CHURCH

Child William, born May 22d, baptized May 27th; parents, Philip and Margaret McBraid.

Child Elizabeth, born April 14th, parents, William and Sarah Baker.

*Child Anne, born June 6, 1750, baptized June 16th; parents, Eric and Mary Stalcop.

*Child Jeremiah, born May 28th, baptized June 16th; parents, William and Christina Swensson Castan.

Child John, born March 29th, baptized April 29th; parents, John and Elizabeth Bishop.

*Child Sarah, born May 17th, baptized June 23d; parents, Matthias and Rebecca Mortenson.

*Child Sarah, born March 21st, baptized May 12th; parents, Joseph and Regina Mortensson.

Child Sylvester, born January 7th, baptized June 23d; parents, Wm. and Anne Welch.

Child John, born August 6th, baptized August 23d; parents, John and Charity Montgomery.

Child John James, born December 24th, baptized June 23d; parents, William and Jane Singletown McDowel.

Child Hannah, born March 25th, baptized June 23d; parents, Adam and Mary Rose.

The following ten were baptized same day in Marlborough Church:

Child George, born February 16, 1744,
Child William, born April 16, 1746,
Child Robert, born October 22, 1748,
Child Elizabeth, born October 2, 1750,
Baptized June 30th; parents, Robert and Elizabeth Tassed.

Child Mary, born August 13, 1750, baptized June 30; parents James and Marta Waldin.

Child Elizabeth, born July 22, 1750, baptized June 30th; parents, Thomas and Mary Wan.

Child William, born April 7, 1749, baptized June 30th; parents, David and Margaret King Breadford.

Child Thomas, born April 15, 1749, baptized June 30th; parents, the last named.

Child Ester, born September 6, 1750, baptized June 30th; parents, Farday and Mary McHew.

Child Joseph, born June 15, 1750, baptized June 30th; parents, Wm. and Margret Gray.

*Child Rebecca, born June 5th, baptized July 1st; parents, Cornelius and Margret Mortenson Van der Weer.

EARLY CHURCH RECORDS OF NEW CASTLE COUNTY

*Child Peter, born June 21st, baptized July 2nd; parents, Andreas and Cathrine Stalcop Stille.

Child John, born May 8th, baptized July 14th; parents, Jacobus and Mary Hein.

Child Amos, born May 10th, baptized July 27th; parents, Wm. and Hannah Nicolas.

Child Mathew, born May 18th, baptized July 27th; parents, Robert and Margaret Klinton.

Child John, born May 26th, baptized July 27th; parents, John and Mary Denin.

Child Elizabeth, born July 12th, baptized July 27th; parents, John and Jane Fisher Baddy.

Child George, born June 25th, baptized July 28th; parents, John and Margret Kees.

Both Illegitimate. { Child John, born April 22nd, baptized July 28th; parents, John Colwell and Mary Kinni. Child Susanna, born May 30th, baptized July 28th; parents, Wm. Bradky and Elizabeth Howell.

Child Timothy, born July 3rd, baptized August 4th; parents, Lulof and Jane Stidham.

Child Anne, born August 15th, baptized August 19th; parents, Swen and Cathrine Hendrickson Walraven.

Child Anne, born April 28th, baptized August 19th; parents, Wm. and Susanna Sharpley.

Child John, born September 30, 1746, baptized August 24th; true father unknown, mother, Rachel Crissen.

Child Jane, born July 16th, baptized August 25th; parents, James and Rose McLaughlin Brochon.

Child Thomas, born August 25th, baptized September 15th; parents, Wm. and Sara Follis.

*Child Jonas, born September ——, baptized September 29th; parents, Gustas and Sara Walraven.

*Child Zachris, born September 7th, baptized October 6th; parents, Zacharias and Sara Derickson.

Child John, born August 21st, baptized October 6th; parents, Mark and Elizabeth Bell Covin.

*Child Willing, born September 21st, baptized October 20th; parents, James and Elenor Willing Minzi.

Child Mary, born August 24th, baptized October 7th; parents, Wm. and Grace Davis.

Child Margret, born January 17th, baptized January 25th; parents, David and Sara Salkeld.

OLD SWEDES CHURCH

Child Hezechiel, born July 3, baptized October 25th; parents, Joseph and Mary Gorby.

Child Ingeborg, born October 14th, baptized October 27th; parents, Jonas and Mary Colsberg Stidham.

Child Thomas, born July 18th, baptized November 3d; parents, Robert and Jane Montgomery Taylor.

Child Edward, born July 27th; parents, Joseph and Mary Pierce.

Child Hannah, born October 4th, baptized November 3d; parents, Wm. and Phœbe Broom.

Child Even, born October 13th, baptized November 10th; parents, John and Annie Cook.

Child John, born July 10th, baptized November 24th; parents, Ephraim and Catharine McCaleb.

Child Sarah, born September 27th, baptized November 24th; parents, John and Mary Meyer.

Child Catharine, born November 3d, baptized November 24th; parents, William and Elenor Culay.

*Child David, born November 15th, baptized December 8th; parents, Moses and Martha White.

Child Margret, born July 1st, baptized December 21st; parents, Edward and Sarah White.

Illegitimate child Charles, born November 3d, baptized December 21st; mother, Sarah Loan; father, Henry Nail.

Child Sarah, baptized December 21st, in a stream of water near Folks Mannor's Church; was sick; parents, James and Jane McKey.

Child James, born December 16, 1750, baptized December 22d; parents, James and Mary Champin Conolly.

Child Mary, born October 12th, baptized December 22d; parents Even and Elizabeth Reece.

Illegitimate child Catharine, born October 17th, baptized December 22d; mother, Sarah Bratton; father, James Thompson.

Child Jacob, born November 18th, baptized December 22d; parents, Richard and Susanna Justis Robbinsson.

ANNO 1752.

Child Peter, born August 19, 1751, baptized January 5; parents, James and Lady McGinnis.

EARLY CHURCH RECORDS OF NEW CASTLE COUNTY

Child John, born May 27, 1750, baptized January 8; parents, Urias and Mary Blew.

Child Susannah, born March 13, 1750, parents George and Johanna King.

Child Rachael, born December 27, baptized January 26; parents, James and Elizabeth Elder.

Child Benjamin, born December 28, baptized February 5; parents, Thomas and Jane Philip.

Child Thomas, born December 26, baptized February 5; parents, Wm. and Jane Miller.

Child James, born October 1, baptized February 5; parents, Patrick and Mary Rion.

Child Mary, born January 14, baptized February 11; parents, Mark and Jane Ellot.

Child Matthew, born January 30, baptized February 16; parents, Thomas and Jane McCord.

Child Henry, born February 17, baptized March 1; parents, Henry and Barbro Ruish.

*Child Anna, born January 14, baptized March 2; parents, Andreas and Maria Justis.

Child Sara, born February 28, baptized March 8; parents, John and Brigite Kirk.

Child Anne, born January 1, baptized March 8; parents, James and Jane Kirk.

Child Emsson, born February 28, baptized, March 21; parents, Emsson and Susannah Bird.

Child Rebecca, born March 7, baptized March 21; parents, James and Catharine Justis McDonald.

Child Anne, born December 26, baptized March 22; parents, John and Anne Hawkey Stuard.

Child Adam, born August 13, 1751, baptized March 22; parents, Adam and Margaret Cooper.

Child Elizabeth, born February 2, baptized March 22; parents, James and Jane Andrew Willsson.

Child James, born January 9, baptized March 22; parents, James and Mary Downard.

Child John, born October 8, baptized March 22; parents, John and Marta Cross Miller.

Child Anne, born September 28, baptized March 22; parents, Alexander and Elizabeth Ramsey.

Child Mary, born January 7, baptized March 29; parents, Eric and Mary Twigg Stalcop.

OLD SWEDES CHURCH

Child Susanna, born December 4, 1751, baptized March 29; parents, Michael and Elizabeth Sigmund.

Child Rachael, born February 17, baptized March 30; parents, Robert and Elizabeth Pierce.

Child Isaac, born March 5, baptized March 30; parents, John and Annie Tossa Lea.

Child James, born March 9, baptized April 5; parents, John and Mary Mortinson Sparry.

Child Elizabeth, born April 3, baptized April 12; parents, Jacob and Mary Loinan Andersson,

*Child Israel, born April 4, baptized April 23; parents, Samuel and Elizabeth Peterson Real.

Child Margret, born April 10, baptized April 23; parents, Thomas and Mary Almond.

Child Samuel, born March 19, baptized April 25; parents, William and Elizabeth Rayl.

Child Jacob, born February 16, baptized in Marlborough, April 25; parents, Jacob and Anne Thompson.

Child Enoch, born February 18, baptized in Marlborough, April 25; parents, Brice and Elizabeth Collins.

Child Jesa, born March 25, baptized in Marlborough, April 25; parents, Henry and Dorothea Fowel.

Child James, born September 18, baptized in Marlborough, April 25; parents, James and Joanna Fitchpatrick.

Child James, born January 4, baptized April 25; parents, James and Mary Shelldon.

Child Hannah, born February 27, baptized April 25; parents, Henry and Brita Clasky.

Child Mary, born February 21, baptized April 25; parents, John and Anne Garritson.

Child Mary, born February 25, baptized in Marlborough, May 6; parents, Daniel and Mary Kain.

Child Antony, born May 10, 1751, baptized in Marlborough, May 6; parents, George and Mary Baldwin.

Child Anne, born May 26, 1751, baptized in Marlborough, May 6; parents, Cornelius and Rachel McWeyer.

Child Levy, born July 14, 1747, baptized in Marlborough, May, 6; parent, James Hall, a Quaker.

Child Mary, born August 23, 1750, baptized in Marlborough, May 6; parent, Mary Cleany.

Child Benjamin, born February 14th, baptized April 26; parents, Thomas and Marget Nott.

EARLY CHURCH RECORDS OF NEW CASTLE COUNTY

Child Paulus, April 12th, baptized May 10th; parents, Paulus and Barbro Hausman.

*Child Senecce, born April 13th, baptized May 10th; parents, James Senecce and Margret Werdeman.

*Child Isaac, born March 16th, baptized April 26th; parents, Lucas and Anna Monson.

*Child Peter, born April 26th, baptized May 17th; parents, John and Sarah Stedham Springer.

*Child Elizabeth, born September 21, 1750, baptized May 21st; parents, Peter and Anne Brunberg.

Child Elenor, born February 2d, baptized May 24th; parents, Michel and Else Meloy.

Child James, born April 17th, baptized May 27th; parents, Moses and Anne White.

Child Mary, born May 9th, baptized May 27th; parents, John and Agnes Howes.

Child Elizabeth, born August 12, 1751, baptized May 28th; parents, Thomas and Anne Garritsson Adams.

Child Rachel, born May 1st, baptized June 2d; parents, William and Anne Robinsson Ball.

IN NEW LONDON.

Child Mary, born August 21st, baptized June 3rd; parents, John and Jane MeKenny.

Child Mary, born April 1st, baptized June 3rd; parents, Robert and Elizabeth Dougherty.

Child John, born December 8th, baptized June 3rd; parents, Frank and Margaret Forster Shiew.

Illegitimate child Jane, born February 10th, baptized June 3rd; parents, Andrew Enochs and Catharine Brion.

Illegitimate child Mary, born August 2, 1750, baptized June 3d; parents, Arthur Molland and Ester Burns.

Illegitimate child Edward, born August 20, 1751, baptized June 3d; parents, John Goldsmidt and Dina a mulatto.

Child James, born May 5th, baptized June 3rd; parents, Jane and James Whitcrust.

Child John, born July 8, 1747, baptized June 3d; parents, Hugh and Mary Thomson McRoy.

Child James, born May 27th, baptized June 7th; parents, Thomas and Jane Johnson.

Child Jacob, born May 3d, baptized June 7th; parents, Hans and Cathrina Nas.

OLD SWEDES CHURCH

Child Isabel, born May 6th, baptized June 7th; parents, Peter and Jane Peterson.

Child Annie, born February 2d, baptized June 14th; parents, Niclas and Margaret Moor.

Child William, born November 7th, baptized June 14th; parents, John and Elizabeth Paulson Kary.

Child Jane, born March 21st, baptized June 14th; parents, Daniel and Anna Carnay.

Child Isaac, born March 23d, baptized June 28th; parents, Henry and Susanna Brachon.

Child Elizabeth, born March 7, 1750, baptized June 28th; parents, James and Elizabeth Matthews.

Child Margret, born June 9th, baptized July 5th; parents, John and Anna Bossord.

*Child Elenor, born June 26th, baptized July 5th; parents, Joseph and Annika Justis Springer.

Child Thomas, born June 3rd, baptized July 12th; parents, John and Elizabeth Dillmore.

*Child Susanna, born July 7th, baptized July 12th; parents, Peter and Cathrina Loinan Andsrson.

Child Susanna, born June 22d, baptized July 19th; parents, John and Susanna Hendrickson Hedge.

Child Lady, born June 11th, baptized July 19th; parents, Peter and Sussanna Paulson Stalcop.

Illegitimate child Ester, born April 12th, baptized July 16th; parents, Henry Lowell and Mary Flatcher.

Child Anna, born May 24th, baptized August 1st; parents, Thomas and Jane Duss.

Child Charles, born July 6th, baptized August 2d; parents, John and Susanna Bauman.

Child John } Twins, born July 31st, baptized August 2d;
Child James } parents, Wm. and Sarah Baker.

*Child Peter, born July 19th, baptized July 20th; parents, Peter and Brita Vander Weer.

*Child William, born June 29th, baptized July 7th; parents, Carl and Johanna Stillman.

*Child Jacob, born July 27th, baptized August 26th; parents, Swen and Maria Justis.

Child Jane, born March 9th, baptized August 26th; parents, James and Else McKoom.

Child Henry, born June 15th, baptized August 26th; parents, Conrad and Barbro Wirth Grey.

EARLY CHURCH RECORDS OF NEW CASTLE COUNTY

*Child Rachel, born July 25th, baptized August 30th; parents, John and Hannah Walraven.

*Child Isaac, born July 9th, baptized September 14th; parents, Hinric and Elizabeth Colesberg.

Child James, born July 14, 1749, } baptized September 14th; Child Elizabeth, born November } parents, Peter and Margret 11th. } Stone.

Child Eleanora, born August 30th, baptized September 24th; parents, Wm. and Johanna Vanneaman.

Child Margret, born September 17th, baptized September 27th; parents, Peter and Rebecca Hopman Peterson.

*Child Benjamin, born October 1st, baptized October 10th; parents, Peter and Isabella Hare Stedham.

*Child Christina, born August 25th, baptized October 10th; parents, Wm. and Christina Swenson Castan.

Child Ann, born July 2nd, baptized October 11th; parents, Abraham and Sarah Twigs.

Child Ann, born July 20th, baptized October 12th, parents, Henry and Mary Watson.

*Child Margret, born October 9th, baptized October 15th; parents, Nils and Mary Springer Justis.

*Child Lady, born October 23, 1751; parents, John and Mary Stedham.

*Child Maria, born August 15th, baptized October 19th; parents, Cornelius and Margret Vander Weer.

Child Maria, born September 28th, baptized October 22nd; parents, Joseph and Hushella Barbro Shaw.

*Child David, born September 20th, baptized October 29th; parents, Matthias and Rebecca Morten.

*Illegitimate child Richard, born April, 1750, baptized November 1st; parents, Richard Barnaby and Rebecca Camp.

Child John, born September 10th, baptized November 4th; parents, Robert and Jane Miller.

*Child Simon, born October 16th, baptized November 23rd; parents, Simon and Elenor Paulson.

*Child William, born November 22nd, baptized 26th; parents, Jesper and Maria Wallraven.

*Child John, born October 20th, baptized November 26th; parents, Jesper and Maria Classon.

Child William, born August 1st, baptized November 29th; parents, Edward and Elizabeth King.

OLD SWEDES CHURCH

Child Hannah, born February 30, 1749; parents, James and Christina Kannathy.

Child Elizabeth, born June 6th, baptized November 29th; parents, Robert and Mary Klinton.

*Child Jacob, born October 26th, baptized December 10th; parents, Jacobus and Mary Hein.

*Child Elenore, born July 26th, baptized December 10th, parents, Wm. and Margret Almond.

Illegitimate child James, born December 6th, baptized 29th; father Matthew and mother Jane Gordon.

ANNO 1753.

Child Catherina, born January 9th, baptized 21st; parents, Edward and Beata Hopman Groahms.

Child Anna, born December 23, 1752, baptized January 21st; parents, James and Lady McGennis.

Child Catherina, born November 19th, baptized January 21st; parents, Wm. and Susanna Sharpley.

Child William, born October 11th, baptized February 1st; parents, Olle and Mary Paulson.

Child Peter, born January 24th, baptized February 6th; parents, Hans and Johanna Jaquet.

Child Christina, born November 24, 1752, baptized February 11th; parents, Jonas and Sara Morten.

Child William, born December 16, 1752, baptized February 11th; parents, Joseph and Margret Abrahams.

Child Susannah, born January 28th, baptized February 11th; parents, Swen Brunberg and Anna Pierce.

Child William, born February 7th, baptized February 25th; parents, William and Sarah Follows.

Child Mary, born April 16, 1752, baptized February 28th; parents, Alexander and Anne Wilson.

Child William, born January 9th, baptized February 28th; parents, Thomas and Elizabeth Borrels.

Child Rachael, born March 4th, baptized March 28th; parents, Wm. and Margret Bell.

Child Cathrina, born March 22nd, baptized April 8th; parents, John and Catharina Didrickson Loinan.

Child John, born February 26th, baptized April 8th; parents, Charles Janson and Anne Ogle Springer.

Child Peter, born February 18th, baptized April 23rd; parents, Wm. and Catharina Justus Paulsson,

EARLY CHURCH RECORDS OF NEW CASTLE COUNTY

Child Ruth, born March 26th, baptized April 23rd; parents, Bartholomew and Eleonora Paulson.

Child Anna Ulrica, born April 28th, baptized May 10th; parents, Mr. Adolph Benzel and Mrs. Rebecca Tranberg Benzel. Witness, Governor and Knight of His Royal Majesty's order of the North Star, Lars Benzelstierna, in whose place stood the Prvost Magister Israel Acrelius, Herr Gostas Hessellius, the Herr Pastor Erric Unander and Morten Justis; the Dean's wife Ulrica Filenia, Mrs. Anna Cathrina Tranberg, the ?astor's wife at Wicacoe, Mrs. Elizabeth Parten and Ingeborg Robinson.

Child Maria, born March 31st, baptized May 9th; parents, Henry and Mary Bishop.

Child Magdalena, born November 9, 1752, baptized May 10th; parents, Daniel and Maria Worms.

Child Maria Eva, born April 14th, baptized May 10th; parents, Johan and Anna Margreta Saader.

Illegitimate child Cathrine, born March 1st, baptized May 13th; father, James Brook, mother, Mary English.

Child Cathrina, born March 7th, baptized March 13th; parents, Henry and Elizabeth Dery.

Child Margret, born February 20th, baptized May 20th; parents, Mark and Elizabeth Caulyn.

Child Ann, born June 10th, baptized July 15th; parents, Tobias and Jane Van der Weer.

Child Eleonora, born June 21st, baptized July 15th; parents, Cloud and Darkes Lyon.

Child Johan, born June 15th, baptized July 15th; parents, James and Maria Springer.

Child Mary, born July 4th, baptized July 17th; parents, Chambers and Rebecca Hall.

Child William, born May 16, 1750,) baptized July 25th; parents, Thomas and Hannah Parkin.
Child Eben Ezer, born December 1, 1752.

Child Rebecca, born June 26th, baptized July 29th; parents, Anders and Maria Justis.

Child Ezechiel, born June 30th, baptized August 19th; parents, John and Elizabeth McKery.

*Child Margreta, born July 22nd, baptized July 26th; parents, Lulof and Jane McDowel.

Child Margretha Dorthea, born August 9th, baptized August 26th; parents, Michael Barbro Wetwer.

OLD SWEDES CHURCH

Child Jonathan, born May 29, 1749, baptized August 29th; parents, William and Martha Taylor.

Child Johannes, born February 7th, baptized September 2nd; parents, George and Anna Maria Grey.

Child Johannes, born April 5th, baptized September 2nd; parents, Christopher and Maria Kraut.

*Child Cathrine, born August 19th, baptized September 16th; parents, Charles and Mary Springer.

*Child James, born August 27th, baptized September 18th; parents, James and Catharina McDonald.

Child Cathrine, born May 18th, baptized September 30th; parents, Charles and Sarah Grahams.

Child Thomas, born July 1st, baptized September 31st; parents, Lewis and Sarah Prees.

Child Sarah, born August 6th, baptized September 30th; parents, James and Jane Willson.

Child William, born May 8th, baptized September 30th; parents, Cornelius and Agnes Bain.

Child Mary, born March 17, 1752, baptized September 30th; parents, Thomas and Martha Mahon.

Child William, born September 2nd, baptized September 30th; parents, Robert and Elizabeth Armstrong.

*Child John, born September 12th, baptized September 26th ; parents, Johan and Sara Springer.

Child Isaac, born September 17th, baptized September 30th; parents, Swen and Cathrina Walraven.

*Child Sarah, born September 30th, baptized October 10th; parents, George and Margret Loinan.

Illegitimate child Susanna, born October 1st, baptized the 8th; father, James Molland, mother, Susanna.

Child Anne, born March 11th, baptized October 16th; parents, William and Anne Morten Welch.

Child, James, born June 23rd, baptized October 18th; parents, Daniel and Christina Few.

Child Wennefrend, born October 24, 1750, parents, Johan and Cathrina Corneliusson.

Child Sarah, born February, baptized, October 21st, parents, Johan and Cathrina Corneliusson.

The following twelve baptized in Marlborough church:

Child James 7 yrs old., baptized October 28th; parents, John and Mary Cookly.

Child Margret, born May 17th, baptized October 28th; parents, John and Mary Denin.

Child Agnes, born June 6th, baptized October 28th; parents, James and Elizabeth Alis.

Child Jane, born March 19th, baptized October 28th; parents, Alexander and Elizabeth Barnsay.

Child John, born June —, baptized October 28th; parents, John and Margret Thomson.

Child William, born March 1st, baptized October 28th; parents, Garret and Elizabeth Dougherthy.

Child Margret, born August 1st, baptized October 28th; parents, Robert and Jane Taylor.

Child Robert, born March 28th, baptized October 28th; parents, Michael and Anne Montgomery.

Child Pheobe, born October 25th, baptized October 28th; parents, William and Jane McDowel.

Child John, born May 3rd, baptized October 28th; parents, John and Mary Breyd.

Child Francis, born August 24, 1750, baptized October 28th.

Child Sarah, born October 28, 1752, baptized October 28th. Parents, Francis and Sarah Chany.

Child Hannah, born October 21st, baptized November 4th; parents, Gustas and Sarah Walraven.

Child Mary, born August 4th, baptized November 6th; parents, Amos and Rachel Erby.

Illegitimate child John, born March 26th, baptized November 22nd; father, John Bratton, mother, Margaret Butler.

Child John, baptized November 25th; parents, Jacob and Anderson.

Child Anna Barbro, born November 30th, baptized December 9th; parents, Philip and Susannah Stalcop.

Child Rachael, born October 21st, baptized December 2nd; parents, Johan and Maria Stedham.

Child Elizabeth, born October 28th, baptized December 23rd; parents, Pierce and Briget Swenson Potat.

Child William, born October 25th, baptized December 26th; parents, William and Sarah Sutton.

Child John, born September 26th, baptized December 26th; parents, Edward and Jamaima Kockhorn.

Child Jane, born July 26th, baptized December 26th; parents, James and Jane Oggle.

OLD SWEDES CHURCH

Child Richard, born November 8th, baptized December 26th ; parents, Joseph and Sarah Tull.

Child Elizabeth, born August 26th, baptized December 26th ; parents, Alexander and Martha Oggle.

Child William, born May 1st, baptized December 26th ; parents, William and Margaret Kean.

Child George, born March 28th, baptized December 29th ; parents, David and Anna Bush.

Child Rebecca, born November 20th, baptized December 30th ; parents, Isaac and Sarah Smidt.

ANNO 1754.

Child Jemaymi, born November 17th, baptized January 10th ; parents, John and Elizabeth Finsh.

*Child John, born January 7th, baptized — 12th ; parents, Samuel and Mary Brunberg Seeds.

Child Mary, born October 9, 1753, baptized January 14th ; parents, John and Elizabeth Bishop.

Child Anne, born December 15, 1753, baptized January 14th ; parents, John and Elizabeth McCollough.

Illegitimate child Johan, baptized January 20th ; father, John Almond, mother, Barbro McMolland.

Child Mary, born December 31, 1753, baptized January 20th ; parents, William and Sarah Baker.

Child Maria Dorothea, born January 2nd, baptized 21st ; parents, Jacob and Maria Barbro Gregg.

Child Henric Christian, born October 1st, baptized January 26th ; parents, Henric and Elizabeth Parsson.

Illegitimate child Hannah, born January 11th, baptized February 17 ; father, John Kelsey, mother Anne.

*Child John, born February 20th, baptized March 3d ; parents Anders and Cathrine Stille.

*Child Isaac, born February 25th, baptized March 17th ; parents Johan and Elizabeth Tummeson.

Child Maria, born September 5th, 1753, baptized March 17th ; parents, James and Jane Kirk.

*Child Peter, born December 28th, baptized March 31st ; parents, Zacharias and Elizabeth Hindricksson.

Child Johan Joseph, born January 31st, baptized March 31st ; parents, Johan and Maria Susanna Bauman.

Child Anna, born February 31st, baptized March 31st ; parents, Jacob and Magdalena Stukley.

113

EARLY CHURCH RECORDS OF NEW CASTLE COUNTY

*Child Sarah, born February 8th, baptized April 7th ; parents, Jonathan and Magdalena Stille.

Child Jacob, born September 13th, baptized April 7th ; parents, Johan and Margret Lewis.

*Child Elizabeth, born January 16, 1753, baptized October 14th ; parents, Thomas and Sarah Morten.

Child Jane, born — 11th, baptized April 15th · parents, Mark and Jane Ellot.

Child Ester, born December 22d, baptized April 15th ; parents, Moses and Martha White.

Child Anne, born January 21st, baptized April 17th ; parents, Conrad and Maria Garritsson.

Child Thomas, born January 9th, baptized April 17th ; parents, William and Phœbe Brown.

Child Cornelia, born November 9th, 1748;
Child William, born October 3th, 1752;
Child Eliakim, born December 11th, 1753;
   Baptized April 1st ; parents, Adam and Sarah Price.

Child Anne, born March 25th, baptized April 21 ; parents, Thomas and Mary Almond.

Child Cathrine, born February 22d, baptized April 21st ; parents, Archibald and Jane Latimore.

Child Mary, born March 24th, baptized April 21st ; parents, Benjamin and Margret Gardner.

Child Samuel, born March 26th, baptized April 28th ; parents, Matthew and Rebecca Tays.

Child Robert, born April 9th, baptized April 28th ; parents, Samuel and Anne Floyd.

Child Elizabeth, born March 28th, baptized April 28th ; parents, Edward and Florentz Ring.

Child Jane, born March 14th, baptized April 28th ; parents, Robert and Mary Douglas.

Child Sarah, born February 12, 1752, baptized May 1st; parents, John and Brigit Collins.

Child Anne, born March 1st, baptized May 23d ; parents, Thomas and Jane Philips.

Child Elihu, born March 25th, baptized May 23d ; parents, William and Rebecca Talley.

Child Richard, born December 29th, baptized May 23d ; parents, Richard and Rebecca Lennard.

OLD SWEDES CHURCH

Child Thomas, 3 years old, } baptized May 23d, parents,
Child Miriam, 2½ years old, } John and Marth Wayd.
Child David, 1 year old,

Child William, 9 years old, baptized May 23d; parents, John and Ester Hopton.

Child John, 1½ years old, baptized May 23d; parents, James and Jane Allen.

Child Elizabeth, 1 year old, baptized May 23d; parents, George and Elizabeth Connel.

Child Robert, born December 16, 1753, baptized May 23d; parents, Robert and Ester Sherred.

*Child John, born April 16th, baptized May 23d; parents, John and Cathrine Jackson.

Child William, born May 17th, baptized May 23rd; parents, Patrick and Mary Royal.

Child Maria Cathrina, born April 18th, baptized May 19th; parents, Paul and Barbro Hausman.

*Child Peter, born May 11th, baptized May 26th;

*Child Cornelius, born May 11th; parents Zacharias and Sarah Derickson.

Child Susannah, born August 10, 1754, baptized June 3rd; parents, Laurents and Comfort Sorely.

Child Samuel, born March 18th, baptized June 3rd; parents, Mattick and Sarah Glain.

Child Rachael, born February 22nd, baptized June 3rd; parents, William and Janet Foot.

Child Mary, born January 23rd, baptized June 3rd; parents, James and Anna Floyd.

Child John, 2½ years old;

Child William, born December 14, 1753;
    Parents, John and Anne Sherlock.

Child Adam, born April 10th, baptized June 3rd; parents, Adam and Anna Marly.

Child Else, born March 9th, baptized June 3rd, parents, Adam and Margret Kelley.

*Child John, born April 2nd, baptized June 5th; parents, Charles and Johannah Stillman.

Child Anna, born May 23rd, baptized June 8th; parents, George and Elizabeth Lewis.

Child Hannah, born May 26th, baptized July 9th; parents, Uriah and Mary Blew.

Child Frances, born July 3rd baptized July 7th; parents, Mr. Samuel and Mrs. Deborah Johnson.

EARLY CHURCH RECORDS OF NEW CASTLE COUNTY

*Child Johan, born June 29th, baptized July 1st; parents, Peter and Brita VanderWeer.

Child Sarah, born November 7, 1757;

Child Anne, born September 26, 1753, baptized August 9th ; parents, Walter and Elizabeth Hogshead.

Child Adam, born May 8th, baptized August 9th; parents, Matthias and Elizabeth Mayer.

Child Balthazar, born July 11, 1754, baptized September 1st; parents, John and Anna Mar Leming Collins.

*Child John, born August 16th, baptized September 15th; parents, Adam and Catherina Sueider.

*Child William, born September 14th, baptized September 22nd; parents, William and Johanna Vanneaman.

*Child Susannah, born August 10th, baptized September 22nd; parents, Peter and Susannah Stalcop.

Child Elizabeth, born November 21, 1753, baptized September 29th; parents, John and Mary Ross.

Child Rebecca, born May 27th, baptized September 29th; parents, Elias and Elizabeth Humphreys.

Illegitimate child Charles, born November 21, 1752, baptized September 29th; father, John Collowel, mother Margret Sandelin.

Illegitimate child Susanna, born August 25th, baptized September 30th; father, Dr. Jacob Ross, mother, Hannah Barbro Owermayerin.

*Child Isaac, born September 2nd, baptized October 20th; parents, Jacob and Mary Heins.

Child James, born September 24th, baptized October 20th; parents, Cloud and Darkes Lyon.

Child Margreta, born November 2nd, baptized November 20th; parents, Matthias and Cathrina Martin.

Child Miriam, born October 25, 1751, baptized 22nd; parents, Jacob and Hindrena Wirth.

Child Anne, born September 18th, baptized October 22nd; parents, Tobias and Margret Poulson.

Child Philip Jacob, born October 24th, baptized October 28th ; parents, Peter and Maria Helfestein.

Child Joseph, born November 14th, baptized December 1st ; parents, Ernest and Lobrina Jacobi.

*Child Maria, born November 25th, baptized December 8th ; parents, Eric and Brita Smidt.

Child Sarah, born October 6th, baptized December 14th ; parents James and Else McKoom.

OLD SWEDES CHURCH

Child William, born November 5th, baptized December 14th ; parents, Wiliam and Elizabeth Philips

*Child Rebecca, born November 23d, baptized December 22d ; parents, Jesper and Maria Wallrave.

Child Anna Barbro, born December 21st, baptized December 22d ; parents, Jacob and Anna Eva Stalley.

Child Maria Barbro, born December 8th, baptized December 22d ; parents, Jacob and Anna Eva Gray.

Child Margret, born March 16th, baptized Decembor 30th; parents, Thomas and Mary Fling.

Mrs. Sarah Falkoner, born April 4th, 1737, baptized December 30th ; the wife of Captain Nathaniel Falkoner, daughter of Robert and Sarah Moulder of Marcus Huik.

Child Robert, born February 11th, 1745;
Child Johan, born April 20th, 1747 ;
Child William, born January 9th, 1748;
Child Joseph, born January 2d, 1751;
Child Margret, born June 17, 1754;
    Parents, Benjamin, and Margret Moulder, of Marcus Hook.

ANNO 1755.

Illegitimate child William, born Nov. 7, 1754, baptized January 1 ; father Isaac Few, mother Rose Gaulanger.

Child David, born October 22d, 1754, baptized January 2d; parents, David and Mary Deric.

Child Henry, born November 16th, 1754, baptized January 2 ; parents, William and Susanna Colgen.

Child Elizabeth, born October 30th, 1754, baptized January 2d ; parents, William and Mary Glean.

Child Mary, born September 6th, 1754, baptized January 2d ; parents, George and Elizabeth Couste.

Child Mary, born April 13th, 1754, baptized January 5th ; parents, Empson and Susanna Bird.

Child Susanna, born December 29th, 1753, baptized January 5th, parents, James and Mary Armstrong.

Child Susanna, born September 22d, 1753, baptized January 5th ; parents, Abraham and Sarah Twigg.

Child Thomas, born October 6th, baptized January 5th ; parents, Walter and Sarah Nugen.

Mrs. Kelly, 54 years old, baptized January 11th ; immediately afterwards took the Lord's supper in New Castle.

EARLY CHURCH RECORDS OF NEW CASTLE COUNTY

Child Joseph, born June 10th, 1754, baptized January 17th ; parents, Samuel and Bachel Barker.
*Child Maria, born January 10th, baptized January 17th ; parents, Anders aud Maria Justis.
*Child Petrus, born January 2d, baptized January 17th ; parents, Magnus and Helena Justis.
Mrs. Lady Robnet, wife of Allen Robenet, 43 years old, baptized March 27th.
Son Joseph, 16 years old,
Daughter Rachel, 12½ years old,
Son David, 9 years old,
Daughter Lady, 5 years old,
baptized March 27th, in Marcus Hook ;
Child Margaret, born February 24th, baptized March 31st ; parents, Peter and Anne Agnew.
Child Elenor, born March 2nd, baptized March 31st ; parents, Joseph and Regina Morton.
Child Levry, born January 20th, baptized March 30th ; parents, Joseph and Jane Pierce.
Daughter Mary, 8 years old; born at Marcus Hook,
Daughter Margaret, 3 years old; born at Marcus Hook,
Child Mails, born January 8th, born at Marcus Hook,
baptized April 5th; parents Mails and Jane McCarty,
Daughter Annie, 5 years old, born at Marcus Hook,
Son John, born September 3, 1752, at Marcus Hook,
baptized April 5th; parents Wm. and Susanna Clark,
Son Joseph, born February 22, 1751, at Marcus Hook,
Daughter Annie, born August 15; 1752; at Marcur Hook,
Son Samuel, born January 15, 1754; at Marcus Hook,
baptized April 5th; parents Samuel and Elizabeth Armor.
Child Mary, born March 1st, baptized April 5th; parents, Wm. and Rebecca Lamplugh.
Child Hannah, born February 4th, baptized April 14th; parents, Wm. and Susanna Sharpley.
Child William, born October 10, 1754, baptized April 13th; parents, Daniel and Christina Few.
Child James, born February 26th, baptized April 13th; parents, James and Elenore Minzy,
Child Johan, born March 26th, baptized May 9th; parents Gabriel and Mary Fought.
Illegitimate, Child Ruth, born December 4th, baptized May 13th; parents, James and Mary McChever.

OLD SWEDES CHURCH

*Child Isaac, born January 12th, baptized May 13th; parents, Wm. and Susanna Stidham

Child William, born March 10th, baptized May 13th; parents, Wm. and Margaret Almond.

Illegitimate child David, born May 29, 1754, baptized May 17th, 1755; parents, David Killpatrick, mother, Mary Montgommery.

*Child Jonas, born April 17th, baptized May 19th; parents, Morten aud Sarah Wallraven.

Child John, born August 29, 1754, baptized June 22nd; parents, John and Jeane Stuart Morten.

*Child James, born April 15th, baptized June 8th; parents, Charles and Annie Springer Johnson.

*Child Henry, born May 7th, baptized June 8th; parents Matthias and Rebecca Morten.

Illegitimate child John, born May 11th, baptized June 8th; parents, John Lokton and Mary Grissith Lokton.

Child James, born May 2nd, baptized June 8th, parents, James and Lady McGinnis.

*Child Mary born May 11th, baptized June 15th; parents William and Mary Dirrickson.

Child Hannah, born September 16, 1749, at Marcus Hook, baptized June 28th; parents, Henry and Mary Stidham.

Child William, born April 12th, at Marcus Hook, baptized June 28th; parents, Ibenhard and Cathrine Steyerwald.

Child Jeane, born May 15th, at Marcus Hook, baptized June 28th; parents, Thomas and Elenor Diric.

Allen, born March 25, 1735, at Marcus Hook, baptized June 28th; son of Allen and Lady Robnet.

*Child Thomas, born June 13th, baptized July 13th; parents, James and Mary Springer.

Child Elizabeth, born December 8th, 1754, baptized July 13th; parents, Chambers and Rebecca Hall.

*Child Cathrina, born June 25th, baptized July 13th; parents, John and Anna Senue.

*Child Rachael born June 6th, baptized July 13th; parents, Peter and Rebecca Springer.

Child Abraham, born June 30th, baptized July 25th; parents, Jacob and Elizabeth Keu.

EARLY CHURCH RECORDS OF NEW CASTLE COUNTY

1755

Child Sarah, born March 31st, baptized July 25th; parents, John and Jane Carter.

Child Rebecca, born May 17th, baptized July 26th; parents, Alexander and Martha Oggle.

Child Edward, born March 18th, baptized August 3d; parents, Thomas and Jane Dufs.

Child Elizabeth, born June 3d, baptized August 3d; parents, James and Jane Alisson.

Child Anne, born March 19th, baptized August 6th; parents, Joseph and Margret Abrahams.

Child Peter, born July 20th, baptized August 10th; parents, Swen and Anna Brunberg.

Child Jeremiah, born July 4th, baptized August 10th; parents, Charles and Mary Springer.

Child Mary, born June 29th, baptized August 23d; parents, William and Sarah Witehead.

Child Thomas, born July 17th, baptized August 24th; parents, Johan and Elizabeth Stille.

Child Elias, born July 22d, baptized September 7th; parents, Johan and Mary King.

Child Rachael, born May 10, 1754, baptized September 9th; parents, Jonathan and Jean Kirk.

Child Tabitha, born August 6th, baptized September 12th; parents, James and Jeane Kirk.

Child Cathrina, born August 30th, baptized September 13th; parents, Cornelius and Sarah Heins.

Child Sarah, born August 27th, baptized September 21st; parents, Hans and Susanna Bauman.

Child Hans George, born August 14th, baptized September 21st; parents, Jacob and Martha Lena Stukel.

Child Adam, born September 23d, baptized September 27th; parents, Jasper and Susanna Justis.

Child Lucas, born July 6th, baptized September 28th; parents, Peter and Sarah Stidham.

Child Prudence, born September 27th, baptized October 2d; parents, Captain Nathaniel and Sarah Falckoner.

Servant girl Mary, born 1741,

Boy Thomas, born 1743,

Boy Aaron, born 1745,

Girl Jeane, born 1750,

Baptized October 8th; parents, Isaac and —— Bullock.

OLD SWEDES CHURCH

Child Elizabeth, born March 27, 1753.
Child Samuel, born July 14th, baptized October 8th.
Child Joseph, born March 4, 1754, baptized October 8th.
Child Thomas, born December 25, 1753, baptized October 8th.
Child John, born October 19, 1754, baptized October 8th ; parents, William and —— Smidt.
Child Richard, born January 19th, baptized October 8th : parents, Banton and Hannah Davis.
Child John, born May 27th, baptized November 5th ; parents, John and Anne Garrit.
Child Sarah, baptized November 7th ; parents, —— Sandes.
*Child Christina, born November 3d, baptized November 16th ; parents, Swen and Cathrina Wallraven.
*Child Anna, born August 16th, baptized November 16th ; parents, William and Cathrina Pålson.
*Child Isaac, born October 25th, baptized November 30th ; ents, Matthias and Maria Petersson.
Child Mary, born August 26th, baptized December 1st ; parparents, John and Elizabeth Carnay.
*Child Brigita, born December 6th, baptized December 7th ; parents, Swen and Maria Justis.
Child Cathrine, born October 23, 1754, baptized December 7th ; parents, Conrad and Barbro Grey.
Child John, born November 26th, baptized December 7th ; parents, Hans and Maria Nebuir.
Child Elizabeth, born January 27th, baptized December 13th ; parents, John and Cathrine Marrow.
Child Isaac, born February 29, 1751, baptized December 13th ; parents, John and Mary Van Neaman.
Child Daniel, born December 19th, baptized December 26th ; parents, Joseph and Mary Jackson.
Child William, born December 12th, baptized December 26th; parents, Lancelot and Margret Johnston.

ANNO 1756.

Child Cathrina Magdalena, born December 5, 1755, baptized, parents, Samuel and Maria Shenk.
*Child Carolus, born December 22, 1755, baptized January 2d; parents, Nils and Maria Justis.
Illegitimate child Barbro, born January 3rd, baptized January 18th; Father, Lewis———Mother, Margreta———

EARLY CHURCH RECORDS OF NEW CASTLE COUNTY

Child John, born December 5, 1755, baptized January 11th, parents, John and Maria Stedham.

Child Cath.ina, born December 29, 1755, baptized January 22d; parents, Moses and Martha White.

Child Judith, born December 3, 1752,
Child Sarah, born June 1754,
   Baptized January 2d; parents, Christopher and Elenor Hendrickson.

Child Maria, born January 7th, baptized January 27th; parents, Fredric and Margret Smidt.

Child Susanna Dorothea, born November 14, 1755, baptized January 26th; parents, Christopher and Barbro Kraut.

Child Rachel, born November 17, 1755, baptized February 18th; parents, James and Maria Smidt.

Child Jane, born April 8, 1754, baptized February 18th; parents, Niclas and Sarah Fling.

Child Isaac, born November 15, 1755, baptized March 6th; parents, Charles and Jeane Galloway.

CONCORD.

Man, John Armen, 31 years old, August 14th, old style.

Woman, Sarah Armen, Jacob Muler's wife, 34 years old the last June, old style.

Elizabeth, born June 3, 1748,
Mary, born October 30, 1750,
Jacob, born November 10, 1753,
   Baptized March 17th; parents, Jacob and Sarah Moth.

Child John, born February 9, 1754, baptized March 17th; parents, John and Ruth Taylor.

Child Barbro, born Februa.y 24th, baptized March 21st; parents Hans and Johannah JaQuette.

Child John, born August 28, 1755, baptized March; parents, John and Elizabeth Kary.

Child Friedrich, born January 13th, baptized March; p rents, Jacob and Margreta Krieg.

Child John, born February 15th, baptized March 28th; parents, Isaac and Sarah Smidt.

Child William, born February 8th, baptized April 9th; parents, Moses and Martha Burns.

Child Elizabeth, born March 27th, baptized April 11th; parents, Philip and Susanna Stalcop.

Child Elijah, born 1st Feb., baptized April 11th; parents, Mark and Jane Ellot,

OLD SWEDES CHURCH

Child, John, bo.n December 17, 1755, baptized April 12th; parents, John and Elizabeth Reese.

Child Susannah, born February 7, 1755, baptized April 12th; parents, Henry and Susanna Brochon.

Illegitimate child Hannah, born February 10, 1755, baptized April 12th; father John McSwine and mother Mary Parmer.

Child Benjamin, born March 29th, baptized April 14th; parents, John and Susannah Hedge.

Child James, born April 8th, baptized April 16th; parents, Daniel and Anne Carnay.

Child Sarah, born March 30th, baptized April 25th; parents, John and Elizabeth Barber.

Child James, born January 28th, baptized April 25th; parents, John and Cathrine Cry.

Child Elizabeth, born March 13th, baptized May 2d: parents, Watkins and Jane Crampton.

Child Elizabeth, born April 13th, baptized May 5th; parents, James and Maria Stidham.

Child Susanna, born February 25th, baptized May 5th; parents, John and Hannah Wallraven.

Child Cathrina Barbro, born April 26th, baptized May 16th; parents, Paul and Barbro Hausman.

Child John Michael, born April 19th, baptized May 6th; parents, Niclas and Anna Cathrina Russel.

Child Isaac, born April 10th, baptized May 19th; parents, Isaac und Margery Bullock.

Child Rachel, born April 10th, baptized May 21st; parents, Tobias and Margret Polson.

Child Elizabeth, born January 17th, baptized May 21st; parents, Edward and Jemmimy Cookhorn.

Child Joseph, born March 7th, baptized May 17th; parents, Samuel and Maria Seeds.

Child James, born April 26th, baptized May 23th; parents, John and Elizabeth Bishop.

Child John, born March 27th, baptized May 23d; parents, Wm. and Mary Allen.

Child Elias, born April 21st, baptized May 23d; parents, Elias and Elizabeth Humphreys.

Child John, born December 16, 1755, baptized May 23d; parents, Isaac and Margret Adams.

*Child Isaac, born May 20th, baptized May 30; parents, Anders and Catharine Stilley.

EARLY CHURCH RECORDS OF NEW CASTLE COUNTY

Child Rebecca, born May 28th, baptized June 6; parents, Joran and Margret Loinan.

*Young woman Christina, 16 years old, parents, Wm. and Mary Hill.

Child Rebecca, born April 17th, baptized June 8th; parents, Benjamin and Margret Larner.

Child Anna Ingeborg, born January 14th, baptized July 4th; parents, Thomas and Sarah Morton.

Child Mary, born December 5, 1753,

Child Arthur, born April 14, 1755,

Child William, born July 3, 1756,

Baptized July 26th; parents, Arthur and Mary Murphy.

Child John, born May 27, 1755, baptized July 28th; parents, Wm. and Catharine Furkes.

Child Joseph, born May 26th, baptized July 11th; parents, Andreas and Dorothea Justis.

Child Elizabeth, born May 10th, baptized July 11th; parents, Robert and Elinor Robinson.

Child Rachael, born June 12th, baptized July 11th; parents, Samuel and Mary Cleany.

Child Amy, born April 3d, baptized July 11th; parents, Wallace and Margaret Bratton.

Child Jacob, born May 5th, baptized July 11th; parents, Hugh and Jane Curfel.

Child John, born April 12th, baptized July 29th; parents, John and Jane Stuart.

Child Maria, born July 23d, baptized August 1st; parents, Gustas and Sarah Walraven.

Child Maria Dorothea,

Child Johan Paul,

Born June 8th, baptized August 1st; parents, Albrecht and Maria Margreta Girchk.

Boy Peter, 10 years old, baptized August 18th; parents, Wm. and Mary Hill.

Child Elizabeth, born July 17th, baptized August 22d; parents, Tobias and Jane Vander Wier.

Child Elenor, born August 31, 1755, baptized August 22d; parents, Thomas and Johannah Shannan.

Child Rachael, born August 22, baptized August 29th; parents, John and Elenor Garretson.

Child Peter, born August 6th, baptized September 3d; parents, Jesper and Maria Classon.

OLD SWEDES CHURCH

Child Anna Margreta, born December 2, 1755, baptized Sept. 4; parents, Balzar and Maria Stelz.

Child Elizabeth, born May 31st, baptized July 4th; parents, Joseph and Martha Simcott.

Child Mary, born August 8th, baptized September 12th; parents James and Catharina McDonald.

Child Catharina, born August 28th, baptized September 12; parents, Michael and Barbro Mezger.

Child Johannes, born September 18th, baptized October 3d; parents, Wm. and Johanna Van Neaman.

Child Jacob, born May 1st, baptized October 2d; parents, Jacob and Anna Cathrina Staley.

Child Johan, born July 31st, baptized October 5th; parents, George and Elinor Hugel.

Child James, born October 10, 1755, baptized October 10th; parents, James and Elizabeth Dornell.

Child Isaac, born July 24th, baptized October 10th; parents, Jacob and Sarah Muthin.

Child John, born January, 1749, batized October 10th; parents, Abraham and Elizabeth Burnet.

Child Amos, born August 4th, baptized October 10th; parents, Wm. and Anne Smidt.

Child Robert, born January 15, 1754, baptized October 10th,
Child Susannah, born December 22, 1754, baptized October 10,
Parents, James and Susannah Porter.

Illegitimate child Richard, baptized October 10th, father —— Hossman, mother, Margreta Paulsson.

Child Elizabeth, born September 10th, baptized October 11th; parents, Daniel and Christina Few.

Annie Grub, Emanuel Grub's wife, baptized October 17th, 21 years old.

Servant Hannah Carter; parents, Ninive and Mary Carter, baptized October 17th, 18 years old.

Child Benjamin, born April 9th, 1753,
Child Susannah, born June 11th, —,
Baptized October 17; parents, Emanuel and Anne Grub.

Child William, born May 29, 1754,
Child James, born May 26th,
Baptized October 17th; parents, James and Mary Curry.

EARLY CHURCH RECORDS OF NEW CASTLE COUNTY

Child John, born April 18th, 1750,
Child James, born April 19th, 1752,
Child William, born April 25th, 1754,
Child George, born Apr. 10-,
  Baptized October 17th ; parents, William and Margret Huston.
Child Elenore, born July 22d, 1754,
Child Phœbe, born November 30th, 1755,
  Baptized October 17th ; parents, Abrah and Elenore Pike.
Record of those who were baptized by Pastor Ereck Unander at Christina Congregation from the commencement of his pastor's office in the month of October, 1756 :
Child Anna, born October 10th, baptized October 15th ; parents, Patrick and Elizabeth Boyd.

Child born in October, baptized November 11th ; parents, Christopher and Hendrickson.

Child Cathrina, born October 21th, baptized October 14th ; parents, Tobias and Maria Smith.

Child Sarah,
Child Rebecca,
  Born November 2d, baptized November 24th ; parents, Thomas and Mary Almond.

Child Margreta, born November 20th, baptized November 24th ; parents, Gloud and Darkeys Lion.

Child Andrew, born July 9th, baptized November 12th ; parents, Joseph and Jane Pearce, from Glouchester County in Jersey.

Child Cathrina, born October 21st, baptized November, 1756 ; arents, Tobias and Maria Smith.

ANNO 1757.

Child Sarah, born December 22, 1756 ; parents, Peter and Cathrine Anderson.

Child Margreta, born November 20th ; parents, Cloud and Darkeys Lion.

Child Sarah, born November 29, 1756, baptized January 30h, 1757 ; parents, John and Anna Sinix.

Child Cathrina, born November 26th, baptized December 5th, 1756 ; parents, Peter and Brita Van Davie.

Child Susannah, born November 23, 1756, baptized January 12th, 1757 ; parents, William and Susanna Sharpley.

OLD SWEDES CHURCH

Child Rachel, born September 25, 1750,
Child Thomas, born May 17, 1756,
 Baptized January 19, 1757 ; parents, William and Rebecca Bratton.

Child Hannah, born November 30, 1756, baptized January 9th; parents, Mounce and Ellen Justis.

Child Peter born January 14th, baptized February 7th; parents, Francis and Anne Cathrine Anthony.

Child Elizabeth, born September 27th, baptized January 5, 1727; mother, Anne Pennington.

Child Bruteena, born February 12th, baptized November 6th; parents, Thomas Rebecca Beason.

Child Joseph, born August 17th, baptized November 6th ; parents, Joseph and Mary Parvis.

Child Jacob, born August 31st, baptized November 2nd; parents, Hance and Rachel Miller.

Child Rebecca, born March 21st, baptized April 2nd; parents, Mathias and Maria Petersson.

Child Elizabeth, born October 3, 1756, baptized March 29th; parents, Conrad and Barbara Grey.

Child John, born December 11, 1756, baptized March 29th; parents, George and Maria Patton.

Child Sarah, born February 1st, baptized April 11th; parents; Paul and Maria Petersson.

Child Elizabeth, born December 13th, baptized April 11th ; parents, Jacobus and Maria Hein.

Child Elizabeth, born March 1st, baptized April 11th; parents, Luluff and Jane Stidham.

Child Hannah, born April 4th, baptized April 14th; parents, Cornelius and Margreta Vandeveers.

Child William, born December 27, 1756, baptized April 14th; parents, John and Cathrina Jackson.

Child Margreta, born October 24, 1756, baptized April 14th; parents, Allen and Anne Robinett.

Child Rebecca, born April 20th, baptized April 23rd; parents, Peter and Rebecca Springer.

Child David, born April 17th, baptized April 24th; parents, Wm. and Margreta Almond.

Jane Peary's illegitimate child Susanna, born March 16th, baptized April 11th.

Barbara Little's illegitimate child Rebecca, born December 14, 1756, baptized April 3rd.

EARLY CHURCH RECORDS OF NEW CASTLE COUNTY

Child David, born November 4, 1756, baptized April 10th; parents, Zacharias and Sarah Dereckson.

Child Jane, born April 11, 1756, baptized May 4th; parents, Samuel and Eliza Reall.

Child Nils, born April 7th, baptized May 2d; parents, Nils and Maria Justis.

Child Hannah, born April 24th, baptized May 13th; parents, Joseph and Hannah Springer.

Child Isaac, born March 17th, baptized May 8th; parents, Calop and Cathrine Parkins.

Child Mary, born August, 1756, baptized May 9th; parents, David and Elizabeth Harris.

Child John Ubrich, born March 15, 1756, baptized May 9th; parents, Ulrich and Catharine Sharmiser.

Child Catharina, born October, 1755, baptized May 9th; parents, Ulrich and Catharine Sharmiser.

Child Anne, born June 9, 1756, baptized May 9th; parents, James and Margreta Maley.

Child Owen, born May 6th, baptized May 19th; parents, John and Anne Sably.

Cathrine Anderson's illegitimate son Jacob, born May 21st, baptized May 27th.

Hannah Pearce's illegitimate son Abner, born May 9, 1756, baptized May 23, 1757.

Child Sarah, born March 3d, baptized May 27, 1757; parents, James and Susanna Porlen.

Child Richard, born May, 1756, baptized May 27, 1757; parents, Will and Jane Trotter.

Child Joseph, baptized August 7th; parents, Joseph and Margreta Bird.

Child Paul, born May 10th, baptized August 7th; parents, John and Susanna Bauman.

Child Susanna, born February 17th, baptized June 12th; parents, Gottfried and Margreta Brown.

Child Rebecca, born August 20th, baptized September 11th; parents, Peter and Rebecca Peterson.

Child William, born July 21st, baptized September 11th; parents, Benjamin and Mary Ford.

Child Rachel, baptized September 11th; parents, Cornelius and Sarah Hein.

Child Martha, born March 2d, baptized September 11th; parents, William and Ruth Braken.

OLD SWEDES CHURCH

Child Anna born December 2, 1752,
Child John, born December 21, 1756,
Baptized September 29th; parents, William and Mary Montgomery.

Child Mary, born March 1st, baptized September 29th; parents, Nathaniel and Elizabeth Lewis.

Child Cathrina, born March 5th, baptized September 29th; parents, John and Anna Reinolds.

Child John, born October 20th, baptized October 21; parents, Eric and Brigits Smidth.

Child Sarah, born September 23d, baptized September 30th; parents, Reading and Elizabeth Young.

Child Lydia, born October 21st, baptized October 29th; parents, John and Elizabeth Stilley.

Child Benjnmin, born May 31, 1751,
Child John, born December 7, 1752,
Elizabeth and Rachel, born December 23, 1754,
Child Samuel, born June 15,
Baptized August 15th, 1757; parents, Henry and Anne Pearce.

Child Andrew, born May 16th, baptized August 14th; parents, George and Susanna Phisik.

Sara Pearce's illegitimate child Robert, born November 7th, baptized December 23d.

Child Thomas, born May 1st, baptized August 13th; parents, Thomas and Mary Barlow.

Child Peter, born October 4th, baptized December 1st; parents, Swen and Cathrina Walraven.

Child Elizabeth, born August 25th, baptized November 5th; parents, Henry and Sara Webster.

Child Lydia, born July 7th, baptized August 26th; parents, William and Sara Whitehead.

Anno 1758.

Child Anne Mary, born December, 1754, baptized January 2d; parents, Niklas and Dorothea Einfass.

Child Hannah, born May 23d, baptized January 2d; parents, Joseph and Margreta Abram.

Child Jacob, born November 13th, baptized January 2d; parents, Jesper and Mary Walraven.

Child Mary, born November 27th, baptized February 3d; parents, John and Mary Stedham.

EARLY CHURCH RECORDS OF NEW CASTLE COUNTY

Child Stephen, born September 4, 1757, baptized March 7th; parents, William and Ester Keeper.

Child John, born January 27th, baptized February 26th; parents, George and Margreta Loinan.

Child Joanna, born March 14th, baptized March 19th; parents, William and Johanna Vaniman.

Child Annable, born February 28th, baptized March 24th; parents, James and Catharine McDonald.

Child Sarah, born 1757, baptized March 27th; parents, Peter and Anne Agnew.

Child Ezekiel, born June 7, 1757, baptized March 24th; parents, John and Elizabeth Rees.

Child Rachel, born January 1st, baptized March 24th; parents, Charles and Mary Springer.

Child Henry, born February 20th, baptized March 1st; parents, Henry and Ann Sinie.

Child Matthias, born October 21, 1757, baptized March 26th; parent, Thomas Morton.

Child Margretta, born November 16th, 1757; parents, Richard and Mary Clark.

Child Lydia, born February 4th, baptized May 1st; parents, Allen and Anne Robinette.

Child Peter, born January 21, 1757, baptized May 3d; parents, Peter and Susanna Slalcop.

Child John, born April 17th, baptized May 4th; parents, Jesper and —— Justis.

Child Benjamin, born January 12th, baptized May 1st; parents, John and Lydia Lazareth.

Child John, born February 16th, baptized April 30th; parents, Swen and Anna Brunberg.

Child Benjamin, born August 1, 1757, baptized May 9th; parents, William and Phœbe Broom.

Child John, born March 26th, baptized May 14th; parents Samuel and Susanna Shank.

Child John Henry, born December 24, 1757, baptized May 14th; parents, John and Cathrina Naff.

Child Mary, born November 26, 1757, baptized May 10th; parents, Hans and Mary Neighbucher.

Child Christopher, born April 5th, baptized May 28th; parents, Christopher and Barbara Kraut.

Child Jacob, born March 14th, baptized June 4th; parents, Jacob and Barbara Kriegen.

OLD SWEDES CHURCH

Child Sarah, born April 27th, baptized June 27th; parents, Thomas and Elizabeth Bowles.

Child Hance Caster Christian, born September 29th, baptized June 18th; parents, Hance and Margreta Heilbrumer.

Child Alexander, born March 15th, baptized June 29th; parents, Joseph and Margreta Thornton.

Child Anna, born June 4th, baptized June 16th; parents, Solomon and Margreta Springer.

Child James, born July 29th, baptized November, parents, Moses and Martha Burns.

Child ——born August 2, 1757, baptized August 12, 1758, parents, Balzar and Margreta Stills.

Child Anna, born July 23rd, baptized August 20th; parents, John and Anna Sininks.

Child Jonathan, born June 15, 1756, baptized September 17th; parents Jonathan and Jane Kirk.

Child Jacob, born July 29th, baptized September, parents Jacob and Maria Anderson.

Child Anna, born June 17th, baptized July 23rd; parents, Wm. and Jane McDowel.

Child Ellenor, born December 4, 1757, baptized March 6th, parents, Christopher and Ellenor Hendrickson.

Child Rebecca, born October 7th, baptized November 7th; parents, John and Lydia Bird.

Child John Fredrick, born December 2nd, baptized December 11th; parents, Nicklas and Dorothea Donnelfass.

Child John, born October 11th, baptized October 23rd; parents, Thomas and Elizabeth Moore.

Child Rudolph, born October 9th, baptized November 12th; parents, Wicklan and Cathrina Guschys.

ANNO 1759.

Child William, born January 3rd, baptiezd February 11th; parents, Tobias and Jane Vandevars.

Child Christina, born February 12th, baptized February 25th, parents, Matthias and Maria Peterson.

Child Susanna, born February 14th, baptized March 8th; parents, Paul and Barbara Hausman.

Child Friedrich, born October 10th, baptized March 18th; parents, Peter and Cathrina Pile.

Child Margaretha, born March 25th, baptized April 1st; parents, Peter and Brigita Vandevar.

EARLY CHURCH RECORDS OF NEW CASTLE COUNTY

Child Hannah, born October 22nd, baptized May 9th; parents, Joseph and Margreta Bird.

Child Isaac, born May 11th, baptized May 11th; parents Gustav and Sarah Wallraven.

Child Susanna, born April 19th, baptized May 22nd; parents, Jonas and Maria Stidham.

Child David, born March 13th, baptized May 22nd; parents, Benjamin and Rebecca Ford.

Child Jesper, born December 7, 1758, baptized May 6th; parents, John and Margaretha Pear.

Child Peter, born January 11th, baptized May 6th; parents, Jacob and Catharine Stadys.

Child William, born April 4th, baptized June 5th; parents, Wm. and Maria Montgommery,

Child John, born June 2nd, baptized June 6th; parents, Robert and Elizabeth Peare.

Child Anna, born July, 1758, baptized June 6th; parents, Moses and Martha White.

Child Joseph, born March 29th, baptized June 17th; parents, Zacharias and Sarah Derrickson.

Mara Magdalena Damarin's illegitimate child John Frederick, born April 3, baptized June 17th.

Child David, born March 17, 1753, baptized June 8th; parents, Lascelly and Margaretha Johnson.

Child Jonathan, born March 1, 1758, baptized June 8th; parents, Lascelly and Margaretha Johnson.

Child Maria, born June 14th, baptized July 8th; parents, Morton and Sarah Morten,

Child Anna, born November 1, 1758, baptized July 15th; parents, Abraham and Catharina Davis.

Child Catharina, born November 15, 1758, baptized July 15th; parents, Joseph and Guine Pearce,

Child Hannah, born May 17th, baptized July 15th; parents, Levi and Mary Pearce.

Child Maria, born June 14th, baptized July 15th; parents, Magnus and Elenora Justice.

Child Elizabeth, born April 12th, baptized August 12th; parents, Ernst and Sabina Jacobi.

Child Hanna, born September 4th, baptized September 27th; parents, Wilhelm and Sara Whitehead.

Child Anna, born August 29th, baptized October 7th; parents, John and Elizabeth Stilley.

OLD SWEDES CHURCH

Child Anders, born September 16th, baptized October 7th; parents, Tobias and Margretha Paulson.

Child William, born October 14, 1757, baptized October 7th, parents, Peter and Helena Monson.

Child Joseph, born July 20th, baptized October 21st; parents, Joseph and Margretha Abram.

Child Thomas, born September 22d, baptized November 2d; parents, Thomas and Brigitta Bird.

Child Robert, born July 21st, baptized November 5th; parents, George and Maria Elliott.

Child Anna, born July 21st, baptized December 17th; parents, Conrad and Barbara Gray.

Child Anna, born October 26th, baptized December 17th; parents, John and Maria Newbeeker.

Child Amos, born September 9th, baptized November 4th; parents, William and Susanna Sharpley.

Child John, born December 4th, baptized December 14th; parents, Cornelius and —— Heins.

ANNO 1760.

Child Anna, born December 17, 1759, baptized January 27th; parents, Jonas and Maria Walraven.

Child Johan Gottfried Michael, born February 3d, baptized February 10th; parents, Nicklas Daniel and Dorothea Foss.

Child Jonas, born February 2d, baptized February 11th; parents, Anders and Dorothea Justis.

Child Jesse, born January 23d, baptized February 17th, parents, Jonas and Catharina Walraven.

Child Maria, born February 16th, baptized March 10th, parents, Nils and Maria Justis.

Child Daniel, born November 19th, baptized March 11th, parents, John and Maria Stedham.

Child Rebecka, born October 1, 1759, baptized March 2d, parents, Cornelius and Maria Evanson Duskill.

Child Lydia, born January 30th, baptized March 16th, parents, Swen and Catharina Walraven.

Catharina Poor's illegitimate child Maria, born November 20, 1758, baptized March 16th.

Child Maria, born October 29th, baptized March 26th, parents, John and Else Cain.

133

EARLY CHURCH RECORDS OF NEW CASTLE COUNTY

Child Maria, born October 2, 1759, baptized April 6th, parents, Thomas and Sarah Morton.

Child John William, born March 15th, baptized April 7th, parents, Wm. and Maria Roberts.

Child Hannah, born March 12th, baptized April 11th, parents, Peter and Christina Springer.

Child Peter, born September 3, 1759, baptized April 23d, parents, Israel and Maria Classon.

Child Maria, born February 13th, baptized April 27, parents, Benjamin and Maria Enock.

Child Susanna, born December 1, 1759, baptized April 29th, parents, Conrad and Maria Garrison.

Child Rebecca, born —— baptized May 7th, parents Wm. and —— McCoy.

Child Maria, born August 6, 1759, baptized May 8th, parents, Zacharias and Elizabeth Hindrickson.

Child Jane, born March 30th, baptized May 9th, parents, Lasselley and Margretha Johnson.

Child Joseph, born November 2, 1759, baptized May 9, parents, James and Maria Bartley.

Child Sarah, born November 22d, baptized May 9th, parents, Samuel and Anna Floyd.

Child John, born February 12th, baptized May 9th, parents, Eliah and Hannah Richie.

Child Benjamin, born March 26th, baptized May 9th; parents, Wm. and Susanna Stidham.

Child William, born September 19th, baptized May 9th, parents, James and Maria McKeaver.

Child Paul, born January 3d, baptized May 10, parents, Hans and Margretha Heilbrunner.

Child Hanna, born January 27th, baptized May 10th, parents, Mark and Jane Elliott.

Child Elizabeth, born October 3, 1755,

Child Maria, born January 23, 1758,

Baptized May 10th, parents, John and Barbara Almond.

Child Maria, born February 9th, baptized April 23d, parents, Wm. and Phoebe Broom.

Child Thomas, born March 4th, baptized May 13th; parents, Wm. and Elizabeth Cartmill.

Child Maria, born May 22nd, baptized June 1st; parents, John and Darkeys Baal.

OLD SWEDES CHURCH

Child Edward, born May 11th, baptized June 7th; parents, John and Cloe Elliott.

Child Rebecca, born——baptized June 8th; parents, Samuel and Magdelena Cleanny.

Child Hans Peter, born September 8 baptized January 8th; parents, Michael and Maria Schwartz.

Child Maria, born May 17th, baptized June 8th; parents, Albrecht and Maria Margaretha Yurgon.

Child Valentin, born February 15th, baptized June 8th; parents, Johan Valentin and Anna Maria Huhlman.

Child William, born July 3rd, baptized July 13th; parents, Wm. and Johanna Vanneaman.

Child Hugh, born December 11, 1759, baptized July 13th; parents, Arthur and Maria Murphey.

RECORD OF THE CHILDREN BAPTIZED BY ANDREW BORRELL. ANNO 1760.

Anna, born June 16th, baptized July 20th; parents, Swen and Maria Justice.

Thomas, born July 6th, baptized August 3rd; parents, William and Elizabeth Philips.

Lydia, born August 5th, baptized August 17th; parents, Charles and Margreta Springer.

Rachel, born July 16th, baptized August 17th; parents, Eric and Susanna Anderson.

Jonas, born August 3rd, baptized August 17th; parents, Charles and Mary Robinson.

Jehu, born September 12th, baptized October 9th; parents, Solomon and Margreta Springer.

Hans George, born October 1st, baptized October 23rd; parents, Jacob and Barbro Craak.

Hanna, born July 13th, baptized October 5th; parents, Richard and Anna Justisson.

Maria, born June 11th, baptized November 4th; parents, John and Anna Senex.

Anna Eva, born October 13th, baptized October 9th; parents Michael and Barbro Matsher.

Johan Niclas, born October 15th, baptized November 16th; parents, John Niclas and Cathrina Bushi.

Anna, born November 9th, baptized November 16th; parents, Peter and Obiah Peterson.

EARLY CHURCH RECORDS OF NEW CASTLE COUNTY

Rachel, born October 29th, baptized December 15th; parents, Jacob and Nancy Stilley.

John, born September 17th, baptized December 7th; parents, Andrew and Cathrina Busheon.

ANNO 1761.

Eleonora, born January 6th, baptized January 12th; parents, Robert and Eleonora Robinson.

John, born February 2nd, baptized February 23rd; parents, John and Debora Ahlmond.

Cathrina, born February 9th, baptized February 25th; parents, Anders and Cathrina Stilley.

Sarah, born May 13, 1757, baptized at St. James,

Moses, born July 14, 1760, baptized at St. James, February 25th; parents, Henry and —— Braehen.

Maria, born September 15, 1760, baptized February 25th; parents, Henry and Maria Bishop.

William, born November 12, 1753, baptized March 14th; parents, Walter and Maria Patterson.

Elizabeth, born February 2nd, baptized March 21st; parents, Jesper and Maria Walraven.

Samuel, born February 24th, baptized March 23rd; parents, Robert and Anna Johns.

Peter, illegitimate, born December 7, 1759, baptized March 25th; parents, Harry Gorden and Hannah.

Jehu, born February 25th, baptized March 29th; parents, Matthias and Maria Peterson.

Anna, born March 14th, baptized April 12th; parents, Henry Senex and his wife.

Hannah, born January 10, 1760, baptized April 19th; parents, Samuel and Anna Strand.

Sarah, born September 29, 1760, baptized April 19th; parents, Peter and Margret Brunberg.

Maria, born April 6th, baptized April 19th; parents, John and Barbro Gaffin.

Lewis, baptized in Penn's Neck.

William, born July 23, 1760, baptized April 26th; parents, Dahaghty and Rebeccah Allen.

Sarah, born August 10, 1760, baptized May 9th; parents, Richard and Elizabeth McManneman.

OLD SWEDES CHURCH

Elizabeth, born April 7th, baptized May 10th ; parents, Philip and Sabina Sleifer.

Jane, born February 11th, baptized May 11th ; parents, Thomas and Maria Ahlmond,

Maria Susanna, born January 25th, baptized May 24th ; parents, Hans and Cathrina Naff.

Samuel, born April 13th, baptized May 24th ; parents, Gottfried and Anna Maria Charley.

John born April 19th, baptized May 24th ; parents, John and Barbro French.

John born April 25th, baptized May 24th ; parents, Matthias. and Anna Eva Skaylor.

Anna, born August 3, 1760, baptized May 24th ; parents, Joseph and Regina Marten.

William, born March 22, 1759, baptized May 12th ; parents, Charles and Jane Galloway.

Deborah, born February 24th, baptized March 2d ; parents, George an Anna Stonmats.

George, born November 26, 1760, baptized March 2d ; parents, William and Catharina Paulson.

Kirck, born December 11, 1759, baptized June 4th ; parents, James and Jane Kirck.

Elizabeth, born June 9, 1758, baptized June 5th ; parents, Jacob and Hindrance Werth.

Susannah, born February 16th, baptized June 7th ; parents, Joseph and Mary Pierce.

Peter, born December 25, 1760, baptized June 7th ; parents, Matthias and Margret Martin,

James, born November 30, 1760, baptized June 11th ; parents, James and Cathrina Clark.

Sarah, born October 10, 1760, baptized June 13th ; parents, Robert and Elizabeth Pierce.

Sarah, born May 23d, baptized June 21st ; parents, Thomas and Martha Barnet.

John, born May 27th, baptized July 5th ; parents, John and Margret Pearce.

Elizabeth, born November 30, 1753, baptized July 11th ; parents, Johnathan and Jane Kirck.

EARLY CHURCH RECORDS OF NEW CASTLE COUNTY

Arcadia, born September 30, 1760 baptized July 29th ; parents, James and Elizabeth Sennex.

Philipina, born February 16th, baptized August 2d; parents, John William and Cathrina Margreta Cob.

Margreta, born June 6th, baptized August 6th ; parents, Christopher and Rachel Lind.

Petrus, born August 16th, baptized September 27th ; parents, John and Maria King.

Elsa, born March 24, 1758, baptized September 27th ; parents, Wallraven Paul and Magdalena Peterson.

Rachel, born January 20, 1758, baptized October 4th : parents, Jacob and Phœbe Maast.

Hannah, born August 8th, baptized October 4th ; parents, Henry and Elenora Hoof.

Thomas, born September 4th, baptized October 4th ; parents, Jonathan and Jane Kirck.

Petrus, born September 9th, baptized October 11th ; parents, Paul and Mary Peterson.

Benjamin, born August 16th, baptized September 20th ; parents, Benjamin and Margreta Bird.

Richard, born May 28th, baptized October 17th ; parents, William and Rachel Runnels.

Jemyme, born September 12th, baptized November 1st ; parents, William and Susannah Sharpley.

Susannah, born October 11th, baptized November 15th ; parents, Anders and Margreta Paulson.

John, born October 19th, baptized November 22d; parents, John and Elizabeth Stilley.

Israel, born October 24th, baptized November 26th ; parents, William and Maria Aston.

Nanny, born October 23d, baptized November 29th ; parents, Caleb and Nanny Parkins.

Maria, born October 22, baptized December 6th ; parents, Michael and Brigitta Mardock.

Jesse, born October 26th, baptized December 6th ; parents, Peter and Catharine Springer.

Rebeccah, born December 16th, baptized December 20th ; parents, Andrew and Annah Vaneman.

William, born October 23, baptized December 26th ; parents, William and Sarah Whithead.

David, born December 22d, baptized December 29th ; parents, James and Jane Kirck.

OLD SWEDES CHURCH

Orphey, born September 25th, baptized December 29th ; parents, —— Houseman.

ANNO 1762.

Robert, born October 13, 1758, baptized January 7th,
Cathrine, born May 14, 1761, baptized January 7th,
Parents, Frederick and Margrete Smidth.

William and Maria, born November 1, 1761, baptized January 28th ; parents, John and Cathrina Cann.

Elizabeth, born January 17th, baptized January 20, parents, John and Elenora Garritson.

Rachel, born April 1, 1760, baptized January 20, parents, Thomas and Annah Adams.

Cathrine, born December 7, 1761, baptized January 4th, parents, Magnus and Elenore JustisJun.

Ephron, born November 14, 1761, baptized February 2, parents, Jonathan and Magdalena Stilley.

Uriel, born December 25, 1761, baptized February 2d, parents, Jacob and Nancy Stilly.

At St. James', Elenora, born September 19, 1761, bapti ed February 24th, parents, John and Anna Mardock.

At St. James', Prudence, born Septemebr 19, 1761, bapti ed February 24th, parents, John and Anna Mardock.

Eleonora, born November 4, 1761, baptized February 24th ; parents, Edward and Briggitta McBride.

At St. James', Harris, born October 4, 1761, baptized February 25, parents, Hannah and Harris Gordon.

At St. James', Andrew Gravenrat, born February 18,th, baptised March 20, Jacob and Cathrine Colesberry.

Annah, born January 24th, baptized March 14th, parents, John and Beata Hendrickson.

Rebeccah, born December 29, 1761, baptized March 25th, parents, Henry and Rebeccah Spencer.

Margrete, born May 19th, baptized March 25th; parents, John and Mary Powel.

John, born March 13th, baptized March 25th; parents, Tobias and Jane Vandevar.

Charles, born March 12, 1761, baptized March 26th; parents, Peter and Eleonore Paulson.

George, born December 14, 1761, baptized March 29th; parents, Hans and Mary Nebukar.

David, born December 4, 1761, baptized April 4th; parents, Benjamin and Mary Enoch.

EARLY CHURCH RECORDS OF NEW CASTLE COUNTY

John, illegitimate, born April 9th, baptized April 10th; father, John Divant, mother, Magdalena Divant.

Rachel, born January 28, baptized April 12th, parents, Thomas and Brita Bird.

Sarah, born January 12th, baptized April 12th, parents, John and Mary Stedham.

William, born February 20th, baptized April 12th, parents, Niclas and Cathrine Bush.

Elizabeth, born July 3, 1755, baptized April 19th,

Cathrine, born September 16, 1757, baptized April 19th,

George, born March 20, 1761, baptized April 19th,

These three children, their parents and T. Michael and Sarah King.

Israel, born March 13th, baptized April 20th, parents, John and Jane Stahlkop.

Annah, illegitimate, born September 13, 1757, baptized December 20th, parents, James Robettson, Elizabeth Rannels.

Jacob, illegitimate, born December 20, 1761, baptized April 20th, parents, Jacob Guns, Elizabeth Rannels.

Peter, illegitimate, born August 10, 1761, baptized April 20th, parents, Christopher and Maria Barbara Croud.

John, born March 20th, baptized May 2d, parents, Peter and Obiah Peterson.

Charles, born April 20th, baptized May 3d, parents, Swen and Mary Justis.

Rebeccah, born December 13, 1761, baptized May 3d, parents, Jonas and Mary Walraven.

Peter, born March 4th, baptized May 3d, parents, Henry and Mary Garritson.

Joseph, born April 6th, baptized May 3d, parents, James and Susanna Enos.

Lydia, born December 29, 1760, baptized May 3d, parents, Samuel and Sarah Reall.

Eli, born December 2, 1761, baptized May 10th, parents, Eric and Brita Anderson.

James, born March 17th, baptized May 10th, parents, Isaac and Sarah Smidt.

Elizabeth, born March 1st, baptized May 22d, parents, Joseph and Hannah Pawl.

George, born February 3d, baptized May 23d, parents, Michael and Maria Swartz.

OLD SWEDES CHURCH

Maria Barbro, born October 15, 1761, baptized May 23d, parents, Albrecht and Margret Geruch.

John, born August 7, 1761, baptized June 20th, parents and wit. John and --- Marshall.

Mary, born April 26th, baptized June 21st, parents, and wit. Jacob & Mary Hines.

Andrew, born June 5th, baptized June 2d, parents, Neils and Mary Justis.

Isaac, born July 12th, baptized August 2d, parents, Jonas and Mary Stedham.

John, born April 4th, baptized August 23d, parents and wit. Jas. and Eleanor Minke.

Eli, born July 30th, baptized September 5th, parents, John and Mary Hendrickson.

William, born August 14th, baptized September 3rd, parents, William and Elenore Kleandenny.

Cathrine, born February 7, 1758, baptized September 11th, parents, James and Elizabeth Hinsel.

Peter, born August 14th, baptized September 16th, parents, Peter and Sarah Stidham.

John, born January 14th, baptized September 23th, parents, John and Margrete Culwell.

Benjaman, born July 14th, baptized October 11th, parents, Cornelius and Margret Vandevar.

John, born January 16th, baptized October 17th, parents, Moses and Catharine Kallom.

Sarah, born April April 27th, baptized November 4th, parents, John and Susannah Springer.

Henry, born May 10th, baptized November 4th, parents, Jacob and Susannah Stedham.

Annah Eva, born February 24th, baptized November 4th, parents, Niclas and Dorotha Foss.

Rebeccah, born October 4th, baptized November 5th, parents, Joseph and Regina Morten.

Philip, born September 22d, baptized November 5th, parents, John and Sarah Dimond.

*Ingeborg, born October 22d, baptized November 22d, parents, John and Annah Senex.

Margrete, born August 15th, baptized December 13th, parents, William and Margrete Moore.

Elizabeth, born June 1, 1761, baptized December 13th, parents, John Bishop and wife.

Catharine, born August 28,th, baptized September 26th, parents, Charles and Margrete Springer.

EARLY CHURCH RECORDS OF NEW CASTLE COUNTY

Sarah, born August 18th, baptized September 26th, parents, Peter and BrigittaV andevar.

ANNO 1763.

Elizabeth, born January 19, 1761, baptized January 14th, parents, James and Ester Brown.

Hannah, born November, 1762, baptized January 15th, parents, John and Elizabeth Stilley.

Mary, born December 24th, 1762, baptized January 25th, parents, Samuel and Mary Cleaney.

William, born October 9th, 1762, baptized January 30th, parents, William and Barbarah Hall.

Sarah, born December 7, 1762, baptized February 1, parents, Eric and Susannah Anderson.

Lydia, born December 23d, 1762, baptized February 1st, parents, Mathias and Mary Peterson.

Annah Mary, born January 10th, baptized February 9th, parents, John and Sarah Bird.

Susannah, born February 14th, baptized February 15th, parents, William and Susannah Stedham.

Robert, born February 12th, baptized February 14th, parents, Robert and Annah Jones.

Mary illegitimate, born August 26th, 1762, baptized March 1st, parents, William Parker and Elizabeth Taylor,

Mary, born September 15th, 1762, baptized April 4th. parents, Louis and Jane Curlet.

Thomas, born, March 12th, baptized April 10th, parents, Robert and Sarah Robinson.

Elizabeth, born January 15th, baptized April 21st, parents, Arthur and Mary Cunningham.

Zacharias, born March 11th, baptized ——, parents, Zacharias Elizabeth Derrickson.

Barbarah, born October 12, 1762, baptized April 4th, parents, Michael and Barbarah Mather.

Elizabeth, born February 18th, baptized April 24th; parents, James and Martha Anderson.

Isaac, born March 3rd, baptized May 14th, parents, Joseph and Margrete Abrahams.

Mary, born February 17th, baptized May 4th; parents, Jacob and Mary Anderson.

Sarah, born March 27th, baptized May 9th, parents, Jesper and Mary Walraven.

OLD SWEDES CHURCH

Alexander, born February 19th, baptized May 9th, parents, George and Mary Elliott.

Timothy, born November 24th, baptized May 15th, parents, Timothy and Lydia Pierce.

Thomas, born February 22nd, baptized May 31st, parents, Jacob and Mary Welch.

—— born February 24th, baptized May 15th, parents, Wm. and Susannah Sharpley.

Sarah, born May 9th, baptized May 31st, parents, Jesper and Cathrine Baat.

George, born November 6, 1762, baptized May 15th, parents, Joseph and Hannah Pierce.

Barbarah, born September 4, 1762, baptied June 5th, parents, Simon and Mary Carlin.

Elizabeth, born June 4th, baptized June 19th, parents, Mathias and Annah Skyler.

Sarah, born March 6th, baptized May 1st, parents, John and Elizabeth Thomelsson.

Barbarah Annah, born March 10th, baptized May 2nd, parents, Israel and Mary Claeson.

Rebecca, born May 13th, baptized July 10th, parents, John and Mary Stedham.

Elizabeth, born May 16th, baptized August 9th, parents, John and Lucia Marshall.

John, born June 30th, baptized September 3rd, parents, Daniel and Margaret Kildee.

Hannah and Thomson, born May 30th, baptized September 12th, parents, Isaac and Elizabeth Bush.

Mary, born September 10th, baptized September 11th, parents, Wm. and Hannah Beats.

John, born June 24th, baptized July 21st, parents, John and Margrete McGenny.

Susannah, born June 16th, baptized July 21st, parents, Richard and Elizabeth McManaMan.

Easter, born July 14th, baptized August 27st, parents, Peter and Obadiah Petersson.

Regina, born February 13th, baptzied August 29th, parents, Jonas and Mary Petersson.

Keark, born April 27th, baptized September 15th, parents, James and Jane Keark.

Thomas, born June——, baptized September ——, parents, Wm. and Hannah Balden.

John, born September 24th, baptized October 10th, parents, Wm. and Rachel Cook.

Peter, born September 29th, baptized October 9th, parents, Wm. and Margreta Stahlkop.

Margrete, born August 21st, baptized October 2nd, parents, John and Margrete Pierce,

John and Dorothea, born June 27, baptized October 20th, parents, Joannes and Anne Sabley.

Rebecca, born September 4th, baptized October 2d; parents, Abraham and Lydy Rose.

Lydia, born October 8, baptized November 5th; parents, Peter and Cathrine Springer.

Margrete, born June 12, 1762, baptized July 22d, parents, James and Elizabeth Senex Jun.

Jacob, born September 19th, baptized October 13th, parents, Simon and Sophia Everlay.

William, born September 19th, baptized November 22d, parents, Tully and Jane Davitt.

Annah, born October 30th, baptized December 27th, parents, Benjamin and Margrete Ford.

James, born August 3, baptized October 19, parents, Harry and Hannah Gordon.

ANNO 1764.

Sarah, born April 5, 1763, baptized January 1st, parents, Arthur and Jane Orr.

Cathrine, born September 26, 1763, baptized January 29th, parents, Caleb and Cathrine Perkins,

Annah, born March 8, 1763, baptized January——parents, Wm. and Rachel Reynolds

John, illegitimate, born November 19th, baptized January 3d, parents, John Bennet and Susanna Vandever.

Hezekiah, born January 24th, baptized January 29th, parents, Andreas and Sarah Peterson.

Uriah, born June 13, 1757,

David, born June 6, 1760,

Solomon, born June 9, 1763,

Baptized June 23rd, parents, Uriah and Mary Blew.

Susannah, born December 13, 1763, baptized January 2d, parents, Jonathan and Mary Hulings.

Rebeccah, born October 19, 1763, baptized January 26th, parents, Wm. and Sarah Whitehead.

OLD SWEDES CHURCH

John, illegitimate, born September 1, 1763, baptized February 12th, father, P. Richards and Mary Hitherton.

John, born January 24, 1764, baptized February 12th, parents, Philip and Mary Staats.

Henry, born September 22, 1763, baptized March 18th, parents, John and Jane Stalcop.

Andrew, born April 5, 1763, baptized May 5th, parents, Michael and Sarah King.

Joseph, born December 21, 1763, baptized May 9th, parents, John and Cathrine Weaver Valentine.

Isaac, born July 14, 1763, baptized May 10th, parents, Isaac and Sarah Smidth.

Cathrine, born December 12, 1763, baptized——parents, John and Mary Husband.

Jane, born November 23, 1760,

Cathrine, born January 16, 1763,

Baptized June 14th, parents, Cornelius and Mary Dirickson.

Margrete, born May 28, baptized June 2, parents, James and Elizabeth Senex.

James, born January 9th, baptized June 6th; parent, Thomas and Henrietta Read.

Jonathan, born May 28th, baptized June 16th; parents, Jacob and Anne Stilley.

Andrew, born May 27th, baptized July 1st; parents, Benjamin and Mary Enoch.

John, born June 10th, baptized July 9th; parents, Henry and Susannah Wynd.

Jacob born October 2, 1759, baptized July 29th, parents, Wm. and Elizabeth Brown.

Margrete born June 27, 1762, baptized July 29th, parents, Wm. and Elizabeth Brown.

Rebeccah, born March 13th, baptized May 11th; parents, Henry and Mary Garrittson.

Mary, born January 10th, baptized July 29th; parents, James and Catharine Cavenau.

William, born June 17th, baptized August 3rd; parents Jonathan and Jane Kirk.

John born April 16th, baptized May 11th; parents, John and Eleanor Garritson.

Abner, born July 28, baptized August 29th; parents Swen and Mary Justis.

EARLY CHURCH RECORDS OF NEW CASTLE COUNTY

Benjamin, born August 23rd, baptized September 2nd; parents Tobias and Mary Wallraven.

Sarah, born January 10th, baptized February 2nd, parents, George and Mary Foy.

Gabriel, born August 28th, baptized September 2nd; parents, Neils and Mary Justis.

Abigail, born July 30th, baptized September 15th; parents, Jacob and Catharine Springer.

Thomas, born July 26th, baptized September 9th; parents, Abraham and Lydia Cox.

James, born December 1st, baptized December 15th, parents Joseph and Hannah Baal.

Mary, born August 23rd, baptized October 5th; parents, Israel and Mary Claesson.

John, born May 3rd, baptized October 5th; parents, John and Eleonora Clerk.

Sarah, born June 19, 1763, baptized October 6th; parents, Wm. and Jane Parker.

Elizabeth, illegitimate born August 1763, baptized October 8th; parents, unknown.

Elizabeth born September 17th, baptized October 13th; parents, George and Margrete Hallis.

John, born April— baptized March 4th; parents, Lewis and Jane Cornet.

Gustave, born May 4th, baptized November 5th; parents, Gustave and Isabel Corneliuson.

Cathrine, born October 3, 1763, baptized November 5th; parents, Michael and Brigetta Mardock.

Lydy, born August 13, baptized November 5th, parents, Elias and Barbarah Reed.

Peter, born November 1st, baptized November 7th; parent Jacob and Barbarah Kriaek.

Mary, born Nov. 1 baptized November 7th; parents, Jacob and Barbarah Kriack.

Jacob and John twins, born October 23rd, baptized November 11th; parents Niclas, and Susannah Zeller.

William, born November 10th, baptized November 24th, parents, James and Martha Anderson.

Eli, born December 7th, baptized December 6th, parents, Mathias and Mary Peterson.

Charlotte, born September —baptized December 9th, parents, John and Reebccah Armstrong.

OLD SWEDES CHURCH

Levy, born November,——baptized December 9th, parents, Charles and Margrete Springer.

John, born November 24th, baptized December 9th, parents, John and Beata Hindrickson.

ANNO 1765.

Margrete, born December 13, 1764, baptized January 14th, parents, John and Sarah Bird.

William, born December 6, 1764, baptized January 15th, parents, John and Elizabeth Stilley.

William, born January 16th, baptized February 9th, parents, Robert and Ann Jones.

Susanna, born July 13, 1754,
Rebecca, born August 6, 1757,
Thomas, born April 2, 1759.
Baptized February 12th, parents, Thomas and Catharine Shepheard.

Tobias, born January 11th, baptized March 1st, parents, Tobias and Jane Vandevar.

David, born March 6th, baptized March 7th, parents, John and Susannah Springer.

Mary, born February 16th, baptized March 17th, parents, Jacob and Judah Hays Ross.

Margarete, born February 24th, baptized March 17th, parents, Jonas and Elizabeth Peterson.

Sarah, born December 13, 1764, baptized March 2nd, parents, Justa and Mary Justis.

Thomas, born January 5th, baptized March 3rd, parents, John and Ann Senex.

Senica, born November 29th, baptized February 28th, parents, John and Ann Senex.

George, born December 12, 1764, baptized February 28th, parents, Edward and Jamyma Cochran.

Rachel, born January 12th, baptized March 9th, parents, Thomas and Cathrine Jones.

Priscilla, born September 1, 1764, baptized March 9th, parents, Paul and Mary Peterson.

Paul, born February 3, baptized April 12th, parents, Paul and Rebeccah Wrolston.

Rachel, born December 28th, baptized April 12th, parents, George and Mary Elliott.

EARLY CHURCH RECORDS OF NEW CASTLE COUNTY

Anne, born March 9th, baptized April 12th, parents, Jacob and Mary Welch.

Mary, born March 5th, baptized April 12th, parents, Richard and Lydia Pierce.

William, born February 25th, baptized April 2nd, parents, George and Margrete Cochran.

Charles, born January 29th, baptized March 28th, parents, Thomas and Elizabeth Owgle.

Cathrine, born February 14th, baptized May 10th, parents, Jacob and Susannah Stedham.

Cathrine, born February 5th, baptized May 12th, parents, Patrick and Elizabeth McClaskey.

Jane, born May 2, 1756, baptized May 14th, parents, Richard and Lydia Claesson.

James, born October, 1761, baptized May 19th, parents, John and Eleonore Morris.

Penelope, born 1745, baptized May 19th, parents, Friedrich and Rebecca Justis.

Sarah, born August 17, 1751,

Thomas, born February 21, 1760,

Anne Frances, born April 12, 1761,

Barna Cozen, born August, 1764.

Baptized May 20th, parents, Robert and Mary Dennis, belonging to St. James Church.

Elizabeth, born May 28th, parents Josiah and Brigitta Loinan Stedham.

John, born September, 1760,

Eleonore, born December 13, 1763,

Baptized May 20, parents, John and Mary Bridly,

Martin, born March 17th, baptized May 24th, parents, Hance and Mary Nabior.

Anne, born March, baptized May 27th, parents, Phillip and Sabina Sleifer.

Willian, born February 19th, baptized May 28th, parents, Robert and Else Slaytor.

Anne, born May 12, baptized June 16th, parents, Robert and Sarah Robbinson.

Elizabeth born March 25th, baptized June 23d, parents, Johnathan and Mary Redman.

Mary, born April 15th, baptized May 4th, parents, John and Mary Husband.

OLD SWEDES CHURCH

Joseph, born August 22d,
James, born March 5th,
Baptized August 6th, parents, George and Hester Martin.

Rebeccah, born February 23d, baptized August 3d, parents, George and Sarah Taylor.

French, born January 3d, baptized August 3d, parents, Moses and Catharine Callom.

Mary, born July 21st, baptized August 3d, parents, John and Anne Nicholson.

Elizabeth, born July 16th, baptized August 13th, parents, Andrew and Margarete Paulson.

Amor, born July 2d, baptized August 13th, parents, John and Jane Stahlkop.

Andrew Christian, born July 8th, baptized August 25th, parents, Matthias and Anne Eve Koeler.

Rebeccah, born August, 30th, baptized August 25th, parents, Hance and Cathrine Naaf.

Mary, born March 11th, baptized October 13th, parents, John and Lydia Parmer.

Benjamin, born May 3d, baptized October 13th, parents, Joseph and Margret Abrahams.

Mary, born September 15th, baptized October 13th, parents, John and Brigitta Garritson.

Catharine Magdalen, born September 4th, baptized October 13, parents, Nicholas and Dorothea Faull.

John, born October 3d, baptized October 9th, parents, John and Margaret Pierce.

Mary, born September 13th, baptized October 11th, parents, Jonas and Mary Stedham.

James, born September 13th, baptized October 19th, parents, Charles and Mary Springer.

Rebeccah, born March 25th, baptized October 19th, parents, John and Elizabeth Bishop.

Eleonore, born October 13th, baptized November 24th, parents, Cornelius and Christiana Stedham.

Isaac, born October 12th, baptized October 24th, parents, Wm. and Margrete Stahlkop.

Eli, born October 30th, baptized December 1st, parents, Magnus and Eleonor Justis.

Jesajah, born September 18th, baptized December 14th, parents, John and Mary Hendrickson.

Peter, born November 8th, baptized December 15th, parents, Wm. and Elizabeth Derickson.

Sarah, born October 14, 1764, baptized December 21st, parents, Samuel and Mary Clark.

Andrew, aorn November 26th, baptized December 21st, parents, Gottfried and Eve Charles.

Mrgrete, born May 3, 1764, baptized December 25th, parents, Arthur and Mary Cunningham.

Susannah, born December 22d, baptized December 29th, parents, Neils and Mary Justis.

Levy, born January 23rd, baptised February 24th, parents, Jonas and Cathrina Walraven.

Peter, born February 15th, baptised April 5th, parents, Eric and Susanna Anderson.

Levy, born February 13th, baptized April 14th, parents, Peter and Eleonore Paulson.

John, born October 6th, baptized April 14th, parents, Joseph and Mary Pierce.

Karon Habits, born December 8, baptized April 14th, parents Wm. and Susannah Sharpley.

Mary, born March 24th, baptized May 19th, parents, Peter and Brita Vandevar.

Children or Older persons, baptized by Lawrence Girelius.

ANNO 1768.
JANUARY.

Sarah, born January 4th, baptized January 11th, parents, Robt. and Else Slater.

Tom, illegitimate, born December 13, 1767, baptized January 14th, mother, Margaret Gallagher.

Peter, born ——baptised January 17th, parents, Peter Springer and . . .

FFBRUARY.

John and Jonas, born   , baptized by Rev. Andrew Borell, January 8th, parents John Stidham and——

Isaac, born October 11, 1767, baptized February 4th, parents, Thomas and Cathrine Quinn.

Anne, born February 3rd, baptized February 12th, parents, Philip and Mary Schlâbs.

Jesper, born November 13, 1767, baptized February 13th, parents, Richard and Lady Peers.

OLD SWEDES CHURCH

Isaac, born January 21st, baptized February 19th, parents, John and Mary Hendrickson.

Thomas, born January 15th, baptized February 19th, parents, Wm. and Elizabeth Elliot.

Mary, born February 16th, baptized February 26th, parents, Martin and Helene Vandever.

Hina, born August 8th, baptized February 26th, parents, Thomas and Cathrine Johns.

MARCH.

Abraham, born February 4th, baptized 3rd, parents, Abraham and Lady Cox.

Margaret, born November 18, 1767, baptized 6th, parents, David and Agnes Louis.

Elizabeth, born September 5, 1767, baptized 13th, parents, John and Anne Haan.

William, born February 29, baptized 6th, parents, Joseph and Cathrine Lawson.

Mary, born September 1, 1766, baptized 14th, parents, Samuel and Mary Clark.

Helena, born December 28th, baptized 27th, parents, John and Rebeccah Armstrong.

APRIL.

Andrew, born March 16th, baptized 13th, parents, Abraham and Elizabeth Brown.

John, born February 28th, baptized 17th, parents, James and Martha Anderson.

Maria, born April 8, 1767, baptized 18th, parents, John and Magdalena Schoreberg.

MAY.

Pauline, born February 6, 1767, baptized 9th, parents, Richard and Anne Justisson.

John, born April 26th, baptized 10th, parents, Mark and Jean Elliott.

Susannah, born——parents,——

Fredrich, born November 7th, baptized 23rd, parents, Richard and Mary Derrick.

John, born April 7th, baptized 29th, parents, Wm. and Hannah Tussey.

EARLY CHURCH RECORDS OF NEW CASTLE COUNTY

JUNE.

Mary, born October 9, 1767, baptized 11th, parents, Andrew and Margrete Paulson.

Jean, born —— baptized 10th, parents, Scheirman and

Robbert, illegitimate, born May 3rd, baptized 12th, parents,

Anne and John, born —— baptized 16th, parents, —— John Welch.

Martha, born February 9th, baptized 21st, parents, Israel and Lydia Hendrickson.

Erick, born March 18th, baptized 27th, parents, James and Mary McKeever.

Mary, born January 15th, baptized 27th, parents, Patrick and Elizabeth McCloskey.

JULY.

Magdalene, born June 1st, baptized tne 17th, parents, Samuel and Mary Cleney.

William, born June 8th, baptized the 31st, parents, Thomas and Sarah Morten.

Joseph, born February 10th, baptized 31st, parents, Niclas and Dorothea Vass.

AUGUST.

Mary, born September 4, 1767, baptized 5th, parents, Adam and Mary Kohl from Jersey.

John, born August 4th, baptized 7th, parents, James and Susannah Hebshir.

Jamimy, born October 28, 1767, baptized 7th, parents, Moses and Cathrine Prellam.

William, born June 13th, baptized 11th, parents, John and Sarah Fresca.

SEPTEMBER.

Sarah, illegitimate, born February 4, 1765, baptized 3rd, mother, Sarah Taylor.

Peter, born August 5th, baptized 11th, parents, John and Beata Hendrickson.

Margaret, born August 2nd, baptized 11th, parents, Caleb and Catharine Perkins.

Samuel, born February 2nd, baptized 18th, parents, Samuel and Anne Floyd.

OLD SWEDES CHURCH

October.

Peter, born September 27th, baptized 4th, parents John and Mary Husband.

Margrete, born August 13th, baptized 16th, parents, Samuel and Sarah Christine.

Hannah Ford, married to Joseph Hedges, born—— baptized 21st.

Phœbe Ford, her sister, born——, baptized 21st.

Benjamin, born—baptized 21st, parents, Joseph and Hannah Hedges.

Isaac and Rebecca, born——, baptized 21st, parents, Peter Vandewer Senior.

John, born June 7th, baptized 22nd, parents, Johnathan and Mary Readman.

Aaron, born 11th, baptized 24th, parents, Swen and Mary Justis.

Henry, born September 21st, baptized 24th, parents, Henry and Susannah Vining.

Susannah, born January 4, 1767, baptized 24th.

Sarah, September 7, 1768.

Parents, Henry and Mary Hiland.

Esther, born October 7th, baptized 3d, parents, James and Lady Penny.

November.

Susannah, born April 16th, baptized 5th, parents, Jacob and Susannah Stedham.

Jacob, born October 7th, baptized 13th, parents, Cornelius and Chistine Stidham.

James, born October 21st, baptized 28th, parents, Arthur and Lady Gool.

Lady, illegitimate, born January 13, 1766, baptised . . . parents, John Broom and Mary McKormach.

Phœbe, born October 19th baptised 28th, parents, Wm. and Agnes Broom.

December.

William, born November 20th, baptised 8th, parents, Jacob and Ingeber Derickson.

Deborah, born November 14th, baptised 19th, parents, John and Margret Peers.

Cathrine, born January 1, 1761,
Elizabeth, born August 15, 1762,
David, born September 5, 1766,
Anne, born July 21, 1768,
  Baptised 7th day September at Augustus.

ANNO 1769.
JANUARY.

John, born December 9, 1768, baptised 4th, parents, Justa and Mary Walraven.

Elizabeth, born October 28, 1768, baptised 15th, parents, John and Ann Sinnex.

Mary, born January 26th, baptised 27th, parents, Thomas and Elizabeth Almond.

FEBRUARY.

Susannah, born ———— baptised 19th, parents, William Derickson Zachary and . . .

William, illegitimate, born June 8, 1768, baptized February 23d, parents, Samuel Hanna and Rebecca Jamison.

MARCH.

Elias, illegitimate, born September 20th, baptised March 25th, parents, Mary Bradford and William Kellowe.

George, born ————, baptised 26th, parents, ———— Hankins and ————.

William, illegitimate, born December 21, 1768, baptised 26th, parents, Elizabeth Walker and William Hemphil.

APRIL.

Solomon, illegitimate, born August 3, 1768, baptised 8th, parents, Brigitte Maly and Solomon Green.

Ally, illegitimate, born March 20th, baptised 13th, parents, Cathrine McClure and Thomas Slater.

Cathrina, born February 3d, baptised 23d, parents, Jonas and Elizabeth Peterson.

MAY.

————, born March 25th, baptised 7th, parents, Joseph Springer Christopherson and lady.

George, born March 26th, baptised 7th, parents, Gabriel and Margret Walker.

John, born April 25th, baptised 8th parents, John and Sarah Bird.

OLD SWEDES CHURCH

Sarah, born September 26, 1767, baptised 8th, parents, Nicholas and Margret Moore.

John and Elizabeth, born March 28, 1768, baptised 9th, parents, John and Elizabeth Stilly.

Mary, born April 2d, baptised 10th, parents, Matthias and Mary Peterson.

Henry, born February 17th, baptised 12th, parents, Henry and Mary Garritson.

Sarah, born January 8th, baptised 12th, parents, Jonas and Mary Wallraven.

Sarah, born October 7, 1768, baptised 12th, parents, Samuel and Ann Roeen.

Elizabeth, born February 17th, baptised 12th, parents, Laughly and Sarah Michnell.

Magdalena, born ——, baptised 14th, parents, Edward and Susannah Parsety.

June.

David, born —— baptised 18th, parents, John Stedham and ——.

August.

Christina Maria, born July 12th, baptised 13th, parents, Matthias and Ann Keller.

Mary, born ——, baptised 17th, parents, —— Willson.

George, born August 12th, baptised 24th, parents, Joseph and Cathrina Lawson.

——, born —— 25th, parents, David and Susanna Tregon.

September.

Sibilla, born April 12th, baptised 17th, parents, Philip and Sabina Sleifer.

James, born August 9th, baptised 23, parents, Thomas and Cathrine Queen.

October.

Helena, born April 31st, baptised 14th, parents, John and Jeane Maneily Shay.

Mary Magdalene, born November 27, 1768, baptised 18th. parents, Henry and Magdalene Mitz.

Ruth, born ——, baptised 19th, parents, —— Almond.

Francis, born July 13, 1768, baptised November 26th, parents, Henry and Jeane Brahin.

John, born . . baptised 31st, parents, Presbyterians, and gave no names to me.

EARLY CHURCH RECORDS OF NEW CASTLE COUNTY

NOVEMBER.

John born January 5th, baptised 4th, parents, Thomas and Hannah Reed.

John born August 25th, baptised 6th, parents, Jonathan and Jeane Kirk.

William, born October 12th, baptised 15th, parents, William Elliott.

Christina, born . . , baptised 19th, parents, Richard Derrick and . . . ,

DECEMBER.

Margret, born November 27th, baptised 3rd, parents, Andrew and Ann Vanneaman.

Benjamin, born October 26th, baptised 10th, parents, Andrew and Sarah Peterson.

Mary, born . . , baptised 17th, parents, Peter Springer.

Ann born . . , baptised 17th, parents, Charles Springer Joseph son and . . ,

Elisabeth, . . ,born baptised 17th, parents, . . ,Elliot.

Hannah Few, 17 years old, baptized 10th.

Isaac born November 19th, baptised 18th, parents, James and Elizabeth Sennex.

Samuel born March 31st, baptised 23rd, parents, Wm. and Mary Ashtin.

Joseph, born . . ,baptised 26th, parents, Francis Day and . . ,

ANNO 1770.
JANUARY.

Fredrick born November 26, 1769, baptised 14th, parents, Wm. Tussey Jr. and Hannah.

FEBRUARY.

Jodiah, born . . , baptised 20th, parents, Christopher and Helena Hendrickson.

William, born December 28, 1769, baptised 3rd, parents, John and Brita Lansale.

Lady, [illegitimate] born October 23, 1769, baptised 7th,

MARCH.

Priscilla, born November 23, 1769, baptised 4th, parents, David and Agnes Louis.

Sarah, born . . ,baptised 25th, parents, . . ,

William, born . . , baptised 22nd, parents, . . ,

OLD SWEDES CHURCH

MAY.

Reese, born March 21st, baptised 6th, parents, Charles and Mary Springer.

Hannah, born April, 7th, baptised 20th, parents, John and Ann Sennex.

Ann, born——, baptised 30th, parents Shierman and. . . ,

Joshua born——, baptised 30th, parents, ——

JUNE.

Debora, born February 20th, baptised 4th, parents, Tobias and Margret Paulson.

Robert, born March 6th, baptised 4th, parents, John and Rebecca Armstrong.

Margret, born February 7, 1769, baptised 9th, parents, Wm. and Mary Glea.

Sarah Robbeson between 20 and 30 years old, baptised the 12th.

Thomas, born February 20th, baptised 17, parents, Thomas and Catharine Jones.

JULY.

Rachel, born July 8th, baptised 26th, parents, Jonas and Mary Stedham.

Elizabeth, born June 20th, baptised 29th, parents, Joseph and Hannah Hedge.

Sarah, born —— ——, baptised 29, parents, Wm. and Susannah Sharpley.

William, born ———, baptised 29, parent, Joseph Pearce.

AUGUST.

Mary, born September 23, 1769, baptised 1st, parents, James and Agnes Steelman.

Barnaba, born July 19, 1769, baptised 7th, parents, Carl and Sarah Etheridge.

Hannah, born August 31, 1768, baptised 19th, parents, Henry and Sarah Webster.

Catharine, born August 14th, baptised 26th, parents, Wm. and Rachel Sharpley.

Rebecca, born ———, baptised 26th, parents Justa Justis and ———.

SEPTEMBER.

Ruth, illegitimate, born April, baptized 19th, parents, Hannah Hughs and Johnathan Readman.

Arthur, born August 23d, baptized 21st, parents, Wm. and Hannah Best.

Margret, born December, 31, 1769, baptized 26th, parents, Jacob and Cathrine Springer.

John, born July 28, 1769, baptized 26th, parents, John and Ann Haan.

OCTOBER.

Ann, born July 22, 1769, baptized 7th, parents, Richard and Ann Justisson.

Caleb, born ——, baptized 7th, parents, Caleb Parkins and ——

George, born August 25th, baptized 10th, parents, Henry Vining and Susannah.

John, born August 21st, baptized 10th, parents, Henry and Mary Hiland.

William, born September 12th, baptized 14th, parents, David and Susanna Tryon.

William and Thomas, born September 28th, baptized 15th, parents, John Foudrey and ——.

Joseph, born October 8th, baptized 21st, parents, Joseph and Susanna Johnson.

Catharine, born ——, baptised 28th, parents, George and Rebecca Righter.

William, born October 16th, baptised 28th, parents, John and Mary Harrison.

Rebecca, born November 18th, baptised 29th, parents, Cornelius and Christina Stedham.

NOVEMBER.

Baptised a sick child called Winny, belonging to —— Lenard.

DECEMBER.

Ruth, born ——, baptised 10th, parents, ——.

Joseph, born October 13th, baptised 15th, parents, John and Ann Lynam.

Beata, born ——, baptised 26th, parents, Wm. Bird and——

ANNO 1771.

JANUARY.

Mary, born December 24, 1770, baptised January —— parents, Israel and Susanna Peterson.

FEBRUARY.

Johnathan, born December 23, 1770, baptised February 24th, parents, John and Cathrine Johnson.

OLD SWEDES CHURCH

March.

John born——baptised March——parents, Andrew Lynam.

Jeane, born February 23rd, baptised 24th, parents, John and Jeane Hawkins.

Jonas, born February 10th, baptised 24th, parents, Cornelius and Christiana Stedham.

Thomas, born January 2d, baptised 27th, parents, John and Jeane Quinn.

April.

Christopher, born——baptised April 6th, parents, John Swing and

Mary, born October 20, 1770, baptised 7th, parents, Arthur and Leady Foot.

Mary, born March 11th, baptised 7th, parents, Wm. and Rebecca Derickson.

Mary, born March 11th, baptised 28th, parents, Swen and Mary Justis.

John, born April 18th, baptised 28th, parents, Jonas and Elenor Walraven.

May.

Rebecca, born——baptised 5th, parents, Wm. Tussy Jr. and . . .

Margaret, born——baptised 5th, parents, Wm. Elliott and . .

George, born January 18th, baptised 10th, parents, Henry and Sarah Webster.

Mary, born February 21, 1770, baptised 20th, parents, Benjamin and Margret Ford.

Mary, born——baptised 26th, parents, John Sperey.

June.

Alexander, born March 17th, baptised 2d, parents, Thomas and Ann Sanford.

Elizabeth, born March 15th, baptised 3rd parents, John and Isabella Lynch.

July.

Andrew, born July 17, baptised 14th, parents, Cornelius and Elisabeth Heins.

Mary and William, born . . . , baptised 28th, parents, Henry Heins and . . . ,

John, born June 26th, baptised 28th, parents, Jonas Peterson and Elizabeth.

EARLY CHURCH RECORDS OF NEW CASTLE COUNTY

AUGUST.

Hannah, born June 20th, baptised 4th, John Hindrickson and . . . .

Morton, born August 5th, baptised 7th, parents, Justa Walraven and . . . .

Jonas, born . . . , baptised 11th, parents, Walraven.

Cathrine, born . . . , baptised 18th, parents, Jacob Derickson and Ingeber.

Elizabeth, born . . . , baptised 22d, parents, ...

James, born July 12th, baptised 25th, parents, Peter and Elizabeth Paulson.

Sarah, born . . . , baptised 25th, parents . . . Webster and

SEPTEMBER.

William, born, June 23d, baptised 2d, parents, John and Cathrine Stedham.

Mary, born July 13th, baptised 21st, parents, Thomas and Elizabeth Kane.

Cathrine, born August 12, baptised 22nd, parents, Joseph Springer Christopherson and Leady.

Mary, born September 12th, baptised 22nd, parents, Joseph and Mary Elliott.

OCTOBER.

Ann, born September 19th, bastised 13th, parents, Andrew and Elizabeth Peterson.

. . . born September 19th, baptised 13th, parents, Charles Springer and ———,

NOVEMBER.

Ann, born June 15th, baptised 17th, parents, George and Mary Warner.

Morton, born December 29th, baptised 3rd, parents, Mathias and Mary Peterson.

DECEMBER.

Sarah, born November 14th, baptised 15th, parents, Andrew and Sarah Peterson.

William, born September 10, 1770, baptised 22nd, parents, Joseph and Hannah Ball.

ANNO 1772.
JANUARY.

Rebecca, born January 20, 1770, baptised———, parents, Jacob and Ingebor Derrickson.

OLD SWEDES CHURCH

Wm. Henry, born December 16, 1769, baptised 15th, parents Henry and Hannah McEntor.

Joseph, born ——, baptised 27th, parents, Charles Springer Josephson and Margret.

FEBRUARY.

Cathrine, born December 6, 1771, baptised 19th, parents, Peter and Cathrine Springer.

William, born February 3, 1769, baptised 22nd, parents, Samuel and Martha Dixon.

David, born September 22, 1771, baptised 22nd, parents, Samuel and Martha Dixon.

William, born November 22, 1671, baptised 22nd, parents, Richard and Mary Derrick.

Gabriel, born December 12, 1771, baptised 29th, parents, Gabriel and Margret Walker.

MARCH.

Henry, born ——, baptised 5th, parents, Henry and Hannah McEntor.

Johnathan, born October 20, 1771, baptised 8th, parents, John and Margret Pearce.

APRIL.

Mary, born . . . baptised 5th, parents, . . .

Mary, born March 17th, baptised 18th, parents, David and Susannah Tryon.

MAY.

Deborah, born . . . baptised 10th, parents, Wm. Derrickson Zachary.

Mary, baptised May 10th, parents Wright

Joseph, baptised May 10th, parents Joseph Lawson.

Rachael, baptised May 10th, parents. Peter Vandever.

JUNE.

Jacob, born ——, baptised 7, parents, William Derrickson, Jr and Rebecca.

William Sharpley, born February 27, 1749.
Mary Sharpley, born ——,
Lea Sharpley, born ——,
Rachel Sharpley, born, ——, .
Daniel Sharpley, born ——,
Danley Sharpley, born ——.

Baptised 4th, parents, Daniel Sharpley, Sr.

EARLY CHURCH RECORDS OF NEW CASTLE COUNTY

Rebecca, born May 14, baptised 14th, William and Isabella Sharpley.

John, born 16th, baptized 25th, parents, Timothy and Johanna Kogg.

JULY.

Margret, born ——, baptised 15th, parents, John and Ann Armstrong.

Peter, born June 12, baptised 2d, parents, Jonas and Gwin Matson.

AUGUST.

Margret, born ——, baptised 3d, parents, —— Broom.

Margret, born ——, baptised 16th, parents, —— Taylor.

Lukas, born May 16th, baptised 19th, parents, Lukas and Mary Neubeuker.

Thomas, born September 20, 1771, baptised 22d, parents, Thomas and Catharine Gwin.

——, born ——, baptised 23d, parents at New Port.

SEPTEMBER.

Elizabeth, born September 13, 1771, baptised 1st, parents, James and Susannah Fletcher.

Mary, born ——, baptised 7th, parents. —— ——.

Elizabeth, born ——, baptised 13th, parents, —— Stockingseacer.

Susannah, born ——, baptised ——, parents, Joseph and Sarah Stidham.

OCTOBER.

Sarah, born September 5th, baptised 10th, parents, William and Mary Hatten.

James, born March 20th, baptised . . . 15th, parents, Bryan and Mary Daily.

NOVEMBER.

Enock, born September 16th, baptised 1st, parents, Andrew Lynam.

Mary, born . . . , baptised 1st, parents, . . . Ashton.

William, born October 14th, baptised 15th, parents, Henry and Ann Sinnex.

DECEMBER.

Benoni, born——, baptised 13th, parents, John and Sarah Bird.

Ann, born ——, baptised 13th, parents, Francis Day and ——.

Thomas, born March 18, 1768, baptised 26th, parents, Edward and Mary Smith.

OLD SWEDES CHURCH

Edward, born December 23, 1771, baptised 26th, parents, Edward and Mary Smith.

Rebecca, born October 14th, baptised 26th, parents, Nicholas and Dorothy Fory.

Anno 1773.
January.

Thomas, born ——, baptised 1st, parents, John Elliott and ——.

David, born ——, baptised April 3d, parents, John and Ann Lynam.

Lady, born December 20, 1772, baptised 10th, parents, Arthur and Lady Tool.

Mary Taylor, wife of George Taylor, baptised 26th.

February.

Joseph Dain, born ——, baptised 12th, between 20 and 30 years old.

Elizabeth, born ——, baptised 14th, parents, John Jontery and ——.

Mary, born December 18, 1772, baptised 21st, parents, Matthias and Elizabeth Gennet.

Martha, born ——, baptised 21st, parents, Andrew Anderson and ——.

March.

Mary, born ——, baptised 7th, parents, Joseph Hedge and Hannah.

Elizabeth, born August, 1772, baptised 20th, parents, Thomas and Margret Rawlings.

Jonas, born January 22d, baptized 28th, parents, Jonas and Elizabeth Peterson.

April.

Susannah, born February 15th, baptised 12th, parents, Michael and Sabilla Wolf.

—— Baptised 12th, child of Elias Tussey.

—— Baptised 20th, child of Peter Springer.

Jacob, baptised 20th, bound to Peter Springer,

Benjamin, born December 25, 1772, baptised 25th, parents, Joseph and Susanna Jackson.

May.

Peter, born March 31, baptised 6th, parents, John Hendrickson and ——.

Rachel, born ——, baptised April 16th, parents,——Justisson and ——.

EARLY CHURCH RECORDS OF NEW CASTLE COUNTY

John, born March 31, baptised 6th, parents, John and Ann Sinnex.

William, born July 25, 1771, baptised 19th, parents, Lars and Sarah Etheridge.

JULY.

—— Baptised 4th, child of William Tussy.
—— Baptised 12th, child of W. Hendrickson.
—— Baptised 19th, sick child.

AUGUST.

Margret, born ——, baptised 2d, parents, Jacob and Ingeber Derrickson.

Elizabeth, illegitimate, born June 14th, baptised 24th, parents, mother, Ester Bines.

Rebecca, born ——, baptized 29th, parents, John and Mary Husbands.

Bird, born ——, baptized 29th, parents, —— Runnels.

SEPTEMBER.

Joseph, born ——, baptised 15th, parents, John Hawkins and ——.

Elizabeth, born ——, baptised 8th, parents, John Welsh and ——.

Mary, born August 15th, baptised 12th, parents, Cornelius and Elizabeth Hines.

William, born ——, baptised 20th, parents, ——.

OCTOBER.

Samuel, born ——. baptised 11th, parents, Johnston.

John, born September 19th, baptised 19th, parents, Thomas and Cathrine Quin.

NOVEMBER.

Solomon, born ——, baptised 7th, parents, Solomon Springer and ——.

Ann, born ——, baptised 7th, parents, Israel Peterson and ——.

John, born . . . , baptised 20th, parents, John Sperry and . . . .

Isaac. born . . . , baptised 20th, parents, John Stidham and . . .

Hannah, born September 24th, baptised 21st, parents, Mathias and Mary Peterson.

William, illegitimate, born July 6th, baptized 25th, parents, Richard Silene and Elizabeth McLane.

—— Baptised 28th, child of William Elliott.

OLD SWEDES CHURCH

Thomas, born November 15 th, baptised 28th, parents, Lukas and Hannah Wallraven.

DECEMBER.

Elizabeth, born . . . , baptised 1st, parents, Charles Springer Jamesson and . . .

Ann, born . . . , baptised 15th, parents, Robert Pierce, Jr., and . . .

Joseph, born . . . , baptised 15th, parents, . . . and Rachel Brown.

Margret, born October 13th, baptised 26th, parents, John and Barbara Rogers.

ANNO 1774.

JANUARY.

Rachel, born——baptised 2nd parents, Wm. and Rebecca Derricson.

John, born December 6, 1773, baptised 3rd, parents, Peter Paulson and . . .

Helena, born October 21, 1773, baptised 20th, parents, Thomas and Leady Lendey.

FEBRUARY.

Mathias, born December 16, 1773, baptised——parents, Fredrich and Barbary King.

Mary, born January 12th, baptised 6th, parents, Isaac and Ann Vanboner.

Martha, born——baptised 27th, parents, Richard and Mary Derrickson.

MARCH.

Thomas, born February 25th, baptised 24th, parents, Justa and Mary Walraven.

James, born April 4, 1772, baptised 27th, parents, James and Martha Anderson.

APRIL.

Thomas, born . . . , baptised 10th, parents, Thomas Kane and . .

. . . . . . 24th, child of Joseph Springer Christopherson and Leady.

MAY.

Samuel, born March 29th, baptised 2nd, parents, John and Ann Jesper.

Philip, born . . , baptised 2nd, parents, Wm. Sharpley, Jr., and Rebecca.

EARLY CHURCH RECORDS OF NEW CASTLE COUNTY

Charlotte, born March 6th, baptised 8th, parents, Gottfried and Mariana Zephernuh.

. . . . , baptised 22nd, a child.

James, born January 28th, baptised 28th, parents, James and Susannah Varney.

David News, born June 15, 1750, baptised 30th, in 24th year of his age.

JUNE.

William, born . . . , baptised 19th, parents, Willson and . . .

William, born . . . , baptised 26th, parents, Jacob and Rebecca Bird.

JULY.

Hannah, born . . . , baptised 7th, parents, Herman and Martha Whiteman.

David, born May 27th, baptised 10th, parents, David and Susannah Tryon.

Cathrina, born . . . , baptised 10th, parents, Jonas Morton and . .

Aaron, born May 27th, baptised 11th, parents, John and Margret Pierce.

Rebecca, illegitimate, born April 2nd, baptised 13th, parents, John Littaer and Mary Harrison.

Mary, born . . . , baptised 17th, parents, Charles Springer Josephson and Margret.

Mary, born February 29, 1772, baptised 26th, parents John and Ann Hahn.

James born January 29, 1772, baptised 26th, parents, John and Ann Hahn.

AUGUST.

Sarah, born March 12th, baptised 26th, parents, Patrick and Margret Carlile.

Alexander, born July 7th, baptised 29th, parents, James and Martha Anderson.

SEPTEMBER.

Sarah, born baptised 12th, parents, . . . ,

OCTOBER.

Fanny, born September 7th, baptised 12th, parents John and Margret Erwin.

Elizabeth born December 7, 1773 baptised 16th, parents, Thomas and Ann Samford.

OLD SWEDES CHURCH

Elizabeth born September 14th, baptised 16th, parents Charles and Susanna Paulson.

Elenor, born baptised 16th, parents, Garner and . . ,

November.

William (illegitimate) born September 23rd, baptised 1st, parents, Erick Anderson and Cathrine Grimes.

Robert, born January 28th, baptised 11th, parents, John and Ruth Peterson.

John Giles, born . . , baptised 12th, parents, Joseph and Elizabeth Gilpin.

Marion, born October 15th, baptised 13th, parents, Robert and Jean Richardson.

December.

Susannah born baptised 26th, parents, John and Mary Foudery.

Anno 1775.
January.

Susanna, born October 22, 1774, baptised 4th, parents, Peter Vandever Jr. and Brita.

Thomas, born . . , baptised 18th, parents, Thomas and Margret Rawlings.

John, born January 2nd, baptised 23rd, parents, Joseph and Susanna Jackson.

February.

Ann, born September 27, 1774, baptised February 2nd, parents, John and Ann Niclason.

Isabelle, born October 28, 1773, baptised 12th, parents, Michael and Isabella Wolf.

Evan Ryle, born . . . baptised 13th, parents, Thomas and Leady Gilpin.

Martha, born January 4th, baptised 27th, parents, Gilbert and Ann McCarter.

Joseph, born January 25th, baptised 28th, parents, John and Beata Hendrickson.

March.

William, born February . . . , baptised 19th, parents, Charles and Cathrine Cooper.

Isaac, born . . . baptised 19th, parents, Wm. Tussey and . .

Mary, born . . . baptised 19th, parents, Thomas and Leady Gilpin.

EARLY CHURCH RECORDS OF NEW CASTLE COUNTY

APRIL.

Elizabeth, born January 5th, baptised 9th, parents, Wm. and Cathrine Husten.

Andrew, born . . . baptised 9th, parents, John Hendrickson Jr., and . .

Joseph, born March 7th, baptised 14th, parents, Joseph and Cathrine Lawson.

Hannah, born . . . baptised 23rd, parents, Robert Pierce, Jr.

MAY.

William, born February 5th, baptised 5th, parents, Brian and Mary Daily.

John, born April 2nd, baptised 5th, parents, Patrick and Elenor Prelly.

Anna, born April 1st, baptised 7th, parents, Joseph and Rachel Brown.

Elizabeth, born April 6th, baptised 14th, parents, Jonas and Elizabeth Peterson.

John, born March 18th, baptised 28th, parents, John and Mary Husband.

John, born April 14th, baptised 28th, parents, Benjamin and Susanna Elliott.

JUNE.

Cathrine, born November 15, 1774, baptised 11th, parents, Jacob and Ann Lessinger.

Joseph, born April 12th, baptised 11th, parents, Cornelius and Christiana Stidham,

Sarah, born April 11th, baptized 13th, parents, Morton and Dorcas Morton.

Mary Sarah Cathrine, born February 21st, baptised 18th, parents, Andrew and Emy Bryan.

Isaac, born May 22, baptised 25th, parents, Wm. Anderson, Jr. and Mary.

John, born December 5, 1774, baptised 27th, parents, David and Rebecca Windel.

JULY.

William, born . . . baptised 5th, parents, Caleb Perkins and

Sarah, born June 11th, baptised 3rd, parents, David and Hannah Stidham.

Mary, born . . . baptised 30th, parents, Wm. Derickson Zacharyson and . .

OLD SWEDES CHURCH

August.

Christina, born . . . baptised 12th, parents, Elias Tursan.
Robeson, born . . . baptised 13th, John Sinex and . .
Henry and Jacob, born August 13th, baptised 25th, parents, Henry and Mary Hiland.

September.

Zacharias, born . . . baptised 10th, parents, Jacob Derrickson Zacharyson and Elenor.
Thomas, born . . . baptised 11th, parents . . .
Ann, born . . . baptised 12th, parents . . .
Mary, born August 17th, baptised 17th, parents, John and Elizabeth Humphries.
William, born May 13th, baptised 18th, parents, Mark and Jeane Elliott.
Jacob, born . . . , baptised 24th, parents, Jacob Derrickson, Williamson and Ingeber.
John, born . . . , baptised 24th, parents, Richard and Hannah Gilome.

October.

Ann, born August 16th, baptised 14th, parents, William and Rebecca Stidham.
John, born . . . , baptised 13th, parents, Charles Springer Jameson and . . . .
Margret, born . . . , baptised 17th, parents.
Sarah, born . . . , baptised 22d, parents, ...
Mary, born September 29th, baptised 29th, parents, John and Sarah Paulson.

November.

George, born August 23d, baptised 4th, parents, Andrew and Margret Lynam.
William, born June 22d, baptised 6th, parents, William Derrickson, Williamson and Rebecca.
Thomas Gilpin, born . . . , two years old, baptised 6th, parents, ...
Mary and Cornelius, born . . . , baptised 8th, parents, Cornelius Derrickson and . . . .

December.

Conrad, born November 17th, baptised 4th, parents, Lukas and Kathrine Wallraven.

EARLY CHURCH RECORDS OF NEW CASTLE COUNTY

Jeane, born . . . , baptised 11th, parents, Andrew Anderson and . . . .

Zacharias, born September 7th, baptised 11th, parents, Isaac and Ann Vanlooner.

James, born . . . , baptised 29th, parents, James and Priscilla McClausky.

ANNO 1776.
JANUARY.

Elizabeth, born . . . , baptised 11th, parents, Peter and Mary Woolbaugh.

Eva, born January 8th, baptised 25th, parents, John and Eva Depolt.

FEBRUARY.

Thomas, born January 18th, baptised ——, Cornelius and Elizabeth Heins.

MARCH.

Elizabeth, born December 25th, baptised 3d, parents, William and Rachel Sharpley.

Andrew, born February 16th, baptised 12th, parents, Andrew and Sarah Peterson.

Elenor, born February 13th, baptised 26th, parents, William and Margret Armer.

Griesey, born March 25th, baptised 29th, parents, ...

Aaron, born . . . , baptised 31st, parents, Charles Paulson and . . . .

Ann, born . . . , baptised . . , parent, Susanna Tryon.

APRIL.

John, born March 11, 1776, baptised 21st, parents, Joseph and Hannah Hedges.

Mary, born . . . , baptised 21st, parents, Griffith Jordan and Phœbe.

MAY.

Andrew, born . . . , baptised 5th, parents, Joseph Springer Christopherson and Lydia.

Mary, born April 29th, baptised 10th, parents, Edward Dawson and . . . .

John, born January 11th, baptised 30th, parents, Robert and Sarah King.

Jacob, born April 14th, baptised 31st, parents, James and Elizabeth Justison.

OLD SWEDES CHURCH

JUNE.

John, born . . . , baptised 2d, parents, John Elliott and . . . .

Mary and Sarah, illegitimate, born Feruary 15th, baptised 2d, parents, James Baily and Elizabeth McKibb.

JULY.

Lancelot Smidt, a soldier in the Continental army, now on his March to New York, baptised 12th, in 25th year of his age.

Sarah, born . . . , baptised 21st, parents, Peter Springer and . . . .

Mary, born . . . , baptised 21st, parents, Peter Paulson and . . . .

John, born June 10th, baptised 26th, parents, Israel Israels and . . . .

Mary, born May 4th, baptised 24th, parents, Theoplufus and Mary Jones.

Elizabeth, born May 4th, baptised 28th, parents, Edward and Mary Bratten.

AUGUST.

. . . , baptised 6th, child of John Price.

Mary, born April 7th, baptised 11th, parents, George and Mary Jackson.

Rebecca, born March 22, 1774, baptised 25th, parents, William and Judah Price.

SEPTEMBER.

Elizabeth, born . . . , baptised 7th, parents, Frederick King.

Rebecca, born . . . , baptised 8th, parents, David and Rebecca Windell.

. . . , born . . . , baptised 22d, parents, John Sperry.

Jane Bralk, born March, 1756, baptised 24th.

Elizabeth, born August 1st, baptised 24th, parents, Barney and Jane Brade.

Isaac, born 7th, baptised 25th, parents, Morton and Dorkas Morton.

OCTOBER.

John, born . . . , baptised 13th, parents, Mathias Peterson and . . . .

John, born September 13th, baptised 13th, parents, Thomas and Cathrine Hogg.

Elizabeth, born July 1st, baptised 26th, parents, Wm. and Elizabeth Elliott.

EARLY CHURCH RECORDS OF NEW CASTLE COUNTY

Mary, born . . baptised 28th, parents, . . McIntire.

James, born . . baptised 28th, parents, Joseph and Elizabeth Gilpin.

NOVEMBER.

Ann, born . . baptised 3rd, parents, Thomas and Isabella Crow.

Margrete, born . . baptised 7th, parents, Mulgrove and . . ,

William, born . . baptised 7th, parents, Fletcher and . . .

John and Fanny, born . . baptised 8th, parents, Robert and Margret Eiles.

David born . . baptised 17th; parents John Hendrickson and . . . ,

Rebecca, born August 14th, baptised 18th, parents, Robert and Elenor Sherman.

John, born . . baptised 24th, parents, Samuel and Mary Landers.

John, born . . baptised 27th, parents Peter Blankshorne and . . . ,

Richard born March 5th, baptised 30th, parents, Richard and Mary Derrick.

DECEMBER.

Elenor, born October . . baptised 3rd, parents, Thomas and Jane Love.

John, born . . baptised 14th, parents, . . . ,

Isaac and Rebecca, born . . baptised 23rd, parents, Gord and . . . ,

Rebecca, born 5th, baptised 29th, parents, Joseph and Mary Elliott.

ANNO 1777.
JANUARY.

John, born . . . baptised 3rd, parents, Hugh and Rachel Montgomery.

Sarah, born . . baptised 4th, parents, Ake Helm and . . . ,

Cathrine born December 11th, baptised 22nd, parents, John and Rebecca Veal.

Colepepper, born . . baptised 29th, parents, Robert Hedges and . . . ,

FEBRUARY.

Sarah born . . baptised 8th, parents, Smith and . . . ,

Johannah born January 10th, baptised 9th, parents, Hans and Susanna Hamcass.

OLD SWEDES CHURCH

John born January 10th, baptised 25th, parents, Wm. and Margret Heagen.

MARCH.

William, born . . baptised 9th, parents, Benjamin Elliott and . . .

Cathrine born January 12th, baptised 16th, parents, Jacob and Elenor Derrickson.

Isaac, born ——, baptised 23d, parents, Israel Peterson and ——.

APRIL.

Margret, born ——, baptised 7th, parents, Morton Vandever and ——.

Tobias, born ——, baptised 7th, parents, Morton Vandever and ——.

Sarah, born ——, baptised 13th, parents, Henry Garritson and ——.

Rebecca, born March 9th, baptised 13th, parents, Jonas and Gwin Matson.

Susanna, born ——, baptised 20th, parents, Robert Peirce, Jr.

MAY.

Jacob born March 12th, baptised 19th, parents, Michael and Isabella Woolf.

Charles, born ——, baptised 25th, parents, Charles Springer Josephson and Margret.

JUNE.

Margret, born February 25th, baptised 14th, parents, Michael and Ann Green.

Margret, born March 25th, baptised 14th, parents, Alexander and Martha Ford.

Margret, born ——, baptised 15th, parents, Thomas Webster.

Elizabeth, born ——, baptised 15th, parents, Thomas Webster.

Jane, born ——, baptised 15th, parents, Thomas Webster.

Strange Backhouse, born November 4, 1750, baptised 17th, parents, John and Mary Backhouse.

Joseph, born September 25, 1776, baptised 17th, parents, Strange and Cathrine Backhouse.

Margret, born April 13th, baptised 22d, parents, John Hendrickson, Jr., and Margret.

JULY.

William, born ——, baptised 13th, parents, Robert and Rachel Armstrong.

Joseph, born ——, baptised 24th, parents, Jacob and Mary Anderson.

AUGUST.

Baptised 2d, a sick child over Brandywine belonging to Presbyterians.

Jacob, born ——, baptised 10th, parents, Caleb Perkins and —— .

Mary, born ——, baptised 10th, parents, Richard and Johanna Silinie.

Cathrine, born ——, baptised 23d, parents, Mary Bradford.

OCTOBER.

Mary, born March 3d, baptised 12th, parents, George and Cathrine Thomas.

Ann, born August 24, baptised 13th, parents, William and Mary Shore.

Elizabeth, born August 25th, baptised 13th, parents, William and Mary Jordan.

Margret, born October 12th, baptised 14th, parents, Charles and Elenor McLaughlin.

Elizabeth, born October 29, 1776, baptised 16th, parents, William and Mary Skott.

Drusilla, born November 28, 1776, baptised 20th, parents, Joseph and Susanna Jackson.

NOVEMBER.

Rachel, born December 27, 1776, baptised 25th, parents, Joseph and Hannah Ball.

DECEMBER.

Mary, born October 5th, baptised 25th, parents, John and Elenor Paulson.

Sarah, born November 25th, baptised 25th, parents, John and Margret Hanah.

ANNO 1778.
JANUARY.

Mary, born December 27, 1777, baptised 9th, parents, John and Abby Ash.

Thomas, born ——, 9 days old, baptised 26th, parents, Thomas and Ann Allison.

FEBRUARY.

Henry, born January 11th, baptised 9th, parents, James and Elenor Birwin.

Cathrine, born . . . , baptised 19th, belonged to a soldier quartered in town.

OLD SWEDES CHURCH

William, born . . . , baptised 19th, parents, Wm. Armor and . . .

John, born December 31, 1777, baptised 21st, parents, Guilbert and Ann M. Vander.

MARCH.

Joel, born . . . , baptised 1st, parents, Charles Paulson and . . .

Sarah, born . . . , baptised 2d, parents, Thomas and Elizabeth Plunket.

. . . . , baptised 20th, child of Morton Morton.

APRIL.

Mary, baptised 6 years old.

Elizabeth, born February 7th, baptised 12th, parents, Arthur and Johannah Dempsey.

MAY.

Charlotta Elenora, born April 24th, baptised 4th, parents, Wm. and Mary Johnson,

Benjamin, born March 24th, baptised 6th, parents, Benjamin and Susannah Elliott.

John, born August 14, 1777, baptised 14th, parents, Zacharias and Sarah Derrickson.

Sarah, born April 5th, baptised 14th, parents, Cornelius and Ann Derrickson.

Robert, born . . . , baptised 17th, parents, ... Bratton and . . .

Elenore, born September 13th, baptised 19th, parents, Thomas and Johannah Afrell.

Elizabeth and Mary, born December 15, 1777, baptised 25th, parents, Patrick and Jane Mooney.

Wm. Owen, born October . , 1777, baptised 24, parents, ...

A child baptised 28th, parents, ...

JUNE.

John, born January 25th, baptised 3d, parents, Theophilus and Mary Jones.

Elizabeth, born . baptised 14th, parents, Grifith and Phoebe Jordan.

Thomas, born April 24th, baptised 17th, parents, John and Persina Vandever.

Adam, born . . . , baptised 28th, parents, Wm. and Rebecca Sharpley.

EARLY CHURCH RECORDS OF NEW CASTLE COUNTY

JULY.

Mary, born January 21, 1777, baptized 2d, parents, John and Mary Fonderey.

Ann, born February 4th, baptised 23rd, parents, John Paulson Johnson and Sarah.

Joseph, born . . . 1768,
Margaret and James, born . . . 1771,
Ruth, born September 20, 1773,
Baptised 26th, parents, Allen and Ann Robinet.

John, born March 31st, baptised 28th, parents, David and Susanna Tryon.

AUGUST.

William, born December 13, 1777, baptised 16th, parents, Abel and Elenor Ghard.

Adolphus, born August 4, 1777, baptised 16th, parents, John and Mary Husband.

SEPTEMBER.

John, born July 15th, baptised 13th, parents, John and Ann Hendrickson.

Anna Maria, born July 24th, baptised 18th, parents, Richard and Mary Derrick.

George Glovier, born . . . baptised 20th, parents, Joseph and Elizabeth Gilpin.

OCTOBER.

Ann, born . . . baptised 16th, parents, Wm. and Margaret Heagen.

Nancy, born August 30, baptised 25th, parents, Andrew and Sarah Peterson.

William, born August 6th, baptised 25th, parents, David and Hannah Stidham.

NOVEMBER.

John, born . . . baptised 2d, parents, John and Elenor Baughman.

Isaac, born October 23rd, baptised 18th, parents, Peter and Elizabeth Paulson.

James, born September 24th, baptised 21st, parents, Samuel and Margret Little.

Joseph, born October 18th, baptised 28th, parents, Joseph Springer Christopherson and Lydia.

OLD SWEDES CHURCH

DECEMBER.

Thomas, born October 14th, baptised 3rd, parents, Mark and Jane Elliott.

Joseph, born November 5th, baptised 14th, parents, Zacharias and Sarah Derickson.

Isabella, born November 31st, baptised 31st, parents, James and Elizabeth Murphey.

ANNO 1779.

JANUARY.

. . . . . . the 4th, baptised a negro chiid.

Enoch, born October 19th, baptised 6th, parents, Andrew and Margret Anderson.

Cathrine, born . . . baptised 7th, parents, John Stilley and . . . . . .

Susanna, born . . . baptised 22d, parents, Cornelius and Christiana Stidham.

. . . child, . . . baptised 31st, parents, Mathias Gennet.

FEBRUARY.

Ely, born January 1, 1778, baptised 5th, parents, John and Ann Sennex.

Rachel, born October 16, 1778, baptised 5th, parents, John Justis and Sarah Sennex.

Cathrine Bratherson baptized 8th, about twenty years old.

Mary, 4 years old, baptised 8th, parents, . . .

Violet, born . . . , baptised 11th, belonging to a free negro woman.

Rachel, born January 23rd, baptised 14th, parents Michael and Isabella Wood.

Ann, born February 1st, baptised 22nd, parents, John H. and Sarah Chair.

MARCH.

Ann Mary, born . . . , baptised 4th, parents Wm. and Rebecca Stidham.

Peter, born . . . , baptised 4th, parents, Wm. and Rebecca Stidham.

John, born March 7th, baptised 14th, parents, Hugh and Susannah McLean.

George, born January 13th, baptised 22nd, parents, Thomas and Elizabeth Harper.

William, born February 16th, baptised 22nd, parents, Christopher and Elizabeth Gennet.

EARLY CHURCH RECORDS OF NEW CASTLE COUNTY

APRIL.

Rebecca, born March 2, 1769, baptised 2nd, parents, Mark and Sarah Morton.

MAY.

Sarah, born March 28, 1769, baptised 2nd, parents, George and Agnes Alkorn.

John, born . . . baptised April 5th, parents, John and Cathrine Pagne.

Thomas, born . . . , baptised April 5th, parents, John and Cathrine Pagne.

William, born . . . , baptised April 5th, parents, John and Cathrine Pagne.

Mary, born April 5th, baptised April 5th, parents, John and Cathrine Pagne.

Thomas, born . . . , baptised 16th, parents, . . Skotshorn and Rebecca.

JUNE.

Mary, born March 14th, baptised 8th, parents, James Peterson and . . .

Mary, born . . , baptised 6th, parents, Edward Smith and . . .

Robert, born December 10, 1778, baptised 10th, parents, Robert and Cathrine Pierce.

John born . . . , baptised 20th, parents . . . Konolly and . . .

Jonas, born . . . , baptised 20th, parents, Wallraven Walraven and . . .

Joseph, born December 20, 1778, baptised 26th, parents, Thomas and Unity Watson.

Henry, born . . . , baptised 27th, parents, George Nelson

JULY.

Thomas, born . . . , baptised 15th, parents, . . . Davis

AUGUST.

James, born May 3rd, baptised 8th, parents, Edward and Ann Dunn.

Esau and Jacob, born . . . , baptised 8th, parents, John Sperey and . . .

Kesia, illegitimate, born February 4th, baptised 14th, parents, Ezekil Eden and Mary Abby.

. . . . baptised 22nd, sick child of Jacob Barnes.

178

OLD SWEDES CHURCH

September.

Jane, born July 18th, baptised 16th, parents, George and Cloe Forsyth.

William, born June 19th, baptised 19th, parents, Hugh and Mary Parker.

October.

Elizabeth, born September 2d, baptised 3d, parents, Hans and Susanna Slameass.

Joseph, born . . . , baptised 3d, parents, Joseph and Elizabeth Gilpin.

David, born March 1, 1778, baptised 14th, parents, David and Ester John.

November.

Ann, born October 5th, baptised 6th, parents, Peter and Cathrine Derickson.

Elizabeth, born October 4th, baptised 28th, parents, John and Elenor Paulson.

December.

Andrew, born October 29th, baptised 7th, parents, John and Ann Lynam.

Anno 1780.
January.

Mary, born January 24th, baptised 25th, parents, Thomas Broom and . . .

February.

Mary and Susanna, born January 5th, baptised 14th, parents, Jacob and Debora Robinson.

William, born December 22d, baptised 27th, parents, William and Mary Anderson.

Ann, illegitimate, born February 17, 1777, baptised 29th, parents, John Kery and Mary Neil.

March.

Peter, born January 7th, baptised 6th, parents, Charles and Susanna Paulson.

Elizabeth, born February 5th, baptised 7th, parents, John and Persina Vandever.

Mary, born November 18, 1779, baptised 27th, parents, Frederick and Barbary King.

EARLY CHURCH RECORDS OF NEW CASTLE COUNTY

Martin, born August, 1777, baptised 27th, parents, Gabriel and Margret Walker.

APRIL.

Sarah, born January 18th, baptised 2d, parents, Jacob and Elenor Derrickson.

Mary, born February 6, 1779, baptised 6th, parents, John and Rebecca Skotshorn.

William, born August 6th, baptised 7th, parents, William and Ester Kiley,

Margret, born March 4th, baptised 8th, parents, Benjamin and Susannah Elliott.

Fanny, born November 16, 1779, baptised 9th, parents, Isaac and Rebecca Cherry.

Martha, born September 19th, baptised 15th, parents, John and Mary Elliott.

John, born August 15, 1779, baptised 15th, parents, John and Sarah Hugis.

Ann, born July 3d, baptised 18th, parents, Jacob and Mary Anderson.

John, born March 12th, baptised 23d, parents, Robert and Rachel Armstrong.

Nancy, born . . . , baptised 30th, parents, . . . Sanderson

MAY.

Mary, born March 11, 1777, baptised 7th, parents, George and Ann Fox.

Frances, born February 4, 1777, baptised 7th, parents, George and Ann Fox.

Susanna, born May . . , baptised 25th, parents, William and Sophia Negly.

Jane, born April 17th, baptised 28th, parents, Samuel and Margret Little

JUNE.

Mary, born November 4, 1779, baptised 3rd, parents, Cornelius and Ann Derickson.

Thomas, born March 30, 1779, baptised 11th, parents, Thomas and Margret Webster.

Peter, born . . . baptised 25th, parents, Peter and Lydia Woolbaugh.

JULY.

James, born December 23, 1779, baptised 8th, parents, Wm. and Jane Flanagan.

OLD SWEDES CHURCH

August.

Cathrine, illegitimate, born November 8, 1779, baptised 14th, parents, James Brindley and Rebecca Smidt.

September.

Andrew, born August 28th, baptised 4th, parents, Jacob and Mary Grebble.

Mary, born November 4, 1779, baptised 25th, parents, George and Martha Nelson.

October.

William, illegitimate, born August 6th, baptised 2nd, parents, Solomon Stockium and Jane Booth.

Anne, born . . . baptised 15th, parents, Joseph and Elenor Baughman.

Daniel, born . . . baptised 22nd, parents, Daniel Janifer Adams and Ann.

John, born September 28th, baptised 23rd, parents, Lukas and Cathrine Wallraven.

Hannah, born February 28th, baptised 25th, parents, Strange and Cathrine Backhouse.

David, born December 25, 1779, baptised 25th, parents, David and Margret Cross.

November.

Thomas, born . . . baptised 2nd, parents, Charles Springer Jamesson and . . .

December.

John Robert, born . . . baptised 1st, parents, . . . Nowlan and . .

Johan Adolph, born October 31st at 4 o'clock in the morning, baptised the 6th of this month by the Rev. Mr. M. Hultgren, parents, Lawrence and Christina Girelius;

Godfathers, The Very Reverend Dr. Charles Magnus Wrangel, chief chaplain to the King and Dean of Sahla in Sweden;

The Very Reverend John Girelius, rector of the Parish, near Averla in Sweden; my dear father;

The Rev. Mathias Hultgren, rector of Wicacoe, Philadelphia.

Godmothers, Dr. Wrangel's Lady, a daughter of Admiral Priusentierna;

Mistress Barbara Helena Girelius my good stepmother, whose maiden name was Borg;

Miss Cathrine Parlen, a daughter of the late Mr. Olof Parlen, rector of Wicacoe, Philadelphia.

EARLY CHURCH RECORDS OF NEW CASTLE COUNTY

ANNO 1781.

JANUARY.

Joanna, born December 17, 1780, baptised 31st, parents, Hans and Hannah Nass.

Benjamin, born . . baptised February 18th, parents, . . . ,

Alexander born . . baptised 21st parents, . . . ,

MARCH.

Sarah, born February 8th, baptised 17th, parents, Wm. and Rebecca Stedham.

APRIL.

Jacob, born . . baptised 2nd, parents, Alexander Carr and .

Lydia, born January 20th, baptised 17th, parents, Joseph Springer Christopherson and Lydia.

Isaac, born March 19th, baptised 23rd, parents, John and Elizabeth Stilly.

Elizabeth, born February 4th, baptised 24th, parents Peter and Elizabeth Paulson.

John, born September 17th, baptised 25th, parents James and Elizabeth Murphey.

Ann, born January 27th, baptised 29th, parents, Cornelius and Christina Stedham.

MAY.

Jonathan, born May 22nd, 1775, baptised 5th, parents, Thomas and Marion Davis.

Susanna, born August 23, 1780, baptised 5th, parents, Thomas and Marion Davis.

Thomas, born April 22nd, baptised 13th, parents, David and Hannah Stedham.

Isaac, born . . , baptised 13th, parents, Charles Springer Josephson and Margret.

JUNE.

Elizabeth, born February 27th, baptised 21st, parents. Robert and Jane Robinson.

JULY

William, born February . . baptised 1st, parents, Thomas and Ann Wilson.

AUGUST.

Ann, born December 25, 1780, baptised 30th, parents Robert and Margret Eccles.

OLD SWEDES CHURCH
SEPTEMBER.

Hannah, born . . , baptised 9th, parents, Joseph and Hannah Hedge.

Levi, born . . , baptised 27th, parents, John and Elizabeth Justis.

Mary, born December 28, 1780, baptised 27th; parents, Henry and Mary Garritson.

OCTOBER.

John, born . . , baptised 7th, parents, Wallraven Wallraven and . . ,

Cathrine, born . . , baptised 14th, parents, Jacob and Mary Anderson.

NOVEMBER.

John Andrew, born August 25th, baptised 17th, parents, John and Ann Han.

George, born November 22nd, baptised 25th, parents Samuel and Cathrine Gass.

DECEMBER.

Isaac, born . . . . , baptised 3d, parents, Samuel and Cathrine Milnor.

Elizabeth, born . . . . , baptised 3d, parents, David and Margret Beeson.

Elizabeth, born . . . . , baptised 3d, parents, Wm. Vandever and . . .

Regina, born . . . . . baptised 4th, parents, Wm. and Lydia Rawson.

William, born Sebtember 1st, baptised 9th, parents, John and Susanna Stilly.

William, born . . . , baptised 29th, parents, Thomas Broom and . . .

ANNO 1782.
JANUARY.

Elizabeth, illegitimate, born December 25, 1772, baptised 6th, parents, Edward Vernon and Ann White.

John, born November 22, 1781, baptised 13th, parents, Hans and Susanna Hamcas.

Jacob, born November 7, baptised 20th, parents, Jacob and Elenor Derrickson.

FEBRUARY.

John, born . . . . , baptised 3d, parents, Henry and Ann Nass.

EARLY CHURCH RECORDS OF NEW CASTLE COUNTY

Joseph, born . . . ,baptised 10th, parents, Joshua and Ann Mortenson.

John, born December 18, 1781, baptised 10th, parents, Samuel and Margret Little.

Sarah, born March 26th, baptised 17th, parents, Jacob and Mary Grebble.

Elenor, born . . . . , baptised 17th, parents, John and Elenor Paulson.

APRIL.

Joseph and Benjamin, born March . . , baptised 9th, parents, John and Sarah Paulson.

Isaac, born February 3d, baptised 13th, parents, Daniel Sharpley, Jr., and Rebecca.

Child baptised 13th, parents, Christopher Gennet and . . . .

Child baptised 29th, parents, Nail Daugherty and . . . . .

Joseph, born January 3, 1782, baptised 29th, parents, Nathaniel and Juliana Philips.

Sarah, born August 6, 1783, baptised . . , parents, Nathaniel and Juliana Phillips.

MAY.

James, born February 11th, baptised 5th, parents, Wm. and Ester Kelley.

Charles, illegitimate, born . . . . , baptised 5th, parents, Thomas Payne and Margret Ferris.

JUNE.

Alexander and James, born . . . , baptised 5th, parents, John Fletcher and . .

John, born March 21st, baptised 22d, parents, Johnathan Kirk, Jr., and Johanna.

JULY.

Mary, born . . . . , baptised 2d, parents, Richard Kean and . . .

Ann, illegitimate, born September 3, 1778, baptised 7th, parents, Andrew Murray and Lydia Londey.

Elizabeth, born February 6th, baptized 7th, parents, John and Lydia May.

Mary, born April 25th, baptized 14th, parents, Andrew Lip and Marelis.

John, born July 29, 1780, baptised 21st, parents, John and Ann Isham.

Sarah, born December 18, 1781, baptised 21st, parents, John and Ann Isham.

OLD SWEDES CHURCH

Mary, born May 31., baptised 28th, parents, Christopher and Hannah Goest.

AUGUST.

Timothy, born ——, baptised 4th, parents, Sanderson and Hannah.

Jacob, born May 26th, baptised 6th, parents, Jacob Virt, Jr., and Mary.

Peter, born May 31st, baptised 8th, parents, John and Persina Vandever.

Reuben, born February 19, 1778, baptised 11th, parents, Nathaniel and Juliana Philips.

SEPTEMBER.

Thomas, born . . . , baptised 15th, parents, Thomas and Sarah Derrick.

Samuel, born . . . , baptised 15th, parents, Charles Paulson.

OCTOBER.

William, born . . . , baptised 15th, parents, . . . Carr.

NOVEMBER.

Sarah, born . . . , baptised 10th, parents, Cornelius Heins.

Ann, born February 14th, baptised 27th, parents, Cornelius and Ann Derrickson.

DECEMBER.

Mary, born September 23d, baptised 4th, parents, Zacharias and Sarah Derickson.

Margret, born August 18th, baptised 4th, parents, Abram and Ann Voores.

James, illegitimate, born . . . , baptised 15th, parents, James Logan and Widow Prevost.

ANNO 1783.

JANUARY.

James, born December 18th, baptised 27th, parents, Edward and Mary Smith.

FFBRUARY.

Rachel, born August 31st, baptised 20th, parents, Joseph and Elenor Baughman.

MARCH.

Thomas, born January 31st, baptised 30th, parents, John and Hannah Flinn.

EARLY CHURCH RECORDS OF NEW CASTLE COUNTY

April.

Henry, born October 23d, baptised 6th, parents, John and Mary Nowlin.

Sarah, born February 7th, baptised 6th, parents, Lukas and Cathrine Wallraven.

Robert, born November 23d, baptised 13th, parents, Robert and Rachel Armstrong.

——, ——, baptised 13th, parents, —— Clishy.

Mary, born February 25th, baptised 22d, parents, George and Elizabeth Weldon.

May.

William Vaneaman, born ——, baptised 1st, parents, Lukas and Joanna Stedham.

David, born April 1st, baptised 25th, parents, Jesse and Rebecca Wallraven.

June.

Child, baptised 9th, parents, Joshua Mortonson.

Ingeber, born . . . , baptised 17th, parents, . . . Lefever.

Mary, born April 17th, baptised 20th, parents, John and Elizabeth Justis.

July.

Richard, born May 24th, baptised 10th, parents, Jacob and Deborah Robeson.

August.

Ann, born May 8th, baptised 2d, parents, Morton and Sarah Morton.

Ann, born August 9, 1782, baptised 3d, parents, John and Elizabeth Bryan.

Isaac, born August 8, 1782, baptised 6th, parents, William and Rebecca Stedham.

Sarah, born March 13th, baptised 6th, parents, Isaac and Anna Mary Stedham.

Mary, born June 13th, baptised 8th, parents, John and Elizabeth Stilley.

Joseph, born January 11th, baptised 17th, parents, Leonard and Lydia Young.

George and John, born . . . , baptised 25th, parents, . . . Carr and . . . .

Elizabeth, born January 1, 1782, baptised 31st, parents, Keto and Rachel Zimmingens (negroes).

September.

John, born August 4, 1782, baptised 18th, parents, John and Ann Veal.

Elizabeth, born . . . , baptised 22d, parents, William and Cathrine Sharpe.

OLD SWEDES CHURCH

Margret, born . . . , baptised 28th, parents, Benjamin Elliott.

Johanna, born August 16th, baptised 28th, parents, Hans and Susannah Hamcast.

OCTOBER.

William, born August 27th, baptised 12th, parents, Samuel and Margret Little.

Samuel, born . . . , baptised 14th, parents, . . . Brown and Rachel.

Elinor, born June 30, 1780, baptised 18th, parents, John and Ann Sinnex.

Elizabeth, born July 21st, baptised 18th parents, Peter and Cathrine Derrickson.

Susanna, born . . . , baptised 22nd, parents, James Brindley and . . . .

James Joseph, born . . . , baptised 22nd, parents, James Brindley and . . . .

Baptised 22d, parents, James Brindley and . . . .

Cathrine, born . . . , baptised 26th, parents, Wallraven Wallraven and . . . .

Brita Cathrina, born September 26th, seven o'clock, P. M.; baptised 2d, parents, Laurence and Christina Girelius; godfather, Rev. Niklas Collin, the present rector of Raccoon and Pennsneck churches, and Rev. Peter Girelius, assistant minister in the parish near Averta Sweden.

Godmother, Anna Maria Girelius, whose maiden name was Fyrshaff.

DECEMBER.

Joseph, born . . . baptized 4th, parents, Jacob and Hannah Justis.

Rebecca, born October 18th, baptised 7th, parents, Charles Springer Josephson and Margret.

Ann, born . . . baptised 15th, parents, Peter Paulson and . .

Samuel Watson, born November 28th, baptised 22nd, parents, Jacob and Mary Grebble.

George, born . . . baptised 11th, parents, Wm. and Lydia Rawson.

ANNO 1784.

JANUARY.

Rachel, baptised 31st, two months old, parents, Jacob and Mary Anderson.

EARLY CHURCH RECORDS OF NEW CASTLE COUNTY

FEBRUARY.

John, born . . . baptised 10th, parents, John Stidham, Jr., and . . .

Mary, born . . . baptised 19th, parents, Daniel and Rebecca Sharpley.

Elizabeth, born February 2nd, baptised 15th, parents, Samuel and Cathrine Gars.

APRIL.

William, born . . . baptised 4th, parents, George Paulson and . . .

Elizabeth, born December, 1783, baptised 12th, parents, Richard and Ann Taylor.

Daniel, born June 2, 1783, baptised 12th, parents, Moses and Sarah McComb.

Peter Haston, born . . twenty-five years old, baptised in sickness, baptised 16th.

John, born . . . sick child belonging to strangers, baptised 16th.

MAY.

Peter, born . . . baptised 13th, parents, Joseph Springer Christopherson and Lydia.

JUNE.

Mary, born September 1783, baptised 6th, parents, John and Elenor Rodgers.

Rebecca, born April 19th, baptised 7th, parents, Wm. and Rebecca Stidham.

Joseph, born May 19th, baptised 20th, parents, Jacob and Elenor Derrickson.

Mary, born May 16th, baptised 27th, parents, Joseph and Cathrine Lawson.

. . . sick child, baptised July, parents, . . . Toest.

JULY.

Archibald, January 2nd, 1777,
Elizabeth, February 27th, 1779,
Mary, May 19 th, 1781,
John, November 23rd, 1783,

Baptised 19th, parents, Robert and Susanna Little.

Ann, born . . . baptised 2nd, parents, Jacob Broom and . .
James, born . . . baptised 2nd, parents, Jacob Broom and . .
Ester, born . . . baptised 2nd, parents, Jacob Broom and . .
Elizabeth, born . . baptised 2nd, parents, Jacob Broom and . .
Elizabeth, born September 20, 1777, baptised April 1778.

OLD SWEDES CHURCH

Mary, born May 29, 1780, qaptised 3rd, parents, Grissie and Phoebe Jordan.

Jonathan, . . . Jannary 2, 1783, baptised 3rd, parents, Grissie and Phoebe Jordan.

Henry Colesburg, born . . . , baptised 6th, parents, . . . Smith and . . .

Nicolas, born . . . baptised 8th, parents, David Stidham and . . .

Hanna, born July 14, 1783, baptised 11th, parents, John and Sarah Wood.

Elizabeth, born February 27th, baptised 11th, parents, Thomas Henry and Mary.

Thomas, born July 4th, baptised 12th, parents, Thomas and Ann Jones.

Susanna, born March 1st, baptised 12th, parents, Joseph and Mary Wagoner.

Sick child . . . baptised 19th, parents, ... Eiles.
Sick child . . . baptised 22d, parents, James Hinson.
Sick child . . . baptised 25th, parents, Jonathan Kirk.
Antony, born 2, 1783, parents, Wynekoop.   26th

OCTOBER.

Rachel, born April 10, 1783, baptised 25th, parents, Thomas and Sara Derrick.

George and Elizabeth, 20 years old, black servants of the Crossans, in Mill Creek Hundred, were baptised in ye church October 10th.

NOVEMBER.

Abraham Few, between 30 and 40 years old; baptised in sickness ye 25th.

ANNO 1785.

JANUARY.

Mary, born November 23, 1784, baptised 7th, parents, Felix and Margret Hanlon.

Thomas, born November 1, 1784, baptised 13th, parents, John and Ann Lynam.

FEBRUARY.

Samuel, born February 3d, baptised 9th, parents, Jesse and Sarah Lewis.

Elizabeth, born April 7, 1784, baptised 12th, parents, John and Elizabeth Bowles.

EARLY CHURCH RECORDS OF NEW CASTLE COUNTY

MARCH.

Mary, born . . . baptised 1st, parents, John and Sarah Springer.

APRIL.

Mary, born January 4th, baptised 16th, parents, Isaac and Mary Stidham.

Elizabeth, born January 20th, baptised 16th, parents, John and Elizabeth Justis.

Nathan, . . . baptised 17th, parents, Charles Paulson.

MAY.

Henry, born . . . baptised 8th, parents, Henry and Ann Nass.

Elenor, born . . . baptised 12th, parents, Jonas Stidham, Jr. and . . .

John, born March 24th, baptised 15th, parents, Daniel Sharpley Jr. and Rebecca.

Peter, born March 25th, baptised 19th, parents, Lucas and Joanna Stidham.

Peter, born February 11th, baptised 22d, parents, John and Ann Flinn.

Samuel, born April 1st, baptised 22d, parents, John and Sarah Wood.

Samuel, illegitimate, born October 27th, baptised 26th, parents, Joseph Day and Elizabeth Clindenone.

Catharine, born December, 1784, baptised 29th, parents, Wm. and Mary Smith.

Baptised 23d, a sick child in town.

JUNE.

William, born March 29th baptised 9th, parents, Jacob and Cathrine Colesberg.

Elizabeth, born October 6, 1784, baptised 9th, parents, James and Mary Eves.

. . . . baptised 28th, sick child, parents, John Fletcher.

JULY.

Anna Ford, born . . . . , baptised in the church 3d.

Baptised a child the 3d.

Gatewell, born October 8, 1784, baptised 7th, parents, Archibald and Margret Croxon.

Margret, born . . . . , baptised 7th, parents, Joshua Mortonson and . .

OLD SWEDES CHURCH
AUGUST.

Mark, born . . . . , baptised 4th, parents, Dr. and Mary Capell.

Peter Tranberg, born July 25th, baptised 8th, parents, Wm. and Cathrine Sharpe

William, born February 27, 1784, baptised 8th, parents, Henry and Ann Haselton.

Rebecca, born . . . . , baptised 11th, parents, Jacob Gribble and . . . ;

Cathrine, born . . . . , baptised 14th, parents, Thomas Cox and , .

Andrew and Christian, born March 17, 1785, baptised 19th, parents, . . . Lyon.

OCTOBER.

Elizabeth, born August 4th, baptised 2d, parents, John and Elinor Rogers.

George, born July 8th baptised 2d, parents, Robert and Rachel Armstrong.

Hannah, born . . . . , baptised 17th, parents, Grissie and Phœbe Jordan.

NOVEMBER.

Mary, born September 30th, baptised 13th, parents, Hans and Susanna Hamcas.

DECEMBER.

Peter and Elizabeth, born November 15th, baptised December 1st, parents, Wallraven Wallraven and . . .

ANNO 1786.
MARCH.

The 20th, baptised Richard Tayla's sick child.

APRIL.

Samuel, born January 29th, baptised 30th, parents, Samuel and Margret Likel.

MAY.

Mary, born December 19, 1785, baptised 21st, parents, Nathaniel and Juliana Phiplis.

JUNE.

Justa, born . . . , baptized 4th, parents, Jacob and Hannah Justis.

Edward Gibson, born . . . , baptized 4th, in the twentieth year of his age.

EARLY CHURCH RECORDS OF NEW CASTLE COUNTY

Rebecca, born January 22d, baptized 11th, parents, Jonas and Sarah Gennet.

Elizabeth, born April 3, baptized 11th, parents, Lukas and Cathrine Wallraven.

Hugh, born February 4, baptized 25th, parents, Hugh and Dolly Biggan, negroes.

JULY.

John, born . . . , baptized 14th, parents, ...

AUGUST.

James, born June 26th, baptized 6th, parents, Peter and Jane Davis.

Peter Abraham, born July 30th, baptized 9th, instant by Rev Charles H. Wharton, D. D., parents, Lawrence and Christina Girelius. This little child was very sick, being born with the whooping cough, and died soon after, the 17th, and was buried in Christine Church the 18th, in afternoon by Dr. Wharton.

SEPTEMBER.

Ann and William, born 1st, baptized 3d, parents, Robert and Mary Shapley.

Sarah, born Apr. 26 and Bapt. 4, Parents Mark and Sarah Morton

Dorothea, Catharine and John, baptized 7th, parent, John Jaquett.

Mary, born . . . , baptized 10th, parents, George Paulson.

OCTOBER.

George, born March 4th, 1783,

Annie, born February, 1785,

Baptized 2d, parents, Robert and Jane Till, negroes, belonging to William Armer.

Anna Brita, born February 26th, baptized 16th, parents, John and Persina Vandever.

James, born September 24th, baptized 16th, parents, William and Maria Ardery.

Susanna, born September 21st, baptized 25th, parents, Hance and Mary Naff.

ANNO 1787.

MARCH.

Sarah, born . . . , baptized 14th, parents, John and Sarah Springer.

APRIL.

John, born February 18th, baptized 1st, parents, John and Sarah Wood.

OLD SWEDES CHURCH

. . . . the 29th, baptized . . . , Willliam Smith's child.

MAY.

Charles, born April 1st, baptised 4th, parents, Charles and Susanna Paulson.

. . . . baptised April 7th, a sick child.

Susanna, born October 14th, baptised 2nd, parents, Isaac and Anna Maria Stedham.

Mary, born . . . , baptised 8th, parents, James and Mary Eves.

* Jonas Stidham, born . . . , baptised 8th, parents, John and Elizabeth Justis.

JUNE.

David, born . . . , baptised 10th, parents, David Stidham and . . .

Ann, born April 30th, baptised 18th, parents, John and Mary Colphos.

JULY.

Susanna and Rebecca, born June 7th, baptised 5th, parents, Leonard and Lydia Young.

Peter Vandever, born . . . , baptised 25th, parents, Winters and Sarah.

Hannah Shallcross, born . . . , baptised 26th, parents, Joseph and Elizabeth Gilpin.

AUGUST.

Ann Cathrine, born May 20th, baptised 2nd, parents, Peter and Ann Wallraven.

Ann, born . . . , baptised 6th, parents, William and Anna Cathrine Sharp.

. . . . , baptised 14th, a sick child.

Peter, born . . . , baptised 19th, parents, Peter Paulson and . .

Elizabeth, born June 12, 1784, baptised 23rd, parents, John and Margret McGlaughlin.

Ann, born July 13, 1786, baptised 23rd, parents, John and Margret McGlaughlin.

SEPTEMBER.

. Sarah and Elenor, born . . . , baptised 17th, parents, Thomas Derrick and . . .

EARLY CHURCH RECORDS OF NEW CASTLE COUNTY

OCTOBER.

Debora, born June 17th, baptised 10th, parents, Joseph and Ann Derrickson.

Mary, born December 5, 1786, baptised 11th, parents, Jonas Stedham, Jr., and Ingeber.

John, born September 8th, baptised 15th, parents, Daniel and Rebecca Hoffman.

Mary, born October 26, 1780, baptised 26th, parents, Timothy and Ann Jackson.

James, born June 22, 1783, baptised 26th, parents, Timothy and Ann Jackson.

Rebecca, born February 16, 1785, baptised 26th, parents, Timothy and Ann Jackson.

NOVEMBER.

William, born . . . , baptised 2nd, parents, Jacob and Mary Anderson.

William, born September 20th, baptised 9th, parents, Zachariah and Sarah Derrickson.

Maria May, born March 24th, baptised 26th, parents, Doctor and Mary Capelle.

DECEMBER.

Aquila, born . . . , baptised 2d, parents, Wallraven Wallraven and . . . .

Hannah, born October 22d, baptised 26th, parents, Thomas and Mary Moore.

Cornelins, born March 26th, baptised 26th, parents, Seneca and Jane Sennex.

ANNO 1788.

JANUARY.

Elizabeth, born . . . , baptised 3d, parents, Peter Justis and . . . .

FEBRUARY.

Elizabeth, born December 19, 1787, baptised 12th, parents, Andrew and Margret Lyon.

Cathrine, born December 24, 1787, baptised 28th, parents, Hance Naff, Jr., and Mary.

OLD SWEDES CHURCH

April.

Baptised Solomon's child.

Elizabeth, born January 22d, baptised 13th, parents, Robert Armstrong and . . . .

Henry, born January 19th, baptised 20th, parents, John and Elizabeth Vining.

May.

Benjamin, born June 6th, baptised . . . , parents, Joseph and Rachel Brown.

Lawrence, born March 20th, baptised 11th, parents, Jacob and Christiana Justis.

. . . , baptised 25th, George Paulson's child.

Lars Gustav, born April 10th, at one o'clock P. M., baptised 29th, by Rev. Dr. Nicholas Collins of Wicacoe, parents, Lawrence and Christina Girelius.

June.

John Beeson, born March 2d, badtised 10th, parents, John and Persina Vandever.

Susanna, born . . . , baptised 15th, parents, Benjamin Elliott and . . . .

Robinson Barrow, born May 12th, baptised 16th, parents, John and Mary Corkshott.

July.

Thomas, born May 16th, baptised 13th, parents, Samuel and Margret Likel.

Mary, born April 1, 1783,

James, born August 20, 1786,

Johann, born Feruary 16, 1788.

Baptised 21st, parents, Richard and Ann Graham.

Elizabeth, illegitimate, born May 15th, baptised 31st, parents, David Colby and Elizabeth Naff.

Peter, born . . . , baptised July 27th, parents, John Justis and . . . .

August.

Caleb, born . . . , baptised 10th, parents, Joshua Mortinson.

Hannah, born . . . , baptised 10th, parents, John Lynam.

Thomas, born . . . , baptised 13th, parents, William Foot and . . . .

September.

Jane, born . . 3rd, baptised 30th, parents, Wm. and Ann Armstrong.

EARLY CHURCH RECORDS OF NEW CASTLE COUNTY

OCTOBER.

. . . , born . . , baptised 10th, the Father Lewis, dead.

John, born July 27th, baptised 16th, parents, George and Elizabeth Weldon.

Jonas, born . . , baptised 31st, parents, Lukas and Johanna Stedham.

DECEMBER.

Daniel, born . . , baptised 14th, parents Daniel Sharpley and . . .

ANNO 1789.

JANUARY.

John, born November 10, 1782, baptised 20th, parents, John and Hannah Flinn.

FFBRUARY.

Eliza, born September 24th, baptised 4th, parents Isaac and Ann Mary Stedham.

. . . , born . . , baptised 27th, child of Sapley.

MARCH.

John, born April 17, 1788, parents, Nathaniel and Juliana Phillips.

Mary, born December 12, 1788; baptised 15th, parents, Peter Walraven and Ann.

Martha, born . . , baptised 15th, parents, English people.

Joseph Stedham, born October 22nd, 1788, parents, Lukas and and Cathrine Wallraven.

APRIL.

Charles, born . . ,baptised 5th, parents, Charles Paulson.

MAY.

William, born . . parents, John Cockshott.

William Hance, born April 11th, parents Hance and Mary Naff.

JUNE.

John, born . . , parents, John and Sarah Springer.

Peter, born February 18th, baptised 3d, parents, Peter and Cathrine Derickson.

JULY.

William, born July, 1787, . . , parents, John and Mary Morris,

Elizabeth illegitimate, born March 31st, parents Sarah Hull.

OLD SWEDES CHURCH

Robert, . . , sick child belonging to some poor Irish people.
Samuel, born . . , parents, Isaac Crawford and . .

AUGUST.

William, born . . parents, Wm. and Anna Cathrine Sharpe.
Mary, 6 years old, baptised 24th, parents, Thomas Smith and . .
John, 3 years old, baptised 24th, parents Thomas Smith.
Johanna, 1 year and 2 months old, baptised 24th, parents, Thomas Smith and . .

SEPTEMBER.

John, born Septemeer 12, 1788, baptised 13th, parents, John and Elenor Rogers.

OCTOBER.

Charles, born May 29th, 1788, baptised 3rd, parents, Charles and Francis Ford.
Isaac, born August 7th, baptised 8th, parents, Isaac and Elizabeth Crawford
John, born May 25, 1788, baptised 12th, parents, John and Sarah Paulson.
Susanna, born . . . baptised 13th, parents, John Brindley

NOVEMBER.

Ann, born October 1st, baptised . . . parents, Thomas and Mary Gun.

DECEMBER.

Joseph, born . baptised 6th, parents, Levi Springer and . .
Cathrine, October 22, 1788, baptised 13th, Peter and Mary Henry.

ANNO 1790.
JANUARY.

Joseph, born October 23, 1789, baptised 3rd, parents, John and Sarah Wood.
Isaac, born August 2nd, baptised 7th, parents, Charles Gransam

FEBRUARY.

Rebecc, illegitimate, born February 14th, baptised 8th, parents, Thomas Westby and Mary.
Susanna, born October 4, 1789, baptised 13th, parents, John and Elizabeth Vining.
Jacob, born . . . six weeks old, baptised 19th, parents, Jonas Stidham, Jr. and . . .

APRIL.

Ann, born . . . baptised 4th, parents, Ray . . .
John, born . . . baptised 6th, parents, John Aul and . .

EARLY CHURCH RECORDS OF NEW CASTLE COUNTY

Rebecca, born December 31, 1789, baptised 8th, parents, John and Elenor Brynberg.

Thomas] born February 9th, baptised 8th, parents, Richard and Margret Runnels.

Robert, born January 31st, baptised 25th, parents, Thomas and Ann Cole.

MAY.

Isaac, born March 12th, baptised 13th, parents Jacob and Mary Anderson.

Susanna, born . . . baptised 19th, parents, Daniel Janifer Adams and . . .

JUNE.

Mary, born January 1, 1784,
Jesse, born August 1, 1789,
Baptised 29th, parents, James and Rachel Husband.

JULY.

Arthur Robinson, born June 10th, baptised 17th, parents, John Mary Cockshott.

Isaac Barrows, born April 1, 1788, baptised 22nd, parents, John and Isabella Bell.

John, born May 23rd, baptised 26th, parents, John and Elizabeth Justis.

Charles Jacob, born July 1st, at 8 o'clock P. M., parents, Lawrence Girelius D. D., Rector of this Church and Commissary of the Swedish Churches in America; mother, Christina Girelius, whose maiden name was Lidenius, daughter of John Abraham Lidenius, formerly Rector of Racoon and Pennsneck congregations, in New Jersey, where he was born, about the year 1714 or 1715, and grand-daughter of Abraham Lidenius the elder, the first minister in Jersey who came in from Sweden, A. D. 1712, and returned to Sweden 1724, where he became Dean of Turnes, in Finland; baptised the 29th by Rev. Dr. Charles Henry Wharton.

SEPTEMBER.

Elizabeth, born June 12th, baptised 19th, parents, John and Elizabeth Stilley.

Marianna, born August 23d, baptised 26th, parents, John and Jane Barnard.

OCTOBER.

Mary, born September 5th, baptised 24th, parents, Samuel and Jane Burnet.

OLD SWEDES CHURCH
NOVEMBER.

George, born May 25th, baptised 19th, parents, David and Elizabeth Bush.

Alexander William Sperey, illegitimate, born October 2d, baptised 23d, parents, John Quam and Mary Sperey.

DECEMBER.

Mary, born November 1st, baptised 5th, parents, Hance and Mary Naff.

ANNO 1791.
JANUARY.

George, born April 10, 1788, baptised 3d, parents, Morton and Sarah Morton.

Samuel, born October 28, 1790, baptised 3d, parents, Morton and Sarah Morton.

Peter Harden's child, baptised 23d.

MARCH.

Cornelius, born December 29, 1790, baptised 3d, parents, John and Rebecca Springer.

APRIL.

Joseph, born December 10, 1789, baptised 6th, parents, Garrit and Elizabeth Lawrence.

John Wants, a negro, 50 years old, baptised 11th.

William Runnels, born ——, baptised in the Church Sunday before Easter, April 17th.

Willam Dushane, born June 13, 1790, parents, James and Mary Eves.

Thomas Runnels, born . . . , brother of William Runnels, baptized 22d.

Mary, born . . . , baptised 27th, parents, Wiclean and Rebecca.

George, born September 5, 1789, parents, George and Unity Johnson.

William, born March 31st, parents, Richard and Margret Runnels.

MAY.

Mary, born November 5, 1790, parents, John and Persina Vandever.

Isaac, born April 6th, baptized 5th, parents, John and Hanna Flin.

Jacob Pierce, born June 7, 1786,

Rachel Maria, born July 20, 1788,

EARLY CHURCH RECORDS OF NEW CASTLE COUNTY

Lavinia, born May 12, 1790,
Baptized 6th, parents, Jacob and Rachel Broom.

Rachel, born October 2, 1790, baptized 7th, parents, Isaac and Mary Stidham.

John, born September 21, 1792, baptized some short time after by the Rev. Dr. Wharton, Dr. Girelius being gone, and now recorded by Rev. Mr. Clarkson at the desire of the parents, who are Hance Naff, Jr., and Mary.

Elizabeth C., daughter of John and Margret Welch, baptized in infancy by Rev. Dr. Wharton.

A RECORD OF BAPTISMS, CONTINUED, BY JOSEPH CLARKSON, FROM THE 25TH OF SEPTEMBER, 1792, TO THE END OF THE YEAR.

Charles, born August 11, 1792, baptized October 11th, parents, Aaron and Sarah Justice.

John, baptized November 17, 1792, parents, Francis and . . . . . . Lafferty.

Thomas, born November 4, 1792, baptized 19th, parents, John and Jane Quandrill.

Sarah, born . . . , baptized November 19, 1792, parents, Moses and Sarah McComb.

Gerardus, born October 13, 1792, baptized November 25th, parents, Joseph and Grace Clarkson.

Anna, born August 5, 1787, baptized December 2, 1792, parents, William and Margret Armar.

Jacob Peter, born September 23, 1792, baptized December 2th, parents, John and Rebecca Springer.

Peter, born October 2, 1792, baptised December 13th, parents, Cope and Mary Anderson.

1793.

Mary, born May 4, 1792, baptised January 11th, parents, James and Mary Springer.

Rebecca, born August 9, 1792, baptised January 13th, parents, Francis and Elizabeth Dunlap.

Joseph, born January 1, 1791, baptised January 4, parents, Ann Lewis.

Thomas, born July 27 1791, baptised January 15th, parents, John and Mary West.

Rebecca, born January 14, 1793, baptised March 10th, parents, John and Parthena Vandever.

Ann, born November 2, 1792, baptised January 15th, parents, John and Mary West.

OLD SWEDES CHURCH

Marian, born March 3, 1793, baptised 25th, parents, Alexander and Jane McKitrick.

Susanna, baptised April 10, 1793,

Mary, baptised April 11th,

Parents, Alexander and Sarah Harvey.

George, born January 31, 1793, baptised May 12, parents, Levi and Mary Wallraven.

Elizabeth, born September 23, 1792, baptised June 9, 1793, parents, David and Elizabeth Bush.

William Murdock, William Hemphill and John Mass, three young men baptised in the church July 21, 1793.

John, born October 1, 1792, baptised July 21, 1793, parents, John and Rachel Robinett.

Thomas, born . . . ., baptised July 21, 1793, in the church, from St. James' Church.

Nicholas Way, born . . . , baptised July 22, 1793, parents, Jacob and Rachel Broom.

Elizabeth, born December 17, 1789, baptized in Philadelphia by Dr. Blacwell with private baptism when sick, received into this church July 28, 1793, parents, Michael and Elizabeth Key.

Michael, born January 16, 1792, baptised July 28, 1793, parents, Michael and Elizabeth Key.

Thomas, born November 5, 1792, baptised August 4, 1793, parents, Thomas and Mary Gunn.

Elizabeth, born February 19, 1793, baptised August . . . , parents, Nathaniel and Juliana Philips.

Jane, born July 8, 1793, baptised August 5th, James and Mary Eves.

Margaret, born . . . , baptised August 8th, parents, . . . Kelley.

Sabina, born April 10, 1792, baptised August 12th, parents, . . . Ann Taylor.

James, born May 28, 1793, baptised August 11th, parents, Jacob and Henry Morgan (negroes).

Henry, a black child belonging to Widow Thomas, of Easton, Md., baptised February 17, 1793, mother's name Phillis . . . .

Ann, born August 8, 1790,

Susanna, born December 8, 1793,

Baptised August 15th, parents, Andrew and Elizabeth Lyons. Dutch people.

Isabella, born September 4, 1792, baptised August 17th, parents, Michael Wolf, Jr., and Elizabeth.

EARLY CHURCH RECORDS OF NEW CASTLE COUNTY

Rebecca, born July 18, 1793, baptised August 19th, parents, Peter and Rebecca Harding.

Elizabeth, born April 27, 1786,

Ann, born March 25, 1790,

Sarah and Aimey, born May 15, 1793,

Baptised September 14th, parents, John and Hannah Nicholas.

Richard, born September 13, 1793, baptised 20th, parents, Jacob and Deborah Robinson.

Zacharias, born June 12, 1793, baptised October 2th, parents, Zacharias and Sarah Derickson.

Margaret, born September 17, 1793, baptised October 7th, parents, George and Sarah Mills.

Williams, born August 31, 1793, baptised October 7th, parents, Peter and Elizabeth Stidham.

Ann, born September 6, 1793, baptised October 7th, parents, Margret Gillin Irish Woman.

David, born . . . baptised October 13th, parents, Jesse and and Margret Pierce.

Ann, born October 18, 1793, baptised October 31st, parents, John and Cathrine Duffy, Irish.

Susan, born June 3, 1792, baptised November 8th, parents, Jonas and Ingeber Stidham, Jr.

Hannah Nicholas, Rachel Dresser; two married women who had been brought up among Quakers, but who, when they came to think for themselves, preferred an outward visible form in baptism to the ideal mode of the Quakers. They were both publicly baptised in church on 17th day of November, 1793.

George, born . . . baptised December 8th, parents, John and Ann Oliver.

Barbary and George, born . . . baptised December 8th, parents, Arthur and Rebecca French.

John, born . . . baptised December 10th, parents, . . .

James, born November 25, 1793, baptised December 16, 1793, parents, . . .

James, born February 27, 1794, baptised February 28, 1794,...

George, born February 3, 1794, baptised February 28, 1794, parents, . . .

Margret, born February 16, 1794, baptised February 28, 1794, parents, . . .

Benjamin, born . . son of Capt. Joseph Stidham, deceased, about 17 years of age; baptised March 21, 1794.

OLD SWEDES CHURCH

William, born July 20, 1793, baptised March 30, 1794.

Alexander, born February 3, 1794, baptised April 7, 1794, parents, Alexander and Sarah Harvey.

Betty Vandever and Jacob her son, wife and child of Peter Vandever vestry-man, baptised September 1, 1792, by Rev. Mr. Turner before I came here, though never entered before.

Peter, born March 13, 1794, baptised April 11, 1794, parents, Peter and Betty Vandever.

1794.

Swain and Morton, born April 12, 1794, baptised April 23rd, parents, Aaron and Sarah Justice.

John, born March 15, 1794, baptised May 4th, parents, Moses and Lettice Hanlin.

Elizabeth, born . . . baptised May 5, 1794, parents, Capt. Andrew and Jane Morris.

David, born January 17, 1790, baptised May 6, 1794, parents, John and Rebecca Patterson from St. James.

Margret, born April 25, 1792, baptised May 6, 1794, parents, John and Rebecca Petterson, from St. James.

Mary, born May 15, 1794, baptised June 22, 1794, parents, Thomas and Margret Cartmell.

Mary Ellison, born June 9, 1794, baptised July 3rd, parents, Abraham and Elizabeth Broom.

William, born May 21, 1794, baptised July 10, 1794, parents, Hance and Mary Naff.

Cathrine, born February 5, 1794, baptised July 28, 1794, parents, Isaac and Mary Morton.

Hugh, born September 25, 1793, baptised August 4, 1794, parents, Edward and Sarah McGonagill.

Rachel, born July 8, 1794, baptised August 17, 1794, parents, Levi and Rebecca Springer.

Ann, born . . . baptised September 8, 1794, parents, John Vandever Jr. and Alse.

John, born November 25, 1792, baptised September 8, 1794, parents, Garret and Elizabeth Lawrence.

Samuel, born December 14, 1793, baptised September 9, 1794, parents, David and Sarah Shutterly.

Michael, born August 8, 1794, baptised September 11th, parents, Michael and Jane Morrow.

Elizabeth, born August 4, 1794, baptised September 12th, parents, John and Hannah, Flin.

EARLY CHURCH RECORDS OF NEW CASTLE COUNTY

John, born December 19th, 1792, baptised September 22, 1794, parents, ... Watson.

Elizabeth, born April 13, 1794, baptised October 12th, parents, Benjamin and Susanna Elliott.

George, born June 29, 1794, baptised October 25th, parents, Richard and Margret Reynolds.

Stewart, born August 18, 1794, baptised October 25th, parents, Robert and Cathrine Henderson.

Eleanor, born August 21, 1794, baptised October 25th, parents, Irish people.

Mary, born February 2, 1794, baptised November 16, 1794, parents, George and Sophia Beatty,

James, illegitimate born September 14, 1793, baptised November 22, 1794, parents, Mildred Gorral and James Booth.

William Henry, born August 14, 1794, baptised November 23rd, parents, John and Mary Vining.

Robert, born ——, baptised December 23, 1794, parents, William and Ann Sharp.

John Paxton, born April 2, 1794, baptised March 2, 1795, parents, George and Elizabeth Hawkins.

Cornelius, born November 20, 1794, baptised March 3, 1795, parents, Peter and Elizabeth Stedham.

James, born July 5, 1794, baptised November 2d, parents, John and Mary West.

1795.

Thomas Hanson Bellach, born February 20, 1794, baptised March 11, 1795, parents, Daniel Jennifer and Ann Adams.

Maria, born August 12, 1794, baptised March 22, 1795, parents, John and Rachel Dresser.

Julian, born November 23, 1794, baptised April 6, 1795, parents, Nathaniel and Juliana Phillips.

Catharine, born January 24, 1795, baptised April 8th, parents, Margret Craig and Charles Hill.

Anna, born November 27, 1794, baptised April 21, 1795, parents, John and Elenor Brynberg.

Ingabar, born . . . , baptised May 30, 1795, parents, Jonas Stedham Jr., and Ingaber.

Charles, born April 25, 1795, baptised June 20th, parents, Benjamin and Mary Rumsey.

James, born August 25, 1794, baptised July 9, 1795, parents, Christopher and Rosina Smith.

OLD SWEDES CHURCH

Esther Cox, born June 3, 1795, baptised July 19th, by Rev. Robert Clay in the Church ; parents, Joseph and Rachel Clarkson.

James, born February 12, 1795, baptised July 29th, parents, John and Ann Gordon, Irish people.

Stephen, born August 19, 1795, baptised September 4, 1795, parents, Abraham and Elizabeth Eves.

Sarah, born August 12, 1795, baptised September 4, 1795, parents, Mr. and Mrs. Grey.

Jacob, born June 16, 1795, baptised September 6th, parents, Jacob Colesberry, Jr., and Margret.

Rachel, born . . . , baptised September 20th, parents, John and Rachel Robinett.

John Clark, born August 14, 1794, baptised September 20, 1795, parents, Samuel and Elizabeth Boots.

Cathrine McBriarty, born October 13, 1779, baptised September 20, 1795, orphan.

Mary, born May 6, 1795, baptised October 11th, parents, John and Sarah German, from St. James'.

George, born September 28, 1795, baptised October 16th, parents, George and Sarah Mills.

James Lewis, born March 28, 1795, baptised October 16th, parents, Richard and Patience Grimes.

Cathrine, born September 12, 1795, baptised October 25th, parents, Richard and Tilly Thompson.

Henry Pearce, born December 31, 1793, baptised November 5, 1795, parents, Joseph and Mary Capelle.

Catharine Garretson, wife of Peter Garretson, born August 22 1770, baptised November 8, 1795.

Henry, born March 14, 1795, baptised November 8th, parents, Peter and Cathrine Garretson.

John Price, born October 14, 1794, baptised November 12, 1795, parents, David and Elizabeth Bush.

John, born July 23, 1791, baptized September 3rd, 1795, parents, Isaac and Elizabeth Crawford.

Sarah, born November 23, 1793, baptized September 3, 1795, parents, Isaac and Elizabeth Crawford.

1796.

John, born November 5, 1795, baptized January 20, 1796, parents, Hugh and Wilhelmina McCulloch.

Alce, wife of John Vandever, Jr., about 31 years of age, baptized January 24, 1796.

EARLY CHURCH RECORDS OF NEW CASTLE COUNTY

John, born November 23, 1794, baptized January 24, 1796, parents, Alce and John Vandever.

Alce, born January 15, 1796, baptized January 24, 1796, parents, Alce and John Vandever.

The following six children of John and Alce Vandever, were baptized by the Rev. Dr. Wharton at different times, but were never entered on the church books, which I am now desired to do.

Rebecca, born March 17, 1785.

Tobias, born December 1, 1786.

Jane, born March 9, 1788.

Thomas, born August 14, 1789.

Mary, born November 16, 1790.

Sarah, born April 13, 1792.

William, born November 6, 1794, baptized January 25, 1796, parents, John and Rebecca Elliott.

Sarah, born March 11, 1795, baptized January 25, 1796, parents, John and Margret Welsh.

Margaret, born May 25, 1795, baptized February 7, 1796, parents, Jacob and Henry Morgan, negroes.

Ann, born December 28, 1795, baptized March 11, 1796, parents, Jacob and Christiana Justice.

Margret Heath, born July 31, 1796, baptized March 20th, parents, Hance and Mary Naff.

Jesse, born . . . , baptized April 3, 1796, parents, Levi and Mary Walraven.

James, born . . . , baptized April 3, 1796, parents, George and Unity Johnson.

Margret, born March 25, 1796, baptized April 12th, parents, Andrew and Isabella Lindsey.

Priscilla, born January 3, 1796, baptized May 1, 1796, parents, Isaac and Elizabeth Crawford.

James, born December 10, 1793, baptized May 11, 1796, parents, Dr. James and Elizabeth Sykes.

William Ennalls, born January 22, 1796, baptized May 11, 1796, parents, Dr. James and Elizabeth Sykes.

Sarah, born March 4, 1796, baptized May 17, parents, David and Sarah Shutterly.

OLD SWEDES CHURCH

Sarah, born April 14, 1796, baptized May 24th, parents, Joseph and Catharine Wallin.

Robert Till, about 36 years of age,
Jane, his wife, about 32 years of age,
Mary, born July 2, 1791,
Elizabeth, born March 21, 1793,
Ann, born February 1, 1796,
 Two black people, free, and their children, baptized May 28, 1796.

John Justa, born Mary 12, 1796, baptized June 2d, parents, John and Mary Wallraven.

Catharine, born September 18, 1789,
Lavianah, born January 30, 1793,
Sarah, born February 19, 1795,
 Baptized June 26, 1796, parents, Jeremiah and Mary Springer.

Bishop, born . . . , baptised September 11, 1796, parents Peter and Betty Vandever.

Rhoda Coram, widow of Robert Coram, born February, 1768, baptized September 19, 1796, with her three children as folfows :
John Robert, born March 4, 1791,
Ann, born July 9, 1793,
Elizabeth, born March 23, 1796,
 Baptized September, 19, 1796.

Lydia Ann, born November 22, 1792,
Elizabeth Mary, born May 1, 1795,
 Baptized September 19, 1796, parents, Henry and Mary Pepper.

Simon, born February 25, 1793,
Margret, born February 20, 1796,
 Baptized September 25, 1796, parents, John and Margret Foote.

Lewis, born February 5, 1789,
John, born July 20, 1790,
 Baptized by Rev. Robert Clay, parents, John and Margret Foote.

Mary, born October 12, 1791,   Samuel, born February 18, 1795,
Jane, born December 19, 1793,   Robert, born June 18, 1796,
 Baptized September 29, 1796, parents, James and Margret Welsh.

EARLY CHURCH RECORDS OF NEW CASTLE COUNTY

James, born September 3, 1796, baptized September 30, 1796, parents, James and Mary Eves.

Sarah, born March 25, 1796, baptized October 2, 1796, parents, Richard and Margret Reynolds.

George, born September 27, 1796, baptized October 10th, parents, George and Sarah Mills.

James, born July 19, 1791, baptized October 23, 1796, parents, James, and Margret Goodfellow, in St. James' Church.

Mary, born December 1, 1793, baptized October 25th, parents, . . . Mary Thompson, in St. James' Church.

Martin, born July 21, 1796, baptized October 25th, parents, Martin and Mary Connor.

Abraham and Elizabeth, born October 4, 1796, baptized October 27th, parents, Abraham and Elizabeth Eves.

John, born September 27, 1796, baptized November 3d, parents, John and Hannah Fling.

Joseph Webb, born April 6, 1760, baptized November 4, 1796.

Rachel, born August 10, 1786, baptized November 4, 1796, parents, John and Margret Reed.

John, born 1796, baptized November 18, 1796. The mother a young black wench belonging to widow Rumsey, father, John Hill, a mulatto.

Elizabeth, born July 5, 1796, baptized November, 30th, parents, Rees and Mary Springer.

Sarah, born September 13, 1793, baptized December 13, 1796, parents, Benjamin and Ann Burrell.

1797.

Catharine, born July 25, 1796, baptized January 1, 1797, parents, Jacob Colesbury, Jr,, and Margret.

Eliza, illegitimate, December 7, 1796, baptized January 11, 1797, parents, Savoy James Ross.

John, born September 27, 1796, baptized January 20, 1797, parents, Henry and Rachel Sinex.

Margret, born February 3, 1777,
James, born March 1, 1779,
Mary, born . . .
William, born January 2, 1783,
Hannah, born January 3, 1785,
Jacob, born January 19, 1789,
John, born February 2, 1792,
Ann, born December 19, 1796,

Baptized January 28, 1797, parents, John and Hannah Welch.

OLD SWEDES CHURCH

Thomas, born May 25, 1796, baptized January 28, 1797, parents, Christopher and Rosina Smith.

Thomas, born November 13, 1796, baptized February 26th, 1797, parents, Thomas and Margret Cartmell.

Mary, born July 4, 1776, baptized August 4, . .
Isaac, born November 8, 1780, baptized January 1, 1781,
Catharine, born July 24, 1785, baptized May 24, 1786,
Gustavas, born May 5, 1792, baptized June 4th,
  parents, Jacob and Christiana Justice or Justison.

Orpah, born July 1, 1791, baptised March 4, 1797, parents, George and Mary Dunn.

Marian, born February 20, 1794, baptised March 4, 1797, parents, George and Mary Dunn.

Nathaniel, born October 8, 1795, baptised March 4, 1797, parents, George and Mary Dunn.

Christiana, born March 1, 1797, baptised March 12th, parents, John and Cathrine Peden.

Judy, born . . , a black woman in my family, about 48 years of age, baptised March 9, 1797.

William, born February 6, 1797, baptised April 2, 1797 parents, Robert and Jane Till.

William, born May 2, 1796, baptised April 4, 1797, parents, Josias and Jane Thompson.

William, born February 8, 1797, baptised May 7, 1797, parents, John and Jane Bernard.

William, born January 16, 1796, baptised 14th, parents, Richard and Mary Edgington.

Thomas, born April 24, 1788, baptised June 5, 1797, parents, Wm. and Mary Smith.

Joseph, born January 14, 1790, baptised June 5, 1797, parents, Wm. and Mary Smith.

Margaret, born March 3, 1792, baptised June 5, 1797, parents, Wm. and Mary Smith.

Rebecca, born September, 21, 1795, baptised June 5, 1797, parents, Wm. and Mary Smith,

George, born January 5, 1797, baptised June 5, 1797, parents, Samuel and Mary Harris.

John, born January 1, 1797, baptised June 26th, parents, James and Hannah Smith.

Isaac, born April 23, 1796,. baptised June 28, 1797, parents, Alexander and Sarah Harvey.

Samuel, born July 18, 1796, baptised July 12, 1797, parents, John and Mary West.

Charles, born June 19, 1797, baptised July 23, 1797, parents, Levi and Rebecca Springer.

Abner, born March 29, 1797, baptised July 30, 1797, parents, Aaron and Sarah Justice.

Eleanor, born September 27, 1793, baptised August, 1797, parents, Richard and Patience Graham.

Sarah, born April 10, 1797, baptised August, 1797, parents, Richard and Patience Graham.

George born March 28, 1796, baptised August 3, 1797, parents, Robert and Catharine Henderson.

Hugh, born June 25, 1797, baptised August 3, 1797, parents, Thomas and Eliza Gifford.

Jane, born July 12, 1797, at sea, baptised August 3, 1797, parents, Matthew and Eleanor Smith.

William, born July 22, 1797, baptised August 3, 1797, parents, Robert and Mary Lennon.

Elias, born June 11, 1797, baptised . . , illegitimate.

Elizabeth born September 20, 1794, baptised September 3, 1797, parents, Thomas and Ann Cole.

Thomas, born June 7, 1797, baptised September 3, 1797, parents Thomas and Ann Cole.

Catharine, born February 27, 1797, baptised October 6, 1797. parents, Lucas and Catharine Wallraven.

Elizabeth, born June 21, 1797, baptised October 31, 1797, parents, Thomas and Ann Bard.

Henry, born September 13, 1797, baptised November 12th, parents, James and Ann Johnston.

Thomas, born May 15, 1797, baptised November 26th, parents, Jacob and Henry Morgan, black people.

Harriot Rumsey, born October 4, 1797, baptised November 26th, parents, Joseph and Grace Clarkson.

Mary, born October 19, 1797, baptised December 3, 1797; parents, Jacob and Margret Colesberry.

ANNO 1798.

Thomas Rumsey, born December 8, 1797, baptised January 8, 1798, parents, Abraham and Elizabeth Broom.

Candice, born October 3, 1779, Orpah, born August 2, 1785, Eunice, born May 7, 1782, Sarah, born November 24, 1787, Baptised January 15, 1798, parents, Joseph and Susanna Jackson.

OLD SWEDES CHURCH

Phillip, born November 19, 1793,
Maria, born February 29, 1796,
William, born October 4, 1797,
Baptised January 15, 1798, parents, Joseph and Catharine Jackson.

Samuel, born December 2d, 1797, baptised February 10, 1798, parents, James and Jane Battersby.

Mary, born June 3, 1793,
Sarah, born April 17, 1795,
George, born April 28, 1797,
Baptised March 6th, 1778, parents, George and Ann Cartmell.

Elizabeth, born November 4, 1797, baptised March 6, 1798, parents, Jacob and Susannah Dick.

These last four grandchildren of William Perkins.

John Harp, born February 13, 1798, baptised March 23d, parents, Jacob and Rachel Morton.

David, born February 6, 1798, baptised April 9th, May 7, 1798, David and Elizabeth Bush.

Isabella and Staton, born December 19, 1796, baptised May 7, 1798, parents Joshua and Susanna Jefferies.

David, born October 12, 1797, baptised May 9, 1798, parents, David and Sarah Shutterly.

Sarah Windsor, born September 5th, 1796,
John, born March 29, 1798,
Baptised June 3, 1798, at St. James, parents, John and Rachel Robinson.

William, born January 17, 1795,
Reuben, born April 27, 1798,
Baptised June 18, 1798, parents, Esau and Rebecca Sharpley.

Eleanor, born January 27, 1794,
Thomas, born October 27, 1796,
Baptised June 24, 1798, parents; James and Eleanor Ray.

Rebecca, born March 29, 1797, baptised July 18, 1798, parents, William and Nancy Sinex.

Elizabeth, born May 24, 1798, baptised July 22, parents, Zachariah and Susanna Derrickson.

Sarah, born January 1, 1798, baptized July 29, parents, Thomas and Isabel McGloghlin.

John, born February 8, 1793,
Alice, born October 8, 1795,
Baptised August 9, 1798, parents, Thomas and Alice Harris.

EARLY CHURCH RECORDS OF NEW CASTLE COUNTY

William Henry, born September 25, 1795,

Margret Eliza, born November 25, 1797,

Baptized August 10, 1798, parents, Tristram and Susanna Thomas.

John, born November 8, 1797, baptized August 23, 1798, parents, John and Sarah Stille.

Mary, born January 31st,

Peter, born February 1st,

Baptized August 23, 1798, parents, Richard and Margret Reynolds.

John, born September 1, 1797, baptized September 3, 1798, parents, John and Rachel Robinett,

James, born October 3, 1797, baptized September 3, 1798, parents, Hugh and Wilhelmina McCulloch.

Esther Serena, born September 29, 1797, baptized October 7, 1798, parents, James and Mary Chestnut.

John, born July 21, 1798, baptized November 11, 1798, in St. James' Church, parents, James and Margret Goodfellow.

James, born September 24, 1798, baptized November 22, 1798, parents, James and Hannah Smith.

Johanna, born November 20, 1798, baptized November 27, 1798, parents, George and Sarah Mills.

Charlotte Mary, born August 16, 1798, baptized December 2, 1798, parents, John Baptist and Ann Orson.

Martha, born . . . , 1798, baptized December 2, 1798, December 2, 1798, also a black child.

Mary Ann, born March 30, 1793,

Benjamin John, born September 25, 1795,

Baptised December 6, 1798, parents, Benjamin and Ann Holmes.

John, born October 9, 1796,   Susan, born October 2, 1798,

Baptized December 25, 1798, parents, James and Sarah McClure.

James, born August 15, 1798, baptized December 31, 1798, parents, James and Mary Eves.

Charles Havens, born September 4, 1798, baptized January 17, 1799, parents, Wm. Chadwick, son of Charles and Catharine, maiden name Oyen.

Arquilla, born January 17, 1795, baptized January 20, 1799, parents, John and Mary Nebeckar.

Hannah, born November, 5, 1796, baptized January 20, 1799, parents, Jonas and Ingaber Stedham.

OLD SWEDES CHURCH

Maria Randolph, born May 11, 1798, baptized February 15, 1799, parents, Roger and Margret McClinchey.

George Washington, born February 1, 1799, baptized February 17, 1799, parents, Thomas and Eleanor Campbell.

Ann, born October 2, 1796,
John, born February 22, 1799,
Baptized March 6, 1799, parents, John and Mary Martin.

Henry Augustus, born June 14, 1793,
Edward Eugene, born November 18, 1795,
Baptized April 22, 1798, parents, Gabriel H. and Frances Ford.

Lewis Dunham, born March 28, 1796, baptized April 22, 1798, parents, Theodorus and Jane Tuthill.

William Alexander, born April 14, 1798,
Sarah . . . . , born August 27, 1796,
Edward . . . . , born February 21, 1794,
Baptized April 22, 1798, parents, William and Hannah Campfield.

ANNO 1799.

Jesse, born June 17, 1798, baptised March 16, 1799, parents, Robert and Jane Till, black people.

Thomas, aged 17 years, baptised October 2, 1798, parents, James and Ann Ogle.

James, aged 14 years, baptised October 2, 1798, parents, James and Ann Ogle.

Martha, aged 10 years, baptised October 2, 1798, parents, James and Ann Ogle.

Patrick, aged 13 years; Jude, aged 3¼ years; Michael, aged 13 months, black children belonging to Dr. McMechen, baptised October 2, 1798,

Christopher, born December 31, 1798, baptised April 30, 1799, parents, Christopher and Catharine Smith.

Maria Robinson, born April 15, 1799, baptised May 12th, parents, Aaron and Sarah Justice.

Andrew, born January 5, 1799, baptised May 16, 1799, parents, John and Jane Bernard.

James, born February 10, 1799, baptised May 16, 1799, parents, John and Isabel McCloskey.

Elizabeth, born November 24, 1797, baptised May 16, 1799, parents, William and Ann Vanneman.

Thomas, born October 15, 1796, baptised May 16, 1799, parents, John and Rebecca Elliott.

John, born August 16, 1798, baptised May 16, 1499, parents, John and Rebecca Elliott.

Mary, born March 10, 1799, baptised May 16, 1799, parents, James and Margret Jacks.

Mary, born September 22, 1799, baptised May 16, 1799, parents, Jeremiah and Elizabeth Branhan.

BAPTISMS CONTINUED, 1799, ENTERED BY HANCE NAFF, WARDEN.

Isabella Welsh, born April 7, 1798, baptised April 7, 1799, by Rev. Mr. Wilmer, parents, —— and Ann Burrell.

Maria Ann, born October 9, 1798, baptised April 28, 1799, by Rev. L. Heath, parents, John and Elizabeth Derrickson.

Eliza Ann, born May 17, 1799, baptised June 30, 1799, by Rev. Mr. Wilmer, parents, Hance and Mary Naff.

MARRIAGES BY ISRAEL ACRELIUS.

(Those designated by a star belong to the congregation. L means license.)

1750.

January.
1. Rudolph Sweitman and Margaret Tespene.
8. Andrew Beard and Elizabeth Connnelly.
23. Alexander McCrackon and Abigail Fail.
23. *Jesper Justice and Susanna Hindrickson,
31. Hesekias Hall and Elizabeth Bemaund.

February.
8. John Keys and Mary Grey.
13. *John Seeds and Bridget Andersson.
18. Philip Welch and Alice Kilbreth.
21. Joseph Fourseides and Mary Dimond.

March.
19. James Toben and Ester Smidt.
20. John Wickers and Alice Kyle.
23. John Maxfield and Ann Patton. L
24. Matthew McLaughlin and Ann Han.
27. Wm. Clendinen and Elenor Ellot.
28. John Wooodward and Hannah Brinton. L

April.
10. Cornelius Hart and Margret Tuker.
17. Joseph Ja Quette and Susanna Ja Quette. L
22. John Greenup and Mary Sarenteen.
28. Timothy Bullock and Cathrine Gray.
30. Benjamin Moore and Elizabeth Patton.

OLD SWEDES CHURCH

May.
    7. William Forquher and Jane Noble.
    9. Jeremiah Cloud and Lady Harlin. L
    9. Wm. McCay and Rebecca Smidt. L
    19. John Mirix and Elizabeth Marton.
    20. Richard Middleton and Rachel Sukorin.
    21. John Boggan and Hannah Grist.
    21. John Tate and Mary Dalle.
    31. James Reed and Mary Worrilow.
    31. Nicolas Norris and Mary Donny.

June.
    3. Thomas Dean and Hannah Hays.
    4. Jacob Jackson and Elizabeth Bollow.
    12. Wm. Bradin and Rebecca Bird. L
    16. Philip Dale and Mary Savin..
    27. John Wills and Elizabeth King.
    27. Wm. Ferguson and Jane Allen. L

July.
    14. Patrick Coyle and Jane Forquar.
    15. George Bate and Tamzin Betts.
    17. John Clarke and Mary Willsson.

August.
    4. John Young and Ann Cowen.
    5. John Pettigrew and Cicely Jones.
    6. Wm. Nooks and Hannah Ericks.
    7. John Jack and Elizabeth Creithon. L
    9. Robert Gilbreth and Jennet Weldin. L
    12. Wm. Goodwind and Huldah Garritsson.
    21. Gabriel Clark and Margret Newman.
    23. Timothy McCheever and Mary Gallion.
    27. John Neely and Elizabeth Dean.
    28. John Erwin and Lady Rudger. L

September.
    3. John Hamilton and Ann Davidsson.
    16. Thomas Herbert and Sara Cartmell.
    26. *Johan Paulsson and Elizabeth Stedham.
    27. Wm. McKey and Martha Peoples.

October.
    1. Wm. Odivars and Mary Egen.
    2. Robert Berney and Margret Hamilton.
    8. James Rowan and Cathrine McGennis.
    18. Thomas Adams and Ann Garritsson.

EARLY CHURCH RECORDS OF NEW CASTLE COUNTY

19. William Paulsson and Mary Tremble. L
22. David Duton and Janna McClasky.
26. Robert Lyon and Mary Crook.
31. James Masters and Susanna Cann.
31. Joseph Perce and Mary Earby.

November.
5. Alexander McKeel and Mary Greer.
7. Benjamin Orin and Elizabeth Sharpe.
11. Mark Cowin and Elizabeth Bell.
12. Justa Justice and Rebecca Hearsson.
14. Thomas Millsson and Martha Way.
19. *Moses White and Marta Hurtehe.

December.
2. Joshua Frost and Ann Linn.
5. Patrick Mullen and Mary Perkins. L
6. Peter Hedge and Elizabeth Seeds. L
11. Charles Holeman and Cathrine Burns.
12. Ephraim McKilleb and Cathrine Sanderson.
18. Wm. Huston and Margret Burns.
18. *Jonas Stedham and Mary Colesberg.
26. John Campbell and Sarah Bowles.
26. John Stedham and Mary Merryman.
27. Daniel Casnay and Ann Moore.

January. 1751.
1. Joseph Jones and Deborah Robinsson. L
1. Adam Sneider and Catharine Breinigern.
4. James Oliver and Cathrine Gordon.
10. James Killen and Anne Duard. L
10. Evan Goss and Hannah Wuker
17. Robert Jackson and Anne McDougle.
22. Justa Walraven and Sarah Wallraven. L
24. Joseph Cloud and Sarah Poile.
30. Isaac Starr and Mary Flower. L
31. Nicholas Moore and Margret Ericks. L

February.
3. Stephen Pyle and Elizabeth Ash.
6. Levy Geogory and Elizabeth Bate.
7. Charles Gordon and Hannah Ward.
7. John Baldwin and Margret York.
21. John Kary and Elizabeth Bisen. L
26. Enos Lewis and Susanna Woodeth.
28. William Bracken and Sarah Garrit. L

OLD SWEDES CHURCH

March.
1. David Loque and Elizabeth Harlin. L
5. John Fisher and Margret Gubbens.
11. Cain McKinni and Mary Hiery.
19. Abel Bork and Sarah Fowlsand.
25. James Bogges and Margret Sharp.
26. James McGarvay and Leane Pettecrow.

April. Apr. 26 Josesph Vernon and Sarah Bennett
4. John Stewart and Mary McDouel. L
8. Harry McCloski and Margret Monagle.
9. Philip McGowen and Mary Preston.
9. Andrew Justis and Mary Justis, L
10. Samuel Brooks and Mary Colains.
13. Charles Porter and Elizabeth Evenson.. L
17. Thomas McDonald and Mary McCorday.
25. Isaac Barton and Sarah Waldon. L
29. William Hews and Rebecca Gregory. L
29. Francis Graham and Juda Carbre.
29. Zebulon Alexander and Hannah Hodgesson. L

May.
4. Charles Cartay and Elizabeth Porter.
5. Thomas Ganday and Elizabeth Colier.
11. William Stuart and Sarah Downing. L
12. Henry Watson and Mary Haycock. L
13. Patrick Fich Patrick and Mary Patterson.
13. Archibald McCollough and Elizabeth Lawson. L
14. Robert Davis and Jane Latta.
18. Isaac Low and Grace Aderthon.
19. John Odiorn and Elizabeth Smidt.
20. Patrick McMollholland and Sarah Baller.

June.
1. Andrew Renceer and Aknes Walles.
2. John Coope and Grace Cloud. L
2. Thomas Duff and Jane Williams. L
5. John Springer and Sarah Walraven. L
6. Thomas Mahan and Marta Ball.
25. Andrew Loinan and Sarah Hall.
25. Jacob Andersson and Mary Loinan.

July.
12. James Mundel and Margaret Garrit. L
20. James Pollyk and Margret Hays.
28. Elias Neeld and Sarah Green. L
30. William Blewit and Sarah Garden.

217

EARLY CHURCH RECORDS OF NEW CASTLE COUNTY

August.
    1. Samuel Dixson and Mary Dixson. L
    2. Joseph Weldin and Margret Robinson. L
    4. Swen Brunberg and Anne Pierce. L
    13. John Sadler and Jane Logan. L
    21. Edward King and Elizabeth Nicols.
    24. John Lean and Jane Howel.
    24. Daniel Finnin and Elinor Dougherty.
    25. John Williams and Anne Carr.

September.
    5. James Kirk and Jane Wessels.
    8. Joseph Seeds and Rachel Proctor. L
    10. Hans Naff and Cathrina Landsbreck.
    12. John Wilson and Margret Sharp. L
    12. John Anderson and Elizabeth Orr. L
    14. James Foreside and Margret Wheel. L
    15. Samuel Ronalds and Grace Woods.
    19. John Brackin and Cathrina Adams. L
    23. John Chevin and Hannah Little.
    26. Edward Richards and Margret Hogin. L
    26. Andrew James and Cathrine Heinman. L
    27. Jacob Bennet and Susanna Born. L

October.
    3. Samuel Beaton and Cathrina Walker.
    7. John McFarlan and Anne Michel.
    8. William Carre and Margret Aspe. L
    13. Isaac England and Anne Evans.
    13. Peter Hatton and Sarah Poyle. L
    14. William Webb and Margret Chartton. L
    15. James Heyd and Anne Woods.
    21. Alexander Wilson and Anne Floyd.
    24. James Humphris and Jane Hill.
    24. Patrick Winters and Elinor Peril.
    24. James Ewing and Jannet Hall.
    24. Swen Justis and Mary Paulsson. L
    24. John Lewis and Margret Lampradin.
    28. Thomas Orkaner and Mary Dow.
    31. Olove Parlin and Elizabeth Tranberg. L

November.
    6. Jeremias Collet and Mary Stedham. L
    17. James Clements and Elizabeth Spencer.
    18. William Ligget and Else Thornberg.
    23. Daniel Welsh and Anne Heald.

OLD SWEDES CHURCH

25. Andrew Crossar and Annable McDonald

December.
2. John Markhon and Mary Skott.
5. William Van Neman and Johanna Hore L
9. John McDerry and Mary Truffis
9. Thomas Babb and Sarah Bishop.
10. Robert Carter and Susanna Sorell. L.
12. William Maxwell and Jane Aken. L
20. Andrew Dickie and Elizabeth McDowel. L
21. Edward Dougherty and Anna Cassidy.
24. James McCombs and Else Lattimore. L
26. John Webster and Hannah Way. L
28. William Ramsey and Susanna Wollaston. L

1752.

January.
7. Robert Nilsson and Elizabeth Lenzy.
24. William Boyce and Mary Carter.

February.
6. John Audley and Anne Claesson. L
11. Richard Morrow and Martha Thomsson.
11. Isaac Gibbs and Ingeborg Stedham. L
12. James Burnside and Grizell Bourges.
16. Mathew Harrow and Elizabeth McNeel.
21. Philip Poyle and Hannah Baldwin.
23. John Barber and Elizabeth Quinn.
24. Charles Higsson and Mary Little
27. Adolph Benzel and Rebecca Tranberg. L

March.
8. George Harris and Bule House.
9. William Haughey and Susanna Pettett.
16. Henry Nail and Catharine Mosseth.
17. Fredrick Boom and Rachel Lawson.
17. James McDonald and Rosina Ross.
30. James Hanly and Elizabeth Hossford.

April.
2. Abraham Stroud and Lucretia Ogle. L
5. John Smidt and Jane McNemee.
6. Charles Bradley and Mary Jefreys.
7. Charles Springer and Susanna Seeds. L
9. Charles Springer and Anne Ogle. L
11. Peter Glansey and Mary McNail.

25. Thomas Williams and Mary Nealy.
May.
  7. Cloud Lyon and Darkes Warden.
  7. John Tossa and Miss Culen.
 10. James Allis and Elizabeth McMullon.
 10. William Krawker and Margret McKoll.
 11. John Gordon and Mary Andrews.
 21. Edward King and Marget Justisson.
 22. Michal Meloy and Else Flean. L
 24. Israel Stalcop and Anne Senex. L
 27. Tobias Paulsson and Margret Walraven. L
June.
  2. John Delap and Elizabeth Fear.
 14. Samuel Rusel and Mary Moore.
 18. John Claesson and Mary Hore. L
 22. James Leatsh and Sarah Johnston.
 22. Davisson Filson and Elinor Clarke. L
 25. Chambears Hall and Rebecca Champion. L
 25. Daniel Few and Christeen Petersson. L
 26. John Carson and Ester Cloud.
 30. Perce Pottitt and Brigit Swensson.
July.
 13. Alexander Miller and Beata Turner. L
 14. John McCoy and Martha Ling.
 26. John Hunt and Hannah Jefreys. L
 26. Joseph Delap and Mary Barker.
 26. Joseph Tull and Sarah Bratton.
 31. John Brown and Mary Heth
August.
  1. Joshua Speakman and Anne Miller. L
  1. Hugh Clark and Martha Jordan
  3. Michael Robertsson and Mary Daugherty.
    David Dean and Elizabeth Weldin.
    Thomas Fling and Mary Flower. L
  6. Benjamin Abraham and Elizabeth Goheen.
    Edward Couchren and Jemymy Garritsson.
    Edward McDonald and Mary Robinson. L
  8. William Montgomery and Mary Hall.
 17. James Reinhold and Mary Clark.
    Edward McSorrly and Mary Cauhoon.
 18. Thomas Bennett and Jane Mathers.
 20. William Armstrong and Mary Mains.
 26. John Isaacs and Rachel Kain.

OLD SWEDES CHURCH

October.
   19. Thomas Swan and Jane Moore. L
   27. John Jackson and Cathrine McFersan. L
   31. John Nisbith and Hannah Wickerson.
November.
   2. William McAllen and Elenor Clerk.
      John Piper and Sarah Busbin.
   4. Thomas Edmund and Mary Jeffrin
      Henry Thomson and Else Cloud. L
      John Wilson and Mary Hall.
   6. William Evans and Elizabeth Mills.
   13. John Harper and Hannah Cloud.
      John Harway and Mary Carson.
   15. Jesper Walraven and Christina Peterson.
   21. Samuel Pennel and Rachel Cobown. L
   29. Timothy Karenoss and Cathy Donolly.
December.
   5. Archibald Wattson and Prudence Richard.
   11. Thomas Gray and Hannah Richardson. L
   16. Abraham Yarnall and Elizabeth James. L
   17. Edward Robinson and Ingebor Sennex. L
   18. James McCulley and Elizabeth Callwell . L
   19. George Alcorn and Rose Anne Adger.
   27. David Broomal and Mary Taylor.
      James Hunter and Sarah Hunter.
      John Marshall and Mary Nickland. L

ANNO 1753.

January.
   4. John Huey and Elizabeth Morgan.
   6. Wm. Sutton and Sarah Turner. L
   7. Hugh Peoples and Abigail Poyle.
   10. John Benderman and Jane Cunningham.
   12. Thomas Bussington and Mary Harlin. L
   14. Wm. Ogglesby and Mary Pierson.
      John Bass and Else Boyd.
   18. Wm. Peton and Hannah Jones.
   19. Joseph Pierce and Jane Hudson. L
   25. Philip Fits Somens and Mary McMolland. L
   30. George Keeth and Ann Melimon. L
February.
   13. Isaac Smidt and Sarah Anderson. L
   19. Philip Truax and Sarah Shaw.

26. John Fox and Mary Hamphill.
27. Charles White and Margret Culen.
28. Patrick Mooney and Jane Beard.

March.
27. John McLewy and Lady Richardson.
28. James Alder and Elizabeth McCook.
29. Edward Gillen and Rebecca Garritson.

April.
5. Mardochay Cloud and Roda Richards.
12. Samuel Seeds and Mary Brunberg.
21. James Donnerthy and Agnes Croshy.
23. Wm. Davis and Cathrine Fraid.
30. John Davis and Jane Lauden.

May.
1. David McJennet and Mary Thomas.
9. John Kimler and Margaret Evans.
10. Robert Hebets and Annie Hunter.
13. George Owens and Mary Stephens.
24. Daniel VanCourt and Mary Jackson. L

June.
6. Samuel Barker and Rachel Ball. L
11. James Stewart and Margret Bently.
    John Marce and Elizabeth Mandee.
12. Matthew Kelly and Jane Stotts.
14. Hugh Stewart and Faithful Walker.
15. Wm. Horn and Ruth Falkinton.
28. James Koll and Susanna Richards.

July.
14. Jonathan Kirk and Jane Proctor.
16. Nathan Scothorn and Mary Thomas. L
17. Laurentz Mannom and Margaret Nichols.
25. Edward Pilkinton and Margret Casy.
26. Christopher Linn and Rachel Mallawedy.
30. James Raily and Jane Richardson.

August.
12. John Engrum and Rebecca Owen.
 . Joseph Hayes and Joanna Pastmore. L
15. John Martin and Anne Carnay.
20. Jeremiah Sulivane and Briget Welch.
21. Joseph Mercer and Jane Swane. L
22. David Pugh and Elizabeth Cloud.
23. Samuel Jaquette and Martha McConnell.

OLD SWEDES CHURCH

30. John Stedham and Mary Won.

September.
 3. Andrew McCaslin and Dorothy Foster.
 18. John Davis and Nanze Fisher.
 21. Francis Johnson and Elizabeth Philips.
 29. Benjamin Tergo and Mary Pyle.

October.
 4. Thomas Morten and Sarah Senecce.
 Peter Jaquette and Margret Ford.
 14. Walter Nugent and Sarah Garitson.
 16. Abraham Pike and Elenore Cobern. L
 . John Steen and Mary Ford.
 21. Charles Justis and Rebecca Robinson. L
 28. Cornelius Waugh and Mary Thomson.

November.
 3. Samuel Forard and Mary Heig.
 5. Wm. White and Susanna Thornberg.
 6. Joseph Rotheram and Lydea Wollaston. L
 22. Eric Smidt and Brigito Andersdotter. L
 25. Adam Grubb and Mary Rossell. L
 Thomas McFadien and Susanna Kirk.

November.
 27. George Brinton and Ester Matlock. L
 30. John Willson and Margret Killen. L.

December.
 9. Samuel Underwood and Mary Kimber.
 11. Joseph McClosky and Agnes Huston.
 16. David Derick and Mary January. L.
 20. Joseph Inloc and Margret Janes. L.
 Joseph Neide and Amalay Bunker. L.
 26. John Newbrough and Elinore McClure.

ANNO 1754.

January.
 2. Matthew Mayer and Elizabeth Fuldam.
 14. James Tully and Nally Holland.
 22. Peter Morton and Hannah Richardson.
 William Ford and Ann Johnson. L.
 24. Joshua North and Susanna Emsson. L.
 27. Daniel McLonen and Darkes McGhee. L.
 31. John Laurentz and Jane Hamilton.

February.
 14. William McKeeson and Elizabeth McPeeck.

17. Joseph McDonald and Elizabeth Oggle. L.
18. John Hargrove and Cathrine Gready.
19. Magnus Justis and Helena Peterson.

March.
8. Archibald Harvey and Cathrine Robinson.
26. John Andrews and Agnes Ewing. L.
30. William Shanklin and Elizabeth Donne.
31. James Collier and Hannah Davis.

April.
2. Hugh Johnson and Eleonor Wilkinson.
William Scaggin and Anne Ratchford.
9. James Barber and Mary Ramsey.
11. John Brock and Mary Moore.
Curtis Grubb and Anne Few.
14. Edward Pain and Margret White. L.
15. Hugh Leach and Jane Forster.
17. Thomas Garritson and Jane Ferris.
18. William Lewis and Anne Montgomery. L.
William Norris and Rebecca White.
29. Joseph Poyl and Ruth Hays.

May.
2. Isaiah Matlock and Mary Hunter. L.
5. Nathaniel Falconer and Sarah Moulder. L.
James Condron and Johanna Allen.
7. William Whetherow and Mary McCloskey.
9. Jacob Richards and Rachel Ruth. L.
William Tunkes and Catharine Cassidy.
Philip Phillips and Barbro Hollingsworth.
12. Thomas Hamilton and Rose Crawssin.
27. John McCalmont and Sarah Latimer. L.
30. James Davis and Patience Bishop.

June.
3. John Chalflint and Else Paul.
James Baxter and Grace Reinolds.
6. Peter Springer and Rebecca Justis.
7. Matthias Peterson and Mary Anderson.
23. George Porter and Rebecca Piloin.
25. John Henderson and Elizabeth Steel. L.
27. Matthias Sullivane and Prudence Gillmore.
29. Thomas Evans and Isabella **Poke.**

July.
Lin McDermott and Mary Wood.
1. James Vaugh and Catharine McNeil.

OLD SWEDES CHURCH

    4. James Johnson and Mary Grist.
   11. David Harris and Elizabeth Springer.
   13. Nathan Roberts and Sarah Eastbourn. L.
   20. Robert Low and Martha Conally.
   31. William Brobson and Judith Dael.

August.
    1. Robert Lowry and Elizabeth Bary.
       Joseph Boyd and Mary Robbinson.
    4. Johann Ernest Jacobi and Sobina Donderin.
    4. John Senece and Anne Robinson. L.
    9. John Ebent Steygerwolt and Anne Cathrine Hummin.
   14. George Martin and Martha Widdows.
   15. Niclas Welch and Ruth Durnel.
   17. John Peak and Mary Wencourtlin.
   18. Peter Biggeley and Margret **Leina**
       James Pillion and Margret Rawson.
   19. Hector Alexander and Margret Young.
   26. John Roberts and Jane Jeffreys.
       Robert King and Sarah Collans.
   28. James Enos and Susanna Van Lewnia.

September.
    1. Henry Senecce and Ann Stalcop.
    2. George Hollis and Margret Sullivane.
    3. John Alexander and Mary Garritson. L
    4. William Durnell and Elizabeth Cleaton.
    5. John Williams Neering and Sarah **Tatlow**
    6. Samuel Hewes and Anne Deer.
    9. James Collet and Margret Smidt.
       Samuel McJunikins and Anne Bogan.
       John Miller and Anne Thomson.
   26. James Camphel and Elenore Lagg.
       John Stille and Elizabeth Ogle. L

October.
    7. John Hans Bad and Sarah Hay.
   15. Stephen Enos and Rebecca Flemmen.
   16. Charles Richardson and Susanna Hayes.
   22. William Brooks and Susanna Willey. L
   18. John Reese and Elizabeth Ball.
   24. William Price and Anne Thomson.
   30. John Lockton and Martha Jacquet. L

November.
    4. John Hopkin and Rachel David.
       Joshua Edwards and Rebecca Ramage.

5. Johnathan Millerson and Anne Mas.
George White and Hannah Welsh.
8. John Powell and Mary Hopes. L
18. William Dixon and Lady Montgomery.

December.
3, James Huston and Jane Ellot.
4. Ferentius Glancy and Elizabeth Collings.
10. James Smidt and Mary Anderson.
11. Joseph Orin and Abigail Kirck.
19. Robert Shannon and Florenz Grahams. L
John Leshley, and Anne Janey. L
23. James Kelly and Sarah McMolland.
24. Richard Sill and Elizabeth Grissell.
25. James English and Mary **Prichard**
26. Laurenz McKlayn and Sarah Griffith.
William Whiteted and Sarah Cleaney.
24. Peter Grubb and Jane Ford.
29. William Stedham and Susanna Breadford.

ANNO 1755.

January.
1. Thomas Clemons and Rebecca **Gennis**
2. Thomas Nelly and Sarah Skott.
13. John Campbell and Margret Downing. L
18. William Smidt and Ann Chandelor. L
20. Christopher Cooper and Elizabeth Henry.
21. Barnabas Sweney and Rebecca Massor.

February.
6. John McClintock and Mary Weir.
10. Ezekiel Bullock and Margret Tool.
13. Peter Wincy and Susanna Patton.
17. Henry Flood and Elizabeth Gordon.
John McCarsley and Elizabeth Curry.
24. James Standley and Bridget Collins.

March.
3. William Martin and Bridget Farell.
4. James McGrady and Margret Colluy.
5. James Burnside and Sarah Pryer.
6. John Hensey and Elizabeth Post.
7. Edward Linwall and Jane Beasley. L
17. Richard White and Mary Naval.
Michael Armstrong and Elenore Daunt.
Daniel Blayr and Mary Price.

OLD SWEDES CHURCH

   20. William Hutchisson and Mary Miller.
   31. John McWay and Mary Thornton.
   David Cushon and Nanzy Landerum.

April.
   1. Isaac Alexander and Jane Ferris.
   19. Isaac Clandonnen and Phœbe Nichols. L
   22. Stephen Smallwood and Mary Hayle.
   John Stuart and Elenore Cook.

May.
   9. Johnathan Valentine and Lady Baldwine. L
   Oliver Cop and Anne McMath.
   Thomas Hutton and Mary Marshall.
   13. Samuel Toon and Mriah Williams.
   14. Joseph Sharp and Franky Willson. L
   16. Moses Burns and Martha Armstrong.
   22. Matthew Lindsay and Mary Logg. L
   31. Robert Thornberry and Ruth Garrman.

June.
   1. James Glasgow and Mary Maffitt. L
   7. John Willson and Anne Underwood. L
   9. Alexander Long and MargretM orison.
   17. Samuel Cleary and Maria Stille. L
   19. William Williams, and Mary Thomson.
   26. James Dunning and Sarah Alrich. L
   29. Edward Wall and Mary Hayns.
   30. William Allen and Mary Patton.

July.
   6. Dennis McCafferty and Susanna Kingkad.
   17. Philip Cauvenah and Cathrine Moothy. L
   Patrick Boyd and Anne George
   19. Richard Clayton and Abigail Powell. L
   26. John Land and Anne Land.
   29. George Adams and Elizabeth Hillis. L
   30. Peter Peterson and Martha White. L
   Robert Robinson and Elenore Poyl. L
   31. Thomas Crawford and Edith Reynolds. L

August.
   3. William Henoch and Hannah Leadley.
   James Donelly and Grace McLaughlin.
   5. Andrew Smidt and Sarah Gregg.
   6. Isaac Adams and Marget Kelly.
   11. William Trotter and Jane Alexander.
   25. William Hunt and Susanna Hutton.
   28. John Swine and Elizabeth Dourthy.

31. John Anderson and Mary Peck.

September.
2. James Nethery and Lady Way.
   Malcom McKnight and Martha Kirryr. L.
3. William Griffith and Else Grant.
10. Richard Jeffrys and Jeane Logan.
13. William White and Sarah Lytur.
    Watkins Crampton and Jeane Morrison.
28. George Avenson and Mary Williamson.
29. Thomas Woods and Mary Martin.
30. John Hemmel and Phœbe Prichet.

October.
5. John Goggin and Lathy McColomay.
9. Samuel Ashmead and Ruth Robinson.
15. John Garrit and Elenore Robinson.
21. Richard Erwin and Elizabeth Sloan.
    John Mun and Margret **Crafford.**
22. Benjamin Hayl and Mary White.
30. John Nebucar and Mary Stilly.

November.
3. Richard Woodward and Abigail Hays.
4. Ulrich Hosteten and Anne Miller.
   John Hook and Elizabeth Strawman.
5. William Bracken and Ruth Gregg. L
7. Henry Sauder and Sarah Frey.
   John Waters and Sarah Thomson.
20. John Hindrickson and Beata Springer.
29. Benjamin Buffington and Mercy Frisdell.

December.
1 John Bently and Thamar Bentley.
  John Cook and Margret Glaine.
4. James Craig and Prudence Holland. L
6. David Davis and Elizabeth Hughs.
7. Richard Clark and Martha Key.
13. Jacob Criss and Mary Elizabeth Ibond.
17. William Hasselton and Anne Lawler.
27. Henry Webster and Sarah Stedham.
28. Timothy Mahoney and Hannah Reily.
30. John William Skop and Cathrine Knakton.

OLD SWEDES CHURCH

ANNO 1756.

January.
- 1. Michael Decroy and Judith Futhrey.
- 2. William Anderson and Margret McChever.
- 3. Stephen Dysurt and Rachel Coswell. L
- Matthew Meloy and Anne Hansson.
- 7. Enoch Dixon and Elizabeth Cloud.
- 8. Joshuah McDowell and Sarah Singleton. L
- 12. Archibald Homes and Elizabeth Land. L
- Allen Robenet and Anne Collins.
- 21. Thomas Haughey and Rose Anna White.
- Richard Meneman and Elizabeth Justisson.

February.
- 3. John McCarlin and Anna Kirgan.
- 9. Arthur Conolly and Jean Wench.
- William Noris and Anne Bowin.
- 10. John Jones and Mary Morgan. L
- 23. James Sheward and Rose Erwin. L

March.
- 3. Joseph Moris and Ester Williams.
- 4. Nathaniel Davis and Margret Davis.
- 5. Israel Pewsy and Sarah Newbery.
- 8. Simon Hadley and Briget Foot. L
- 17. James McCausland and Jeane Ramage. L
- John Headin and Sarah Headon. L
- 24. Job Ward and Rachel Battin.
- 28. Francis Mechem and Sarah Underwood.
- 29. William Ruston and Tacy Sincock.

April.
- 4. Daniel Evans and Hannah Dillworth.
- 5. Jacob Taylor and Elizabeth Walter.
- Michael Metzger and Barbro Gedlin.
- 6. Moris Willims and Ester Jatton.
- John Rawson and Anne Grub. L
- 8. John Register and Hannah Green. L
- James Dell and Mary Hutchison.
- 12. Herman Hoffman and Hannah Miller.
- 22. Thomas Beeson and Rebecca Kallem.
- 29. William Cunningham and Mary Weldin. L

May.
- 3. Henry Law and Unity Ready.
- 10. Thomas Kellum and Rachel Taylor. L

11. John Bird and Lady Stilley. L
20. Alexander Chestnut and Mary Roial.
26. Caleb Perkins and Cathrine Derickson.
29. Thomas Barlow and Mary Grace.
    Joseph Wood and Cathrine Curry.

June.
2. Peter Vander Weer and Mary Vander Weer. I.
6. John Redden and Anne Cleane.
7. Robert Broom and Francis Jacobs.
    Henry Jones and Anne Morgan. L
9. Isaac Malin and Elizabeth Traygot.
    Cornelius Derickson and Mary Van Neaman. I.
    Wm. McKnight and Margret Jordan.

July.
11. John Harding and Mary Vaneman. L
12. Abel Whitaker and Charity Jeffrys.
26. Joshua Benthley and Susanna Davis. L

August.
1. John Glasky and Elizabeth Gamble. L
3. James Glaskow and Mary Masset. L
8. Moris Justis and Cathrine Senecka. L
    Mardochay Mercer and Abigail Eachey.
22. Joseph Clist and Mary McCahan.
    Thomas Shannan and Johanna Carey,
28. Israel Taylor and Elizabeth Beamond.
29. John Fleming and Elizabeth Bathon.

September.
1. William Foot and Ester Ball. L
    Benjamin Judah and Rebecca Hawerd.
5. Alexander Cummins and Mary Barber. L
12. James Dickie and Cathrine Means. L
14. Andrew Vaneaman and Mary Jones.
21. Benjamin Ford and Margret Derickson. L
28. William Sinclair and Mary Grandy.

October.
2. Joseph Mendinhall and Abigail Hary.
    Thomas Reed and Henrietta Won.
10. William Crowley and Johannah Runnels.
16. Hans Miller and Rachael Paulson.
11. James Hannums and Anne Norset.
18. James McBoyd and Elizabeth Buckley.

OLD SWEDES CHURCH

MARRIED BY ERICK UNANDER.

ANNO 1756.

William Glackon and Anne Hannah.

November.
- 4. **Isaac** Williams and Elizabeth Thatcher. L
- 15. Jonathan Richards and Hannah Dutton.
- 16. John Ross and Isabell Smith. L
  James Fleming and Jane Henderson. L
- 20. Calop Hays and Mary Bailey.
- 22. Michael Plaster and Thamar Hewston.
  John Kay and Elizabeth Smart.

December.
- 6. Samuel Alexander and Elizabeth Wilson. L
  Joseph Bird and Margreta Rutter.
- 9. William Longwill and Margreta Glann. L
  Patrick Duffee and Christian Barthelson.
- 27. Kingsman Dutton and Ruth Watson. L
- 20. George Moor and Esther Dinney.
  Wm. Ashton and Mary Emlerer,
- **30.** Adam Richardson and Jane Karnes.

ANNO 1757.

January.
- 6. Jacob Richards and Susanna Wills. L
- 13. Joseph Parke and Mary Davis. L
- 20. Richard Few and Jane Chalfin. L
  Samuel Floyd and Elizabeth Willson.
- 31. Thomas Brakin and Martha Machan.

February.
- 1. Peter Murphy and Margreta O'Neil. L
  Thomas Barnet and Martha Derickson.
- 12. John M'Colly and Mary McCord.
- 13. John Long and Rebecca Wallace.
- 21. John Armstrong and Anne Erwin.
- 22. Edward Maghan and Margreta Welch.
- 27. Wm. Hebron and Elizabeth Ceane.
- 26. Wm. Armour and Jane Cann.

March.
- 7. John Arment and Cathrina Tilly.
- **14.** Samuel Carson and Sarah Wallace.
  James Doudle and Martha McCall.
- 16. John Rushton and Catharina Massen.

EARLY CHURCH RECORDS OF NEW CASTLE COUNTY

    19. Joseph Burris and Mary Nickolson.
    29. Daniel Ragin and Mary Strong.
        John McNamie and Martha Lea.

April.
    15. Martin Adams and Elizabeth Stabs.
        Owen Evans and Mary Baily.
        Wm. English and Martha Miller.

May.
    3. James Hames and Anne Hays.
        Andrew Mitchell and Phanny Phassath.
    28. Robert Scott and Mary Hamilton.

June.
    6. Luke Whalley and Mary **Partty.**
        James Camell and Mary Jackson.
    13. Caleb Whame and Sara McManumie.
    23. Joseph Wood and Rachel Harris.
        James Harris and Rachel Wood.
    24. George Martin and Mary Nickols.

July.
    4. Edward Brown and Engellest Lowecell.
        George Elliott and Mary Henry.
    5. Wm. Grant and Mary Willson.
    19. Thomas Marshall and Susanna Taylor.
        John Scott and Margreta Willson.
    26. John Dayly and Elsa Voghan.

August.
    14. Barnet Miles and Susanna Brownwood.
    24. James Dodd and Anne Dodd, not paid.
    27. Robert Eachus and Mary Griffith.
    28. Eberhardt **Steigerwalt &** Susanna Engel.

September.
    15. Dennis McKoy and Mary Davis.
    15. Samuel McMullon and Agnes McVan.
    15. James Hutchison and Margreta Ross.
    15. John Kell and Agnes Pharas.
    15. John Simons and Rebecca Rolls.

October.
    24. Jacob Reily and Mary Miller.
        John Red and Salome Danbergin.
        Lorance Dahlbo and Cathrine Tussey,
    30. John Sparry and Rachel Seeds.

OLD SWEDES CHURCH

November.
- 2. Wil Durnell and Margreta Melon.
- 3. James Hamilton and Elizabeth Carter.
- 4. Francis Philpot and Mary Murdock.
- 5. Will Peperall and Elizabeth Tangerin, John M'Carmack and Sara Hughs.
- 23. Will Murfy and Jane Morrison.
- 23. John Woodward and Mary Sharpe. L
  Patrick **McLean** and Elizabeth Lingin.

December.
- 3. Solomon Springer and Margreta Kelly.
  John Gray and Elizabeth Fox.
- 14. Wm. Keach and Hannah Bauldin.
  Mark Cunningham and Margreta Voghan.

April.
- 3. Isaac Howell and Mary Harris. L
- 30. Thomas Hanmun and Sara Bonsel. L

May.
- 6. Moses Montgomery and Elizabeth **Roa** L
- 30. William Wilson and Jane Canby, L

June.
- 14. John Dick and Mary Culen. L

August.
- 1. James Clarke and Frances Hill. L

September.
- 12. Samuel Thomson and Phœbe Allen. L

October.
- 20. Lorance **MacMarie** and Catharina **McCaffity** L
- 27. Robert Bratton and Margrete Huston. L

November.
- 3. Adam Henry Prince and Mary Cloud. L
- 30. Wm. Ronolds and Rachel Bird. L

May.
- 25. Emmor Jeffrys and Elizabeth Taylor. L

June 28. Benjamin Foot and Mary Robinson. L

November.
- 8. Charles Willson and Hannah Booner. L
- 9. David Jackson and Elizabeth Day. L

ANNO 1758.

January.
- 9. John Twigg and Mary Philips. L
  John Finney and Ruth Lloid.
- 10. Thomas Flowers and Prudence Moulders.

EARLY CHURCH RECORDS OF NEW CASTLE COUNTY

February.
    4. John Morton and Mary Hogg.
    13. Joseph Parkins and Anne Dougharty.
    16. James Woodward and Alice Thornburg.
    13. Thomas Dutton and Anna Ruth.
    13. Wm. Griffith and Cathrina Salvage. L
        Jacob Stahlman and Anne Mary Lemmerin.
    27. Christopher Majer and Cathrina Burns.

March.
    6. James Shearon and Agnes Armstrong.
    9. Thomas Hunter and Elizabeth Witherow.
    9. John Long and Christian Paulson.
    15. Fredrick Carpenter and Anne Lowmake.
    10. Hugh Gibson and Jane Grahams.
    16. Moses Minor and Mary Broadshaw. L
    31. John Toulson and Sarah Richison.

April.
    1. Charles Rawlins and Elizabeth Lorce.
       John Johnson and Elizabeth Dennis.
       Samuel Tally and Margreta Cloud. L
    13. David Eckhof and Elizabeth Pyle. L
    16. Abraham John on and Mary Oran.
    18. Niklas More and Barbara Reading.
    19. John Todd and Sarah Lindsay. L
    20. Johnathan Groves and Elsa Millikin.
    21. John McPeter and Jane Scott. L
    25. John McEasie and Briget McLean.
       Henry Mannik and Hannah Cook.
    26. John Armstrong and Isabella Willson.

May.
    1. John Taniers and Prudence Dericks.
    3. Jonas Canby any Latischee Pickle.
    15. James Duggan and Cathrina Elliott.
    16. Robert Edwards and Jane McMichall.
    16. James Stevens and Priscilla Jackson.

June.
    6. Fredrick Miller and Cathrina Graubein.
    8. James Wilson and Mary Wilson.
    29. Samuel Paterson and Hannah Clayton.

July.
    11. Robert Shillingford and Cathrine Vanlewvanaugh.
    25. James Longhead and Cathrine Finney. L
    28. Steven Mandenhall and Rebecca M'Collock.

OLD SWEDES CHURCH

August.
    15. Richard More and Elizabeth Smith. L
    16. John Howard and Rachel Evans. L
    10. Enoch Passmore and Mary Laughnaugh. L
September.
    4. Stephen Anderson and Sarah Jackson. L
October.
    10. Stephen Hurd and Elizabeth Burns. L
    17. John Carter and Anne Whippoe. L
    19. William McCullach and Deborah Hope. L
    24. John Armstrong and Mary Springer. L
    25. Benjamin Nickolson and Mary Ashton. L
November.
    4. John Henderson and Mary Chapman. L
    4. James Chandler and Elizabeth Ring. L
    7. John Johnson and Anne Gay. L
    9. William Robeson and Martha Huston. L
    23. John Kallum and Hannah Cartmill. L
December 6. Vincent Gilpon and Abigail Woodward. L
    June
    8. Joseph Harway and Ruth Fisher.
       Timothy Conley and Anne Gibson.
       James Limbur and Elinor Simond
August.
    3. Alexander Carson and Margret Mack.
       James James and Elizabeth Owens.
    9. John Clyde and Margret Scott.
    12. David Alexander and Mary Carter.
    13. Philip McLaughlin and Cathrine O'Neal.
    14. Abraham Hutson and Cathrine Hutson
       Eliah Richey and Hannah Ball.
    24. Jonas Walraven and Mary Carry.
       James Hughs and Jane Ainsworth.
    27. Charles Hopkins and Mary Vandavier.
September.
    4. Archibald Miller and Jane Boyd.
       Joseph Taylor and Cathrine Hendrickson.
October.
    12. Benjamin Hartly and Mary Rowen.
       John Barnet and Margret Willis.
    23. James Shore and Elizabeth Sanders.
    25. Adam Andreas and Cathrine Borshorford.

EARLY CHURCH RECORDS OF NEW CASTLE COUNTY

November.
    6. Richard Justice and Anne Webster.
   12. William Booth and Anne Brilton.
   23. John Otlay and Mary Hays.
       John Hatton and Rebecca Black.
       Joseph Ball and Agnes Adams,
   26. Roger McGally and Jane Rimson.

December.
    5. John O'Freel and Margret Farmer.
       Timothy Williams and Susanna Minor.

ANNO 1759.

January.
   10. William Coles and Phœbe Calamay.
       Stephen Maden and Margery Diling.
   17. Isaac Roman and Hannah Roman. L
   23. Thomas Lasselley and Sarah Thomas. L

February.
    1. David Frame and Cathrine Miller. L
   21. William Atkins and Martha Buttington.

March
    8. Charles McClair and Agnes McRea.
       Robert Banefil and Esther Camel.
   13. Thomas Bird and Brigitta Seeds. L
   25. James Rowan and Elizabeth Connol. L
   26. Ludwig Leonard Londgrov and Anne Ernest.
   28. John Hendrickson and Mary Justice.
   29. George Spence and Sarah **Fasetty**
       James Mills and Johannah Neals.

April.
    2. Joseph Passmore and Elizabeth Martin. L
       William Turner and Anne Rayl.
       John Johns and Thamar Johnson.
    6. Henry Christopher and Kennet Dorothea.
    7. James Craig and Jane Wetherow.
    8. John Nash and Judith Bailly.
   12. Benjamin Kallum and Mary Beaton. L
   13. James Ramage and Elizabeth More. L
   24. John Ball and Darkeys Springer. L
   26. John Druitt and Mary Ingolls. L
   28. Abraham Taylor and Rebecca Way. L

OLD SWEDES CHURCH

May.
   3. Valentine Bullord and Elizabeth Ridnua.
   9. John Harper and Phoebe Vernon.
      John Martin and Anne Larken.
      John Smith and Hannah Otlay. L

June.
   2. James Bennet and Jane Henry.

June.
   3. John Skelton and Mary Bush.
   4. Mathew Wilson and Cathrine Kerson.
   7. Stephen Bennet and Margret Buddon.
 17. Francis Rock and Mary Pryer. L
  19. George Chandler and Jane Connelly.
     Abert Skeer and Patience Trevel.
  21. Peter Springer and Cathrine Anderson. L
  23. William Miller and Sarah Hall. L

July.
   2. Evan Morgan and Margret Morgan.
   3. Francis McMullon and Margret Gallohun.
   9. Edward Taylor and Rebecka McClour.
  22. Joseph Satford and Susanna Wooliston.

August.
   1. Joseph Buttington and Mary Few. L
     John L'Loyd and Mary Moore.
   3. Patrick Kelly and Anne Hide.
   5. John Crampton and Sarah Barnet.
     Peter Gallorhon and Flora Camel.
     Alexander Moore and Elizabeth Moore.
   6. David Anderson and Agnes Mitchel.
  13. John Bell and Mary Straw.
     Andrew Rees and Anne Alderwood.
     William Cook and Rachel Morgan.
     James Underwood and Ester Matson.
   9. James Buttington and Mary Blackly.
     James Kear and Else Taylor.
  21. George Stalker and Sarah Thornburry.
  22. George Hall and Phœbe Thomas. L

July.
  30. James Carr and Else Taylor. L

September.
  13. Jacob Dawson and Anne **Harris** L

16. Thomas Barclay and Mary Chapman. L
John Elliott and Cloe FitsRandel. L
Barne Miles and Martha Moore.
8. John Wollarlou and Mary Gray.
26. John Bell and Margret Mayer.
Thomas Williams and Martha Rowland.
Robert Wilson and Mary Wilson.
James Shields and Margret Bently.
Thomas Monks and Mary Mace.
27. James Little and Sarah Laird. L
28. William Henry and Sarah Ralston. L
26. Valentine Ofwerdoff and Agnes Pepperell.

October.
16. John Cann and Cathrine James. L
28. Charles Springer and Margret Springer.
29. Nathan Scuttaron and Hannah Twigg. L
31. James Gibson and Mary Thomson.

November.
1. Evan Lewis and Margret Davis.
2. German Davis and Sarah Carrigan. L
5. Michael Murduck and Brigit Springer. L
William Clark and Anne Bauldin. L
Christopher Kariland Cathrine Faril.
Joseph Baston and Jannet Barton.
John Lawler and Darkeys Barker. L
Jacob Staahlman and Cathrine Chersherin.
Charles Garra and Anne Saulter.
6. Ezekiel Currey and Elizabeth Brownlees. L
21. Patrick Gamble and Jane Nosette. L
Abraham Springer and Christine Anderson.

ANNO 1760.

January.
1. William Chapman and Elizabeth Bishop.
12. James Wilson and Mary Moore. L
15. Peter Peterson and Abaah Garrison. L
22. William Peoples and Jane Haag.
John Siddon and Jane Robert.
29. Francis McCulley and Susanna Patton.
Friedrich Warner and Rebecca Robeson. L

February.
2. James Hasting and Susanna Justice. L
5. Jacob Stilley, Jr., and Anne French. L
6. John Dixson and Susanna Pryer. L

OLD SWEDES CHURCH

    7. Thomas Wilson and Agnes Young.
  25. Joseph Mea and Martha Hill.

March.
    3. Mardechay Woodward and Bridgette Knowles.
       James Garman and Phœbe Bradford.
    6. Lawrence Flinn and Elizabeth Gordon. L
  17. William McKea and Sarah Smith.
  22. Thomas Allen and Cathrine Vaneman.
  24. Robert Adair and Isabel Douglas.
       Johnathan Hays and Elizabeth Horlen.
       John Gottfried Charley and Anne Mary Reilerin.

April 14. Abraham Swange and Alse Pyle.
  28. Samuel Heald and Ruth Harlan.
  29. Thomas David and Rebecca Long.
       Peter Gallohar and Mary Halom.

May.
    9. Joseph Cloud and Charity Tally. L

June.
    5. Swen Colesburg and Annie Torner. L
  26. Joseph Paerce and Beata Grimes. L
  27. Andrew Hall and Anna Maxel. L
  12. John Webb and Sarah Green. L

           MARRIED BY ANDREW BORELL.
July.
  30. Joseph Ball and Hannah Brachin. L
  30. John Chalfant and Matire.

August.
    4. Matthias Kaler and Anna Euklingen.
    5. Hans Peter Harald and Margrete Leana.
  14. Samuel Nail and Margrete Brownly.
  18. Cornelius McDannel and Cherry Dely.
  18. Archibald Grey and Chatrine Clark.
  10. Abraham Woodward and Anna Tarnbery.
  13. George Thomson and Rachel Lewden. L
  20. Aaron Evan and Ruth M'Charson. L
  27. Benjamin Pain and Cathrine Gibson.
       John Buffington and Annah Clayton.

September.
    7. Matthias Martin and Margrete Brown.
  22. John Shreve and Deborah Mounsell. L
  23. John French and Barbro Jagerin. L

October.
> 10. Joseph Cloud and Margrete Brady.
> 23. George Brinton and Christine Hill. L
> 24. Joseph Chandlor and Elizabeth Forman. L

November.
> 4. Joseph Woodward and Rebecca Martin. L
> 16. Stephen Harris and Sarah Taylor L
> 24. George Danevan and Elizabeth Rees.
> 25. Anthony Turnantz and Mary Grimes.
> 26. Richard Robinson and Sarah Pail L
> 9. Richard Woodward and Hannah Taylor. L
> 10. Seth Evanson and Hannah Davis. L

December.
> 1. Archibald Gardner and Mary Patterson L
> 16. John Carr and Penelope Hual.
> 16. Robert Bennet and Elizabeth Garny.
> 18. Robert Woodcock and Deborah Jonas. L
> 25. James Harper and Mary Sharp.
> 26. Andrew Polson and Margrete Robinson. L

ANNO 1761-2. F. F. D. O. M.

January.
> 1. Peter Polson and Eleonorah Justis. L
>> 1. James Moy and Sarah Ross.
>> 22. Robert Balden and Hannah Houss.
>> 26. John Scarlet and Mary O'Neal.
>> 26. David Crawford and Mary Harrison.

February.
> 2. John Bird and Sarah Tossey. L
> 15. Thomas Davis and Jane Elliott.

March.
> 10. John Stalcop and Jane Snicker.
> 30. John Morris and Eleonore **Fargesson** L
> 30. Samuel Way and Elizabeth McClean.

April.
> 2. Nathaniel Way and Sarah Taylor. L.
> 21. James Clark and Mary Davis. L

May.
> 5. John Valentin Wieber and Cathrine Bernhard.
> 9. Jacob Stedham and Susannah Justisson.
> 11. Philip Stats and Mary Peterson.
> 30. Thomas Barnard and Mary Collet. L

June.
> 11. Henry Janes and Mary **Parm**. L

OLD SWEDES CHURCH

    11. James Keitly and Elizabeth **Durnal**
June 22. John Ward and Elizabeth McMaghan L
July.
    23. Caleb Dicksson and Hannah Gradel.
August.
    4. Niclas Hoy and Mary Lampley.
    5. James Marcer and Sarah Lyle. L
    6, Henry Garritson and Mary Spraig. L
    8. Abraham Davis and Lydia Jeffrys. L
    25. Benjamin Shadweck and Margret Johnson.
    31. Hans Plassart and Annah Genkens. L
Sept. 9. John McCutchen and Mary Bogs.

September.
    10. James McKnight and Susannah Maxel. L
    16. Christopher Gun and Margrete **Sanderine**
    20. Moses Callon and Cathrine Paulson. L
August.
    17. Alexander Skalton and Rachel Maris. L
October.
    5. Isaac Williams and Elizabeth Durnal. L
    6. Isaac Taylor and Susannah Rowles. L
    8. George Fryar and Margrete Green.
    9. George Martin and Annah Cloud.
    17. Joseph Dickson and Eleonore Cammel. L
    22. Michael Lightbody and Sarah Langley.
    25. George Lewis and Anna Wheighth.
    26. Joshua Falkenton and Susannah Persons. L
    26. Thomas Marshal and Ursilla Bradley. L
November.
    5. William Moore and Elizabeth Moore.
    9. Thomas Jonson and Margrete Rarden. L
    13. Samuel Vernon and Elizabeth Hays.
    19. William Merchant and Jane Armstrong. L
    27. George McDowal and Jane **Purtal**L
        John Tarbox and Eleonore Stephenson.
    30. Thomas Spakman and Jane Wollaston.
December.
    11. Samuel Heath and Ruth Barnat.
    24. Lewis Purlat and Jane Latymore. L
    25. Koheath **Huse** and Martha Palding.
    30. Charles Gallower and Cathrine **Crafort**
    31. Richard Keallom and Elizabeth Cartmal.

EARLY CHURCH RECORDS OF NEW CASTLE COUNTY
ANNO 1762.

January.
2. William Groub and Rachel Groub. L
6. Thomas Nicols and Eleonore Butler.
7. James McClaskey and Patience Rouse.
14. Gabriel Springer and Elizabeth Parlin. L
14. Robert Buffington and Elizabeth Martin.
14. John Martin Deaver and Mary Cathrine Celyona.
14. Joseph Taylor and Eleonore Mulay. L
19. Simon Carlin and Elizabeth Naff.
22. Robert Robinson and Sarah Hindrickson. L

February.
4. James Miller and Jane Enklan.
11. Nathan Heald and Rebecca McBride.
19. Joseph Robinet and Annah Taylor. L
18. John Springer and Susannah Springer. L
23. Daniel Cloud and Sarah Walley. L.
24. John Fitz Jarel and Mary Hews.

March.
2. William Stalkop and Margrete Anderson. L
4. John Beazen and Mary Carter. L.
3. Edward Jones and Annah Warl.
2. George Sharp and Abigail Craig. L
9. William Hunt and Latty James. L
13. John Nathary and Mary Lyan.
17. James Moore and Elizabeth Warlé.
James Meleehan and Mary Taylor.
18. Melchior Stile and Cathrine Ziegleni.
19. Joseph Park and Margrete Cloud. L

April.
14. John McKlean and Margrete Hackat.
26. Jacob Graig and Susanna Anderwood.
26. Charles Booth and Jane Whitby.
29. John Starr and Mary Barrans.
29. James Anderson and Martha Elliott. L

May.
6. William Didrickson and Elizabeth Brunberry, L
8. John Harper and Sarah Rowles.
10. Christopher Cromet and Elizabeth Ay.
11. James Firth and Jane Peet.
11. Caleb Stroud and Hannah Hackman. L
21. Jonas Matsson and Gwine Owen.

June.
2. Francis Adams and Elizabeth Clankenhorm.

OLD SWEDES CHURCH

 21. David Rees and Martha Morgan.
 23. Joseph Barlow and Annah Chatfin.
 23. Richard Allen and Hannah Vaneman.
 20. Benjamin Black and Annah Ralson.

July.
  1. Neal Curry and Rebeccah Wallis.
  1. James Harlon and Dina Davis.
  1. Caleb Oanes and Jane Robinson.
  18. Elias Jones and Hanna Frikman.

August.
  7. John Maguire and Jane Bate.
  14. Daniel Kilda and Margrete Brason.
  17. William Dilworth and Cathrine Gooden.

September.
  1. Alexander Spear and Sarah Tomson.
  13. Robert McDonal and Eleonore Powel.
  26. Thomas Gibbon and Anna Bealy.
  28. Jesper Bach and Cathrine Sneiker. L

October.
  3. James Young and Barbara White. L
  5. Thomas Joanes and Margrete Kelly.
   Richard Pierce and Lydia Paulson. L
  9. James Harry and Margrete Seed.
  11. John Pyl and Phœbe Dornal.
  14. William Jones and Hannah Eals. L
  21. Elisel Garons and Susanna Stedham. L

November.
  4. William Spear and Anna McSooly.
   James Smidth and Martha May.

November.
  4. David Weily and Annah Stedham. L
  4. George Clark and Mary Brooks. L
  4. Joseph Steel and Margrete Philips. L
  4. William Gray and Mary Coburn. L
  11. William Shay and Mary Latimore.
  17. William Carlin and Cathrine Johnson.
  27. Caleb Way and Rebecca Mendinghall. L
  25. Cornelius Hines and Elizabeth Peterson. L

December.
  2. Joseph Smidth and Mary Morgan.

EARLY CHURCH RECORDS OF NEW CASTLE COUNTY

 22. Adam Ekman and Mary Ryan.
 29. Thomas Lesly and Rachel Allen.
 23. Wilson Parker and Jane Bratchen.
 2. Joseph Loyd and Elizabeth Brown.
 22. John Way and Ruth Hallonsworth.
 23. Andrew Justis and Anna Garritson.
 23. John Husbands and Mary Woolbutt.
 30. George Gun and Margrete Miles.

   ANNO 1763. Q. F. F. J. D. O. M,

January.
 4. Abraham Cox and Lydia Hendrickson.
 11. William Warner and Margery Farron. L
 26. George Passmore and Ann Mansell.
 28. Tully Davitt and Jane Means.
 29. William Armstrong and Rebecka Ervin. L

February.
 2. John Jones and Annah Trees,
 3. Andrew Peterson and Sarah Ford. L
 3. Jacob Hedge and Cathrine Justis. L
 14. John Ford and Margret Morgan.

March.
 10. Peter Glancy and Jane King.
 31. Andrew Vandavar and Annah Cirl. L

April.
 4. Ludwig Laybobt and Margrete Black.

February.
 3. Jesse McCullough and . . . McPhaerson.

April
 18. David Wadle and Sarah Mase.

February.
 13. William Beats and Hannah McCafforty.

April.
 24. Thomas Hayes and Ruth Jones. L
 25. John Robeson and Elizabeth Spencer. L
 28. Amor Chandler and Elizabeth Harlen. L

May.
 2. Alexander Dick and Christiana Hews. L
 4. Harry Gordon and Hannah Meredith. L
 9. Roland Burk and Hannah Carter.
 9. Thomas Jones and Cathrine Allen.
 16. John Barber and Hannah Barns.
 16. John Shadd and Jane Williams.
 19. Henry Wyna and Susanna Justis. L

OLD SWEDES CHURCH

June.
   16. Jacob Pritchett and Elizabeth Stafford.

July.
   2. Jacob Brinton and Cathrine McCoy.
   4. Andrew Crips and Hannah Stahlkop. L
   9. Matthias Jannet and Sarah Hill.
  10. John Nickols and Ann Peterson. L
  17. Martin Doyle and Rose Brogen.
  18. Enoch Hallonsworth and Hannah Smith.
      John Gunn and Sarah Gordon.
  28. John Karran and Hannah Miller.

August.
   7. Peter Osborne and Elizabeth Stephens.
  10. John Baxley and Mary Sproul.
  17. Robert Anderson and Margrete Neily. L.
  26. James Sayre and Elizabeth Dyatt.
  29. Walter Welsh and Mary Rely.

September.
   5. William Johnson and Cathrine Royal.

October.
  11. Peter Babb and Mary Beasen. L
  15. Joseph Lobb and Francis Strange. L

November.
   3. Thomas Coburn and Martha Hartley. L
   4. James Means and Sarah Barnet. L
   4. Charles Barnet and Phœbe White. L
   4. Robert Hudgeon and Mary Dottan.
   5. John Houlden and Jane Bullow. L
  10. Matthew Giffin and Mary Ball.
  14. John Stilly and Sarah French: L
  20. Patrick McCloskey and Elizabeth Oversiller.
  24. Patrick Brady and Mary Gore.
  25. Joseph Glassan and Sarah Warl. L

December.
   8. Cornelius Stidham and Christina Justice.
  10. Abraham Flaharty and Rachel Ferris.
  22. Amos Hope and Ann Marshall. L
  26. John Boggs and Mary Cummings. L
  26. Thomas Wilson and Elizabeth Dunn. L
  26. William Watson and Chrisy Owens.

EARLY CHURCH RECORDS OF NEW CASTLE COUNTY

ANNO 1764. Q. F. F. I. D. T. O. M.

January.
- 6. John Walker and Jane Miles. L
- 14. John Rodgers and Elizabeth Ranolds. L
- 26. William Anderson and Sarah Evans. L

February.
- 2. John Grow and Anne Danely.
- 3. William Reath and Susanna Doyle.

March.
- 4. William McCab and Sarah White.
- 5. William Lovis and Elizabeth Wood.
- 8. William Smidth and Anne Peterson.
- 13. Joseph Scott and Margret Caughlan.
- 15. Jesse Canby and Lydy Davis. L

April.
- 2. John Tussey and Sarah James. L
- 4. Wm. Dennon and Elizabeth Hely.
- 12. Richard Thornberry and Mary Guersley.
- 12. Moses Fraeser and Anne Ails
  Jonas Peterson and Elizabeth Hines. L

May.
- 3. Thomas Ogle and Elizabeth Davis.
- 5. John Howell and Elizabeth Cookin.
- 7. Joseph McCullough and Elizabeth Hopes.
- 7. Paul Wrelson and Rebecca Anderson.
- 7. Rees Enock and Jane Carter.
- 9. Robert Jack and Mary Sheerer.
- 10. John Armstong and Rebecca Springer.
- 22. John Richardson and Sarah Carter.

June.
- 5. Henry Garritson and Anne Mack.
- 5. Jonathan Redman and Mary Hendrickson.
- 14. Charles Springer and Mary Baal.
- 20. Abel Way and Else Taylor.

July.
- 19. Richard Garner and Elenor Derrickson.
- 26. Thomas Hopes and Sarah Harlen.
- 30. John Gapin and Mary Williams.

August.
- 2. James Moore and Mary Canley.
  Thomas Charleton and Elizabeth Cook.
- 6. James Hinman and Elizabeth Jonson.
- 10. John Corkran and Mary Carr.

OLD SWEDES CHURCH

September.
   10. Jesse Harlan and Sarah Harlen.
   27. John Bullock and Sarah Bartley.
October.
   10. Robert Barker and Deborah Jordan.
   10. George Heald and Rachel Nickols.
   18. Nickolas Hay and Cathrine Cantbine.
      John Beeson and Mary Gregg.
   25. Wm. Cleany and Elizabeth Gilpin.
November.
   1. John Clerk and Sarah Bird.
   5. Wm. Glover and Mary Baker.
   5. Thomas Newark and Anne Cannoway.
   6. Aaron Hackeney and Lydy Rees. L
   13. John James and Mary Lovis.
   16. John Dottan and Rachel Collet.
   22. Thomas Roman and Cathrine Douglas
   24. Adam Diat and Mary Nailson.
   25. John McFairlamb and Sarah Heald.
   26. Joseph Moll and Sarah Mackendear.
December.
   4. Philip Shaaf and Mary Thanker.
      George Liggit and Anne Chalfin.
   13. Moses Montgomery and Annable Robertson.
   20. Robert Eyre and Anne Preis.
   20. George Greiff and Cathrine Simmers.
   24. Wm. Moore and Mary Agnew.
   24. Wm. Simons and Ruth Bird.
   29. John Shee and Cathrine Lawrence.

Anno 1765, Q F. F. J. D. F. O. M.

January.
   3. Benjamin Jones and Else Temple.
   7. Bernhard Rodgers and Martha Enos.
   12. Israel **Gilpin** and Elizabeth Hannums.
February.
   12. Wm. Leonard and Jamima Mabaly.
   21. Simon Kaaron and Mary Morgan.
   21. John Foresight and Elizabeth Way.
   21. Wm. Baldwin and Debora Benet.
   25. Thomas Brown and Elizabeth Berber.
   26. Joseph Taylor and Ann Woodward.
      James Nicholson and Sarah Miller.

EARLY CHURCH RECORDS OF NEW CASTLE COUNTY

March.
    4. John Wilson and Mary Fogner.
  13. Francis Simonson and Elizabeth Johnson.
  14. Robert Shearman and Elenore Derrickson.
  20. John Welch and Eleonor Kildennin.
  20. Jethro Baker and Ann Johnson.

April.
    3. Wm. Askew and Mary Jones.
    9. James Dunning and Lydia Aldridge.
  13. John Darlington and Mary Way.
  19. Stephen Hall and Elizabeth Mounsell.
  21. Charles Harrison and Ann Timewell. Negroes.
  22. George Jeffeys and Ann Butler.

June.
    5. David Chandler and Mary Wayrom.
    5. Samuel Clark and Mary Farrill.
  10. John Kembole and Lydia Charleton.
  17. Isaac Berry and Elizabeth House.
  17. John Nichols and Ann Greist.

July.
    3. George Valantine and Mary Cohoon.
    7. John Burns and Elizabeth Hill.
    7. John McCafferty and Mary Proier.
  10. Allen Cunningham and Elizabeth Hackett.
  20. Wm. Cummings and Mary Kirk.
  22. Jacob Way and Phœbe Pennock.
  31. George Gorden and Mary Culbertson.

August.
  22. Eneas Foulk and Mary Guest.
  30. James Ervin and Elizabeth Tardey.

September.
    1. Charles McNeal and Elizabeth Paulson.
    6. John McKea and Abigail McDonald.
  11. John Barker and Miriam Graig.
  16. Joseph Sawwil and Mary Pemroy.
  19. John Hays and Rachel Hall.
  19. Edward Pegman and Margarete . . .
  26. Thomas Barnet and Agnes Carter.

October.
    3. Henry Kinnen and Elizabeth Gordon.
       Isaac England and Sarah Hill.
       Wm. Sample and Ann Robinson.

OLD SWEDES CHURCH

    5. Joseph Dickin and Grisell Rowells.
   11. Thomas Mahaffy and Elizabeth Linsay,
   18. Stephen Harlen and Lydia Greenfield.
   25. John Jordan and Rachel Robinson.
   30. Enoch Graig and Hannah Bason.
November.
    5. Charles Rely and Sarah Dawson.
   17. Matthew Case and Elizabeth Hinkley.
      Benjamin Dottan and Elizabeth Vandovar.
December.
   23. Matthew Johnson and Elizabeth Burrows
   24. Andrew Anderson and Mary Conelly.
   ,24. Abraham Brown and Elizabeth Loynan.
   25. James Boggs and Hannah Rees.
   30. James Flatcher and Susanna Young.
      Wm. Barnet and Mary Barlow.
May.
    9. George Hall and Sarah Black
September.
    4. Robert Meers and Sarah Wood.

        ANNO 1766. Q. F. F. J. D. T. O. M.

January.
    1. Samuel Dickson and Martha Barnet.
    3. James Way and Mary Parr.
   13. John Peterson and Mary Heburns.
   23. John Watson and Mary Williams.
   23. Magnus Schrouder and Isabella Allison.
   28. Laughlin McNeal and Sarah Parks.
February.
    5. John Foudrey and Mary Derick.
    6. Henry Gray and . . . Waterson.
   12. Wm. Leonard and Jamaymy Mabaly.
   20. George Mardock and Ann Mascall.
   22. Thomas Cartmell and Mary Taylor.
   24. Walter Sweeny and Susan Stewart.
March.
   11. Andrew Red and Elizah Hallonsworth.
   11. Matthias Branberry and Mary Anderson.
   13. John Naaly and Martha Culbertson.
   13. Wm. Headen and Ann Vernon
      Wm. Hays and Mary Langlay.
   16. John Niclan and Mary Underwood.

EARLY CHURCH RECORDS OF NEW CASTLE COUNTY

    17. George McCleod and Jane Johnson
    20. Samuel Smidth and Mary Lyle.
    27. Isaac Houlton and Margrete Poldon.
    31. Robert Dunlap and Cathrine Dennary.
April.
    7. Wm. Spotswood and Elizabeth . . .
       Alexander McMollan and . . . Hestins.
       Edmund Dougherty and . . . .
    17. James Ross and Eleonore Runnels.
    29. Jesper Camp and Margrete Hedinghan.
May.
    7. Cornelius Truax and Elizabeth Tobin.
    15. Robert Way and Hannah Lea.
    29. John Gleann and Margrete Craig.
June.
    4. Edward Crangetton and Mary Darby.
       Daniel McNeal and Rebecca Dunlap.
    7. Wm. Willis and Susannah Guest.
July.
    4. James Montgomery and Mary Sterlin.
    11. Thomas Deglish and Anne Muster.
    14. David Martin and Eleonore Kirklan.
August.
    17. Robert James and Sarah Way.
    19. Robert Welsh and Cathrine Stidham.
September.
    1. —— Barnet and Mary White.
October.
    7. Casper Brown and Rebecca Haston.
November.
    4. William Glenn and Brigitta Dunn.
    4. Samuel Feer and Ann Dilling.
    4. Thomas Tally and Hannah Grubb.
    4. Thomas Bradford and Hannah Barnet.
    5. Israel Hendrickson and Lydia Hewell.
    25. David Ford and Mary Parlen.
December.
    2. John Carle and Sarah Gates.
    11. Joseph Chaffin and Susanna Robinet.
    17. James Craig and Charity Craven.
    18. Jacob Derickson and Ingeborg Stidham.
    21. David Johnson and Mary Brinton.

OLD SWEDES CHURCH

  22. Samuel Stahlkey and Elizabeth Faulken.
  22. John Montgomery and Mary Guest.
      Thomas Shannahan and Rebecca Wallace.
  24. John Harrison and Mary Peterson.
  27. Isaac Welding and Sarah Dearman.
  29. George Laurence and Lady Derick.

MARRIAGES BY LAWRENCE GIRELIUS.
ANNO 1767.

November.
  19. Matthias Ginnet and Elizabeth Masters.
  21. Jacob Craig and Mary West.
  22. John Minner and Phoebe Larkin.
  24. Joseph Bonsall and Jean Frame.
  26. Joseph Hedges and Hannah Ford.

December.
  17. Joshua Woodrow and Elizabeth Wilson.
  22. John Kesler and Christine Aman.
  28. Joseph Moony and Elizabeth Taylor.
  31. Nathaniel Brown and Elizabeth Lamply.

ANNO 1768.

January.
  6. Archibald McDonald and Margret Smidt.
  9. John Wilson and Margret Justis.
  12. Christopher Rich and Dina Hays.
  13. George Harlen and Elizabeth Chandler.
  14. Gabe Walker and Margret Brown.

February.
  7. Abraham Jonson and Magdalene James.
  8. Antony Baldwin and Mary Harlin.
  29. Jacob Morfy and Elizabeth Welch.

March.
  16. Garret Covead and Mary Maggy.
  21. Nathaniel Williams and Mary Sennex.   19.

All these were married by orders and directions of the Rev. Andrew Borell, Ordinary, who died the 4th day of April, as during this space of time he married several himself which have not yet been recorded. The record is not complete.

ANNO 1768.

April.
  12. Nathan Jefris and Beninah Wall. L
  13. Elias Tussey and Anne McKeever.
  27. Joseph Cowperthwait and Susanna Hellings. L
  28. Isaac Colbert and Elizabeth Gart.

EARLY CHURCH RECORDS OF NEW CASTLE COUNTY

28. Abel Way and Sarah Reech.

May.
  5. John Taylor and Mary Crother.
  9. John Wallace and Mary Page. L
 16. John Tallbot and Sarah Lowys. L
 19. Thomas Almond and Elizabeth Craig. L
 22. James Way and Mary Moran.

June.
 13. David Waddle and Mary Ratbew. L
 13. Edward **McCaffety** and **Susanna Stedham.**
 16. David Jameson and Anne Springer. L

July.
 16. John Runolds and Mary Paulson. L
 20. Wm. Jordan and Rebecca Robertson. L
 31. Thomas Richardson and **Mary Jompferson.**

August.
  1. Wm. **McEathran and Hannah Thomas.**
  7. John File and Elizabeth Burgass. L
 10. Thomas Wilson and Elizabeth Roberson.
 14. Hugh Ferrel and Sarah Grime.
    Michael **Schivel** and Sarah Caring.
 18. Robert Armstrong and Hannah Richardson.
 29. George Harn and Sarah West.

September.
  4. Benjamin Tempel and Sarah Broomer.
  8. Andrew Pollen and Jennet Willson.
 15. David Tryon and Susanna Tussey. L
 17. Oliver Bursall and Elizabeth Simons. L
 17. Joseph Marshall and Elizabeth Grubb. L
 21. Wm. Conner and Helena **Schnohill.**
 22. Benjamin Montgomery and Mary McFersson.
 29. Samuell Rett and Elizabeth Fredd.

October.
  6. James Kean and Jean Kott.
 13. Owen Donelly and Sarah Andrewwood.
 13. John Shay and Jean Manelly.
 14. John Askew and Elizabeth Colbert. L
 20. George Rendy and Elizabeth Litla. L
 26. Robert Means and Rachel Cunningham.

November.
  4. Wm. Talley and Judith Fitzsimmons.
  5. Wm. **Talley Crossin and Dina Stille.**
 10. Robert Cooper and Hannah Walter.

OLD SWEDES CHURCH

    22. Frend Gray and Sarah Batten.
    25. Elias Nilson and Deborah Edwards.
December.
    11. Isaac Pennel and Ester Dicks.
    22. John Armot and Susanna McLaughlin.
    22. Wm. Addy and Elenor Clark.
    22. Peter Paulson and Elizabeth Springer.
    23. Thomas Beal and Jean Gold.
    27. Nathaniel Carter and Sarah Edwards.
    29. Thomas **Powell and Jean Porter.**
    29. James Oarr and Sarah Eynon.
    30. Tobias Peterson and Mary McCarty.

ANNO 1769.

January.
    3. John Pyle and Beaulah Beaukley. L
    9. John Starr and Elizabeth Williams.
    18. Abraham Darlington and Mary Nuklan.
    20. Jacob England and Rhoda Forton. L
    28. Cornelius McCashey and Cathrine Fisher.
February.
    1. Wm. Karser and Elizabeth VanLooner. L
       John Brown and Hannah Nickols. L
    14. Henry McElnois and Hannah Broom.
    15. Adam Hall and Sarah Barr.
    21. Moses Mendenhall and Bethsheba Hope.
    23. Wm. Baker and Elizabeth Herny.
    28. David Boid and Mary Johns.
       Married by Presbyterian minister Mr. McKinnan, but published in my church.
March
    8. John Proctor and Sarah Johnson. L
      George Taylor and Mary Few.
    23. Nathaniel Cloud and Mary Steen. L
       Abraham Jerd and Elizabeth Millner. L
    28. Thomas Samferd and Ann **Broom**
       John Neely and Jane Huston. L
    29. John York and Cathrine Don. L
       Caleb Pyle and Sophia House.
April 10. Andrew Creater and Ann Davis.
    11. Joseph Springer and Ann Hendrickson.
    20. Amor McGlaughland and Mary Weldon.
    21. John Stalkop and Cathrine Fitzgerald.
       Published in New Castle Church.

EARLY CHURCH RECORDS OF NEW CASTLE COUNTY

 27. George Walter and Dina Nichols.

May.
- 9. Henry Collins and Elizabeth Mendenhall.
- 9. David Johns and Elizabeth McCafferty.
- 10. John Newlin and Susannah Richards.
- 11. John Hay and Jean Steen.
  Henry Thomson and Elizabeth Bon.
- 15. Edward Burn and Else Alligon.
- 16. Francis Day and Mary Morton. L
- 22. William Lee and Susannah Weakons.
- 24. Jacob Dingee and Hannah Sumption.
- 27. Robert Woodward and Jean Sure. L
- 29. Peter Harford and Marget Pog.

June.
- 1. William Firth and Jean Olls. L
- 1. John Sperey and Catharine Walraven. L
- 1. Josiah White and Susanna Lodge. L
- 7. William McClure and Jean Dunlap. L
  Frederick Wilterslain and Cathrine Charles.
- 19. James Pyle and Abigail Boldon.
- 20. James McKnight and Lydia Morgan.

July.
- 29. Peter Baker and Hannah Seal L

August.
- 4. Archibold Stewart and Ann Russell. L
- **14. Benjamin Whiteall and Elizabeth Hopper.** L
- 15. John Gackhagen and Cathrine Bryan.
- 24. Sylvanus Day and Mary Baldwin. L
- 27. George McFarlen and Sarah Clements.
- **31. Robert Hentzler and Mary Shiars.**
- 31. Isaac Brakin and Rachel Stalkop.

September.
- 8. Philip Halter and Sarah Philips.
- 12. Robert Chalfant and Phœbe Chalfant. L
- 14. William Walch and Cathrine Davis.
- 16. John Cunningham and Rachel Zebley.
- 18. Thomas Jeffs and Mary Wilson.
- 21. John Rafferty and Elizabeth Bryan. L
- 29. Joseph Thomson and Ann Hollongsworth.

October.
- 1. Michael Kenrian and Rosanna Smidth.
- 2. Matthew Doile and Cathrine Grimes.
  Joseph Taylor and Mary Caringten.

OLD SWEDES CHURCH

    5. John Simonten and Frances Armatage.
    7. Samuel Bowler and Margret Moore. L
  12. William Burns and Mary Ennys.
      Thomas Kane and Elizabeth Elliott L.
      Sigfridus Alrich and Rachel Colesberry.
      Robert Armstrong and Mary Emore.
  15. Patrick Mullon and Cathrine Wilky.
  17. Thomas Morgan and Ann McHicken.
  28. Joseph Beal and Frances Kirgen.
      William Hatton and Mary Quin.
  30. John Wasten and Ann England.
  30. Aaron Pottle and Martha **Fowler**
      Thomas Gandy and Cathrine Pradle. **/Croak?**

November.
    1. William Sharpley and Rachel Vandever. L
    3. William Jones and Mary Dilward. L
    4. John Fredrick and Jean Maguire.
    8. Thomas Johnston and Margret Baldwin.
  13. Henry Maclear and Mary Bentley.
  30. John Bruce and Lady Paulson. L

December.
    7. William Arthur and Hannah Gooden.
  10. James **Ferguson and Ann Few.**
  25. Edward Beeson and Mary Stedham.
      John Johnson and Cathrine Philips.
 ·28. John Hedrich and Ann Emit.
      John Loynam and Ann Springer. L

ANNO 1770.

January.
    1. Tobias Henderson and Phœbe Backsler.
    2. Matthew Treazey and Mary Walter.
    5. John Taylor and Jean McCoom.
    6. Michael Young and Mary Barent.
    9. Joseph Garrisson and Sarah Abrams. L
  10. David Jenkins and Hannah O'Danel. L
  17. Benjamin McCall and Abigail Harlan.

February.
    7. Israel Peterson and Susanna Peterson.
  13. John Crosby and Ann Pearce. L
  15. James Walter and Sarah Dickson.
  26. Thomas Webster and Margret Clarke.

EARLY CHURCH RECORDS OF NEW CASTLE COUNTY

March.
- 5. Henry Harlan and Phœbe Starr. L
- 6. Israel Pyle and Margery Robertson.
- 12. Robert Hindman and Margaret Walker.
- 14. John Davis and Ann Davis.
- 15. Robert File and Ruth Cling. L
    Bezaller Bentley and Catharine Little.
- 26. Johnathan Steely and Debora Shaw.
- 27. Andrew Loynam and Ann Walraven.

April.
- 2. James Woolson and Mary Roberson.
- 5. Jonas Walraven and Elenor Justis. L
- 9. Aaron Musgrave and Rachel Woodrow.
    James Garritson and Mary Abrams.
- 16. Robert Eccles and Margret Robb.
    John Henley and Martha McKeever.
- 17. Ellis Bently and Else Edmonds.
- 17. James Skott and Elizabeth Willson. L

May.
- 3. Samuel Brays and Elizabeth McMikel. L
- 9. Andrew Morten and Mary Post.
- 10. John Martin and Mary Craft.
    Isaac Hollingsworth and Hannah Skott.
- 31. Jacob Shreves and Elizabeth Cremer.

June.
- 4. William Wiley and Margret White.
- 5. Brian Daily and Mary Morphy.
- 12. Harman Whiteman and Elizabeth Junkins. L
- 17. Jeremia Flemon and Ann Byrns
- 18. John Stack and Mary Darlington.
- 19. William Derickson and Rebecca Springer. L

July.
- 1. Conrad Saesa and Susanna Henderson.
- 2. John Linch and Isabella Walker.
- 25. Eliah Hooten and Sarah Bird. L

August.
- 6. William Bell and Hester Richy.
- 8. Dennis McGee and Susanna Roberson.
- 9. Joseph Smidth and Frances Barrington.
- 13. Andrew McIntire and Mary Lampley,
- 16. Jacob Derrickson, Jr., and Susanna Sennex.
- 22. John Webster and Sarah Vanneaman.

OLD SWEDES CHURCH

27. John Orr and Elizabeth Henry.
26. Benjamin Way and Mary Bolden.

September.
11. James Masters and Cathrine Ellis.
    William Robbins and Mary Forgerson.
13. Samuel Huston and Elizabeth Maxfield.
24. John Chard and Susanna Shanks.
28. Hugh Russel and Mary Buckingham,

October.
2. James Walker and Agnes Miley. L
5. John Dunsmore and Guenny Morgan. L
9. Evan Evan and Hannah Sullivon. L
13. John Brogan and Mary Chalfant. L
22. Alexander Walker and Mary McIntire.

November.
1. William Nichols and Hannah Chalfant.
5. John Black and Martha Steward.
   Matthew Smidth and Sarah Cunningham.
   William Dunn and Elizabeth Pike.
   Joseph Day and Elizabeth Wood. L
6. Richard Troushon and Lydia Underwood.
20. James McArthur and Margret Clemens.
22. James Cann and Rachel Chandlor.
23. Edward Crow and Mary Adertown.
29. Joseph Brown and Susanna Davis.
30. Robert Ryan and Mary Wilson.

December.
4. Andrew Peterson, Jr., and Elizabeth Brunberg.
7. James Woodward and Jane Bullock.
10. James Maxwell and Elizabeth McDougal.
13. Samuel Durnal and Elizabeth McCartor.
    James Elliott and Sarah Gise.
18. William Login and Jane Way.
19. Samuel Kirkpatrick and Mary Sutton.
20. Joseph Gorby and Hannah Stilley. L

ANNO 1771.

January.
2. John Gest and Rebecca Davis. L
   Lawrence Woods and Mary Kelly.
3. Isaac Powell and Hannah Bealy.
17. John McKellway and Frances McBride.

EARLY CHURCH RECORDS OF NEW CASTLE COUNTY

18. Francis Hestis and Elizabeth Skott.
24. Thomas Edwards and Hannah Philips.

February.
2. Jacob Greave and Rebecca Langley. L
14. Thomas Burtington and Leady Woodward.
18. John Wilkins and Susanna Webb.
21. Joseph Baker and Mary Garnel. L

March.
4. Isaac Johnson and Leady Miller.
5. Robert Hugh and Ann McBride. L
7. Job Meyer and Margret Gordon.
21. Joseph Wiley and Elizabeth Johnson. L
25. James Solgrave and Cathrine Suttin.
25. Abner Meyer and Jean Brown.
26. Nathaniel Maguire and Sara Collins.
27. John Flinn and Jeane Parker.
28. John Dunlap and Sarah Melaun. L

April.
4. Jerssey Bentley and Leady Chalfant.
9. Johnathan Rumford, Jr., and Sarah Way.
9. George Witzel and Mary Stedham.
16. John Knight and Elizabeth Henderson.
21. Abraham Clark and Hannah Chamberlain.

May.
4. John Waterson and Jean Coldwell.
9. Robert Gunn and Mary Paterson.
10. Samuel Lenard and Elizabeth Parkisson.
11. George Caldwell and Prudence Maahon.
22. Robert Edward and Mary Crook. L
30. John Clark and Mary Clark. L

June.
2. Andrew Anderson and Mary Guthrie.
22. John Barlow and Elizabeth Barnet.
24. Thomas Sharp and Elizabeth Rotch.
25. John Richmot and Margret Parker.
27. Johnathan Evans and Hannah Robertson.
30. Edmund Daugherty and Leady Pyle.

July.
1. Stephen Allis and Elizabeth Swayon. L
16. Christopher Sayers and Cathrine McDouglas. L
28. Jacob Pyle and Sarah Hurford. L
29. James Cambel and Elizabeth McCollock.
30. Benjamin Miller and Hannah Martin.

258

OLD SWEDES CHURCH

    31. John Hays and Phœbe Huston. L

August.
    9. Thomas Baldwin and Mary Starr. L
    15. James Brown and Margret Maxfield. L
    19. James Logan and Leah Victory.

September.
    3. Archibald McMurphy and Juliana Rickets.
    10. Ledom Ingrom and Ann Ford.
    19. Michael Nelson and Barbara Bratten.
    26. Collins Hamor and Sarah Smidth.
    28. Christopher Gowing and Ann Murphy.

October.
    5. Wm. Karran and Rebecca Owen.
    6. Joseph Bursington and Cathrine Dixon. L
    13. Timothy Hanson and Mary Way. L
    17. Abraham Vanneaman and Ann Paulson.

November.
    1. Allen Key and Mary Mote.
    4. John Wates and Hannah Mitchel.
    Gilbert Bradley and Mary Woolly.
    Joseph Borman and Elenor Bartley.
    25. John Hennings and Mary Ford.
    David Chandlor and Leady Henderson.

December.
    1. John Faddes and Hannah Tremble.
    2. John Nails and Sarah Woodward.
    16. Gilbert McCarter and Ann Spence.
    19. Joseph Stedham and Sarah Hedge.
    22. Thomas Davis and Mary Bird.
    23. John Floyd and Hannah Thomson.
    26. Mathias Gennet and Elizabeth Justis. L

ANNO 1772.

January.
    15. John Warrel and Sarah Goolder. L
    16. George Rich and Hannah McDonald.
    27. Johnathan Johnson and Elizabeth Richards.
    William Elliott and Elizabeth Kimbler

February.
    5. Johnathan Dutton and Martha Beeson.
    6. Robert Bryon, Jr·, and Ingeber Stedham.
    8. John Taylor and Elizabeth Moulder.
    16. Abraham Heald and Mary Heald.
    20. John Savill and Mary Langley. L
    23. Jacob Sanders and Mary Dorothy.

EARLY CHURCH RECORDS OF NEW CASTLE COUNTY

    27. Charles MGonigale and Elizabeth Lyle.

March.
    19. Isaiah Hoops and Jean Martin.
        Michael King and Mary Garrison.
    30. Daniel Dealy and Elizabeth Pitman.

April.
    6. Charles Whitelock and Hannah Gray. L
    8. James Wilson and Catharine Peterson. L
    21. Gottlieb Snider and Catharine Lytieker.
    23. John Bratten and Margret McEntire.
    28. Henry Deal and Margret Little.

May.
    4. Samuel Richardson and Rachel Harlen.
    6. Thomas Savadge and Hannah Woodward.
    9. John Creag and Else Alfred. L
    9. Robert McCullah and Mary Robertson. L
    11. James Murphey and Ann Zebley.
    18 Thomas Gandy and Barbara Hollingsworth.
    18. Timothy Kogg and Johanna Taylor.
    25. Barry Cossins Harris and Margret Marshall.

June.
    9. Abner Cloud and Elizabeth Rummond. L
    18. John Hendrickson and Margret Sennex. L
    23. Robert Black and Margret Tardey.
    24. Samuel Chandler and Mary Welch.
    27. Daniel Grimes and Mary Seed. L

July.
    9. Archibald McDonald and Hannah Springer.
    30. George Beale and Mary Middleton.

August.
    1. Richard Jamison and Elizabeth Smidt. L
       Joseph Dain and Rachel Bratten. L
    20. Thomas Londey and Lydia Derrick.

September.
    1. Thomas McKingley and Lucrecy Evans.
    1. James McCollah and Hannah Eves
    12. Thomas Gilpin and Leady Rise. L
    19. John Young and Rebecca Sheward. L
    20. Samuel Tussey and Sarah Sparks.
    24. Isaac Vanloaner and Ann England.
    29. William Hannum and Ruth Evans.
       John Fred and Ann Davis.

OLD SWEDES CHURCH

October.
    26. Caleb Golleher and Martha Jones.
November.
    2. Joseph Latta and Sussanna Steen.
    4. John Thomson and Mary Clayton.
        Samuel Conn and Ann Bullock. L
    5. John Dealy and Jean Gray.
    9. Daniel Davis and Mary Pearce.
    12. Nathanael Wilkinson and Elinor Dunihoo.
        Gideon Clark and Sarah Jaquette.
    16. John Dehanor Dunham and Rebecca Rockerel. L
    17. George Groes and Ann Fisher,
    18. John McCarter and Margret Thomson.
December.
    3. John Kersin and Hannah Booth.
    24. Thomas Smith and Susanna Talley.
        Thomas Moore and Ann Stephenson.
    28. Thomas Littler and Leady Feelding. L

ANNO 1773.

January.
    4. William Clayton and Mary Harlan.
    5. Joseph Stroda and Cathrine Smith.
    7. George Thomas and Cathrine Paulson.
    9. Solomon Gregg and Isabel McCracken.
    20. Benjamin Rothwell and Margret Abrams. L
    21. Lukas Walraven and Cathrine Gray. L
    21. Walter Meredith and Rachel Lea. L
    22. John Huggins and Mary Marshall. L
    28. Stephen Mendenhall and Margret Farlo. L
February.
    2. Michael Ravel and Ann Dain.
    2. Henry Fri and Sarah Hendrickson.
    4. Joseph Gilpin and Elizabeth Malean. L
    6. John Darlington and Elenor Armstrong.
    9. John White and Elenor Karney. L
        Michael McCrea and Mary Sulliven.
    18. Peter Whiteaker and Frances Bethel.
    22. Robert Love and Ann Moore.
March.
    10. James Crosely and Hannah Moore.
    15. Joshua Pierce and Rachel Hays. L
    23. John Maguire and Margret Shute. L
April.
    1. William Anderson and Mary Bird. L

EARLY CHURCH RECORDS OF NEW CASTLE COUNTY

   7. Francis Williams and Mary Taylor. L
   8. Arthur Gennoi and Hannah Huston. L
 13. John Burns and Sarah Derrick.
 15. John Wilson and Margret Monteith.
 22. John Fisher and Ann Taylor.

May.
   1. William Pennock and Mary Martin. L
   6. John Williams and Mary Whitting. L
 20. Joseph Gray and Ann Miller. L
      Benjamin Pierce and Mary Folk.
 21. John Lowis and Mary Krawson.
 26. Joseph Baldwin and Rebecca Elliott.
 29. David Philips and Ann Igelsten.

June.
   3. Joshua Harlan and Mary Whitey.
      Richard Denny and Mary Cummins.
   9. Henry Cubbin and Christiana Dugen.
 10. Christopher Gennet and Elizabeth Penn.
 11. Robert Pierce and Cathrine Sharpley.
 14. Peter Green and Rebecca Grispe.
 17. David Stedham and Hannah Knott.
 18. Daniel Kenney and Mary Alford.
 20. John Rodgers and Barbary Sanders.
 24. Jacob Bird and Rebecca Justis.
 26. David Chandler and Hannah Buckingham.
      John Martin and Mary Hicklin.

July.
   4. James Frith and Phœbe Thomsen.
   9. John Peterson and Ruth Pyles.
 27. William Winnet and Sarah Strainge. L
      Hugh Mitchell and Sarah Koll.
      John Barret and Margret When. L

August.
   2. Jeremiah Underwood and Elizabeth Hutton.
   9. John Davis and Mary Loury.
 10. James Sim and Margret Calahan.
      Henry Fuller and Hannah Backster.
 23. Isaac Cherrey and Rebecca Bird.
 27. John McClary and Mary Wallace. L

September.
   1. Peter Woolbough and Mary Smidt.
   2. James McKean and Ann Wilson.

OLD SWEDES CHURCH

7. Nathan Johnson and Ruth Webb.
8. John Peter and Balty Robbeson. L
30. Thomas Wade and Nancy Hamilton.

October.
4. Isaac Allen and Rachel Sharp. L
5. Joseph Jonson and Martha House
9. Jacob Berndt and Else Brothers.
14. James Alford and Elizabeth Welch.
18. Richard Silenie and Johanna Few. L
21. David McCausland and Sarah Holms. L
31. John Johnson and Sarah Shiels. L.

November.
15. Samuel Grundow and Rebecca Rouse.
21. Richard Derrick, Jr., and Leady Cloud. L
John Chamberlain and Batty Mole. L
23. Jacob Bennet and Mary Tood.
24. Evan Philips and Mary Harlan.
25. David Brown and Hannah Martin.
29. Joseph Fisher and Susanna Gray.

December.
2. David Windell and Rebecca Lynam.
10. John Henry Wagner and Elizabeth Hilden.
14. Jacob Broom and Rachel Pierce. L
15. Thomas Treacy and Sarah Coplind.
23. John Churchman and Jean Taylor.
Joshua Dickson and Phœbe Heald. L
30. Charles Paulson and Susanna Woolbough.

ANNO 1774.

January.
6. James Dougherty and Livina Lawrence.
10. David Denny and Leady Nelson.
27, John Spragg and Mary Garrison. L
31. Wm. Craig and Margret Holahan.

February.
1. Peter Ingram and Elizabeth Taylor.
14. iMchael Higgins and Cathrine Menzener.
14. Archibald Sherer and Ann Hall.

March.
3. Henry Philips and Rebecca Gillbreath. L
10. John Hunter and Mary Cochlin.
11. James Law and Elizabeth Kennoi.

263

EARLY CHURCH RECORDS OF NEW CASTLE COUNTY

    15. Wm. Sturges and Jean Devor.
    16. Wm. Chamberlain and Sarah Goss.
    26. Wm. Martin and Jean McCarty.

April.
    3. John McLaughlin and Jean Dunlap. L
    9. Robert Richardson and Jean Davison.
    14. Isaac Gregg and Sarah Galloher. L.
    14. James Currey and Rachel Kirk. L
    18. Wm. Wright and Margret Keith.
       Samuel Moore and Sarah Thomson.

May.
    17. John Hague and Sarah Collins.
    19. Andrew Lynam and Margret Hall. L
    19. Robert Chalfant and Rachel Walter.
    27. Thomas Wilson and Rachel Chalfant.
    30. Thomas Bullock and Elizabeth Nelson.

June.
    3. John Gold and Cathrine McBride. L
    12. Thomas Morton and Elizabeth Thompson.
    16. John Gritsie and Hannah Daly.
       George Dennis and Elenor ?eterson.
    23. David Hews and Rosanna Hugile.
    30. Daniel Brown and Mary Wagner.

July.
    6. John Humphreys and Elizabeth Woodside. L
    15. John stall and Mary Pyle.
    16. John Paulson and Sarah McCallem.
    19. Wm. Moore and Margret McLouin.
    31. Charles Bewgles and Margret Byrnes.

August.
    1. Robert McIntire and Rachel Floyd.
    9. Joseph Savill and Martha Farra.

September.
    12. Joseph stunton and Agnes Hendrickson.
    13. Edward Woods and Sarah Heaveren.
    19. Joseph Sill and Elizabeth Ford.
    22. Jacob Hews and Rachell Perkins.
    29. Wm. Stidham and Rebecca Tussaw.

October.
    14. George Williamson and Mary Page.
    20. John Reed and Agnes Brakin. L
       John Stern and Hester Heald.

OLD SWEDES CHURCH

 24. Isaac Ryan and Hannah Townsand.
 26. Isaac Hearshy and Jean McEntire. L
 27. Jacob Derrickson and Elenor Stidham.
November.
  1. Wm. Willson and Ann Bill.
  4. Mentor Pimperdue and Jemima Farle.
  9. John Danielson and Mary Jinkins.
 10. Griffit Jordan and Phœbe Ford. L
 14. Robert Grunde and Elizabeth Neil.
 17. Robert Armstrong and Rachel Springer.
 21. Samuel Landers and Mary Welch.
December. 15. **Daniel Coghran and Cathrine Wilson.**
  3. John Brinton and Mary Rogers. L
  7. Enoch Chandler and Hannah Baldwin.
 12. Thomas Williams and Rachel Woodward.
 14. Christopher Chandler and Phœbe Kirk. L
 15. Joseph Griss and Margret Aberdain.
   Thomas Heins and Elenor Willison.
 22. Hugh Montgomery and Rachel Peterson. L
 27. Thomas Dennison and Jean Cunningham.

     ANNO 1775.
January.
  3. Samuel Steel and Leah Elliott. L
  8. Shesh Cazzar Bentley and Hannah Baldwin. L
  9. Aaron Grubb and Priscilla Cloud. L
 11. Henry Jeffrey and Emy Bennet.
 16. Edward Willison and Elizabeth Hanley.
 19. Samuel McSavan and Cathrine McDowel.
February.
 27. Robert Allen and Cathrine Manough.
March.
  2. Day Branson and Margret Freeman.
   Thomas Hogg and Cathrine Heens. L
  8. George Andrews and Mary Bradford. L
 20. Moses Johnson and Rachel Johnson.
   Andrew McKee and Mary Almond. L.
 28. Samuel Shipley and Jane Bennet.
   Robert Taylor and Mary Hastings.
   Samuel Gibson and Margret Almond.
 29. William Simonson and Martha Russel.
   James Veech and Rebecca Jemison.
April.
  8. Nathan Millner and Mary Sharpley.
 13. David Evans and Elizabeth Todd.

EARLY CHURCH RECORDS OF NEW CASTLE COUNTY

17. Francis Dutton and Hannah Talbert.
18. John Stoop and Elenor McCallen.
24. Samuel O'Hughs and Mary Baiard.
26. David Caldwell and Martha Thompson.
29. Jonathan Jordan and Susanna Flupen.

May.
4. Theophilus Jones and Mary Eccles.
7. James Moore and Margret Ramsay.
9. Philip Ward and Mary Hall.
9. Edward Bratten and Mary Harris.
9. James Ford and Mary Eldridge.
21. John Wiley and Sarah Morgan.
25. George Key and Martha Simons.
26. Wm Mann and Jean Brown.

June.
5. Peter Hendrickson and Mary Leard.
10. Samuel Hollingsworth and Hannah Rondle.
15. George Lauerbeck and Rebecca East.
19. Francis Cluggage and Jean Nixon.
22. William Hutchins and Ann Bennet.

July.
6. Richard January and Mary Thomas.
8. John Martin and Rebecca Runnels.
11. Robert Huggins and Hannah Bennet.
13. Joseph Moorestrand and Hannah Enis.
17. Aron Job and Barbara Jacobus.
22. Joseph Hollis and Hannah Sheward.
27. Joseph Gregg and Rachel Hicklin.

August.
3. Thomas Moores and Jemima Derrick.
" Nicklas Tailleuh and Juda Price.
17. George Nixon and Sarah Seeds.
28. Richard Marer and Elenor Perkins.

September.
7. Israel Israels and Hanna Erwin.
14. Thomas Knight and Mary Tayler.

October.
4. Richard Richards and Jeane McCowel
5. John Alford and Rebecca Welch.
10. Daniel Walker and Margret Walker.
14. Amos Davis and Elenor Ferrel.
" William Park and Elizabeth McBride.
16. Abel Sherwood and Elenor Johnson.

OLD SWEDES CHURCH

24. John Gars and Mary Mahane.
25. Samuel Marshall and Elizabeth Vandever.
26. James Eves and Phœbe Brinton.

November.
4. John Parry and Hannah Diliwerd.
7. Archibald Hocks and Jean McKee.
8. Ebenezer Tally and Elizabeth Brown.
19. Thomas Hanson and Elenor Digdon.
22. Thomas Love and Jean Clindelon.
23. William Calvert and Jean Craig.

December.
4. John Branen and Margret Pingelton
6. George Sellers and Sarah Clifferd.
7. Joseph Elliott and Mary Lampley.
" William Hanby and Elizabeth Konelly.
19. David Irvin and Isabel Adams.
" David Huston and Elenor Sheerer.

ANNO 1776

January.
7. John Askew and Elizabeth Jackson.
6. John Jacobs Falkoner and Ann Harlon.
9. Strainge Backhouse and Cathrine Springer.
11. John Hanna and Leady McDannel.
13. John Spenees and Mary Holahan.
15. Robert Russel and Jennet Allen.
22. Thomas Ewart and Phœbe Woodward.
23. John Veall and Rebecca Stilley.
24. Abraham Ritchee and Elizabeth Clark.

February.
10. David Leech and Mary Jordan.
13. Robert McWilkin and Mary Bradford.
22. James Hickman and Sarah Owens.

March.
5. John Welch and Hanna Darty.
5. James Pyle and Lydia Dilworth.
6. Daniel Foresman and Susanna Downing.
8. Joshua Bussington and Ann Marshall.
21. Wm. Dixon and Dorcas Eyon.
24. Joseph Carter and Margret Cloud.
27. John Bratton and Mary Huston.

April.
2. Hans Stameast and Susanna Cling.
4. John Ward and Mary Taylor.

EARLY CHURCH RECORDS OF NEW CASTLE COUNTY

    6. James McKeever and Susanna McCafferty.
  16. Ephriam Russel and Elizabeth Simonson.
  18. James Russell and Margret Bratten.
  28. John Highfield and Martha Bailiss.

May.
  27. Andrew Towers and Charity Frames.
  29. John Grined and Debora Robeson.
  29. James Cohoon and Ann Nedrick.

June.
    9. Thomas Watson and Jane America.

July.
  28. Robert Garrett and Jane Colber.

August. 1. Zacharius Derickson to Sarah Sullivan
    1. David Derrickson and Leady Sullivan.
       James Robinson and Agnes Johnson.
       Lewis Janney and Mary Pennock.
    4. James Murphy and Mary Jackson.
  12. John Middleton and Elizabeth Porter
  15. Solomon Hays and Mary Craig
  17. Ely Baily and Ruth Taylor.

September.
    3. Adam Truman and Elizabeth Talbot.
    9. John Cashedy and Mary Myers.
  10. Thomas Thomson and Prudence Jefferis.
  23. John Freiczer and Martha Swain.
  26. Peter Harden and Rebecca Peterson.
  30. Philip Otley and Hanna Baker.

October.
  14. George Roads and Hanna Mercer.
  15. Alexander Brown and Hanna Ritchie.
  28. John Hickman and Elizabeth Jeffries.
  30. Thomas Robinson and Sara Baldwin.

November.
    4. Wm. Fletcher and Jane McChesney.
    4. Archibald McWicker and Dorcas Dickson.
    4. James McClyde and Martha Chalfant.
    6. Wm. Pluright and Rachel Walraven.
  21. Philip Sellars and Hannah Gordon.
  28. Peter Blankcharr and Martha McCann.

December.
    2. George Bradley and Mary Taylor.
    7. Lampson Barnet and Phoebe Grissie.

OLD SWEDES CHURCH

16. Benjamin Grubb and Leady Larkin.
18. John Paulson and Elenor Armstrong.
13. Benjan Brown and Ann Trevillo.

Anno 1777.

January.
2. John Hendrickson, Jr., and Ann **Lessenger**.
16. James Hughs and Margret McClane.
23. James Walker and Mary Downing.
26, Bartram Donde and Mary Campbell.

February.
5. John Richardson and Hannah McEntois.
6. Thomas Broom and Margret Morton.
6. James Brown and Rebecca Warden.
8. Thomas **Plunket** and Elizabeth Brown.
10. Wm. **Eccles** and Jane Ross.
12. Joseph Cloud and Elizabeth Folk.
20. Wm. Smith and Elizabeth Cambel.
23. Wm. Heagens and Margret Daugherty.
24. James Burrough and Alice Jordan.
27. John Wilkesson and Jane Robeson.

March. 24. **Jas. Tague and Margaret Paro.**
3. John Spassy and Ann Harrison.
10. Samuel Davidson McCaplin and Elizabeth Buckley.
11. Stephen **Pyke** and Jane Conner.
12. Richard Strode and Hannah Batten.
   Wm. Husbands and Margret Megarrough.
14. Wm. Johnson and Cathrine Shanks.
19. Matthew Anderson and Elizabeth Mickebroi.
18. Jacob Anderson and Mary Johnson.
20. Jesse Crossman and Elizabeth Ridge.
24. Robert Bryan and Rebecca Hall.
    Stephen League and Hannah Nickols.
    Richard Moore and Ann Brown.
27. David Ford and Jemima Ford.
31. John McKaghuen and Hannah Moore.

April.
1. Cornelius Derrickson and Ann Almond.
2. Peter Durnal and Hannah Wilson.
14. Thomas Carr and Mary Owen.
14. Walter Clark and Martha Adamson.
15. Wm. Loudon and Charity Davis.
25. Robert Forgreave and Sarah Young.
26. John McGrashan and Ann Olding.

EARLY CHURCH RECORDS OF NEW CASTLE COUNTY

May.
  1. Thomas Neill and Elisabeth Bush.
  9. Abner Broadford and Rachel Baldwin.
    John Flahen and Alse **Eccles**
 12. John Dougherty and Ann Proctor.
    John Williams and Sarah Pyle.
 14. Matthew McConnel and Margret Williams.
 19. John Robinson and Alse McDernot.
 29. James Wallace and Elizabeth Shaw.

June.
 18. Samuel Brown and Mary Ellwel.
 27. John Tolan and Mary Laferty

July.
  1. James Motlay and Elizabeth Cruden.
  3. Thomas Mathews and Ann Kirk.
  5. John Jones and Elizabeth Johnson.
 16. James McKeever and Mary Edwards.
 20. George Stanton and Mary Stedham.

August.
 11. Thomas Berry and Mary Harrison.
 22. John Bernard and Hannah Davis.
 27. Wm. Hanby and Hannah Hanby.

September.
  2. John Disney and Cathrine Miller.
 25. James Shofield and Mary Job.

October.
 10. Robert Robeson and Elizabeth Sleifer.
 15. Wm. Jones and Hannah Casson.
 29. **Matthew Everite and Mary Wilson.**
    Thomas Watson and Unity Dugal.

November.
  4. Samuel Little and Margret McCollan.
 15. Daniel Howard aud Sara Porter.
 20. James McFadren and Martha Carlton.
 25. Samuel Hodges and Mary Miller.

December.
 11. John Stilley and Elizabeth Gray.
 23. Francis Harbeson and Hanhah Hannum.
 27. Hugh McKeever and Elizabeth Talbert.

ANNO 1778.

January.
  6. John Baughman and Mary Gilbreath.
 10. Wm. Saunders and Hanna Richardson.

OLD SWEDES CHURCH

    John Vandever and Persina Beeson.
- 12. John Maylark aud Jane Killpatrick,
- 19. Patrick Burk and Susanna Fielding.
- 22. Joseph Baughman and Elenor Springer.
- 28. William Rosny and Margret Farme.
- 31. George Neilson and Martha Colesbery.

February.
- 21. Isaac Griffie and Ann Moore.
- " John Roberts and Philis May.

March.
- 8. John Emeson and Mary Green.
- 11. Henry Glack and Ann Carpenter.
- 24. Christopher Brown and Alse Stuart.
- 26. John Scothorn and Rebecca Walraven.

April.
- 2. William McKee and Elizabeth Miles.
  James McGustin and Elenore Hines.
- 8. Joseph Hall and Mary Forsyth.
- 19. Samuel Bowjer and Susanna Hall.
- 20. Thomas Stanley and Ann Greenacre.
- 21. Thomas Harper and Elizabeth Wood.
- 27. George Stuart and Mary White.
  William Gaskin and Carina Tussey.
  Benjamin Yarnel and Mary William.
- 29. Joseph Wilde and Rachel Jacquet.
  William Bright and Johanna Parfis.
  Samerlain Spencer and Mary Ayres.
- 30. Isaac Sumption and Ann Mason.
  Andrew Vanneaman and Cathrine Andey.

May.
- 4. Joseph Burk and Eleanore McGin.
- 7. Hugh McLean and Susanna Pendelgrass.
- 9. John Welshe and Cathrine Campbel.
- 12. Francis Thomson and Mary Taylor.
- 14. Laurence Conely and Rebecca Almond.
  Thomas Jones and Ann McCarter.
- 16. Caleb Seal and Sarah Brown.

June.
- 18. Edward Dunn and Ann Stalcop.
- 25. Thomas Brogth Hugan and Elizabeth Morgan.

July.
- 7. Ambrose William and Cathrine Johnson.

EARLY CHURCH RECORDS OF NEW CASTLE COUNTY

    7. Walraven Walraven and Elizabeth Slaughter.
    7. Hezekiel Carey and Rosanna McCafferty.
   14. Samuel Dixon and Sarah Woodward.
   18. William Mould and Elizabeth Fritch,
   23. John Strawbridge and Hannah Evans.

August.
    9. John Malcolm and Cathrine Brotherton.
   23. Edward Fielden and Rebecca Anderson.

September.
   14. Andrew Calderwood and Mary Campbell,
   17. John Justis and Elizabeth Stidham.

October.
    1. David Dutton and Hannah Rodgers.
   13. Samuel Horner and Elizabeth Ferrey
   22. Daniel Meginnis and Catharine Mallen.

November.
    4. William McNail and Sarah Bailey.

December.
    7. William Jones and Mary Ghislin.
   16. Timothy Collins and Sarah Stewart,
   17. Jacob Robinson and Debora Justis.
   20. Daniel Boyle and Elizabeth Enis.
   25. Peter McDonald and Margaret Fox.

ANNO 1779.

January.
   14. Thomas Glenn and Lydia Cox.
   17. Richard Lampley and Prudence Derrick,

February.
   15. Jacob Butler and Ann Chalfant.

March.
    1. James Biggs and Mary Gordon.
    3. Bryan McNally and Jane McFarlan.
    4. Joseph Sommerlin and Sarah Stidham.
    9. James McWay and Sarah Woods.
   24. James Johnson and Jane Anderson.
   26. John Brown and Elizabeth McWesten.

April.
    3. Elisha Adkisson and Patience Chapman.
    8. Henry Colesberry and Ann Lynam.
   28. Robert Hues and Ann Gartigen.
   29. James Brindley and Elizabeth Ogle.

OLD SWEDES CHURCH

May.
    4. Ely Woodward and Alice Pyle.
    4. Lawrence Girelius and Christina Lidenius, married by Rev. N. Collin, rector of Raccoon and Pennsneck Churches.
    9. Daniel Brown and Sarah Seals.

June.
    16. Samuel Greave and Elizabeth Bishop.
    20. Daniel Janifer Adams and Ann Hanson.
    25. Thomas Jurden and Amelia Davy, negroes.
    26. Thomas Morgan and Elizabeth Dougherty.
    27. Arthur Dempsey and Johanna Riley.

July.
    16. James Gaskey and Rachel Wallace.
    22. William Smith and Orphey Cloud.

August.
    4. Peter Woolbough and Lydia Morton.
    16. William Alcorn and Alice Means.
    19. George Willis and Elizabeth Moore.
    30. Stephen Anderson and Elizabeth Farrell.

September.
    18. William Tinsley and Mary Greenfield.
    20. Joseph Hilton and Mary Alcott.
    29. William Armoth and Sarah Amystid.

October.
    7 Robert Keith and Mary Adams.

November.
    16. Thomas Robinson and Elizabeth Murdock.
    20. Thomas Durner and Mary Collett.

December.
    2. Peter Brynberg and Lydia Walraven.
    7. Timothy Cook and Ann Nelson.
    29. Richard Webster and Mary Thomas.
    30. William Wood and Elizabeth McBride.

ANNO 1780.

January.
    15. Nicholas Foss and Elenor Conolly.
    25. David Denny and Susanna O'Neile.

February.
    1. Samuel Faries and Rachel Hanson.
    3. Leonard Young and Lydia Flood.
    12. Marshall Battin and Susanna Hoode.

EARLY CHURCH RECORDS OF NEW CASTLE COUNTY

March.
    2. Thomas Hall and Hannah Marshall.
    14. Francis Liss and Margret Moore.
    21. James Blair and Ruth Peterson.

April .
    1. Gideon Williamson and Rachel Taylor.
    6. Joseph Coleman and Rebecca Windel.
       William Chamberlin and Ann Hampton.
    8. Benjamin Langley and Hannah Colon, negroes.
    9. Willlam Hewes and Cathrine Conelly.
    13. Andrew Peterson and Elizabeth Thomson.
    24. James Seeds and Isabella Donaldson.
    29. James Fowler and Ann English.

May.
    16. William Hague and Ruth Mndenhall.
    31. William Miller and Hannah Haney.

June.
    1. John Hawthorn and Margret Phillips.
    18. Robert Morrison and Sarah McClan.
    21. William Lockheart and Rebecca Farle.
    29. William McGlaughlin and Susanna Ford.
       John Nowlin and Mary Gray.

July.
    8. Joseph Wilkeson and Margret Muckelvain.
    19. Frederick Hall and Sarah Dublin.
    25. George Barnet and Margret Montgomery.
    25. Neil Toy and Cathrine Black.
    29. Andrew Cunningham and Ann Farrel.

August.
    6. William Dixon and Susanna Tryon.
    19. Casperus Meginnis and Elizabeth **Lajorge**

September
    30. Frederick Steen and Mary Woodward.

October.
    2. David Ray and Esther Jeffries.
    11. Thomas Williams and Phœbe Worrel.
    15. Isaac Brown and Mary **Bine**

November.
    4. Jonathan Kirk and Johanna Lewis.
    30. William Vandever and Johanna Milliner.

December.
    7. John Saunders and Johanna Silence.

OLD SWEDES CHURCH
ANNO 1781.

January.
- 14. Israel Brown and Ann Adkinson.
- 28. Samuel Taylor and Mary Miller.
- 30. Joseph Ashton and Leah Sharpley.

February.
- 11. Joshua Mortenson and Nancy Perkins.
- 13. Jacob Bratten and Rachel Sharpley.
- 27. George Weldin and Elizabeth Almond.

March.
- 7. Daniel Sharpley and Rebecca Vandever.
- 8. David Beeson and Margret Vandever.
- 10. Samuel Millner and Catharine Vandever.
- 26. Louis Jones and Catharine Budget,
- 25. Jonas Stidham, Jr., and Elenor Derickson.

April.
- 8. John Crampton and Hester Connel.
- 9. David Marshall and Mary Bussington.
- 9. Richard Bussington and Rachel Baker.
- 14. William Rawson and Lydia Woolbaugh.
- 25. William Thomson and Mary Hall.

May.
- 8. James Cannon and Debora McCullough.
- 17. John Veal and Ann Springer.
- 23. John Milton and Rachel Thomson.
    Caleb Way and Sarah Pierce.

June.
- 20. Benjamin Tilton and Margret Bailey.
- 24. Jeremiah Carter and Sarah Chew.

July.
- 17. Bernard Diamond and Mary Carr.

September,
- 8. Robert Rue and Elenor Vandever.
- 29. Robert McKnight and Rachel Nield.

October.
- 1. Isaac Sharp and Margret Johnson.
- 10. Anthony Redman and Elizabeth Brinton.
- 16. James Chalfant and Jane McCarty.
- 24. Jonathan Harlan and Abigal McCall

November.
- 3. Samuel Skott and Phœbe Edwards.
- 17. Philip Dwire and Margret Sullivan.

EARLY CHURCH RECORDS OF NEW CASTLE COUNTY

December.
   12. Eli Weldon and Mary Kellam.
   26. Jacob Justis and Hannah Springer.

ANNO 1782.

January.
   24. John Hansson and Rachel Hendrickson.
       Richard Taught and Mary Parkison.
   28. Thomas Smith and Jane Welch.

February.
   21. William Ford and Catharine Golden.

March.
   14. James Terney and Elizabeth **McCaffety**
   23. Israel Rambo and Margret Kellam.
   26. Jesse Walraven and Rebecca Hendrickson.
   28. Thomas Neilds and Mary Fling.

April.
   9. John Butler and Jane Philips.
   18. Joshua Marshall and Rachel Baily.
      John Ford and Rachel Johnson.

May.
   20. John Flin and Hannah Justis.
   28. John Allardice and Ann Baid.
   30. William Elliott and Elizabeth Clark.
      Elis Evanson and Rachel Seal.

June.
   5. John Taylor and Mary Smith
   11. Casper Camp and Margret Allen.
   12. Joseph Cocks and Elizabeth Twining.
   20. Lucas Stidham and Joanna Vaneaman.

July.
   7. William Sharpe and Cathrine Parlin.
   25. Thomas Nixon and Elizabeth Mason Adams.

August.
   1. William Cowly and Margret Heagans.

September.
   9. Henry Garritson and Sarah Robinson.
      John Rodgers and Elenor Dirrick.

October.
   2. John Baldwin and Ruth Way.
   4. James Gibson and Agnes Topping.
   8. Garret McQuillen and Jane McGloien.
   12. John Crosan and Mary Bishop.

OLD SWEDES CHURCH

 22. Be jamin Bentley and Mary Baldwin.
 23. John Barber and Rebecca Vining.

November.
 14. Richard Tagla and Ann Sleifer.
 23. Israel Hendrick Johnson and Sara Cappel.

December.
 15. Lulof Peterson and Rachel **Dain**
 24. George Vansandt and Cathrine King.
 31. John Vandever and Alse Beeson.

ANNO 1783.

January.
 1. Thomas Gilpin and Sarah **Council**
 2. Joseph Suttou and Magdalena Sleifer.
 5. William Alley and Mary Burris.
 16. James Killen and Elizabeth Lightbody.
 21. Joshua Todd and Mary Allen.
 23. William Smith and Mary Husbands.
   Jonas Stidham and Ingebor Sinnex
 27. Allen McKee and Ledda Canby.

February.
 2. John Hasselton and Ann Paulson.
 27. Simon Paulson and Ann Patton.

March.
 3. Andrew McUlvain and Rachel Montgomery.
 15. John Wood and Sarah Arey.

April.
 10. Archibald Philips and Elizabeth O'Donnelly.
 13. George Brown and Mary Tate.
 19. Isaac Moote and Ann Smidth.
 22. Oliver Evans and Sarah Tomlinson.

May.
 1. Joseph Robeson and Cathrine McDonnald.
 3. John Bowls and Elizabeth Kirk.
 6. Andrew Smith and Rachel Alrich.
 10. George Paulson and Rachel Bird.
 29. Joseph Coleman and Alice Jordan.

June.
 8. William Glasgow and Milchit Wroth.
 9. John Fanrod and Martha Gallaher.
 21. George Hamilton and Rachel Morgan.
 17. David Brown and Dinah Allen.

EARLY CHURCH RECORDS OF NEW CASTLE COUNTY

11. Abraham Johnson and Mary Chaney.

July.
16. Griffith Owen and Jane Sherman.

August.
7. John Springer and Sarah Horner.
9. Peter Davis and Jane Stinson.
18. Joseph McAsfey and Elizabeth Adamson.
25. Philip Ellick and Rachel Pashall.

October.
1. Joseph Brown and Rachel Cooper.
11. Casperus Meginnis and Mary Craw.
11. Benjamin Laforge and Margret Ervin.
15. Absalom Baird and Susanna Brown.
27. John Hewes and Hannah Conolly.

November.
4. John Vernon and Phœbe Marsh.
13. Joseph Capell and Mary Pearce.
20. John Robinson and Ann Vandever.
26. The Honorable William Killen, Chief Justice of Delaware State, and Mrs. Rebecca Bonzel.

December.
18. Mitchel Kinkead and Ann Ramsey.
25. Harlen Cloud and Debocah Canby.
31. John Yates and Lettice Davis.

Anno 1784.

January.
1. Robert Crangal and Susanna Steward.
6. Andrew Ray and Mary Taylor.

February.
5. John White and Elizabeth Richardson.
13. Wm. Richard and Margaret Simpson.
19. Thomas Tally and
19. Robert Wilson and Elizabeth Gibbons.
19. Andrew King and Rachel Ford.
26. John Jobbley and Eve Livingston.

March.
4. John Clark and Hannah Holte.
6. Jacob Ford and Jane Maul.
23. Thomas McDawel and Ruth McEntire.

April.
1. Samuel Lewis and Lydia Pearson.
3. James McWay and Elizabeth Mackey.

5. John Cossey and Elizabeth Sample.
14. John Williams and Hannah Garritson.
16. Nathaniel Jaquett and Mary Jaquett.

May.
26. Thomas Almond and Cathrine Derickson.

June.
3. Wm. Edwards and Elizabeth Rudolph.
10. Thomas Bird and Mary Babb.
17. James Reed and Phœbe Barnet.
24. Wm. Woodcock and Letitia Means.

July.
22. Joseph Meredith and Ann Ford.
23. John Price and Jemima Hansey.

August.
12. John Brawn and Hannah Jones.
17. Thomas Tyler and Susanna Wesley.
19. Alexander Harvey and Sarah Bird.
Edward McKeone and Ann Duugherty.
26. Wm. Colwell and Martha Newel
31. John Kitts and Rachel Peterson.

September.
9. John Cockran and Mary Smidt.
Jacob Moore and Grace Linch.

October.
9. Samuel Temple and Elizabeth Clemens.
13. Thomas Wilson and Mary Peirce.
21. Hance Naff and Mary Colligan.
28. Nathan Cummins and Mary Milben.

November.
9. Jessey Sharpless and Joanna Townsend.
11. Wm. Cosure and Rachel May.
17. John Holton and Cathrine Corridon.

December.
15. Owen McBraiherly and Ann Conner.
25. Jeremiah Brown and Phœbe Booth.
27. Thomas Griffin and Jane Spencer.

ANNO 1785.

January.
6. Alexander Hall and Sarah Heavens.
John Adair and Mary Hews.
12. Nicholas Richardson and Bell Jane Cambel.
17. Philip Jackson and Isabella Almond.

18. Briant Montague and Elenor Welsh.
February.
27. Moses Draper and Eve Williams.
March.
1. James Robinson and Cathrine Augustus.
17. Andrew McIntosh and Margret Claeson.
24. Isaac Abraham and Janet Smidth.
28. Abraham Hughes and Sara Brynberg.
April.
4. Daniel McBride and Rachel Bird.
7. John Shanks and Hannah Ghiseline.
May.
1. Wm. Moore and Rebecca Robinson.
19. Charles Savin and Mary McGinnis.
July.
7. Abel Green and Prudence Sidwel.
10. Thomas Smith and Debora Ward.
14. Israel Peterson and Jane Bratten.
25. James Fairbrother and Cathrine Barret.
August.
11. Joseph Enos and Ann Morton.
18. Wm. Pennock and Lydia Jackson.
23. Robert Culbertson and Mary Ogle.
September.
29. John Armstrong and, Elizabeth Peterman.
October.
13. John Brown and Ann Alardice.
16. William Cassidy and Martha McHenry.
November.
3. Joseph Justis and Ann Justis.
10. John **Kirk** and Mary Bishop.
16. Joseph Mungan and Sarah Alling.
16. Richard Graham and Patience Lewis.
27. Elva Valentine and Lovy Morgan.
28. Jeremiah Shadd and Amelia Sishe.
December.
13. Robert Leslie and Lydia Baker.

ANNO 1786.

January
5. Peter Walraven and Anna Hendrickson.
   Daniel Hossman and Rebecca Crampton.
29. Thomas Philpot and Brita Anderson.

OLD SWEDES CHURCH

February.
- 27. John Bogs and Elizabeth Carr.

March.
- 8. Samuel Harris and Mary Hall.
- Zadi Davis and Elenor Norris.
- 30. Benjamin Hall and Sara Arven.

April.
- 2. John Watson and Susanna Keepers.
- 10. Thomas Clark and Cathrine Floyd.
- 10. Patrick Roney and Mary Bicket.

May.
- 4. Joseph Jenkins and Sabina Sleifers.
- 23. Charles Thomas and Susanna McCallmont.
- 25. George Plank and Elizabeth Horn.

June.
- 4. John Green and Mary Hayhes.
- 21. Thomas Barrows and Ann HenriettalSmith.
- 24. Jacob Barnet and Sarah Ford.
- 25. Benjamin Hartley and Sarah Canby.
- 27. Timothy Pierce and Sarah Ashmead.

August.
- 2. Joseph Der.ickson and Ann Sullivan.
- 14. Henry Debooh and Martha Lawrence.
- 24. Abraham Brown aud Sarah Sinnex.

September.
- 7. James Davis and Johanna Mullen.
- 14. Kirk Kirk and Margret Megill.
- Daniel Sharpley and Isabella Weldon.
- 16. Francis Mendenhall and Mary Quine.
- 22. Peter D. Evermon and Anna Sinnex.

October.
- 11. Seneca Sinnex and Jane Derrickson.
- 13. Thomas Sharp and Elizabeth Harvey.
- 26. Peter Grubb and Hannah White,
- 31. John Smidt and Sarah Weldon.

1786.

Novembr.
- 5. The Rev. Charles Henry Wharton and Miss Mary Weems.
- 9. John McBeath and Margret Montgomery.
- 13. John McConnel and Mary Giffen.
- 27. Peter Justis and Sarah Hersey.

EARLY CHURCH RECORDS OF NEW CASTLE COUNTY

December.
    6. George Sellars and Ann Matson.
    9. Henry Likel and Isabella Stuard.
    27. Aaron James and Mary Messer.
    28. Benjamin Burrill and Ann Welsh.

ANNO 1787.

January
    4. Thomas Moore and Mary Lawrence.
    20. Benjamin Barnet and Mary Justison by order of a Justice of Peace in Presence of the Constable,

February.
    7. Moses Bullock and Ester Faulk.
    27. John Faulk and Jemima Sharpley.

March.
    1. Abner Dickinson and Jane Friar.
    12. John Bell and Isabella Dundas.
    27. John Kinsman and Margaret Weldon.

April.
    4. James Ball and Mary Evans.

May.
    13. Timothy Reed and Rebecca Monro.
    23. Isaac Justisson and Sarah Tossawa

June.
    10. Charles Stewart and Sarah Rawlins, from London England.

July.
    7. John Abrams and Jane French, from Madeira.
    12. **Michael** England and Rebecca Brown.
    18. Wm. Kirk and Susanna Anderson.

August.
    11. Joseph Webb and Sarah Fowser.
    15. Jacob Dick and Susanna Perkins.

September.
    2. Nathaniel Williams and Ann Sinnex.
    4. Samuel Kelly and Margret Gray.
    12. Ezekiel Grissit and Ann Sumption.
    13. James Delavon and Jemmima Rain.
    20. My Servant, Solomon Camper and Grace Timor, black.
    24. James Grubb and Sarah Ford.

October.
    16. Hugh Melagan and Margret McGaughey.
    27. John Lary and Ann Combs.

December.
    11. John Allinsser and Hannah McCarter.

OLD SWEDES CHURCH

29. Robert Taylor and Martha Haynes.

ANNO 1788

February.
    25. Christopher Crawford and Margaret Jaquett.

March.
    19. Caleb Johnson and Betty Nickols.
    20. Andrew Justis and Susanna Ball.

April.
    1. John Adams and Catharine Cochran.
    24. Samuel Wallace and Ann Laferty.

May.
    6. John Foot and Margret Lewis.
    15. Ebenezer Augustus Smith and Mary Stidham.

June.
    16. Robert McCaskey and Mary Hewes.
    17. James Ross and Priscilla Lewis.

July.
    16. Peter Henry and Mary Stonemety.

August.
    9. Charles McLean and Sarah McColly.
    14. John Francis Lefevre and Isabella Sanderson.
    26. Joseph Lamborn and Catharine Shivery.

September.
    16. James Delaplain and Mary Kirk.
    17. David Graham and Martha Parket.
    25. John Hall and Margret Elliot.

October.
    14. Isaiah Chester and Mary Peterson.
    17. Thomas Baxter and Rachel Ersley.
    21. Barnaby Kelly and Onore Suraney.

November.
    22. Edward Gilpin and Lydia Grubb.

December.
    17. James Maxfield and Mary Armstrong.
    24. Wm. Sanders and Letitia Jeffrey.

ANNO 1789.

January.
    6. Joseph Harris and Cathrine Righter.
    8. Cornelius Stidham and Rebecca Derrickson.
    Isaac Woodcock and Mary McCallem.

EARLY CHURCH RECORDS OF NEW CASTLE COUNTY

Robert Cauzine and Anne Sanders.
February.
    5. Levi Springer and Rebecca Hendrickson.
   11. Richard Millason and Ann Millason
March.
   19. Richard Runnels and Margret Lynam.
April.
    2. John Brynberg and Elenor Stedman.
   16. Edward Oldhman and Mary McDaniels.
July. 25. Neil Kellog and Magdaline McCassity
    7. John Stoops and Martha Moore.
   20. Charles Gelly and Ann Crosby.
   30. Valentine Robeson and Charity Cloud.
August.
    6. William Hawk and Mary Fallows.
   25. Malachia John and Martha Addy.
September.
   21. Abraham Baily and Phœbe Carpenter.
   22. Joshua Perkins and Rachel Preston.
October.
   22. John Robnell and Rachel Dingee
       Robert Nickols and Sarah Gennet.
   24. Neil Gallagher and Elizabeth Ball.
   29. Joseph Webb and Grace Parke.
November.
   23. John Banhare and Jane Boyd.
December.
    2. William Cooke and Jane Gaust
   15. Samuel Daas and Mary Purly.

ANNO 1790.

January.
   10. John Benderman and Bridget Fletcher.
   14. Cornelius Cripps and Hannah Hays.
February.
   11. Jacob Peterman and Brita Springer.
   20. Richard Few and Mary Tayler.
March.
    1. Memutan Howels and Elizabeth Taylor.
    4. Ephraim Bussington and Rebecca Framey.
   11. Nathan Boyce and Susanna Hiland.
   18. Jacob Weld and Mary Almond.
       John Welsh and Margret Elliott

25. John Springer and Rebecca Stidham.
29. George Butler and Elizabeth Conner.

April.
6. Alexander McKever and Susanna Stidham.
14. Sy Smith and Sarah Donaldson.
15. William Tolon and Sarah Bennet.
25. Thomas Delap and Elizabeth Stuart.

May.
6. John Stedham and Abigail Springer.
17. Jacob Smith and Isabella Sharpley.
27. Samuel Bolin and Ruth Butler.

June.
11. Michael King and Ann Sutton.
24. Joshua McClean and Rebecca Morton.

July.
22. George Pierce and Martha Chalfant.
24. Thomas Smith and Hannah Kirk.

August.
5. Nicholas Quinn and Elizabeth Runnels.
7. Bloomfield Grier and Lydia Harriot.
16. Thomas Smith and Margret Colbreth.

September.
2. Zacharias Garner and Lea Rue.
25. James Lackey and Mary Goddaid.
27. Joseph Smith and Phœbe Bail.
29. John Prerie and Debora Prerie.

October.
11. Thomas Pearce and Hanna Collins.
21. Charles Kelly and Debora Cobbs.
25. John McCennaugh and Rachel McCarnaughie.

November.
11. David Vanneman and Dorothy Runnels.
23. Thomas McKee and Mary Jordan.

December.
9. David Ford and Martha Gissin.
16. Thomas Elliott and Martha Anderson.

ANNO 1791.

January.
2. Robert Swan and Elizabeth Hamilton.
13. Abraham Chandler and Ann Cochran.
20. Caleb Marshall and Mary Marshall.

February.
3. Josiah Anderson and Rachel Derickson.

10. Benjamin Springer and Lydia McEntire.
April.
7. Auron Justis and Sarah Hiland.
15. John Withrow and Susanna Elliott.
21. Silas Bailey and Margret Harlan.
23. William Hazlett and Elizabeth Pyle.
27. Andrew Moore and Elizabeth Bines.
May.
4. William Dixon and Susanna Pearson.

MARRIAGES WHICH HAVE BEEN CELEBRATED IN THIS STATE (DELAWARE) AGREEABLY TO THE LAWS OF THE SAME RESPECTING MARRIAGES, BY JOSEPH CLARKSON.

1792.

December.
30. Tristram Thomas and Susan Geddes.

1793.

January.
12. Cadwalader Morris and Maria Leuden.
March.
17. Andrew Colesberry and Mary Allrich.
April.
4. Thomas Cartmell and Margret Perkins.
16. Joseph Walden and Rebecca Tussey.
May.
11. David Logan and Mary Long.
June.
9. William Wickersham and Elizabeth Green
15. Alexander McIntosh and Elizabeth Low.
24. Michael Morrow and Jane Robinson.
July.
3. George Shields and Hannah Walker.
9. Frederick Tussey and Catharine Springer.
17. John Gears and Anna Marley.
18. Thomas Mullin and Susan Readus.

OLD SWEDES CHURCH

August.
    12. George Henderson and Rachel Dampsey.
    16. Samuel Wilson and Cathrine Rother am.
    27. John Cannon and Ann Downs.
September.
    11. Alexander Tussey and **Margaret** Welch
    12. John Sinex and Margaret Ford.
    23. Thomas Watson and Mary Watson.
October.
    16. Francis Gurney and Mary ———.
    16. William Clark and Jane Lankin Branson.
    23. John Picket and Elenor McClaskey.
November.
    16. George Spain and Elizabeth Reynold.
    21. Nathaniel Grubb and Margret Babb.
        Philip Ford and Catharine Perkins.
    26. Berkely McClain and Ann Jane Townley.
December.
    3. William Currie and Lydia Tool.
    12. George Bush and Ann James.
    19. Jonathan Beson and Elizabeth Shipley.
    28. Charles Collins and Giles McNultey.

1794.

January.
    7. John Walraven and Mary Colesberry.
    13. William Lenderman and Elizabeth Stidham.
February.
    15. Nicholas Haney and Margret Backster.
    25. Jonas Stedham and Elizabeth Nebeker.
March.
    26. Peter Jaquet and Elizabeth Price.
April.
    6. Manasseh Dougherty and Cathrine Dougherty.
    21. John Valentine Webber and Sarah Chapman,
    24. John S. Lettler and Ann Broom,
June.
    30. John Crumpton and Sarah Harden, "no fee."
July.
    17. Thomas Daugherty and Mary Ford.
August.
    18. John Mills and Isabella Lindey, "ne fee."
September.
    15. Michael Mullin and Mary Culbertson.

EARLY CHURCH RECORDS OF NEW CASTLE COUNTY

    16. William Rice and Sarah Bracken.
    Samuel Kennedy and Tamazin Downing.
October.
    22. Edward Clois and Cathrine McGonagil.
November.
    15. Thomas Baily and Mary Heiser.
December.
    4. Isaac Tyson and Hannah Lobb.

February.   1795.
    19. Henry Logan and Mary McCalla.
    26. John Price and Elizabeth Smith.
    27. John Jeffries and Rachel Bale.
March.
    12. Henry Crawford and Hester Beeson.
    17. Ralph Lotton and Mary Hannah.
    21. George Weaver and Mary McWorter.
    28. William Hemmingway and Sarah Hayes.
April.
    20. Cornelius McDade and Mary Carr.
May.
    16. Louis Tousard and Ann Geddes.
June.
    4. Jacob Morton and Rachel Harp.
    18. Isaac Culin and Hannah Carter.
    25. Henry Barry and Elizabeth Rice.

July.
    9. Jacob Richards and Elizabeth James.
    8. William Hart and Margret Mikeljohn.
    15. Adam Talley and Rebecca Day.

October.
    8. John Rumford and Priscilla Jeffries.
    16. James McMullen and Cathrine Bryans.
    29. James D. Ross and Elizabeth M. Bancroft.

December.
    31. Patrick McNeil and Elizabeth Jeffries.
    1796.
January.
    10. Enoch Moore and Elizabeth Harris.
    17. Francis Dunlap and Honor Stidham.
    John Byrnes and Mary Cox.

27. William Foot and Kitty Matson.
27. Richard Hancock and Rebecca Matson.

February.
4. Francis O'Daniel and Isabella French.
11. Robert McCall and Elizabeth Calahan.
18. John Warner and Mary Lea.

March.
6. Samuel Sevel and Ann Golden.
31. William Wilson and Jane Bail.
31. Robert Montgomery Graham and Sarah Connell.

April.
10. Thomas Hancock and Ann Taylor.
12. James McClure and Sarah Rogers.
12. Daniel Coningham and Sarah Walker.

July.
19. William Gloss and Phœbe Jones.

August.
16. William Taylor and Martha Osborne.

September.
21. Samuel Tally and Mary Russell.
27. Henry Bridle and Christiana Gilmer.

October.
6. Worrick Martin and Ruth Miller.
6. Nathan Brown and Mary Mie.
13. William Taylor and Mary Murdock.
15. James Latham and Sarah Pritchett.
21. William Miller and Elizabeth Chamberlain.
25. John Guin and Rachel Dunlap.

November.
1. Ezra Lewis and Sarah Ford.
2. Edward Davis and Mary Taylor.
William Cloud and Ann Davis.
3. William Stedham and Elizabeth Poulson.
23. Neil Campbel and Sarah Smith.

1797.

January.
7. Patrick Nugent and Elianor Nugent.

March.
30. Frederick Obedeer and Fredrica Nultanius.

April.
 6. John D. Thompson and Sophia Baxter.
 20.' William Pluright and Eliza Stidham.
  Jonathan Davis and Elizabeth Boggs.
May.
 4. John Dawson and Elizabeth Jennet.
 9. James Wiltbank and Sally Cooper.
June.
 8. Zachariah Derickson and Susanna Johnson.
 11. Andrew Morris and Elizabeth Wott.
 18. David Alrich and Elizabeth Harvey.
 21. John Baptist Orso and Ann Ramsey.
July.
 5. Christopher Smith and Cathrine Sperry.
 6. Thomas Preston and Ann Sellars.
 26. John Johnson and Mary Powell.
August.
 3. Jesse Plankenton and Jane Robbins.
 10. Gilbert Fox and Sarah Loutit Veazy.
 22. James Boyle and Mary Anderson.
 31. Thomas Hunter and Cathrine Watson.
September.
 7. Thomas Warren Clark and Ann Trent Jacquett.
 16. John Henry Dobelbower and Edith Jones.
 24. John Job and Eleanor Galloway.
 28. John Gilpin and Mary Hollingsworth.
October.
 9. Clotworthy Barber and Elizabeth Given.
 12. James McConnal and Mary Harp.
 18. Wm. Dothat and Elizabeth Houstan.
 26. Jacob Brinton and Sarah Broom.
 28 John Morrow and Sarah Pyle.
 29. Lancelot L.' Smith and Ann Morton.
November.
 1. Daniel McDaniel and Susanna Loone.
 21. Garret Headen and Catharine Pain.
November,
 28. Robert Pyle and Hannah Clark.
December.
 18. James Mortemore and Margret Gregg.
 21. Joseph Stidham and Ann Gregg.

OLD SWEDES CHURCH

1798.

January,
1. James Foot and Margret Boyd.
11. Thos R. Gregg and Rachel Walters·
Adam Ayres and Sarah Larken.
14. Abraham Mendenhall and Eliznbeth Wells.
20. Thomas Rice and Ann Ball.

February.
1. Peter Vandever and Elizabeth Clandening.
14. Thomas E. Rumsey and Harriet Sykes.
18. Thomas Ellison and Harriet Rumsey.

March.
8. George Matson and Elizabeth Walters.
18. Michael Snodey and Lena Sutton.
31. Matthew Perry and Lydia Carothers.

April.
5. Joseph Hoops and Eleanor Hamilton.
30. Anthony W. Robinson and Mary Ogle.

May.
14 Wm. Hannah and Cathrine McDaniel.

June.
14. Aaron Pike and Rachel Killom.
21. Samuel Ford and Mary Snmption.

July.
14. James Cochran and Elenor P. Barclay·
26. Jacob Wolf and Rebecca Taylor.

August.
11. George Davis and Hester Griffith.
29. John Niels and Hannah Backhouse.

September.
3. Barnard Barrow and Eleanor Tolan.

November.
1. John Gallaher and Margrete Hedrick,
8. Harmon Savill and Sarah Thomson.
10. James Jack and Margret Marlarney.
25. George Gillaspey and Mary Geddes.

December.
8. Benjamin Masson and Ruth Dingee
9. Daniel Dingee and Mary Mooney.
15. James Ball and Isabella McKnight.
20. John Hansley and Mary McClaskey.
27. Wm. Hamilton Boyd and Elizabeth Mitchel.

EARLY CHURCH RECORDS OF NEW CASTLE COUNTY

1799.

January:
  12. Thomas Ring and Elizabeth Good.

February.
  14. Henry Bracken and Susanna Davis.
  28. John Gelespe and Mary Derrickson.

March.
  12. John Landers and Sarah Garretson.

April.
  11. Peter Walraven and Ann Fussel.
  15. Benjamin Derrickson and Sarah Reynolds.

May.
  16. Thomas Cryea and Rebecca Sellars.

INDEX

LAST NAME UNKNOWN:
  Alexander, 182
  Ann, 169, 197
  Anne, 113, 154
  Barbro, 121
  Benjamin, 182
  Cathrine, 154, 174
  Christian (negro), 8
  Daniel (servant), 11
  David, 154
  Davis, 178
  Dina, 106
  Easter, 90
  Edward, 100, 106
  Eleanor, 204
  Elenor, 167
  Elias, 210
  Elizabeth, 41, 90,
    146, 154, 160,
    189, 250
  Garner, 167
  George, 189, 202
  Gord, 172
  Griesey, 170
  Hannah, 113, 136
  Henry, 201
  Isaac, 172
  James, 202
  Jean, 152
  John, 100, 141, 155,
    172, 188
  Joshua, 157
  Jude, 213
  Judy, 209
  Lewis, 121, 136
  Magdalena, 88
  Margaretta, Widow, 9
  Margret, 100, 169,
    202
  Margreta, 121
  Margrete, 248
  Martha, 212
  Mary, 90, 120, 161,
    162, 175, 177,
    199, 287
  Michael, 213
  Patrick, 213
  Peggy, 35, 41
  Peter, 35, 136
  Phillis, 201
  Phoebe, 95
  Rachel, 88
  Ray, 197
  Rebecca, 172, 199
  Robbert, 152
  Robert, 197
  Ruth, 158
  Sarah, 156, 166,
    169, 192
  Scheirman, 152
  Susanna, 111
  Susannah, 151
  Thomas, 169, 201
  Violet, 177
  Wiclean, 199
  William, 88, 156,
    164, 166, 203
  Willson, 166

-A-

AAR, Mary, 60
ABBY, Kesia, 178
  Mary, 178
ABERDAIN, Margret, 265
ABRAHAM, Agnes, 88
  Benjamin, 220
  Isaac, 280
  Joseph, 12, 79, 84,
    88, 94, 100
  Margaret, 94, 100
  Margret, 84, 88
  Maria, 12, 16
  Mary, 84
  Sara, 94
  William, 5, 12, 16
ABRAHAMS, Anne, 120
  Benjamin, 149
  Isaac, 142
  Joseph, 109, 120,
    142, 149
  Margret, 109, 120,
    149
  Margrete, 142
  William, 109
ABRAM, Hannah, 129
  Joseph, 129, 133
  Margreta, 129
  Margretha, 133
ABRAMS, John, 282
  Margret, 261
  Mary, 256
  Sarah, 255
ACRELIUS, Isarel, 96,
    110
ADAIR, John, 279
  Robert, 239
ADAMS, Agnes, 236
  Ann, 181, 204
  Annah, 139
  Anne Garritsson, 106
  Cathrina, 218
  Daniel, 181, 198

Daniel Janifer, 181,
  273
Daniel Jennifer, 204
Elizabeth, 106
Elizabeth Mason, 276
Francis, 242
George, 227
Isaac, 123, 227
Isabel, 267
Janifer, 198
John, 123, 283
Margret, 123
Martin, 232
Mary, 273
Rachel, 139
Susanna, 198
Thomas, 106, 139,
  215
Thomas Hanson
  Bellach, 204
ADAMSON, Elizabeth,
  278
  Martha, 269
ADARE, Jane, 86
  Margaret, 89
ADDY, Martha, 284
  William, 253
ADERTHON, Grace, 217
ADGER, Rose Anne, 221
ADKINSON, Ann, 275
ADKIS, Richard, 82
ADKISSON, Elisha, 272
AFRELL, Elenore, 175
  Johannah, 175
  Thomas, 175
AGGOR, Margret, 100
  Robert, 100
  Sarah, 100
AGNEW, Anne, 118, 130
  David, 118
  Joseph, 118
  Lady, 118
  Margaret, 118
  Mary, 247
  Peter, 118, 130
  Rachel, 118
  Sarah, 130
AGORSEN, Rachel, 82
AHLFORD, Charles, 84
AHLMOND, Debora, 136
  Jane, 137
  John, 136
  Maria, 137
  Thomas, 137
AILS, Anne, 246
AINSWORTH, Jane, 235
AISTRIN, Anna Maria,
  16

AKEN, Jane, 219
AL, Elizabeth, 242
ALARDICE, Ann, 280
ALCORN, George, 221
  William, 273
ALCOTT, Mary, 273
ALDER, James, 222
ALDERWOOD, Anne, 237
ALDRIDGE, Lydia, 248
ALEXANDER, David, 235
  Garsheam, 90
  Hector, 225
  Isaac, 227
  James, 92
  Jane, 227
  John, 225
  Samuel, 231
  Zebulon, 217
ALFORD, James, 263
  John, 266
  Mary, 262
ALFRED, Else, 260
ALIS, Agnes, 112
  Elizabeth, 112
  James, 112
ALISSON, Elizabeth,
  120
  James, 120
  Jane, 120
ALKORN, Agnes, 178
  George, 178
  Sarah, 178
ALLARDICE, John, 276
ALLEN, Cathrine, 244
  Dahaghty, 136
  Dinah, 277
  Isaac, 94, 263
  James, 115
  Jane, 115, 215
  Jennet, 267
  Johanna, 224
  Johannes, 32
  John, 94, 115, 123
  Jonas, 41
  Margareta, 32
  Margret, 276
  Mary, 123, 277
  Phoebe, 233
  Rachel, 244
  Rebeccah, 136
  Richard, 243
  Robert, 265
  Thomas, 239
  William, 32, 41,
    123, 136, 227
ALLEY, William, 277
ALLIGON, Else, 254
ALLIN, Jonas, 42

INDEX

Margaretta, 42
William, 42
ALLING, Sarah, 280
ALLINSSER, John, 282
ALLIS, James, 220
Stephen, 258
ALLISON, Ann, 174
Isabella, 249
Thomas, 174
ALLMOND, Benjamin, 31
Rachel, 31
Susanna, 31
ALLOWER, John, 44
ALLRDIGE, Mary, 76
Peter, 76
Susanna, 76
ALLRICH, Mary, 286
ALLRIDCH, Andrew, 286
ALMOND, Ann, 269
Anne, 114
Barbara, 134
David, 127
Elenore, 109
Elizabeth, 134, 154, 275
Isabella, 279
John, 98, 113, 134
Joseph, 28
Margaret, 98, 119
Margaretta, 28
Margret, 105, 109, 265
Margreta, 127
Maria, 134
Mary, 105, 114, 126, 154, 265, 284
Rebecca, 126, 271
Ruth, 155
Sarah, 126
Solomon, 28
Thomas, 105, 114, 126, 154, 252, 279
William, 98, 109, 119, 127
ALRICH, David, 290
Peter Sigfreedus, 69
Rachel, 277
Sarah, 227
Sigfridus, 255
ALY, Mary, 86
AMAN, Christine, 251
AMERICA, Jane, 268
AMMET, Elizabeth, 80
Mary, 80
AMYSTID, Sarah, 273
ANDERS, Johan, 3
Margareta, 3
ANDERSON, ---, 112

Alexander, 166
Andreas, 74
Andrew, 95, 163, 170, 177, 249, 258
Ann, 90, 180
Brigita Loinan, 95
Brigitta, 79
Brita, 11, 64, 73, 140, 281
Brita Loinan, 75, 88
Britta, 79
Catharina, 33, 74
Catharina Loinan, 84, 94, 107
Catharina Lorena, 78
Catharine, 11
Cathrine, 126, 128, 183, 237
Christina, 78
Christine, 238
Cope, 200
David, 237
Eli, 140
Elizabeth, 8, 63, 142
Enoch, 177
Eric, 11, 135, 140, 142, 150
Erick, 167
George, 33
Isaac, 168, 198
Jacob, 112, 128, 131, 142, 174, 180, 183, 187, 194, 198, 269
Jacobus, 48
James, 1, 8, 63, 64, 73, 75, 79, 88, 95, 142, 146, 151, 165, 166, 242
James Joransson, 10
Jane, 272
Jeane, 170
Johan, 8, 11
John, 112, 151, 218, 228
Joran, 16
Joseph, 174
Josiah, 285
Kerstin, 48, 63, 72, 74
Lady, 88
Magdalena, 1, 10
Mans, 8
Margareta, 33
Margret, 177
Margrete, 242
Margrita, 84

EARLY CHURCH RECORDS OF NEW CASTLE COUNTY

Maria, 64, 131
Martha, 142, 146, 151, 163, 165, 166, 285
Mary, 94, 142, 168, 174, 179, 180, 183, 187, 194, 198, 200, 224, 226, 249, 290
Matthew, 269
Matz, 8
Ole, 63
Peter, 1, 3, 7, 10, 48, 63, 68, 72, 74, 78, 84, 94, 107, 126, 150, 200
Rachel, 135, 187
Rebecca, 246, 272
Robert, 245
Sara, 8
Sarah, 126, 142, 221
Stephen, 235, 273
Susanna, 107, 135, 150, 282
Susannah, 142
Thomas, 66
Wife, 1
William, 73, 74, 83, 146, 168, 179, 194, 229, 246, 261
ANDERSSEN, Brita, 71
  Catharina, 71
  James, 71
  Kerstin, 71
  Ole, 71
  Peter, 71
ANDERSSON, Bridget, 214
  Brita, 48, 57
  Catharina, 55
  Catharine Loinan, 98
  Christeen, 97
  Elizabeth, 7, 105
  Eric, 70, 97
  Jacob, 105, 217
  Johan, 17
  Jonas, 61
  Joran, 7
  Kerstin, 48, 54, 55, 57, 61, 70
  Magdalena, 7
  Mans, 10, 34
  Maria, 7, 54
  Mary, 21
  Mary Loinan, 105
  Olle, 48, 57, 97
  Peter, 7, 47, 55, 57, 58, 59, 70, 98
  Sara, 57
  Wiljam, 54
  William, 30
ANDERWOOD, Susanna, 242
ANDESDOTTER, Brigito, 223
ANDEY, Cathrine, 271
ANDREAS, Adam, 235
ANDREW, Elizabeth, 83
ANDREWS, George, 265
  John, 224
  Mary, 220
ANDREWWOOD, Sarah, 252
ANHEDSON, Catharina, 93
ANNIKA, Kerstin, 3
  Mrs., 3
ANSTEL, Sara, 81
ANTHONY, Anne
  Cathrine, 127
  Francis, 127
  Peter, 127
ARCHER, Margareta, 44
ARDERY, James, 192
  Maria, 192
  William, 192
AREY, Sarah, 277
ARMAR, Anna, 200
  Margret, 200
  William, 200
ARMATAGE, Frances, 255
ARMEN, John, 122
  Sarah, 122
ARMENT, John, 231
ARMER, Ann, 89
  Elenor, 170
  Margret, 170
  William, 170, 192
ARMOR, Annie, 118
  Elizabeth, 118
  Joseph, 118
  Samuel, 118
  William, 175
ARMOT, John, 253
ARMOTH, William, 273
ARMOUR, William, 231
ARMSTRONG, Agnes, 234
  Ann, 162, 195
  Archibald, 81
  Charlotte, 146
  Elenor, 261, 269
  Eleonora, 97
  Elizabeth, 111, 195
  Elizabeth Robinson, 97
  George, 191
  Hanna, 69

INDEX

Helena, 151
James, 60, 117
Jane, 195, 241
John, 146, 151, 157,
  162, 180, 231,
  234, 235, 246, 280
Margret, 162
Martha, 227
Mary, 89, 117, 283
Michael, 226
Rachel, 173, 180,
  186, 191
Ready, 91
Rebecca, 157
Rebeccah, 146, 151
Robert, 97, 111,
  157, 173, 180,
  186, 191, 195,
  252, 255, 265
Susanna, 117
William, 91, 111,
  173, 195, 220, 244
ARTHUR, William, 255
ARVEN, Sara, 281
ASBON, David, 67
ASH, Abby, 174
  Elizabeth, 216
  John, 174
  Mary, 174
ASHFORD, Mary, 83
ASHMEAD, Samuel, 228
  Sarah, 281
ASHTIN, Mary, 156
  Samuel, 156
  William, 156
ASHTON, Joseph, 275
  Mary, 162, 235
  Susanna, 84
  William, 231
ASKEW, John, 252, 267
  William, 248
ASMUND, Margaretta, 6
ASPE, Margret, 218
ASTON, Israel, 138
  Maria, 138
  William, 138
ATHERSON, Mary, 82
ATKINS, William, 236
ATKINSON, Isabel, 13
  Michael, 50
  Sara, 26
AUDLEY, John, 219
AUGUSTUS, Cathrine,
  280
AUL, John, 197
AUSTLE, Ann, 92
AVENSON, George, 228
AVERY, Daniel, 85

AYRES, Adam, 291
  Mary, 271

-B-
BAAL, Darkeys, 134
  Hannah, 146
  James, 146
  John, 134
  Joseph, 146
  Maria, 134
  Mary, 246
BAAT, Cathrine, 143
  Jesper, 143
  Sarah, 143
BAB, Thomas, 49
BABB, Margret, 287
  Mary, 279
  Peter, 245
  Thomas, 219
BABBER, Robert, 66
BACH, Jesper, 243
BACKHOUSE, Cathrine,
  173, 181
  Hannah, 181, 291
  John, 173
  Joseph, 173
  Mary, 173
  Mr., 65
  Strainge, 267
  Strange, 173, 181
BACKSLER, Phoebe, 255
BACKSTER, Hannah, 262
  Margret, 287
BAD, John Hans, 225
BADDEN, Henry, 89
BADDY, John, 102
BADIN, Catharina, 76
  Maria, 76
  Reinold, 76
BADRILL, Maria, 78
  Thomas, 78
BAIARD, Mary, 266
BAID, Ann, 276
  Mary, 66
BAIL, Jane, 289
  Phoebe, 285
BAILEY, Margret, 275
  Mary, 231
  Sarah, 272
  Silas, 286
BAILISS, Martha, 268
BAILLY, Judith, 236
BAILY, Abraham, 284
  Ely, 268
  Isaac, 93
  James, 171
  Mary, 232
  Rachel, 276

297

EARLY CHURCH RECORDS OF NEW CASTLE COUNTY

Thomas, 288
BAIN, Agnes, 111
  Cornelius, 111
  William, 111
BAIRD, Absalom, 278
BAKER, Elizabeth, 101
  Hannah, 268
  James, 107
  Jethro, 248
  John, 107
  Joseph, 50, 258
  Lydia, 280
  Mary, 83, 113, 247
  Peter, 254
  Rachel, 275
  Sara, 70
  Sarah, 101, 107, 113
  William, 101, 107, 113, 253
BALDEN, Hannah, 143
  Robert, 240
  Thomas, 143
  William, 143
BALDON, Cathreen, 68
BALDWIN, Antony, 105, 251
  Francis, 86, 87
  George, 105
  Hannah, 219, 265
  John, 216, 276
  Joseph, 262
  Margret, 255
  Martha, 80
  Mary, 105, 254, 277
  Rachel, 270
  Sara, 81, 268
  Thomas, 259
  William, 85, 247
BALDWINE, Lady, 227
BALE, Rachel, 288
BALL, Ann, 291
  Anne Robinsson, 106
  Elizabeth, 225, 284
  Ester, 230
  Hannah, 160, 174, 235
  James, 282, 291
  Jeremy, 24
  John, 236
  Joseph, 160, 174, 236, 239
  Marta, 217
  Mary, 24, 92, 245
  Rachel, 106, 174, 222
  Sarah, 89
  Susanna, 283

William, 24, 106, 160
BALLER, Sarah, 217
BALLMAN, Dorothy, 82
BANCROFT, Elizabeth M., 288
BANE, Samuel, 67
BANEFIL, Robert, 236
BANHARE, John, 284
BANN, Johan, 56
BAPTIST, Ann Orson, 212
  Charlotte Mary, 212
  John, 212
BAR, David, 53
BARBER, Clotworthy, 290
  Elizabeth, 89, 123
  James, 224
  John, 123, 219, 244, 277
  Mary, 230
  Sara, 90
  Sarah, 123
BARBOR, Abram, 87
  Isaac, 86
BARCLAY, Elenor P., 291
  Thomas, 238
BARD, Ann, 210
  Elizabeth, 210
  Johyn, 90
  Thomas, 210
BARDEN, Lucy, 85
BARENT, Mary, 255
BARET, Mary, 100
  Nelly, 100
  Thomas, 100
BARK, Charles, 86
BARKER, Darkeys, 238
  Johanna, 19, 24
  John, 248
  Joseph, 12, 19, 24, 118
  Kerstin, 43
  Maria, 19
  Mary, 220
  Rachel, 118
  Robert, 247
  Samuel, 15, 16, 23, 24, 118, 222
  Susanna, 80
BARLOW, John, 258
  Joseph, 243
  Mary, 129, 249
  Thomas, 129, 230
BARN, Martha, 50
BARNABY, Richard, 108

INDEX

BARNARD, Jane, 198
  John, 198
  Marianna, 198
  Thomas, 240
BARNAT, Ruth, 241
BARNES, Jacob, 178
  Ruth, 85
BARNET, ---, 250
  Abram, 68
  Benjamin, 282
  Carl, 17
  Charles, 245
  Elizabeth, 258
  George, 274
  Hannah, 250
  Jacob, 281
  Jeremia, 17
  Johan, 17
  John, 235
  Lampson, 268
  Margareta, 17
  Margaretta, 17
  Martha, 137, 249
  Mary, 79
  Phoebe, 279
  Robert, 17
  Sarah, 137, 237, 245
  Thomas, 17, 137, 231, 248
  William, 249
BARNS, Elias, 66
  Eliha, 67
  Hannah, 244
  Immanuel, 87
  Rachel, 94
BARNSAY, Alexander, 112
  Elizabeth, 112
  Jane, 112
BARR, Sarah, 253
BARRANS, Mary, 242
BARRELL, Marie Catharine, 60
BARRET, Cathrine, 280
  John, 262
BARRINGTON, Frances, 256
BARROW, Barnard, 291
BARROWS, Thomas, 281
BARRY, Henry, 288
BARTELSON, Andrew, 85
  Richard, 86
BARTHELSON, Christian, 231
BARTLEY, Elenor, 259
  James, 134
  Joseph, 134
  Maria, 134
  Sarah, 247
BARTON, Isaac, 217
  Jannet, 238
BARY, Elizabeth, 225
BASE, Elizabeth, 49
BASON, Hannah, 249
BASS, John, 221
BASTON, Joseph, 238
BATE, Elizabeth, 216
  George, 215
  John, 243
BATEMAN, Johan, 23
  Susanna, 23
  William, 23
BATERTEN, Mary, 66
BATES, Ann, 81
  Humphrey, 59
BATHON, Elizabeth, 230
BATSON, Elizabeth, 90
BATTEL, Cornelia, 36
  France, 36
  Pernilla, 60
  W., 36
BATTEN, Hannah, 269
  Sarah, 253
BATTERSBY, James, 211
  Jane, 211
  Samuel, 211
BATTIN, Marshall, 273
  Rachel, 229
BATY, Robert, 81
BAUDIN, Johan, 62
  Maria Chatrina, 62
  Reynold, 60
  Rienold, 62
BAUDWIN, Catharina, 64, 72, 74
  Fredrick, 74
  Jacob, 64
  Mary, 61
  Niclas, 72
  Reinold, 64, 72
  Reynold, 74
BAUGHMAN, Anne, 181
  Elenor, 176, 181, 185
  John, 176, 270
  Joseph, 181, 185, 271
  Rachel, 185
BAULDIN, Anne, 238
  Hannah, 233
BAUMAN, Charles, 107
  Hans, 120
  Johan, 113
  Johan Joseph, 113
  John, 107, 128
  Maria Susanna, 113

Paul, 128
Sarah, 120
Susanna, 107, 120, 128
BAVERLIN, Robert, 85
BAXLEY, John, 245
BAXTER, James, 89, 224
  Joan, 90
  Sophia, 290
  Thomas, 283
  William, 66
BAYLEY, James, 60
BAYLY, Ann, 88
  Rachel, 87
BEAL, Joseph, 255
  Thomas, 253
BEALE, George, 260
BEALY, Anna, 243
  Hannah, 257
BEAMOND, Elizabeth, 230
BEAN, Daniel, 89
  Hannah, 89
  Martha, 90
  William, 88
BEANS, Mary, 81
BEARD, Andrew, 214
  Jane, 222
  Jean, 47
  John, 80
  William, 82, 83
BEASEN, Mary, 245
BEASLEY, Jane, 226
BEASON, Benjamin, 81
  Bruteena, 127
  Rebecca, 127
  Thomas, 127
BEATON, Mary, 236
  Samuel, 218
BEATS, Hannah, 143
  Mary, 143
  William, 143, 244
BEATTY, George, 204
  Mary, 204
  Sophia, 204
BEATY, Ann, 88
BEAUKLEY, Beaulah, 253
BEAZEN, John, 242
BEEBY, Dan, 69
BEEN, Joseph, 70
BEESON, Alse, 277
  David, 183, 275
  Edward, 255
  Elizabeth, 183
  Hester, 288
  John, 247
  Margret, 183
  Martha, 259

  Persina, 271
  Thomas, 229
BEHESKEI, Bathi, 67
BELIS, Hannah, 69
BELL, Elizabeth, 216
  Hannah, 93
  Isaac Barrows, 198
  Isabell, 89
  Isabelle, 198
  John, 198, 237, 238, 282
  Margret, 109
  Mary, 83
  Rachael, 109
  William, 109, 256
BELLEF, Thomas, 81
BEMAUND, Elizabeth, 214
BENDERMAN, John, 221, 284
BENET, Debora, 247
BENNET, Ann, 266
  Edward, 86
  Emy, 265
  Hannah, 266
  Jacob, 218, 263
  James, 237
  Jane, 265
  John, 144
  Robert, 240
  Sarah, 217, 285
  Stephen, 237
BENNETT, Thomas, 220
BENTHLEY, Joshua, 230
BENTLEY, Benjamin, 277
  Bezaller, 256
  Jerssey, 258
  Mary, 255
  Shesh Cazzar, 265
BENTLY, Ellis, 256
  John, 228
  Margret, 222, 238
  Thamar, 228
BENZEL, Adolph, 219
  Rebecca Tranberg, 110
BENZELSTIERNA, Lars, 110
BERBER, Elizabeth, 247
BERNARD, Andrew, 213
  Jane, 209, 213
  John, 209, 213, 270
  William, 209
BERNDT, Jacob, 263
BERNEY, Robert, 215
BERNHARD, Cathrine, 240
BERRY, Elizabeth, 29

INDEX

Isaac, 248
John, 93
Thomas, 47, 270
BERTETSSON, Sara, 3
  Zackarias, 3
BERTILSON, Sara, 6
  William, 6
  Zacharias, 6
BERTILSSON, Grenilla, 9
  Johan, 6
  Sara, 9
BESLY, Prishilla, 93
BESON, Jonathan, 287
BEST, Arthur, 157
  Hannah, 157
  William, 157
BETHEL, Frances, 261
BETHIEM, Carin, 4
BETTEL, Sara, 90
BETTS, Tamzin, 215
BEWGLES, Charles, 264
BIARD, James, 70
BICKET, Mary, 281
BIGGAN, Dolly, 192
  Hugh, 192
BIGGELEY, Peter, 225
BIGGS, James, 272
BILL, Ann, 265
BILLERBACK, Albert, 3
  Margaretta, 8
BILTERBACK, Daniel, 3
BINE, Mary, 274
BINES, Elizabeth, 164, 286
  Ester, 164
BIORK, Eric, 2, 4, 23, 31
  Erick, 3
  Maria, 2
  Petrus, 13
  Provost, 13
  Wife, 4
BIRD, ---, 76
  Anna, 47
  Annah, 142
  Anne, 91
  Beata, 158
  Benjamin, 36, 138
  Benoni, 162
  Brigitta, 133
  Brita, 140
  Elizabeth, 18
  Empson, 117
  Emsson, 104
  Francis, 46
  Hanna, 35
  Hannah, 36, 132

  Jacob, 166, 262
  James, 83
  Johan, 35, 39
  John, 47, 131, 142, 147, 154, 162, 230, 240
  Joseph, 128, 132, 231
  Lydia, 131
  Margareta, 47, 132
  Margreta, 128, 138
  Margrete, 147
  Maria, 32, 41
  Mary, 29, 50, 60, 117, 259, 261
  Rachael, 39
  Rachel, 140, 233, 277, 280
  Rebecca, 29, 43, 131, 166, 215, 262
  Robin, 29, 32
  Ruth, 247
  Sara, 18, 51, 90
  Sarah, 142, 147, 154, 162, 247, 256, 279
  Susanna, 32, 80, 117
  Susannah, 104
  Thomas, 18, 35, 36, 39, 41, 133, 140, 236, 279
  William, 158, 166
BIRK, Ellenor, 87
BIRWIN, Elenor, 174
  Henry, 174
  James, 174
BISCHOP, Esther, 89
BISEN, Benjamin, 99
  Elizabeth, 216
  Elizabeth Paulsson, 99
  Jesper, 99
  Mary, 99
BISHOP, Dorcas, 19, 24
  Elizabeth, 101, 113, 123, 141, 149, 238, 273
  Henry, 100, 110, 136
  James, 123
  Johan, 19
  John, 86, 101, 113, 123, 141, 149
  Maria, 110, 136
  Mary, 100, 110, 113, 276, 280
  Nicholas, 24
  Niclas, 19
  Nicol, 70

Patience, 224
Rebeccah, 149
Sarah, 219
Susanna, 24
BLACK, Benjamin, 243
  Cathrine, 274
  David, 66
  Jane, 85
  John, 257
  Margrete, 244
  Mary, 69, 85
  Rebecca, 236
  Robert, 260
  Sarah, 249
BLACKLY, Mary, 237
BLACWELL, Dr., 201
BLAGER, Elizabeth, 82
BLAIR, James, 274
  Mary, 66
BLAN, Mary, 44
BLANKCHARR, Peter, 268
BLANKSHORNE, John, 172
  Peter, 172
BLAYR, Daniel, 226
BLEW, David, 144
  Hannah, 115
  John, 104
  Mary, 87, 104, 115, 144
  Solomon, 144
  Uria, 89
  Uriah, 115, 144
  Urias, 104
BLEWIT, William, 217
BLOAIR, Sara, 50
BLOOMER, Ellinor, 85
BOALS, Barbara, 67
BODLY, John, 85
BOGAN, Anne, 225
BOGGAN, John, 215
BOGGES, James, 217
BOGGS, Elizabeth, 290
  James, 249
  John, 245
BOGS, John, 281
  Mary, 241
BOID, David, 253
BOLDEN, Mary, 257
BOLDON, Abigail, 254
BOLE, Batty, 263
BOLIN, Samuel, 285
BOLLOW, Elizabeth, 215
BOLTON, Robert, 93
BOMAN, Andrew, 97
  Johannes, 97
  Susanna, 97
BON, Elizabeth, 254
BOND, Joseph, 50, 65

BONNY, Johan, 28
  Mary, 28
BONSALL, Joseph, 251
BONSEL, Sara, 233
BONZEL, Rebecca, 278
BOOM, Fredrick, 219
BOON, Peter, 91
BOONER, Hannah, 233
BOOTH, Charles, 242
  Hannah, 261
  James, 204
  Jane, 181
  Phoebe, 279
  William, 181, 236
BOOTS, Elizabeth, 205
  John Clark, 205
  Samuel, 205
BORCH, Ann, 83
BORD, Anna, 65, 73
  Rebecca, 73
  Thomas, 65, 73
BORELL, Andrew, 150, 239, 251
BORK, Abel, 217
  William, 92
BORMAN, Joseph, 259
BORN, Susanna, 218
BORRELS, Elizabeth, 109
  Thomas, 109
  William, 109
BORSHORFORD, Cathrine, 235
BOSSARD, Margret, 107
BOSSORD, Anna, 107
  John, 107
BOULDING, William, 59
BOURGES, Grizell, 219
BOWIN, Anne, 229
BOWJER, Samuel, 271
BOWLER, Samuel, 255
BOWLES, Elizabeth, 131, 189
  John, 189
  Mary, 100
  Sarah, 131, 216
  Thomas, 84, 100, 131
BOWLS, John, 277
BOWRING, Henry, 50
BOYCE, Nathan, 284
  William, 219
BOYD, Agnis, 92
  Anna, 126
  Elizabeth, 126
  Else, 221
  Jane, 235, 284
  Joseph, 225
  Margret, 291

INDEX

Patrick, 126, 227
Susanna, 68
William Hamilton, 291
BOYLE, Daniel, 272
James, 290
BRACHIN, Hannah, 239
BRACHON, Henry, 107
Isaac, 107
Susanna, 107
BRACKEN, Henry, 292
Sarah, 288
William, 216, 228
BRACKIN, Hanna, 26
John, 218
Thomas, 23
BRACKSTINE, William, 81
BRADE, Barney, 171
Elizabeth, 171
Jane, 171
BRADFORD, Cathrine, 174
David, 80
Elia, 82
Elias, 154
Mary, 154, 174, 265, 267
Phoebe, 239
Thomas, 250
BRADIN, William, 215
BRADKY, Susanna, 102
William, 102
BRADLEY, Catharina, 26
Charles, 219
Elizabeth, 26, 90
George, 268
Gilbert, 259
Henry, 26
Ursilla, 241
BRADY, Margrete, 240
Patrick, 245
BRAEHEN, Henry, 136
Moses, 136
Sarah, 136
BRAHIN, Francis, 155
Henry, 155
Jeane, 155
BRAKEN, Martha, 128
Ruth, 128
William, 128
BRAKIN, Agnes, 264
Isaac, 254
Thomas, 231
BRALK, Jane, 171
BRANBERRY, Matthias, 249
BRAND, John, 86

BRANDEN, John, 68
BRANEN, John, 267
BRANHAN, Elizabeth, 214
Jeremiah, 214
Mary, 214
BRANIN, Annika, 20
Edward, 20
Mary, 20
BRANNIN, Annika, 21
Edward, 21
BRANSON, Day, 265
Lankin, 287
BRANTON, Jane, 67
Mary, 68
Samuel, 82
BRASON, Margrete, 243
BRATCHEN, Jane, 244
BRATHERSON, Cathrine, 177
BRATSON, Valentin, 82
BRATTEN, Barbara, 259
Edward, 171, 266
Elizabeth, 171
Jacob, 275
Jane, 280
John, 260
Margret, 268
Mary, 171
Rachel, 260
BRATTON, Amy, 124
Catharine, 103
John, 112, 267
Margaret, 124
Rachel, 127
Rebecca, 127
Robert, 175, 233
Sarah, 103, 220
Thomas, 127
Wallace, 124
William, 127
BRAUN, Elizabeth, 100
Maria, 6, 7, 10
Marte, 59
Mary, 100
William, 100
BRAWN, John, 279
Rachel, 69
BRAYS, Samuel, 256
BREADFORD, David, 101
Margaret King, 101
Susanna, 226
Thomas, 101
William, 101
BREDIN, James, 87
BREINIGERN, Catharine, 216
BRENNEN, Edward, 19

EARLY CHURCH RECORDS OF NEW CASTLE COUNTY

BRETT, Elizabeth, 37
BREYD, John, 112
  Mary, 112
BREYEN, Margaret, 60
BRICKER, Peter, 83
BRIDLE, Henry, 289
BRIDLY, Eleonore, 148
  John, 148
  Mary, 148
BRIGHT, William, 271
BRILTON, Anne, 236
BRINBURG, Christiern, 10
BRINDLEY, James, 181, 187, 272
  James Joseph, 187
  John, 197
  Susanna, 187, 197
BRINTON, Elizabeth, 275
  George, 223, 240
  Hannah, 214
  Jacob, 245, 290
  John, 265
  Mary, 250
  Phoebe, 267
BRION, Catharine, 106
  Jane, 106
BRIOND, Anna, 90
BRISTOL, Isabel, 83
BROADFORD, Abner, 270
BROADSHAW, Mary, 234
BROBSON, William, 225
BROCHON, Henry, 123
  James, 102
  Jane, 102
  Rose McLaughlin, 102
  Susanna, 123
  Susannah, 123
BROCK, John, 224
BROGAN, John, 257
BROGEN, Rose, 245
BROGGAN, John, 97
BROOK, James, 110
BROOKS, Joseph, 70
  Mary, 243
  Samuel, 217
  William, 225
BROOM, Abraham, 203, 210
  Agnes, 153
  Ann, 188, 253, 287
  Benjamin, 130
  Elizabeth, 188, 203, 210
  Ester, 188
  Hannah, 89, 103, 253

  Jacob, 188, 200, 201, 263
  Jacob Pierce, 199
  James, 188
  John, 153
  Lavinia, 200
  Margret, 162
  Maria, 134
  Mary, 67, 179
  Mary Ellison, 203
  Nicholas Way, 201
  Pheobe, 103
  Phoebe, 130, 134, 153
  Rachel, 200
  Rachel Maria, 199
  Rebecca, 201
  Robert, 230
  Sarah, 290
  Thomas, 50, 179, 183, 269
  Thomas Rumsey, 210
  William, 103, 130, 134, 153, 183
BROOMAL, David, 221
BROOMER, Sarah, 252
BROTHERS, Else, 263
BROTHERTON, Cathrine, 272
BROUNFIELD, Mary, 67
BROWN, Abraham, 75, 151, 249, 281
  Alexander, 268
  Andrew, 151
  Ann, 269
  Anna, 168
  Benjamin (Benjan.), 195, 269
  Casper, 250
  Christina Mounson, 75
  Christopher, 271
  Daniel, 264, 273
  David, 263, 277
  Edward, 232
  Elizabeth, 142, 145, 151, 244, 267, 269
  Ester, 142
  George, 277
  Gottfried, 128
  Isaac, 274
  Jacob, 145
  James, 142, 259, 269
  Jean, 258, 266
  Jeremiah, 279
  John, 220, 253, 272, 280

INDEX

Joseph, 165, 168, 195, 257, 278
Margret, 251
Margreta, 128
Margrete, 145, 239
Maria, 57
Mary, 66, 85
Nathan, 289
Nathaniel, 251
Phoebe, 114
Rachel, 165, 168, 187, 195
Rebecca, 282
Samuel, 187, 270
Sarah, 271
Susanna, 128, 278
Thomas, 114, 247
William, 65, 69, 75, 114, 145
BROWNLESS, Elizabeth, 238
BROWNLY, Margrete, 239
BROWNWOOD, Susanna, 232
BRUCE, John, 255
BRUCKS, James, 69
BRUNBERG, Anna, 120, 130
Anne, 106
Christiern, 51, 52, 72, 75
Christina, 17, 72
Elizabeth, 75, 106, 257
John, 51, 52, 130
Margret, 136
Maria, 51, 72, 75
Mary, 222
Matthias, 52
Peter, 86, 106, 120, 136
Sarah, 136
Susanna, 79
Swen, 120, 130, 218
BRUNBERRY, Elizabeth, 242
BRUNTON, Thomas, 66
BRUSE, Debora, 80
BRYAN, Andrew, 168
Ann, 186
Cathrine, 254
Elizabeth, 52, 186, 254
Emy, 168
John, 186
Mary Sarah Cathrine, 168
Robert, 269

William, 52
BRYANS, Cathrine, 288
BRYARLY, Hugh, 85
BRYNBERG, Anna, 204
Christian, 28
Christiern, 19, 20, 23, 33, 39, 64
Elenor, 198, 204
Elizabeth, 20, 23
John, 198, 204, 284
Karia, 20
Maria, 23, 28, 33, 39, 64
Matthew, 64
Matthias, 39
Peter, 28, 273
Rebecca, 198
Sara, 280
Susanna, 33
Swen, 23
BRYNES, Margret, 264
BRYON, Robert, 259
BUCKINGHAM, Hannah, 262
Mary, 257
BUCKLEY, Ann, 81
Elizabeth, 230, 269
Hanna, 46
BUDDLE, Claytor, 91
BUDDON, Margret, 237
BUDGET, Catharine, 275
BUFFINGTON, Abigail, 70
Anna, 68
Benjamin, 228
John, 239
Mary, 70
Richard, 68
Robert, 242
BUFFINTON, Alie, 81
BULLERWARD, James, 86
BULLOCK, Aaron, 120
Ann, 261
Ezekiel, 226
Isaac, 120, 123
Jane, 257
Jeane, 120
John, 247
Margaret, 93
Margery, 123
Moses, 282
Thomas, 120, 264
Timothy, 214
BULLORD, Valentine, 237
BULLOW, Jane, 245
BUNKER, Amalay, 223

BURGASS, Elizabeth, 252
BURK, Edmund, 68
  Joseph, 271
  Patrick, 271
  Roland, 244
BURN, Edward, 254
BURNET, Abraham, 125
  Elizabeth, 125
  Henry, 89
  Jane, 198
  John, 125
  Mary, 198
  Samuel, 198
BURNS, Catharina, 93
  Cathrina, 234
  Cathrine, 216
  Elizabeth, 235
  Ester, 106
  James, 131
  Johan, 40
  John, 248, 262
  Margret, 216
  Martha, 122, 131
  Mary, 106
  Moses, 122, 131, 227
  Patrick, 93
  William, 122, 255
BURNSIDE, Ellenor, 80
  James, 219, 226
BURRELL, Ann, 208, 214
  Benjamin, 208
  Isabella Welsh, 214
  Sarah, 208
BURRILL, Benjamin, 282
BURRIS, Joseph, 232
  Mary, 277
BURROUGH, James, 269
BURROWS, Elizabeth, 249
BURSINGTON, Joseph, 259
BURTINGTON, Thomas, 258
BUSBIN, Sarah, 221
BUSH, Anna, 113
  Anne, 99
  Cathrine, 140
  David, 93, 99, 113, 199, 201, 205, 211
  Elisabeth, 270
  Elizabeth, 143, 199, 201, 205, 211
  George, 113, 199, 287
  Hannah, 143
  Isaac, 143
  John, 46

  John Price, 205
  Lewis, 99
  Mary, 237
  Miriam, 80
  Niclas, 140
  Thomson, 143
  William, 140
BUSHELL, Alki, 27
  Ann, 27
  Catharina, 27
  Magdalena, 27
  Mary, 27
  Samuel, 27
  Susanna, 27
BUSHEON, Andrew, 136
  Cathrina, 136
  John, 136
BUSHI, Cathrina, 135
  Johan Niclas, 135
  John Niclas, 135
BUSSINGTON, Ephraim, 284
  Joshua, 267
  Mary, 275
  Richard, 275
  Thomas, 221
BUTCHER, John, 26
  Mary, 19
BUTLER, Ann, 248
  Eleonore, 242
  George, 285
  Jacob, 272
  John, 112, 276
  Margaret, 112
  Mary, 91
  Ruth, 285
BUTTINGTON, James, 237
  Joseph, 237
  Martha, 236
BYRNES, John, 288
BYRNS, Ann, 256

-C-

CABNER, Cornelius, 80
  Samuel, 83
CABY, Ellinor, 93
CADIE, Elizabeth, 2
CAFFOR, Patrick, 90
CAIN, Else, 133
  John, 133
  Maria, 133
CALAHAN, Elizabeth, 289
  Margret, 262
CALAMAY, Phoebe, 236
CALDERWOOD, Andrew, 272

INDEX

CALDWELL, David, 266
  George, 258
CALHOUN, Margaret, 92
CALLIERT, Elizabeth, 33
  Rebecca, 33
CALLOM, Catharine, 149
  French, 149
  Moses, 149, 241
CALLWELL, Elizabeth, 221
CALVERT, William, 267
CAMBEL, Bell Jane, 279
  Elizabeth, 269
  James, 258
CAMEL, Elizabeth, 85, 93
  Esther, 236
  Flora, 237
CAMELL, James, 232
CAMMEL, Eleonore, 241
CAMP, Casper, 276
  Jesper, 250
  Rebecca, 108
  Richard, 108
CAMPBEL, Cathrine, 271
  Neil, 289
CAMPBELL, Archibald, 65
  Eleanor, 213
  George Washington, 213
  John, 216, 226
  Mary, 269, 272
  Thomas, 213
CAMPER, Solomon, 282
CAMPFIELD, Edward, 213
  Hannah, 213
  Sarah, 213
  William, 213
CAMPHEL, James, 225
CANADA, George, 43
  James, 43
  Nathaniel, 86
  Tabitha, 43
CANADY, Briget, 60
  James, 91
  Thomas, 82
CANAPY, Peter, 7
CANBY, Debocah, 278
  Enoch, 10
  Jane, 233
  Jesse, 246
  Jonas, 234
  Ledda, 277
  Sarah, 281
CANIDA, James, 51
  Jane, 51

Wilyam, 51
CANLEY, Mary, 246
CANLY, Enok, 5
CANN, Ann, 92
  Cathrina, 139
  James, 257
  Jane, 25, 231
  John, 139, 238
  Maria, 139
  Susanna, 216
  William, 25, 139
CANNADY, Archibald, 80
CANNAWAY, Mary, 93
CANNERS, Timothy, 92
CANNON, James, 275
  John, 287
CANNOWAY, Anne, 247
CANPANY, Andreas, 56
  Annika Petersson, 49
  Helena, 7, 36, 52
  Hellena, 6
  Johannes, 6
  Magdalena, 36, 43, 52, 56
  Maria, 43
  Peter, 6, 7
  Peter Petersson, 6, 11, 35, 36, 43, 52, 56
  Susanna, 52
CANPONY, Anders, 4
  Catharina, 72
  Helena, 2, 4, 7
  Johan, 75
  Magdalena, 72, 75
  Peter, 4, 6, 72
  Peter Peters, 75
CANTBINE, Cathrine, 247
CANTREL, Catharina, 22
  Hanna, 22
  Joseph, 22
CAPELL, Dr., 191
  Joseph, 278
  Mark, 191
  Mary, 191
CAPELLA, Henry Pearce, 205
  Joseph, 205
  Mary, 205
CAPELLE, Doctor, 194
  Maria May, 194
  Mary, 194
CAPON, William, 89
CAPPEL, Sara, 277
CARBRE, Juda, 217
CAREY, Elizabeth, 49
  Johanna, 230

EARLY CHURCH RECORDS OF NEW CASTLE COUNTY

John, 179
CARING, Sarah, 252
CARINGTEN, Mary, 254
CARLE, John, 250
CARLILE, Margret, 166
  Patrick, 166
  Sarah, 166
CARLIN, Barbarah, 143
  Mary, 143
  Simon, 143, 242
  William, 243
CARLTON, Martha, 270
CARNAY, Anna, 107
  Anne, 123, 222
  Daniel, 107, 123
  Elizabeth, 121
  James, 123
  Jane, 107
  John, 121
  Mary, 121
CAROTHERS, Lydia, 291
CARPENTER, Ann, 271
  Fredrick, 234
  Phoebe, 284
CARR, Alexander, 182
  Anne, 218
  Elizabeth, 281
  George, 186
  Jacob, 182
  James, 237
  John, 186, 240
  Mary, 246, 275, 288
  Thomas, 269
  William, 185
CARRE, William, 218
CARREL, Edward, 80
  Elizabeth, 84
  Hugh, 82
CARRIGAN, Sarah, 238
CARRY, Mary, 235
CARSHIN, Moses, 68
CARSON, Alexander, 235
  James, 92
  John, 220
  Mary, 221
  Samuel, 231
CARTAY, Charles, 217
CARTELL, Margaret, 80
CARTER, Agnes, 248
  Elizabeth, 233
  Hannah, 125, 244, 288
  Jane, 29, 120, 246
  Jeremiah, 275
  John, 85, 120, 235
  Joseph, 80, 267
  Mary, 2, 125, 219, 235, 242

Nathaniel, 60, 253
Ninive, 125
Robert, 219
Sarah, 120, 246
CARTMAL, Elizabeth, 241
CARTMELL, Ann, 211
  Anna, 98
  George, 211
  Joseph, 98
  Margret, 203, 209
  Mary, 203, 211
  Sara, 215
  Sarah, 211
  Sarah Gepson, 98
  Thomas, 203, 209, 249, 286
CARTMILL, Elizabeth, 134
  Hanna, 75
  Hannah, 235
  Joseph, 75
  Sara, 75
  Thomas, 134
  William, 134
CASE, Matthew, 249
CASHEDY, John, 268
CASNAY, Daniel, 216
CASPARSON, Ann, 93
CASPARSSON, Anthony, 2
  John, 2
CASSEL, Christina, 27
  Johan, 27
CASSIDY, Anna, 219
  Catharine, 224
  William, 280
CASSITY, Madaline, 284
CASSON, Hannah, 270
CASTAN, Andreas, 91
  Christina, 108
  Christina Swenson, 108
  Christina Swensson, 91, 101
  Jeremiah, 101
  William, 91, 101, 108
CASY, Margret, 222
CATHI, Malii, 68
CATORI, Elizabeth, 93
CAUGHLAN, Margret, 246
CAUHOON, Mary, 220
CAULYN, Elizabeth, 110
  Margret, 110
  Mark, 110
CAUVENAH, Philip, 227
CAUZINE, Robert, 284

INDEX

CAVENAU, Catharine, 145
  James, 145
  Mary, 145
CEANE, Elizabeth, 231
CELYONA, Mary Cathrine, 242
CERTAIN, Esther, 43
  Hester, 61
  Maria, 43
  Martha, 43
  Richard, 43
CHAD, Anna, 42
  Francis, 42
  Grace, 42
CHADWICK, Catharine Oyen, 212
  Charles Havens, 212
  William, 212
CHAFFIN, Joseph, 250
CHAIR, Anna, 177
  John H., 177
  Sarah, 177
CHALFANT, Ann, 272
  Catharine, 83
  Hannah, 257
  James, 275
  John, 239
  Leady, 258
  Martha, 268, 285
  Mary, 257
  Phoebe, 254
  Rachel, 264
  Robert, 254, 264
CHALFIN, Anne, 247
  Jane, 231
CHALFLINT, John, 224
CHALFON, Robert, 91
  Thomas, 92
CHALMERS, Andrew, 68
CHAMBELL, Thomas, 60
CHAMBERLAIN, Elizabeth, 289
  Hannah, 258
  John, 263
  William, 264
CHAMBERLIN, William, 274
CHAMBERS, Rebecca, 89
CHAMPELL, Eleanor, 70
CHAMPION, Joseph, 25
  Mary, 25
  Rebecca, 220
CHANDELOR, Ann, 226
CHANDLER, Abraham, 285
  Amor, 244
  Christopher, 265
  David, 248, 262

  Elizabeth, 251
  Enoch, 265
  George, 237
  James, 235
  John, 49
  Samuel, 260
CHANDLOR, David, 259
  Joseph, 240
  Rachel, 257
CHANEY, Mary, 278
CHANTRILL, Catharina, 39
  Catherina, 38
  John, 38
  Joseph, 38, 39
CHANY, Francis, 112
  Sarah, 112
CHAPMAN, Mary, 235, 238
  Patience, 272
  Sarah, 287
  William, 238
CHARD, John, 257
CHARLES, Andrew, 150
  Eve, 150
  Gottfried, 150
CHARLETON, Lydia, 248
  Thomas, 246
CHARLES, Cathrine, 254
CHARLEY, Anna Maria, 137
  Gottfried, 137
  John Gottfried, 239
  Samuel, 137
CHARTTON, Margret, 218
CHATFIN, Annah, 243
CHATSON, Elizabeth, 68
CHERREY, Isaac, 262
CHERRY, Fanny, 180
  Isaac, 180
  Rebecca, 180
CHERSHERIN, Cathrine, 238
CHESTER, Isaiah, 283
  Thomas, 50
CHESTNUT, Alexander, 230
  Esther Serena, 212
  James, 212
  Mary, 212
CHEVIN, John, 218
CHEW, Sarah, 275
CHIAFIN, Elizabeth, 68
CHRISTINE, Margrete, 153
  Samuel, 153
  Sarah, 153

CHRISTOPHER, Henry,
   236
CHRISTOPHERSON,
   Andrew, 170
   Cathrine, 160
   Joseph, 176
   Joseph Springer,
      154, 160, 165,
      170, 176, 182, 188
   Leady, 160, 165
   Lydia, 170, 176,
      182, 188
   Peter, 188
CHURCHMAN, John, 263
CIRL, Annah, 244
CLAESON, Barbarah
   Annah, 143
   Israel, 143
   Margret, 280
   Mary, 143
CLAESSON, Anne, 219
   Isarel, 146
   Jane, 148
   John, 220
   Lydia, 148
   Mary, 146
   Richard, 148
CLANDENING, Elizabeth,
   291
CLANDONNEN, Isaac, 227
CLANKENHORM,
   Elizabeth, 242
CLARK, Abraham, 258
   Annie, 118
   Annika, 54
   Benjamin, 65
   Cathrina, 137
   Chatrine, 239
   Cornelius, 85, 90
   Elenor, 253
   Elizabeth, 89, 267,
      276
   Gabriel, 215
   George, 243
   Gideon, 261
   Hannah, 290
   Hugh, 220
   James, 137, 240
   John, 118, 258, 278
   Margretta, 130
   Maria, 54
   Mary, 130, 150, 151,
      220, 258
   Richard, 130, 228
   Samuel, 150, 151,
      248
   Sarah, 83, 150
   Susanna, 118

   Thomas, 54, 60, 281
   Thomas Warren, 290
   Walter, 269
   William, 60, 65,
      118, 238, 287
CLARKE, Elinor, 220
   James, 233
   John, 215
   Margret, 255
CLARKSON, Esther Cox,
   205
   Geradus, 200
   Grace, 200, 210
   Harriot Rumsey, 210
   Joseph, 200, 205,
      210, 286
   Rachel, 205
   Rev. Mr., 200
CLASKY, Brita, 105
   Hannah, 105
   Henry, 105
CLASSON, Anna, 28
   Dorothea, 4
   Elizabeth, 51
   Isarel, 134
   Israel, 55
   Jesper, 12, 59, 108,
      124
   Joanna, 42
   Johan, 9
   Johannes, 22
   John, 108
   Magaretta, 5
   Margaretta, 4, 17
   Maria, 34, 108, 124,
      134
   Oney, 9
   Peter, 4, 10, 12,
      17, 22, 28, 34,
      42, 51, 55, 57,
      124, 134
   Walberg, 51
   Walborg, 10, 12, 17,
      22, 28, 34, 42, 55
   Wolborg, 10
CLATT, Elizabeth, 87
CLAWSON, Elizabeth, 79
   Jesper, 79
   Johanna, 91
   Maria, 79
CLAY, Robert, 207
CLAYTON, Ambrous, 50
   Annah, 239
   Ella, 11
   Hannah, 234
   Johan, 30
   Johanna, 12
   Joseph, 11, 30

INDEX

Lydia, 65
Mary, 261
Richard, 227
Rosamunda, 30
Thomas, 46
William, 261
CLEANE, Anne, 230
CLEANEAY, Maria, 62
Sarah, 62
William, 62
CLEANEY, Mary, 142
Samuel, 142
Sarah, 226
CLEANNY, Magdelena, 135
Rebecca, 135
Samuel, 135
CLEANY, Carolus, 25
Maria, 16, 19, 25
Mary, 105, 124
Rachael, 124
Rebecca, 16
Samuel, 124
William, 16, 19, 25, 247
CLEARY, Samuel, 227
CLEATON, Elizabeth, 69, 225
CLEESTER, Michel, 86
CLEMENS, Brita, 3
Elizabeth, 279
Gabriel, 31
Joseph, 31
Margret, 257
Sara, 31
CLEMENTS, James, 218
Sarah, 254
CLEMMY, Jane, 53
Maria, 53
Wiljam, 53
CLEMONS, Thomas, 226
CLENDINEN, William, 214
CLENEY, Magdalene, 152
Mary, 152
Samuel, 152
CLENNY, Hanna, 46
Jane, 32
Kerston, 70
Maria, 32, 38, 46
Mary, 86
Rebecca, 65
William, 32, 38, 46, 70
CLERK, Elenor, 221
Eleonora, 146
John, 146, 247
CLIFFERD, Sarah, 267

CLINDELON, Jean, 267
CLINDENONE, Elizabeth, 190
Samuel, 190
CLING, Ruth, 256
Susanna, 267
CLISHY, ---, 186
CLIST, Joseph, 230
CLOIS, Edward, 288
CLOOD, Gertrude, 2
Lydia, 2
Robin, 2
CLOSE, Catharine, 83
CLOUD, Abner, 260
Anna, 44
Annah, 241
Charity, 284
Daniel, 242
Edward, 46
Elizabeth, 222, 226, 229
Else, 221
Ester, 220
Grace, 217
Hannah, 221
Harlen, 278
James, 41
Joseph, 216, 239, 240, 269
Leady, 263
Mardochay, 222
Margret, 267
Margreta, 234
Margrete, 242
Mary, 233
Nathan, 94
Nathaniel, 253
Orphey, 273
Phoebe, 41
Priscilla, 265
Rebecca, 40
Robbert, 41
Sara, 41, 91
Susanna, 65, 90
William, 289
CLUGGAGE, Francis, 266
CLYDE, John, 235
COB, Cathrina
Margreta, 138
John William, 138
Philipina, 138
COBBS, Debora, 285
COBERN, Elenore, 223
COBOWN, Rachel, 221
COBURN, Mary, 243
Thomas, 245
COCHLIN, Mary, 263
COCHRAN, Ann, 285

Catharine, 283
Edward, 147
George, 147, 148
James, 291
Jamyma, 147
Margrete, 148
Richard, 148
William, 82
COCK, Abigail, 34
Adam, 26
Anders, 3, 7, 10, 16, 20, 26, 34, 40, 49
Andreas, 20, 22
Andrew, 95
Anna, 6, 12, 28
Annika, 3, 22
Augustin, 28
Bille, 13
Brita, 10, 40
Carolus, 34
Catharina, 12, 21, 26, 40
Elizabeth, 50
Emi, 45
Emma, 13
Emy, 22, 30, 38
Gustaf, 6, 12, 22
Hanna, 22
Helena, 16
Johan, 4, 13, 28
Magnus, 11
Margareta, 30
Peter, 11
Regner, 45
Sara, 7, 10, 16, 20, 26, 34, 49
William, 22, 30, 38, 40, 45
COCKRAN, John, 279
COCKS, Joseph, 276
COCKSHOTT, Arthur Robinson, 198
John, 196, 198
Mary, 198
William, 196
COGHRAN, Daniel, 265
COHOON, Ellinor, 93
James, 268
Mary, 248
Thomas, 80
COLAINS, Mary, 217
COLBER, Jane, 268
COLBERSON, Jane, 86
COLBERT, Elizabeth, 252
Isaac, 251
COLBRETH, Margret, 285

COLBY, David, 195
COLDWELL, Jean, 258
COLE, Ann, 198, 210
Elizabeth, 210
Robert, 198
Stephen, 50
Thomas, 198, 210
COLEBURG, Elizabeth, 5
COLEMAN, Joseph, 274, 277
COLEN, Jacob, 22
John, 22
Kerstin, 22
COLES, William, 236
COLESBERG, Cathrine, 190
Elizabeth, 2, 5, 56, 79, 96, 108
Henrick, 56
Henry, 79, 96
Hinric, 108
Isaac, 108
Jacob, 190
Margareta, 44
Marta, 96
Mary, 216
Susanna, 79
William, 190
COLESBERRY, Andrew, 286
Andrew Gravenrat, 139
Cathrine, 139
Henry, 272
Jacob, 139, 205, 210
Margret, 205, 210
Martha, 271
Mary, 210, 287
Rachel, 255
COLESBURG, Bette, 62
Elizabeth, 70, 73
Hendric, 73
Henrick, 62, 70, 73
Jacob, 62
Swen, 70, 239
COLESBURY, Catharine, 208
Jacob, 208
Margret, 208
COLGEN, Henry, 117
Susanna, 117
William, 117
COLIER, Elizabeth, 217
COLLANS, Sarah, 225
COLLET, Charles, 90
James, 225
Jeremias, 218
Mary, 240

INDEX

Rachel, 247
William, 90
COLLETT, Mary, 273
COLLIER, Hanna, 82
  James, 224
  Martha, 86
  Susanna, 83
COLLIGAN, Mary, 279
COLLIN, Niklas, 187
  Rev. N., 273
COLLINGS, Elizabeth, 226
COLLINS, Anna Mar Leming, 116
  Anne, 229
  Balthazar, 116
  Brice, 90, 105
  Bridget, 226
  Brigit, 114
  Charles, 287
  Elizabeth, 105
  Enoch, 105
  Hanna, 285
  Henry, 254
  John, 114, 116
  Mary, 83
  Nicholas, 195
  Sara, 258
  Sarah, 114, 264
  Timothy, 272
COLLOWEL, John, 116
COLLUY, Margret, 226
COLN, John, 65
COLON, Hannah, 274
COLPHOS, Ann, 193
  John, 193
  Mary, 193
COLSBERRY, Elizabeth, 76
  Henry, 76
  William, 76
COLTER, George, 83
  Rebecca, 82
COLWELL, John, 102
  William, 279
COMBS, Ann, 282
CONALLY, Martha, 225
CONDRON, James, 224
CONELLY, Cathrine, 274
  Mary, 249
CONGTTUN, Mary, 96
  Robert, 96
  William, 96
CONINGHAM, Daniel, 289
CONLEY, Laurence, 271
  Timothy, 235
CONN, Samuel, 261
CONNEL, Elizabeth, 115

George, 115
Hester, 275
CONNELL, Sarah, 289
CONNELLY, Eleanor, 68
  Elizabeth, 214
  Jane, 237
CONNER, Ann, 279
  Elizabeth, 285
  Jane, 269
  William, 252
CONNOL, Elizabeth, 236
CONNOR, Martin, 208
  Mary, 208
CONOLLY, Arthur, 229
  Elenor, 273
  Hannah, 278
  James, 103
  Mary Champin, 103
CONPONY, Anna, 63
  Magdalena, 63
  Peter Petersson, 63
CONRAD, Constantine, 6
  Dau., 2
  Kiastin, 5
  Maria, 2
CONRI, Jane, 85
CONSTANTIN, ---, 2
  Augustin, 78
  Conrad, 4, 6, 7, 9, 23, 47
  Constianins, 9
  Kerstin, 4, 23
  Maria, 5, 9
  Mary, 6
  Miss, 5
  Sara, 78
CONSTANTINE,
  Augustine, 75
  Conrad, 2, 11
  Kustin, 6
  Maria, 75
  Mary, 2
COOK, Annie, 103
  Benjamin, 80
  Eleanor, 53
  Elenore, 227
  Elizabeth, 246
  Even, 103
  Hannah, 234
  John, 103, 144, 228
  Rachel, 144
  Timothy, 273
  William, 144, 237
COOKE, William, 284
COOKHORN, Edward, 123
  Elizabeth, 123
  Jemmimy, 123
COOKIN, Elizabeth, 246

COOKLY, James, 111
  John, 111
  Mary, 111
COOPE, John, 217
COOPER, Adam, 104
  Cathrine, 167
  Charles, 167
  Christopher, 226
  Jane, 69
  John, 79
  Margaret, 104
  Rachel, 278
  Robert, 252
  Sally, 290
  William, 167
COP, Oliver, 227
COPLIND, Sarah, 263
CORAM, Ann, 207
  Elizabeth, 207
  John Robert, 207
  Rhoda, 207
  Robert, 207
CORCORAN, Thomas, 95
CORDERY, Elizabeth, 44
CORDEY, Thomas, 40
CORDREAT, Peter, 29
CORDREY, John, 46
  Maria, 46
  Thomas, 46
CORKRAN, John, 246
CORNELII, Carl, 63
  Manni, 63
  Samuel, 63
CORNELIISSON,
  Cornelius, 1, 9
  Jacob, 9
CORNELIUS, Anders, 6
  Andreas, 53
  Anna, 53
  Carl, 50, 53, 58, 62
  Charles, 58
  Cornelius, 11
  Elizabeth, 22, 62
  Gierkie, 34
  Gustaf, 13
  Johan, 82
  Nanne, 62
  Richard, 86
  Staffan, 6, 11, 13
  Stephen, 22
  Wilhelmina, 6
  Wiliaminka, 22
  Williminka, 13
CORNELIUSON, Gustave, 146
  Isabel, 146
CORNELIUSSON,
  Cathrina, 111
  Johan, 111
  Sarah, 111
  Wennefrend, 111
CORNELLISSON,
  Williaminke, 9
CORNER, Judith, 69
CORNET, Jane, 146
  John, 146
  Lewis, 146
CORREL, Mary, 92
CORRELL, John, 99
  Mary, 99
  Rachel, 99
CORRIDON, Cathrine, 279
CORRY, Mary, 81
CORSINE, Niclas, 85
CORSKSHOTT, John, 195
  Mary, 195
  Robinson Barrow, 195
CORY, Judith, 83
COSSEY, John, 279
COSURE, William, 279
COSWELL, Rachel, 229
COUCHREN, Edward, 220
COULTER, Jenny, 60
COUNCIL, Sarah, 277
COUSTE, Elizabeth, 117
  George, 117
  Mary, 117
COVE, James, 65
COVEAD, Garret, 251
COVIN, Elizabeth Bell, 102
  John, 102
  Mark, 102
COWEN, Ann, 215
COWIN, Mark, 216
COWINS, John, 85
COWLY, William, 276
COWPER, Mary, 60
COWPERTHWAIT, Joseph, 251
COX, Abraham, 146, 151, 244
  Andrew, 92
  Cathrine, 191
  John, 92
  Joseph, 27
  Lady, 151
  Lydia, 146, 272
  Mary, 27, 288
  Richard, 27
  Thomas, 146, 191
COXE, Joseph, 20
  Margarita, 20
  Maria, 20
COYLE, Patrick, 215

INDEX

CRAAK, Barbro, 135
    Hans George, 135
    Jacob, 135
CRACKON, Archibald, 82
CRAFFORD, Jean, 93
    Martha, 228
    Mary, 90
    Sara, 79
CRAFORD, Cathrine, 241
CRAFT, Mary, 256
CRAIG, Abigail, 242
    Elizabeth, 252
    Jacob, 251
    James, 228, 236, 250
    Jean, 267
    Margret, 228
    Margrete, 250
    Mary, 268
    William, 263
CRAMPTON, Elizabeth, 123
    Jane, 123
    John, 237, 275
    Rebecca, 280
    Watkins, 123, 228
CRANGAL, Robert, 278
CRANGETTON, Edward, 250
CRASHER, John, 66
CRAVEN, Charity, 250
CRAW, Mary, 278
CRAWFORD,
    Christopher, 283
    David, 240
    Elizabeth, 197, 205, 206
    Henry, 288
    Isaac, 197, 205, 206
    John, 205
    Priscilla, 206
    Samuel, 197
    Sarah, 205
    Thomas, 227
CRAWSSIN, Rose, 224
CREAG, John, 260
CREATER, Andrew, 253
CREGG, Margery, 81
CREID, John, 66
CREIG, Margret, 85
CREITHON, Elizabeth, 215
CREMER, Elizabeth, 256
CRIPPS, Cornelius, 284
CRIPS, Andrew, 245
CRISS, Jacob, 228
CRISSEN, John, 102
    Rachel, 102

CROAK(?), Cathrine, 255
CROCKER, Anna, 46
    John, 46
    Maria, 46
CROCKERT, Mary, 80
CROKER, William, 87
CROMET, Christopher, 242
CROOK, Mary, 216, 258
CROSAN, John, 276
CROSBY, Ann, 284
    John, 69, 255
CROSELY, James, 261
CROSHEE, William, 49
CROSHY, Agnes, 222
CROSS, David, 181
    Margaret, 181
    William, 90
CROSSAR, Andrew, 219
CROSSIN, William
    Talley, 252
CROSSMAN, Jesse, 269
CROTHER, Mary, 252
CROUD, Christopher, 140
    Maria Barbara, 140
    Peter, 140
CROW, Ann, 172
    Edward, 257
    George, 87
    Isabella, 172
    Thomas, 172
CROWLEY, James, 84
    William, 230
CROXON, Archibald, 190
    Gatewell, 190
    Margret, 190
CRUDEN, Elizabeth, 270
CRUMPTON, John, 287
CRY, Cathrine, 123
    James, 123
    John, 123
CRYEA, Thomas, 292
CUBBIN, Henry, 262
CULAY, Catherine, 103
    Elenor, 103
    William, 103
CULBERTSON, Martha, 249
    Mary, 248, 287
    Robert, 280
CULEN, Anders, 26
    Annika, 56
    Bryan, 67
    Christina, 32
    Daniel, 78
    Elizabeth, 78

EARLY CHURCH RECORDS OF NEW CASTLE COUNTY

Johan, 4, 26, 32
Kerstin, 26, 32
Margaretta, 2
Margret, 222
Maria, 78
Mary, 233
Miss, 220
Rachel, 78
Regner, 56
William, 56, 78
CULFORD, Philip, 90
CULIN, Eleanor, 69
Isaac, 288
CULWELL, John, 141
Margrete, 141
CUMMINGS, Mary, 245
William, 248
CUMMINS, Alexander, 230
Hugh, 93
Mary, 262
Nathan, 279
Timothy, 50
CUNNINGHAM, Allen, 248
Andrew, 274
Arthur, 142, 150
Elizabeth, 142
Jane, 221
Jean, 265
John, 254
Margrete, 150
Mark, 233
Mary, 69, 142, 150
Rachel, 252
Sarah, 257
William, 229
CURFEL, Hugh, 124
Jacob, 124
Jane, 124
CURLE, Thomas, 81
CURLET, Jane, 142
Louis, 142
Mary, 142
CURREY, Ezekiel, 238
James, 264
CURRIE, William, 287
CURRY, Anna, 66
Cathrine, 230
James, 125
Mary, 125
Neal, 243
William, 125
CURSENG, Magdalena Stedham, 96
Niclas, 96
Sarah, 96
CURSINE, Nicolaus, 43
CURTLO, John, 66

CUSHON, David, 227

-D-

DAAS, Samuel, 284
DACKEYNE, William, 82
DADS, Jane, 69
DAEL, Judith, 225
DAHLBO, Lorance, 232
DAILY, Brian, 168, 256
Bryan, 162
James, 162
Mary, 162, 168
William, 168
DAIN, Ann, 261
James, 87
Joseph, 163, 260
DAKRILL, Mary, 87
DALE, Philip, 215
DALLE, Mary, 215
DALY, Hannah, 264
DAMARIN, John
Frederick, 132
Mara Magdalena, 132
DAME, Magdalen, 90
DAMPSEY, Rachel, 287
DAMSEL, Henry, 60
DANALLY, James, 91
DANBERGIN, Salome, 232
DANELY, Anne, 246
DANEVAN, George, 240
DANIEL, Breyer Meg, 42
Catharina, 42
Thomas, 82
DANIELSON, John, 265
DARBY, Mary, 250
DARLINGTON, Abraham, 253
John, 248, 261
Mary, 256
DARRAN, Elizabeth Stedham, 94
Henry, 94
Susanna, 94
DARRAYN, Elizabeth Stedham, 99
Henry, 99
Margaret, 99
DARTY, Hanna, 267
DASON, John, 46
Sara, 46
DASSON, James, 46
John, 46
Sara, 46
DAUGHERTY, Ann, 279
Edmund, 258
Margret, 269
Mary, 220
Nail, 184

INDEX

Thomas, 287
DAUNT, Elenore, 226
DAVID, James, 224
  Johyn, 223
  Rachel, 225
  Robert, 217
  Thomas, 239
DAVIDSON, Alexander, 90
DAVIDSSON, Ann, 215
DAVIS, Abraham, 132, 241
  Amos, 266
  Ann, 253, 256, 260, 289
  Anna, 132
  Banton, 121
  Catharina, 132
  Catharine, 81
  Cathrine, 254
  Charity, 269
  Daniel, 261
  David, 47, 228
  Dina, 243
  Edward, 289
  Elizabeth, 246
  George, 291
  German, 238
  Grace, 75, 102
  Hannah, 80, 121, 224, 240, 270
  Isaac, 49
  James, 11, 192, 281
  Jane, 192
  John, 43, 222, 256, 262
  Jonathan, 182, 290
  Lettice, 278
  Lydy, 246
  Margret, 93, 229, 238
  Marion, 182
  Mary, 19, 75, 102, 231, 232, 240
  Nathaniel, 229
  Peter, 192, 278
  Rebecca, 257
  Richard, 121
  Susanna, 230, 257, 292
  Thomas, 14, 182, 240, 259
  William, 75, 102, 222
  Zadi, 281
DAVISON, Jean, 264
DAVITT, Jane, 144
  Tully, 144, 244
  William, 144
DAVY, Amelia, 273
DAWSON, Edward, 170
  Jacob, 237
  Johan, 33
  John, 290
  Margret, 82
  Maria, 33
  Mary, 170
  Sara, 33
  Sarah, 249
DAWSY, Eliza, 84
DAY, Ann, 162
  Elizabeth, 233
  Francis, 156, 162, 254
  John, 60, 190
  Joseph, 156, 257
  Rebecca, 288
  Sylvanus, 254
DAYLY, John, 232
DE FOSS, Anne, 13
  Elizabeth, 46
  Hanna, 17, 22, 46
  Hannah, 13
  Johan, 17
  Johanna, 6
  Johannes, 6, 13, 17, 22, 23, 46
  Mattias, 6
  Sara, 47
  Thomas, 22
DEAL, Henry, 260
DEALY, Daniel, 260
  John, 261
DEAN, David, 220
  Elizabeth, 215
  Thomas, 215
DEARMAN, Sarah, 251
DEARON, Henry, 89
DEAVER, John Martin, 242
DEBOOH, Henry, 281
DECROY, Michael, 229
DEDRICHSON, Ellinor, 77
  Zachariah, 77
DEDRICKSON, Mary, 76
  Susanna, 76
  William, 76
DEEBLE, Jane, 70
DEER, Anne, 225
DEGLISH, Thomas, 250
DEGNEN, Helena, 64
  John, 64
  Maria, 64
DEGUNN, John, 60
DELANY, Elizabeth, 60

DELAP, John, 220
  Joseph, 220
  Thomas, 285
DELAPLAIN, James, 283
DELAVON, James, 282
DELL, James, 229
DELY, Cherry, 239
DEMPSEY, Arthur, 175, 273
  Elizabeth, 175
  Johannah, 175
DEMSY, Mary, 65
DENIN, John, 102, 112
  Margret, 112
  Mary, 102, 112
DENNARY, Cathrine, 250
DENNEY, Martha, 89
DENNIS, Anne Frances, 148
  Barna Cozen, 148
  Elizabeth, 234
  George, 264
  Mary, 148
  Robert, 148
  Sarah, 148
  Thomas, 148
DENNISON, Thomas, 265
DENNON, William, 246
DENNY, Ann, 90
  David, 263, 273
  Richard, 262
DENNYS, Margaret, 88
DEPOLT, Eva, 170
  John, 170
DERECKSON, David, 128
  Sarah, 128
  Zacharias, 128
DERIC, David, 117
  Mary, 117
DERICK, David, 223
  Lady, 251
  Mary, 249
DERICKS, Prudence, 234
DERICKSON, Ann, 179, 180
  Cathrine, 179, 196, 230, 279
  Cornelius, 115, 180, 230
  Elenor, 275
  Elizabeth, 150
  Ingeber, 153, 160
  Jacob, 153, 160, 250
  Joseph, 177, 281
  Margret, 230
  Martha, 231
  Mary, 159, 180, 185
  Peter, 115, 150, 179, 196
  Rachel, 285
  Rebecca, 159, 169
  Sara, 102
  Sarah, 115, 177, 185, 202
  William, 150, 153, 159, 169, 256
  Williamson, 169
  Zachariah, 290
  Zacharias, 102, 115, 177, 185, 202
  Zachris, 102
DERICSSON, Helena, 44
DERMOTT, Lin, 224
DERRICK, Anna Maria, 176
  Christina, 156
  Elenor, 193
  Fredrich, 151
  Jemima, 266
  Lydia, 260
  Mary, 151, 161, 172, 176
  Prudence, 272
  Rachel, 189
  Richard, 151, 156, 161, 172, 176, 263
  Sara, 189
  Sarah, 185, 193, 262
  Thomas, 185, 189, 193
  William, 161
DERRICKSON, Ann, 175, 185, 194
  Benjamin, 292
  Cathrine, 173, 187
  Cornelius, 169, 175, 185, 269
  David, 268
  Debora, 194
  Elenor, 173, 180, 183, 188, 246
  Elenore, 248
  Elizabeth, 142, 187, 211, 214
  Ingeber, 164, 169
  Ingebor, 160
  Jacob, 160, 161, 164, 169, 173, 180, 183, 188, 256, 265
  Jane, 281
  John, 175, 180, 214
  Joseph, 132, 188, 194
  Margret, 164

INDEX

Maria Ann, 214
Martha, 165
Mary, 165, 169, 292
Peter, 187
Rebecca, 160, 161, 283
Richard, 165
Sarah, 132, 175, 180, 194
Susanna, 211
William, 194
Williamson, 169
Zachariah, 194, 211
Zacharias, 132, 142, 175, 268
DERRICSON, Rachel, 165
Rebecca, 165
William, 165
DERY, Cathrina, 110
Elizabeth, 110
Henry, 110
DEVENEY, Aaron, 65
DEVOR, Jean, 264
DIAMOND, Bernard, 275
DIAT, Adam, 247
DICK, Alexander, 244
Elizabeth, 211
Jacob, 211, 282
John, 233
Susannah, 211
DICKEY, George, 83
DICKIE, Andrew, 219
James, 230
DICKIN, Joseph, 249
DICKINSON, Abner, 282
DICKMAN, Johan, 8
Mariah, 8
DICKS, Ester, 253
DICKSON, Dorcas, 268
Joseph, 241
Joshua, 263
Samuel, 249
Sarah, 255
DICKSSON, Caleb, 241
DICKY, James, 81
DIDRICH, Martha, 70
DIDRICK, Thomas, 68
DIDRICKSON, Catharina, 63
Jacob, 71, 74
Margarita, 74
Maria, 63, 71
Peter, 69, 74
Sara, 64
Wiljam, 61
William, 63, 64, 71, 242
Zacharias, 64

Zachrison, 92
DIDRICSSON, Cornelius, 15
Helena, 10, 15
Peter, 10
Zacharias, 10, 15
DIDRIKSSON, Hellena, 1
Zacharias, 1
DIGDON, Elenor, 267
DILING, Margery, 236
DILIWERD, Hannah, 267
DILLING, Ann, 250
DILLMORE, Elizabeth, 107
John, 107
Susanna, 107
DILLWORTH, Hannah, 229
DILMORE, Edward, 95
Elizabeth Aldrichson, 95
John, 95
DILWARD, Mary, 255
DILWORTH, James, 81
Lydia, 267
Richard, 81
William, 243
DIMOND, John, 141
Mary, 214
Philip, 141
Sarah, 141
DINGEE, Daniel, 291
Jacob, 254
Rachel, 284
Ruth, 291
DINNEY, Esther, 231
DIRIC, Elenor, 119
Jeane, 119
Thomas, 119
DIRICKSON, Cathrine, 145
Cornelius, 145
Jane, 145
Mary, 145
DIRICSON, Jacobus, 47
DIRICSSON, Elizabeth, 44
DIRIXON, Annika, 50
Elizabeth, 47
DIRIXSON, Jacobus, 46
DIRRICK, Elenor, 276
DIRRICKSON, Mary, 119
William, 119
DISNEY, John, 270
DIVANT, John, 140
Magdalena, 140
DIX, Mary, 60
DIXON, Cathrine, 259
David, 161

EARLY CHURCH RECORDS OF NEW CASTLE COUNTY

Enoch, 229
Martha, 161
Samuel, 161, 272
William, 83, 161, 226, 267, 274, 286
DIXSON, Mary, 218
Samuel, 218
DOBBIN, Peter, 81
DOBELBOWER, John
Henry, 290
DOBSON, John, 89
DOCHERTY, Ann, 80
DOCKRIA, Sara, 83
DODD, Anne, 232
James, 232
DOILE, Matthew, 254
DOLBOY, John, 93
DON, Cathrine, 253
DONALDSON, Isabella, 274
Margaret Townsend, 98
Sarah, 285
William, 98
DONDERIN, Sobina, 225
DONDLE, Bartram, 269
DONE, Daniel, 92
Elizabeth, 51
Patrick, 51
Susanna, 51
DONELLY, James, 227
Owen, 252
DONNE, Elizabeth, 224
DONNELFASS, Dorothea, 131
John Fredrick, 131
Nicklas, 131
DONNELLY, Arthur, 69
DONNERTHY, James, 222
DONNY, Mary, 215
DONOLLY, Cathy, 221
DORNAL, Phoebe, 243
DORNELL, Elizabeth, 125
James, 125
DOROTHY, Mary, 259
DOTHAT, William, 290
DOTTAN, Benjamin, 249
John, 247
Mary, 245
DOUDLE, James, 231
DOUGHARTY, Anne, 234
DOUGHERTHY, Elizabeth, 112
Garret, 112
William, 112
DOUGHERTY, Cathrine, 287

Edmund, 250
Edward, 219
Elinor, 218
Elizabeth, 106, 273
James, 263
John, 270
Manasseh, 287
Mary, 106
Robert, 106
DOUGLAS, Cathrine, 247
Isabel, 239
Jane, 114
Mary, 114
Robert, 114
DOUN, Rachel, 277
DOURTHY, Elizabeth, 227
DOW, Mary, 218
DOWLING, Mary, 93
DOWNARD, James, 104
Mary, 104
DOWNART, James, 83
DOWNING, Margret, 226
Mary, 269
Sarah, 217
Susanna, 267
Tamazin, 288
DOWNS, Ann, 287
Thomas, 92
DOYLE, Martin, 245
Susanna, 246
DRAPER, Moses, 280
DRESSER, John, 204
Maria, 204
Rachel, 202, 204
DRUITT, John, 236
DUARD, Anne, 216
DUBLIN, Sarah, 274
DUCKERTY, Edward, 84
DUFF, Thomas, 217
DUFFEE, Patrick, 231
DUFFY, Ann, 202
Cathrine, 202
John, 202
DUFS, Edward, 120
Jane, 120
Thomas, 120
DUGAL, Unity, 270
DUGEN, Christiana, 262
DUGGAN, James, 234
DUGLAS, Elizabeth, 93
DULLY, John, 80
DUNDAS, Isabella, 282
DUNHAM, John Dehanor, 261
DUNIHOO, Elinor, 261
DUNKEN, Brita, 2, 29
DUNKIN, Brita, 7

320

INDEX

DUNLAP, Elizabeth, 200
  Francis, 200, 288
  Jean, 254, 264
  John, 258
  Rachel, 289
  Rebecca, 200, 250
  Robert, 250
DUNN, Ann, 178
  Brigitta, 250
  Edward, 178, 271
  Elizabeth, 245
  George, 209
  James, 178
  Marian, 209
  Martha, 65
  Mary, 209
  Nathaniel, 209
  Orpah, 209
  William, 257
DUNNING, James, 227, 248
DUNSMORE, John, 257
DURNAL, Elizabeth, 241
  Grashon, 53
  Peter, 269
  Samuel, 257
DURNEL, Ruth, 225
DURNELL, Wil, 233
  William, 225
DURNEY, Thomas, 273
DURRHAM, John, 85
DURROM, Richard, 82
DUSKILL, Cornelius, 133
  Maria Evanson, 133
  Rebecka, 133
DUSS, Anna, 107
  Jane, 107
  Thomas, 107
DUTON, David, 216
DUTTON, David, 70, 272
  Francis, 266
  Hannah, 231
  Johnathan, 259
  Kingsman, 231
  Thomas, 234
DWIRE, Philip, 275
DYATT, Elizabeth, 245
DYER, Henry, 28
  Mr., 28
DYKE, Hannah, 90
DYSURT, Stephen, 229

-E-

EACHEY, Abigail, 230
EACHUS, Robert, 232
EALS, Hannah, 243
EARBY, Amos, 87
  Anna, 48
  Edward, 48
  Maria, 48
  Mary, 216
  Susanna, 92
EARLY, Edward, 50
  Titus, 60
EAST, Rebecca, 266
EASTBOURN, Sarah, 225
EATON, Johan, 17, 18
ECCLES, Alse, 270
  Anna, 182
  Margret, 182
  Mary, 266
  Robert, 182, 256
  William, 269
ECKHOF, David, 234
ECKMAN, Christina, 41
  Johan, 41
  Robbert, 41
EDEN, Ezekil, 178
EDGINGTON, Mary, 209
  Richard, 209
  William, 209
EDMONDS, Else, 256
EDMUND, Thomas, 221
EDMUNDSON, Susanna, 80
EDWARD, Robert, 258
EDWARDS, Deborah, 253
  Elizabeth, 70
  Joshua, 225
  Mary, 270
  Phoebe, 275
  Robert, 234
  Sarah, 253
  Thomas, 258
  William, 279
EGEN, Mary, 215
EGLESTON, Richard, 86
EICTKEN, Goran, 3
  Kerstin, 3
EILES, ---, 189
  Fanny, 172
  John, 172
  Margret, 172
  Robert, 172
EINFASS, Anne Mary, 129
  Dorothea, 129
  Niklas, 129
EKMAN, Adam, 244
ELDARE, Joseph, 87
ELDER, Elizabeth, 104
  James, 104
  Rachael, 104
ELDERS, James, 89
ELDRICH, James, 66
ELDRIDGE, Mary, 266

ELLESON, Margret, 92
ELLET, James, 81, 83
  Jane, 78
  Margret, 78
  Martin, 78
  Mary, 83
  Thomas, 90
ELLICK, Philip, 278
ELLIOT, Benjamin, 195
  Elisabeth, 156
  Elizabeth, 151
  George, 232
  Margret, 283
  Thomas, 151
  William, 151
ELLIOTT, Alexander, 143
  Benjamin, 168, 173, 175, 180, 187, 204
  Cathrina, 234
  Cloe, 135
  Edward, 135
  Elizabeth, 171, 204, 255
  Francis, 83
  George, 133, 143, 147
  Hanna, 134
  James, 257
  Jane, 134, 177, 240
  Jean, 151
  Jeane, 169
  John, 135, 151, 163, 168, 171, 180, 206, 213, 214, 238
  Joseph, 160, 172, 267
  Leah, 265
  Margaret, 159
  Margret, 180, 187, 284
  Maria, 133
  Mark, 134, 151, 169, 177
  Martha, 180, 242
  Mary, 143, 147, 160, 172, 180
  Rachel, 147
  Rebecca, 172, 206, 213, 214, 262
  Robert, 133
  Susanna, 168, 195, 204, 286
  Susannah, 175, 180
  Thomas, 163, 177, 213, 285
  William, 156, 159, 164, 169, 171, 173, 206, 259, 276
ELLIS, Catherine, 257
  Hannah, 17
  Persanna, 70
ELLISON, Thomas, 291
ELLOT, Elenor, 214
  Elijah, 122
  Jane, 104, 114, 122, 226
  Mark, 104, 114, 122
  Mary, 104
ELLWEL, Mary, 270
ELLY, Benjamin, 78
  Margaret, 78
  William, 78
ELNES, Ellenor, 92
ELROD, Elizabeth, 17
  George Arendt, 26
  Johan Didrick, 7, 17, 26
  Maria Magdalena, 17
  Sara, 26
ELWILL, Joseph, 86
ELWOOD, Elizabeth, 17
  Thomas, 17
  William, 17
EMESON, John, 271
EMIT, Ann, 255
EMLERER, Mary, 231
EMORE, Mary, 255
EMPSON, Aben Ezer, 28
  Abenezer, 23
  Charles, 43
  Ebenezer, 40
  Jonathan, 40
  Maria, 23
  Rebecca, 28
  Susanna, 23, 28
EMPSSON, Aben Ezer, 29
  Ebenezer, 33, 40
  Rebecca, 29
  Susanna, 33, 40
EMSSON, Joshua, 223
ENGEL, Susanna, 232
ENGLAND, Ann, 255, 260
  Benjamin, 83
  Isaac, 218, 248
  Jacob, 253
  Michael, 282
ENGLISH, Ann, 274
  Catherine, 110
  James, 226
  Mary, 110
  William, 232
ENGRUM, John, 222
ENIS, Elizabeth, 272

INDEX

Hannah, 266
ENKLAN, Jane, 242
ENNYS, Mary, 255
ENOCH, Andreas, 28
  Andrew, 145
  Benjamin, 139, 145
  David, 28, 54, 139
  Gertrude, 54
  Helena, 28, 54
  Mary, 139, 145
ENOCHS, Andrew, 106
ENOCK, Benjamin, 134
  Maria, 134
  Rees, 246
ENOS, Elizabeth, 12
  James, 140, 225
  Joseph, 5, 16, 140, 280
  Maria, 18
  Martha, 247
  Richard, 5, 12, 16, 18, 24
  Stephen, 225
  Susanna, 5, 12, 18, 24, 140
ERBY, Amos, 112
  Anna, 42
  Edward, 42
  Mary, 112
  Rachel, 112
  Susanna, 42
ERICKS, Hannah, 215
  Margret, 216
ERICSON, Eric, 13
ERICSSON, Annika, 8
  Catharina, 2
  Elizabeth, 35
  Emma, 3
  Eric, 3, 8
  Maria, 34
  Matz, 7
ERNEST, Anne, 236
ERRICSON, Eric, 10
ERSHELOT, Margareta, 38
  Robert, 38
  Samuel, 38
ERSLEY, Rachel, 283
ERVIN, James, 248
  Margret, 278
  Rebecca, 244
ERWIN, Anne, 231
  Fanny, 166
  Hanna, 266
  John, 166, 215
  Margret, 166
  Richard, 228
  Rose, 229

ESPY, Mary, 92
ETHERIDGE, Barnaba, 157
  Carl, 157
  Lars, 164
  Sarah, 157, 164
  William, 164
EUKLINGEN, Anna, 239
EVAN, Aaron, 239
  Evan, 257
EVANS, Anne, 218
  Daniel, 229
  David, 83, 265
  Elinor, 35
  Elizabeth, 89
  Hannah, 272
  John, 60
  Johnathan, 258
  Lucrecy, 260
  Margaret, 67, 88, 222
  Martha, 93
  Mary, 94, 282
  Oliver, 277
  Owen, 232
  Rachel, 235
  Rees, 37
  Ruth, 260
  Sarah, 246
  Thomas, 67, 224
  William, 35, 221
EVANSON, Elis, 276
  Phoebe, 81
  Seth, 240
EVARS, Rebecca, 82
EVENSON, Elizabeth, 217
EVERITE, Matthew, 270
EVERLAY, Jacob, 144
  Simon, 144
  Sophia, 144
EVERMON, Peter D., 281
EVES, Abraham, 205, 208
  Elizabeth, 190, 205, 208
  Hannah, 260
  James, 190, 193, 199, 201, 208, 212, 267
  Jane, 201
  Mary, 190, 193, 199, 201, 208, 212
  Stephen, 205
  William Dushane, 199
EWART, Thomas, 267
EWING, Agnes, 224
  James, 218

EYNON, Sarah, 253
EYON, Dorcas, 267
EYRE, Robert, 247

-F-
FADDES, John, 259
FAIL, Abigail, 214
  Hannah, 89
  Mary, 85
FAIRBROTHER, James, 280
FALCKONER, Nathaniel, 120
  Prudence, 120
  Sarah, 120
FALCONER, Nathaniel, 224
FALKENTON, Joshua, 241
FALKINTON, Ruth, 222
FALKNER, Jassay, 81
FALKONER, John Jacobs, 267
  Nathaniel, 117
  Sarah, 117
FALLOWS, Mary, 284
FANDRIC, Annika, 55
  Maria, 55
  Samuel, 55
FANROD, John, 277
FARELL, Bridget, 226
FARGESSON, Eleonore, 240
FARIES, Samuel, 273
FARIL, Cathrine, 238
FARLE, Jemima, 265
  Rebecca, 274
FARLO, Margret, 261
FARLON, Judith, 65
FARLOU, Catharina, 68
FARLOW, Elizabeth, 61
  Michel, 67
FARME, Margret, 271
FARMER, Margret, 236
FARNISS, William, 93
FARR, Catharina, 2
  John, 2
FARRA, Martha, 264
FARRAYS, Margaret, 79
FARREL, Ann, 274
  Jean, 87
FARRELL, Bridget, 226
  Elizabeth, 273
FARRILL, Mary, 248
FARRON, Margery, 244
FASETTY, Sarah, 236
FASSAL, Richard, 82
FAULK, Ester, 282

FAULKEN, Elizabeth, 251
FAULL, Catharine
  Magdalen, 149
  Dorothea, 149
  Nicholas, 149
FEAR, Elizabeth, 220
FEELDING, Leady, 261
FEER, Margaretta, 59
  Samuel, 250
FEGEN, Brigget, 50
FELLOWS, John, 96
  Mary, 96
  William, 96
FERGUSON, William, 215
FERREL, Elenor, 266
  Hugh, 252
FERREY, Elizabeth, 272
FERRIS, Charles, 184
  Jane, 68, 224, 227
  Margret, 184
  Rachel, 245
FEW, Abraham, 189
  Anne, 224
  Christina, 111, 118, 125
  Daniel, 111, 118, 125, 220
  Elizabeth, 44, 125
  Hannah, 156
  Isaac, 117
  James, 111
  Johanna, 263
  Mary, 237, 253, 255
  Richard, 231, 284
  William, 118
FEWLER, Judith, 81
FIELDEN, Edward, 272
FIELDING, Susanna, 271
FILE, John, 252
  Robert, 256
FILENIA, Ulrica, 110
FILLPOT, John, 93
FILSON, Davisson, 220
FINLEY, Samuel, 87
FINNEY, Cathrine, 234
  John, 233
FINNIN, Daniel, 218
FINSH, Elizabeth, 113
  Jemaymi, 113
  John, 113
FIPS, Mary, 82
FIRTH, James, 242
  William, 254
FISHER, Amy, 261
  Cathrine, 253
  Elizabeth, 39
  George, 39

INDEX

John, 217, 262
Joseph, 263
Nanze, 223
Ruth, 235
FITCHGIRL, Ann, 85
FITCHPATRICK, James, 105
  Joanna, 105
FITSRANDEL, Cloe, 238
FITZGERALD, Cathrine, 253
FITZIMMON, Marget, 53
  Maria, 53
FITZSIMMON, James, 53
  Margret, 53
  Maria, 53
FITZSIMMONS,
  Elizabeth, 56
  James, 56
  Judith, 252
  Margareta, 56
FLAHARTY, Abraham, 245
FLAHEN, John, 270
FLANAGAN, James, 180
  Jane, 180
  William, 180
FLAREGAN, Thomas, 89
FLATCHER, Ester, 107
  James, 249
  Mary, 107
FLEAN, Else, 220
FLEMING, James, 231
  John, 230
FLEMMEN, Hanna, 80
  Rebecca, 225
FLEMON, Jeremia, 256
FLETCHER, Alexander, 184
  Bridget, 284
  Elizabeth, 162
  James, 162, 184
  John, 60, 184, 190
  Susannah, 162
  William, 172, 268
FLIN, Elizabeth, 203
  Hanna, 199
  Hannah, 203
  Isaac, 199
  John, 199, 203, 276
FLING, Hannah, 208
  Jane, 122
  John, 208
  Margaret, 117
  Mary, 117, 276
  Niclas, 90, 122
  Sarah, 122
  Thomas, 117, 220
FLINN, Ann, 190

Christopher, 69
Hannah, 185, 196
John, 185, 190, 196, 258
Lawrence, 239
Peter, 190
Thomas, 185
FLINTHAM, John, 61
FLOOD, Henry, 226
  Lydia, 273
FLOWER, Mary, 216, 220
FLOWERS, Thomas, 233
FLOYD, Anna, 115, 134
  Anne, 114, 152, 218
  Cathrine, 281
  James, 79, 115
  John, 259
  Mary, 115
  Rachel, 264
  Robert, 114
  Samuel, 114, 134, 152, 231
  Sarah, 134
  William, 83
FLUPEN, Susanna, 266
FLYED, James, 65
FOARD, Hanna, 84
FOCKER, Joshua, 81
FODREY, Alis, 48
  Anna, 48
  Samuel, 48
FOGNER, Mary, 248
FOLEK, Sara, 49
FOLK, Elizabeth, 269
  Mary, 262
FOLLIS, Sara, 102
  Thomas, 102
  William, 94, 102
FOLLOWS, Sarah, 109
  William, 109
FOLTON, John, 90
  Richard, 81
FONDEREY, John, 176
  Mary, 176
FOOT, Arthur, 159
  Benjamin, 233
  Briget, 229
  James, 291
  Janet, 115
  John, 283
  Leady, 159
  Mary, 159
  Rachael, 115
  Thomas, 195
  William, 115, 195, 230, 289
FOOTE, John, 207
  Lewis, 207

Margret, 207
Simon, 207
FORARD, Samuel, 223
FORD, Abraham, 68
 Alexander, 173
 Ann, 259, 279
 Anna, 66, 190
 Annah, 144
 Benjamin, 50, 128,
  132, 144, 159, 230
 Charles, 197
 David, 132, 250,
  269, 285
 Edward Eugene, 213
 Elizabeth, 264
 Frances, 213
 Francis, 197
 Gabriel H., 213
 Hannah, 153, 251
 Henry Augustus, 213
 Jacob, 278
 James, 266
 Jane, 226
 Jemima, 269
 John, 67, 244, 276
 Margaret, 287
 Margret, 159, 173,
  223
 Margrete, 144
 Martha, 173
 Mary, 71, 87, 128,
  159, 223, 259, 287
 Philip, 287
 Phoebe, 153, 265
 Rachel, 278
 Rebecca, 132
 Robin, 71
 Samuel, 291
 Sarah, 46, 244, 281,
  282, 289
 Susanna, 274
 William, 66, 128,
  223, 276
FOREHEAD, Johan, 20
 Margaretta, 15
 Maria, 20, 25, 38,
  45
 Mary, 15
 Rebecca, 38
 Samuel, 45
 William, 12, 15, 20,
  25, 38, 45
FOREMER, ---, 82
FORESIDE, James, 218
FORESIDES, Prudence,
 95
FORESIGHT, John, 247
FORESMAN, Daniel, 267

FORGERSON, Mary, 257
FORGESON, Elizabeth,
 81
FORGREAVE, Robert, 269
FORGUSON, James, 255
FORKINEAR, Catherine,
 66
FORMAN, Elizabeth, 240
FORQUAR, Jane, 215
FORQUHER, William, 215
FORSTER, Jane, 224
FORSYTH, Cloe, 179
 George, 179
 Jane, 179
 Mary, 271
FORTON, Rhoda, 253
FORWOOD, Rebecca, 85
FORY, Dorothy, 163
 Nicholas, 163
 Rebecca, 163
FOSS, Annah Eva, 141
 Dorothea, 133, 141
 Johan Gottfried
  Michael, 133
 Nicholas, 273
 Nicklas Daniel, 133
 Niclas, 141
FOSTER, Dorothy, 223
 Thomas, 82
FOSTON, Ann, 83
FOUDERY, John, 167
 Mary, 167
 Susannah, 167
FOUDREY, John, 158
 Thomas, 158
 William, 158
FOUGHT, Gabriel, 118
 Johan, 118
 Mary, 118
FOULK, Eneas, 248
FOUNDREY, John, 249
FOURSEIDES, Joseph,
 214
FOWDREY, Anna, 38
 Samuel, 35, 38
 Susanna, 38
FOWEL, Dorothea, 105
 Henry, 105
 Jesa, 105
FOWLER, Henry, 20
 James, 274
 Martha, 255
 Mary Andersson, 20
 William, 20
FOWLSAND, Sarah, 217
FOWSER, Sarah, 282
FOX, Ann, 180
 Elizabeth, 233

INDEX

Frances, 180
George, 180
Gilbert, 290
John, 222
Margaret, 272
Mary, 180
FOY, George, 146
Mary, 146
Sarah, 146
FRAESER, Moses, 246
FRAID, Cathrine, 222
FRAME, David, 236
Jean, 251
Nathan, 83
FRAMES, Charity, 268
FRAMEY, Rebecca, 284
FRANCE, John, 7
FRANSSEN, Christina, 3
FRANSSON, Olof, 2
Peter, 2
FRANTSSEN, Anna, 3, 9
FRANTSSON, John Mink
Olof, 2
FRED, John, 260
FREDD, Elizabeth, 252
FREDERICK, John, 255
Samuel, 58
FREEMAN, Margret, 265
Sarah, 65
FREICZER, John, 268
FRENCH, Anne, 238
Arthur, 202
Barbro, 137
Barnaby, 202
Isabella, 289
Jane, 282
John, 83, 137, 239
Rebecca, 202
Sarah, 245
FRESCA, John, 152
Sarah, 152
William, 152
FRESHER, Mary, 81
FREST, Mary, 98
Mary Ann McMary, 98
Richard, 98
FREY, Jane, 67
Sarah, 228
FRI, Henry, 261
FRIAR, Jane, 282
FRIKMAN, Hanna, 243
FRILL, Johan
Garrisson, 21
FRISDELL, Mercy, 228
FRITCH, Elizabeth, 272
FRITH, James, 262
FROST, Joshua, 216
FRYAR, George, 241

FUDRIE, Nanny, 70
Samuel, 70
FULDAM, Elizabeth, 223
FULLER, Henry, 262
FULTREY, Susanna, 80
FURKES, Catharine, 124
John, 124
William, 124
FUSSEL, Ann, 292
FUTHREY, Judith, 229

-G-
GACKHAGEN, John, 254
GAFFIN, Barbro, 136
John, 136
Maria, 136
GALLAGHER, Margaret, 150
Neil, 284
Tom, 150
GALLAHER, John, 291
Martha, 277
GALLION, Mary, 215
GALLOHAR, Peter, 239
GALLOHER, Sarah, 264
GALLOHUN, Margret, 237
GALLORHON, Peter, 237
GALLOWAY, Charles, 122, 137
Eleanor, 290
Isaac, 122
Jane, 137
Jeane, 122
Mary, 100
Peter, 100
Sarah, 100
William, 137
GALLOWER, Charles, 241
GAMBLE, Elizabeth, 230
Patrick, 238
GANDAY, Thomas, 217
GANDOUCT, Mary, 87
GANDY, Thomas, 255, 260
GANTHONY, Peter, 89
GAPIN, John, 246
GARDEN, Gen, 33
Sarah, 217
GARDNER, Archibald, 240
Benjamin, 114
John, 87
Margret, 114
Mary, 114
GARISSONS, Hendrick, 23
Johanney, 23
Kustin, 23

EARLY CHURCH RECORDS OF NEW CASTLE COUNTY

GARITSON, Sarah, 223
GARITSSON, Conrad, 98
  Maria, 98
  Maria Johnson, 98
GARMAN, James, 239
GARNEL, Mary, 258
GARNER, Richard, 246
  Zacharias, 285
GARNY, Elizabeth, 240
GARONS, Elisel, 243
GARRA, Charles, 238
GARRESSON, Hindric, 18
  Johan, 9
  Kerstin, 18
  Maria, 18
GARRET, John, 50
GARRETSON, Catharine, 205
  Conrad, 66
  Elenor, 124
  Henry, 205
  John, 124
  Peter, 205
  Rachael, 124
  Sarah, 292
GARRETSSON, Anna, 25
  Catharina, 37
  Ester, 35
  Garret, 35, 37
  Garrit Palsson, 35
  Johan, 25
GARRETT, Robert, 268
GARRISON, Abaah, 238
  Conrad, 134
  Henric, 4
  John, 80
  Kerstin, 6, 7
  Maria, 134
  Mary, 82, 260, 263
  Susanna, 134
GARRISSON, Anna, 30
  Catherine, 36
  Conrad, 13
  Elizabeth, 30, 36
  Esther, 30
  Garret, 30, 77
  Garrit, 36, 61
  Hendric, 9
  Hendrick, 9
  Henry, 29
  Hindric, 13
  Hindrick, 26, 29
  Johan, 29
  John, 77
  Joseph, 255
  Kerstin, 9, 13
  Mary, 77
  Peter, 77
  Richard, 29
  Sara, 77
GARRIT, Anne, 121
  Annika, 75
  John, 121, 228
  Margaret, 75, 217
  Morton, 75
  Sarah, 216
GARRITFSSON,
  Elizabeth, 45
  Ester, 45
  Garrit, 45
  Garrit Palsson, 45
  Hindric, 45
  John, 45
  Rebecca, 45
GARRITSON, Anna, 244
  Anne, 105
  Brigitta, 149
  Christina, 73
  Conrad, 73
  Elenora, 139
  Elizabeth, 52, 58, 139
  Hannah, 279
  Henry, 140, 155, 173, 183, 241, 246, 276
  James, 256
  John, 52, 105, 139, 149
  Mary, 73, 105, 140, 149, 155, 183, 225
  Peter, 140
  Rebecca, 222
  Sarah, 173
  Thomas, 52, 224
GARRITSSEN, Elizabeth, 61
  Garrit, 61
  Maria, 61
GARRITSSON, Ann, 215
  Anna, 34, 49, 54
  Anne, 114
  child, 39
  Conrad, 114
  Elizabeth, 49, 54
  Garrit, 39, 54, 64
  Huldah, 215
  Jemymy, 220
  John, 49, 50
  Maria, 64, 114
  Rebecca, 64
GARRITTSON, Eleanor, 145
  Henry, 145
  John, 145
  Mary, 145

INDEX

Rebeccah, 145
GARRMAN, Ruth, 227
GARRON, Eleanora, 68
GARS, Cathrine, 188
  Elizabeth, 188
  John, 267
  Samuel, 188
GART, Elizabeth, 251
GARTIGEN, Ann, 272
GARTISSON, Garrit, 99
  Jacob, 99
  Mary, 99
GASKEY, James, 273
GASKIN, William, 271
GASS, Cathrine, 183
  George, 183
  Samuel, 183
GASSERT, Elizabeth, 97
  Emma Kallamiller, 97
  Johannes, 97
  John, 97
  Nannie, 97
GATES, Sarah, 250
GAULANGER, Rose, 117
  William, 117
GAUST, Jane, 284
GAVIN, William, 60
GAY, Anne, 235
GEARS, John, 286
GEDDES, Ann, 288
  Mary, 291
  Susan, 286
GEDLIN, Barbro, 229
GEENS, Mary, 14
GELASPY, Jane, 53
GELESPE, John, 292
GELLY, Charles, 284
GENKENS, Annah, 241
GENNET, Christopher, 177, 184, 262
  Elizabeth, 163, 177
  Jonas, 192
  Mary, 163
  Mathias, 177, 259
  Matthias, 163
  Rebecca, 192
  Sarah, 192, 284
  William, 177
GENNETT, Michael, 97
GENNIS, Rebecca, 226
GENNOI, Arthur, 262
GENNY, Jacob, 84
  Michael, 84
  Susanna Morton, 84
GEOGORY, Levy, 216
GEORGE, Anne, 227
  Hanna, 82
  Sarah, 93

GERMAN, John, 205
  Lewis, 35
  Mary, 205
  Sarah, 205
GERUCH, Albrecht, 141
  Margret, 141
  Maria Barbro, 141
GEST, John, 257
GHARD, Abel, 176
  Elenor, 176
  William, 176
GHISELINE, Hannah, 280
GHISLIN, Mary, 272
GIARGE, Elizabeth, 66
GIBBON, Thomas, 243
GIBBONS, Elizabeth, 278
GIBBS, Isaac, 219
GIBRETH, Robert, 215
GIBS, Mary, 80
GIBSON, Anne, 235
  Cathrine, 239
  Edward, 192
  Hugh, 234
  James, 238, 276
  John, 86
  Samuel, 265
GIFFIN, Martha, 285
  Mary, 281
  Matthew, 245
GIFFING, Thomas, 50, 93
GIFFORD, Eliza, 210
  Hugh, 210
  Thomas, 210
GILBORG, Mary, 86
GILBREATH, Mary, 270
GILLASPEY, George, 291
GILLBREATH, Rebecca, 263
GILLEN, Edward, 222
GILLIN, Ann, 202
  Margret, 202
GILLMORE, Prudence, 224
GILMER, Christina, 289
GILOME, Hannah, 169
  John, 169
  Richard, 169
GILPIN, Edward, 283
  Elizabeth, 167, 172, 176, 179, 193, 247
  Evan Ryle, 167
  George Glovier, 176
  Hannah Shallcross, 193
  Israel, 247
  James, 172

EARLY CHURCH RECORDS OF NEW CASTLE COUNTY

John, 290
John Giles, 167
Joseph, 167, 172, 176, 179, 193, 261
Leady, 167
Mary, 167
Thomas, 167, 169, 260, 277
GILPON, Vincent, 235
GINNET, Matthias, 251
GIODING, Anna, 2
  Annika, 1, 3, 34
  Catharina, 35
  Johan, 1, 3, 23, 34
  Mr., 14
GIRCHK, Albrecht, 124
  Johan Paul, 124
  Maria Dorothea, 124
  Maria Margreta, 124
GIRELIUS, Abraham Peter, 192
  Anna Maria, 187
  Barbara Helena, 181
  Brita Cathrina, 187
  Charles Jacob, 198
  Christina, 181, 187, 192, 195, 198
  Dr., 200
  Johan Adolph, 181
  John, 181
  Lars Gustav, 195
  Laurence, 187
  Lawence, 195
  Lawrence, 150, 181, 192, 198, 251, 273
  Peter, 187
GISE, Sarah, 257
GIVEN, Elizabeth, 290
GLACK, Henry, 271
GLACKON, William, 231
GLAIN, Mattick, 115
  Samuel, 115
  Sarah, 115
GLAINE, Margret, 228
GLANCY, Ferentius, 226
  Peter, 244
GLANN, Margareta, 231
GLANSEY, Peter, 219
GLANSY, Jane, 83
GLASGLOW, James, 227
GLASGOW, William, 277
GLASKOW, James, 230
GLASKY, John, 230
GLASON, Patrick, 83
GLASSAN, Joseph, 245
GLEA, Margret, 157
  Mary, 157
  William, 157

GLEAN, Elizabeth, 117
  Mary, 117
  William, 117
GLEANN, John, 250
GLENN, Thomas, 272
  William, 250
GLINN, Ann, 80
  William, 95
GLOSS, William, 289
GLOVER, William, 247
GODDARD, Mary, 285
GODFREY, Jerem, 83
  John, 79
GOEST, Christopher, 185
  Hannah, 185
  Mary, 185
GOFARD, Nannie, 67
GOGGIN, John, 228
GOHEN, Elizabeth, 220
GOLD, Jean, 253
  John, 264
GOLDEN, Ann, 289
  Catharine, 276
GOLDSMIDT, John, 106
GOLDSMIT, James, 84
GOLDTROP, Susan, 85
GOLLEHER, Caleb, 261
GOLLFEY, Charles, 92
GOOD, Benjamin, 35
  Elizabeth, 292
  Eschiel, 35
  Ingrid, 35
GOODBODY, Ann, 65
GOODEN, Cathrine, 243
  Hannah, 255
GOODFELLOW, James, 208, 212
  John, 212
  Margret, 208, 212
GOODWIND, William, 215
GOOL, Arthur, 153
  James, 153
  Lady, 153
GOOLDER, Sarah, 259
GORAHMS, Edward, 109
GORBY, Hezechiel, 103
  Joseph, 82, 103, 257
  Mary, 103
GORDEN, George, 248
  Harry, 136
GORDON, Ann, 205
  Cathrine, 216
  Charles, 216
  Elizabeth, 226, 239, 248
  Hannah, 139, 144, 268

INDEX

Harris, 139
Harry, 144, 244
James, 109, 144, 205
Jane, 109
John, 205, 220
Margret, 83, 258
Mary, 272
Matthew, 109
Robert, 60
Sarah, 245
GORE, Mary, 245
GORRAL, James, 204
Mildred, 204
GOSS, Evan, 216
Sarah, 264
GOTHREY, Mary, 89
Samuel, 83
GOUN, Sarah, 66
GOWING, Christopher, 259
GRACE, Mary, 230
GRADEL, Hannah, 241
GRAGAN, Mary, 80
GRAHAM, Ann, 195
Arthur, 81
David, 283
Eleanor, 210
Francis, 217
James, 195
Johann, 195
Mary, 195
Patience, 210
Richard, 66, 195, 210, 280
Robert Montgomery, 289
Sarah, 210
GRAHAMS, Cathrina, 111
Charles, 111
Florenze, 226
Jane, 234
Sarah, 111
GRAIG, Enoch, 249
Jacob, 242
Miriam, 248
GRAIMS, Letes, 68
GRAN, Jeremiah, 91
GRANDY, Mary, 230
GRANSAM, Charles, 197
Isaac, 197
GRANT, Else, 228
William, 232
GRANTIEM, Catharina, 5
GRANTREM, Ambrosius, 10
Carl, 10
Helena, 10
Johan, 10
Widow, 10
GRAUBEIN, Cathrina, 234
GRAVENROD, Hannah, 90
GRAVES, Cicily, 83
GRAY, Anna, 133
Anna Eva, 117
Barbara, 133
Cathrine, 214, 261
Conrad, 133
Elizabeth, 270
Frend, 253
Hannah, 260
Henry, 249
Jacob, 117
Jean, 261
John, 67, 233
Joseph, 101, 262
Margret, 101, 282
Maria Barbro, 117
Mary, 92, 238, 274
Susanna, 263
Thomas, 221
William, 101, 243
GREADY, Cathrine, 224
GREAVE, Jacob, 258
Samuel, 273
GREBBLE, Andrew, 181
Jacob, 181, 184, 187
Mary, 181, 184, 187
Samuel Watson, 187
Sarah, 184
GREEDY, John, 43
GREEN, Abel, 280
Abigail, 61
Ann, 173
Elizabeth, 286
Hannah, 229
Isachar, 50
John, 49, 281
Margaret, 53
Margret, 92, 173
Margrete, 241
Martha, 23
Mary, 271
Michael, 173
Peter, 262
Robert, 69
Sara, 50
Sarah, 217, 239
Solomon, 154
William, 66
GREENACRE, Ann, 271
GREENFIELD, Lydia, 249
Mary, 273
GREENUP, Isabella, 96
John, 96, 214
Mary, 96

EARLY CHURCH RECORDS OF NEW CASTLE COUNTY

GREER, John, 66
  Mary, 216
GREGG, Ann, 290
  Isaac, 264
  Jacob, 113
  Joseph, 266
  Margret, 290
  Maria Barbro, 113
  Maria Dorothea, 113
  Mary, 247
  Ruth, 228
  Sarah, 227
  Solomon, 261
  Thomas, 65
  Thomas R., 291
GREGORY, Rebecca, 217
  William, 65
GREIFF, George, 247
GREIST, Ann, 248
GRELSSON, Anders Mink, 3
GREW, Elizabeth, 100
  James, 100
  Matthews, 100
GREY, Anna Maria, 111
  Archibald, 239
  Barbara, 127
  Barbro, 121
  Barbro Wirth, 107
  Cathrine, 121
  Conrad, 107, 121, 127
  Elizabeth, 127
  George, 111
  Henry, 107
  Johannes, 111
  Mary, 214
  Sarah, 205
GRIBBLE, Jacob, 191
  Rebecca, 191
GRICE, Joseph, 50
GRIER, Bloomfield, 285
GRIFFIE, Isaac, 271
GRIFFIN, James, 31
  Margareta, 31
  Samuel, 31
  Thomas, 279
  William, 31
GRIFFIS, Jean, 34
  Margareta, 34
  Mary, 65
  Sara, 34
GRIFFIT, Ezekiel, 282
GRIFFITH, Cadwalet, 83
  Hester, 291
  Mary, 232
  Sarah, 226
  William, 228, 234

GRIFFY, Mary, 79
  William, 85
GRIFIN, Brigit, 76
  Hannah, 76
  Peter, 76
GRIME, Sarah, 252
GRIMES, Beata, 239
  Cathrine, 167, 254
  Daniel, 260
  James Lewis, 205
  Mary, 240
  Patience, 205
  Richard, 81, 205
  William, 167
GRINDALL, Thomas, 53
GRINED, John, 268
GRISPE, Rebecca, 262
GRISS, Joseph, 265
GRISSELL, Elizabeth, 226
GRISSIE, Phoebe, 268
GRIST, Hannah, 97, 215
  Jacob, 97
  Mary, 225
  Rachel, 46
GRITSIE, John, 264
GROAHMS, Beata Hopman, 109
  Catherina, 109
GROES, George, 261
GROOMS, Jean, 86
GROUB, Rachel, 242
  William, 242
GROUDT, Richard, 66
GROVES, Johnathan, 234
GROW, John, 246
GRUB, Annie, 125
  Benjamin, 125
  Emanuel, 125
  Susannah, 125
GRUBB, Aaron, 265
  Adam, 223
  Anne, 229
  Benjamin, 269
  Curtis, 224
  Elizabeth, 252
  Hannah, 250
  James, 282
  Joseph, 84
  Lydia, 283
  Nathaniel, 287
  Peter, 226, 281
  Rachel, 93
GRUKEN, Henrie, 6
GRUNDE, Robert, 265
GRUNDOW, Samuel, 263
GUBBENS, Margret, 217
GUERSLEY, Mary, 246

INDEX

GUEST, Henry, 50
  James, 81
  Mary, 248, 251
  Susannah, 250
GUILLIAMSON, Carin, 8
  Catharina, 3
  Karin, 9
  Thomas, 3
GUIN, John, 289
GUN, Ann, 197
  Christopher, 241
  George, 244
  Mary, 197
  Thomas, 197
GUNN, John, 245
  Mary, 201
  Robert, 258
  Thomas, 201
GUNS, Jacob, 140
GURNEY, Francis, 287
GUSCHYS, Cathrina, 131
  Rudolph, 131
  Wicklan, 131
GUST, Jonathan, 93
GUSTAF, Anders, 6, 7, 11, 14
  Annika, 14
  Brita, 1, 6, 7, 9, 10, 11, 23
  Catharina, 9, 14
  Catharine, 6
  Johan, 6, 12, 23
  John, 10
  Mans, 6, 9, 14
  Martin, 7
  Swen, 12
GUSTAFF, Catharina, 1
  Christina, 1
  Mons, 1
GUSTAFFAS, Andreas, 31
  Brita, 31
  Marten, 31
GUSTAFFSON, Martin, 1
GUSTAFSON, Anders, 23
  Brita, 23
  Catharina, 28
  Gustaf, 8
  Joseph, 63
  Karin, 8
  Mans, 28
  Pafuel, 63
  Paul, 8
  Sara, 28
GUSTAFSSON, Anders, 3, 11, 13, 40, 58
  Beata, 18
  Brita, 3, 4, 6, 7, 9, 10, 12, 18, 24, 34, 38, 43
  Catharina, 4, 7, 15, 18, 22, 33, 41, 45, 56
  Catharine, 3, 13
  Christina, 31
  Gustaf, 7, 9, 12, 15, 22, 31, 54
  Gustaf Johan, 14
  Gustaf Mans, 14
  Gustafwus, 47
  Gustavus, 54
  Hans, 18
  Helena, 41
  Hindric, 43
  Jesper, 22
  Johan, 4, 7, 9, 11, 14
  Johannes, 11
  John, 47
  Jonas, 6, 11, 24
  Kerstin, 15, 22, 31, 54
  Mans, 3, 4, 6, 7, 13, 22, 33, 41, 45, 56
  Maria, 7, 11
  Marten, 24, 38
  Martin, 2, 6, 7, 9, 10, 12, 18
  Morton, 11
  Pal, 15
  Paul, 4
  Peter, 15
  Peter Johan, 14
  Rebecca, 33
  Susanna, 22
  Swen, 7, 15, 38, 45
GUSTASS, Britta, 1
  Johan, 1
GUSTASSON, Gustaf, 6
  Kerstin, 6
  Martin, 6
  Nils, 6
GUTHRIE, Mary, 258
GUTREY, Cornelius, 94
GWIN, Catharine, 162
  Thomas, 162

-H-

HAAG, Jane, 238
HAAN, Ann, 158
  Anne, 151
  Elizabeth, 151
  John, 151, 158
HACKAT, Margrete, 242

EARLY CHURCH RECORDS OF NEW CASTLE COUNTY

HACKENEY, Aaron, 247
HACKET, Prudence, 31
  Sara, 31
  William, 31
HACKETT, Elizabeth, 248
HACKMAN, Hannah, 242
HACKNEY, Charity, 87
HADLEY, Simon, 229
HAGGORN, Edward, 85
HAGTON, Thomas, 87
HAGUE, John, 264
  William, 274
HAHN, Ann, 166
  James, 166
  John, 166
  Mary, 166
HAKA, Andrew, 59
HALEY, Edward, 44
  Eleonora, 28
  James, 28
  Mary, 28
HALL, Adam, 253
  Alexander, 279
  Andrew, 239
  Ann, 263
  Anna Elizabeth, 16, 37
  Barbarah, 142
  Benjamin, 281
  Caleb, 30
  Chambears, 220
  Chambers, 110, 119
  Charles, 79
  Dina, 37
  Elizabeth, 2, 119
  Frederick, 274
  George, 237, 249
  Hannah, 79
  Hesekias, 214
  Isabella, 87
  James, 86, 105
  Jannet, 218
  John, 283
  Joseph, 271
  Levy, 105
  Liddy, 89
  Margaret, 90
  Margret, 264
  Mary, 110, 220, 221, 266, 275, 281
  Rachel, 248
  Rebecca, 82, 110, 119, 269
  Samuel, 2, 16, 37, 86
  Sarah, 217, 237
  Stephen, 248
  Susanna, 271
  Thomas, 274
  William, 93, 142
HALLANGER, Hugh, 69
HALLINGSWORTH,
  Elizabeth, 82
HALLIS, Elizabeth, 146
  George, 146
  Margrete, 146
HALLOER, John, 65
HALLONSWORTH, Elizah., 249
  Enoch, 245
  Ruth, 244
HALOM, Mary, 239
HALS, Anna Elizabeth, 8
  George, 8
  Samuel, 8
HALTER, Philip, 254
HAMCAS, Hans, 183, 191
  John, 183
  Mary, 191
  Susanna, 183, 191
HAMCASS, Hans, 172
  Johannah, 172
  Susanna, 172
HAMCAST, Hans, 187
  Johanna, 187
  Susannah, 187
HAMELIN, Anna, 16
  Ingeborg, 16
  Matz, 16
  Michael, 30
HAMES, James, 232
HAMILTON, Archibald, 81
  Eleanor, 291
  Elizabeth, 285
  George, 277
  James, 79, 233
  Jane, 60, 223
  John, 215
  Margret, 215
  Mary, 232
  Nancy, 263
  Sara, 91
  Thomas, 224
HAMOR, Collins, 259
HAMPHILL, Mary, 222
HAMPTON, Ann, 274
HAN, Ann, 183, 214
  John, 183
  John Andrew, 183
HANAH, John, 174
  Margret, 174
  Mary, 174
HANBY, Hannah, 270

INDEX

Richard, 43, 50
William, 267, 270
HANCE, Ann, 82
HANCOCK, Richard, 289
  Thomas, 289
HANDLEY, Muxtey, 85
HANEY, Hannah, 274
  Nicholas, 287
HANKINS, George, 154
HANLEY, Elizabeth, 265
HANLIN, John, 203
  Lettice, 203
  Moses, 203
HANLON, Felix, 189
  Margret, 189
  Mary, 189
HANLY, James, 219
HANMUN, Thomas, 233
HANNA, John, 267
  Samuel, 154
HANNAH, Anders, 50
  Anne, 231
  Mary, 288
  William, 291
HANNELKIN, James, 53
HANNONS, John, 89
HANNUM, Hanhah, 270
  William, 260
HANNUMS, Elizabeth, 247
  James, 230
HANS, Nas, 106
HANSEY, Jemima, 279
HANSLEY, John, 291
HANSON, Ann, 273
  John, 87
  Rachel, 273
  Thomas, 267
  Timothy, 259
HANSSON, Anne, 229
  John, 276
HARALD, Hans Peter, 239
HARBESON, Francis, 270
HARDAY, John, 83
HARDEN, Peter, 199, 268
  Sarah, 287
HARDING, John, 230
  Peter, 202
  Rebecca, 202
HARFORD, Peter, 254
HARGROVE, John, 224
HARLAN, Abigail, 255
  Henry, 256
  Jesse, 247
  Jonathan, 275
  Joshua, 262
  Margret, 286
  Mary, 261, 263
  Ruth, 239
  Samuel, 82
  Sarah, 247
HARLAY, Aaron, 85
HARLEN, Elizabeth, 244
  George, 251
  Rachel, 260
  Sarah, 246
  Stephen, 249
HARLIN, Debora, 67
  Elizabeth, 217
  Lady, 215
  Mary, 221, 251
HARLOG, Aaron, 85
HARLON, Ann, 267
  James, 243
  Sara, 92
HARN, George, 252
HARP, Mary, 290
  Rachel, 288
HARPER, Alexander, 92
  Ann, 86
  Elizabeth, 29, 177
  George, 177
  Jacob, 65
  James, 29, 240
  John, 221, 237, 242
  Moses, 61
  Robert, 44
  Samuel, 91
  Thomas, 29, 177, 271
HARRIOT, Lydia, 285
HARRIS, Alice, 211
  Anne, 237
  Barry Cossins, 260
  David, 128, 225
  Edward, 80
  Elizabeth, 80, 128, 288
  George, 209, 219
  James, 232
  John, 211
  Joseph, 283
  Mary, 128, 209, 233, 266
  Rachel, 66, 232
  Samuel, 209, 281
  Stephen, 240
  Thomas, 211
HARRISON, Ann, 269
  Charles, 248
  John, 80, 158, 251
  Mary, 158, 166, 240, 270
  Rebecca, 166
  William, 158

HARROW, Mathew, 219
HARRY, James, 243
HART, Cornelius, 214
　William, 288
HARTLEY, Benjamin, 281
　Martha, 245
HARTLY, Benjamin, 235
HARVEY, Alexander,
　　201, 203, 209, 279
　Ann, 92
　Archibald, 224
　David, 37
　Elizabeth, 281, 290
　Isaac, 209
　Mary, 89, 201
　Sarah, 201, 203, 209
　Susanna, 201
　Thomas, 89
HARWAY, John, 221
　Joseph, 235
HARY, Abigail, 230
HASELTON, Ann, 191
　Henry, 191
　William, 191
HASFORD, Elizabeth, 81
HASSELTON, John, 277
　William, 228
HASTING, James, 238
HASTINGS, Mary, 265
HASTON, Peter, 188
　Rebecca, 250
HATTEN, Mary, 162
　Sarah, 162
　William, 162
HATTON, John, 236
　Peter, 218
　William, 255
HAUGHEY, Thomas, 229
　William, 219
HAUL, William, 53
HAUSMAN, Barbara, 131
　Barbro, 106, 115, 123
　Cathrina Barbro, 123
　Maria Cathrina, 115
　Paul, 115, 123, 131
　Paulus, 106
　Susanna, 131
HAUSSMAN, Barbro, 96
　Jacob, 96
　Saul, 96
HAWERD, Rebecca, 230
HAWK, William, 284
HAWKINS, Edward, 27
　Elizabeth, 204
　Esther, 27
　George, 204
　Jeane, 159

　John, 159, 164
　John Paxton, 204
　Joseph, 164
　Mary, 27
HAWTHORN, John, 274
HAY, Francis, 98
　John, 254
　Nickolas, 247
　Sarah, 225
　William, 98
HAYCOCK, Mary, 217
HAYES, Joseph, 222
　Samuel, 85
　Sarah, 288
　Susanna, 225
　Thomas, 244
HAYHES, Mary, 281
HAYL, Benjamin, 228
HAYLE, Mary, 227
HAYNES, Martha, 283
HAYNS, Mary, 227
HAYS, Abigail, 228
　Anne, 232
　Calop, 231
　Catharinne, 92
　Dina, 251
　Elizabeth, 241
　Hannah, 67, 215, 284
　John, 248, 259
　Johnathan, 239
　Margret, 217
　Mary, 236
　Rachel, 261
　Ruth, 224
　Solomon, 268
　William, 249
HAYWARD, Johan, 28
　Margareta Howel, 28
　Rachel, 28
HAZLETT, William, 286
HEADEN, Garret, 290
　William, 249
HEADIN, John, 229
HEADON, Sarah, 229
HEAGANS, Margret, 276
HEAGEN, Ann, 176
　John, 173
　Margaret, 176
　Margret, 173
　William, 173, 176
HEAGENS, William, 269
HEALD, Abraham, 259
　Anna, 218
　George, 247
　Hester, 264
　Joseph, 87
　Mary, 259
　Nathan, 242

INDEX

Phoebe, 263
Samuel, 239
Sarah, 247
HEARNEY, Elizabeth, 85
HEARRSON, Rebecca, 216
HEARSHY, Isaac, 265
HEART, Johanna, 80
HEATH, Rev. L., 214
  Samuel, 241
HEAVENS, Sarah, 279
HEAVEREN, Sarah, 264
HEBETS, Robert, 222
HEBRON, William, 231
HEBSHIR, James, 152
  John, 152
  Susannah, 152
HEBURNS, Mary, 249
HEDGE, Benjamin, 123
  Elizabeth, 96, 157
  Hannah, 157, 163, 183
  Jacob, 244
  John, 96, 107, 123
  Joseph, 2, 157, 163, 183
  Mary, 163
  Peter, 216
  Sarah, 259
  Susanna, 107
  Susanna Hendrickson, 107
  Susanna Hindrickson, 96
  Susannah, 123
HEDGES, Benjamin, 153
  Charles, 65, 74
  Colepepper, 172
  Hannah, 153, 170
  Johan, 74
  John, 68, 75, 77, 84, 94, 170
  Joseph, 77, 153, 170, 251
  Robert, 172
  Samuel, 94
  Sara, 84
  Susanna, 74, 77
  Susanna Hendrickson, 75, 84
  Susanna Hindricsson, 94
HEDINGHAN, Margrete, 250
HEDRICH, John, 255
HEDRICK, Margrete, 291
HEELD, John, 93
HEENS, Cathrine, 265
HEIG, Mary, 223

HEILBRUMER, Hance, 131
  Hance Caster Christian, 131
  Margreta, 131
HEILBRUNNER, Hans, 134
  Margretha, 134
  Paul, 134
HEIN, Cornelius, 37, 128
  Elizabeth, 127
  Jacob, 37, 57, 109
  Jacobus, 102, 109, 127
  John, 102
  Kerstin, 37
  Maria, 127
  Mary, 102, 109
  Nicklas, 57
  Rachel, 128
HEINE, Jacob, 33
  Kerstin, 33
HEINMAN, Cathrine, 218
  Helena, 60
HEINS, Andrew, 159
  Cathrina, 120
  Cornelius, 120, 133, 159, 170, 185
  Elisabeth, 159
  Elizabeth, 170
  Henry, 159
  Isaac, 116
  John, 133
  Mary, 116, 159
  Sarah, 120, 185
  Thomas, 170, 265
  William, 159
HEIRS, Jacobus, 87
HEISER, Mary, 288
HELENA, Magdalena Springer, 97
  Marten, 97
HELFESTEIN, Maria, 116
  Peter, 116
  Philip Jacob, 116
HELLINGS, Susanna, 251
HELM, Ake, 172
  Sarah, 172
HELY, Elizabeth, 246
HEMMEL, John, 228
HEMMINGWAY, William, 288
HEMPHIL, William, 154
HEMPHILL, William, 201
HENCOCK, Annika, 36
  David, 36, 44
  Debora, 42
  Helena, 36, 44
  Hindric, 44

EARLY CHURCH RECORDS OF NEW CASTLE COUNTY

Richard, 42
Susanna, 42
HENDERSON, Becky, 69
  Brita, 8
  Catharine, 210
  Cathrine, 204
  Elizabeth, 258
  George, 210, 287
  Jane, 231
  Johan, 8
  John, 224, 235
  Leady, 259
  Robert, 204, 210
  Stewart, 204
  Susanna, 256
  Tobias, 255
HENDRICKSON, Agnes, 264
  Anders, 74, 84
  Andrew, 63, 71, 94
  Ann, 176, 253
  Anna, 75, 280
  Beata, 152, 167
  Brita, 2
  Catharina, 71
  Cathrine, 235
  Christopher, 122, 126, 156
  David, 75, 172
  Elenor, 122
  Eli, 141
  Helena, 156
  Isaac, 151
  Israel, 63, 152, 250
  Jesajah, 149
  Jodiah, 156
  Johan, 2
  John, 141, 149, 151, 152, 163, 167, 172, 173, 176, 236, 260, 269
  Jonas, 74
  Joseph, 167
  Judith, 122
  Lydia, 152, 244
  Margret, 173
  Maria, 63, 71, 74, 94
  Martha, 152
  Mary, 141, 149, 151, 246
  Peter, 75, 152, 163, 266
  Rachel, 276
  Rebecca, 284
  Sarah, 65, 84, 122, 261
  Susanna, 2, 68

Tobias, 94
W., 164
HENDRICKSSON,
  Christopher, 68
HENDRICSON, Anders, 2
  Catharine, 9
HENDRICSSON, Anders, 8
  Christina, 19
  Hendric, 7, 8, 19
  Jacob, 8
  Judith, 8, 19
  Peter, 8
HENEKLY, Francis, 80
HENLEY, John, 256
HENNINGS, John, 259
HENOCH, William, 227
HENOCK, David, 48
  Helena, 48
  Margareta, 48
HENRICHSON, Peter, 79
  Sara, 79
HENRICKSON, Anders, 78
  Frances, 67
  Leddy, 78
  Mary, 78
HENRICSON, John, 76
  Rebecca, 76
HENRY, Cathrine, 197
  Elizabeth, 189, 226, 257
  Jane, 86, 237
  Mary, 189, 197, 232
  Peter, 197, 283
  Thomas, 189
  William, 85, 238
HENSEY, John, 226
HENTZLER, Robert, 254
HERBERT, Thomas, 215
HERNY, Elizabeth, 253
HERSEY, Sarah, 281
HERSMAN, James, 90
HESSELIUS, Brita, 36, 52
  Samuel, 36, 52
  Sara, 2, 36
HESSELLINS,
  Margaretta, 9
  Pastor, 5, 10
  Sara, 10
HESSELLIUS, Andreas, 12, 23, 30, 31
  Anna Maria, 31
  Brita, 31, 43
  Christiern, 43
  Christina, 55
  Emmanuel, 17, 21
  Gertrude, 54
  Gostas, 110

INDEX

Gustaf, 12, 17
Jonas, 22
Lydia, 12, 17
Maria, 30
Maria Bergia, 7
Pastor, 3, 6, 7, 8,
  11, 13, 17, 21
Pastor Magister, 2,
  4
Peter, 21
Petrus, 13
Probost Magister, 22
Samuel, 21, 31, 43,
  50, 54, 55
Sara, 3, 4, 6, 8,
  10, 13, 17, 22, 30
HESSILLIUS, Andreas, 6
  Pastor Andreas, 6
  Sara, 6
HESTINS, ---, 250
HESTIS, Francis, 258
HETH, Mary, 220
HEWELL, Lydia, 250
HEWES, John, 278
  Mary, 283
  Samuel, 225
  William, 274
HEWS, Christiana, 244
  David, 264
  Jacob, 264
  Mary, 242, 279
  William, 217
HEWSTON, Thamar, 231
HEYD, James, 218
HICKLIN, Mary, 262
  Rachel, 266
HICKMAN, James, 267
  John, 268
HICKS, Anna, 16
  William, 16
HIDE, Anne, 237
HIERY, Mary, 217
HIGGINS, Michael, 263
  Michel, 67
HIGGSON, Charles, 219
HIGHFIELD, John, 268
HILAND, Henry, 153,
  158, 169
  Jacob, 169
  John, 158
  Mary, 153, 158, 169
  Sarah, 153, 286
  Susanna, 284
HILD, Hannah, 87
HILDEN, Elizabeth, 263
HILL, Catharine, 204
  Charles, 204
  Christina, 124

Christine, 240
Elizabeth, 248
Frances, 233
Jane, 218
Job, 29
John, 53, 208
Margret Craig, 204
Martha, 239
Mary, 29, 53, 124
Peter, 124
Sarah, 245, 248
William, 124
HILLE, Elizabeth, 78
  Jonathan, 78
HILLIS, Elizabeth, 227
HILLYARD, Marget, 79
HILTON, Joseph, 273
HINDERSON, Beata, 3
  Jacob, 4
  Maline, 4
HINDERSSON, Beata, 3
HINDMAN, Robert, 256
HINDRESSON, Brita, 3
  Hindri, 3
  Judith, 3
HINDRICKSDOTTER,
  Kerstin, 61
HINDRICKSON, Andrew,
  168
  Anna, 62
  Annah, 139
  Beata, 139, 147
  Christopher, 131
  Elizabeth, 134
  Elizabeth Howel, 84
  Elizabeth Howell, 96
  Ellenor, 131
  Hannah, 160
  John, 96, 139, 147,
    160, 168, 228
  Maria, 134
  Peter, 62
  Rebecca, 276
  Sarah, 242
  Susanna, 214
  William, 84
  Zacharias, 84, 96,
    134
HINDRICKSSON, Anders,
  30, 34
  Christopher, 98
  Elenora, 98
  Elizabeth, 113
  Jacob, 3
  Johan, 3
  Maria, 30, 34
  Peter, 113
  Samuel, 98

339

Susanna, 34
Zacharias, 113
HINDRICSON, Johan, 2, 9
HINDRICSSON, Anders, 41, 48, 56, 61
  Anna, 29, 55
  Brigitta, 37
  Brita, 2, 18
  Hindric, 15, 29, 40
  Ingrid, 3
  Johan, 2, 3, 18, 55, 56
  Judith, 15
  Maria, 40, 41, 48, 56
  Peter, 55
  Tobias, 53
  Zacharias, 15
HINDRIESSON, Anders, 3
  Beata, 3
  Ingrid, 3
HINES, Cornelius, 164, 243
  Elenore, 271
  Elizabeth, 164, 246
  Jacob, 141
  Mary, 141, 164
HINKLEY, Elizabeth, 249
HINMAN, James, 246
HINSEL, Cathrine, 141
  Elizabeth, 141
  James, 141
HINSON, James, 189
HINSTON, Lille, 59
HITHERTON, John, 145
  Mary, 145
HIUS, Martin, 60
HOCKS, Archibald, 267
HODGES, Catharina, 8
  Joseph, 8
  Joshua, 8
  Samuel, 270
HODGESON, Isabel, 81
HODGESSON, Hannah, 217
HOE, Anna, 48
  Jean, 48
  Richard, 47, 48
HOFFMAN, Daniel, 194
  Herman, 229
  John, 194
  Rebecca, 194
HOGG, Cathrine, 171
  John, 171
  Margaret, 79
  Mary, 234
  Thoma, 265

Thomas, 171
HOGIN, Margret, 218
HOGLY, John, 84
HOGSHEAD, Anne, 116
  Elizabeth, 116
  Sarah, 116
  Walter, 116
HOLAHAN, Margret, 263
  Mary, 267
HOLEMAN, Charles, 216
HOLLAND, Joseph, 87
  Nally, 223
  Prudence, 228
  Van, 26
HOLLEYS, Elizabeth, 80
HOLLIN, Christopher, 23
  Eleanor, 23
  Elizabeth, 23
HOLLINGSWORTH,
  Barbara, 260
  Barbro, 224
  Isaac, 256
  James, 89
  Mary, 290
  Rachel, 67
  Samuel, 266
  Sara, 85
HOLLIS, George, 225
  Henry, 92
  Joseph, 266
HOLLONGSWORTH, Ann, 254
HOLMES, Ann, 212
  Benjamin, 212
  Benjamin John, 212
  Mary Ann, 212
HOLMS, Sarah, 263
HOLOWAY, Mary, 61
HOLSTEN, Lars, 80
  Maria, 31
  Peter, 8, 31
  Sara, 31
HOLSTON, Peter, 8
HOLTE, Hannah, 278
HOLTON, John, 279
HOLYDAY, Henry, 85
HOMES, Archibald, 229
HOMESPOKER, Catharina, 53
HOODE, Susanna, 273
HOOF, Elenora, 138
  Hannah, 138
  Henry, 138
HOOK, John, 228
HOOKER, Helena, 30
HOOPER, Elizabeth, 43
  Ellenor, 90

INDEX

Mary, 93
HOOPS, Isaiah, 260
  Joseph, 291
HOOTEN, Eliah, 256
HOOTON, Samuel, 65
HOPE, Amos, 245
  Bethsheba, 253
  Deborah, 235
HOPES, Elizabeth, 246
  John, 79, 94
  Mary, 226
  Thomas, 246
HOPKIN, John, 225
HOPKINS, Charles, 235
HOPMAN, Catharine, 86
  Mounce, 82
HOPPER, Elizabeth, 254
HOPPMAN, Margareta, 68
HOPTON, Ester, 115
  John, 115
  William, 115
HORE, Johanna, 219
  Mary, 220
HORLEN, Elizabeth, 239
HORN, Elizabeth, 281
  William, 222
HORNER, Samuel, 272
  Sarah, 278
HORSEY, Joseph, 47
HOSEN, Susanna, 92
HOSLIP, Ellenor, 87
HOSSFORD, Elizabeth, 219
HOSSMAN, ---, 125
  Catharine, 85
  Daniel, 280
HOSSY, Rebecca, 69
HOSTETEN, Ulrich, 228
HOULDEN, John, 245
HOULTON, Isaac, 250
HOUSE, Bule, 219
  Elizabeth, 248
  Hanna, 80
  James, 69
  Martha, 263
  Sophia, 253
  Susanna, 81
HOUSEMAN, Orphey, 139
HOUSS, Hannah, 240
HOUSTAN, Elizabeth, 290
HOUSTON, David, 267
HOWARD, Daniel, 270
  John, 235
  Margret, 93
  Rachel, 68
HOWD, Margaretta, 24
  William, 24

HOWEL, Jane, 218
HOWELL, Elizabeth, 102
  Isaac, 233
  John, 246
  Margaretta, 15
  Patience, 15
  William, 15
HOWELS, Elizabeth, 86
  Memutan, 284
HOWES, Agnes, 106
  John, 106
  Mary, 106
HOWL, Margaret, 40
HOY, Niclas, 241
HUAL, Penelope, 240
HUDGEON, Robert, 245
HUDGESON, Ann, 90
HUDSON, George, 49
  Jane, 221
HUES, Robert, 272
HUESTON, Robert, 93
HUEY, John, 221
HUGAN, Thomas Brogth, 271
HUGEL, Alki, 30
  Anna, 30
  Elinor, 125
  George, 30, 125
  Johan, 125
HUGGINS, John, 261
  Robert, 266
HUGH, Robert, 258
HUGHES, Abraham, 280
  Barney, 82
HUGHS, Elizabeth, 228
  Hannah, 157
  James, 235, 269
  Ruth, 157
  Sara, 233
HUGILE, Rosanna, 264
HUGIS, John, 180
  Sarah, 180
HULINGS, Jonathan, 144
  Mary, 144
  Susannah, 144
HULL, Elizabeth, 196
  Sarah, 196
HULTGREN, M., 181
  Mathias, 181
HUMAHRG, Mary, 82
HUMMIN, Anne Cathrine, 225
HUMPHREYS, Elias, 80, 100, 116, 123
  Elizabeth, 100, 116, 123
  John, 264
  Rebecca, 116

HUMPHRIES, Elizabeth, 169
  John, 169
  Mary, 169
HUMPHRIS, James, 218
HUMPRIES, Elias, 99
  Elizabeth, 99
  Hannah, 99
  Johanna, 99
  Thomas, 99
HUNT, John, 220
  William, 227, 242
HUNTER, Alexander, 50
  Annie, 222
  James, 221
  John, 263
  Mary, 224
  Sarah, 221
  Thomas, 234, 290
HURD, Stephen, 235
HURFORD, Sarah, 258
HURFURD, Mary, 89
HURTEHE, Marta, 216
HUSBAND, Adolphus, 176
  Cathrine, 145
  James, 198
  Jesse, 198
  John, 145, 148, 153, 168, 176
  Mary, 145, 148, 152, 168, 176, 198
  Peter, 153
  Rachel, 198
HUSBANDS, John, 164, 244
  Mary, 164, 277
  Rebecca, 164
  William, 269
HUSE, Koheath, 241
HUSTEN, Cathrine, 168
  Elizabeth, 168
  James, 24
  Mary, 24
  William, 168
HUSTON, Agnes, 223
  George, 126
  Hannah, 262
  James, 126, 226
  Jane, 253
  John, 126
  Margret, 126
  Margrete, 233
  Martha, 235
  Mary, 267
  Mathiew, 67
  Phoebe, 259
  Samuel, 257
  Thomas, 85
  William, 126, 216
HUTCHINS, William, 266
HUTCHINSON, James, 232
HUTCHINSSON, William, 227
HUTCHISON, Mary, 229
HUTSON, Abraham, 235
  Cathrine, 235
HUTTON, Elizabeth, 262
  Susanna, 227
  Thomas, 227
HWEITMAN, Jacob, 98
  Margaret Thespen, 98
  Rudolph, 98
HYLAND, Johan, 77
  Mary, 77
HYNES, Hynes, 79
  Rebecca, 79

-I-

IBARD, Elizabeth, 32
  Emmy, 32
IBOND, Mary Elizabeth, 228
IGELSTEN, Ann, 262
INGLISBY, Rose, 93
INGOLLS, Mary, 236
INGRAM, Peter, 263
INGROM, Ledom, 259
INLOC, Joseph, 223
IRVIN, David, 267
ISAACS, John, 220
ISAC, John, 68
ISHAM, Ann, 184
  John, 184
  Sarah, 184
ISRAEL, Brown, 275
ISRAELS, Israel, 171, 266
  John, 171
ISSARD, Elizabeth, 40
IVARS, Catharina, 10
  Maria, 10
IVARSDOTTER, Walborg, 8
IVARSON, Elizabeth, 7
  Johan, 7
  John, 7
  Kasin, 7
  Maria, 7
IVARSSON, Catharine, 14
  John, 8
  Maria, 8
IVES, Thomas, 69
IWARSON, Johan, 11
IWARSSEN, Elizabeth, 17

INDEX

-J-

JA QUETT, Anton, 41
  Casparus, 20
  Catharina, 41
  Christina, 60
  Cornelius, 19, 20,
    25, 47, 58
  Elizabeth, 41
  Johan, 19
  Maria, 20, 23, 25
  Peter, 23
  Susanna, 47
JA QUETTE, Cornelius,
    14
  John, 60
  Joseph, 214
  Susanna, 214
JACK, James, 291
  John, 215
  Robert, 246
JACKS, James, 214
  Margret, 214
  Mary, 214
JACKSON, Ann, 194
  Benjamin, 86, 94,
    163
  Candice, 210
  Catharine, 211
  Cathrina, 127
  Cathrine, 115
  Daniel, 121
  David, 233
  Drusilla, 174
  Elizabeth, 79, 267
  Eunice, 210
  George, 26, 42, 71,
    171
  Honor, 42
  Jacob, 215
  James, 194
  John, 46, 85, 94,
    115, 127, 167, 221
  Joseph, 66, 71, 73,
    79, 94, 121, 163,
    167, 174, 210, 211
  Judith, 85
  Katharina, 42
  Liddy, 94
  Lydia, 280
  Malin, 71, 73
  Maria, 211
  Mary, 26, 79, 94,
    121, 171, 194,
    222, 232, 268
  Onar, 26
  Orpah, 210
  Philip, 73, 279
  Phillip, 211
  Priscilla, 234
  Rebecca, 194
  Robert, 216
  Sarah, 210, 235
  Susanna, 163, 167,
    174, 210
  Timothy, 194
  William, 127, 211
JACKSSON, Catharina,
    49
  Joseph, 99
  Mary Vanderweer, 99
  Rachel, 99
JACOBI, Elizabeth, 132
  Ernest, 116
  Ernst, 132
  Johann Ernest, 225
  Joseph, 116
  Lobrina, 116
  Sabrina, 132
JACOBS, Catharine, 85
  Francis, 230
JACOBUS, Barbara, 266
JACQUET, Elizabeth, 90
  Martha, 225
  Peter, 90
  Rachel, 271
JACQUETT, Ann Trent,
    290
JAGERIN, Barbro, 239
JALEY, Joseph, 68
JAMES, Aaron, 282
  Andrew, 218
  Ann, 287
  Cathrine, 238
  Elizabeth, 221, 288
  Isaac, 37
  James, 235
  John, 247
  Latisha, 83
  Latty, 242
  Magdalene, 251
  Mary, 92
  Robert, 250
  Sara, 79
  Sarah, 246
JAMESON, Charles
    Springer, 169
  David, 252
  John, 169
JAMESSON, Charles
    Springer, 165, 181
  Elizabeth, 165
  Thomas, 181
JAMISON, Margaretta, 6
  Rebecca, 154
  Richard, 260

Thomas, 6
William, 154
JANE, Lolof, 102
JANES, Henry, 240
　Margret, 223
JANEY, Anne, 226
JANNET, Matthias, 245
JANNEY, Lewis, 268
JANSON, ---, 11
　Johan, 11
　Susanna, 11
JANSSON, Jane, 37
　William, 37
JANUARY, Mary, 223
　Richard, 266
JAQUET, Anton, 35
　Catharina, 35
　Hans, 109
　Johan, 35
　Johanna, 109
　John, 91
　Mary, 86
　Peter, 93, 109, 287
JAQUETT, Anton, 48, 35
　Catharina, 48
　Catharine, 192
　Cornelius, 36, 43, 18
　Dorothea, 192
　Hans, 44
　Johan, 17, 18
　Johannes, 43
　John, 192
　Kerstin, 44
　Margaret, 283
　Maria, 22, 36, 43, 44, 18
　Marta, 22, 48
　Mary, 279
　Nathaniel, 279
　Paulus, 48
　Peter, 22, 48
　Petrus, 36
　Susanna, 43
　Thomas, 48
JAQUETTE, Barbro, 122
　Elizabeth, 44
　Hans, 122
　Jane, 100
　Johannah, 122
　John, 100
　Peter, 223
　Samuel, 222
　Sarah, 261
JAQUETTES, Mariah, 1
　Peter, 1
JAREL, John Fitz, 242
JATTON, Ester, 229

JAZUETT, Sussanna, 21
JEANS, Brita, 40
　Mary, 43
JEFFERIES, Isabella, 211
　Joshua, 211
　Susanna, 211
JEFFERIS, Prudence, 268
　Richard, 40
　Thomas, 68
JEFFEYS, George, 248
JEFFREY, Henry, 265
　Letitia, 283
JEFFREYS, Jane, 225
JEFFRIES, Elizabeth, 268, 288
　Esther, 274
　John, 288
　Priscilla, 288
JEFFRIN, Mary, 221
JEFFRYS, Charity, 230
　Emmor, 233
　Lydia, 241
　Richard, 228
JEFFS, Thomas, 254
JEFREYS, Hannah, 220
　Mary, 219
JEFRIS, Nathan, 251
JEFRYS, Mary, 83
JEMISON, Rebecca, 265
JENKINS, David, 255
　Joseph, 281
JENNET, Elizabeth, 290
JERD, Abraham, 253
JESPER, Ann, 165
　John, 165
　Samuel, 165
JINKINS, Mary, 60, 265
JOANES, Thomas, 243
JOB, Aron, 266
　John, 290
　Mary, 270
JOBBLEY, John, 278
JOHAN, Bertil, 8
　Maria, 8
JOHANNSON, Peter Stalcop, 14
JOHANSON, Hanna, 9
　Johan, 9
　Lydia, 9
JOHANSSON, Aaron, 21
　Anders Gustafsson, 12
　Anna, 13
　Annika, 8
　Barbro, 21
　Bertil, 15

INDEX

Eskel, 5
Johan, 8
Laurentz, 8
Maria, 13, 15
Matz, 8
Olof, 8
Simon, 8, 13
Susanna, 15
JOHN, Abraham, 234
  Anna, 3
  David, 179
  Ester, 179, 282
  Malachia, 284
  Thomas, 3
JOHNS, Anna, 136
  Catharina, 89
  Cathrine, 151
  David, 254
  Hina, 151
  John, 236
  Mary, 253
  Robert, 136
  Samuel, 136
  Thomas, 151
JOHNSON, Abraham, 278
  Agnes, 268
  Ann, 176, 223, 248
  Annie Springer, 119
  Caleb, 283
  Cathrine, 158, 243, 271
  Charles, 119
  Charlotta Elenora, 175
  David, 132, 250
  Deborah, 115
  Elenor, 266
  Elizabeth, 248, 258, 270
  Frances, 115
  Francis, 223
  George, 199, 206
  Henry, 49
  Hugh, 224
  Isaac, 258
  Israel Hendrick, 277
  James, 106, 119, 206, 225, 272
  Jane, 106, 134, 250
  John, 158, 234, 235, 255, 263, 290
  John Paulson, 176
  Johnathan, 158, 259
  Jonathan, 132
  Joseph, 158
  Lascelly, 132
  Lasselley, 134
  Margareta, 10
  Margaretha, 132
  Margaretta, 6
  Margret, 241, 275
  Margretha, 134
  Martin, 9
  Mary, 66, 175, 269
  Matthew, 249
  Moses, 265
  Nathan, 263
  Rachel, 265, 276
  Samuel, 115
  Sarah, 176, 253
  Susanna, 158, 290
  Thamar, 236
  Thomas, 6, 10, 106
  Unity, 199, 206
  William, 175, 245, 269
JOHNSSON, Jennet Hamilton, 98
  Martin, 8
  Thomas, 4, 98
JOHNSTON, Ann, 210
  Elizabeth, 94
  Henry, 210
  James, 210
  Lancelot, 121
  Margret, 121
  Samuel, 164
  Sarah, 220
  Thomas, 255
  William, 121
JOHNSTONE, John, 79
JOMPFERSON, Mary, 252
JONAS, Deborah, 240
JONES, Ann, 147, 189
  Annah, 142
  Benjamin, 247
  Catharine, 157
  Cathrine, 147
  Cicely, 215
  Edith, 290
  Edward, 31, 242
  Elias, 243
  Elizabeth, 31
  Hannah, 221, 279
  Henry, 230
  John, 90, 175, 229, 244, 270
  Joseph, 86, 216
  Louis, 275
  Margaretta, 59
  Martha, 261
  Mary, 31, 92, 171, 175, 230, 248
  Morgan, 35
  Phoebe, 289
  Rachel, 81, 147

EARLY CHURCH RECORDS OF NEW CASTLE COUNTY

Robert, 142, 147
Ruth, 244
Samuel, 92
Sara, 67
Theophilus, 175, 266
Theoplufus, 171
Thomas, 82, 147,
  157, 189, 244, 271
William, 68, 147,
  243, 255, 270, 272
JONSON, Abraham, 251
  Elizabeth, 246
  Joseph, 263
  Thomas, 241
JONSSON, Anna, 11
  Thomas, 11
JONSTON, Lanty, 99
  Margaret, 99
  Roda, 99
JONTERY, Elizabeth, 163
  John, 163
JORAN, Christian, 1
  Christiern, 15
  Elizabeth, 1, 15
  Margaretta, 15
  Sophia, 1
JORANSSON, Christiern, 6
  Christina, 6
  Elizabeth, 6, 21
  Jons, 7
  Jons Anders, 7
  Sara, 7
JORDAN, Alice, 269, 277
  Anna, 42
  Catharina, 80
  Deborah, 247
  Elizabeth, 42, 86, 174, 175
  Griffith, 170, 175
  Grissie, 189, 191
  Grissit, 265
  Hannah, 191
  James, 26, 42
  John, 249
  Jonathan, 189, 266
  Jonnathan, 92
  Margret, 230
  Martha, 220
  Mary, 170, 174, 189, 267, 285
  Phoebe, 170, 175, 189, 191
  William, 174, 252
JORDON, Mary, 89
JOSEPHSON, Ann, 156

Charles, 173
Charles Springer,
  156, 161, 166,
  173, 182, 187
Isaac, 182
Joseph, 161
Margret, 161, 166,
  173, 182, 187
Mary, 166
Rebecca, 187
JUDAH, Benjamin, 230
JUNKINS, Elizabeth, 256
JURDEN, Thomas, 273
JURGEN, Hans, 23
  Maria, 23
  Peter, 23
JURY, Margareta, 35
JUSTAFSSON, Annika, 56
  Brigitta, 56
  Marten, 56
JUSTICE, Aaron, 200,
  203, 210, 213
  Abner, 210
  Andrew, 97
  Ann, 206
  Anna, 135
  Annika, 46
  Brita, 51
  Catharine, 209
  Charles, 79, 200
  Christina, 94, 206, 209
  Dorothea Paulson, 97
  Elenora, 132
  Gustavas, 209
  Isaac, 209
  Jacob, 206, 209
  Jesper, 98, 214
  John, 97
  Judith, 49
  Lydia, 51
  Magnus, 132
  Maria, 132, 135
  Maria Robinson, 213
  Marten, 51, 97
  Martin, 91
  Mary, 66, 79, 209, 236
  Mary Springer, 94, 99
  Morton, 203
  Nils, 79, 94, 99
  Rebecca, 98
  Richard, 236
  Sara, 85
  Sarah, 200, 203, 210, 213

INDEX

Susanna, 238
Susanna
  Hindricksson, 98
Swain, 203
Swen, 99, 135
William, 45, 49
JUSTIS, Aaron, 153
  Abner, 145
  Adam, 120
  Anders, 110, 118,
    133
  Andrea, 104
  Andreas, 124
  Andrew, 217, 244,
    283
  Ann, 280
  Anna, 104
  Anron, 286
  Beata, 68
  Brigita, 121
  Brita, 64, 72
  Carolus, 121
  Catharina, 29
  Cathrine, 139, 244
  Charles, 140, 223
  Christiana, 195
  Christina, 245
  Christine, 60
  Debora, 272
  Dorothea, 124, 133
  Elenor, 256
  Elenorah, 240
  Elenore, 139
  Eleonor, 149
  Eli, 149
  Elizabeth, 183, 186,
    190, 193, 194,
    198, 259
  Ellen, 127
  Friedrich, 148
  Gabriel, 146
  Gustaf, 59, 72
  Hannah, 127, 187,
    191, 276
  Helena, 118
  Israel, 58
  Jacob, 107, 187,
    191, 195, 276
  Jasper, 120
  Jesper, 130
  Johan, 64, 73
  John, 66, 130, 183,
    186, 190, 195,
    198, 272
  Jonas, 81, 133
  Jonas Stidham, 193
  Joseph, 124, 187,
    280

Justa, 88, 147, 157,
  191, 216
Justas, 66
Kerstin, 73
Lawrence, 195
Levi, 183
Magnus, 118, 139,
  149, 224
Margret, 108, 251
Maria, 44, 72, 104,
  107, 110, 118,
  121, 128, 133
Maria Springer, 88
Mary, 140, 141, 145,
  146, 147, 150,
  153, 159, 186, 217
Mary Springer, 96,
  108
Moris, 230
Morten, 64, 110
Morton, 72
Mounce, 127
Neils, 141, 146, 150
Nils, 88, 96, 108,
  121, 128, 133
Penelope, 148
Peter, 194, 195, 281
Petrus, 118
Rebecca, 110, 148,
  157, 224, 262
Sara, 72
Sarah, 147
Susanna, 69, 72, 73,
  120, 244
Susannah, 150
Swen, 92, 96, 107,
  121, 140, 145,
  153, 159, 218
JUSTISON, Catharina,
  74
  Elizabeth, 170
  Gustaf, 74
  Jacob, 170
  James, 170
  Mary, 282
  Susanna, 74
JUSTISSON, Ann, 158
  Anna, 135
  Anne, 151
  Elizabeth, 229
  Hanna, 135
  Isaac, 282
  Margret, 220
  Pauline, 151
  Rachel, 163
  Richard, 135, 151,
    158
  Susannah, 240

347

-K-
KAARON, Simon, 247
KAGLAY, Susanna, 83
KAIN, Daniel, 105
  Mary, 105
  Rachel, 220
KALER, Matthias, 239
KALLEM, Rebecca, 229
KALLOM, Benjamin, 45
  Catharine, 141
  John, 141
  Maria, 45
  Moses, 141
  William, 45
KALLUM, Benjamin, 236
  John, 235
KALSBERG, Christina, 37
KALSBURG, Elizabeth, 52
  Hindric, 52
  Maria, 52
KALTON, Jane, 83
KAMPSTER, John, 86
KANE, Elizabeth, 160
  Mary, 160
  Thomas, 160, 165, 255
KANNATHY, Christina, 109
  Hannah, 109
  James, 109
KANOTS, Margaret, 83
KARENOSS, Timothy, 221
KARIL, Christopher, 238
KARLIN, Elizabeth, 60
KARNES, Jane, 231
KARNEY, Elenor, 261
KARRAN, John, 245
  William, 259
KARY, Elizabeth, 122
  Elizabeth Paulson, 107
  John, 107, 122, 216
  William, 107
KATHI, Hannah, 66
KAY, Hannah, 67
  John, 231
  Zacheus, 93
KEACH, William, 233
KEALLOM, Richard, 241
KEAN, James, 252
  Margaret, 113
  Mary, 184
  Richard, 184
  William, 113

KEAR, James, 237
KEARK, James, 143
  Jane, 143
  Keark, 143
KEEN, Catharina, 69
KEEPER, Ester, 130
  Stephen, 130
  William, 130
KEEPERS, Susanna, 281
KEES, George, 102
  John, 102
  Margret, 102
KEETH, George, 221
KEITH, Margret, 264
  Robert, 273
KEITLY, James, 241
KELL, John, 232
KELLAM, Margret, 276
  Mary, 25, 276
  Parthenia, 25
  William, 21, 25
KELLE, Catharina, 51
  Maria, 51
  Martin, 51
KELLER, Ann, 155
  Christina Maria, 155
  Matthias, 155
KELLEY, Adam, 115
  Else, 115
  Margaret, 201
  Margret, 115
KELLOG, Neil, 284
KELLOWE, William, 154
KELLUM, Thomas, 229
KELLY, Barnaby, 283
  Charles, 285
  Daniel, 81
  Ester, 184
  James, 184, 226
  John, 93
  Margret, 227
  Margreta, 233
  Margrete, 243
  Martha, 91
  Mary, 257
  Matthew, 222
  Mrs., 117
  Patrick, 237
  Samuel, 282
  Sara, 67
  William, 184
KELSEY, John, 113
KEMBOLE, John, 248
KENNEDY, Samuel, 288
KENNET, Dorothea, 236
KENNEY, Daniel, 262
KENNOI, Elizabeth, 263
KENRIAN, Michael, 254

INDEX

KENT, Elizabeth, 31
  William, 31
KERSIN, John, 261
KERSON, Cathrine, 237
KESLER, John, 251
KET, Cornelius, 55
  Judith, 55
  Marick, 55
KETLY, Agnes, 92
KETRICK, Robert, 87
KEU, Abraham, 119
  Elizabeth, 119
  Jacob, 119
KEY, Allen, 259
  Elizabeth, 201
  George, 266
  Lydy, 67
  Martha, 228
  Michael, 201
KEYS, John, 214
KIABBIN, Elizabeth, 68
KIDD, Jacob, 90
KILBRETH, Alice, 214
KILDA, Daniel, 243
KILDEE, Daniel, 143
  John, 143
  Margaret, 143
KILDENNIN, Eleonor, 248
KILEY, Ester, 180
  William, 180
KILLEN, James, 216, 277
  Margret, 223
  William, 278
KILLOM, Rachel, 291
KILLPATRICK, David, 119
  Jane, 271
KILPOS, Catharine, 20
  Gustaf Palsson, 22
  Johan, 20
  Marta, 22
  Paul, 20
  Peter, 22
KIMBER, Mary, 223
KIMBLER, Elizabeth, 259
KIMLER, John, 222
KING, Andrew, 145, 278
  Barbary, 165, 179
  Benjamin, 67, 82
  Cathrine, 140, 277
  Christina, 66, 85
  Daniel, 89
  Edward, 108, 218, 220
  Elias, 61, 81, 120
  Eliza, 98
  Elizabeth, 108, 140, 171, 215
  Frederick, 171, 179
  Fredrich, 165
  George, 104, 140
  Jane, 244
  Johanna, 104
  John, 87, 98, 100, 138
  Margret, 100
  Maria, 138
  Mary, 120, 179
  Mathias, 165
  Michael, 145, 260, 285
  Petrus, 138
  Rebecca, 98
  Robert, 170, 225
  Samuel, 100
  Sarah, 140, 145, 170
  Susannah, 104
  T. Michael, 140
  Walled, 100
  William, 108
KINGKAD, Susanna, 227
KINKEAD, Mitchel, 278
KINNEN, Henry, 248
KINNI, Mary, 102
KINSMAN, John, 282
KIOLN, Jacob, 55
  Jonas, 55
  Rener, 55
KIRCK, Abigail, 226
  David, 138
  Elizabeth, 137
  James, 137, 138
  Jane, 137, 138
  Johnathan, 137
  Jonathan, 138
  Kirck, 137
  Thomas, 138
KIRGAN, Anna, 229
KIRGEN, Frances, 255
KIRGIAN, Hugh, 68
KIEK, John, 280
KIRK, Abigail, 22, 56
  Alphonsi, 22
  Ann, 270
  Anne, 104
  Brigite, 104
  Dorothea, 97
  Elizabeth, 31, 277
  Hannah, 285
  James, 25, 85, 104, 113, 120, 218
  Jane, 104, 113, 131, 145

Jeane, 120, 156
Joathan, 25
Johan, 120
Johanna, 184
John, 104, 156, 184, 280
Johnathan, 21, 184
Jonathan, 22, 31, 36, 42, 54, 56, 94, 97, 120, 131, 145, 156, 189, 222, 274
Josiah, 97
Josua, 54
Kirk, 281
Maria, 36, 42, 54, 56, 113
Mary, 25, 31, 81, 248, 283
Phoebe, 265
Rachael, 120
Rachel, 264
Samuel, 21
Sara, 104
Susanna, 42, 223
Tabitha, 120
William, 145, 282
KIRKLAN, Eleonore, 250
KIRKPATRICK, Donald, 29
  Samuel, 257
KIRRYR, Martha, 228
KISER, Mary, 83
KITTEL, Zacharias, 60
KITTS, John, 279
KLEANDENNY, Elenore, 141
  William, 141
KLENNY, William, 81
KLINTON, Elizabeth, 109
  Margaret, 102
  Mary, 109
  Mathew, 102
  Robert, 102, 109
KNAKTON, Cathrine, 228
KNIGHT, John, 258
  Judith, 65
  Thomas, 266
KNOCHS, Jane, 68
KNOCKS, Margret, 85
KNOT, Marjory, 80
  Thomas, 80
KNOTT, Hannah, 262
KNOTTS, John, 91
KNOWLES, Bridgette, 239
KOCK, Anders, 8
  Anna, 1
  Francina, 1
  George, 80
  Gustass, 1
  Valentine, 21
KOCKHORN, Edward, 112
  Jamaima, 112
  John, 112
KOELER, Andrew Christian, 149
  Anne Eve, 149
  Matthias, 149
KOGG, Johanna, 162
  John, 162
  Timothy, 162, 260
KOHL, Adam, 152
  Elizabeth, 44
  Mary, 152
KOLL, James, 222
  Sarah, 262
KONELLY, Elizabeth, 267
KONOLLY, John, 178
KRANSTON, Isabel, 65
KRASER, William, 253
KRAUT, Anna Maria, 20
  Barbara, 130
  Barbro, 122
  Christopher, 111, 122, 130
  George, 20
  Johannes, 20, 111
  Maria, 111
  Susanna Dorothea, 122
KRAWKER, William, 220
KRAWSON, Mary, 262
KREY, Hezekiel, 272
KRIACK, Barbarah, 146
  Jacob, 146
  Mary, 146
  Peter, 146
KRIEG, Friedrich, 122
  Jacob, 122
  Margreta, 122
KRIEGEN, Barbara, 130
  Jacob, 130
KYLE, Alice, 214
KYNLER, Owen, 66

—L—

LA QUETT, Ingeburg, 5
  Marta, 33
  Peter, 33
LACHAERD, Jacob, 69
LACKEY, James, 285
LADLY, Mary, 82

INDEX

LAFERTY, Ann, 283
  Mary, 270
LAFFERTY, Francis, 200
  John, 200
LAFORGE, Benjamin, 278
LAGG, Elenore, 225
LAIRD, Sarah, 238
LAITON, Francis, 46
LAJORGE, Elizabeth, 274
LALSHIELD, Jane, 69
LAMBERT, John Casper, 68
LAMBORN, Joseph, 283
LAMMON, Mary, 79
LAMPLEY, Mary, 241, 256, 267
  Richard, 272
LAMPLIGH, William, 80
LAMPLUGH, Mary, 118
  Rebecca, 118
  William, 118
LAMPLY, Elizabeth, 251
LAMPRADIN, Margret, 218
LAND, Ann, 227
  Elizabeth, 229
  John, 227
  Samuel, 81
LANDER, Samuel, 265
LANDERS, John, 172, 292
  Mary, 172
  Samuel, 172
LANDERUM, Nanzy, 227
LANDSBRECK, Cathrina, 218
LANE, Henry, 67
LANGLAY, Mary, 249
LANGLEY, Benjamin, 274
  Mary, 259
  Rebecca, 258
  Sarah, 241
LANGLY, Mary, 67
LANSALE, Brita, 156
  William, 156
LAQUETT, Cornelius, 32
  Ingeberg, 6
  Johannes, 32
  Maria, 32
LAQUETTE, Ingeborg, 8
LARKEN, Anne, 237
  Sarah, 291
LARKIN, Leady, 269
  Phoebe, 251
LARNER, Benjamin, 124
  Margret, 124
  Rebecca, 124

LARY, John, 282
LASSELLEY, Thomas, 236
LATHAM, James, 289
LATHEMORE, John, 83
LATIMER, Sarah, 224
LATIMORE, Archibald, 114
  Cathrine, 114
  Jane, 114
  Mary, 243
LATTA, Jane, 217
  Joseph, 261
LATTIMON, Arthur, 67
LATTIMORE, Else, 219
LATTON, Ann, 86
LATTY, Elizabeth, 84
LATYMORE, Jane, 241
LAUDEN, Jane, 222
LAUERBECK, George, 266
LAUGHEAD, Charles, 89
LAUGHLIN, Hugh, 94
LAUGHNAUGH, Mary, 235
LAUGHTON, Elizabeth, 84
  Ellinor, 93
LAURENCE, George, 251
LAURENTZ, John, 223
LAURIS, Elizabeth, 66
LAW, Henry, 229
  James, 263
LAWELL, Johanna, 66
LAWLER, Anne, 228
  John, 238
LAWRENCE, Cathrine, 247
  Elizabeth, 199, 203
  Garret, 203
  Garrit, 199
  John, 70, 203
  Joseph, 199
  Livina, 263
  Martha, 281
  Mary, 282
LAWSON, Cathrina, 155
  Cathrine, 151, 168, 188
  Daniel, 80
  Elizabeth, 217
  George, 155
  Joseph, 151, 155, 161, 168, 188
  Mary, 188
  Rachel, 219
  William, 151
LAYBOBT, Ludwig, 244
LAZARETH, Benjamin, 130
  John, 130

Lydia, 130
LEA, Annie Tossa, 105
　Hannah, 250
　Isaac, 105
　John, 105
　Martha, 232
　Mary, 289
　Rachel, 261
LEACH, Hugh, 224
LEADLEY, Hannah, 227
LEAGUE, Stephen, 269
LEAN, John, 218
LEANA, Margaret, 225
　Margrete, 239
LEARD, Mary, 266
LEAT, Mary, 87
LEATSH, James, 220
LEE, James, 81
　William, 254
LEECH, David, 267
　Mary, 66
LEFEVER, Ingeber, 186
LEFEVRE, John Francis, 283
LEGARE, Jane, 83
LEICESTNER, Adam, 29
　Johannes, 29
　Magdalena, 29
LEIKAN, Brita, 21
LEINA, Catharina, 68
LEMMERIN, Anne Mary, 234
LENARD, Samuel, 258
　Winny, 158
LENDERMAN, William, 287
LENDEY, Helena, 165
　Leady, 165
　Thomas, 165
LENNARD, Rebecca, 114
　Richard, 114
LENNON, Mary, 210
　Robert, 210
　William, 210
LENZY, Elizabeth, 219
LEONARD, William, 247, 249
LERCHENZEILER, Johan Wilhelm, 21
　Johan William, 11, 21
　Susanna, 21
LESHLEY, John, 226
LESLIE, Robert, 280
LESLY, Thomas, 244
LESSENGER, Ann, 269
LESSINGER, Ann, 168
　Cathrine, 168

　Jacob, 168
LETTLER, John S., 287
LEUDEN, Maria, 286
LEWDEN, Rachel, 239
LEWIS, Ann, 200
　Anna, 115
　David, 81
　Elizabeth, 44, 98, 115, 129
　Ellenor, 87
　Enoch, 98
　Enos, 216
　Evan, 238
　Even, 81
　Ezra, 289
　George, 115, 241
　Jacob, 114
　James, 98
　Jesse, 189
　Johan, 114
　Johanna, 274
　John, 44
　Joseph, 200
　Margret, 114, 283
　Maria, 54
　Mary, 129
　Nathaniel, 129
　Patience, 280
　Priscilla, 283
　Samuel, 54, 89, 189, 278
　Sara, 44
　Sarah, 89, 189
　Wiljam, 54
　William, 47, 224
LEY, Rebecca, 60
LIDENIUS, Abraham, 8
　Christina, 273
　John Abraham, 198
　Mr., 2, 3, 4
　Rev., 2
　Rev. Abraham, 2, 5
LIDEUIUS, Rev Abraham, 8
LIGGET, William, 218
LIGGIT, George, 247
LIGHTBODY, Elizabeth, 277
　Michael, 241
LIKAN, Annika, 42
　Elizabeth, 42
LIKEL, Henry, 282
　Margret, 191, 195
　Samuel, 191, 195
　Thomas, 195
LIKON, Maria, 50
LIMBUR, James, 235
LINAN, John, 82

INDEX

LINCH, Grace, 279
  John, 256
LIND, Christopher, 138
  Margreta, 138
  Mary, 70
  Rachel, 138
LINDEY, Isabella, 287
LINDMEYER, Christ, 73
  Joran, 73
LINDSAY, Matthew, 227
  Sarah, 234
LINDSEY, Alexander, 83
  Andrew, 206
  Isabella, 206
  Margret, 206
LING, Martha, 220
LINGIN, Elizabeth, 233
LINK, Anna, 10
  Johan, 10
  John, 81
  Mary, 92
LINMEYER, George, 53
LINMEYERS,
  Christopher, 59
LINN, Christopher, 222
  Mary, 216
LINSAY, Elizabeth, 249
LINVEL, Lydia, 65
LINWALL, Edward, 226
LION, Cloud, 126
  Darkeys, 126
  Margreta, 126
  Thomas, 86
LIP, Andrew, 184
  Marelis, 184
  Mary, 184
LISS, Francis, 274
LITIEN, George, 4
  Kerstin, 4
LITLA, Elizabeth, 252
LITLE, John, 90
LITLER, Liddy, 81
LITTAER, John, 166
LITTLE, Archibald, 188
  Barbara, 127
  Catharine, 256
  Elizabeth, 188
  Hannah, 218
  James, 176, 238
  Jane, 100, 180
  John, 100, 184, 188
  Margret, 86, 100,
    176, 180, 184,
    187, 260
  Mary, 188, 219
  Rebecca, 127
  Robert, 188
  Samuel, 176, 180,
    184, 187, 270
  Susanna, 188
  William, 187
LITTLEJOHN, John, 42,
    49
  Maria, 42
  Mary, 40, 49
LITTLER, Thomas, 261
LITTOL, Elizabeth, 91
LIVINGSTON, Eve, 278
LLOID, Ruth, 233
L'LOYD, John, 237
LOAN, Charles, 103
  Mary, 82
  Sarah, 103
LOBB, Hannah, 288
  Joseph, 245
LOBUM, Thomas, 44
LOCKHART, Mary, 82
LOCKHEART, William,
    274
LOCKTON, John, 225
LODGE, Susannah, 254
LOFTON, Mary, 82
LOFTUS, Isabella, 68
LOGAN, David, 286
  Henry, 288
  James, 185, 259
  Jane, 218
  Jeane, 228
LOGG, Mary, 227
LOGIN, William, 257
LOINAM, Anders, 16
  Brita, 16
  Maria, 16
LOINAN, Anders, 12,
    16, 19, 23, 32,
    36, 43, 59, 94
  Andreas, 23
  Andrew, 217
  Annika, 32
  Brita, 12, 19, 23,
    61, 84
  Catharina, 19, 84,
    94
  Catharine, 88
  Cathrina, 109
  Cathrina Didrickson,
    109
  Elizabeth, 88
  George, 111, 130
  Goran, 99
  Johan, 32
  John, 109, 130
  Joran, 12, 84, 88,
    94, 124
  Margret, 111, 124

Margret Stalcop, 99
Margreta, 130
Maria, 16, 36
Philip, 99
Rebecca, 124
Sarah, 111
LOKTON, John, 119
　Mary Grissith, 119
LONDEY, Ann, 184
　Lydia, 184
　Thomas, 260
LONDGROV, Ludwig
　Leonard, 236
LONDON, Ambrosius, 15, 19, 26
　Brita, 15, 19, 26
　Helena, 19
　Joseph, 25
LONG, Alexander, 227
　Jacob, 83
　John, 231, 234
　Mary, 286
　Mathew, 80
　Rebecca, 239
　Thomas, 49, 61
LONGHEAD, James, 234
LONGWILL, William, 231
LONIAN, Mary, 217
LOODON, Ambrosius, 24
　Brita, 24
　Joseph, 24
LOONE, Susanna, 290
LOQUE, David, 217
LORCE, Elizabeth, 234
LOTTON, Ralph, 288
LOUDON, Ambrosius, 10
　Brita, 10
　Jesper, 10
　William, 269
LOUIS, Agnes, 151, 156
　David, 151, 156
　Margaret, 151
　Priscilla, 156
LOURY, Mary, 262
LOVE, Elenor, 172
　Jane, 172
　Robert, 261
　Thomas, 172, 267
LOVIS, Mary, 247
　William, 246
　Robert, 225
LOW, Elizabeth, 286
　Isaac, 217
　Robert, 224
LOWE, Marget, 65
LOWECELL, Engellest, 232
LOWELL, Henry, 107

LOWIS, John, 262
LOWMAKE, Anne, 234
LOWNES, James, 65
LOWRY, Anne, 70
　Elizabeth, 70
　Robert, 225
LOWYS, Sarah, 252
LOYD, Joseph, 244
　Lucretia, 94
LOYNAM, Andrew, 256
LOYNAN, Elizabeth, 249
LOYNMAN, John, 255
LUCASSON, ---, 2
LUFFIRTY, Sara, 87
LY(LEE), Elizabeth, 97
　Sarah, 97
　Thomas, 97
LYAN, Mary, 242
LYLE, Elizabeth, 260
　Mary, 250
　Sarah, 241
LYNAM, Andrew, 158, 159, 162, 169, 179, 264
　Ann, 163, 179, 189, 272
　David, 163
　Enock, 162
　George, 169
　Hannah, 195
　John, 158, 159, 163, 179, 189, 195
　Joseph, 158
　Margret, 169, 284
　Rebecca, 263
　Thomas, 189
LYNCH, Elizabeth, 159
　Isabella, 159
　John, 159
LYON, Andrew, 191, 194
　Christian, 191
　Cloud, 110, 116, 220
　Darkes, 110, 116
　Eleonora, 110
　Elizabeth, 194
　James, 116
　Margret, 194
　Robert, 216
LYONS, Andrew, 201
　Ann, 201
　Elizabeth, 201
　Susanna, 201
LYTIEKER, Catharine, 260
LYTUR, Sarah, 228
　　　　-M-
MAAHON, Prudence, 258
MAAST, Jacob, 138

INDEX

Phoebe, 138
Rachel, 138
MABALY, Jamaymy, 249
  Jamima, 247
MAC GRA, Mortin, 83
MCALLEN, William, 221
MACARTHER, Robert, 81
MCARTHUR, James, 257
MCASFEY, Joseph, 278
MCBEATH, John, 281
MCBOYD, James, 230
MCBRAID, Margaret, 101
  Philip, 101
  William, 101
MCBRAIHERLY, Owen, 279
MCBRIARTY, Cathrine, 205
MCBRIDE, Ann, 258
  Briggita, 139
  Cathrine, 264
  Daniel, 280
  Edward, 139
  Eleonora, 139
  Elizabeth, 266, 273
  Frances, 257
  Rebecca, 242
MCBRIGHT, John, 90
MCCAB, William, 246
MCCAFFERTY, Dennis, 227
  Elizabeth, 254
  John, 248
  Rosanna, 272
  Susanna, 268
MCCAFFETY, Elizabeth, 276
MCCAFFITY, Catharina, 233
MCCAFFORTY, Hannah, 244
MCCAHAN, Mary, 230
MCCALEB, Catharine, 103
  Ephraim, 103
  John, 103
MCCALL, Abigal, 275
  Benjamin, 255
  Martha, 231
  Robert, 289
MCCALLA, Mary, 288
MCCALLEM, Mary, 283
  Sarah, 264
MCCALLEN, Elenor, 266
MCCALLMONT, Susanna, 281
MCCALMONT, John, 224
MACCALSHONDER, Martha, 69

MCCANN, Martha, 268
MCCAPLIN, Samuel
  Davidson, 269
MCCARLIN, John, 229
M'CARMACK, John, 233
MCCARNAUGHIE, Rachel, 285
MCCARSLEY, John, 226
MCCARTER, ---, 86
  Ann, 167, 271
  Gilbert, 167, 259
  Hannah, 282
  John, 261
  Martha, 167
MCCARTOR, Elizabeth, 257
MCCARTSY, Robert, 80
MCCARTY, Edward, 252
  Elizabeth, 83
  Jane, 118, 275
  Jean, 264
  Mails, 118
  Margaret, 118
  Mary, 118, 253
MCCARY, Esther, 27
  Jane, 27
  Richard, 27
MCCASHEY, Cornelius, 253
MCCASKEY, Robert, 283
MCCASLIN, Andrew, 223
MCCAUSLAND, David, 263
  James, 229
MCCAY, William, 215
MACCDADE, Mary, 69
MCCENNAUGH, John, 285
M'CHARSON, Ruth, 239
MACCHASLIN, Annika, 72
  James, 72
  Johan, 72
MCCHEEVER, Timothy, 215
MCCHESNEY, Jane, 268
MCCHESTNEY, Isabel, 81
MCCHEVER, James, 100, 118
  Margret, 229
  Martha, 100
  Mary, 100, 118
  Ruth, 118
MCCLAIN, Berkely, 287
MCCLAIR, Charles, 236
MCCLAN, Sarah, 274
MCCLANE, Margret, 269
MCCLARE, Anna, 89, 174
MCCLARY, John, 69, 262
MCCLASKEY, Cathrine, 148

355

Elenor, 287
Elizabeth, 148
James, 242
Mary, 291
Patrick, 148
MCCLASKY, Janna, 216
MCCLAUGHLIN, Charles,
MCCLAUSKY, James, 170
Priscilla, 170
MCCLEAN, Elizabeth, 240
Joshua, 285
Patrick, 233
MCCLEAVE, George, 86
MCCLEOD, George, 250
MCCLINCHEY, Margret, 213
Maria Randolph, 213
Roger, 213
MCCLINTOCK, John, 226
MCCLOSKEY, Elizabeth, 152
Isabel, 213
James, 213
John, 213
Mary, 152, 224
Patrick, 152, 245
MCCLOSKI, Harry, 217
MCCLOSKY, Joseph, 223
MCCLOUD, Jeremiah, 215
MCCLOUR, Rebecka, 237
MCCLURE, Ally, 154
Cathrine, 154
Elinore, 223
James, 212, 289
John, 212
William, 254
MCCLYDE, James, 268
MCCOLLAN, Margret, 270
MCCOLLOCK, Elizabeth, 258
Rebecca, 234
MCCOLLOH, James, 260
MCCOLLOUGH, Anne, 113
Archibald, 217
Elizabeth, 113
John, 113
M'COLLY, John, 231
MCCOLLY, Sarah, 283
MCCOLOMAY, Lathy, 228
MCCOMB, Daniel, 188
Moses, 188, 200
Sarah, 188, 200
MCCOMBS, James, 219
MCCONNAL, James, 290
MCCONNEL, Hugh, 89
John, 281
Matthew, 270

N., 89
MCCONNELL, Martha, 222
MCCOOK, Elizabeth, 222
MCCOOM, Jean, 255
MCCORD, Jane, 104
Mary, 231
Matthew, 104
Thomas, 104
MCCORDAY, Mary, 217
MCCORMICK, Sara, 86
MCCOWEL, Jeane, 266
MCCOY, Cathrine, 245
Jane, 83
John, 220
Rebecca, 134
William, 134
MCCRACKEN, Isabel, 261
MCCRACKON, Alexander, 214
MCCREA, Michael, 261
MCCULLACH, William, 235
MCCULLAH, Robert, 260
MCCULLEY, Francis, 238
James, 221
MCCULLOCH, Hugh, 205, 212
James, 212
John, 205
Wilhelmina, 205, 212
MCCULLON, Samuel, 232
MCCULLOUGH, Debora, 275
Jesse, 244
Joseph, 246
MCCUTCHEN, John, 241
MCDADE, Cornelius, 288
MCDANIEL, Cathrine, 291
Daniel, 290
MACDANIEL, Mary, 60
MCDANIELS, Mary, 284
MCDANNEL, Cornelius, 239
Leady, 267
MCDAWEL, Thomas, 278
MCDERNOT, Alse, 270
MCDERRY, John, 219
MCDOEL, Amy, 84
Ann, 84
MCDONAL, Robert, 243
MCDONALD, Abigail, 248
Annable, 130, 219
Archibald, 251, 260
Catharina, 111
Catharine, 125, 130
Catharine Justis, 104

INDEX

Edward, 220
Hannah, 259
James, 104, 111, 125, 130, 219
Joseph, 25, 224
Mary, 25, 125
Peter, 272
Rebecca, 104
Thomas, 217
William, 25
MCDONNALD, Cathrine, 277
MCDOUEL, Mary, 217
MCDOUGAL, Elizabeth, 257
MCDOUGLAS, Cathrine, 258
MCDOUGLE, Anne, 216
MCDOUL, Mary, 93
MCDOWAL, George, 241
Isaac, 91
MCDOWEL, Anna, 131
Cathrine, 265
Elizabeth, 219
Jane, 110, 112, 131
Jane Singletown, 101
John James, 101
Lulof, 110
Phoebe, 112
William, 101, 112, 131
MCDOWELL, Joshuah, 229
MCDUEL, Jane, 26
Mary, 26
Sanders, 26
MCDUNOLD, Archdibald, 94
MACE, Mary, 238
MCEACHAN, William, 252
MCEASIE, John, 234
MCELNOIS, Henry, 253
MCENTIRE, Jean, 265
Lydia, 286
Margret, 260
Ruth, 278
MCENTOIS, Hannah, 269
MCENTOR, Hannah, 161
Henry, 161
William Henry, 161
MCFADIEN, Thomas, 223
MCFADREN, James, 270
MCFAIRLAMB, John, 247
MCFALL, Frances, 91
Indy, 92
MCFARLAN, Jane, 272
John, 218
MCFARLEN, Ann, 80
George, 254

MCFARN, James, 82
MCFARSON, William, 90
MCFERSAN, Cathrine, 221
MACFERSSON, Anna, 60
MCFERSSON, Mary, 252
MCGALLY, Roger, 236
MCGARROUT, Robert, 92
MCGARVAY, James, 217
MCGARVY, Sara, 91
MCGAUGHEY, Margret, 282
MCGAWEB, Jane, 266
MCGEARY, Nail, 80
MCGEE, Dennis, 256
Mary, 92
MCGENNIS, Anna, 109
Anne, 98
Cathrine, 215
James, 88, 98, 109
Laddy Kobb, 88
Lady, 109
Lady Kob, 98
William, 88
MCGENNY, John, 143
Margrete, 143
MCGERY, Catharine, 80
MCGHEE, Darkes, 223
MCGIN, Eleanore, 271
MACGINNIE, Bryan, 67
MCGINNIS, James, 103, 119
Lady, 103, 119
Mary, 280
Peter, 103
MCGINNYS, John, 89
MCGLAUGHLAND, Amor, 253
MCGLAUGHLIN, Ann, 193
Elizabeth, 193
John, 193
Margret, 193
William, 274
MCGLOGHLIN, Isabel, 211
Sarah, 211
Thomas, 211
MCGLOIEN, Jane, 276
MCGONAGIL, Cathrine, 288
MCGONAGILL, Edward, 203
Hugh, 203
Sarah, 203
MCGONIGALE, Charles, 260
MCGOWEN, Philip, 217
MCGRADY, James, 226

357

MCGRASHAN, John, 269
MACGRAU, James, 60
MCGRUB, John, 90
MCGUKY, Elizabeth, 81
MCGUSTIN, James, 271
MACHAN, Martha, 231
MCHENRY, Martha, 280
MCHEW, Ester, 101
  Farday, 101
  Mary, 101
MCHICKEN, Ann, 255
MCINTIRE, Mary, 172, 257
  Robert, 264
MCINTOSH, Alexander, 286
  Andrew, 280
MCINTYRE, Andrew, 256
MCJENNET, David, 222
MCJUNIKINS, Samuel, 225
MACK, Anne, 246
  Margret, 235
MCKAGHUEN, John, 269
MACKARFOSS, Daniel, 89
MACKDONALD, Mary, 61
MCKEA, John, 248
  William, 239
MCKEAN, James, 262
MCKEAVER, James, 134
  Maria, 134
  William, 134
MCKEE, Allen, 277
  Andrew, 265
  Jean, 267
  Thomas, 285
  William, 271
MCKEEL, Alexander, 216
MCKEESON, William, 223
MCKEEVER, Anne, 251
  Erick, 152
  Hugh, 270
  James, 152, 268, 270
  Martha, 256
  Mary, 152
MACKELHENNY, Jennet, 46
MCKELLWAY, John, 257
MCKELWHAY, David, 97
  John, 97
  Mary, 97
MACKENDEAR, Sarah, 247
MCKENY, Jane, 106
  John, 106
  Mary, 106
MCKEONE, Edward, 279
MCKERY, Elizabeth, 110
  Ezechiel, 110

  John, 110
MCKEVER, Alexander, 285
MACKEVER, James, 90
MACKEY, Elizabeth, 278
MCKEY, James, 103
  Jane, 83, 103
  Sarah, 103
  William, 215
MACKFADIEN, Mary, 65
MACKGINLEY, Denis, 61
MACKGREIO, Fenly, 66
MCKIBB, Elizabeth, 171
  Mary, 171
  Sarah, 171
MCKILLEB, Ephraim, 216
MCKINGLEY, Thomas, 260
MCKINNAN, Mr., 253
MCKINNI, Cain, 217
MCKITRICK, Alexander, 201
  Jane, 201
  Marian, 201
MACKKARTY, Elsa, 61
MACKLAUER, Mary, 60
MCKLAYN, Laurenz, 226
MCKLEAN, John, 242
MACKMATH, Anna, 43
MACKMULLEN, James, 61
MACKNEL, Anna, 47
MCKNIGHT, Isabella, 291
  James, 241, 254
  Malcom, 228
  Robert, 275
  William, 230
MCKOLL, Margret, 220
MCKOOM, Else, 107, 116
  James, 107, 116
  Jane, 107
  Sarah, 116
MCKORMACH, Lady, 153
  Mary, 153
MCKOY, Dennis, 232
MACKSEN, Francis, 68
MCLACKLON, Catharine, 96
  William, 96
MCLAGHLIN, ---, 85
MCLALY, Marget, 79
MCLANE, Elizabeth, 164
  William, 164
MCLARY, John, 262
  Elenor, 174
  Grace, 227
  John, 264
  Margret, 174
  Matthew, 214

INDEX

Philip, 235
Susanna, 253
MCLEAN, Anna, 52
  Briget, 234
  Charles, 283, 2832
  Hugh, 177, 271
  John, 177
  Laughlin, 52
  Sara, 52
  Susannah, 177
MACLEAR, Henry, 255
MACLECLAN, Martha, 69
MCLEWEY, John, 222
MCLONEN, Daniel, 223
MCLOUIN, Margret, 264
MCMAGHAN, Elizabeth, 241
MCMANAMAN, Elizabeth, 143
  Richard, 143
  Susannah, 143
MCMANNEMAN, Elizabeth, 136
  Richard, 136
  Sarah, 136
MCMANUMIE, Sara, 232
MACMARIE, Lorance, 233
MCMATH, Anne, 227
MCMECHEN, Dr., 213
MCMICHALL, Jane, 234
MCMIKEL, Elizabeth, 256
MCMOLLAN, Alexander, 250
MCMOLLAND, Barbro, 113
  Johan, 113
  Mary, 221
  Sarah, 226
MCMOLLHOLLAND, Patrick, 217
MCMULLEN, James, 288
MACMULLIN, Sarah, 68
MCMULLON, Elizabeth, 220
  Francis, 237
MCMURPHY, Archibald, 259
MCNAIL, Elizabeth, 89
  Mary, 219
  William, 272
MCNALLY, Bryan, 272
MCNAMIE, John, 232
MCNEAL, Charles, 248
  Daniel, 250
  Laughlin, 249
MCNEEL, Elizabeth, 219
MCNEIL, Catharine, 224
  Patrick, 288

MCNEMEE, Jane, 219
MCNULTEY, Giles, 287
MCOLLERN, Cornelius, 86
MCPEECK, Elizabeth, 223
MCPETER, John, 234
MCPHAERSON, ---, 244
MCQUILLEN, Garret, 276
MCREA, Agnes, 236
MCRICHY, John, 88
MCROY, Hugh, 106
  John, 106
  Mary Thompson, 106
MCSAVAN, Samuel, 265
MCSOOLY, Anna, 243
MCSORRLY, Edward, 220
MCSWEANY, Cornelius, 87
MCSWINE, John, 123
MCTEAR, Margret, 85
MCULVAIN, Andrew, 277
MCVAN, Agnes, 232
MCWAY, James, 272, 278
  John, 227
MCWESTEN, Elizabeth, 272
MCWEYER, Anne, 105
  Cornelius, 105
  Rachel, 105
MCWICKER, Archibald, 268
MCWILKIN, Robert, 267
MCWILLIAMS, John, 87
MCWORTER, Mary, 288
MADDOCK, Henry, 67
MADEN, Stephen, 236
MADGIER, John, 51
  Richard, 51
  Sara, 51
MAFFITT, Mary, 227
MAG CURDE (MCGURDY), Catharina, 53
MAGDALENA, Agneta, 7
  Maria, 7
MAGGEE, Jane, 86
MAGGY, Mary, 251
MAGHAN, Edward, 231
MAGUIRE, John, 243, 261
  Nathaniel, 258
MAHAFFY, Thomas, 249
MAHAN, John, 93
  Thomas, 217
MAHANE, Mary, 267
MAHATI, John, 67
MAHON, Martha, 111
  Mary, 111

Thomas, 111
MAHONEY, Timothy, 228
MAINS, Mary, 220
MAJER, Christopher, 234
MAKEN, Anna, 66
MAKER, Sara, 94
MALCOLM, John, 272
MALEAN, Elizabeth, 261
MALEY, Anne, 128
  James, 128
  Margreta, 128
MALIN, Isaac, 230
MALLAWEDY, Rachel, 222
MALLEN, Catharine, 272
MALY, Brigitte, 154
  Solomon, 154
MAN, Johan, 56
  Kerstin, 56
MANDEE, Elizabeth, 222
MANDENHALL, Steven, 234
MANELLY, Jean, 252
MANKIN, Richard, 11
MANLY, Debora, 17
MANN, William, 266
MANNELY, Anna, 60
MANNIK, Henry, 234
MANNOM, Laurentz, 222
MANNSON, Peter, 30
MANOUGH, Cathrine, 265
MANSELL, Ann, 244
MANSON, Anna, 12, 15
  Annika, 37, 74
  Ingeborg, 16, 26
  Johannes, 12, 15, 16, 26
  Jonathan, 74
  Lucas, 16, 74
  Margaret, 34
  Maria, 26
  Olle, 37
  Olof, 12
  Peter, 15
  Petrus, 37
MANSSEN, Annika, 44
  Johan, 44
  Olle, 44
MANSSION, Karin, 49
  Peter, 49
MANSSON, Anna, 26
  Annika, 6, 7, 10, 20, 31, 32
  Bengt, 20, 30
  Catharina, 32, 33, 47
  Catharina Ester, 39
  Hindric, 49
  Ingeborg, 10, 22, 44
  James, 27
  Johan, 11
  Johan Peter, 1
  Johanes, 10
  Johannas, 33
  Johanneas, 39
  Johannes, 4, 6, 22, 30, 39
  Johanny, 34
  Karin, 6
  Kerstin, 7
  Margaret, 21
  Margareta, 27
  Maria, 31, 34
  Olle, 32, 40, 47, 49
  Olof, 1, 4, 6, 26
  Paul, 39
  Peter, 2, 4, 6, 7, 9, 10, 11, 19, 20, 27, 30, 31, 49
  Petrus, 30
  Sara, 9, 10, 12
  Susanna, 26, 40
MANSSONS, Carin, 4
MAQUIRE, Jean, 255
MARCE, John, 222
MARCER, James, 241
MARDOCK, Anna, 139
  Brigetta, 146
  Brigitta, 138
  Cathrine, 146
  Elenora, 139
  George, 249
  John, 139
  Maria, 138
  Michael, 138, 146
  Prudence, 139
MARER, Richard, 266
MARIS, Rachel, 241
MARKHON, John, 219
MARLARNEY, Margret, 291
MARLEY, Anna, 286
MARLY, Adam, 115
  Anna, 115
MARROW, Cathrine, 121
  Elizabeth, 121
  John, 121
MARSH, Phoebe, 278
  William, 83
MARSHALL, Ann, 245, 267
  Caleb, 285
  David, 275
  Hannah, 274
  John, 141, 221
  Joseph, 252

INDEX

Joshua, 276
Margret, 260
Mary, 227, 261, 285
Samuel, 267
Thomas, 232, 241
MARTEN, Anna, 137
  Christina, 46
  John, 46, 54, 58, 59
  Joseph, 137
  Margareta, 54
  Margaretta, 46
  Marten, 59
  Petrus, 54
  Rachael, 30
  Regina, 137
MARTENS, Kerstin, 21
MARTENSSON, Andreas, 30
  Anna, 52
  Cornelius, 57
  Elizabeth, 54
  Johan, 37
  Johannes, 45
  Jonas, 24
  Kersten, 20
  Kerstin, 24, 30, 36, 45, 52, 57
  Marten, 20, 24, 30, 36, 45, 52, 57
  Matthias, 20, 54
  Sara, 36
  Thomas, 54
MARTIN, Ann, 213
  Cathrina, 116
  David, 250
  Elizabeth, 48, 236, 242
  George, 149, 225, 232, 241
  Hannah, 258, 263
  Hester, 149
  Hugh, 81
  James, 149
  Jean, 260
  John, 65, 85, 213, 222, 237, 256, 262, 266
  Joseph, 149
  Liddy, 81
  Margret, 137
  Margreta, 116
  Martin, 58
  Mary, 213, 228, 262
  Matthias, 116, 137, 239
  Peter, 137
  Rachel, 89
  Rebecca, 240

  Ruth, 86
  Susanna, 48
  Thomas, 40, 48
  William, 226, 264
  Worrick, 289
MARTINS, Martin, 58
  Matthias, 50
MARTINSSON, Martin, 16
MARTON, Elizabeth, 215
MARY, Nuklan, 253
MAS, Anne, 226
MASCALL, Ann, 249
MASHALL, Elizabeth, 143
  John, 143
  Lucia, 143
MASLANDER, Abraham, 18
  Elizabeth, 23
  Helekin, 3, 23
  Helena, 8, 13, 18
  Maria, 8
  William, 8, 13, 18, 23
MASON, Ann, 271
MASS, John, 201
MASSEN, Catharina, 231
MASSET, Mary, 230
MASSON, Benjamin, 291
MASSOR, Rebecca, 226
MASTEN, Johan, 38, 57
  Ledi, 57
  Margareta, 38
  Marget, 57
  Matthias, 38
MASTERS, Elizabeth, 251
  James, 216, 257
MATHER, Barbarah, 142
  James, 50
  John, 50
  Michael, 142
MATHERS, Jane, 220
MATHEW, Hanna, 40
MATHEWS, Thomas, 270
MATIRE, ---, 239
MATLOCK, Ester, 223
  Isaiah, 224
MATSHER, Anna Eva, 135
  Barbro, 135
  Michael, 135
MATSON, Ann, 282
  Britta, 82
  Ester, 237
  George, 291
  Gwin, 162, 173
  Jonas, 162, 173
  Kitty, 289
  Peter, 162

Rebecca, 173, 289
MATSSON, Jonas, 242
MATTHEW, Hanna, 39
  Sara, 39
MATTHEWS, Edward, 39
  Elizabeth, 15, 107
  James, 107
  Mary, 40
  Oliver, 15
  William, 15
MAUL, Jane, 278
MAXEL, Anna, 239
  Susannah, 241
MAXFIELD, Elizabeth, 257
  James, 283
  John, 214
  Margret, 259
MAXWELL, James, 93, 257
  William, 219
MAY, Andrew, 76
  Elizabeth, 184
  John, 184
  Lydia, 184
  Martha, 243
  Philis, 271
  Rachel, 279
  Robert, 76
  Susanna, 76
MAYER, Adam, 116
  Annika, 33
  Elizabeth, 116
  Margret, 80, 238
  Matthew, 223
  Matthias, 116
  Michael, 6, 33
  Peter, 5
  Sara, 5
  Susanna, 33
MAYLARK, John, 271
MEA, Joseph, 239
MEAD, Anna, 54
  Samuel, 54
  Wiljam, 54
MEANS, Alice, 273
  Cathrine, 230
  James, 245
  Jane, 244
  Letitia, 279
  Mary, 81
  Robert, 252
  Samuel, 60
MEASON, Christian, 91
MEASOR, Thomas, 60
MECHASLIN, Annika, 62, 63
  James, 62, 63

  Kethi, 63
MECHEM, Francis, 229
MECKANAPPIT, Indians, 18
MEERS, Robert, 249
MEGARROUGH, Margret, 269
MEGILL, Margret, 281
MEGINNIS, Casperus, 274, 278
  Daniel, 272
MEHAN, Prudence, 96
  Sara, 96
  Thomas, 96
MELAGEN, Hugh, 282
MELAUN, Sarah, 258
MELEEHAN, James, 242
MELIMON, Ann, 221
MELLOR, James, 96
  Jane, 96
  Robert, 96
MELON, Margareta, 233
MELOY, Elenor, 106
  Else, 106
  Matthew, 229
  Michal, 220
  Michel, 106
MENDENHALL, Abraham, 291
  Elizabeth, 254
  Francis, 281
  Moses, 253
  Stephen, 261
MENDINGHALL, Rebecca, 243
MENDINHALL, Joseph, 230
MENEMAN, Richard, 229
MENZENER, Cathrine, 263
MERCER, Hanna, 268
  Joseph, 222
  Mardochay, 230
MERCHANT, William, 241
MEREDITH, Hannah, 244
  Joseph, 279
  Mary, 89
  Walter, 261
MERRYMAN, Mary, 216
MESSER, Mary, 282
METZGER, Michael, 229
MEYER, Abner, 258
  Abraham, 10
  Anna, 25, 28
  Aron, 23
  Barbara, 83
  Christopher, 11, 15, 20

INDEX

Eleizer, 59
Job, 258
John, 103
Jonathan, 29
Margareta, 25, 26
Margaretta, 15
Maria, 28
Mary, 103
Matta, 15, 20
Michael, 10, 11, 25
Michal, 28
Michel, 26
Peter, 10, 23
Philip, 20
Sara, 10, 23, 29, 55
Sarah, 103
MEYERS, Anna, 6, 13, 18
Christopher, 6
David, 18
Michael, 6, 13, 18
William, 13
MEZGER, Barbro, 125
Catharina, 125
Michael, 125
MICHEL, Anne, 218
John, 66
Mary, 87
MICHNELL, Elizabeth, 155
Laughly, 155
Sarah, 155
MICKEBROI, Elizabeth, 269
MICKEL, Daniel, 53
MIDDLETON, John, 268
Mary, 260
Richard, 215
MIE, Mary, 289
MIES, Barnet, 232
MIKELJOHN, Margret, 288
MILBEN, Mary, 279
MILES, Barna, 238
Elizabeth, 271
Jane, 246
Margrete, 244
MILEY, Agnes, 257
MILLASON, Ann, 284
Richard, 284
MILLEGAN, Edward, 80
MILLER, Agnes, 83
Alexander, 220
Ann, 262
Anne, 220, 228
Archibald, 235
Benjamin, 258
Cathrine, 236, 270

Dorothy, 27
Fredrick, 234
George, 80
Hance, 127
Hannah, 229, 245
Hans, 230
Jacob, 127
James, 80, 242
Jane, 104, 108
Johan, 27
John, 104, 108, 225
Killian, 27
Leady, 258
Marta Cross, 104
Martha, 232
Mary, 80, 87, 227, 232, 270, 275
Rachel, 27, 127
Robert, 108
Ruth, 289
Sarah, 247
Tholly, 65
Thomas, 104
William, 86, 104, 237, 274, 289
MILLERSON, Johnathan, 226
MILLESON, Anna, 69
MILLIKIN, Elsa, 234
MILLINER, Johanna, 274
MILLNER, Elizabeth, 253
Nathan, 265
Samuel, 275
MILLS, Elizabeth, 221
George, 202, 205, 208, 212
James, 236
Johanna, 212
John, 287
Margaret, 202
Mary, 82
Sarah, 202, 205, 208, 212
MILLSSON, Thomas, 216
MILNOR, Cathrine, 183
Isaac, 183
James, 70
Samuel, 183
MILOVE, Johanna, 82
MILTON, John, 275
MINER, Elizabeth, 66
Thomas, 66
MINK, Elizabeth, 8
Gertrude, 4
Johan, 3, 8
MINKE, Eleanor, 141
James, 141

John, 141
MINNER, John, 251
MINOR, Moses, 234
  Susanna, 236
MINSHALL, Griffith, 67
  Sarah, 67
  Thomas, 69
MINSSON, Abraham, 22
  Annika, 22
  Olof, 22
MINZI, Edai, 94
  Elenor Willing, 102
  Ellenor Willing, 94
  James, 94, 102
  Willing, 102
MINZY, Elenore, 118
  James, 118
MIRIX, John, 215
MISMAN, John, 87
MITCHEL, Agnes, 237
  Elizabeth, 291
  Hannah, 259
MITCHELL, Andrew, 232
  Hugh, 262
MITZ, Henry, 155
  Mary, 155
  Mary Magdalene, 155
MOLL, Joseph, 247
MOLLAND, Arthur, 106
  James, 111
MOLLIN, Jane, 90
MOLOUGHNY, Daniel, 53
MONAGAN, Patrick, 79
MONAGLE, Margret, 217
MONDE, Debora, 91
MONKS, Thomas, 238
MONRO, Rebecca, 282
MONROE, Catharina, 27
  Mary, 27
  William, 27
MONSON, Anna, 106
  Annika, 77
  Helena, 133
  Isaac, 106
  Lucas, 106
  Olle, 77
  Peter, 133
  William, 133
MONTAGUE, Briant, 280
MONTEITH, Margret, 262
MONTGOMERY, Anna, 129
  Anna Hallowday, 25
  Anne, 112, 224
  Benjamin, 252
  Charity, 101
  David, 119
  Hugh, 172, 265
  James, 250
  Johan, 25
  John, 93, 101, 129, 172, 251
  Lady, 226
  Margret, 274, 281
  Mary, 119, 129
  Michael, 112
  Michel, 84
  Moses, 233, 247
  Rachel, 172, 277
  Robert, 112
  William, 84, 129, 220
MONTGOMMERY, Maria, 132
  William, 132
MOONEY, Elizabeth, 175
  Jane, 175
  Mary, 175, 291
  Patrick, 175, 222
MOONY, Joseph, 251
MOOR, Annie, 107
  George, 231
  Margaret, 107
  Niclas, 107
MOORE, Alexander, 237
  Andrew, 286
  Ann, 216, 261, 271
  Anna, 69
  Anna, 53 (Anna Moose?, Moore?)
  Benjamin, 86, 214
  Elizabeth, 131, 237, 241, 273
  Enoch, 288
  Hannah, 194, 261, 269
  Jacob, 279
  James, 242, 246, 266
  Jane, 221
  John, 60, 83, 131
  Margaret, 155
  Margret, 255, 274
  Margrete, 141
  Martha, 238, 284
  Mary, 194, 220, 224, 237, 238
  Nicholas, 155, 216
  Richard, 269
  Samuel, 89, 264
  Sarah, 155
  Thomas, 131, 194, 261, 282
  William, 141, 241, 247, 264, 280
MOORES, Thomas, 266
MOORESTRAND, Joseph, 266

INDEX

MOOSE – See Moore
MOOTE, Isaac, 277
MOOTHY, Cathrine, 227
MORAN, Mary, 252
MORE, Andrew, 90
  Dorothy, 94
  Elizabeth, 236
  Martha, 89
  Niklas, 234
  Patrick, 85
  Richard, 235
  Robert, 85
MORFY, Jacob, 251
MORGAN, Abel, 86
  Anna, 68
  Anne, 230
  Catharina, 25
  David, 25, 46
  Elizabeth, 221, 271
  Evan, 237
  Guenny, 257
  Henry, 201, 206, 210
  Hugh, 90
  Jacob, 201, 206, 210
  James, 201
  Lovy, 280
  Lydia, 254
  Margaret, 206
  Margret, 237, 244
  Martha, 243
  Mary, 229, 243, 247
  Michael, 70
  Morgan, 25
  Rachel, 237, 277
  Sarah, 266
  Thomas, 210, 255, 273
  William, 68
MORGON, Darby, 87
MORIS, Joseph, 229
MORISON, Margret, 227
MORLHOUSEN, Margery, 59
MORNEY, Jane, 92
MORNS, Nail, 87
MORPHEY, Catharina, 85
MORPHY, Mary, 256
  Timothy, 90
MORRIS, Andrew, 203, 290
  Cadwalader, 286
  Catharina, 15
  Eleonora, 15
  Eleonore, 148
  Elizabeth, 203
  George, 2
  James, 148
  Jane, 203
  John, 49, 148, 196, 240
  Marj., 81
  Mary, 196
  William, 196
MORRISON, Jane, 233
  Jeane, 228
  Robert, 274
MORRISS, Helena, 40
  Johan, 40
MORROW, Jane, 203
  John, 290
  Mary, 91
  Michael, 203, 286
  Richard, 59, 219
MORSCHEY, Esther, 82
MORSE, Catharina, 34
MORTEMORE, James, 290
MORTEN, Andrew, 256
  Bette, 62
  Brita, 67
  Carl, 54
  Christina, 71, 109
  David, 108
  Elizabeth, 76, 114
  Erasmus, 65
  Henry, 119
  Jacob, 62
  Jeane Stuart, 119
  Johan, 75
  John, 119
  Jonas, 109
  Joseph, 141
  Kerstin, 63, 71, 75
  Marget, 54
  Maria, 54, 132
  Mary, 89
  Mathew, 62
  Mathias, 76, 119
  Matthias, 108
  Morten, 63, 71, 75, 132
  Rebecca, 108, 119
  Rebeccah, 141
  Regina, 141
  Sara, 109
  Sarah, 114, 132, 152
  Susanna, 63
  Thomas, 114, 152, 223
  William, 152
MORTENSON, Ann, 184
  Joseph, 84, 95, 184
  Joshua, 84, 184, 275
  Mary, 95
  Matthias, 101
  Rebecca, 101

EARLY CHURCH RECORDS OF NEW CASTLE COUNTY

Regina Peterson, 84, 95
Sarah, 101
MORTENSSON, Jonas, 99
  Joseph, 101
  Rebecca, 99
  Regina, 101
  Sarah, 99, 101
MORTIN, Brigita, 90
  Johan, 71
  John, 71
  Marget, 71
MORTINSON, Caleb, 195
  Joshua, 195
MORTOL, Jeanet, 61
MORTON, Andrew, 82
  Ann, 186, 280, 290
  Anna Ingeborg, 124
  Cathrina, 166
  Cathrine, 203
  Dorcas, 168
  Dorkas, 171
  Elenor, 118
  Erasmus, 89
  George, 199
  Isaac, 171, 203
  Jacob, 211, 288
  John, 234
  John Harp, 211
  Jonas, 85, 166
  Joseph, 118
  Lydia, 273
  Marget, 67
  Margret, 269
  Maria, 134
  Mark, 178
  Mary, 203, 254
  Mathias, 82
  Matthias, 130
  Morton, 168, 171, 175, 186, 199
  Peter, 223
  Rachel, 211
  Rebecca, 178, 285
  Regina, 118
  Samuel, 199
  Sarah, 124, 134, 168, 178, 186, 199
  Susanna, 97
  Thomas, 124, 130, 134, 264
MORTONSON, Joshua, 186, 190
  Margret, 190
MOSSETH, Catharine, 219
MOTE, Jacob, 80
  Mary, 259

MOTH, Elizabeth, 122
  Jacob, 122
  Mary, 122
  Sarah, 122
MOTLAY, James, 270
MOULD, William, 272
MOULDER, Benjamin, 117
  Elizabeth, 259
  Johan, 117
  Joseph, 117
  Margret, 117
  Robert, 117
  Sarah, 117, 224
  William, 117
MOULDERS, Elizabeth, 80
  Prudence, 233
MOUNSELL, Deborah, 239
  Elizabeth, 248
MOUNSON, Christina, 69
MOUNSSON, Judith, 53
MOUSLEY, Hannah, 66
MOY, James, 240
MUCKELVAIN, Margret, 274
MUDENHALL, Ruth, 274
MULAY, Eleonore, 242
MULER, Jacob, 122
MULGROVE, Margrete, 172
MULLEN, Johanna, 281
  Patrick, 216
MULLIN, Michael, 287
  Susanna, 87
  Thomas, 286
MULLON, Patrick, 255
MUN, John, 228
MUNDAY, Henry, 50
MUNDEL, James, 217
MUNGAN, Joseph, 280
MURDOCK, Elizabeth, 273
  Mary, 233, 289
  William, 201
MURDUCK, Michael, 238
MURFY, Will, 233
MURPHEY, Arthur, 135
  Elizabeth, 177, 182
  Hugh, 135
  Isabella, 177
  James, 177, 182, 260
  Maria, 135
MURPHY, Ann, 259
  Arthur, 124
  James, 268
  John, 70
  Mary, 124
  Peter, 231

INDEX

William, 124
MURRAY, Andrew, 184
MUSGRAVE, Aaron, 256
  John, 66
MUSTER, Anne, 250
MUTHIN, Isaac, 125
  Jacob, 125
  Sarah, 125
MYERS, Mary, 268

-N-

NAAF, Cathrine, 149
  Hance, 149
  Rebeccah, 149
NAALY, John, 249
NABIOR, Hance, 148
  Martin, 148
  Mary, 148
NADGER, Sara, 60
NAF, Elizabeth, 195
NAFF, Cathrina, 130, 137
  Cathrine, 194
  Eliza Ann, 214
  Elizabeth, 242
  Hance, 192, 194, 196, 199, 200, 203, 206, 214, 279
  Hans, 137, 218
  John, 130, 200
  John Henry, 130
  Margret, 206
  Maria Susanna, 137
  Mary, 192, 194, 196, 199, 200, 203, 206, 214
  Susanna, 192
  William, 203
  William Hance, 196
NAIL, Henry, 103, 219
  Samuel, 239
NAILS, John, 259
NAILSON, Mary, 247
NAS, Catharina, 106
  Jacob, 106
NASH, John, 236
NASS, Ann, 183, 190
  Hannah, 182
  Hans, 182
  Henry, 183, 190
  Joanna, 182
NATHARY, John, 242
NATT, Johanna, 94
  Margareta Mayer, 94
  Thomas, 94
NAVAL, Mary, 226
NEAL, Mary, 46
  Thomas, 53

NEALS, Elizabeth, 90
  Johannah, 236
NEALY, James, 68
  Mary, 220
NEBECKAR, Arquilla, 212
  John, 212
  Mary, 212
NEBEKER, Elizabeth, 287
NEBUCAR, John, 228
NEBUIR, Hans, 121
  John, 121
  Maria, 121
NEBUKAR, George, 139
  Hans, 139
  Mary, 139
NECKLYN, Ellenor, 80
NEDRICK, Ann, 268
NEELD, Elias, 217
NEELY, John, 253
  Joyhn, 215
NEEMAN, Beata, 73
  Johan, 73
  Maria, 73
  Olof Van, 6
NEERING, John Williams, 225
NEGLY, Sophia, 180
  Susanna, 180
  William, 180
NEIDE, Joseph, 223
NEIGHBUCHER, Hans, 130
  Mary, 130
NEIL, Ann, 179
  Elizabeth, 265
  Mary, 179
NEILDS, Thomas, 276
NEILL, Thomas, 270
NEILSON, George, 271
NEILY, Margrete, 245
NELLY, Thomas, 226
NELSON, Ann, 273
  Edward, 6
  Elizabeth, 264
  George, 181
  Henry, 178
  Leady, 263
  Maria, 6
  Martha, 181
  Mary, 181
  Michael, 259
  Sara, 6
NETHERY, James, 228
NEUBEUKER, Lukas, 162
  Mary, 162
NEWARK, Thomas, 247
NEWBEEKER, Anna, 133

EARLY CHURCH RECORDS OF NEW CASTLE COUNTY

John, 133
Maria, 133
NEWBERY, Sarah, 229
NEWBROUGH, John, 223
  Josua, 82
NEWDEN, Alexander, 65
NEWEL, Martha, 279
NEWLIN, John, 254
NEWMAN, Margret, 215
NEWPORT, ---, 84
NEWS, David, 166
NEWWORK, Margret, 87
NICHER, Lara, 80
NICHOLAS, Aimey, 202
  Ann, 202
  Elizabeth, 202
  Hannah, 202
  John, 202
  Sara, 26
  Sarah, 202
NICHOLS, Dina, 254
  John, 248
  Margaret, 222
  Phoebe, 227
  Thomas, 242
  William, 257
NICHOLSON, Anne, 149
  James, 247
  John, 149
  Mary, 149
NICKLAND, Mary, 221
NICKLIN, John, 67
  Sarah, 67
NICKOLS, Betty, 283
  Hannah, 253, 269
  Mary, 232
  Rachel, 247
  Robert, 284
NICKOLSON, Benjamin, 235
  Mary, 232
NICLAN, John, 249
  Patience, 86
NICLASON, Ann, 167
  John, 167
NICLES, Richard, 80
NICOLAS, Amos, 102
  Hannah, 102
  William, 102
NICOLS, Elizabeth, 218
NICOLSON, Margret, 86
NICSSEN, Elizabeth, 18
  Maria, 18
NIELD, Rachel, 275
NIELS, John, 291
NIKOLS, John, 245
NILSON, David, 66
  Elias, 253

NILSSON, Elias, 40
  Margaretta, 4
  Olof, 4
  Robert, 219
NISBITH, John, 221
NIXON, George, 266
  Jean, 266
  Thomas, 276
NOBLE, Jane, 215
NOELS, Jane, 66
NOOKS, William, 215
NORIS, William, 229
NORMAN, John, 93
NORRIS, Elenor, 281
  Nicholas, 215
  William, 224
NORSET, Anne, 230
NORTH, Joshua, 223
NOSETTE, Jane, 238
NOTT, Benjamin, 105
  Marget, 105
  Thomas, 105
NOWELL, Christina, 75
  Joseph, 75
  Mary, 75
NOWLAN, John Robert, 181
NOWLIN, Henry, 186
  John, 186, 274
  Mary, 186
NUGEN, Sarah, 117
  Thomas, 117
  Walter, 117
NUGENT, Elianor, 289
  Patrick, 289
  Walter, 223
NULTANIUS, Fredica, 289

-O-

OANES, Caleb, 243
OARR, James, 253
OBEDEER, Frederick, 289
OBIYAN, Neal, 61
OBORN, Hanna, 47
OBRYAN, Cornelius, 80
O'DANEL, Hannah, 255
O'DANIEL, Francis, 289
ODIORN, John, 217
ODIVARS, William, 215
O'DONNELLY, Elizabeth, 277
O'FREEL, John, 236
OFWERDOFF, Valentine, 238

INDEX

OGDEN, Catharine, 88
OGGLE, Alexander, 113, 120
  Elizabeth, 113, 224
  James, 112
  Jane, 112
  Martha, 113, 120
  Rebecca, 120
OGGLESBY, William, 221
OGLE, Ann, 213
  David, 90
  Edward, 93
  Elizabeth, 225, 272
  Grissel, 60
  James, 213
  Joseph, 49
  Lucretia, 219
  Martha, 213
  Mary, 24, 280, 291
  Thomas, 24, 92, 213, 246
O'HUGHS, Samuel, 266
OINS, Catharine, 9
  Elizabeth, 9, 19
  Johan, 9, 14
OLDHMAN, Edward, 284
OLDING, Ann, 269
OLIN, Elizabeth, 12
  Johan, 12
OLIVER, Ann, 202
  George, 202
  James, 216
  John, 202
OLLS, Jean, 254
ONAIL, Catharine, 68
ONAYLE, Francis, 66
O'NEAL, Cathrine, 235
  Mary, 240
O'NEIL, Margareta, 231
O'NEILE, Susanna, 273
ORAN, Mary, 234
ORCHARD, Johan, 28
  Margaretta, 28
  Mary, 28
ORETON, Patrick, 81
ORHAN, Hindric, 7
ORIN, Benjamin, 216
  Joseph, 226
ORKAN, Hindric Johanson, 11
ORKANER, Thomas, 218
ORR, Arthur, 144
  Elizabeth, 218
  Jane, 144
  John, 257
  Sarah, 144
ORSO, John Baptist, 290

ORSON, George, 47
OSBORNE, Martha, 289
  Peter, 245
OTLAY, Hannah, 237
  John, 236
OTLEY, Johnathan, 17
  Philip, 268
OTTLAY, James, 92
OVERSILLER, Elizabeth, 245
OWEN, Catharine, 59
  Griffith, 278
  Gwine, 242
  John, 59
  Mary, 269
  Rebecca, 222, 259
  Sarah, 267
  William, 175
OWENS, Ann, 86
  Chrisy, 245
  Elizabeth, 235
  George, 222
  Margury, 65
  Mary, 90
OWERMAYERIN, Hannah Barbro, 116
  Susannah, 116
OWGLE, Charles, 148
  Elizabeth, 148
  Thomas, 148
OWIN, Elizabeth, 29
  John, 40
  Sara, 40
OWINS, Dorothea, 35
  Elizabeth, 35
  James, 35
OYEN, Catharine, 212

-P-

PAALSON, Peter, 9
PACKERTON, Elizabeth, 80
PADRICK, Michael, 51
PAERCE, Joseph, 239
PAFWELSON, Carl, 70
  Magdalena, 70
  Powel, 70
PAGE, Mary, 252, 264
PAGNE, Cathrine, 178
  John, 178
  Mary, 178
  Thomas, 178
  William, 178
PAIL, Sarah, 240
PAIN, Benjamin, 239
  Catharine, 290
  Edward, 224

PALATINUS, Casparus, 21
PALDING, Martha, 241
PALLSSON, Debora, 20
  Gustaf, 20
  Marita, 20
  Sara, 20
PALSON, Anna, 121
  Cathrina, 121
  Elizabeth, 16
  Gustaf, 57
  Margareta, 57
  Mariah, 5
  Olof, 5, 16
  Peter, 5
  Susanna, 67
  William, 121
PALSSON, Anders, 29, 32
  Andreas, 30, 55
  Anna, 21
  Berget, 47
  Catharina, 25, 30, 35, 41, 42, 48, 54, 57
  Christina, 4
  Dorothea, 51
  Elizabeth, 8, 10, 12, 20, 32, 38, 54
  Geikie, 47
  Geisee, 9
  Geisie, 9
  Gustaf, 29, 38, 42, 53, 72
  Ingeborg, 38
  Jacob, 24, 32, 34
  Jacobus, 19
  Jean Benjaminsson, 34
  John, 55
  Kerstin, 4, 57, 72
  Magdalena, 51
  Mans, 9
  Margaret, 53
  Margareta, 38, 42, 47
  Margaretta, 9, 72
  Marget, 41
  Maria, 4, 14, 35, 53
  Mary, 10, 24
  Olle, 32, 34, 59
  Olof, 8, 12, 20
  Pal, 9, 10, 41, 47, 51, 57
  Paulus, 57
  Pawel, 25
  Peter, 20, 21, 24, 25, 30, 35, 38, 42, 47, 48, 49, 52, 54, 55, 57, 59
  Rebecca, 58
  Richard, 41
  Sophia, 55
  Susanna, 12, 38
  Swen, 42, 49
  Tobias, 32
  William, 42
PARFIS, Johanna, 271
PARK, Joseph, 242
  Rachel, 44
  William, 266
PARKE, Grace, 284
  Joseph, 231
PARKER, Edward, 83
  Hugh, 179
  Jane, 146
  Jeane, 258
  Johan, 30
  Margret, 258
  Mary, 179
  Sara, 92
  Sarah, 146
  Susanna, 67
  William, 142, 146, 179
  Wilson, 244
PARKET, Martha, 283
PARKIN, Eben Ezer, 110
  Hannah, 110
  Thomas, 110
  William, 110
PARKINS, Caleb, 138, 158
  Calop, 128
  Cathrine, 128
  Isaac, 128
  Joseph, 234
  Nanny, 138
PARKINSON, Mary, 276
PARKISSON, Elizabeth, 258
PARKS, Sarah, 249
PARLEN, Catrine, 181
  Mary, 250
  Olof, 181
PARLIN, Cathrine, 276
  Elizabeth, 242
  Olove, 218
PARM, Mary, 240
PARMER, Hannah, 123
  John, 149
  Lydia, 149
  Mary, 123, 149

PARO, Margaret, 269
PARR, Mary, 249

INDEX

PARRY, John, 267
PARSETY, Edward, 155
  Magdalena, 155
  Susannah, 155
PARSONS, Daniel, 50
PARSSON, Elizabeth, 113
  Henric, 113
  Henric Christian, 113
PARTEN, Elizabeth, 110
PARTTY, Mary, 232
PARVIS, Joseph, 127
  Mary, 127
PASHALL, Rachel, 278
PASMORE, Augustine, 65
PASSMORE, Enoch, 235
  George, 244
  Joseph, 236
PASTMORE, Joanna, 222
PATERSON, Mary, 258
  Samuel, 234
PATERSSON, Elizabeth, 99
  Mary, 99
  William, 99
PATRICK, ---, 86
  Patrick Fich, 217
PATTERSON, David, 203
  John, 203
  Margret, 203
  Maria, 136
  Mary, 217, 240
  Rebecca, 203
  Walter, 136
  William, 136
PATTON, Ann, 214, 277
  Elizabeth, 214
  George, 127
  John, 127
  Maria, 127
  Mary, 227
  Sara, 92
  Susanna, 226, 238
  William, 92
PAUELSON, Magdalena, 63
  Pafuel, 63
PAUL, Else, 224
PAULSON, Aaron, 170
  Anders, 133, 138
  Andrew, 149, 152
  Ann, 187, 259, 277
  Bartholomew, 77, 110
  Batholomew, 77
  Benjamin, 184
  Catharina, 77, 137
  Cathrine, 241, 261
  Charles, 139, 167, 170, 175, 179, 185, 190, 193, 196, 263
  Christian, 234
  Debora, 157
  Eleanor, 77
  Elenor, 108, 174, 179, 184
  Eleonora, 110
  Eleonore, 139, 150
  Elizabeth, 149, 160, 167, 176, 179, 182, 248
  George, 137, 188, 192, 195, 277
  Isaac, 176
  James, 160
  Joel, 175
  John, 165, 169, 174, 179, 184, 197, 264, 269
  Joseph, 184
  Lady, 255
  Levy, 150
  Lydia, 243
  Margarete, 149
  Margret, 157
  Margreta, 138
  Margrete, 152
  Margretha, 133
  Mary, 77, 109, 152, 169, 171, 174, 192, 252
  Nathan, 190
  Olle, 109
  Paul, 4
  Peter, 77, 139, 150, 160, 165, 171, 176, 179, 182, 187, 193, 253
  Rachael, 230
  Ruth, 110
  Samuel, 185
  Sarah, 184, 197
  Simon, 108, 277
  Susanna, 167, 179, 193
  Susannah, 138
  Tobias, 133, 157
  William, 109, 137, 188
PAULSSON, Catharina Justus, 109
  Elizabeth Stedham, 99
  Gustaf, 34
  Johan, 215

EARLY CHURCH RECORDS OF NEW CASTLE COUNTY

John, 99
Margreta, 125
Mary, 218
Peter, 109
Richard, 125
Tobias, 220
William, 109, 216
PAWL, Elizabeth, 140
Hannah, 140
Joseph, 140
PAYNE, Thomas, 184
PEAK, John, 225
PEAR, Jesper, 132
John, 132
Margaretha, 132
PEARCE, Abner, 128
Andrew, 126
Ann, 255
Anne, 129
Benjamin, 129
Catharina, 132
Elizabeth, 129
Guine, 132
Hannah, 128, 132
Henry, 129
Jane, 126
John, 129, 137, 161
Johnathan, 161
Joseph, 126, 132, 157
Levi, 132
Margaret, 161
Margret, 137
Mary, 132, 261, 278
Rachel, 129
Samuel, 129
Sara, 129
Thomas, 285
William, 157
PEARE, Elizabeth, 132
John, 132
Robert, 132
PEARS, Johan, 71
Joseph, 26, 63, 71
Mari, 63
Maria, 65, 71
Timotheus, 63
PEARSON, Lydia, 278
Susanna, 286
PEARY, Jane, 127
Susannah, 127
PEAST, Mary, 83
PEAXE, Henry, 88
PECK, Mary, 228
PEDEN, Cathrine, 209
Christina, 209
John, 209
PEDRICK, John, 93

PEERS, Jesper, 150
John, 153
Joseph, 74
Lady, 150
Margret, 153
Mary, 74
Richard, 74, 150
Robin, 5
PEERSSON, George, 38
Henry, 38
Joseph, 38
Maria, 38
PEET, Jane, 242
PEGMAN, Edward, 248
PEIRCE, Robert, 173
Susanna, 173
PEITTERSON, Hans, 4
Sara, 4
PEMROY, Mary, 248
PENDELGRASS, Susanna, 271
PENN, ELizabeth, 262
William, 60
PENNEL, Isaac, 253
Samuel, 221
PENNINGTON, Anne, 127
Elizabeth, 127
PENNOCK, Mary, 268
Phoebe, 248
William, 262, 280
PENNY, Esther, 153
James, 153
Lady, 153
PEOPLES, Hugh, 221
Martha, 215
William, 238
PEPERALL, Will, 233
PEPPER, Elizabeth
Mary, 207
Henry, 207
Lydia Ann, 207
Mary, 207
PEPPERELL, Agnes, 238
PERCE, Joseph, 216
PERIL, Elinor, 218
PERKINS, Caleb, 144, 152, 168, 174, 230
Catharine, 152, 287
Cathrine, 144
Elenor, 266
Jacob, 174
Jean, 49
Joshua, 284
Margaret, 152
Margret, 286
Mary, 79, 216
Nancy, 275
Rachell, 264

INDEX

Susanna, 282
William, 168, 211
PERRY, Mary, 25
  Matthew, 291
  Samuel, 25
  Thomas, 25
PERSONS, Susannah, 241
PERSSEN, Anna, 6
PERSSON, Anna, 9
  Lars, 2
PETER, John, 263
PETERMAN, Elizabeth, 280
  Jacob, 284
PETERS, Charity, 66
  Susanna, 82
PETERSDOTTER, Magdalena, 11
PETERSON, Andreas, 75, 144
  Andrew, 84, 98, 156, 160, 170, 176, 244, 257, 274
  Ann, 160, 164, 245
  Anna, 2, 135
  Anne, 246
  Benjamin, 156
  Brita, 81
  Captain Hans, 5
  Catharina, 75
  Catharine, 260
  Cathrina, 154
  Christina, 39, 62, 131, 221
  Ei, 146
  Elenor, 264
  Elizabeth, 63, 147, 154, 159, 160, 163, 168, 243
  Elsa, 138
  Gabriel, 2, 4
  Hannah, 164
  Hans, 63, 75
  Helena, 224
  Hezekiah, 144
  Ingrid, 2
  Isaac, 173
  Isabel, 107
  Israel, 13, 62, 77, 158, 164, 173, 255, 280
  James, 98, 178
  Jane, 94, 107
  Jehu, 136
  Johan, 63
  John, 140, 159, 167, 171, 249, 262
  Jonas, 62, 147, 154, 159, 163, 168, 246
  Kerstin, 4, 24, 39
  Lulof, 77, 277
  Lydia, 142
  Lylof, 13
  Magdalena, 87, 138
  Margarete, 147
  Margaretta, 13, 62
  Margret, 108
  Maria, 24, 88, 131, 136
  Mary, 17, 84, 138, 142, 146, 147, 155, 158, 160, 164, 178, 240, 251, 283
  Mathias, 142, 160, 171
  Matthias, 131, 136, 146, 155, 164, 224
  Morton, 160
  Nancy, 176
  Obiah, 135, 140
  Paul, 138
  Peter, 11, 67, 87, 88, 95, 107, 108, 128, 135, 140, 227, 238
  Petrus, 138
  Philip, 147
  Priscilla, 147
  Rachel, 95, 265, 279
  Rebecca, 128, 268
  Rebecca Hoffman, 88, 95
  Rebecca Hopman, 108
  Robert, 167
  Ruth, 167, 274
  Samuel, 21, 24, 39, 62, 84
  Sarah, 98, 144, 156, 160, 170, 176
  Susanna, 62, 158, 255
  Tobias, 253
  Wallraven Paul, 138
PETERSSON, Abraham, 8
  Anders, 24
  Andreas, 57, 76
  Anna, 8, 33, 41
  Annika, 7, 46, 53, 64
  Brita, 72
  Catharina, 46, 47, 64, 72, 76
  Catharine, 56
  Chatrina, 61

Christeen, 220
Christian, 4
Christina, 56, 74
Easter, 143
Elizabeth, 21, 28, 41, 51
Hance, 30, 56
Hans, 2, 5, 7, 41, 51, 61, 64, 72, 76
Helena, 9, 10, 12, 61
Hellena, 5
Isaac, 121
Isarel, 5, 30, 35
Israel, 10, 24, 30, 31, 45, 53
Jonas, 56, 74, 143
Joseph, 41
Kerstin, 28, 33, 48
Lars, 59
Lucas, 3, 8
Magdalena, 21, 45
Margareta, 24, 31, 59
Margaretta, 45, 46
Margarita, 35
Marget, 53
Marguretta, 5
Maria, 7, 19, 61, 70, 121, 127
Mary, 143
Mathias, 72, 127
Matthias, 48, 121
Matz, 6, 7, 21
Obadiah, 143
Paul, 127
Peter, 5, 6, 7, 41, 46, 47, 53, 57, 58, 64, 72, 143
Petrus, 64
Rebecca, 127
Regina, 35, 143
Regner, 41
Rubin, 51
Samuel, 28, 33, 48, 56, 58, 64, 70, 74
Sara, 56
Sarah, 127
Susanna, 30, 31, 53, 72
PETETT, Susanna, 219
PETLES, Samuel, 84
PETON, William, 221
PETTECROW, Leane, 217
PETTERSON, Hindric, 9
 Israel, 18
 Margareta, 18
 Petrus, 18

PETTERSSON, Catharina, 72
 Elizabeth, 72
 Hans, 72
PETTIGREW, John, 215
PETTIGRUE, William, 59
PEW, Foster, 34
PEWSY, Israel, 229
PHARAS, Agnes, 232
PHASSATH, Phanny, 232
PHILIP, Benjamin, 104
 Jane, 104
 Thomas, 104
PHILIPS, Anna, 35, 56
 Anne, 114
 Archibald, 277
 Cathrine, 255
 Charles, 56, 96
 David, 262
 Elizabeth, 135, 201, 223
 Evan, 263
 Hannah, 258
 Henry, 263
 Jane, 96, 114, 276
 Joseph, 184
 Juliana, 184, 185, 191, 201
 Mary, 191, 233
 Nathaniel, 184, 185, 191, 201
 Reuben, 185
 Sarah, 184, 254
 Susanna, 56, 86
 Thomas, 96, 114, 135
 William, 135
PHILLIPS, Elizabeth, 117
 John, 196
 Julian, 204
 Juliana, 196, 204
 Margret, 274
 Nathaniel, 196, 204
 Philip, 224
 William, 117
PHILPOT, Anna, 3
 Francis, 233
 John, 92
 Margaretta, 3
 Thomas, 280
 William, 3
PHISIK, Andrew, 129
 George, 129
 Susanna, 129
PICKET, John, 287
PICKLE, Latischee, 234
PICKMAN, Anna, 9
 Robin, 9

INDEX

Sara, 9
PIDGET, Mary, 80
PIERCE, Aaron, 166
  Ann, 92, 165
  Anna, 91, 109
  Anne, 218
  Benjamin, 262
  Cathrine, 178
  Charles, 92
  David, 202
  Edward, 103
  Elizabeth, 105, 137
  George, 143, 285
  Hannah, 143, 168
  Henric, 91
  Henry, 50
  Jane, 118
  Jean, 47
  Jesse, 202
  John, 144, 149, 150, 166
  Joseph, 91, 103, 118, 137, 143, 150, 221
  Joshua, 261
  Levry, 118
  Lydia, 143, 148
  Margaret, 149
  Margret, 166, 202
  Margrete, 144
  Mary, 92, 103, 137, 148, 150, 279
  Rachael, 105
  Rachel, 263
  Richard, 148, 243
  Robert, 76, 105, 137, 165, 168, 178, 262
  Sara, 49
  Sarah, 137, 275
  Susannah, 109, 137
  Swen Brunberg, 109
  Timothy, 143, 281
PIERSON, Mary, 221
PIETTERSON, Anna, 9
  Hans, 7, 9
PIETTERSSON, Annika, 7
  Hans, 7, 36, 39
  Sara, 36, 39
PIGGOTTE, Mary, 40
PIKE, Aaron, 291
  Abrah, 126
  Abraham, 223
  Elenore, 126
  Elizabeth, 257
  John, 50
  Phoebe, 126
PILE, Cathrina, 131

  Friedrich, 131
  John, 81
  Peter, 131
  Rachel, 87
  Ralph, 50
  William, 50
PILES, Robert, 87
PILKINGTON, Edward, 222
PILLON, James, 225
PILOIN, Rebecca, 224
PIMPERDUE, Mentor, 265
PINGELTON, Margret, 267
PIPER, John, 221
PIPPIN, John, 42
  Joseph, 42
  Rebecca, 42
PITMAN, Elizabeth, 260
PLANK, George, 281
PLANKENTON, Jesse, 290
PLASSART, Hans, 241
PLASSON, Maria, 14
PLASTER, Michael, 231
PLATE, Elizabeth, 80
PLUMMER, John, 89
PLUNKET, Elizabeth, 175
  Sarah, 175
  Thomas, 175, 269
PLURIGHT, William, 290
POG, Marget, 254
POHLSON, Elizabeth, 81
  Magdalena, 91
POIL, Sarah, 66
POILE, Sarah, 216
POKE, Isabella, 224
POLDON, Margrete, 250
POLLEN, Andrew, 252
POLLYK, James, 217
POLSEN, Gustaf, 64
  Marget, 64
  Susanna, 64
POLSON, Anders, 62
  Andreas, 62
  Andrew, 240
  Catharina, 63, 72, 73
  Elizabeth, 62, 89, 92
  Margret, 123
  Ole, 63
  Peter, 63, 72, 73, 240
  Rachel, 123
  Susanna, 73
  Tobias, 123
POOR, Catharina, 133

John, 61
Maria, 133
PORLEN, James, 128
　Sarah, 128
　Susanna, 128
PORTER, Charles, 217
　Elizabeth, 217, 268
　George, 224
　James, 125
　Jean, 253
　Robert, 125
　Sara, 270
　Susannah, 125
PORTMAN, Elizabeth, 86
POST, Elizabeth, 226
　Mary, 256
POTAT, Briget Swenson, 112
　Elizabeth, 112
　Pierce, 112
POTTITT, Perce, 220
POTTLE, Aaron, 255
POTTS, Elizabeth, 59
POUEL, David, 68
POULESON, Magdalena, 73
　Paul, 73
　Petrus, 73
POULSEN, Magdalena, 61
　Pouel, 61
　Rebecca, 61
POULSON, Anne, 116
　Catharine, 76
　Elizabeth, 289
　Justa, 76
　Margareta, 76
　Margret, 116
　Tobias, 116
POWEL, Dorothea, 97
　Eleonore, 243
　Henry, 97
　John, 85, 139
　Joseph, 83
　Margrete, 139
　Mary, 139
　Persilla, 69
　Sarah, 97
POWELL, Abigail, 227
　Anna Prudens, 15
　Elizabeth Kent, 15
　Henry, 15
　Isaac, 257
　John, 226
　Mary, 290
　Thomas, 253
POWELSON, Powel, 79
　Sara, 79
POYL, Elenore, 227

Joseph, 224
POYLE, Abigail, 221
　Philip, 219
　Sarah, 218
PREES, Lewis, 111
　Rees, 15
　Sarah, 111
　Thomas, 111
PREIS, Anne, 247
　Esther, 65
PRELLAM, Cathrine, 152
　Jamimy, 152
　Moses, 152
PRELLY, Elenor, 168
　John, 168
　Patrick, 168
PRERIE, Debora, 285
　John, 285
PRESTON, Mary, 217
　Rachel, 284
　Thomas, 290
PREVOST, James, 185
　Widow, 185
PRICE, Adam, 114
　Catharina, 49
　Cornelia, 114
　Eliakim, 114
　Elizabeth, 37, 287
　Ester, 43
　Helena, 60
　John, 83, 171, 279, 288
　Juda, 266
　Judah, 171
　Mary, 226
　Rebecca, 171
　Sara, 53
　Sarah, 114
　William, 85, 114, 171, 225
PRICHARD, Mary, 226
PRICHET, Phoebe, 228
PRINCE, Adam Henry, 233
PRITCHETT, Jacob, 245
　Sarah, 289
PRIUSENTIERNA, Admiral, 181
PROCTOR, Ann, 270
　Jane, 222
　John, 253
　Rachel, 218
PROIER, Mary, 248
PRYER, Mary, 237
　Sarah, 226
　Susanna, 238
PUGH, David, 222
PULRIGHT, William, 268

INDEX

PURLAT, Lewis, 241
PURLY, Mary, 284
PURTAL, Jane, 241
PYKE, Stephen, 269
PYL, John, 243
PYLE, Alice, 273
  Alse, 239
  Caleb, 253
  Elizabeth, 234, 286
  Israel, 256
  Jacob, 258
  James, 92, 254, 267
  John, 253
  Leady, 258
  Mary, 223, 264
  Robert, 290
  Sarah, 270, 290
PYLES, Ruth, 262

-Q-
QUAM, John, 199
QUANDRILL, Jane, 200
  John, 200
  Thomas, 200
QUEEN, Cathrine, 155
  James, 155
  Thomas, 155
QUIGHLY, William, 83
QUIN, Cathrine, 164
  John, 164
  Mary, 255
  Susanna, 53
  Thomas, 164
QUINE, Mary, 281
QUINN, Cathrine, 150
  Elizabeth, 219
  Isaac, 150
  Jeane, 159
  John, 159
  Nicholas, 285
  Thomas, 150, 159

-R-
RACEN, Andrew, 95
  Anna Petersson, 95
  John, 95
RAFFERTY, John, 254
RAGIN, Daniel, 232
RAILY, James, 222
RAIN, Jemmima, 282
RAIS, Johan, 38
  Margaretta, 38
  Thomas, 38
RALSON, Annah, 243
RALSTON, Sarah, 238
RAMAGE, James, 236
  Jeane, 229
  Marrian, 65

  Rebecca, 225
RAMBO, Israel, 276
RAMSAY, Margret, 266
RAMSEY, Alexander, 104
  Ann, 278, 290
  Anne, 104
  Elizabeth, 104
  Josiah, 80
  Mary, 224
  William, 219
RANNELS, Annah, 140
  Elizabeth, 140
  Jacob, 140
RANOLDS, Elizabeth, 246
RARDEN, Margrete, 241
RASERMAN, Nater, 68
RASSEN, William, 50
RATBEW, Mary, 252
RATCHFORD, Anne, 224
RAVEL, Michael, 261
RAWLINGS, Elizabeth, 163
  Margret, 163, 167
  Thomas, 163, 167
RAWLINS, Charles, 234
  Sarah, 282
RAWSON, George, 187
  John, 229
  Lydia, 183, 187
  Margret, 225
  Regina, 183
  William, 183, 187, 275
RAY, Andrew, 278
  David, 274
  Eleanor, 211
  James, 211
  Thomas, 211
RAYL, Anne, 236
  Elizabeth, 105
  Samuel, 105
  William, 105
REA, Robert, 92
READ, Charles, 62
  George, 62
  Henrietta, 145
  Ingeborg, 59, 62
  James, 145
  Jane, 61
  John, 69
  Samuel, 86
  Thomas, 145
READING, Barbara, 234
READMAN, John, 153
  Johnathan, 157
  Jonathan, 153
  Mary, 153

READUS, Susan, 286
READY, Unity, 229
REAL, Elizabeth
  Peterson, 105
  Israel, 105
  Samuel, 105
REALL, Eliza, 128
  Jane, 128
  Lydia, 140
  Samuel, 128, 140
  Sarah, 140
REATH, William, 246
RED, Andrew, 249
  John, 232
REDDEN, John, 230
REDLY, Rebecca, 2
REDMAN, Anthony, 275
  Elizabeth, 148
  Johnathan, 148
  Jonathan, 246
  MAry, 148
REECE, Elizabeth, 87, 103
  Even, 103
  Mary, 103
  Rachel, 81
REECH, Sarah, 252
REED, Barbarah, 146
  Charity, 93
  Elias, 72, 146
  George, 2, 25, 37, 39, 44, 45, 47, 50, 52, 72
  Hannah, 156
  Ingeborg, 45, 52, 72
  James, 215, 279
  John, 156, 208, 264
  Lydia, 52
  Lydy, 146
  Margret, 208
  Mary, 2
  Rachel, 208
  Robbert, 47
  Robert, 37, 85
  Sara, 2, 25, 37, 39
  Thomas, 156, 230
  Timothy, 282
  William, 45, 93
REES, Andrew, 237
  David, 243
  Elizabeth, 130, 240
  Ezekiel, 130
  Hannah, 249
  John, 130
  Lydy, 247
  Maria, 30
  Rachel, 37
  Rees, 53

REESE, Elizabeth, 123
  John, 79, 123, 225
  Lewis, 89
REGISTER, John, 229
REILERIN, Anne Mary, 239
REILY, Hannah, 228
  Jacob, 232
  William, 53, 88
REINHOLD, James, 220
  Richard, 49
  Sara, 29
REINOLDS, Anna, 129
  Cathrina, 129
  Grace, 224
  John, 129
REKMAN, Robert, 2
  Thomas, 2
RELY, Charles, 249
  Mary, 245
RENCEER, Andrew, 217
RENDY, George, 252
REOUGH, Ellinor, 84
RETT, Samuel, 252
REYAL, Elizabeth, 93
REYNOLD, Elizabeth, 287
REYNOLDS, Annah, 144
  Edith, 227
  George, 204
  Margret, 204, 208, 212
  Mary, 21, 212
  Peter, 212
  Rachel, 144
  Richard, 204, 208, 212
  Sarah, 208, 292
  William, 144
REYON, Cornelius, 85
RIARD, Elizabeth
  Peterson, 97
  Jacob, 97
  Samuel, 97
RICE, Barney, 93
  Catharine, 44
  Elizabeth, 288
  Thomas, 291
  William, 288
RICH, Christopher, 251
  George, 259
RICHARD, Prudence, 221
  William, 278
RICHARDS, Amos, 87
  Catharine, 80
  Edward, 218
  Elizabeth, 259
  Jacob, 224, 231, 288

INDEX

Jonathan, 231
Joseph, 50
P., 145
Richard, 266
Roda, 222
Susanna, 222
Susannah, 254
RICHARDSON, Adam, 231
  Anna, 15
  Cahrles, 225
  Elizabeth, 278
  Hanna, 270
  Hannah, 221, 223, 252
  Jane, 222
  Jean, 167
  John, 246, 269
  Lady, 222
  Marion, 167
  Mary, 15, 16
  Nicholas, 279
  Robert, 167, 264
  Samuel, 260
  Thomas, 252
  William, 15, 16
RICHARDSSON, Edward, 41
  Sara, 41
RICHEY, Eliah, 235
RICHIE, Eliah, 134
  Hannah, 134
  John, 134
  Samuel, 65
RICHISON, Sarah, 234
RICHMOT, John, 258
RICHY, Hester, 256
RICKETS, Juliana, 259
RICKRI, Margaret, 40
RIDGE, Elizabeth, 269
RIDNUA, Elizabeth, 237
RIGHT, Anna, 52
  Annika, 45
  John, 44, 45, 52
  Matthias, 52
  Sara, 45
RIGHTER, Catharine, 158
  Cathrine, 283
  George, 158
  Rebecca, 158
RILEY, Johanna, 273
  Mary, 93
RIMSON, Jane, 236
RINBERG, Anders, 50
RING, Edward, 114
  Elizabeth, 114, 235
  Florentz, 114
  Thomas, 292

RION, James, 104
  Mary, 104
  Patrick, 104
RISE, Leady, 260
RITCHEE, Abraham, 267
RITCHIE, Hanna, 268
ROA, Elizabeth, 233
ROADS, Ann, 86
  George, 268
  Mary, 85
ROBB, Margret, 256
ROBBERSSON, Josua, 39
  Maria, 39
  William, 44
ROBBESON, Balty, 263
  Sarah, 157
ROBBESSON, Anna, 32, 51
  Carl, 38
  Edward, 47, 51, 52
  Elizabeth, 32, 38, 52
  Israel, 32, 38
ROBBINS, Jane, 290
  William, 257
ROBBINSON, Anne, 148
  Mary, 225
  Robert, 148
  Sarah, 148
ROBBINSSON, Jacob, 103
  Jesper, 43
  Magdalena, 43
  Richard, 103
  Susanna Justis, 103
ROBBISSON, Elizabeth, 53
  Israel, 53
  Magdalena, 47
ROBENET, Allen, 229
ROBERSON, Elizabeth, 252
  Mary, 256
  Susanna, 256
ROBERSSON, Catharina, 57
  Robert, 57
  William, 39
ROBERT, Jane, 238
ROBERTS, Ann, 92
  John, 225, 271
  John William, 134
  Maria, 134
  Nathan, 225
  William, 134
ROBERTSON, Annable, 247
  Hannah, 258
  Jonas, 65

Margery, 256
Mary, 260
Rebecca, 252
Robert, 58
ROBERTSSON, Catharina, 54
  Elizabeth, 54
  Joshua, 36
  Maria, 36
  Michael, 220
  Robert, 54
ROBESON, Andrew, 78
  Catharina, 71
  Catharine, 92
  Debora, 268
  Deborah, 186
  Edward, 76
  Elizabeth, 77, 92
  Isarel, 77
  Jacob, 186
  Jane, 269
  John, 244
  Jonas, 76
  Joseph, 277
  Mary, 68, 81
  Rebecca, 238
  Richard, 71, 78, 186
  Robert, 71, 270
  Sara, 77
  Susanna, 78
  Valentine, 284
  William, 235
ROBESSON, Catharina, 64
  Charles, 71
  Elizabeth, 63
  Israel, 63, 64
  Jesper, 37, 40
  Jonas, 71
  Joseph, 63
  Rebecca, 71
  Robert, 64
ROBETTSON, James, 140
ROBINET, Allen, 176
  Ann, 176
  James, 176
  Joseph, 176, 242
  Margaret, 176
  Ruth, 176
  Susanna, 250
ROBINETT, Allen, 127
  Anne, 127
  John, 201, 205, 212
  Margareta, 127
  Rachel, 201, 205, 212
ROBINETTE, Allen, 130
  Anne, 130
  Lydia, 130
ROBINSON, Ann, 248
  Anna, 62
  Anne, 225
  Anthony W., 291
  Catharina, 24, 62, 82
  Cathrine, 224
  Charles, 135
  Debora, 179
  Deborah, 202
  Edward, 1, 4, 8, 221
  Elenore, 228
  Eleonora, 136
  Elinor, 124
  Elizabeth, 56, 65, 124, 182
  Henry, 88
  Ingeborg, 110
  Israel, 56
  Jacob, 179, 202, 272
  James, 24, 68, 268, 280
  Jane, 182, 243, 286
  John, 61, 211, 270, 278
  Jonas, 135
  Margareta, 74
  Margaretta, 8
  Margret, 218
  Margrete, 240
  Maria, 56
  Mary, 84, 135, 179, 220, 233
  Phoebe, 24
  Rachel, 211, 249
  Rebecca, 223, 280
  Richard, 69, 74, 84, 202, 240
  Robert, 62, 124, 136, 142, 182, 227, 242
  Ruth, 228
  Sarah, 142, 276
  Susanna, 74, 179
  Susanna Justice, 84
  Thomas, 142, 268, 273
ROBINSSON, Catharina, 21, 56
  Deborah, 216
  Edward, 10, 17, 21
  Eleonore, 56
  Elizabeth, 55
  Jacob, 17
  Johan, 11
  Margareta, 17
  Margaretta, 10, 21

INDEX

Richard, 10
Robert, 55, 56
ROBISON, Anna, 60
ROBNELL, John, 284
ROBNET, Allen, 118, 119
  Lady, 118, 119
ROCK, Anna, 2
  Daniel, 49
  Francis, 237
  Gustaf, 2
ROCKEREL, Rebecca, 261
RODGERS, Bernhard, 247
  Elenor, 188
  Hannah, 272
  John, 188, 246, 262, 276
  Mary, 44, 188
ROEEN, Ann, 155
  Samuel, 155
  Sarah, 155
ROGERS, Barbara, 165
  Elenor, 197
  Elinor, 191
  Elizabeth, 191
  John, 165, 191, 197
  Margret, 165
  Mary, 265
  Sarah, 289
ROGIS, Cornelius, 55
  Jacob, 55
  Johanna, 55
  Johanne, 55
ROIAL, Mary, 230
ROISKO, Henric, 4
ROLLS, Rebecca, 232
ROMAGE, Hugh, 86
ROMAN, Hannah, 236
  Isaac, 236
  Josua, 87
  Mary, 87
  Ruth, 65
  Thomas, 247
RONALDS, Samuel, 218
RONDLE, Hannah, 266
RONEY, Patrick, 281
RONOLDS, William, 233
RONOLS, Martha, 89
ROSE, Abraham, 144
  Adam, 101
  Hannah, 101
  Lydy, 144
  Mary, 101
  Rebecca, 144
ROSNY, William, 271
ROSS, Eliza, 208
  Elizabeth, 116
  Jacob, 116, 147

  James, 250, 283
  James D., 288
  Jane, 70, 269
  John, 116, 231
  Judah Hays, 147
  Margreta, 232
  Mary, 147
  Mr., 61
  Rosina, 219
  Sarah, 240
  Savoy James, 208
ROSSELL, Mary, 223
ROSSEN, Andrew, 50
  Johan, 41
  Marget, 41
  Maria, 41
ROTCH, Elizabeth, 258
ROTHERAM, Cathrine, 287
  Joseph, 85, 223
ROTHWELL, Benjamin, 261
ROTTER, Mary, 93
ROUSE, Patience, 242
  Rebecca, 263
ROWAN, James, 215, 236
ROWELLS, Grisell, 249
ROWEN, Mary, 235
ROWLAND, Martha, 238
ROWLES, Sarah, 242
  Susannah, 241
ROYAL, Cathrine, 245
  Mary, 115
  Patrick, 115
  William, 115
ROYLY, Ann, 81
RUDGER, Lady, 215
RUDOLPH, Elizabeth, 279
RUE, Lea, 285
  Robert, 275
RUISH, Barbro, 104
  Henry, 104
RULEDSON, William, 93
RUMFORD, John, 288
  Johnathan, 258
RUMMOND, Elizabeth, 260
RUMSEY, Benjamin, 204
  Charles, 204
  Harriet, 291
  Mary, 204
  Thomas E., 291
RUNNELS, Bird, 164
  Dorothy, 285
  Eleonore, 250
  Elizabeth, 285
  Johannah, 230

Margret, 198, 199
Rachel, 138
Rebecca, 266
Richard, 138, 198, 199, 284
Thomas, 198, 199
William, 138, 199
RUNOLDS, John, 252
RUSEL, Samuel, 220
RUSHOCKEN, Catharina, 95
  Hans Gorgen, 95
  Mary Frey, 95
RUSHTON, John, 231
RUSSEL, Anna Cathrina, 123
  Ephraim, 268
  Hugh, 257
  John Michael, 123
  Martha, 265
  Mary, 289
  Niclas, 123
  Robert, 267
RUSSELL, Ann, 254
  James, 268
  Oliver, 252
RUSTON, William, 229
RUTH, Anna, 234
  Rachel, 224
RUTTER, Margreta, 231
RYAN, Isaac, 265
  Mary, 244
  Robert, 257

      -S-
SAADER, Anna Margreta, 110
  Johan, 110
  Maria Eva, 110
SABLEY, Anne, 144
  Johannes, 144
  John, 144
SADLER, John, 218
SAESA, Conrad, 256
SALBY, Anne, 128
  John, 128
  Owen, 128
SALKELD, David, 102
  Margret, 102
  Sara, 102
SALLOVAIN, Dennys, 87
SALVAGE, Cathrina, 234
SAMFERD, Thomas, 253
SAMFORD, Ann, 166
  Elizabeth, 166
  Thomas, 166
SAMPLE, Elizabeth, 279
  William, 248

SAMUELDOTTER,
  Margareta, 4
SANDELANDS, Rebecca, 67
SANDELIN, Charles, 116
  Margaret, 116
SANDERINE, Margrete, 241
SANDERS, Ann, 284
  Barbary, 262
  Elizabeth, 235
  Jacob, 259
  William, 283
SANDERSON, Cathrine, 216
  Hannah, 185
  Isabella, 283
  Nancy, 180
  Timothy, 185
SANDES, Sarah, 121
SANFORD, Alexander, 159
  Ann, 159
  Thomas, 159
SANKEY, Giles, 92
SAP, Johan, 30
  Martha, 30
SAPLEY, ---, 196
SARENTEEN, Mary, 214
SARIN, Mary, 215
SARR, Margret, 87
SAUDER, Henry, 228
SAULTER, Anne, 238
SAUNDERS, John, 274
  William, 270
SAVADGE, Thomas, 260
SAVAGE, Mary, 80
SAVILL, Harmon, 291
  John, 259
  Joseph, 264
SAVIN, Charles, 280
SAVOY, Abraham, 9
  Carin, 3
  Ingrid, 3
  Jean, 9
SAWWIL, Joseph, 248
SAYERS, Christopher, 258
SAYRE, James, 245
SCAGGIN, William, 224
SCARLET, John, 240
SCHAFFENHAUSER,
  Kirsten, 59
SCHLABS, Anne, 150
  Mary, 150
  Philip, 150
SCHNOHILL, Helena, 252
SCHOOWEK, Michael, 252

INDEX

SCHOREBERG, John, 151
  Magdalena, 151
  Maria, 151
SCHROUDER, Magnus, 249
SCHWARTZ, Hans Peter, 135
  Maria, 135
  Michael, 135
SCOGGEN, Mary, 89
SCOTHORN, John, 271
  Nathan, 222
SCOTT, Catharina, 33, 42, 47
  Elizabeth, 70
  Jane, 234
  John, 232
  Joseph, 246
  Margret, 235
  Maria, 33
  Mary, 80
  Robert, 232
  Sara, 42, 47
  Thomas, 29, 33, 41, 42, 47
SCOTTMAN, Elizabeth, 28
  Marten, 28
  Mary, 28
SCUTTARON, Nathan, 238
SEAD, Brita, 63
  John, 63
  William, 63
SEAL, Caleb, 271
  Hannah, 254
  Rachel, 276
SEALS, Sarah, 273
SEED, Anna, 71
  Brita, 29, 36, 41, 45, 52, 55, 57, 71
  Edward, 70
  Elizabeth, 45
  Johan, 26, 29, 36
  John, 41, 45, 52, 55, 57, 71
  Joseph, 29
  Margrete, 243
  Mary, 260
  Nicklos, 55
  Rebecca, 41
  Samuel, 57
  Sara, 26
  Susanna, 52
SEEDS, Brigitta, 236
  Brita, 32
  Elizabeth, 216
  James, 274
  Jan, 32
  Johan, 21

  John, 113, 214
  Joseph, 123, 218
  Maria, 32, 123
  Mary Brunberg, 113
  Rachel, 232
  Samuel, 113, 123, 222
  Sarah, 266
  Susanna, 219
SELLARS, Ann, 290
  George, 282
  Philip, 268
  Rebecca, 292
SELLERS, George, 267
SENECA, Anders, 2
  Widow, 1
SENECCE, Henry, 225
SENECE, John, 225
SENECEE, Sarah, 223
SENECH, Anna Ingeborg, 71
  Ingeborg, 71
  John, 71
SENECK, Anna, 61
  Brewer, 63
  Brita, 63
  Catharina, 64
  Ingeborg, 61, 64
  James, 62, 63, 64, 76, 95
  John, 61, 62, 64
  Margaret, 76
  Margaret Werdeman, 95
  Marget, 62, 64
  Morina, 95
  Sara, 76
SENECKA, Cathrine, 230
SENECKS, Ingeborg, 74, 76
  Isaac, 79
  James, 72, 79, 88
  John, 74, 76
  Magdalena, 85
  Margaret, 79
  Margaret Werdeman, 88
  Margaretha, 72
  Margret, 88
  Maria, 76
  Susanna, 72, 74
SENEKE, Anders, 3
  Anna, 35
  Brewer, 35, 40, 43, 49, 52, 57
  Brita, 35, 43, 52, 57
  Darkis, 43

Darkish, 30
Ingeberg, 43
James, 30
Johan, 3, 40
John, 43
Maria, 57
SENEKESSON, Anders, 3
  Seneke, 3
SENEPON, Ingeborg, 51
  John, 51
SENEX, Ann, 147
  Anna, 135, 136
  Annah, 141
  Anne, 220
  Elizabeth, 144, 145
  Henry, 136
  Ingeborg, 141
  James, 144, 145
  John, 135, 141, 147
  Margrete, 144, 145
  Maria, 135
  Senica, 147
  Thomas, 147
SENEXON, James, 50, 53
  Margareta, 53
SENNECKSON, Henry, 55
  James, 55
  Margaret Werdman, 55
SENNEX, Ann, 157, 177
  Arcadia, 138
  Cornelius, 194
  Elizabeth, 138, 156
  Ely, 177
  Hannah, 157
  Ingebor, 221
  Isaac, 156
  James, 138, 156
  Jane, 194
  John, 157, 177
  Justis, 177
  Margret, 260
  Mary, 251
  Rachel, 177
  Sarah, 177
  Seneca, 194
  Susanna, 256
SENNEXEN, Ingeborg, 55
  John, 55
  Sara, 55
SENUE, Anna, 119
  Cathrina, 119
  John, 119
SERGEANT, Edward, 61
SEVEL, Samuel, 289
SHAAF, Philips, 247
SHADD, Jeremiah, 280
  John, 244

SHADWECK, Benjamin, 241
SHAGAN, Annika, 35
  Elizabeth, 35
  Jonas, 35
SHANK, John, 130
  Samuel, 130
  Susanna, 130
SHANKLIN, William, 224
SHANKS, Cathrine, 269
  John, 280
  Susanna, 257
SHANNAHAN, Thomas, 251
SHANNAN, Elenor, 124
  Johannah, 124
  Thomas, 124, 230
SHANNON, Margret, 86
  Robert, 226
SHAPLEY, Ann, 192
  Mary, 192
  Robert, 192
  William, 192
SHARMISER, Catharine, 128
  John Ulrich, 128
  Ulrich, 128
SHARP, Ann, 193, 204
  Anna Cathrina, 193
  George, 242
  Isaac, 275
  Jane, 81
  Joseph, 227
  Margret, 217, 218
  Mary, 240
  Rachel, 263
  Robert, 204
  Thomas, 258, 281
  William, 193, 204
SHARPE, Anna Cathrine, 197
  Cathrine, 186, 191
  Elizabeth, 186, 216
  Mary, 233
  Peter Tranberg, 191
  William, 186, 191, 197, 276
SHARPLESS, David, 69
  Jessey, 279
SHARPLEY, Adam, 175
  Amos, 133
  Anne, 102
  Catharine, 157
  Catherina, 109
  Cathrine, 262
  Daniel, 92, 184, 188, 190, 196, 275, 281
  Elizabeth, 170

INDEX

Esau, 211
Hannah, 118
Isaac, 184
Isabella, 162, 285
Jemima, 282
Jemyme, 138
John, 190
Karon Habits, 150
Lea, 161
Leah, 275
Mary, 161, 188, 265
Philip, 165
Rachel, 157, 161, 170, 275
Rebecca, 162, 165, 175, 184, 188, 190, 211
Reuben, 211
Sarah, 157
Susanna, 102, 109, 118, 126, 133
Susannah, 126, 138, 143, 150, 157
William, 92, 102, 109, 118, 126, 133, 138, 143, 150, 157, 161, 162, 165, 170, 175, 211, 255
SHAW, Debora, 256
  Elizabeth, 270
  Hushella Barbro, 108
  Joseph, 108
  Marie, 108
  Sarah, 221
SHAY, Helena, 155
  Jeane Maneily, 155
  John, 155, 252
  William, 243
SHEARMAN, Robert, 248
SHEARON, James, 234
SHEE, John, 247
SHEERER, Elenor, 267
  Mary, 246
SHEGEL, Christopher, 16
SHELLDON, James, 105
  Mary, 105
SHENK, Cathrina Magdalena, 121
  Maria, 121
  Samuel, 121
SHEPARD, Rosannah, 80
SHEPHEARD, Catharine, 147
  Rebecca, 147
  Susanna, 147
  Thomas, 147

SHER, Ana, 9
  Anna, 3, 4
  Annika, 8
  Hans, 3, 4, 8
  Isaiah, 8
  Kerstin, 28
  Maria, 28
  Marten, 28
SHERER, Archibald, 263
SHERLOCK, Anne, 115
  John, 115
  William, 115
SHERMAN, Elenor, 172
  Jane, 278
  Margaret, 50
  Rebecca, 172
  Robert, 172
SHERRED, Ester, 115
  Robert, 115
SHERWOOD, Abel, 266
SHEWARD, Hannah, 266
  James, 229
  Rebecca, 260
SHIARS, Mary, 254
SHIELDS, George, 286
  James, 238
SHIELS, Sarah, 263
SHIERMAN, Ann, 157
SHILLINGFORD, Robert, 234
SHIPLEY, Elizabeth, 287
  Samuel, 265
SHIREW, Frank, 106
  John, 106
  Margaret Foster, 106
SHIVERY, Catharine, 283
SHLIGEL, Christopher, 24
  Hanna, 24
  Mary, 24
SHOFIELD, James, 270
SHORE, Ann, 174
  James, 235
  Mary, 174
  William, 174
SHORT, Miriam, 46
SHOW, Daniel, 93
SHREVE, John, 239
SHREVES, Jacob, 256
SHUGGART, John, 85
SHUTE, Margret, 261
SHUTTERLY, David, 203, 206, 211
  Samuel, 203
  Sarah, 203, 206, 211
SIDDON, John, 238

SIDWEL, Prudence, 280
SIGMUND, Cornelius, 95
  Elizabeth, 105
  Elizabeth Walraven, 88, 95
  John William, 88
  Michael, 95, 105
  Michel, 88
  Susanna, 105
SILENCE, Johanna, 274
SILENE, Richard, 164
SILENIE, Richard, 263
SILINIE, Johanna, 174
  Mary, 174
  Richard, 174
SILL, Joseph, 264
  Richard, 226
  Thomas, 50
SIM, James, 262
SIMCOTT, Elizabeth, 125
  Joseph, 125
  Martha, 125
SIMMERS, Cathrine, 247
SIMMONS, Charles, 9
  Francina, 9
  Hugh, 9
  Mary, 9
  Samuel, 60
SIMOND, Elinor, 235
SIMONS, Christina, 9
  Elizabeth, 252
  Francina, 9
  Hugh, 9
  John, 232
  Martha, 266
  Mary, 5
  William, 247
SIMONSON, Elizabeth, 268
  Francis, 60, 248
  Henry, 70
  William, 265
SIMONTEN, John, 255
SIMPSON, Joseph, 67
  Margaret, 34, 278
SIMSON, Mary, 81
SINCLAIR, William, 230
SINCOCK, Elizabeth, 67
  Tacy, 229
SINEX, Henry, 208
  John, 169, 208, 287
  Nancy, 211
  Rachel, 208
  Rebecca, 211
  Robeson, 169
  Sara, 92
  William, 211

SINGLETON, Sarah, 229
  Thomas, 93
SINIE, Ann, 130
  Henry, 130
SININKS, Anna, 131
  John, 131
SINIX, Anna, 126
  John, 126
  Sarah, 126
SINNEX, Ann, 154, 162, 164, 187, 282
  Anna, 281
  Elinor, 187
  Elizabeth, 154
  Henry, 162
  Ingebor, 277
  John, 154, 164, 187
  Sarah, 281
  Seneca, 281
  William, 162
SISHE, Amelia, 280
SKAGAN, Elizabeth, 11
  Mary, 6, 17
  William, 11
SKAGEN, Elizabeth, 2
  Johan, 2
  Jonas, 26, 31
  Matthias, 5
SKAGGEN, Anna, 43, 47
  Jonas, 43, 47
SKAGGIN, Annika, 32
  Johan, 32
  Jonas, 32
SKAIL, Alki, 27
  Catherie, 27
  Henry, 27
  Peter, 27
SKALTON, Alexander, 241
SKAYLOR, Anna Eva, 137
  John, 137
  Matthias, 137
SKEER, Abert, 237
SKELTON, John, 237
SKOP, John William, 228
SKOTSHORN, ---, 178
  John, 180
  Mary, 180
  Rebecca, 178, 180
  Thomas, 178
SKOTT, Elizabeth, 174, 258
  Hannah, 256
  James, 256
  Jean, 252
  Mary, 174, 219
  Samuel, 275

INDEX

Sarah, 226
William, 174
SKREEN, Robert, 66
SKUTE, Jacob, 60
SKYLER, Annah, 143
  Elizabeth, 143
  Mathias, 143
SLAMEASS, Elizabeth, 179
  Hans, 179
  Susanna, 179
SLATER, Else, 150
  Robert, 150
  Sarah, 150
  Thomas, 154
SLAUGHTER, Elizabeth, 272
SLAYTOR, Else, 148
  Robert, 148
  William, 148
SLEIFER, Ann, 277
  Elizabeth, 137
  Elizabth, 270
  Magdalena, 277
  Philip, 137, 155
  Sabina, 137, 155
  Sibilla, 155
SLEIFERS, Sabina, 281
SLIEFER, Anne, 148
  Phillip, 148
  Sabina, 148
SLOAN, Elizabeth, 228
SLOBY, Annika, 74
  William, 74
SMALLWOOD, Stephen, 227
SMART, Elizabeth, 231
SMIDT, Amos, 125
  Andrew, 227
  Anna Springer, 94, 98
  Anne, 125
  Brita, 116
  Cathrine, 181
  Elizabeth, 121, 217, 260
  Eric, 116, 223
  Ester, 214
  Fredric, 122
  Isaac, 113, 122, 140, 221
  James, 122, 140, 226
  John, 94, 98, 121, 122, 219, 281
  Joseph, 121
  Lancelot, 171
  Margret, 122, 225, 251
  Maria, 116, 122
  Mary, 262, 279
  Rachel, 94, 122
  Rebecca, 98, 113, 181, 215
  Samuel, 121
  Sarah, 113, 122, 140
  Thomas, 121
  William, 121, 125, 226
SMIDTH, Ann, 277
  Brigits, 129
  Cathrine, 139
  Eric, 129
  Frederick, 139
  Isaac, 145
  James, 243
  Janet, 280
  John, 129
  Joseph, 243, 256
  Margrete, 139
  Matthew, 257
  Robert, 139
  Rosanna, 254
  Samuel, 250
  Sarah, 145, 259
  William, 246
SMIT, Hans, 74
  Maria, 74
SMITH, Andreas, 53
  Andrew, 277
  Ann, 94
  Ann Henrietta, 281
  Annika, 39
  Catharina, 31
  Catharine, 190, 213
  Cathrina, 126
  Cathrine, 261
  Charity, 27
  Christopher, 204, 209, 213, 290
  Ebenezer Augustus, 283
  Edward, 163, 178, 185
  Eleanor, 210
  Elizabeth, 24, 31, 83, 90, 235, 288
  Elizabeth Wandewer, 88
  Ericus, 62
  Fredric, 42
  Hannah, 209, 212, 245
  Hans, 31, 42, 53, 59, 71
  Hans Georg, 62
  Hans George, 29

EARLY CHURCH RECORDS OF NEW CASTLE COUNTY

Hans Peterson, 55
Hans Petersson, 24
Hans Piettersson, 19
Henry Colesburg, 189
Hester, 70
Isabell, 231
Jacob, 285
James, 185, 204, 209, 212
Jane, 210
Johan, 27, 29
Johanna, 197
John, 44, 47, 79, 197, 209, 237
Jonas, 71
Joseph, 209, 285
Lancelot L', 290
Mans, 35
Margaret, 209
Maria, 24, 35, 42, 53, 71, 126
Marias, 62
Martha, 81
Mary, 27, 29, 76, 88, 163, 178, 185, 190, 197, 209, 276
Matthew, 210
Peter, 88
Peter Petersson, 37, 39
Rebecca, 209
Reuben, 55
Robert, 76
Rosina, 204, 209
Samuel, 82
Sarah, 172, 239, 289
Sy, 285
Thomas, 80, 163, 197, 209, 261, 276, 280, 285
Tobias, 35, 39, 126
William, 70, 76, 89, 190, 193, 209, 269, 273, 277
SNECKER, Catharina, 38
Hindric, 38
Maria, 6, 7, 12
Mary, 2
SNEIDER, Adam, 216
SNEIKER, Cathrine, 243
SNEKE, Anders, 3
SNEKINS, Mary, 68
SNICKER, Hindrick, 21
Jane, 240
SNIDER, Gottlieb, 260
SNODEY, Michael, 291
SOLGRAVE, James, 258

SOMENS, Philip Fits, 221
SOMMERLIN, Joseph, 272
SORBORG, Barbro, 98
Henry, 98
SORELL, Susanna, 219
SORELY, Comfort, 115
Laurents, 115
Susannah, 115
SPAIN, George, 287
SPAKMAN, Thomas, 241
SPARI, John, 96
Mary Mortonson, 96
Prudence, 96
SPARK, Catharina, 80
SPARKS, Sarah, 260
SPARRY, James, 105
John, 105, 232
Mary Mortinson, 105
SPASSY, John, 269
SPEAKMAN, Joshua, 220
SPEAR, Alexander, 243
William, 243
SPENCE, Ann, 259
George, 236
SPENCER, Elizabeth, 218, 244
Henry, 139
Jane, 279
Rebeccah, 139
Samerlain, 271
SPENEES, John, 267
SPEREY, Alexander William, 199
Esau, 178
Jacob, 178
John, 159, 178, 254
Mary, 159, 199
SPERRY, Cathrine, 290
John, 164, 171
SPOTSWOOD, William, 250
SPRAGG, Elizabeth, 49
Henry, 70
John, 263
SPRAIG, Mary, 241
SPRINGER, Abigail, 146, 285
Abraham, 64, 238
Andreas, 55, 58, 62
Andrew, 97
Ann, 79, 255, 275
Anna, 41, 76, 77, 91, 131
Anna Justice, 91
Anna Justis, 97
Anne, 252
Anne Ogle, 109

INDEX

Annika, 56, 62, 63, 71, 73
Annika Justis, 107
Beata, 63, 228
Benjamin, 286
Brigit, 238
Brita, 39, 284
Carl, 8, 9, 31, 40, 44, 46, 54
Carl Christopher, 58
Caroli, 61
Carolus, 29, 36, 41, 46, 75, 77, 88, 91
Catharina, 29, 34, 39, 54, 64, 72, 76
Catharine, 48, 61, 138, 141, 146, 207, 286
Cathrine, 111, 144, 158, 161, 267
Charl, 56
Charles, 6, 58, 63, 70, 73, 92, 111, 120, 130, 135, 141, 147, 149, 157, 160, 210, 219, 238, 246
Charles Janson, 109
Chatarine, 54
Christina, 134
Christopher, 29, 34, 39, 48, 54, 61, 64, 72, 76
Cornelius, 199
Darkeys, 236
Darkis, 57
David, 147
Edward, 61
Elenor, 107, 271
Elizabeth, 91, 208, 225, 253
Gabriel, 73, 242
Hannah, 128, 134, 260, 276
Israel, 55
Jacob, 70, 96, 146, 158, 163
Jacob Peter, 200
James, 57, 58, 63, 71, 73, 77, 110, 119, 149, 200
Jehu, 135
Jeremiah, 120, 207
Jesse, 138
Johan, 34, 36, 110, 111
Johannas, 65
Johannes, 46, 55, 64

John, 78, 91, 97, 106, 109, 111, 141, 147, 190, 192, 196, 199, 200, 217, 242, 278, 285
Josef, 58
Joseph, 56, 62, 63, 64, 71, 72, 73, 76, 77, 91, 97, 107, 128, 197, 253
Lavianah, 207
Levi, 197, 203, 210, 284
Levy, 147
Lydia, 135, 144
Magdalena, 37
Margaret, 46, 77
Margaret Robinson, 88, 91
Margareta, 31, 41
Margaretta, 73
Margarita, 36, 75, 91
Marget, 54, 61
Margret, 70, 158, 238
Margreta, 131, 135
Margrete, 141, 147
Maria, 8, 9, 31, 40, 46, 55, 57, 63, 64, 71, 110
Mary, 55, 73, 77, 78, 91, 97, 111, 119, 120, 130, 149, 156, 157, 190, 200, 207, 208, 235
Mary Bishop, 96
Mr., 15
Niclas, 77
Peter, 48, 106, 119, 127, 134, 138, 144, 150, 156, 161, 163, 171, 224, 237
Rachael, 119
Rachel, 77, 97, 130, 203, 265
Rebecca, 88, 119, 127, 199, 200, 203, 210, 246, 256
Rees, 208
Reese, 157
Sara, 77, 111
Sarah, 141, 171, 190, 192, 196, 207
Sarah Stedham, 106

Solomon, 61, 131, 135, 164, 233
Susanna, 54, 71
Susannah, 141, 147, 242
Thomas, 119
SPROUL, Mary, 245
SPRUCE, Catharine, 70
SPRUS, John, 65
STAAHLMAN, Jacob, 238
STAAL, Adam, 52
Christina, 52
STAATS, John, 145
Mary, 145
Philip, 145
STABS, Elizabeth, 232
STACK, John, 256
STADYS, Catharine, 132
Jacob, 132
Peter, 132
STAFFEN, Anders Cock, 9
STAFFORD, Elizabeth, 245
STAFORD, Joseph, 237
STAHLKEY, Samuel, 251
STAHLKOP, Amor, 149
Hannah, 245
Isaac, 149
Israel, 140
Jane, 140, 149
John, 140, 149
Margreta, 144
Margrete, 149
Peter, 144
William, 144, 149
STAHLMAN, Jacob, 234
STALCOP, Anders, 1, 9, 14, 17, 20, 25, 34, 36, 42, 78
Andreas, 20, 32, 52, 70, 74, 77, 78
Ann, 225, 271
Anna Barbrie, 32
Anna Barbro, 17, 42, 112
Anne, 101
Annika, 18, 48
Antille, 41
Antilli, 42, 52
Barbara, 20
Barbro, 25, 36, 42
Brita, 4, 6
Carl, 24, 34
Catharina, 8, 17, 24, 68
Christina, 7, 12
Dorothea, 99

Elizabeth, 33, 52, 122
Eric, 85, 101, 104
Ericus, 31
Helena, 33, 38, 48
Henry, 145
Isarel, 220
Israel, 21, 25, 31, 37, 38, 39
Jane, 145
Joanna, 74
Johan, 2, 7, 12, 13, 17, 18, 24, 25, 31, 37, 57, 58, 73
Johannes, 41, 74
John, 48, 58, 70, 145, 240
Jonas, 6, 8, 9, 12, 18, 24, 26, 33, 34, 38, 48, 52
Joseph, 30
Judith, 12, 18, 24, 26
Lady, 107
Margareta, 30
Margaretta, 14, 37
Margarita, 36
Maria, 3, 4, 7, 13, 18, 23, 24, 31, 37, 39, 48, 57, 70
Maria Christina, 32, 34
Mary, 78, 101, 104
Mary Twigg, 104
Matthias, 13
Peter, 14, 67, 73, 75, 78, 107, 116, 130
Philip, 25, 78, 79, 99, 112, 122
Susanna, 25, 31, 73, 75, 78, 122, 130
Susanna Brunberg, 99
Susannah, 112, 116
Sussanna Paulson, 107
Tobias, 18, 58, 78
William, 75
STALEY, Anna Cathrina, 125
Jacob, 125
STALKER, George, 237
STALKOP, John, 253
Rachel, 254
William, 242
STALL, John, 264
STALLEY, Anna Eva, 117
Jacob, 117

INDEX

Maria Barbro, 117
STAMEAST, Hans, 267
STANDLEY, James, 226
STANLEY, Thomas, 271
STANNINGS, Margareta, 30
STANTON, George, 270
STARDGER, Jeremiah, 65
STARDGES, John, 66
STARK, Matthias, 37
  Matz, 3
STARR, Isaac, 216
  John, 242, 253
  Mary, 259
  Phoebe, 256
STARRET, Margaret, 53
STATS, Philip, 240
STEDDOM, Timotheus, 70
STEDHAM, Abraham, 57
  Adam, 20, 30, 51, 71, 74
  Anders, 40
  Andreas, 13
  Ann, 182
  Ann Mary, 196
  Anna, 33, 38, 41, 48, 186
  Anna Maria, 37, 193
  Annah, 243
  Annika, 22, 26, 77
  Asmond, 61
  Asmund, 64, 76, 88, 94, 97
  Benjamin, 108
  Brigitta Loinan, 148
  Carin, 10
  Catharina, 16, 19, 25, 28, 32, 41, 44, 45, 51, 54, 62, 64, 82
  Catherine, 36
  Cathrine, 148, 160
  Christeen Hendrickson, 97
  Christiana, 159
  Christina, 16, 52, 60, 71, 149, 158, 182
  Christina Hendrickson, 88
  Christina Hindrickson, 76, 94
  Christopher, 14, 16, 19, 20, 27, 34, 41, 48, 58
  Cornelius, 22, 45, 70, 91, 94, 149, 158, 159, 182, 204
  Daniel, 133
  David, 155, 182, 262
  Elenor, 284
  Eleonore, 149
  Eliza, 196
  Elizabeth, 10, 16, 22, 31, 36, 48, 49, 51, 55, 58, 62, 77, 89, 148, 204, 215
  Engelke, 13, 18
  Engilke, 7
  Erasmus, 12, 13, 19, 25, 26, 34, 40, 43, 48, 71, 75
  Gertrude, 57
  Hanna, 20, 27, 48
  Hannah, 182, 212
  Helen, 19, 25
  Helena, 13, 34, 45, 52, 56, 57, 63, 70, 73, 78
  Hendric, 8, 12
  Hendrich, 16
  Hendrick, 32, 54
  Henric, 72
  Henrich, 74
  Henrick, 58, 62, 65
  Henry, 28, 77, 79, 141
  Hindric, 16, 19, 33, 36, 41, 45, 51
  Hindrick, 25, 57, 59
  Ingaber, 204, 212
  Ingeber, 194, 259
  Ingeberg, 5
  Ingeborg, 2, 5, 12, 16, 23, 28, 32, 37, 45, 51, 55, 57, 219
  Ingeburg, 4
  Isaac, 141, 186, 193, 196
  Isabella Hare, 95, 108
  Isarel, 18, 19
  Israel, 90
  Jacob, 22, 62, 141, 148, 153, 240
  Jane, 79
  Johan, 27, 36, 63, 112
  Johanna, 16, 34, 186, 196
  Johannes, 16

John, 108, 122, 129,
    133, 140, 143,
    155, 160, 216,
    223, 285
John Wallace, 96
Jonas, 32, 44, 45,
    56, 57, 63, 73,
    78, 141, 149, 157,
    159, 194, 196,
    204, 212, 216, 287
Jones, 52, 70
Joseph, 44, 79, 259
Josiah, 148
Judith, 54
Karin, 7, 70
Kerstin, 64
Lady, 108
Lucas, 5, 7, 10, 16,
    23, 28, 32, 34,
    37, 39, 45, 51,
    55, 96
Lucas Lucasson, 12
Lucus Lucasson, 7
Lukas, 186, 196
Lulof, 93
Lylof, 30, 31, 33,
    38, 48, 79
Magdalena, 13, 35
Margaret, 77
Margareta, 34
Margaretta, 14, 28,
    72
Margery, 74, 77
Marget, 55
Maria, 2, 7, 12, 23,
    25, 26, 32, 34,
    43, 48, 112, 122,
    133
Mary, 91, 108, 129,
    140, 141, 143,
    149, 157, 194,
    218, 255, 258, 270
Peter, 12, 95, 108,
    204
Rachael, 112
Rachel, 157
Rebecca, 143, 158,
    182, 186
Samuel, 6, 19, 22,
    64
Sara, 45, 64, 72,
    86, 88
Sarah, 96, 140, 182,
    186, 228
Susanna, 28, 48, 91,
    193, 243, 252
Susannah, 141, 142,
    148, 153

Thomas, 182
Timothei, 62
Timothens Adamsson,
    7
Timothens Lylofson,
    10
Timotheus, 31, 49,
    55, 62, 64, 77
Timotheus Adamsson,
    13, 18
Timotheus
    Benedictus, 6
Timotheus Bengtsson,
    5, 34
Timotheus Benjamin,
    36, 44
Timotheus Llyofson,
    10
Timotheus Lylofson,
    8
Timotheus Lylofsson,
    5, 9, 11, 22
Timothy Lucas, 75
Timothy Lulofson, 75
Timothy Lylofson, 2
Tobias, 97
William, 95, 142,
    160, 182, 186,
    226, 289
Zacharias, 41, 56,
    76
STEDNAM, Eramus, 21
    Israel, 21
STEDPAM, Lucas, 2
STEEL, Elizabeth, 224
    John, 83
    Joseph, 243
    Samuel, 265
STEELMAN, Agnes, 157
    Charles, 66
    James, 157
    Mary, 157
STEELY, Johnathan, 256
STEEN, Frederick, 274
    Jean, 254
    John, 223
    Mary, 253
    Sussanna, 261
STEFENSON, John, 67
STEIGERWALT,
    Eberhardt, 232
STEIN, John, 83
STELLE, Jacob, 9
    Maria, 9
    Rebecca, 9
STELZ, Anna Margreta,
    125
    Balzar, 125

INDEX

Maria, 125
STENNOP, William, 67
STEPHANSON, Jane, 76
  John, 76
STEPHEN, Elizabeth, 245
STEPHENS, Mary, 222
STEPHENSON, Ann, 261
  Eleonore, 241
STERLIN, Mary, 250
STERLING, Johan, 27
  Mary, 27
  Rachel, 27
STERN, John, 264
STEVENS, James, 234
STEVENSON, James, 92
STEWARD, Adam, 91
  James, 93
  Martha, 257
  Susanna, 278
STEWART, Archibold, 254
  Charles, 282
  Hugh, 222
  James, 222
  John, 217
  Sarah, 272
  Susan, 249
  William, 67
STEYERWALD, Cathrine, 119
  Ibenhard, 119
  William, 119
STEYGERWOLT, John Ebent, 225
STIDDOM, Anders, 69
STIDHAM, Ann, 169, 177
  Benjamin, 134, 202
  Cathrine, 250
  Chistine, 153
  Christiana, 168, 177
  Cornelius, 153, 168, 177, 245, 283
  David, 168, 176, 189, 193
  Elenor, 190, 265
  Eliza, 290
  Elizabeth, 123, 127, 202, 272, 287
  Hannah, 119, 168, 176
  Henry, 119
  Honor, 288
  Ingeber, 202
  Ingeborg, 103, 250
  Isaac, 119, 164, 190, 200
  Jacob, 153, 197
  James, 123
  Jane, 127
  Joanna, 190
  John, 150, 164, 188, 191, 202
  Jonas, 103, 132, 150, 190, 197, 202, 275, 277
  Joseph, 162, 168, 202, 290
  Lucas, 120, 190, 276
  Luluff, 127
  Maria, 123, 132
  Mary, 119, 190, 200, 283
  Mary Colsberg, 103
  Nicholas, 189
  Peter, 120, 141, 177, 190, 202
  Rachel, 200
  Rebecca, 169, 177, 188, 285
  Sarah, 120, 141, 162, 168, 272
  Susan, 202
  Susanna, 69, 119, 132, 134, 177, 285
  Susannah, 162
  Timothy, 102
  William, 119, 134, 169, 176, 177, 188, 264
  Williams, 202
STILE, Melchior, 242
STILLE, Anders, 113
  Andreas, 84, 102
  Catharina, 84
  Cathrine, 113
  Cathrine Stalcop, 102
  Dina, 99, 252
  Elizabeth, 24, 120
  Gertrude, 50
  Jacob, 15, 19, 24, 29, 35, 42, 55, 73, 84
  Johan, 120
  John, 42, 113, 212, 225
  Jonathan, 58, 61, 99, 114
  Jonothan, 73
  Leddie, 55
  Magdalena, 73, 114
  Magdalena Vandeveer, 99
  Margaretta, 29
  Maria, 227

Peter, 15, 102
  Rebecca, 15, 19, 24,
    29, 35, 42, 55, 79
  Sarah, 114, 212
  Susanna, 19
  Thomas, 120
STILLEY, Anders, 123,
    136
  Anna, 132
  Anne, 145
  Catharine, 123
  Cathrina, 136
  Cathrine, 177
  Elizabeth, 129, 132,
    138, 142, 147,
    186, 198
  Ephron, 139
  Hannah, 142, 257
  Isaac, 123
  Jacob, 136, 145, 238
  John, 129, 132, 138,
    142, 147, 177,
    186, 198, 270
  Jonathan, 64, 139,
    145
  Lady, 230
  Lydia, 129
  Magdalena, 64, 139
  Mary, 186
  Nancy, 136
  Rachel, 136
  Rebecca, 64, 267
  Susanna, 66
  William, 147
STILLMAN, Carl, 97,
    107
  Charles, 115
  Johanna, 107
  Johanna Lavel, 97
  Johannah, 115
  John, 97, 115
  William, 107
STILLS, Anna, 131
  Balzar, 131
  Margreta, 131
STILLY, Andreas, 68
  Elizabeth, 155, 182
  Isaac, 182
  Jacob, 139
  John, 155, 182, 245
  Jonathan, 71
  Magdalena, 71
  Margareta, 69
  Maria, 71
  Mary, 65, 228
  Nancy, 139
  Susanna, 183
  Uriel, 139

  William, 183
STINSON, Jane, 278
STITLY, Anders, 74
  Catharina, 74
  Maria, 74
STOANE, James, 60
STOBBY, Magdalena, 79
  William, 79
STOBY, William, 67
STOCKINGSEACER,
    Elizabeth, 162
STOCKIUM, Solomon, 181
STOLE, Adam, 46
  Catharina, 46
  Johannes, 46
STOLT, Mary, 82
STONE, Elizabeth, 108
  James, 108
  Margret, 108
  Peter, 108
STONEMETY, Mary, 283
STONMATS, Anna, 137
  Deborah, 137
  George, 137
STOOP, John, 266
STOOPS, John, 284
STOTTS, Jane, 222
STOUBEI, Anna
    Ifvarson, 98
  Isabelle, 98
  Willian, 98
STOUT, Anna, 15, 19,
    28
  Cornelius, 28
  Johan, 15, 19, 28
  Joseph, 15
STRAINGE, Sarah, 262
STRAND, Anna, 136
  Hannah, 136
  Samuel, 136
STRANGE, Francis, 245
STRAW, Mary, 237
STRAWBRIDGE, John, 272
STRAWMAN, Elizabeth,
    228
STRODA, Joseph, 261
STRODE, Richard, 269
  William, 95
STRONG, Mary, 232
STROUD, Abraham, 219
  Caleb, 242
  George, 69
  Isaac, 70
STROUT, Samuel, 50
STUARD, Anne, 104
  Anne Hawkey, 104
  Isabella, 282
  John, 104

INDEX

STUART, Alse, 271
  Elizabeth, 285
  George, 271
  Jane, 124
  John, 124, 227
  William, 217
STUBBY, Magdalena, 11
STUBY, Anna, 77
  James, 77
  William, 77
STUERDE, Margaret, 65
STUKEL, Hans George, 120
  Jacob, 120
  Martha Lena, 120
STUKLEY, Anna, 113
  Jacob, 113
  Magdalena, 113
STUNTON, Joseph, 264
STURGES, William, 264
SUEIDER, Adam, 116
  Catherina, 116
  John, 116
SUKORIN, Rachel, 215
SULLIVAN, Ann, 281
  Leady, 268
  Margret, 275
  Sarah, 268
SULLIVANE, Jeremiah, 222
  Margret, 225
  Matthias, 224
SULLIVEN, Mary, 261
SULLIVON, Hannah, 257
SUMPTION, Ann, 282
  Hannah, 254
  Mary, 291
SUMPTION, Ann, 282
  Isaac, 271
SUPINGAM, Christina, 86
SURANEY, Onore, 283
SURE, Jean, 254
SUTTIN, Cathrine, 258
SUTTON, Ann, 285
  Joseph, 277
  Lena, 291
  Mary, 257
  Sarah, 112
  William, 112, 221
SWAIN, Martha, 268
SWAN, Margret, 87
  Robert, 285
  Thomas, 221
SWANE, Jane, 222
SWANGE, Abraham, 239
SWANSON, Christina, 89
SWARTZ, George, 140
  Maria, 140
SWAYON, Elizabeth, 258
SWEDBERG, Emmanuel, 17
  I., 6
SWEDBURG, Bishop, 6
SWEENEY, Myles, 70
SWEENY, Walter, 249
SWEITMAN, Rudolph, 214
SWEN, Christina, 78
  Justice, 78
  Mary, 78
SWENEY, Barnabas, 226
SWENSSON, Brigit, 220
SWINE, John, 227
SWING, Christopher, 159
  John, 159
SYKES, Elizabeth, 206
  Harriet, 291
  James, 206
  William Ennalls, 206

-T-

TAGLA, Richard, 277
TAGUE, James, 269
TAILLEUH, Nicklas, 266
TAKNET, Elizabeth, 91
TALBERT, Elizabeth, 270
  Hannah, 266
TALBOT, Elizabeth, 268
TALKINTON, Susanna, 85
TALLBOT, John, 252
TALLEY, Adam, 288
  Elihu, 114
  Hanna, 50
  Rebecca, 114
  Susanna, 261
  William, 114, 252
TALLY, Charity, 239
  Ebenezer, 267
  Samuel, 234, 289
  Thomas, 250, 278
TANGERIN, Elizabeth, 233
TANIERS, John, 234
TANNER, Hanna, 85
TARBOX, John, 241
TARDEY, Elizabeth, 248
  Margret, 260
TARNBERY, Anna, 239
TARRAT, Sussanna, 70
TARRINGTON, Joseph, 69
TASSA, Anna, 73
  Christina, 73
  Elias, 73
  Fredrick, 70
  Maria, 70

Olle, 70
TASSAWA, Annika, 4
TASSAWAS, Annika, 5
　Elias, 5
　Johan, 5
　Karin, 5
　Stafan, 5
TASSE, Ally, 79
　Elias, 79
TASSED, Elizabeth, 101
　George, 101
　Robert, 101
　William, 101
TASSEY, Charles, 80
TATCHER, Mary, 49
TATE, John, 215
　Mary, 277
　Sara, 85
TATHEN, Andrew, 78
　Elizabeth, 78
　Henry, 78
TATLOW, Sarah, 225
TAUGHT, Richard, 276
TAYLA, Richard, 191
TAYLER, Mary, 266
TAYLOR, Abraham, 236
　Ann, 188, 201, 262, 289
　Annah, 242
　Archibald, 80
　Edward, 237
　Elizabeth, 98, 142, 188, 233, 251, 263, 284
　Ellinor, 85
　Else, 237, 246
　George, 149, 163, 253
　Hannah, 240
　Isaac, 241
　Israel, 230
　Jacob, 229
　Jane, 112
　Jane Montgomery, 103
　Jean, 263
　Johanna, 260
　John, 98, 122, 252, 255, 259, 276
　Jonathan, 111
　Joseph, 235, 242, 247, 254
　Margret, 112, 162
　Martha, 111
　Mary, 142, 163, 221, 242, 249, 262, 267, 268, 271, 278, 284, 289
　Philip, 93

　Rachel, 98, 229, 274
　Rebecca, 291
　Rebeccah, 149
　Richard, 188
　Robert, 103, 112, 265, 283
　Ruth, 122, 268
　Sabina, 201
　Samuel, 275
　Sarah, 149, 152, 240
　Susanna, 232
　Thomas, 103
　William, 111, 289
TAYS, Matthew, 114
　Rebecca, 114
　Samuel, 114
TEETH, Elizabeth, 60
TEMPEL, Benjamin, 252
TEMPLE, Else, 247
　Samuel, 279
TERGO, Benjamin, 223
TERNEY, James, 276
TESPENE, Margaret, 214
THANKER, Mary, 247
THATCHER, Elizabeth, 231
　Martha, 61
THEALS, John, 87
THETFORD, Elizabeth, 97
　Mary, 97
　Simon, 97
THOMAS, Cathrine, 174
　Charles, 281
　Davis, 178
　George, 174, 261
　Hannah, 252
　Helena, 23
　Jana, 90
　Margret Eliza, 212
　Mary, 174, 222, 266, 273
　Phoebe, 237
　Rachel, 61
　Samson, 61
　Sara, 29
　Sarah, 236
　Susanna, 212
　Tristram, 212, 286
　Widow, 201
　William, 89
　William Henry, 212
THOMASON, Joseph, 80
　Thomas, 93
THOMELSSON, Elizabeth, 143
　John, 143
　Sarah, 143

INDEX

THOMPSON, Anne, 105
  Cathrine, 205
  Elizabeth, 264
  Jacob, 105
  James, 69, 103
  Jane, 209
  John, 100
  John D., 290
  Josias, 209
  Martha, 266
  Mary, 100, 208
  Rachel, 79
  Richard, 205
  Tilly, 205
  William, 100, 209
THOMSEN, Phoebe, 262
THOMSON, Anne, 225
  Elizabeth, 93, 274
  Francis, 271
  George, 239
  Hannah, 259
  Henry, 221, 254
  Jane, 67
  John, 112, 261
  Joseph, 83, 254
  Margret, 112, 261
  Mary, 81, 83, 223, 227, 238
  Rachel, 275
  Samuel, 233
  Sarah, 228, 264, 291
  Susanna, 91
  Thomas, 268
  William, 275
THOMSSON, Martha, 219
THORNBERG, Else, 218
  Susanna, 223
  Thomas, 80
THORNBERRY, Richard, 246
  Robert, 227
THORNBURG, Alice, 234
THORNBURRY, Sarah, 237
THORNTON, Alexander, 131
  Joseph, 131
  Margreta, 131
  Mary, 227
TIBS, Adam, 29
  Mary, 29
TILL, Ann, 207
  Annie, 192
  Elizabeth, 207
  George, 192
  Jane, 192, 207, 209, 213
  Jesse, 213
  Mary, 207
  Robert, 192, 207, 209, 213
  William, 209
TILLY, Cathrina, 231
TILTON, Ann, 69
  Benjamin, 275
TIMEWELL, Ann, 248
TIMOR, Grace, 282
TINN, John, 92
TINSLEY, William, 273
TOBE, Elizabeth, 65
TOBEN, James, 214
TOBIN, Elizabeth, 250
TODD, Elizabeth, 265
  John, 234
  Joshua, 277
TOENE, Gertrude, 18
  Philip, 18
TOILES, Anna, 34
  Elizabeth, 34
  Jean, 34
TOLAN, Eleanor, 291
  John, 270
TOLON, William, 285
TOMLINSON, Sarah, 277
TOMPLEN, Joseph, 50
TOMSON, Sarah, 243
TOOD, Mary, 263
TOOL, Arthur, 163
  Lady, 163
  Lydia, 287
  Margret, 226
  Mary, 95
TOON, Samuel, 227
TOPPING, Agnes, 276
TORNER, Annie, 239
TOSAWA, Maria, 4, 78
  Matz, 4
  William, 78
TOSSA, Alexander, 71
  Christina, 71
  Elias, 66, 71
  Frederick, 65
  Isaac, 95
  John, 220
  Mary, 65, 84
  Mary Scapenhois, 84
  Mary Schapenhois, 95
  Mary Shapenhoise, 62
  Olaf, 95
  Rebecca, 95
  Sarah, 62
  William, 62, 65, 84
TOSSAWA, Anders, 1
  Anna, 15, 44, 54
  Annika, 1, 8, 19
  Catharina, 1, 10, 45, 60

EARLY CHURCH RECORDS OF NEW CASTLE COUNTY

Christina, 54
Elizabeth, 12, 46
Gertrude, 5, 6, 13
Hindric, 15, 16
Ingeborg, 40
Johan, 8, 15, 16, 29, 39, 40
John, 48
Kerstin, 30
Mans, 47
Margareta, 39
Margaretta, 46
Marget, 54
Maria, 40, 45, 48, 54
Olle, 45, 48, 59
Olof, 6, 13, 29
Peter, 39, 46, 54
Sarah, 282
Staffan, 10, 11
Staffin, 1
Wiljam, 54
TOSSEY, Sarah, 240
TOULSON, John, 234
TOUNSEN, Anna, 68
TOUSARD, Louis, 288
TOWEL, Henry, 82
TOWERS, Andrew, 268
TOWNLEY, Ann Jane, 287
TOWNSAND, Hannah, 265
TOWNSEN, James, 68
TOWNSEND, Joanna, 279
TOY, Neil, 274
TRANBERG, Anna Catharina, 43
 Anna Cathrina, 110
 Catharina Rudman, 78, 88
 Elizabeth, 218
 Peter, 78, 88, 95
 Petrus, 43
 Rebecca, 219
 Theophilius, 88
TRAUX, Philip, 221
TRAYGOT, Elizabeth, 230
TRAYNER, Gasper, 81
TREACY, Thomas, 263
TREAHAME, William, 50
TREAZEY, Matthew, 255
TREES, Annah, 244
TREGO, Margaret, 90
TREGON, David, 155
 Susanna, 155
TREHEARNE, William, 44
TREMBLE, Hannah, 259
 John, 67
 Mary, 216

TREVEL, Patience, 237
TREVILLO, Ann, 269
TROTTER, Jane, 128
 Richard, 128
 Will, 128
 William, 227
TROUSHON, Richard, 257
TRUAX, Cornelius, 250
TRUFFIS, Mary, 219
TRUMAN, Adam, 268
TRYON, Ann, 170
 David, 166, 176, 252
 John, 176
 Susanna, 176, 274
 Susannah, 166
TUCKER, Nathaniel, 14
TUCKNEY, Mary, 65
TUFFS, Margret, 87
TUKER, Margret, 214
TULL, Joseph, 113, 220
 Richard, 113
 Sarah, 113
TULLY, James, 223
TUMMELSSON, Elizabeth, 99
 John, 99
TUMMESON, Elizabeth, 113
 Isaac, 113
 Johan, 113
TUNGBERG, Jonas, 80
TUNKES, William, 224
TURNANTZ, Anthony, 240
TURNER, Beata, 75, 76, 99, 220
 Maria, 75
 Martha, 60
 Mary, 76
 Niclos, 76
 Rev. Mr., 203
 Robert, 83
 Sarah, 99, 221
 Thomas, 68, 75, 99
 William, 236
TURNS, David, 79
TURSAN, Christina, 169
 Elias, 169
TUSSAW, Rebecca, 264
TUSSE, Maria, 62
 Olle, 62
 Sara, 62
TUSSEY, Alexander, 287
 Carina, 271
 Cathrine, 232
 Elias, 163, 251
 Frederick, 286
 Fredrick, 156
 Hannah, 151, 156

INDEX

Isaac, 167
John, 151, 246
Rebecca, 286
Samuel, 260
Susanna, 252
William, 151, 156, 167
TUSSEY (TOSSAWA),
  Annika, 61
TUSSY, Catharina, 66
  Maria, 73
  Mathias, 73
  Rebecca, 159
  William, 73, 159, 164
TUTHILL, Jane, 213
  Lewis Dunham, 213
  Theodorus, 213
TWIGG, Abraham, 90, 117
  Hannah, 238
  John, 233
  Sarah, 117
  Susanna, 117
TWIGGS, Abraham, 99
  Joahn, 23
  John, 99
  Sarah, 99
TWIGS, Abraham, 108
  Ann, 108
  Mary, 85
  Sarah, 108
TWINING, Elizabeth, 276
TYLER, Thomas, 279
TYRON, David, 158, 161
  Mary, 161
  Susanna, 158
  Susannah, 161
  William, 158
TYSON, Isaac, 288

—U—
ULRICA, Anna, 110
UNANDER, Ereck, 126
  Erric, 110
UNDERWOOD, Anne, 227
  Benjamin, 80
  James, 237
  Jeremiah, 262
  Lydia, 257
  Mary, 249
  Samuel, 223
  Sarah, 229

—V—
VAINAM, Anton, 11
  Catharina, 3

Elizabeth, 11
Lars, 9
Hendric, 9
Nannie, 67
VAINAN, Anders, 22, 23
  Andes, 17
  Ante, 13, 14
  Jacob, 22, 23
  Lars, 14
  Margareta, 17, 22
  Peter, 17
  Staphan, 13
VAINANS, Andreas, 5
  Aute, 5
  Marguretta, 5
VALANTINE, George, 248
VALENTIN, Anna Maria
  Huhlman, 135
  John, 135
VALENTINE, Cathrine
  Weaver, 145
  Elva, 280
  John, 145
  Johnathan, 227
  Joseph, 145
VAN DAVIE, Brita, 126
  Cathrina, 126
  Peter, 126
VAN DE VER, Alice, 21
  Andreas, 20
  Anna, 35
  Catharina, 2, 19, 25
  Cornelius, 18, 19
  Coruelius, 9
  Elizabeth, 5, 9, 15, 18, 20, 29, 33, 35, 43, 47
  Hana, 18
  Helena, 6
  Jacob, 2, 4, 7, 18, 25, 33, 40, 43, 11
  Jacob Jabsson, 21
  Jacobus, 5, 9
  Johan, 1, 4
  Judith, 1, 4, 8, 11, 12
  Magdalena, 18
  Margareta, 21
  Margaretta, 19
  Maria, 15, 25, 33, 11
  Peter, 9
  Philip, 1, 3, 9, 15, 18, 19, 20, 29, 35, 40, 43, 47
  Susanna, 43
  Tobias, 29
  Wife, 2, 4

EARLY CHURCH RECORDS OF NEW CASTLE COUNTY

William, 5, 8, 19, 44
VAN DE VERR, William, 2
VAN DE WEER, Breta Hoffman, 94
  Philip, 94
  Rebecca, 94
VAN DER CULLEN,
  Johanna, 14
  Regner, 38
VAN DER VER,
  Elizabeth, 43
  Philip, 43
VAN DER WEER, Ann, 110
  Cornelius, 101
  Jane, 110
  Margret Mortenson, 101
  Rebecca, 101
  Tobias, 110
VAN LEWNIA, Susanna, 225
VAN NEAMAN, Isaac, 121
  Johanna, 125
  Johannes, 125
  John, 121
  Mary, 121, 230
  William, 125
VAN NEAMAN, Elizabeth, 2
VAN NEEMEEN, John, 8
VAN NEMAN, Abraham, 91
  Mary, 96
  Mary Scott, 91
  William, 91, 96, 219
VANBONER, Ann, 165
  Isaac, 165
  Mary, 165
VANCOURT, Daniel, 222
VANDAVAR, Andrew, 244
VANDAVIER, Mary, 235
VANDER, Ann M., 175
  Guilbert, 175
  John, 175
VANDER WEER, Brita, 107, 116
  Cornelius, 108
  Johan, 116
  Margret, 108
  Maria, 108
  Mary, 230
  Peter, 107, 116, 230
VANDEVAR, Benjamin, 141
  Brigita, 131
  Brigitta, 142
  Brita, 150

  Cornelius, 141
  Jane, 139, 147
  John, 139
  Margaretha, 131
  Margret, 141
  Mary, 150
  Peter, 131, 142, 150
  Sarah, 142
  Tobias, 139, 147
VANDEVARS, Jane, 131
  Tobias, 131
  William, 131
VANDEVEERS, Cornelius, 127
  Hannah, 127
  Margareta, 127
VANDEVER, Adam, 58
  Alce, 205, 206
  Alse, 203
  Andreas, 73
  Ann, 203, 278
  Anna Brita, 192
  Beata Hoffman, 84
  Betty, 203, 207
  Bille, 59
  Bishop, 207
  Brigitta, 77
  Brita, 52, 74, 167
  Catharina, 64, 67
  Catharine, 275
  Cornelius, 54, 67, 73, 74, 75, 77
  Elenor, 275
  Elizabeth, 46, 84, 179, 183, 267
  Helene, 151
  Henry, 90
  Jacob, 45, 51, 56, 58, 59, 75, 203
  Jane, 206
  John, 51, 66, 144, 175, 179, 185, 192, 195, 199, 200, 203, 205, 206, 271, 277
  John Beeson, 195
  Kerstin, 57
  Magdalena, 61
  Mali, 66
  Margaret, 73, 75
  Margareta, 51
  Margaretha, 72
  Margaretta, 46, 73
  Margarita, 74, 77, 84
  Marget, 54, 64
  Margret, 173, 275

INDEX

Maria, 45, 51, 56, 70
Martin, 151
Mary, 151, 199, 206
Morton, 173
Parthena, 200
Persina, 175, 179, 185, 192, 195, 199
Peter, 68, 73, 77, 161, 167, 185, 193, 203, 207, 291
Petrus, 56
Philip, 52, 57, 77, 81, 84
Rachael, 161
Rachel, 84, 255
Rebecca, 84, 200, 206, 275
Sarah, 193, 206
Stina, 59
Susanna, 51, 57, 58, 73, 144, 167
Swen, 72
Thomas, 175, 206
Tobias, 45, 173, 206
Wiljam, 54
William, 51, 46, 58, 59, 64, 72, 183, 274
Winters, 193
VANDEVOIR, Elizabeth, 81
  Jacob, 93
VANDEWEER, Cornelius, 97
  Margaret Morton, 97
  Philip, 97
VANDEWER, Isaac, 153
  Marget, 61
  Peter, 153
  Rebecca, 153
  William, 153
VANDOVAR, Elizabeth, 249
VANEAMAN, Andrew, 230
  Joanna, 276
VANEMAN, Andrew, 138
  Annah, 138
  Cathrine, 239
  Hannah, 243
  Mary, 230
  Rebeccah, 138
VANIMAN, Catharina, 78
  Joanna, 130
  Johanna, 130
  Magdalena, 78
  William, 78, 130

VANLEWVANAUGH, Cathrine, 234
VANLOANER, Isaac, 260
VANLOONER, Ann, 170
  Elizabeth, 253
  Isaac, 170
  Zacharias, 170
VANNEAMAN, Abraham, 259
  Andrew, 156, 271
  Anna, 156
  Eleanora, 108
  Johanna, 108, 116, 135
  Margret, 156
  Sarah, 256
  William, 108, 116, 135
VANNEMAN, Ann, 213
  Beata, 81
  David, 285
  Elizabeth, 213
  Johan, 79
  John, 59
  William, 80, 213
VANSANDT, George, 277
VANSANT, Ann, 87
VARNEY, James, 166
  Susannah, 166
VASS, Dorothea, 152
  Joseph, 152
  Niclas, 152
VATHAN, James, 81
VAUGH, James, 224
VAUGHAM, Mary, 92
VEAL, Ann, 186
  Cathrine, 172
  John, 172, 186, 275
  Rebecca, 172
  Thomas, 89
VEALL, John, 267
VEALS, Thomas, 81
VEAZY, Sarah Loutit, 290
VEECH, James, 265
VER DE MAN, William, 21
VERDEMAN, Margareta, 33
  Maria, 33
  William, 33
VERNON, Ann, 249
  Edward, 183
  Elizabeth, 183
  Ester, 70
  John, 278
  Joseph, 217
  Mordecay, 83

Phoebe, 237
Prishilla, 86
Samuel, 241
VICKRY, Thomas, 92
VICTORY, Leah, 259
VINAN, Elizabeth, 51
  Hindric, 51
  Lars, 49, 51
VINING, Elizabeth,
  195, 197
  George, 158
  Henry, 153, 158, 195
  John, 195, 197, 204
  Mary, 204
  Rebecca, 277
  Susanna, 197
  Susannah, 153, 158
  William Henry, 204
VIRT, Jacob, 185
  Mary, 185
VOGHAN, Elsa, 232
  Margreta, 233
VOLBACH, Alberti, 7
  Barbro, 7
  Peters, 7
VON CALEN, Capt.
  Johan, 2
VON CULEN, Andreas, 75
  Anna, 49
  Christina, 5
  George, 32
  Helena, 32
  Ingrid, 5
  Johan, 4, 5, 10, 18, 38
  Johanna, 14
  Kerstin, 5, 10, 18, 38
  Margareta, 32, 49
  Maria, 18, 75
  Peter, 38
  Regner, 5, 47, 49
  William, 75
VON CULLEN, Regner, 8
VON DE CULEN, Regner, 40
VON NAEMAN, Elizabeth, 2
  Olof, 2
VON NEEMAN, Elizabeth, 3, 5
  Johan, 3
  Magdalena, 6
  Magdelena, 8
  Olof, 8
VON NEMAN, Magdalena
  Von Dever, 96
  Olle, 96

William, 96
VON NIEMEN, Beata, 64
  Johan, 64
  John, 64
VONIMAN, Magdalena, 87
  William, 85
VOORES, Abram, 185
  Ann, 185
  Margret, 185
VOUMAN, John, 87

-W-
WADDINGTON, Jonathan, 44
WADDLE, David, 252
WADLE, David, 244
  John, 50, 70
  Thomas, 69, 263
WAGNER, John Henry, 263
  Mary, 264
WAGONER, Joseph, 189
  Mary, 189
  Susanna, 189
WAINAM, Anna, 3
  Henrin, 3
WAINAN, Ante, 12
  Margaretta, 12
  Maria, 12
WAKA, Anna, 44
WALCH, William, 254
WALDEN, Joseph, 286
WALDIN, James, 101
  Marta, 101
  Mary, 101
WALDON, Sarah, 217
WALKER, Alexander, 257
  Anna, 66
  Cathrina, 218
  Daniel, 266
  Elizabeth, 154
  Faithful, 222
  Gabe, 251
  Gabriel, 154, 161, 180
  George, 154
  Hannah, 286
  Isabella, 256
  James, 257, 269
  John, 80, 246
  Margaret, 161, 256
  Margret, 154, 180, 266
  Martin, 180
  Mary, 85
  Sarah, 289
  Thomas, 60
  William, 154

INDEX

WALL, Beninah, 251
  Edward, 227
WALLACE, James, 270
  John, 252
  Mary, 262
  Rachel, 273
  Rebecca, 231, 251
  Samuel, 283
  Sarah, 231
WALLES, Aknes, 217
WALLEY, Sarah, 242
WALLIN, Catharine, 207
  Joseph, 207
  Sarah, 207
WALLIS, Rebeccah, 243
WALLRAVEN, Ann, 193
  Ann Cathrine, 193
  Aquila, 194
  Benjamin, 146
  Catharine, 210
  Cathrina, 121
  Cathrine, 181, 186, 187, 192
  Christina, 121
  Conrad, 169
  David, 186
  Elizabeth, 191, 192
  George, 201
  Gustav, 132
  Hannah, 123, 165
  Isaac, 132
  Jesper, 108, 117
  Jesse, 186
  John, 123, 181, 183, 207
  John Justa, 207
  Jonas, 119, 155
  Kathrine, 169
  Levi, 201
  Lucas, 210
  Lukas, 165, 169, 181, 186, 192
  Maria, 108, 117
  Mary, 146, 155, 201, 207
  Morten, 119
  Peter, 191, 193
  Rebecca, 117, 186
  Sarah, 119, 132, 155, 186, 216
  Susanna, 123
  Swen, 121
  Thomas, 165
  Tobias, 146
  Wallraven, 183, 187, 191, 194
  William, 108
WALRAVEN, Anders, 56
  Ann, 196, 256
  Anna, 36, 39, 133
  Anne, 102
  Annika, 3, 7, 9, 17, 44, 45, 52, 56
  Benjamin, 36, 49
  Brita, 3
  Britta, 1
  Catharina, 33, 38, 133
  Catharina Hindrickson, 95
  Catharine, 254
  Catherine Hendrickson, 102
  Cathrina, 111, 129, 150
  Cathrine, 196
  Christina, 20, 82
  Cornelius, 3, 10, 33
  Elias, 82
  Elenor, 159
  Elizabeth, 3, 17, 33, 62, 136
  Gustafsson, 45
  Gustas, 102, 124
  Gustus, 112
  Hannah, 108, 112
  Isaac, 111
  Jacob, 129
  Jasper, 12
  Jesper, 1, 8, 17, 20, 25, 30, 32, 34, 36, 37, 39, 45, 49, 52, 56, 99, 129, 136, 142, 221
  Jesse, 133, 206, 276
  Johan, 64
  Johannas, 10
  Johannes, 95
  John, 6, 86, 90, 91, 108, 154, 159, 287
  Jonas, 1, 2, 3, 7, 9, 17, 34, 44, 45, 51, 52, 56, 91, 102, 133, 140, 150, 159, 160, 178, 235, 256
  Jonas Jespersson, 33, 38, 40
  Joseph Stedham, 196
  Justa, 154, 165, 216
  Justas, 160
  Kerstin, 16, 37, 39, 47, 53, 56, 64
  Kirstin, 66
  Kristen, 62

Levi, 206
Levy, 150
Lukas, 196, 261
Lydia, 133, 273
Margareta, 45
Margret, 220
Maria, 17, 20, 25, 30, 32, 38, 39, 45, 47, 51, 124, 133, 136
Mary, 81, 99, 129, 140, 142, 154, 165, 196, 206
Morton, 160
Olle, 58
Pastor, 8
Peter, 129, 196, 280, 292
Rachel, 99, 108, 268
Rebecca, 271
Rebeccah, 140
Sara, 39, 49, 51, 53, 102
Sara Jespersdotter, 21
Sara Jespesdotter, 10
Sara Stedham, 91
Sarah, 112, 124, 142, 217
Swen, 39, 95, 102, 111, 129, 133
Thomas, 165
Tobias, 56
Walborg, 33
Walla, 56
Wallraven, 178
Walraven, 37, 39, 47, 53, 62, 64, 272
Wolborg, 10
WALSON, Catharina, 67
WALTER, Elizabeth, 23, 229
George, 254
Hannah, 252
James, 23, 255
Joseph, 67
Mary, 255
Rachel, 264
WALTERS, Agnes Andersson, 72
Cunningham, 72
Edward, 72
Elizabeth, 291
Rachel, 291
WAN, Elizabeth, 101
Mary, 101

Thomas, 101
WANSFORD, Anna, 66
WANTS, John, 199
WARD, Deborah, 280
Hannah, 216
Job, 229
John, 241, 267
Marris, 81
Philip, 266
Sara, 68
WARDEN, Darkes, 220
Rebecca, 269
WARL, Annah, 242
Sarah, 245
WARLE, Elizabeth, 242
WARNER, Ann, 160
Friedrich, 238
George, 160
John, 289
Mary, 160
William, 244
WARREL, John, 259
WASE, Sarah, 244
WASTEN, John, 255
WATERS, John, 228
WATERSON, ---, 249
John, 258
WATES, John, 259
WATKINS, James, 2
John, 2
WATSON, Ann, 108
Cathrine, 290
Henry, 108, 217
John, 204, 249, 281
Joseph, 178
Mary, 108, 287
Ruth, 231
Thomas, 178, 268, 270, 287
Unity, 178
William, 245
WATTSON, Archibald, 221
WAUGH, Cornelius, 223
WAY, Abel, 246, 252
Ann, 79
Benjamin, 257
Caleb, 243, 275
Elizabeth, 247
Hannah, 219
Jacob, 248
James, 249, 252
Jane, 257
John, 92, 244
Lady, 228
Martha, 216
Mary, 248, 259
Nathaniel, 240

INDEX

Rebecca, 236
Robert, 250
Ruth, 276
Samuel, 240
Sarah, 250, 258
WAYD, David, 115
John, 115
Marth, 115
Miriam, 115
Thomas, 115
WAYROM, Mary, 248
WEAKONS, Susannah, 254
WEAVER, George, 288
WEBB, James, 89
John, 239
Joseph, 208, 282, 284
Margret, 81
Ruth, 263
Susanna, 258
William, 218
WEBBER, John Valentine, 287
WEBSTER, Anne, 236
Elizabeth, 129, 173
George, 159
Hannah, 157
Henry, 129, 157, 159, 228
Jane, 173
John, 219, 256
Margret, 173, 180
Richard, 273
Sara, 129
Sarah, 157, 159, 160
Thomas, 173, 180, 255
WEEMS, Mary, 281
WEIGHT, Catharina, 90
WEILI, Sarah, 66
WEILY, David, 243
William, 68
WEIR, Mary, 226
WELCH, Ann, 208
Anne, 101, 111, 148, 152
Anne Morten, 111
Briget, 222
Elizabeth, 251, 263
Elizabeth C., 200
Hannah, 208
Jacob, 143, 148, 208
James, 208
Jane, 276
John, 81, 152, 200, 208, 248, 267
Margaret, 287
Margret, 200, 208

Margreta, 231
Mary, 143, 148, 208, 260, 265
Niclas, 225
Philip, 214
Rebecca, 266
Sylvester, 101
Thomas, 143
William, 101, 111, 208
WELD, Jacob, 284
WELDIN, Elizabeth, 92, 220
George, 275
Jennet, 215
Joseph, 218
Mary, 229
WELDING, Isaac, 251
WELDOM, Isabella, 281
WELDON, Eli, 276
Elizabeth, 186, 196
George, 186, 196
John, 196
Margaret, 282
Mary, 186, 253
Sarah, 281
WELK, Rebecca, 90
WELLCOCK, Elizabeth, 86
WELLDON, Sara, 93
WELLS, Elizabeth, 291
WELSH, Ann, 93, 282
Daniel, 218
Elenor, 280
Elizabeth, 164
Hannah, 226
Helena, 47
James, 207
Jane, 207
John, 70, 164, 206, 284
Margret, 206, 207
Mary, 37, 67, 91, 207
Robert, 207, 250
Samuel, 207
Sarah, 206
Walter, 245
WELSHE, John, 271
WENCH, Jean, 229
WENCOURTLIN, Mary, 225
WERDEMAN, James Senecce, 106
Margaret, 50, 106
Senecce, 106
WERTH, Elizabeth, 137
Hindrance, 137
Jacob, 137

WESLEY, Susanna, 279
WESSELS, Jane, 218
WEST, Ann, 200
  Christina, 51
  James, 204
  John, 200, 204, 209
  Kerstin, 51
  Mary, 200, 204, 209, 251
  Samuel, 209
  Sarah, 252
  Thomas, 30, 51, 200
WESTBY, Mary, 197
  Rebecc, 197
  Thomas, 197
WETHEROW, Jane, 236
WETWER, Barbro, 110
  Dorthea Margreta, 110
  Michael, 110
WHALLEY, Luke, 232
WHAME, Caleb, 232
WHARTON, Charles H., 192
  Charles Henry, 198, 281
  Rev. Dr., 200
WHEALON, Dennis, 68
WHEATFIELD, Henry, 44
WHEEL, Margret, 218
WHEIGHTH, Anna, 241
WHELAN, Darby, 5
  Richard, 5
  Susa, 5
WHELCH, John, 79
WHEN, Margret, 262
WHETHEROW, William, 224
WHIPPLE, John, 60
WHIPPOE, Anne, 235
WHITAKER, Abel, 230
WHITBY, Jane, 242
WHITCRUST, James, 106
  Jane, 106
WHITE, Ann, 183
  Anna, 132
  Anne, 106
  Barbara, 243
  Carolus, 46
  Cathrina, 122
  Charles, 222
  David, 34, 36, 46, 103
  Edward, 103
  Elizabeth, 35, 89
  Ester, 114
  George, 90, 226
  Gierkie, 36
  Hannah, 80, 281
  Hierkie, 46
  James, 106
  John, 261, 278
  Josiah, 254
  Margret, 103, 224, 256
  Maria, 35, 39, 42, 51
  Martha, 103, 114, 122, 132, 227
  Mary, 67, 90, 228, 250, 271
  Moses, 36, 92, 103, 106, 114, 122, 132, 216
  Phoebe, 245
  Rebecca, 224
  Richard, 226
  Rose Anna, 229
  Sara, 60
  Sarah, 103, 246
  Stephanius, 36
  Susanna, 42
  Thomas, 40, 51
  William, 34, 35, 39, 42, 51, 228
WHITEAKER, Peter, 261
WHITEALL, Benjamin, 254
WHITECKER, James, 80
WHITEHEAD, Hanna, 132
  Lydia, 129
  Rebeccah, 144
  Sara, 129, 132
  Sarah, 144
  Wilhelm, 132
  William, 129, 144, 223
WHITELOCK, Charles, 260
WHITEMAN, Hannah, 166
  Harman, 256
  Herman, 166
  Martha, 166
WHITEROUS, Robert, 89
WHITESIDE, George, 10
  Rebecca, 67
WHITETED, William, 226
WHITEY, Mary, 262
WHITHEAD, Sarah, 138
  William, 138
WHITHERS, Ralph, 50
WHITLETA, David, 89
WHITLOCK, Isaac, 90
WHITTAKER, Abel, 82
WHITTIKER, Anna, 42
  Maria, 42

INDEX

Robert, 42
WHITTING, Mary, 262
WHOLOHAN, Cain, 91
WICKERS, John, 214
WICKERSHAM, William, 286
WICKERSON, Hannah, 221
WIDDOWS, James, 50
  Martha, 225
WIEBER, John Valentin, 240
WIER, Elizabeth, 124
  Jane Vander, 124
  Tobias, 124
WIGHT, William, 44
WILCOCKS, Thomas, 44
WILDE, Joseph, 271
WILDER, Elizabeth, 36
  Johan, 22, 32, 34, 36, 41
  John, 19, 26, 43
  Margareta, 22, 32, 41, 43
  Margaretta, 26
  Margarita, 36
  Richard, 32, 34
  William, 22, 26
WILEY, John, 266
  Joseph, 258
  William, 256
WILHELMS, George, 6
  James, 6
  Kustin, 6
WILKESON, Joseph, 274
WILKESSON, John, 269
WILKINS, John, 258
WILKINSON, Ann, 85
  Eleonor, 224
  Nathanael, 261
WILKY, Cathrine, 255
WILLEY, Mattie, 65
  Susanna, 225
WILLIAM, Ambrose, 271
  Mary, 271
WILLIAMS, Benjamin, 60
  Elizabeth, 253
  Ester, 229
  Eve, 280
  Francis, 262
  George, 27
  Hannah, 93
  Isaac, 231, 241
  Jane, 217, 244
  Johan, 40
  John, 82, 218, 262, 270, 279
  Joseph, 80
  Margret, 270

  Mary, 83, 246, 249
  Mriah, 227
  Nathaniel, 251, 282
  Ralph, 69
  Richard, 27, 37
  Sara, 27
  Thomas, 220, 238, 265, 274
  Timothy, 236
  William, 227
WILLIAMSON, George, 264
  Gideon, 274
  Joseph, 67, 69
  Mary, 88, 228
WILLIMS, Moris, 229
WILLING, Anna, 74
  Catharina, 49, 74
  Cathrina, 56
  Helena, 49
  Rebecca, 56
  Thomas, 47, 49, 56, 74
WILLIS, George, 273
  Joseph, 80
  Margret, 235
  William, 250
WILLISON, Edward, 265
  Elenor, 265
WILLS, John, 215
  Susanna, 231
WILLSON, Charles, 233
  Elizabeth, 231, 256
  Franky, 227
  Isabella, 234
  Jennet, 252
  John, 223, 227
  Margreta, 232
  Mary, 155, 232
WILLSSON, Elizabeth, 104
  James, 104
  Jane Andrew, 104
  Mary, 215
WILMER, Rev. Mr., 214
WILSON, Alexander, 109, 218
  Ann, 182, 262
  Anne, 109
  Cathrine, 265
  Elizabeth, 41, 231, 251
  Hannah, 269
  James, 111, 234, 238, 260
  Jane, 66, 111
  John, 218, 221, 248, 251, 262

EARLY CHURCH RECORDS OF NEW CASTLE COUNTY

Joseph, 88
Josia, 41
Mary, 109, 234, 238, 254, 257, 270
Mathew, 237
Rebecca, 41, 80
Robert, 238, 278
Samuel, 287
Sarah, 89, 111
Thomas, 67, 182, 239, 245, 252, 264, 279
William, 182, 233, 265, 289
WILSSON, Edward, 11
Elizabeth, 43
John, 48
Margareta, 48
Maria, 48
Sara, 11
WILTERSLAIN, Frederick, 254
WINCY, Peter, 226
WINDEL, David, 168
John, 168
Rebecca, 168, 274
WINDELL, David, 171, 263
Rebecca, 171
WINDRUFVA, Andreas, 44
WINDRUFWA, Andreas, 43
Elizabeth, 43
WINDSOR, Sarah, 211
WINEY, Mary, 66
WINNET, William, 262
WINS, Martie, 65
WINTERS, Patrick, 218
Sara, 49
WINTWORTH, Ezekiel, 86
WIRTH, Hindrena, 116
Jacob, 116
Miriam, 116
WITBANK, James, 290
WITEHEAD, Mary, 120
Sarah, 120
William, 120
WITHAL, Johanna, 82
WITHEROW, Elizabeth, 234
WITHETAN, David, 98
Mary Kein, 98
Stephen, 98
William, 98
WITHROW, John, 286
WITTEN, Elizabeth, 45
Isaac, 45
WITTERTON, Sara, 87
WITZEL, George, 258

WOLBACK, Albertus, 11
Barbro, 14
WOLF, Elizabeth, 201
Isabella, 201
Isabelle, 167
Jacob, 291
Michael, 163, 167, 201
Sabilla, 163
Susannah, 163
WOLFSBACH, Adolph, 100
Catharine, 100
Rebecca, 100
WOLLARLOU, John, 238
WOLLASTON, Jane, 241
Lydea, 223
Susanna, 219
WOLLESTON, Ebenezer, 88
William, 89
WOLLOWS, Elizabeth, 83
WOLSTEN, John, 80
WOLTERS, Elizabeth, 82
WON, Henrietta, 230
Mary, 223
WOOD, Elizabeth, 246, 257, 271
Hanna, 189
Isabella, 177
John, 189, 190, 192, 197, 277
Joseph, 197, 230, 232
Mary, 86, 224
Michael, 177
Rachel, 177, 232
Samuel, 190
Sarah, 189, 190, 192, 197, 249
William, 273
WOODARD, Ann, 88
WOODCOCK, Isaac, 283
Robert, 240
William, 279
WOODETH, Susanna, 216
WOODLAND, Johan, 33
WOODROW, Joshua, 251
Rachel, 256
WOODS, Anne, 218
Edward, 264
Grace, 218
Jane, 100
John, 100
Joseph, 100
Lawrence, 257
Sarah, 272
Thomas, 228
William, 69

INDEX

WOODSIDE, Elizabeth, 264
WOODWARD, Abigail, 235
  Abraham, 239
  Ann, 247
  Deborah, 95
  Ely, 273
  Hannah, 260
  James, 234, 257
  John, 214, 233
  Joseph, 240
  Leady, 258
  Mardechay, 239
  Mary, 274
  Phoebe, 267
  Rachel, 265
  Richard, 86, 228, 240
  Robert, 254
  Sarah, 259, 272
WOOLBAUGH, Elizabeth, 170
  Lydia, 180, 275
  Mary, 170
  Peter, 170, 180
WOOLBOUGH, Peter, 262, 273
  Susanna, 263
WOOLBUTT, Mary, 244
WOOLCOCKS, Hannah, 93
WOOLF, Isabella, 173
  Jacob, 173
  Michael, 173
WOOLISTON, Susanna, 237
WOOLLY, Mary, 259
WOOLSON, James, 256
WORMS, Daniel, 110
  Magadalena, 110
  Maria, 110
WORREL, Phoebe, 274
WORRILOW, Mary, 215
WORT, Judith, 46
  Kerstin, 46
  Thomas, 46
WOTT, Elizabeth, 290
WRANGEL, Charles Magnus, 181
  Dr., 181
WRELSON, Paul, 246
WRIGHT, John, 5
  Mary, 69, 161
  Samuel, 92
  Sarah, 5
  William, 264
WROLSTON, Paul, 147
  Rebeccah, 147
WROTH, Milchit, 277

WUHLBACH, Adolph, 73
  Catharina, 73
  Maria, 73
WUKER, Hannah, 216
WULBACK, Adolph, 67
WYNA, Henry, 244
WYND, Henry, 145
  John, 145
  Susannah, 145
WYNEKOOP, Antony, 189

-Y-

YARNALL, Abraham, 221
YARNEL, Benjamin, 271
YATES, John, 278
YETMAN, Mary, 86
YORK, John, 48, 253
  Marget, 48
  Margret, 216
  Maria, 48
YOUNG, Agnes, 239
  Elizabeth, 129
  James, 243
  Jane, 87
  John, 215, 260
  Joseph, 186
  Leonard, 186, 193, 273
  Lydia, 186, 193
  Margret, 225
  Michael, 255
  Reading, 129
  Rebecca, 193
  Sarah, 129, 269
  Susanna, 193, 249
  William, 68
YOUNGBLOOD, Jacob, 67
  John, 66
YUNG, Ann, 83
YURGON, Albrecht, 135
  Maria, 135
  Maria Margaretha, 135

-Z-

ZACHARY, Deborah, 161
  Susannah, 154
  William Derickson, 154
  William Derrickson, 161
ZACHARYSON, Elenor, 169
  Jacob Derrickson, 169
  Mary, 168
  William Derickson, 168

Zacharias, 169
ZEBLEY, Ann, 260
　Rachel, 254
ZELLER, Jacob, 146
　John, 146
　Niclas, 146
　Susannah, 146
ZEPHERNUH, Charlotte,
　166
　Gottfried, 166
　Mariana, 166
ZIEGLENI, Cathrine,
　242
ZIMMINGENS, Elizabeth,
　186
　Keto, 186
　Rachel, 186

www.ingramcontent.com/pod-product-compliance
Lightning Source LLC
Chambersburg PA
CBHW071941220426
43662CB00009B/950